EXAM/CRAM

MCTS 70-640

Windows Server 2008 Active Directory, Configuring

Don Poulton

MCTS 70-640 Exam Cram: Windows Server 2008 Active Directory, Configuring

Copyright © 2009 by Pearson Education, Inc.

ISBN-13: 978-0-7897-3791-5
ISBN-10: 0-7897-3791-4

Library of Congress Cataloging-in-Publication Data

Poulton, Don.

  MCTS 70-640 exam cram : Windows server 2008 active directory, configuring / Don Poulton. -- 1st ed.

     p. cm.

  ISBN 978-0-7897-3791-5 (pbk. w/cd)

  1. Electronic data processing personnel--Certification. 2. Microsoft software-- Examinations--Study guides. 3. Directory services (Computer network technology)-- Examinations--Study guides. I. Title.

  QA76.3.P667 2008

  005.7'1376--dc22

                    2008034083

Printed in the United States of America

Fourth Printing: July 2011

Trademarks

Warning and Disclaimer

Bulk Sales

Que Publishing offers excellent discounts on this book when ordered in quantity for bulk purchases or special sales. For more information, please contact

  U.S. Corporate and Government Sales

  1-800-382-3419

  corpsales@pearsontechgroup.com

For sales outside of the U.S., please contact

  International Sales

  international@pearson.com

Associate Publisher
Dave Dusthimer

Executive Editor
Betsy Brown

Development Editor
Deadline Driven
Publishing

Managing Editor
Patrick Kanouse

Project Editor
Amanda Gillum

Copy Editor
Gill Editorial Services

Indexer
Tim Wright

Proofreader
Leslie Joseph

Technical Editors
David Camardella
Pawan J. Bhardwaj

Publishing Coordinator
Vanessa Evans

Book Designer
Gary Adair

Composition
Louisa Adair

Contents at a Glance

Table of Contents

About the Author

Don Poulton, MCSA, MCSE, A+, Network+, Security+, has been involved with computers since the days of 80-column punch cards. After a career of more than 20 years in environmental science, Don switched careers and trained as a Windows NT 4.0 MCSE. He has been involved in consulting with a couple of small training providers as a technical writer, during which time he wrote training and exam prep materials for Windows NT 4.0, Windows 2000, and Windows XP.

In addition, Don has worked on programming projects, both in his days as an environmental scientist, and more recently with Visual Basic to update an older statistical package used for multivariate analysis of sediment contaminants.

When not working on computers, Don is an avid amateur photographer who has had his photos displayed in international competitions and published in magazines such as *Michigan Natural Resources Magazine* and *National Geographic Traveler*. Don also enjoys traveling and keeping fit.

Don lives in Burlington, Ontario, with his wife, Terry.

Dedication

I would like to dedicate this work to the memory of my first wife Elaine, who passed away exactly 20 years ago this spring. She was an inspiration not just to our two children but also to the hundreds of children she touched in her too-brief teaching career.

—*Don Poulton*

Acknowledgments

I would like to thank all the staff at Que, and in particular, Betsy Brown, for giving me the opportunity to produce this work. Thanks also to Kim Lindros, who connected me to the wonderful Que staff in Indianapolis, and thanks to both for their hospitality during my 2007 visits. I would also like to thank my development editor, Ginny Bess Munroe, and my tech editors, Pawan Bhardwaj and David Camardella, for their helpful comments that greatly improved the final product.

We Want to Hear from You!

As the reader of this book, *you* are our most important critic and commentator. We value your opinion and want to know what we're doing right, what we could do better, what areas you'd like to see us publish in, and any other words of wisdom you're willing to pass our way.

As an associate publisher for Que Publishing, I welcome your comments. You can email or write me directly to let me know what you did or didn't like about this book as well as what we can do to make our books better.

Please note that I cannot help you with technical problems related to the topic of this book. We do have a User Services group, however, where I will forward specific technical questions related to the book.

When you write, please be sure to include this book's title and author as well as your name, email address, and phone number. I will carefully review your comments and share them with the author and editors who worked on the book.

Email: feedback@quepublishing.com

Mail: Dave Dusthimer
            Associate Publisher
            Que Publishing
            800 East 96th Street
            Indianapolis, IN 46240 USA

Reader Services

Visit our website and register this book at informit.com/register for convenient access to any updates, downloads, or errata that might be available for this book.

Introduction

Welcome to *MCTS 70-640 Exam Cram: Windows Server 2008 Active Directory, Configuring*. This book aims to help you get ready to take—and pass—Microsoft Certification Exam 70-640: TS: Windows Server 2008 Active Directory, Configuring. This book contains information to help ensure your success as you pursue this Microsoft exam and the Technology Specialist or IT Professional certification.

This Introduction explains the new generation of Microsoft certifications centering on Windows Server 2008 and how the *Exam Cram* series can help you prepare for Exam 70-640. This chapter discusses the basics of the MCTS and MCITP certifications, including a discussion of test-taking strategies. Chapters 1 through 9 are designed to remind you of everything you need to know to take and pass the exam. The two sample tests at the end of this book should give you a reasonably accurate assessment of your knowledge and, yes, I've provided the answers and their explanations to the tests. Along with the explanations are some particularly useful links to more information on each topic. Each answer also includes a reference to the chapter in the book that covers the topic.

Read this book and understand the material, and you'll stand a very good chance of passing the test. Use the additional links to the other materials and points of reference, and along with actual product use, you will be in excellent shape to do well on the exam.

Exam Cram books help you understand and appreciate the subjects and materials you need to pass Microsoft certification exams. These books are aimed strictly at test preparation and review. They do not teach you everything you need to know about a topic. Instead, they present and dissect the questions and problems that you're likely to encounter on a test. These books work to bring together as much information as possible about Microsoft certification exams.

The MCTS (Microsoft Certified Technology Specialist) certification requires you to have a strong knowledge of the features of Active Directory in Windows Server 2008, in particular the newer features. To move on to the next level, you have to drill down into each feature significantly. The MCITP (Microsoft Certified IT Professional) Windows Server 2008 Administrator and Windows Server 2008 Enterprise Administrator certifications require considerable in-depth information about the particulars of each of the Windows Server 2008 features.

Traditional MCP Program Tracks

The traditional program tracks that Microsoft has followed for a number of years certify individuals on technologies up to and including Windows Server 2003:

▶ **MCSE (Microsoft Certified Systems Engineer)**— Anyone who has a current MCSE is warranted to possess a high level of networking expertise with Microsoft operating systems and products. This credential is designed to prepare individuals to plan, implement, maintain, and support information systems, network, and internetworks built around Microsoft Windows 2000 or Windows Server 2003 and its BackOffice Server family of products.

The Windows Server 2003 MCSE is the last certification that Microsoft plans to award on this program. Obtaining this credential requires an individual to pass six core exams and one elective exam. The core exams include four networking system exams, one operating system exam, and one design exam. Beginning with Windows Server 2008, the MCSE has been replaced by the MCITP credential already mentioned.

▶ **MCSA (Microsoft Certified Systems Administrator)**— This certification program is designed for individuals who are systems administrators but have no need for network design skills in their current career path. An MCSA on Windows Server 2003 candidate must pass three core exams plus one elective exam. Beginning with Windows Server 2008, the MCSA has been replaced by the MCTS and MCITP credentials already mentioned.

▶ **MCP (Microsoft Certified Professional)**—This is the least prestigious of all the certification tracks from Microsoft. Passing one of the major Microsoft exams qualifies an individual for the MCP credential. Individuals can demonstrate proficiency with additional Microsoft products by passing additional certification exams.

▶ **MCSD (Microsoft Certified Solution Developer)**—The MCSD credential reflects the skills required to create multitier, distributed, and COM-based solutions, in addition to desktop and Internet applications, using new technologies. An MCSD must pass three core exams and one elective exam. The last iteration of the MCSD program validated competency in the 6.0 level of Microsoft Visual C++, Microsoft Visual FoxPro, or Microsoft Visual Basic. Beyond this level, this certification has been replaced with the MCPD already mentioned.

▶ **MCDBA (Microsoft Certified Database Administrator)**—The MCDBA credential reflects the skills required to implement and administer Microsoft SQL Server databases. To become an MCDBA, you must pass a total of three core exams and one elective exam. The core exams involve SQL Server administration, SQL Server design, and networking systems. Beginning with SQL Server 2005, this certification has been replaced with the MCITP: Database Developer and the MCITP: Database Administrator certifications.

▶ **MCT (Microsoft Certified Trainer)**—Microsoft Certified Trainers are deemed able to deliver elements of the official Microsoft curriculum, based on technical knowledge and instructional ability. Therefore, it is necessary for an individual seeking MCT credentials (which are granted on a course-by-course basis) to pass the related certification exam for a course and complete the official Microsoft training in the subject area, as well as to demonstrate an ability to teach.

This teaching skill criterion may be satisfied by proving that you have already attained training certification from Novell, Banyan, Lotus, the Santa Cruz Operation, or Cisco, or by taking a Microsoft-sanctioned workshop on instruction. Microsoft makes it clear that MCTs are important cogs in the Microsoft training channels. Instructors must be MCTs before Microsoft allows them to teach in any of its official training channels, including the Certified Technology Education Centers (CTEC) and its online training partner network.

After a Microsoft product becomes obsolete, MCPs typically have to recertify on current versions. (If individuals do not recertify, their certifications become invalid; a current exception to this rule is the MCSE on Windows NT 4.0.) Because technology keeps changing and new products continually supplant old ones, this recertification requirement should come as no surprise.

The best place to keep tabs on the various certification programs is on the Web. The URL for these programs is http://www.microsoft.com/learning/default.mspx. But the Microsoft website changes often, so if this URL doesn't work, try using the Search tool on the Microsoft site with "MCP," "MCTS," or the quoted phrases "Microsoft Certified Professional" or "Microsoft Certified Technology Specialist" as a search string. This can help you find the latest and most accurate information about Microsoft's certification programs.

About the Exam and Content Areas

Exam 70-640: Windows Server 2008 Active Directory, Configuring, includes a variety of content. For specifics on the exam, check the exam guide on the Microsoft website at http://www.microsoft.com/learning/en/us/exams/70-640.mspx.

The broad topic areas covered by the exam include the following:

▸ **Configuring Domain Name System (DNS) for Active Directory**— You should be able to configure DNS zones, DNS server settings, zone transfers, and replication.

▸ **Configuring the Active Directory Infrastructure**—You are expected to be able to configure Active Directory forests, domains, trusts, sites, replication, global catalog, and operations masters.

▸ **Configuring Additional Active Directory Server Roles**—You are expected to be able to configure Windows Server 2008 as a Server Core domain controller and a read-only domain controller, and to use the new Server Manager console to configure services related to Active Directory in Windows Server 2008.

▸ **Creating and Maintaining Active Directory Objects**—You should be able to configure and maintain Active Directory accounts, including automatic creation of user and group accounts. You should also be able to configure Group Policy objects (GPO), including creating and applying GPOs and configuring GPO templates, software deployment GPOs, account policies, and audit policies.

▸ **Maintaining the Active Directory Environment**—You should be familiar with how to monitor and maintain Active Directory and be able to recover from various types of failures.

▸ **Configuring Active Directory Certificate Services**—You must be able to install Certificate Services and configure server settings, certificate templates, and certificate enrollments and revocations in Active Directory.

Each of the task areas represents important components of Active Directory management that an individual responsible for the task must be familiar with. You will be able to plan and implement an Active Directory installation and perform the essential day-to-day management and troubleshooting tasks.

How to Prepare for the Exam

Preparing for any Windows Server 2008–related exam requires that you obtain and study materials designed to provide comprehensive information about the product and its capabilities that will appear on the specific exam for which you are preparing. The following list of materials will help you study and prepare:

▶ The Windows Server 2008 product DVD-ROM, which includes comprehensive online documentation and related materials; it should be a primary resource when you are preparing for the test.

▶ The exam preparation materials, practice tests, and self-assessment exams on the Microsoft Certified Professional and Office Specialist Exams page at http://www.microsoft.com/learning/mcpexams/default.mspx; the Testing Innovations page (http://www.microsoft.com/learning/mcpexams/policies/innovations.mspx) offers examples of the new question types found on the Windows Server 2008 MCTS and MCITP exams. Find the material, download it, and use it!

▶ The exam-preparation advice, practice tests, questions of the day, and discussion groups on the ExamCram.com e-learning and certification destination website (http://www.informit.com/imprint/index.aspx?st=61087).

In addition, you'll probably find any or all of the following materials useful in your quest for Active Directory configuration expertise:

▶ **Microsoft training kits**—Microsoft Press offers a training kit that specifically targets Exam 70-640. For more information, visit http://www.microsoft.com/MSPress/books/11754.aspx. This training kit contains information useful in preparing for the test.

▶ **Microsoft TechNet Subscriptions**—This Microsoft resource delivers comprehensive resources that assist IT professionals in resolving problems and issues, implementing technologies, and enhancing their skills. Included are product facts, technical notes, tools and utilities, and access to training materials for all aspects of Windows Server 2008, Windows Vista, and other Microsoft products. Beta software and evaluation versions of released software packages are also included. A subscription to TechNet costs anywhere from $349 to $999 per year, but it is well worth the price. Visit http://technet.microsoft.com/en-us/subscriptions/default.aspx and check out the information under the TechNet Plus Subscriptions menu entry for more details.

▶ **Study guides**—Several publishers, including Que, offer Windows Server 2008 titles. Que Certification includes the following:

  ▶ The *Exam Cram* series—These books provide information about the material you need to know to pass the tests.

  ▶ The *Exam Prep* series—For some Microsoft exams, Que also offers *Exam Prep* books, which provide a greater level of detail than the *Exam Cram* books and are designed to teach you everything you need to know from an exam perspective. Each book comes with a CD-ROM that contains interactive practice exams in a variety of testing formats.

▶ **Multimedia**—The MeasureUp Practice Tests CD-ROM that comes with each *Exam Cram* and *Exam Prep* title features a powerful, state-of-the-art test engine that prepares you for the actual exam. MeasureUp Practice Tests are developed by certified IT professionals and are trusted by certification students around the world. For more information, visit www.measureup.com.

▶ **Classroom training**—CTECs and third-party training companies (such as Learning Tree International, Global Knowledge, New Horizons, triOS College, and others) offer classroom training on Windows Server 2008. Although such training runs upward of $350 per day in class, most of the individuals lucky enough to partake find it to be quite worthwhile.

▶ **Other publications**—There's no shortage of materials available about Active Directory configuration. The resource sections in Appendix A, "Need to Know More?" should give you an idea of where you should look for further discussion.

You cannot adequately prepare for this exam or other Microsoft certification exams by simply rote-memorizing terms and definitions. You need to be able to analyze a scenario and answer by combining various knowledge points from various topic areas. Successfully completing this exam requires a great deal of thought and analysis to properly choose the "best" solution from several "viable" solutions in many cases.

As stated and restated, this exam is best prepared for by doing. You must work with Active Directory and all of its features to be comfortable with the material being addressed by the exam.

Taking a Certification Exam

After you've prepared for your exam, you need to register with a testing center. Each computer-based MCP exam costs $125, and if you don't pass, you may retest for an additional $125 for each try. In the United States and Canada, all tests after January 1, 2008, are administered by Prometric. You can sign up for an exam through the company's website at securereg3.prometric.com, or you can register by phone at 800-755-3926 (within the United States and Canada) or at 410-843-8000 (outside the United States and Canada).

To sign up for a test, you must possess a valid credit card, or you can contact Prometric for mailing instructions to send in a check (in the United States). Only when payment is verified or your check has cleared can you actually register for a test.

To schedule an exam, call the number or visit the web page at least one day in advance. To cancel or reschedule an exam, you must call before 7 p.m. Pacific Standard Time the day before the scheduled test time (or you may be charged, even if you don't appear to take the test). When you want to schedule a test, have the following information ready:

- ▶ Your name, organization, and mailing address.

- ▶ Your Microsoft Test ID. (Inside the United States, this means your Social Security Number and in Canada, it means your Social Insurance Number. Citizens of other nations should call ahead to find out what type of identification number is required to register for a test.)

- ▶ The name and number of the exam you want to take.

- ▶ A method of payment. Besides the methods already mentioned, you might be able to purchase a voucher online before registering.

After you sign up for a test, you are informed as to when and where the test is scheduled. Try to arrive at least 15 minutes early. You must supply two forms of identification—one of which must be a photo ID—to be admitted into the testing room.

All exams are completely closed book. In fact, you are not permitted to take anything into the test area, but you are furnished with a blank sheet of paper and a pen, or in some cases, an erasable plastic sheet and an erasable pen. Immediately write down on that sheet of paper all the information you've memorized for the test. In *Exam Cram* books, this information appears on a tearcard inside the front cover of each book. You are allowed some time to compose yourself, record this information, and take a sample orientation exam before you begin the real thing. It's best to take the orientation test before taking your first exam, but because they're all more or less identical in layout, behavior, and controls, you probably don't need to do this more than once.

When you complete a Microsoft certification exam, the software tells you whether you've passed or failed. If you need to retake an exam, you have to schedule a new test with Prometric and pay another $125.

> **NOTE**
>
> The first time you fail a test, you can retake it the next day. However, if you fail a second time, you must wait 14 days before retaking that test. The 14-day waiting period remains in effect for all retakes after the second failure.

What This Book Will Do

This book is designed to be read as a pointer to the areas of knowledge you will be tested on. In other words, you might want to read this book one time just to get insight into how comprehensive your knowledge of this topic is. The book is also designed to be read shortly before you go for the actual test. You can use this book to get a sense of the underlying context of any topic in the chapters or to skim-read for Exam Alerts, bulleted points, summaries, and topic headings.

This book draws on material from Microsoft's own listing of knowledge requirements, from other preparation guides, and from the exams. It also draws from a battery of technical websites, as well as from my own experience with Microsoft servers and the exam. The goal is to walk you through the knowledge you will need. By reading this book, you will gain from the experience of real-world professional development.

What This Book Will Not Do

This book will not teach you everything you need to know about Active Directory in Windows Server 2008. The scope of the book is exam preparation. It is intended to ramp you up and give you confidence heading into the exam. This book is not intended as an introduction to Active Directory configuration. It reviews what you need to know before you take the test, with its fundamental purpose dedicated to reviewing the information needed on the Microsoft certification exam.

This book uses a variety of teaching and memorization techniques to analyze the exam-related topics and to provide you with everything you need to know to pass the test.

About This Book

Read this book from front to back. You won't be wasting your time because nothing written here is a guess about an unknown exam. I have had to explain certain underlying information on such a regular basis that I have included those explanations here.

After you have read this book, you can brush up on a certain area by using the index or the table of contents to go straight to the topics and questions you want to re-examine. I have tried to use the headings and subheadings to provide outline information about each given topic. After you have been certified, you will find this book useful as a tightly focused reference and an essential foundation of Active Directory configuration and management.

Each *Exam Cram* chapter follows a regular structure and offers graphical cues about especially important or useful material. The structure of a typical chapter is as follows:

- ▶ **Opening hotlists**—Each chapter begins with lists of the terms you need to understand and the concepts you need to master before you can be fully conversant in the chapter's subject matter. The hotlists are followed with a few introductory paragraphs, setting the stage for the rest of the chapter.

- ▶ **Topical coverage**—After the opening hotlists, each chapter covers the topics related to the chapter's subject.

- ▶ **Exam Alerts**—Throughout the text, the material that is most likely to appear on the exam is highlighted by using a special Exam Alert that looks like this:

EXAM ALERT

This is what an Exam Alert looks like. An Exam Alert stresses concepts, terms, or best practices that will most likely appear in at least one certification exam question. For that reason, any information presented in an Exam Alert is worthy of unusual attentiveness on your part.

Even if material is not flagged as an Exam Alert, all the content in this book is associated in some way with test-related material. What appears in the chapter content is critical knowledge.

▶ **Notes**—This book is an overall examination of Active Directory configuration, management, and troubleshooting. As such, it delves into many aspects of computer networks. Where a body of knowledge is deeper than the scope of the book, this book uses Notes to indicate areas of concern.

NOTE

Cramming for an exam will get you through a test, but it will not make you a competent Active Directory professional. Although you can memorize just the facts you need to become certified, your daily work in the field will rapidly put you in water over your head if you do not know the underlying principles.

▶ **Tips**—This book provides Tips that will help you build a better foundation of knowledge or to focus your attention on an important concept that reappears later in the book. Tips provide a helpful way to remind you of the context surrounding a particular area of a topic under discussion.

TIP

This is how Tips are formatted. Keep your eyes open for them, and you'll become an Active Directory configuration guru in no time!

▶ **Practice questions**—These present a short list of test questions related to the specific chapter topic. Following each question is an explanation of both correct and incorrect answers. The practice questions highlight the areas that are the most important on the exam.

The bulk of this book follows this chapter structure, but I would like to point out a few other elements:

▶ **Details and resources**—Appendix A at the end of this book is titled "Need to Know More?" This appendix provides direct pointers to Microsoft and third-party resources offering more details on each chapter's subject. If you find a resource you like in this collection, use it, but don't feel compelled to use all the resources. On the other hand, I recommend only resources that I use regularly, so none of my recommendations will be a waste of your time or money (but purchasing them all at once probably represents an expense that many network administrators and would-be MCTSs and MCITPs might find hard to justify).

▶ **Glossary**—This book has an extensive glossary of important terms used throughout the book.

▶ **The Cram Sheet**—This appears as a tearcard inside the front cover of this *Exam Cram* book. It is a valuable tool that represents a collection of the most difficult-to-remember facts and numbers you should memorize before taking the test. Remember, you can dump this information out of your head onto a piece of paper as soon as you enter the testing room. This tearcard has facts that require brute-force memorization. You need to remember this information only long enough to write it down when you walk into the test room. Be advised that you will be asked to surrender all personal belongings other than pencils before you enter the exam room.

You might want to look at the Cram Sheet in your car or in the lobby of the testing center just before you walk into the testing center. It is divided into exam objective headings, so you can review the appropriate parts just before each test.

Increasing numbers of people are attaining Microsoft certifications, so the goal is within reach. You can get all the real-world motivation you need from knowing that many others have gone before, so you can follow in their footsteps. If you're willing to tackle the process seriously and do what it takes to obtain the necessary experience and knowledge, you can take—and pass—all the certification tests involved in obtaining an MCITP certification. If you're willing to tackle the preparation process seriously and do what it takes to gain the necessary experience and knowledge, you can take and pass the exam. In fact, the *Exam Crams* and the companion *Exam Preps* are designed to make it as easy as possible for you to prepare for these exams, but prepare you must!

The Ideal MCITP Candidate

To give you some idea of what an ideal candidate is like, following is relevant information about the background and experience such an individual should have. Don't worry if you don't meet these qualifications or don't even come close—this is a far-from-ideal world, and where you fall short is simply where you have more work to do:

► Academic or professional training in network theory, concepts, and operations. This includes everything from networking media and transmission techniques to network operating systems, services, and applications.

► Three-plus years of professional networking experience, including experience with various types of networking media, including Ethernet and wireless. This must include installation, configuration, upgrading, and troubleshooting experience.

► Two-plus years in a networked environment that includes hands-on experience with Windows Server 2000/2003/2008, Windows 2000 Professional, Windows XP Professional, and Windows Vista Business/ Enterprise/Ultimate. A solid understanding of each system's architecture, installation, configuration, maintenance, and troubleshooting is also essential.

► Knowledge of the various methods for installing Windows Server 2008, including manual and automated installations and server virtualization. Appendix C, "Installing Windows Server 2008," takes a quick look at manual installation and use of virtual servers.

► A thorough understanding of networking protocols, most specifically versions 4 and 6 of TCP/IP. Knowledge of how Windows-based computers network with non-Windows computers such as Macintosh, UNIX, and Linux is also helpful.

▶ Familiarity with key Windows Server 2008–based TCP/IP-based services, including HTTP (web servers), DHCP, WINS, and DNS, plus familiarity with one or more of the following: Internet Information Services (IIS), Index Server, and Internet Security and Acceleration Server.

▶ An understanding of how to implement security for key network data in a Windows Server 2008 environment.

▶ A good working understanding of Active Directory. Obviously, this book prepares you for the Active Directory configuration exam, but it is helpful if you have real-world exposure to an Active Directory environment. The more you work with Windows Server 2008, the more you'll realize that this operating system is quite different from Windows NT. Newer technologies such as Active Directory have really changed the way that Windows is configured and used. Find out as much as you can about Active Directory, and acquire as much experience using this technology as possible. The time you take learning about Active Directory is time well spent!

Although a bachelor's degree in computer science can be helpful, a strong willingness to learn new techniques and technologies combined with as many of these qualifications as possible is key to your success. Well under half of all certification candidates possess such experience, and most meet less than half of these requirements—at least when they begin the certification process. But because all the people who already have been certified have survived this ordeal, you can survive it, too, especially if you heed what this Self-Assessment can tell you about what you already know and what you need to learn.

Put Yourself to the Test

The following series of questions and observations are designed to help you figure out how much work is ahead in pursuing your Microsoft certification and what kinds of resources you can consult on your quest. Be absolutely honest in your answers, or you'll end up wasting money on an exam you're not ready to take. There are no right or wrong answers—only steps along the path to certification. Only *you* can decide when you're ready.

Two things should be clear from the outset, however:

▶ Even a modest background in computer science will be helpful.

▶ Hands-on experience with Microsoft products and technologies is an essential ingredient for success.

ISBN 0-7897-3687-x) to guide your activities and studies, or you can work straight from Microsoft's test objectives if you prefer.

For any and all of these Microsoft exams, the *Resource Kits* for the topics involved are a good study resource. You can purchase soft cover *Resource Kits* from Microsoft Press. Along with the *Exam Cram* and *Exam Prep* series, *Resource Kits* are among the best tools you can use to prepare for Microsoft exams.

TIP

If you have the funds or your employer is willing to pay your way, consider taking a class led by a professional instructor. In particular, those just starting out or with limited knowledge or access to state-of-the-art computer systems should take a class. Microsoft has designed very good courses that are available in most communities. In addition, the course includes trial versions of the software that is the focus of your course, along with the operating system that it requires.

Testing Your Exam Readiness

Whether you attend a formal class on a specific topic to get ready for an exam or use written materials to study on your own, some preparation for the certification exams is essential. You pay for your exam attempts pass or fail, so you want to do everything you can to pass on your first try. Not only can failed attempts be expensive to your pocketbook, but they can be very discouraging.

This book includes *Exam Cram* questions at the end of each chapter as well as two practice exams, so if you don't score well on the chapter questions, you can study more and then tackle the practice exams at the end of the book.

For any given subject, consider taking a class if you've tackled self-study materials, taken the practice test, and failed anyway. If you can afford the privilege, the opportunity to interact with an instructor and fellow students can make all the difference in the world. For information about systems auditing classes, visit the Microsoft Learning page at http://learning.microsoft.com/Manager/Catalog.aspx.

If you can't afford to take a class, visit the Microsoft Learning page anyway, because it also includes pointers to free practice exams and to Microsoft Certified Professional Approved Study Guides and other self-study tools. Even if you can't afford to spend much, you should still invest in some low-cost practice exams from commercial vendors.

6. Have you taken a practice exam on your chosen test subject? (Yes or No)

If Yes and you scored 90 percent or better, you're probably ready to tackle the real thing. If your score isn't above that crucial threshold, keep at it until you break that barrier. If you answered No, go back and study the book some more, and repeat the practice exams. Keep at it until you can comfortably break the passing threshold.

TIP

There is no better way to assess your test readiness than to take a good-quality practice exam and pass with a score of 90% or better. When I'm preparing, I shoot for 95%, just to leave room for the "weirdness factor" that sometimes shows up on Microsoft exams.

One last note: I hope it makes sense to stress the importance of hands-on experience in the context of the exams. As you review the material for the exams, you'll realize that hands-on experience with server configuration and best practices is invaluable.

Well, Let's Get to It

After you've assessed your readiness, undertaken the right background studies, obtained the hands-on experience that will help you understand the products and technologies at work, and reviewed the many sources of information to help you prepare for a test, you'll be ready to take a round of practice tests. When your scores come back positive enough to get you through the exam, you're ready to go after the real thing. If you follow our assessment regimen, you'll not only know what you need to study, but you'll know when you're ready to take the exam. Good luck!

Beginning with Windows 2000, Microsoft completely revolutionized its concept of Windows domains. Gone was the limited size, flat namespace of Windows NT domains, and in its place was the hierarchical Active Directory domain structure built upon the concepts of X.500 and Lightweight Directory Access Protocol (LDAP). Active Directory has matured since its beginnings with Windows Server 2003 and now Windows Server 2008's new features, improved functionality, and ease of configuration and management. Those of you who have worked with Active Directory in Windows 2000 or Windows Server 2003 will be familiar with much of the content of this book. For those of you who are new to server and network management or who have worked with only Windows NT networks, this book begins with a brief introduction to the concepts that Microsoft used to put Active Directory together.

The Building Blocks of Active Directory

In creating the hierarchical database structure of Active Directory, Microsoft facilitated locating resources such as folders and printers by name rather than by physical location. These logical building blocks include domains, trees, forests, and organizational units (OU). The physical location of objects within Active Directory is represented by including all objects in a given location in its own site.

Domains

Similar to the case in Windows NT, the *domain* represents the core unit of the network structure. As in Windows NT, the domain is a logical grouping of computers that shares a common directory database and security. However, whereas in Windows NT each domain was a unit unto itself with no default trust relationship with other domains, in Active Directory you can have a series of domains organized into larger units called trees and forests, with inherent trust relationships already built into them. Individuals can be designated with administrative powers over a single domain or across an entire forest, and you can even configure trust relationships to external forests. Furthermore, Active Directory domains can hold millions of objects, as opposed to the Windows NT domain structure, which was limited to approximately 40,000 objects.

Trees

A tree is a group of domains that shares a contiguous namespace. In other words, a tree consists of a parent domain plus one or more sets of child domains whose name reflects that of a parent. For example, a parent domain named examcram.com can include child domains with names such as products. examcram.com, sales.examcram.com, and manufacturing.examcram.com. Furthermore, the tree structure can contain grandchild domains such as america.sales.examcram.com or europe.sales.examcram.com, and so on, as shown in Figure 1.1. All domains in a tree are linked with two-way, transitive trust relationships; in other words, accounts in any one domain can access resources in another domain and vice versa. See Chapter 5, "Active Directory Objects and Trusts," for more information on trust relationships.

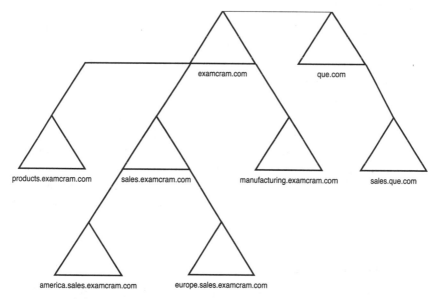

FIGURE 1.1 A forest can contain multiple trees, and trees can contain multiple levels of child domains.

Forests

A forest consists of a group of domain trees that do not share a contiguous namespace. For example, you can have two trees with parent domains named examcram.com and que.com, as shown in Figure 1.1. Each tree can contain its own child domains within its namespace. Again, two-way transitive trust relationships exist between domains in the trees of a single forest. When you create a new Active Directory structure, the first domain created is the *forest root* domain.

Organizational Units

An *organizational unit (OU)* is a logical subgroup within a domain. It is convenient for locating resources used by a single work group, section, or department in a company and applying policies that apply to only these resources. You can create a hierarchy of OUs and child OUs organized in much the same way as that of a hierarchy of folders, subfolders, and sub-subfolders on a disk. You can also delegate control of administrative activities to users within a single OU, such as creating and working with user accounts, groups, and printers. Further, you can control users and computers within an OU by means of Group Policy; this is the smallest unit to which you can deploy Group Policy.

Sites

In contrast to the logical grouping of Active Directory into forests, trees, domains, and OUs, Microsoft includes the concept of *sites* to group resources within a forest according to their physical location or subnet. A site can contain objects from more than one tree or domain within a single forest, and individual trees and domains can encompass more than one site. The use of sites enables you to control the replication of data within the Active Directory database as well as to apply policies to all users and computers or delegate administrative control to these objects within a single physical location. In addition, sites enable users to be authenticated by domain controllers in the same physical location rather than a distant location as often as possible. You should configure a single site for all work locations connected within a high-speed, always-available local area network (LAN) link and designate additional sites for locations separated from each other by a slower wide area network (WAN) link.

Domain Controllers

Any server that has Active Directory installed is a *domain controller*. These servers authenticate all users logging on to their domain, and they serve as centers where you can administer Active Directory in Windows Server 2008. A domain controller stores a complete copy of all objects contained within the domain, plus the schema and configuration information relevant to the forest where the domain is located. Unlike Windows NT, Active Directory has no primary or backup domain controllers. Similar to Windows 2000 and Windows Server 2003, all domain controllers hold a master, editable copy of the Active Directory database.

Global Catalog

The *global catalog* is a subset of domain information created for the purpose of enabling domain controllers in other domains in the same forest to locate resources in any domain. Users searching for objects such as files, folders, or printers in another domain are directed to a global catalog for searching the entire directory database. A global catalog server provides information on universal group membership, which can include users or groups from any domain in the forest. The global catalog server also enables users to log on to a domain other than their home domain by using their *user principal name (UPN)*, which is a username constructed in the format of an email address (for example, user@products.examcram.com).

Operations Masters

Microsoft designed Active Directory in such a fashion that you can perform most configuration activities from any domain controller. However, certain functions within the directory are restricted to specific domain controllers, which are known as *flexible single-master operations (FSMO) servers*, or simply *operations masters*. These functions include the following:

* ▶ **Schema master**—Holds the only writable copy of the Active Directory Schema. This is a configuration database that describes all available object and function types in the Active Directory forest. Only one domain controller in the forest holds this role.

* ▶ **Domain naming master**—Ensures that any newly created domains are uniquely identified by names that adhere to the proper naming conventions for new trees or child domains in existing trees. Only one domain controller in the forest holds this role.

* ▶ **PDC emulator**—Serves as a primary domain controller (PDC) for Windows NT 4.0 client computers authenticating to the domain and processes any changes to user properties on these clients, such as password changes. This server also acts as a time synchronization master to synchronize the time on the remaining domain controllers in the domain. One domain controller in each domain holds this role.

* ▶ **Infrastructure master**—Updates references in its domain from objects such as domain group memberships to objects in other domains. This server processes any changes in objects in the forest received from global catalog servers and replicates these changes to other domain controllers in its domain. One domain controller in each domain holds this role.

▶ **RID master**—Assigns security identifiers (SIDs) to objects created in its domain. A SID consists of a domain identifier common to all objects in its domain and a relative identifier (RID) that is unique to each object. This server ensures that no two objects have the same RID and hands out pools of RIDs to every domain controller in its domain. One domain controller in each domain holds this role.

New Features of Active Directory in Windows Server 2008

As with each previous version of Windows Server, Microsoft has introduced many new components that improve the functionality and manageability of Active Directory and of Windows Server 2008 as a whole. This section briefly summarizes these components, most of which you will learn about later in this book:

▶ **Server roles and features**—Microsoft has organized the capabilities of a computer into various roles and features. Simply put, a *role* is a specific function that a server can perform on the network, including file services, terminal services, and certificate services. Active Directory Domain Services (AD DS) is the server role that encompasses all domain control functions. A *feature* is an optional component that adds a specific function, such as .NET Framework 3.0, BitLocker Drive Encryption, Network Load Balancing, and so on. Certain roles require specific features to be installed, and these are automatically installed when you add this role. You can add roles and features from the Initial Configuration Tasks window, the Server Manager, or the command line. These are discussed later in this chapter.

▶ **Read-only domain controller**—A *read-only domain controller (RODC)* is a domain controller that contains a read-only copy of the directory database. It can perform all client-based actions, such as authenticating users and distributing group policies to clients, but administrators cannot make changes to the database directly from the RODC. It is particularly useful for branch office deployment, where security might not be as high as in the central office and no administrative personnel are present for day-to-day operations.

▶ **Server Core**—A *Server Core* is a stripped-down version of Windows Server 2008 that does not contain a GUI, the taskbar, or the Start menu.

After logging on, you are presented with a command prompt window, where you perform all administrative actions. A Server Core computer uses less hardware and memory resources than a normal server, and it is able to perform most (but not all) of the roles that a normal server performs. Furthermore, a Server Core computer is more secure because it presents a smaller attack footprint than a normal server.

▶ **Restartable Active Directory Domain Services**—You can now perform many actions, such as offline defragmentation of the database, simply by stopping Active Directory. This reduces the number of instances that you must restart the server in Directory Services Restore Mode; thereby, it reduces the length of time the domain controller is unavailable to serve requests from client computers.

▶ **Active Directory Certificate Services (AD CS)**—Certificate Services has been enhanced considerably from Windows Server 2003. For example, you can enroll network devices such as routers for certificates, you can use new certificate templates that support new cryptographic algorithms, you can designate several limited roles for delegating administrative tasks to different individuals, and you can use the online responder service as an alternative to traditional certificate revocation lists.

▶ **Active Directory Lightweight Directory Services (AD LDS)**— Microsoft has enhanced and modified the previous Active Directory Application Mode (ADAM) feature introduced in Windows Server 2003 Release 2 (R2).

▶ **Active Directory Rights Management Services (AD RMS)**—Microsoft has added numerous features, such as a new interface, delegation of administration, and integration with Active Directory Federation Services (AD FS).

▶ **Enhancements to Group Policy**—Microsoft has added many new policy settings. In particular, these settings enhance the management of Windows Vista client computers. All policy management is now handled by means of the Group Policy Management Console (GPMC), which was an optional feature first added to Windows Server 2003 R2. In addition, Microsoft has added new auditing capabilities to Group Policy and added a searchable database for locating policy settings from within GPMC.

▶ **Fine-Grained Password Policies**—Microsoft has added the capability to apply granular password and account lockout policy settings to different sets of users within the same domain.

TIP

If you do not want Server Manager to open when you start your domain controller, select the check box labeled Do Not Show Me This Console at Logon, found on the Server Summary page of Server Manager.

Adding Roles and Features

Server Manager facilitates the adding of roles and features. To add a role, right-click Roles in the console tree and choose Add Roles. This starts the Add Roles Wizard. Figure 1.3 shows the roles you can add to the server using this wizard. To add a feature, right-click Features and choose Add Features. Simply follow the instructions provided by the wizard, and reboot the server if requested.

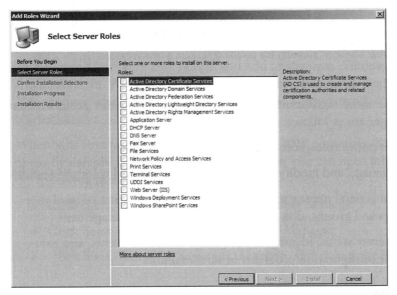

FIGURE 1.3 The Add Roles Wizard enables you to select from a series of roles that you can add to your server.

This book discusses Active Directory–related uses of Server Manager throughout. For further information on other uses of Server Manager, refer to Appendix A, "Need to Know More?" or refer to the *Exam Cram* books for Exams 70-642, 70-643, 70-646, or 70-647.

Command-Line Server Management

Server Manager also provides a command-line version, `ServerManagerCmd.exe`. You can perform many tasks without the GUI, such as adding or removing roles, role services, and features. You can use the command-line version from either the full version of Windows Server 2008 or from Server Core. To obtain information on the available commands, open a command prompt and type `ServerManagerCmd /?`.

Configuring Forests and Domains

As already mentioned, the domain is the primary administrative unit in Active Directory. Windows Server 2008 uses the concept of domains to separate available resources among registered users. Therefore, all activities of planning and implementing an Active Directory namespace arise from the viewpoint of the domain structure.

The first domain installed in any Active Directory setup is always the forest root domain. All subdomains in the forest root domain tree contain the root domain name in their own domain name. Domains in another tree contain a different domain name structure. In addition, the top-level domain names are defined in the DNS hierarchy that will be established in the forest.

> **CAUTION**
>
> Before installing Active Directory for the first time on any company network, you need to plan the proposed domain namespace. Decide how many domains your forest needs and whether multiple trees or child domains are needed. Refer to *Exam Cram* or *Exam Prep* books on Exams 70-298, 70-646, or 70-647 for details of planning a domain namespace.

Requirements for Installing Active Directory Domain Services

Before you can install AD DS, you must have at least one server that meets the following requirements:

- **Operating system**—The server must be running the Standard, Enterprise, or Datacenter edition of Windows Server 2008. Note that a server running the Web edition cannot act as a domain controller.

- **Adequate hard disk space**—Beyond the space used for installing Windows Server 2008, the server must have a minimum of 500MB of

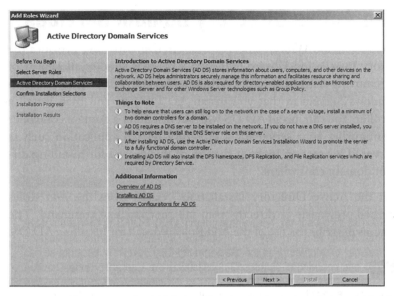

FIGURE 1.4   You can use the Add Roles Wizard to begin the installation of AD DS.

3. Note the information provided on the Confirm Installation Selections page, and then click Install to begin installing Active Directory.

4. The wizard displays an Installation Progress page that charts the progress of installation. After a few minutes, it informs you that the AD DS role has been installed successfully. Click Close to exit the wizard and return to Server Manager.

5. Scroll down to the Roles Summary section of Server Manager. Note that Active Directory Domain Services is shown as having been installed. It is marked with a red *X* because Active Directory itself has not yet been installed. Click the Active Directory Domain Services link.

6. You are informed that the server has not been promoted to a domain controller. Click the link provided to run the AD DS Installation Wizard.

7. This wizard opens with a Welcome page. Click Next.

8. On the Choose a Deployment Configuration page shown in Figure 1.5, select Create a New Domain in a New Forest, and then click Next. On this page, you would select the Existing Forest option when creating a new domain in an existing forest or adding a domain controller to an existing domain. These options are discussed later in this chapter.

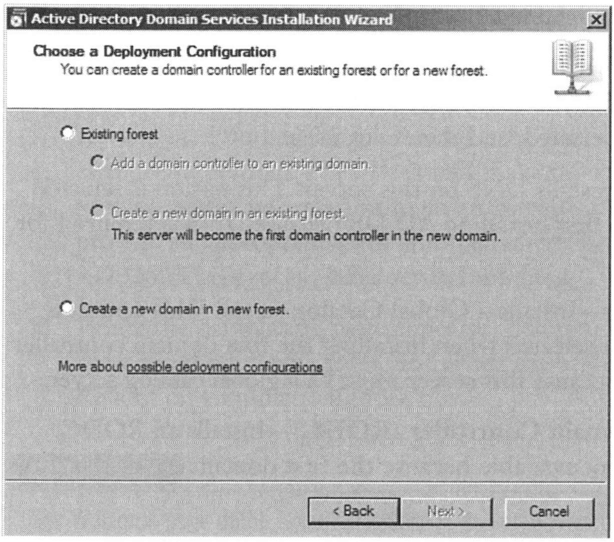

FIGURE 1.5 The wizard provides options for installing a domain controller in an existing forest or a new one.

9. Type the full DNS name of the forest root domain, and then click Next.

10. The wizard verifies the forest and NetBIOS names and then displays the Forest Functional Level page shown in Figure 1.6. Select the appropriate forest functional level, and then click Next. The available domain and forest functional levels are discussed later in this chapter.

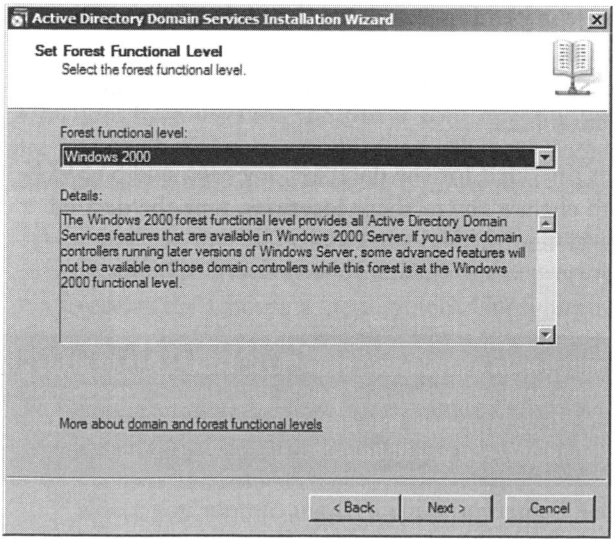

FIGURE 1.6 The wizard enables you to select from one of three forest functional levels.

4. On the Name the New Domain page shown in Figure 1.7, type the name of the parent and child domains in the spaces provided. The new domain will be created as a child domain or new tree automatically depending on the name you provide. Then click Next.

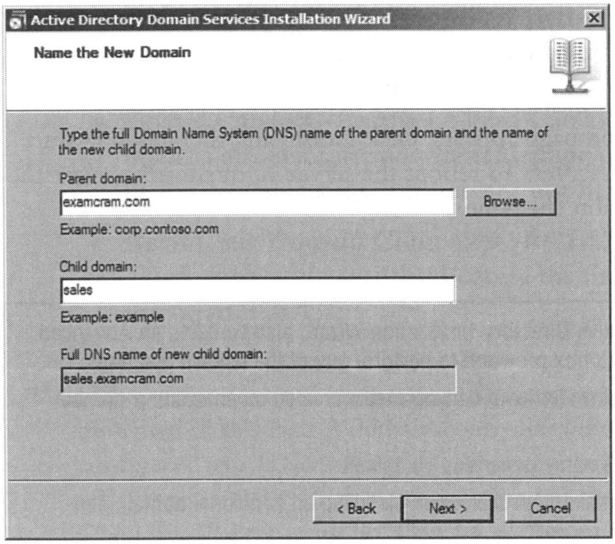

FIGURE 1.7 You create a child domain name from the name of the parent domain and the new top-level name on the Name the New Domain page.

5. On the Set Domain Functional Level page, select the required functional level and then click Next. Domain functional levels are discussed later in this chapter.

6. On the Select a Site page, select an appropriate site and then click Next. Sites are discussed in Chapter 3, "Active Directory Sites and Replication."

7. Complete the installation of the domain controller according to steps 13 to 18 of the previous procedure.

Existing Domains

Installing additional domain controllers in an existing domain is important for the following reasons:

▶ Doing so adds fault tolerance and load balancing to the domain. In other words, additional domain controllers help share the load and improve performance.

- ▶ Users logging on to the domain can connect to any available domain controller for authentication.

- ▶ Users at a remote location can connect to a domain controller at their site rather than making a slow connection across a WAN link.

- ▶ If a domain controller should become unavailable because of a network or hardware failure, users can still log on to the domain.

To install an additional domain controller in an existing domain, follow the same procedure as in the previous section, except select the Add a Domain Controller to an Existing Domain option shown in Figure 1.5. Then select the proper domain from the Select a Domain page. (This page displays all available domains in the forest.) The remainder of the procedure is the same as that for creating a new domain in an existing forest, except that the Set Domain Functional Level page does not appear.

Verifying the Proper Installation of Active Directory

After you have installed Active Directory, you should perform several steps to verify that the proper components have been installed. Click Start, Administrative Tools. You should see links to three Active Directory management tools: Active Directory Domains and Trusts, Active Directory Sites and Services, and Active Directory Users and Computers. You should also see a link to the DNS snap-in, unless you have specified another server as the DNS server for your domain.

Open Active Directory Users and Computers. You should see the default containers Builtin, Computers, ForeignSecurityPrincipals, and Users under the domain you have created. You should also see a default Domain Controllers OU. Select this OU and verify that computer accounts for all domain controllers in the domain are present, as shown in Figure 1.8.

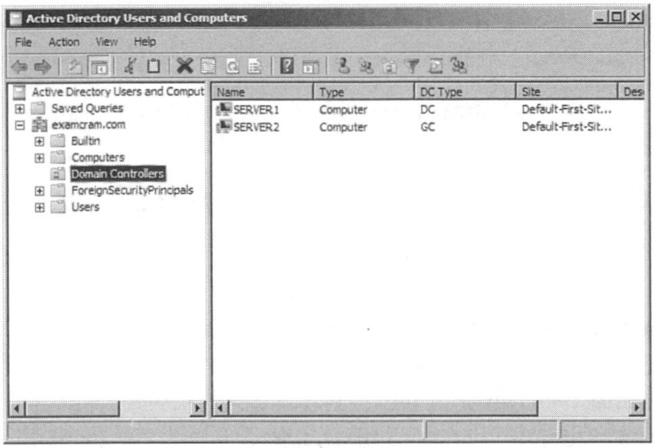

FIGURE 1.8 After installing Active Directory, you should see a default set of containers in the Active Directory Users and Computers, together with domain controller computer accounts in the Domain Controllers OU.

Performing Unattended Installations of Active Directory

Windows Server 2008 enables you to specify parameters for Active Directory installation in an answer file that you can use to facilitate the installation of multiple domain controllers. This file is formatted as a simple text file containing the statement [DCINSTALL] on the first line followed by statements in the form *option=value*. Table 1.1 describes several of the more common options you can use in this file.

TABLE 1.1   Several Options Used for Unattended Domain Controller Installation

Option	Value	Meaning
UserName	Username of administrative user	Installs the domain controller in the context of this user.
Password	User's password | *	Password of user installing the domain controller. Use * to prompt for the password.
ReplicaOr NewDomain	Domain | Replica | ReadOnlyReplica	Specifies whether to install a new domain, an additional domain controller (replica) in an existing domain, or an RODC in an existing domain.
ReplicaDomain DNSName	Existing domain name	Specifies the fully qualified domain name (FQDN) of the domain where you are installing an additional domain controller.

TABLE 1.1 *Continued*

Option	Value	Meaning
NewDomain	Forest | Tree | Child	Specifies whether to install a new forest, a new tree in an existing forest, or a child domain.
NewDomainDNSName	Domain name to be created	Specifies the FQDN for a new domain.
ParentDomain DNSName	Parent domain name	Specifies the FQDN of the parent domain when creating a child domain.
ChildName	Child domain name	Specifies the top-level DNS name of the child domain. This name is prefixed to the parent name to create the FQDN of the child domain.
ForestLevel	0 | 2 | 3	Specifies the forest functional level of a new forest: 0 = Windows 2000 2 = Windows Server 2003 3 = Windows Server 2008
DomainLevel	0 | 2 | 3	Specifies the domain functional level of a new domain. Parameters have the same meaning as above.
InstallDNS	Yes | No	Specifies whether a DNS server is installed.
ConfirmGC	Yes | No	Specifies whether the domain controller is installed as a global catalog server.
DatabasePath	Path to database folder	Default is %systemroot%\NTDS.
LogPath	Path to log folder	Default is %systemroot%\NTDS.
SysvolPath	Path to SYSVOL folder	Default is %systemroot%\ SYSVOL.
RebootOn Completion	Yes | No	Specifies whether to restart the computer on completion, regardless of success.

Many additional options are available, including options specific to the demotion of domain controllers. For additional information, consult "Appendix of Unattended Installation Parameters" in Appendix A.

To perform an unattended installation of a domain controller, open a command prompt and type the following command:

```
Dcpromo /answer:<path_to_answer_file>
```

In this command, *<path_to_answer_file>* specifies the complete path to the unattended answer file containing the parameters specified in Table 1.1. You can also include any of these parameters in the command line by prefixing each of them with the / character. The output to the command prompt tracks the progress of promotion, and then the server automatically reboots if the RebootOnCompletion parameter has been specified.

Server Core Domain Controllers

You cannot use Server Manager or a simple execution of dcpromo to promote a Server Core machine to a domain controller. You must use an unattended installation answer file in a similar manner to that described in the previous section. This file must include the information required to identify the domain being joined, including the username and password for a domain administrator account.

For further information on the use of Server Core, including its use as a domain controller, refer to "Server Core Installation Option of Windows Server 2008 Step-by-Step Guide" in Appendix A.

Active Directory Migration Tool (ADMT) v.3.1

ADMT v.3.1, a utility available for download from the Microsoft website (http://www.microsoft.com/downloads/details.aspx?FamilyID=ae279d01-7dca-413c-a9d2-b42dfb746059&DisplayLang=en), enables you to move users, groups, computers, and other objects from a Windows NT 4.0 domain to an Active Directory domain or to move objects between Active Directory domains in the same or different forests. It requires trust relationships between the domains in use to ensure data security during the migration process.

ADMT is particularly useful when restructuring a series of Windows NT 4.0 domains (such as account and resource domains structured into a multiple trust model) into a single Active Directory domain. Actions performed by ADMT include the following:

▶ Migrates objects in a Windows NT domain to an OU in the Active Directory domain

▶ Ensures security of objects being migrated by using 128-bit encryption with the Passport Export Server (PES) service

▶ Preserves the SID history of objects being migrated

▶ Enables migration of user profiles

▶ Migrates computer accounts, including domain controllers

▶ Enables the restructuring of Active Directory domains between forests

▶ Enables you to use a preconfigured SQL database to hold migration information

▶ Enables you to perform test migrations so you can ensure that the actual migration will run properly

▶ Provides a log file that you can check for migration errors and other problems

▶ Provides for rollback options if the migration does not proceed properly

▶ Facilitates the decommissioning of old domains, both NT 4.0 and Active Directory domains in forests to be removed

Alternate User Principal Name (UPN) Suffixes

As mentioned earlier in this chapter, a UPN is a logon name specified in the format of an email address, such as user@examcram.com. It is a convenient means of logging on to a domain from a computer located in another domain in the forest or a trusted forest. Two types of UPNs are available:

▶ **Implicit UPN**—This UPN is always in the form user@domain, such as peter@sales.examcram.com. It is defined on the Account tab of a user's Properties dialog box in Active Directory Users and Computers.

▶ **Explicit UPN**—This UPN is in the form string1@string2, where an administrator can define values for each string. For example, a user named Peter in the sales.examcram.com domain could have an explicit UPN in the form peter@sales. Using explicit UPNs is practical when an organization does not want to reveal its internal domain structure.

Windows Server 2008 supports the principle of the *UPN suffix*, introduced in Windows Server 2003. This is the portion of the UPN to the right of the at (@) character. By default, the UPN suffix is the DNS domain name of the user account.

Adding an alternate UPN suffix provides several advantages:

▸ You can use a common UPN suffix across all users in a forest. This is especially useful if some users have long domain names.

▸ The UPN suffix enables you to conceal the actual domain structure of the forest from external users.

▸ You can use separate UPN suffixes when different divisions of a company have separate email domain names, thereby enabling users to log on with a name that matches their email address.

To define an alternate UPN suffix, access Active Directory Domains and Trusts from the Administrative Tools folder. Right-click Active Directory Domains and Trusts and click Properties. From the Properties dialog box shown in Figure 1.9, type the name of the alternate UPN suffix desired, click Add, and then click OK. After you have done this, the alternate UPN suffix is available when you are configuring new or existing user accounts. For more information on configuring user accounts, see Chapter 5.

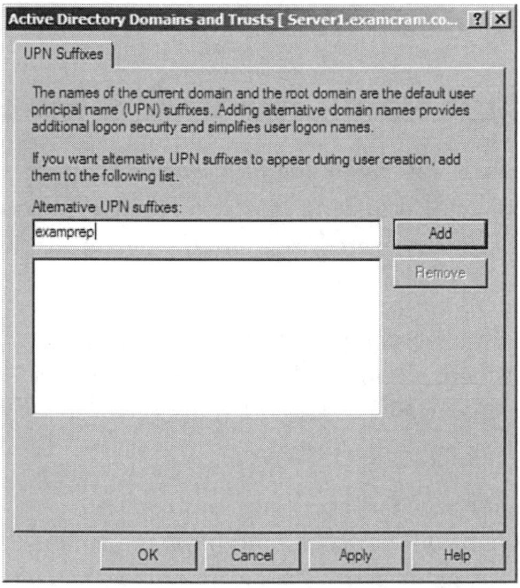

FIGURE 1.9 You can configure alternate UPN suffixes from the Active Directory Domains and Trusts Properties dialog box.

Removing Active Directory

The Active Directory Installation Wizard also enables you to remove Active Directory from a domain controller, thereby demoting it to a member server. Proceed as follows:

1. Click Start, Run, type **dcpromo**, and then press Enter.

2. Windows checks if Active Directory Domain Services is installed; then it displays the Welcome page. Click Next.

3. If you receive a message warning you of the effects of removing a global catalog server, click OK.

4. You receive the Delete the Domain page shown in Figure 1.10. Note all the warnings displayed about the effects of removing a domain. Select the check box only if you are removing the last domain controller from its domain, and then click Next.

5. You receive the Application Directory Partitions page if the server holds the last replica of any application directory partitions. Click Next, select the check box labeled Delete All Application Directory Partitions on This Domain Controller, and then click Next again to remove the application directory partitions.

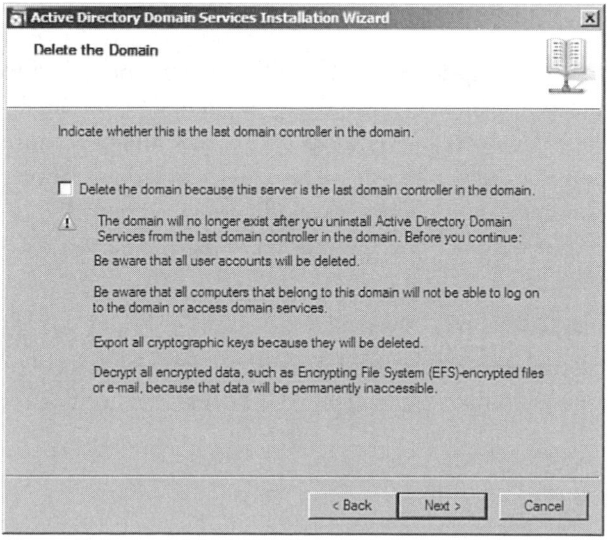

FIGURE 1.10 When you demote a domain controller, you are warned of the effects of deleting the domain.

6. Type and confirm a password for the local Administrator account on the server, and then click Next.

7. Read the information provided on the Summary page. If you need to make changes, click Back. When ready, click Next to demote the server.

8. When the demotion is finished, click Finish, and then click Restart Now to restart the server. To reboot the server automatically, select the Reboot on Completion check box.

NOTE

While this procedure demotes the computer to a member server, it does not remove AD DS. If you want to remove AD DS after demoting the server, use the Remove Roles Wizard available from Server Manager after restarting the server.

Upgrading from Windows Server 2003

Many organizations have created Active Directory domains based on Windows 2000 or Windows Server 2003 domain controllers and are now in a position to take advantage of the new features of Windows Server 2008 Active Directory. You can add new Windows Server 2008 domain controllers to an existing older Active Directory forest or upgrade all domain controllers in the forest to Windows Server 2008.

You can also upgrade an existing Windows Server 2003 domain controller to Windows Server 2008. Refer to Appendix C, "Installing Windows Server 2008," for information on upgrading Windows Server 2003 computers; the procedure outlined in this chapter automatically upgrades AD DS to Windows Server 2008. However, you cannot upgrade a Windows 2000 domain controller to Windows Server 2008 directly; you must first upgrade to Windows Server 2003 and then to Windows Server 2008.

Note that to upgrade a Windows Server 2003 domain controller to Windows Server 2008, you must first run the Adprep utility to upgrade the schema for accepting Windows Server 2008 domain controllers. We discuss this utility later in this chapter.

Interoperability with Previous Versions of Active Directory

As summarized earlier in this chapter, Active Directory in Windows Server 2008 introduces numerous additional features not supported by previous versions of Windows Server. Many of these features limit the interoperability of Windows Server 2008 with previous versions, and Microsoft has extended the concept of domain and forest functional levels to define the actions that can be done on a network that includes older domain controllers.

This section looks at these functional levels and the tools used for upgrading an older Active Directory network to Windows Server 2008.

Forest and Domain Functional Levels

Table 1.2 summarizes the forest and domain functional levels supported by Active Directory in Windows Server 2008.

TABLE 1.2   Forest and Domain Functional Levels in Windows Server 2008 Active Directory

Forest Functional Level	Domain Functional Levels Supported	Domain Controllers Supported
Windows 2000	Windows 2000	Windows 2000
	Windows Server 2003 native	Windows Server 2003
	Windows Server 2008 native	Windows Server 2008
Windows Server 2003 native	Windows Server 2003 native	Windows Server 2003
	Windows Server 2008 native	Windows Server 2008
Windows Server 2008 native	Windows Server 2008 native	Windows Server 2008

To use the functionality provided by Windows Server 2008 Active Directory, you must upgrade all domain controllers to Windows Server 2008 and upgrade the functional levels accordingly. A domain running at the Windows Server 2008 domain functional level located in a forest running at a lower functional level supports domain-based Windows Server 2008 Active Directory features but not forest-based ones.

> **NOTE**
>
> You can deploy an RODC to a domain in which the domain and forest functional levels are set to either Windows Server 2003 or Windows Server 2008.

EXAM ALERT

Remember that you must run `adprep /forestprep` on the schema master, and you must run it before you run `adprep /domainprep`. Also remember that you must run `adprep /domainprep` on the infrastructure master of each domain where you want to introduce a Windows Server 2008 domain controller and that you must complete these commands before promoting or upgrading an existing domain controller.

Upgrading a Windows Server 2003 Domain Controller

You can upgrade a Windows Server 2003 domain controller to Windows Server 2008, provided the server meets the hardware requirements discussed in Appendix C.

Before upgrading the first Windows Server 2003 domain controller, ensure that you have run the `Adprep /forestprep` and `Adprep /domainprep` commands and that these commands have completed without error. Then select the Install Now command from the Welcome screen displayed by the Windows Server 2008 DVD-ROM, and follow the instructions provided by the Installation Wizard and summarized in Appendix C.

Configuring Global Catalog Servers

A global catalog (GC) server maintains a subset of information pertaining to all objects located in its domain, plus summary information pertaining to objects in other domains of its forest. In doing so, a GC server enables the following features:

- ▶ It validates universal group memberships at logon.

- ▶ It enables users to search the entire forest for resources they might need to access.

- ▶ It validates UPNs across the entire forest, thereby enabling user logon in other domains.

CAUTION

You should have at least two GC servers in each domain for fault tolerance purposes.

Promotion of Domain Controllers to Global Catalog Servers

By default, the first domain controller in each domain is automatically designated as a GC server. You can designate additional GCs from the Active Directory Sites and Services snap-in, by performing the following steps:

1. Expand the Sites container, and expand the site in which the domain controller is located.

2. Expand the Servers container, and expand the entry for the domain controller to be designated as a GC.

3. Right-click NTDS Settings and choose Properties.

4. In the General tab of the NTDS Settings Properties dialog box, select the Global Catalog check box and click OK or Apply, as shown in Figure 1.12.

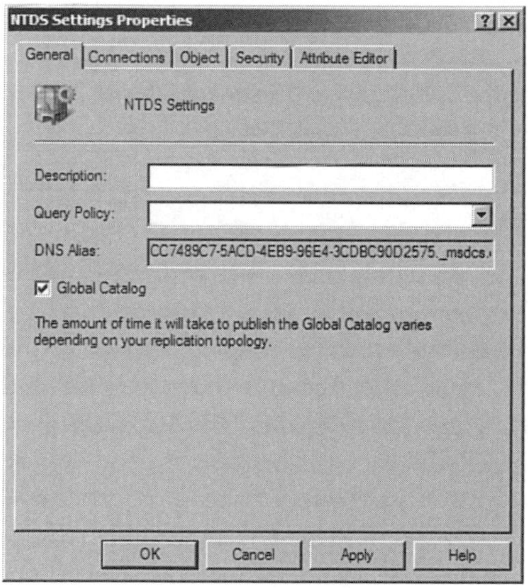

FIGURE 1.12 Designating an additional global catalog server.

You can also remove a GC server; simply clear the Global Catalog check box shown in Figure 1.12.

Universal Group Membership Caching (UGMC)

A universal group is a group that can contain users or global groups from any domain in the forest. You can use this group scope to grant permissions for accessing resources in any domain in the forest, either directly or by adding the group to domain local groups in other domains.

As already mentioned, GC servers store universal group membership information. It is important that this information is available so that a user receives a complete access token upon logon. The logon fails if a GC server is unavailable for any reason. Microsoft provides another mechanism for obtaining universal group information in the absence of a GC server—universal group membership caching (UGMC). When you configure UGMC, any domain controller that services a user's logon stores the user's universal group information when he logs on to that domain controller for the first time. At subsequent logons, the domain controller can verify the user's universal group membership information without contacting a GC server. This speeds up the logon process and ensures that it will complete successfully even if a GC server is unavailable.

> **CAUTION**
>
> You should be aware that the GC server still must be available if the user has never logged on to this particular domain controller previously. UGMC then caches this user's universal group membership information.

It is most practical to employ UGMC in a small branch office connected to the head office with a low-bandwidth WAN connection and low-end servers, where the replication load might place an undesirable load on either the server or the connection. You can enable UGMC from the Active Directory Sites and Services snap-in. Select the site where you want to enable UGMC, right-click the NTDS Site Settings object in the details pane of this snap-in, and choose Properties. On the Site Settings tab of the NTDS Site Settings Properties dialog box shown in Figure 1.13, select the Universal Group Membership Caching check box, and click OK or Apply. If you want to select a specific site where UGMC data is replicated, select the site from the Refresh Cache From drop-down list.

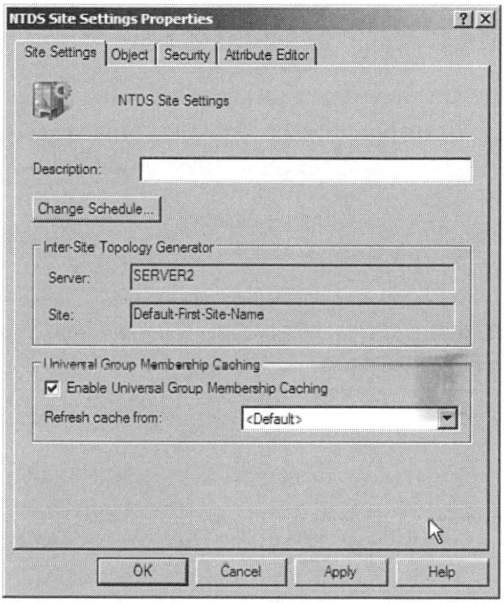

FIGURE 1.13 Enabling universal group membership caching.

EXAM ALERT

An exam question might offer the choice between designating additional global GC servers or enabling UGMC. If the question informs you that logons are slow and does not mention slow resource access, the most likely answer is to enable UGMC. If the question informs you that resource access across a WAN is slow, you should configure a GC server. Also remember that you do not need to enable both a GC and a UGMC at the same site. Furthermore, in a single domain forest, neither additional GC servers nor UGMC provides benefit.

Partial Attribute Sets

The *partial attribute set* is a schema attribute that tracks the internal replication status of partial replicas, such as those found on GC servers. Attributes included in the partial attribute set are those that are required by the schema plus the attributes most commonly utilized during user search activities. Storing these attributes in the global catalog improves the efficiency of user searches by reducing the amount of network activity required.

The Active Directory Schema and its configuration are discussed later in this chapter.

Configuring Operations Masters

Earlier in this chapter, you read about the five operations masters roles, which are initially held on the first domain controller in each domain. This section looks at configuring these roles as well as several problems that might arise if these roles become unavailable.

> **NOTE**
>
> An RODC cannot host any of the operations masters roles, because the nature of these roles requires the capability to write to the AD DS database.

Schema Master

The schema master holds the only writable copy of the Active Directory Schema. Briefly stated, the schema is a set of rules that define the classes of objects and their attributes that can be created in the directory. All domains in the forest share a common schema, which is replicated to all domain controllers in the forest. Only one schema master is present in the forest.

You should be aware of the following definitions as they relate to the schema:

- **Object**—A specific item that can be cataloged in Active Directory. Some types of objects include OUs, users, computers, folders, files, and printers. When you first install Active Directory, the default schema contains definitions of commonly used objects and their properties.

- **Container**—A type of object that can hold other objects. The schema contains the Classes and Attributes containers. Default containers are also created when you first install Active Directory.

- **Attribute**—A distinct characteristic held by a specific object. For example, a user object holds attributes such as the username, full name, and email address. In general, objects in the same container have the same type of attributes but are characterized by different values of these attributes. The extent of attributes that can be specified for any object is defined by an `attributeSchema` object in the schema.

- **Class**—A series of attributes associated with each object. The attributes associated with each class are defined by a `classSchema` object in the schema.

For further information on object classes, their characteristics, and a description of the key attributes of a `classSchema` object, see "Characteristics of Object Classes" in Appendix A. For similar information for attributes, see "Characteristics of Attributes" in Appendix A.

> **CAUTION**
>
> Improper modifications of the schema can cause irreparable harm to Active Directory. For this reason, Microsoft created a global group called Schema Admins, and only members of this group can perform such modifications. As a best practice to avoid unauthorized modifications, you should remove all users from this group and add a user only when it is necessary to modify the schema. In addition, it is strongly advisable to create a test forest in a lab environment and test schema modifications here before deploying them to a production forest.

Configuring the Schema

You use the Active Directory Schema snap-in to configure the schema. This snap-in is not present on domain controllers by default; you must register and install it before you can perform any modifications to the schema.

To register the Active Directory Schema snap-in, open a command prompt and type **regsvr32 schmmgmt.dll**. You then receive the following message box: `DllRegisterServer in schmmgmt.dll succeeded.`

After registering the snap-in, perform the following steps to install it:

1. Click Start, Run, type **mmc**, and press Enter. This opens a blank MMC console.

2. Click File, Add or Remove Snap-In to display the Add or Remove Snap-Ins dialog box.

3. Select Active Directory Schema from the Available Snap-Ins field, and click Add to display this snap-in in the Selected Snap-Ins field, as shown in Figure 1.14. Then click OK.

4. Save the console with a descriptive name such as Active Directory Schema. By default, it is stored in the Administrative Tools folder.

FIGURE 1.14   Installing the Active Directory Schema snap-in.

EXAM ALERT

An exam question might ask you why you are unable to locate this snap-in. Remember that you must be a member of the Schema Admins group and that you must first register the snap-in so that it appears in the Add or Remove Snap-Ins dialog box.

Extending the Schema

After you have installed the Active Directory Schema snap-in, you can extend the schema to include any classes or attributes not defined by default. To extend the schema, proceed as follows:

1. Open the Active Directory Schema snap-in.

2. To create a new class, right-click Classes and choose Create Class. You then receive the warning shown in Figure 1.15 informing you of the seriousness of this action.

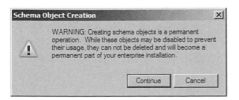

FIGURE 1.15   You are warned that creating schema objects is a permanent operation.

3. Click Continue, and in the Create New Schema Class dialog box shown in Figure 1.16, supply the following information that describes the class you are creating:

   ▸ **Common Name**—A unique name related to the LDAP display name.

   ▸ **LDAP Display Name**—A unique display name that programmers and system administrators can use to programmatically reference the object.

   ▸ **Unique X.500 Object ID**—A required, unique identifier associated with all object classes or attributes defined in the schema.

   ▸ **Description**—An optional description for the class or attribute.

   ▸ **Parent Class**—Defines the hierarchy of each class. Every class must have exactly one parent, except at the root of the directory hierarchy.

   ▸ **Class Type**—Select from Structural (the only class type that can have instances in AD DS), Abstract (a template that is used to derive new abstract, auxiliary, and structural classes and can include auxiliary classes in its definition), or Auxiliary (an additional class that can be included in the definition of another class and can be a subclass of an abstract or auxiliary class).

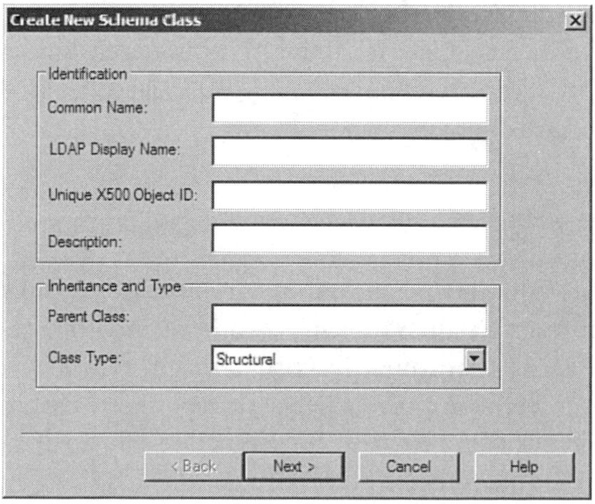

FIGURE 1.16 Creating a new schema class.

4. Click Next, and in the Create New Schema Class dialog box, add mandatory or optional attributes to this class by clicking Add under either Mandatory or Optional. In either case, select the desired object from the Select Schema Object dialog box that appears, and then click OK.

5. When you are finished, click Finish. The class is added and can be found by expanding the Classes folder in the console tree of the snap-in.

Creating attributes in the schema is similar. Right-click Attributes and choose Create New Attribute. You need to supply similar information, which also includes the syntax (type of information stored by this attribute, such as a case-insensitive string, a distinguished name, an integer, or a numerical string), as well as minimum and maximum values according to the syntax type.

CAUTION

After you have added a class or attribute to the schema, it is permanently added. You cannot delete a class or attribute; you can only deactivate it. Improper additions or modifications of schema classes or attributes might cause severe problems to Active Directory that can be solved only by completely reinstalling Active Directory. This is one reason Microsoft is so restrictive about using the Schema snap-in.

To deactivate a class or attribute, right-click it in the Schema Manager snap-in and choose Properties. On the General tab of the Properties dialog box that appears, clear the check box labeled Attribute Is Active. If this check box is unavailable (grayed out), it means that the class or attribute is essential for Active Directory functionality and cannot be disabled.

Domain Naming Master

The domain naming master comes into play whenever an administrator creates a new domain anywhere in the forest or renames or removes an existing domain. Failure of the domain naming master is not ordinarily a problem and comes into play only if an administrator wants to perform any of these activities. There is only one domain naming master in the entire forest, and by default it is located on the first domain controller installed in the forest. Microsoft recommends that you keep the domain naming master and schema master roles on the same computer.

PDC Emulator

In Windows 2000 and Windows Server 2003 Active Directory, the PDC Emulator served as a primary domain controller (PDC) for any Windows NT 4.0 backup domain controllers (BDC) in the domain. This role is no longer significant in Windows Server 2008 because Windows NT BDCs can no longer be supported on the network. However, pre-Windows 2000 computers such as Windows 98 and Windows NT 4.0 can still exist on the network, and the PDC emulator handles account management activities such as password changes for users at these computers. It also processes error messages and lockout actions for users entering incorrect passwords at these computers. In addition, the PDC emulator acts as a time synchronization master for all computers in the domain. This role is discussed further in the next section. There is one PDC emulator in each domain in the forest.

> **TIP**
>
> Microsoft recommends that you leave the PDC emulator role in the forest root domain on a Windows Server 2008 domain controller.

Should the PDC emulator become unavailable, users of pre-Windows 2000 computers will be unable to change their passwords. If their passwords expire, they will be unable to log on until the PDC emulator is brought back online.

> **TIP**
>
> In an environment containing a large number of pre-Windows 2000 computers, the PDC emulator can receive a large workload. You can reduce the number of authentication requests processed by this server by adjusting its weight or priority in the DNS environment. To reduce the number of authentication requests, adjust its weight. To ensure that it does not receive client authentication requests, adjust its priority. We discuss DNS in detail in Chapter 2. Also, see "Configuring Operations Master Roles" in Appendix A.

Time Service

On a network in which all member servers and client computers are running Windows 2000 or higher, the sole function of the PDC emulator is that of the time synchronization master. It uses the Windows Time Service (W32time) to perform this activity.

By default, the Windows Time Service uses the PDC emulator's local clock for providing time to client computers. You should utilize one of the following best practices for ensuring accurate time on the PDC emulator:

▶ Install a hardware clock such as a radio or global positioning service (GPS) device on the PDC emulator.

▶ Configure the Windows Time Service to synchronize with an external time source such as the Microsoft time server at time.windows.com. You can use the w32tm utility to perform this task. Type w32tm /? at a command prompt to obtain information on using this command.

For further information, refer to "Configure the Windows Time Service" in Appendix A.

If you have deployed an RODC at a branch office, the PDC emulator for the domain must be running Windows Server 2008. Otherwise, the RODC will be unable to act as a time source for client computers in the branch office. Client computers will be unable to synchronize their time with the RODC, and a time difference (clock skew) between their time and that of the RODC might develop. Should the clock skew exceed five minutes, client computers will be unable to receive new Kerberos tickets, which can prevent users from accessing resources.

Another solution to this problem is available. You can configure a writable Windows Server 2008 domain controller in the domain to act as GTIMESERV for the domain. A GTIMESERV is a domain controller or member server running Windows Server 2008 that acts as an authoritative time server within the domain. Client computers can use this server as a time synchronization master.

A server acting as GTIMESERV in the forest root domain acts as the authoritative time source for the entire forest. You should configure this server to receive time from an external time server and configure the PDC emulator in this domain to synchronize time with this server. In domains that are not the forest root domain, the GTIMESERV server can synchronize time from the PDC emulator or a GTIMESERV server higher up in the domain hierarchy. You can also configure this server to receive time from an external time server.

EXAM ALERT

If an exam question states that a user is unable to log on and the time on his computer is incorrect, the most likely reason for this problem is that the PDC emulator or GTIMESERV computer is unavailable.

Infrastructure Master

The infrastructure master performs two critical actions in multidomain forests:

▶ It updates references to objects in other domains in the forest. In doing so, it ensures that changes made by different administrators from different locations are not in conflict. Such changes include adding users or groups or modifying group memberships. For example, if two administrators in two different cities were to create a user named Mary at the same time, a problem would occur. In this case, the infrastructure master would generate a uniqueness error. Further, if you were to create a user account in one domain from a domain controller in another domain, you would need to contact the infrastructure master in the domain where the account will be created.

▶ It tracks group membership changes that cross domain boundaries within the forest. For example, domain local groups can contain users and global groups in other domains, and global groups can be made members of domain local groups in other domains. In addition, these groups can be members of universal groups and vice versa. The infrastructure master ensures that these changes occur properly and without conflict.

If the infrastructure master were to fail, an administrator would notice a problem if she attempted to perform either of these actions. She would be unable to move or rename a large number of accounts. Users might be unable to access objects in other domains because their references would not be updated.

> **CAUTION**
>
> You should not place the infrastructure master role on a domain controller that is configured as a global catalog server unless all domain controllers are configured as global catalog servers. Otherwise, the infrastructure master would be unable to update its references to objects in other domains properly. New to Windows Server 2008, when you create an additional domain controller in a child domain, `dcpromo` checks whether the infrastructure master is on a global catalog server. If so, it prompts you to transfer this role to the new domain controller.

RID Master

As mentioned earlier in this chapter, all objects such as user or group accounts defined in a forest must have a SID, which uniquely identifies the object to Active Directory and contains a domain identifier plus a domain-specific RID.

The RID master keeps track of all RIDs assigned within its domain and issues blocks of 500 RIDs to all other domain controllers in the domain so that administrators can create accounts. The RID master issues a new block of RIDs after the existing block is down to 20 percent of its original value. You can modify registry keys to allow larger pools if desired in a large environment. If the RID master were to fail, administrators at other domain controllers would be able to create accounts until the existing pool of RIDs at that domain controller became exhausted, after which account creation would fail.

> **EXAM ALERT**
>
> Remember that an RODC cannot be either a global catalog server or an operations master. An exam question might trick you into believing that you can install a GC server or transfer an operations master role to an RODC.

Placement of Operations Masters

I have already touched on the fact that the first domain controller installed in a new forest holds all five operations master roles and that the first domain controller installed in a new child domain or tree in an existing forest holds all three domainwide operations master roles. The placement of operations masters affects the performance of your network, both in single domain and multiple domain situations. Here are several factors you should be aware of when designing a strategy for placing operations masters or transferring them at a later date:

- When you create a new tree or child domain in an existing forest, the server you are promoting must be able to contact the domain naming master, or the promotion will fail.

- If you need to modify the schema, the server you are working from must be able to contact the schema master. This includes the installation or configuration of server applications such as Exchange Server that add classes or attributes to the schema.

- Client computers running pre-Windows 2000 operating systems must be able to contact the PDC emulator if users on these computers want to perform account modifications such as password changes.

- The PDC emulator ensures that clocks on all computers in the domain remain synchronized. You can also configure another domain controller with GTIMESERV to ensure clock synchronization.

▶ When creating new users or groups, you must be able to contact the infrastructure master to ensure that conflicting changes are not occurring elsewhere in the domain. Remember that this server also tracks changes in group membership that can cross domains, and that these changes cannot occur if the infrastructure master is unavailable.

▶ When creating new user, group, or computer accounts, the server on which you are performing these tasks must have RIDs available. When this server exhausts its pool of RIDs, it must be able to contact the RID master, or you won't be able to create additional new accounts.

Transferring and Seizing of Operations Master Roles

When you create a new domain or forest, all the operations master roles are located on the first domain controller by default. You might want to *transfer* these roles to other domain controllers for any of several reasons, or if an operations master role holder becomes unavailable, you might want to *seize* this role. This section looks at these actions.

TIP

It is recommended that you back up the system state on your domain controllers before performing a transfer of operations master roles. Backup of servers, including operations master roles, is discussed in Chapter 8.

Transferring Operations Master Roles

You can transfer operations master roles to another domain controller when the original role holder is still available and functioning. The following are several reasons why you might want to do this:

▶ You might want to perform load balancing; in other words, you might distribute the processing load among more than one server to avoid overloading a single machine.

▶ You might need to perform scheduled maintenance on the computer holding one or more of these roles.

▶ A role holder located on a WAN might be creating excessive replication traffic that hinders other network traffic.

- ▶ You might want to move role holders to locations near the administrators who are responsible for them.

- ▶ You need to ensure that the infrastructure master is not held on a computer that hosts the global catalog.

- ▶ In general, you should host the schema master and domain naming master roles on the same server. This server should be close to another server that you can use as a backup if required.

You can transfer the three domainwide operations masters roles from the Active Directory Users and Computers console. While logged on as a member of the Domain Admins group, right-click Active Directory Users and Computers at the top of the console tree and select Change Domain Controller. In the Change Domain Controller dialog box, select the server where you want to transfer one or more roles, and then click OK, All Tasks, Operations Masters. In the Operations Masters dialog box shown in Figure 1.17, select the tab corresponding to the role you want to transfer and click Change; then click Yes on the confirmation message box that appears.

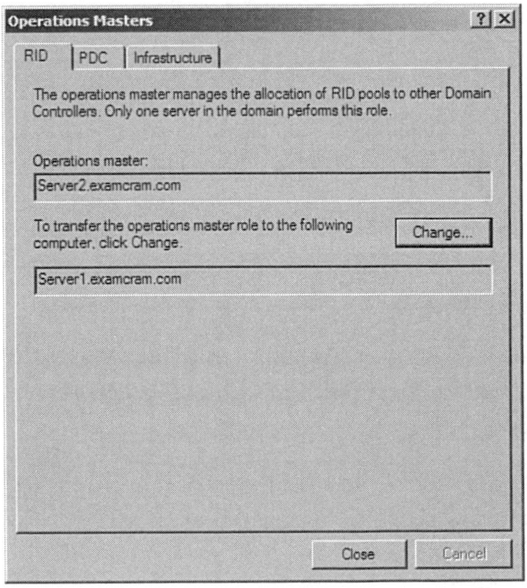

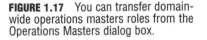

FIGURE 1.17 You can transfer domain-wide operations masters roles from the Operations Masters dialog box.

To transfer the domain naming master role, access the Active Directory Domains and Trusts console on the server where you want to transfer this role. Right-click Active Directory Domains and Trusts and select Operations

Masters. Then follow a procedure similar to that described earlier. To transfer this role, you must be logged on as a member of the Enterprise Admins group.

To transfer the schema master role, perform this task in a similar manner from the Active Directory Schema console. To transfer this role, you must be logged on as a member of the Schema Admins group.

Seizing Operations Masters Roles

Should an operations master role become unavailable due to a network or computer crash, you cannot use the preceding procedures to transfer its roles to an operational server. You can use the ntdsutil command-line utility to seize the role at another domain controller. Use the following procedure:

1. Open a command prompt and type **ntdsutil**.

2. At the ntdsutil command prompt, type **roles**.

3. At the FSMO maintenance command prompt, type **connection**.

4. At the server connections command prompt, type **connect to server <*server*>**, where <*server*> is the name of the server to which you want to seize the role.

5. At the server connections command prompt, type **quit**.

6. At the FSMO maintenance command prompt, type **seize <*role*>**, where <*role*> is the operations master role you want to seize.

7. Click Yes on the confirmation message box that appears.

8. ntdsutil first attempts to connect to the server and confirms that it is unavailable. After receiving an error message, it seizes the role, displaying the output shown in Figure 1.18. If it finds that the server hosting the role is online, it transfers the role rather than seizing it.

9. Type **quit** twice to exit ntdsutil.

In general, once you have seized an operations master role, you should never bring back online the server originally holding this role. You should reformat this server's hard disk and reinstall Windows Server 2008. However, you can transfer the infrastructure master or PDC emulator role back to the original holder after you have restored it and brought it back online without having to rebuild its operating system completely.

FIGURE 1.18 Seizing an operations master role.

NOTE

Many additional options are available with the `ntdsutil` utility. Some of the more important ones include creating application directory partitions, restoring AD DS, performing an online compaction of the AD DS database, and cleaning up of metadata left behind by decommissioned domain controllers. For more information, type **ntdsutil /?** at a command prompt. You can also type **help** or **?** at a subcommand to see a description of the available options.

Exam Cram Questions

1. You install Active Directory on a server. You want it to be a separate domain that is part of an existing forest but containing a namespace separate from the forest where you are installing it. What is this type of domain called?

   ○ **A.** A replica

   ○ **B.** A child domain

   ○ **C.** A forest root

   ● **D.** A tree root

2. You are installing Active Directory on a new domain controller and selecting options for placing the database and log files. Which of the following options would produce the optimum performance of these files? (Each answer represents part of the solution. Choose two.)

   ○ **A.** Placing them on the same NTFS partition

   ● **B.** Ensuring plenty of hard disk space for these files to expand

   ● **C.** Placing them on NTFS partitions located on separate physical disks

   ○ **D.** Restricting them to small partitions to control their size

3. Which of the following represent valid requirements for installing Active Directory Domain Services on a Windows Server 2008 computer? (Choose all that apply.)

   ○ **A.** A disk volume formatted with the FAT32 file system

   ● **B.** A disk volume formatted with the NTFS file system

   ● **C.** The Standard, Enterprise, or Datacenter edition of Windows Server 2008

   ○ **D.** Any available edition of Windows Server 2008

   ● **E.** A DNS server

   ○ **F.** A WINS server

   ● **G.** Administrative privileges on the server

4. Which of the following is the most appropriate scenario where you would want to install a read-only domain controller?

   ● **A.** In a branch office where physical security might be less than optimum

   ○ **B.** In the head office near the receptionist's desk

   ○ **C.** In the server room where the forest root domain is located and you need an optimum location for the schema master and domain naming master

   ○ **D.** In a branch office server room where you need to place the infrastructure master, RID master, and PDC emulator close to clients requiring their services

5. Peter is a network administrator for a company that operates an Active Directory forest consisting of two domains in separate trees. The company has offices in Chicago and Rome, which are connected by a 236kbps WAN link. Each office is represented by a separate Active Directory site as well as its own domain.

   Peter's company stores resource location data in Active Directory so that users can perform searches to locate the appropriate resources on their client computers, which run either Windows XP Professional or Windows Vista Business. However, users in the Rome office report that search times for resources are unacceptably slow.

   Which of the following should Peter do to improve search times at the Rome office?

   ○ **A.** Enable universal group caching at the Rome office.

   ● **B.** Configure a global catalog server at the Rome office.

   ○ **C.** Configure a domain controller for the Chicago domain in the Rome office.

   ○ **D.** Configure a domain controller for the Rome domain in the Chicago office.

6. Sharon is the IT manager of a community college whose administrative staff is planning the college's new Windows Server 2008 domain infrastructure. Ten domain controllers will be located in various campus buildings. The college's administrators and technical support staff are to be based in an annex to the computer sciences department that would include a powerful server acting as the forest root domain controller. The administrative staff presented Sharon with a proposal that this server would incorporate the roles of global catalog server, schema master, domain naming master, and infrastructure master. Servers in other buildings would take on the other operations master roles.

   After studying the proposal carefully, Sharon asks the administrative staff to modify the operations master setup. Which of the following should the staff change?

    ○ **A.** The college's computer help center, which is staffed by students who work part-time shifts and is located in the student union building, needs frequent access to the infrastructure master. The administrative staff should locate this role there.

    ○ **B.** The infrastructure master does not need to be located close to the IT staff. A more sensible change would be for the administrative staff to move this role elsewhere and have the PDC emulator located close to the support staff.

    ○ **C.** The schema master and domain naming master roles cannot function properly if they are hosted by the same computer.

    ● **D.** The global catalog server and infrastructure master roles cannot function properly if they are hosted by the same computer.

7. Ryan has installed Windows Server 2008 on a new server using the Server Core option. He would like to install AD DS and promote the server to be a replica domain controller in his company's single domain network. What should he do?

    ○ **A.** Run Server Manager from the command prompt and select the AD DS role.

    ○ **B.** Run Server Manager from the command prompt and select the dcpromo option.

    ○ **C.** Execute the dcpromo command from the command prompt and specify the appropriate answers when prompted.

    ● **D.** Execute the dcpromo command from the command prompt and specify an unattended answer file containing the required information.

8. Which of the following are valid domain and forest functional levels for a Windows Server 2008 domain? (Choose all that apply.)

    ○ **A.** Windows 2000 mixed

    ● **B.** Windows 2000 native

    ○ **C.** Windows Server 2003 mixed

    ● **D.** Windows Server 2003 native

    ● **E.** Windows Server 2008 native

9. Karen is the network administrator for a company that operates an Active Directory domain whose domain controllers run Windows Server 2003. The company wants to upgrade the domain controllers to Windows Server 2008. Karen's user account is a member of the Domain Admins, Enterprise Admins, and Schema Admins groups in her company's domain.

Which of the following actions does Karen need to perform before upgrading any of the domain controllers to Windows Server 2008? To answer, select the two required actions from the list that follows in the sequence in which she must execute them.

- ○ **A.** Run the Adprep /domainprep command on the PDC emulator.
- ○ **B.** Run the Adprep /forestprep command on the PDC emulator.
- ● **C.** Run the Adprep /domainprep command on the infrastructure master.
- ○ **D.** Run the Adprep /forestprep command on the domain naming master.
- ○ **E.** Run the Adprep /domainprep command on the schema master.
- ● **F.** Run the Adprep /forestprep command on the schema master.

10. Jason is a support technician who is creating user accounts for a series of new employees that your company has hired. After creating several dozen user accounts successfully, he suddenly receives an error message informing him that Active Directory cannot create the account. He comes to you for assistance.

Which of the following should you do first?

- ○ **A.** Check the operational status of the infrastructure master.
- ● **B.** Check the operational status of the RID master.
- ○ **C.** Check the operational status of the PDC emulator.
- ○ **D.** Check the amount of disk space on the computer Jason is using.

Answers to *Exam Cram* Questions

1. **D.** A tree root is the top domain in a new tree, which exists parallel to the forest root domain and possesses a disjointed namespace. In other words, its namespace is completely separate from that of the forest root domain; for example, Examcram.com versus Que.com. A replica represents an additional domain controller in an existing domain. This is not a separate domain, so answer A is incorrect. A child domain exists under a forest or tree root and contains the parent's name in its domain name, so answer B is incorrect. A forest root is the first domain created in a new forest, so answer C is incorrect.

2. **B, C.** The best way to ensure an optimum database and log file configuration is to provide plenty of room and separate physical disks. Placing the files on the same NTFS partition does not enhance performance, so answer A is incorrect. Limiting the growth of the database and log files would hinder proper Active Directory operation because these files grow normally, so answer D is incorrect.

3. **B, C, E, G.** To install Active Directory, you must have a partition formatted with the NTFS file system. You must be using the Standard, Enterprise, or Datacenter edition of Windows Server 2008, you must have DNS available, and you must have administrative privileges on the server. You do not need a FAT32 partition (in fact, Windows Server 2008 automatically formats its partition with NTFS when you install it), so answer A is incorrect. You cannot use the Web edition of Windows Server 2008, so answer D is incorrect. You do not need a WINS server to install Active Directory, so answer F is incorrect.

4. **A.** The RODC is especially useful for deploying to a branch office where security might be less than optimum. The RODC contains a read-only copy of the directory database, and users or intruders at this location cannot make modifications, such as adding new user accounts or granting administrative privileges. A head office would certainly contain a server room where you would place all domain controllers for this location. It would be unwise to place a domain controller behind the receptionist's desk, so answer B is incorrect. It is not possible to host operations master roles on an RODC, so answers C and D are incorrect.

5. **B.** Peter should configure a global catalog server at the Rome office. A GC server contains directory information about all objects in the forest, including the location of resources in each domain. Universal group membership caching stores information about universal group membership in the domain controller where it is implemented, but it does not store information about resources in Active Directory, so answer A is incorrect. Installing a domain controller for each domain in the other office would increase replication traffic across the WAN link. This is unnecessary for solving this problem, so answers C and D are incorrect.

6. **D.** The infrastructure master should not be hosted on the same domain controller as the global catalog server unless all domain controllers are configured as global catalog servers. This is because the infrastructure master would be unable to update its references to objects in other domains properly. The students at the help center do not need access to the infrastructure master, so answer A is incorrect. It is possible to administer the servers remotely, including the infrastructure master. Consequently, the location of this server does not matter, so answer B is incorrect. The domain naming master and schema master can operate on the same computer without problems, so answer C is incorrect.

7. **D.** Ryan should execute the `dcpromo` command from the command prompt and specify an unattended answer file containing the required information. Server Core does not contain a GUI, and you must supply all required information in the form of the answer file. You can execute Server Manager using the command line (`ServerManagerCmd.exe`), but you cannot select roles or options in this manner because there is no GUI, so answers A and B are incorrect. Also, `dcpromo` on a Server Core machine cannot run the GUI, so answer C is incorrect.

8. **B, D, E.** Windows 2000 native, Windows Server 2003 native, and Windows Server 2008 native are valid domain or forest functional levels for Active Directory in Windows Server 2008. Windows 2000 mixed functional level was formerly available in Windows Server 2003 Active Directory to support Windows NT 4.0 domain controllers; however, this mode is not available in Windows Server 2008, so answer A is incorrect. A functional level called Windows Server 2003 mixed never existed, so answer C is incorrect.

9. **F, C.** Karen must run the `Adprep /forestprep` command on the schema master, and then she must run the `Adprep /domainprep` command on the infrastructure master. She cannot run the `Adprep /domainprep` command on the PDC emulator or the schema master, so answers A and E are incorrect. She also cannot run the `Adprep /forestprep` command on the PDC emulator or the domain naming master, so answers B and D are incorrect.

   You should note that in an "ordered list" or "build list and reorder" exam question, you must place the required items in the proper order for the answer to be scored correct. Therefore, specifying the answer to this question as "C, F" is incorrect. A question of this type would appear as a drag-and-drop question type on the exam.

10. **B.** You should check the operational status of the RID master. In this case, Jason was able to create several dozen user accounts before he encountered a problem, which suggests that the computer he was using ran out of RIDs and has been unable to contact the RID master to obtain more. The infrastructure master updates references to objects in other domains but is not involved in account creation, so answer A is incorrect. The PDC emulator services account changes from pre-Windows 2000 client computers but is not involved in account creation, so answer C is incorrect. It is possible that disk space could create a problem, but this is not likely the cause here, so answer D is incorrect. Always select the answer that is the *most likely* solution to the problem.

CHAPTER 2

Active Directory and DNS

Terms You'll Need to Understand

- ✓ Active Directory–integrated zone
- ✓ Application directory partition
- ✓ Conditional forwarding
- ✓ Dnscmd
- ✓ DNS Notify
- ✓ Dynamic DNS (DDNS)
- ✓ Forward lookup
- ✓ Forwarding
- ✓ Full zone transfer (AXFR)
- ✓ Fully qualified domain name (FQDN)
- ✓ Incremental zone transfer (IXFR)
- ✓ Master server
- ✓ Non-dynamic DNS (NDDNS)
- ✓ Primary zone
- ✓ Resource record
- ✓ Reverse lookup
- ✓ Root hints
- ✓ Round robin
- ✓ Scavenging
- ✓ Secondary server
- ✓ Secondary zone
- ✓ Secure dynamic DNS (SDDNS)
- ✓ Stub zone
- ✓ Time to Live (TTL)
- ✓ Zone
- ✓ Zone delegation

Concepts/Techniques You'll Need to Master

- ✓ Creating forward and reverse lookup zones
- ✓ Configuring zone types
- ✓ Configuring dynamic updates
- ✓ Configuring forwarding and conditional forwarding
- ✓ Configuring zone delegation
- ✓ Configuring debug logging
- ✓ Understanding and configuring advanced DNS server options
- ✓ Configuring zone transfers and replication

Since Active Directory was introduced in Windows 2000, the Domain Name System (DNS) has served as the premier name resolution service for all Windows computers and has been fully integrated with Active Directory Domain Services (AD DS). As you learned in Chapter 1, "Getting Started with Windows Server 2008 Active Directory," you must have DNS to install a domain controller; the Active Directory Installation Wizard automatically installs it for you if it is not present. If DNS is not working properly, client computers cannot resolve domain controller names to IP addresses, and users cannot log on unless cached credentials are available. In the latter case, they still cannot access network resources by computer names. So you can see how vital DNS is to the proper functioning of your network.

DNS uses a hierarchical namespace that contains several levels of information. For example, an Internet name such as www.sales.examcram.com has four levels of data. Here, com represents the top level, examcram represents a second-level domain, sales is a subdomain, and www is a web server name. The DNS naming scheme is used to create the structure of the Active Directory namespace, permitting interoperability with Internet technologies; therefore, the concept of namespaces is central to Active Directory.

In Windows Server 2008, DNS is present as a server role. You can install DNS on any server, including one that you do not want to add the Domain Controller role to, using the Add Roles Wizard. DNS now provides complete support for IP version 6 (IPv6). After you have installed DNS (whether as part of Active Directory installation or separately on a member server), the DNS Manager MMC snap-in is available in the Administrative Tools folder, where you can perform all configuration activities associated with DNS.

Configuring DNS Zones

Each DNS name server stores information about a discrete portion of the Internet namespace. Such a portion is known as a *zone*, and the DNS server that is primarily responsible for each zone is considered to be authoritative for that zone. In other words, the DNS server is the main source of information regarding the Internet addresses contained within the zone. A zone can be considered part of the big database that is DNS and can contain information on one or more AD DS domains. Zones are defined by who looks after maintaining the records that they contain. In Windows Server 2008, DNS stores its zone data in one or more *application directory partitions*, each of which is an AD DS partition that contains application-specific data (in this case, DNS) that needs to be replicated throughout specified portions of the forest.

When you install AD DS, a default set of zones and subzones is installed, as
shown in Figure 2.1. DNS Manager provides the New Zone Wizard that can
assist you in creating new zones.

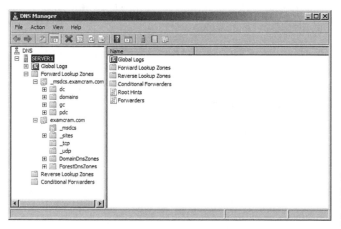

FIGURE 2.1 A default
set of zones is included
in DNS Manager when
you create your domain.

DNS Zone Types

Each DNS server provides several types of zones, including primary, secondary,
stub, and Active Directory integrated. As shown in Figure 2.1, you can have forward
and reverse lookup zones in each of these zone types. A *forward lookup* zone
resolves a computer's *fully qualified domain name (FQDN)* to its IP address, whereas
a *reverse lookup* zone resolves an IP address to the corresponding FQDN.

Primary Zones

A *primary zone* is a master copy of zone data hosted on a DNS server that is the
primary source of information for records found in this zone. This server is considered to be authoritative for this zone, and you can update zone data directly
on this server. It is also known as a *master server*. If the zone data is not integrated with AD DS, the server holds this data in a local file named `zone_name.dns`
that is located in the %systemroot%\system32\DNS folder. The server that
hosts this zone is frequently called the *master server*.

Secondary Zones

A *secondary zone* is an additional copy of DNS zone data hosted on a DNS server that is a secondary source for this zone information. This server obtains the zone information from the server hosting the corresponding primary zone. Using secondary zones improves name resolution services on the network by providing redundancy and load balancing. The server that hosts a secondary zone is frequently called the *secondary server*.

Stub Zones

A *stub zone* contains source information about authoritative name servers for its zone only. The DNS server hosting the stub zone obtains its information from another server that hosts a primary or secondary copy of the same zone data. The following are several purposes of stub zones:

▶ Maintain a current list of delegated zone information within a hierarchy of DNS zones. A DNS server can host a parent zone at the primary or secondary level with stub zones for its child zones, and thereby have a list of authoritative DNS servers for the child zones.

▶ Enable improved name resolution by enabling a DNS server to rapidly locate the stub zone's list of name servers without the need for querying other servers to locate the appropriate DNS server.

▶ Simplify the administration of DNS by enabling the distribution of the list of authoritative DNS servers throughout a large enterprise network without the need for hosting a large number of secondary zones.

✱ Active Directory–Integrated Zones

An Active Directory–integrated zone stores data in one or more application directory partitions that are replicated along with other AD DS directory partitions. This helps to ensure that zone data remains up to date on all domain controllers hosting DNS in the domain. Using Active Directory–integrated zones also provides the following benefits:

▶ It promotes fault tolerance because data is always available and can always be updated even if one of the servers fails. If a DNS server hosting a primary zone outside of AD DS fails, you cannot update its data because no mechanism exists for promoting a secondary DNS zone to primary.

▶ Each writable domain controller where DNS is installed acts as a master server and allows updates to the zones where they are authoritative; no separate DNS zone transfer topology is needed.

▶ Security is enhanced because you can configure dynamic updates to be secured; by contrast, zone data not integrated with AD DS is stored in plain text files that unauthorized users can access, modify, or delete.

You can integrate either primary or stub zones with AD DS. You cannot create an Active Directory–integrated secondary zone.

> **EXAM ALERT**
>
> Keep in mind the properties of the various zone types. In particular, remember that you must have an Active Directory–integrated zone if you want to enable secure dynamic updates. Also remember that you can configure a secondary server with a copy of an Active Directory–integrated zone, but this secondary zone copy is stored locally on that server and is not integrated with Active Directory. An exam question might ask which type of DNS zone is appropriate in a given scenario.

Creating DNS Zones

One of the first activities you perform when configuring a new DNS server is to specify forward and reverse lookup zones.

The following two types of DNS lookup zones exist:

▶ **Forward lookup**—This is the usual action in which a client requires the IP address of a remote computer as found in the DNS server's A or AAAA (host) *resource record*.

▶ **Reverse lookup**—This occurs when a client computer knows the IP address of another computer and requires its host name, which can be found in the DNS server's PTR (pointer) resource record.

By creating primary forward and reverse lookup zones, you create a primary name server that is authoritative for the zone that you have created. Or you can create a secondary name server for any zone that you have already created on another DNS server. Note that you can create any number of zones on a single DNS server and that one DNS server can contain any combination of primary and secondary zones.

Forward Lookup Zones

As you already have seen, DNS creates forward lookup zones when you install it as part of creating a new domain. When you install DNS by itself, it does not create lookup zones. DNS provides the New Zone Wizard to facilitate the creation of all types of zones. It is simple to create a new forward lookup zone, as follows:

1. In the DNS Manager snap-in, right-click Forward Lookup Zones and choose New Zone.

2. Click Next, and on the Zone Type page, select the zone type from the options described earlier in this chapter. Then click Next again.

3. If you select the option to create an Active Directory–integrated zone, you see the Active Directory Zone Replication Scope page shown in Figure 2.2, which asks you how you want the data in the zone replicated. (The available options are discussed later in this chapter; the default is To All DNS Servers in this Domain.) Make an appropriate choice, and then click Next.

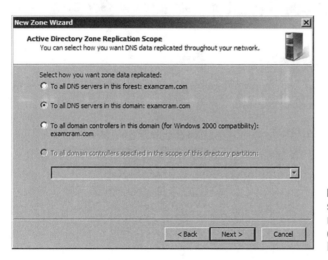

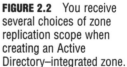

FIGURE 2.2 You receive several choices of zone replication scope when creating an Active Directory–integrated zone.

4. On the Zone Name page, type the name of the zone to be created, and then click Next.

5. If you have selected the Secondary zone type, you receive the Master DNS Servers page. On this page, provide the IP addresses of one or more DNS servers from which the zone information will be copied to create the secondary zone, and then click Next.

6. The Zone File page provides a default filename consisting of the zone name with a .dns extension. You can modify this if you need to or choose the option of using an existing file that has been saved to the %systemroot%\ system32\dns folder. Make your choice, and then click Next.

7. The Dynamic Update page shown in Figure 2.3 provides a choice of dynamic update types, as discussed earlier in this section. Make your selection, and then click Next.

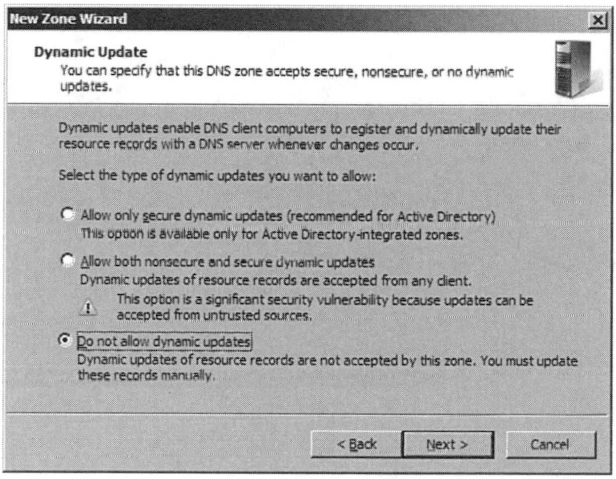

FIGURE 2.3 The New Zone Wizard enables you to specify the type of dynamic update desired.

8. Review the information provided on the Completing the New Zone Wizard page. When you are done, click Finish. If you need to make modifications, click Back. The zone is created and added to the list in the console tree of the DNS Manager snap-in.

Reverse Lookup Zones

The reverse lookup files map IP addresses to host names by using a special domain name that ends in `in-addr.arpa` and contains the octets of the network portion of the IP address in reverse sequence, such as `0.168.192.in-addr.arpa` for the Class C network address range of `192.168.0.0/24`. It is a database file that is used for reverse lookups; in other words, a client can provide an IP address and request a matching host name. Pointer (PTR) records mentioned previously are used to provide a static mapping of IP addresses to host names within a reverse-lookup zone. They can be created either manually or automatically when A or AAAA records are added to the forward lookup zone file.

You can use the New Zone Wizard to create a reverse lookup zone, as follows:

1. In the DNS Manager snap-in, right-click Reverse Lookup Zones, and choose New Zone.

2. Click Next, and on the Zone Type page, select the zone type from the options described earlier in this chapter. Then click Next again.

3. If creating an Active Directory–integrated zone, select your choice of replication scope, as described earlier and shown in Figure 2.2, and then click Next.

4. Choose whether you want to create an IPv4 or IPv6 reverse lookup zone, and then click Next.

5. In the Reverse Lookup Zone name page, type the network ID portion of the IP addresses that will belong to the zone in normal sequence. As you can see in Figure 2.4, this creates a reverse lookup zone name, as described earlier in this section. Click Next.

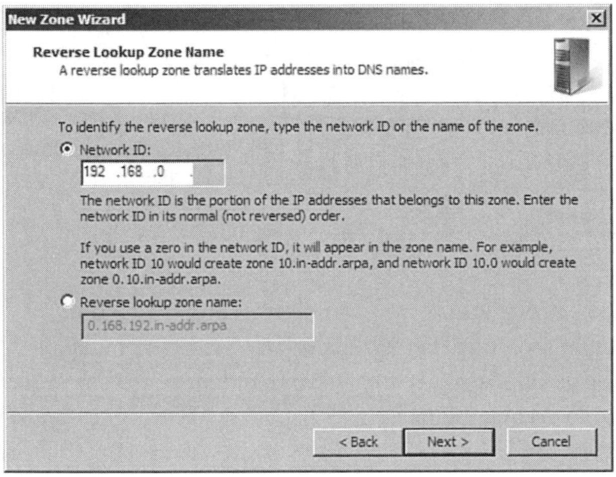

FIGURE 2.4 Specifying the name of the reverse lookup zone.

6. Select the appropriate option on the Dynamic Update page as previously described, and then click Next.

7. Review the summary information, and click Finish to create the zone. The new zone appears under the Reverse Lookup Zones node of the DNS Manager snap-in.

After you have created either type of DNS zone, you can specify additional zone properties. We discuss various zone properties in the sections that follow.

TIP

You can create a pair of forward and reverse lookup zones at the same time from the Configure a DNS Server Wizard. To access this wizard, right-click your server at the top of the DNS Manager console tree and choose Configure a DNS Server. Then select the Create Forward and Reverse Lookup Zones (Recommended for Large Networks) option.

DNS Records

Each zone file contains a series of entries known as resource records for a DNS domain. If your zone is examcram.com, your database file is called examcram.com.dns. A copy of this database is stored at %systemroot%\ System32\dns\backup. Windows Server 2008 supplies a sample database file called place.dns, located in the %systemroot%\System32\dns\Samples folder, as a template. This file is duplicated and renamed whenever you create a new zone using the New Zone Wizard.

Table 2.1 contains descriptions of the most common resource records found in the zone file.

TABLE 2.1 Common DNS Resource Records

Resource Record	Description
SOA (start of authority)	Is the first record in any zone file. It identifies the primary name server within the domain. It also Includes other properties, such as an administrator email address and caching properties for the zone.
A and AAAA (host)	Contains computer name to IPv4 (A) or IPv6 (AAAA) address mappings for all hosts found in the domain, thereby identifying these host names.
NS (name server)	Contains the DNS servers that are authoritative in the domain. This includes both the primary DNS servers and any secondary DNS servers.
SRV (service)	Stores information about where computers that provide a specific service are located on the network. Information in these records includes the name of the service and the DNS name of the host that provides the service. A computer still needs to access the A or AAAA record for a service provider to resolve the name to an IP address. Examples can include web services associated with a web server or logon services associated with a domain controller on an AD DS domain.
CNAME (alias)	Provides aliases (canonical names), which are additional names that point to a single host. Machines respond to either the original name or the alias. This facilitates doing such things as hosting both an FTP server and a web server on the same machine or for server migrations.
PTR (pointer)	Allows reverse lookups by containing IP address-to-name mappings.
MX (mail exchanger)	Identifies preferred mail servers on the network. When more than one mail server exists, they are listed in order of precedence.

You can create new DNS resource records if required. Right-click your DNS zone and choose the appropriate option from those shown in Figure 2.5. Provide the requested information in the dialog box that appears, and then click OK. The Other New Records option enables you to select from a complete list of available resource record types and provides a description of each of the available record types.

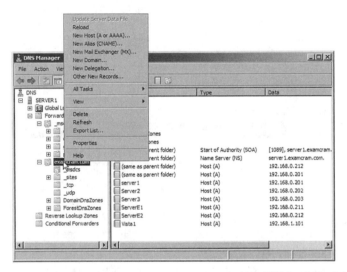

FIGURE 2.5 You can create new resource records in DNS by right-clicking your zone name and choosing the appropriate option.

Configuring DNS Zone Properties

The Properties dialog box for each DNS zone enables you to configure a large number of properties, including the following:

▶ Zone types

▶ Dynamic updating

▶ Aging/scavenging and time to live

▶ Additional DNS server properties

Right-click the zone in the console tree of DNS Manager and choose Properties to display the dialog box shown in Figure 2.6. The sections that follow outline the configuration of the more important properties of which you should be aware.

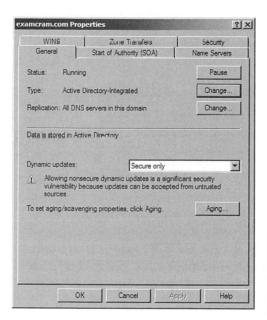

FIGURE 2.6 The General tab of a zone's Properties dialog box provides several important details on the zone and enables you to configure zone types, replication, dynamic updates, and aging/scavenging properties.

Configuring Zone Types

The Properties dialog box for a DNS zone enables you to change the zone type and determine whether the zone files are stored in Active Directory. In DNS Manager, right-click the zone and choose Properties. On the General tab of the zone's Properties dialog box shown in Figure 2.6, click the Change button opposite the Type entry. This brings up the Change Zone Type dialog box shown in Figure 2.7, which displays the current zone type. It also enables you to change the zone type and determine whether the zone data is stored in Active Directory. Click OK when you are finished.

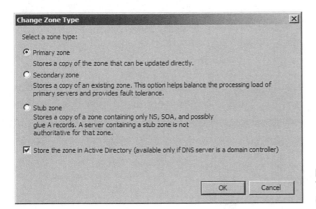

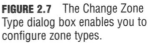

FIGURE 2.7 The Change Zone Type dialog box enables you to configure zone types.

Dynamic, Non-Dynamic, and Secure Dynamic DNS

Dynamic DNS (DDNS) enables DNS zone files to be updated "on the fly," so to speak, whenever DNS client computers update their TCP/IP configuration information. In other words, DNS clients can dynamically update their A and PTR records in the master zone file on startup or whenever their configuration changes. Introduced in Windows 2000, client computers automatically report their TCP/IP information to the DNS server. If your network is using Dynamic Host Configuration Protocol (DHCP), the DHCP server can update the DDNS server with each client computer's current IP address whenever it renews client IP address leases.

Non-dynamic DNS (NDDNS) was the default prior to Windows 2000. At that time, the administrator was required to enter A records manually to keep the DNS database up to date, although it was possible to integrate DNS with Windows Internet Name Service (WINS) to provide a "pseudo" dynamic version of DNS.

Secure dynamic DNS (SDDNS) is an enhancement that enables you to permit dynamic updates only from authorized client computers in an Active Directory–integrated zone. Secure dynamic updates are defined by Request for Comment (RFC) 2137 and offer the following benefits:

▶ Only computers with existing domain accounts can update DNS records.

▶ Only computers that create (and therefore own) a DNS record can update the record.

▶ Only authorized users can modify zones and resource records, thereby protecting them from unauthorized modification.

▶ You can specify which users and groups are authorized to modify zones and resource records.

You can configure the type of update being used from the General tab of the zone's Properties dialog box, previously shown in Figure 2.6. From the Dynamic Updates drop-down list, select None for NDDNS, Nonsecure and Secure for DDNS, or Secure Only for SDDNS. The default for Active Directory–integrated zones is Secure Only.

CAUTION

You cannot have secure dynamic updates on a zone that is not integrated with Active Directory. Microsoft recommends that you not allow dynamic updates when creating such a zone, because dynamic updates can be accepted from untrusted sources. The New Zone Wizard cautions you to this fact when creating such a zone.

EXAM ALERT

Know the purpose of the various dynamic update options available here. An exam question might present a scenario in which your DNS server's primary zone contains entries for unknown computers. You must select the Secure Only option to prevent this problem from occurring. Also remember that the zone must be Active Directory–integrated to enable this option.

For more information on dynamic updates and their use, refer to "Understanding Dynamic Update" in Windows Server 2008 Help and Support.

Time to Live

Client computers often request the same FQDNs. Upon receipt of a successful resolution of an iterative query with another DNS server, the server places the query results in its cache. This information is stored in memory and is available to the client (or any other client on the network requesting the same FQDN) without the need to send an external query. It is retained for the time known as the *time to live* (TTL), which is a configurable retention time interval that specifies the length of time that the server will retain cached information for a zone. This value and the next one are both specified as days:hours:minutes:seconds.

Increase this value if zone information does not change frequently. A longer TTL reduces the amount of network traffic but consumes more memory utilization on the DNS server. The TTL for This Record entry immediately beneath specifies the TTL for the SOA record.

You can configure a DNS zone's TTL property from the Start of Authority (SOA) tab of the zone's Properties dialog box, as shown in Figure 2.8. In the list box labeled Minimum (default) TTL, type a number and select a unit (days, hours, minutes, or seconds). By default, this TTL is one hour.

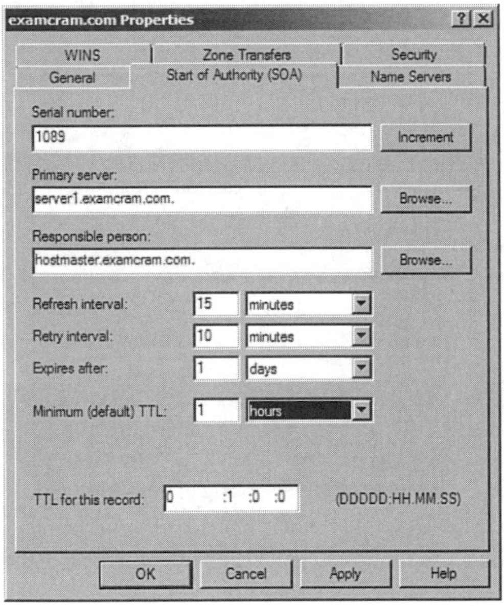

FIGURE 2.8 The Start of Authority (SOA) tab enables you to configure several zone properties, including the TTL for caching externally resolved queries.

NOTE

DNS cache information is also lost whenever the server is rebooted. For this reason, it is best to avoid rebooting the DNS server unless absolutely necessary.

The Start of Authority (SOA) tab contains the following additional settings you should be aware of; all these are related to the information contained in the server's SOA resource record:

▶ **Serial Number**—Starts at 1 and is incremented every time a change to some property of the zone occurs. You normally do not change this number. A secondary server that queries the primary server for updates uses this number to determine if changes to the zone file have occurred. If they have, the data is replicated to the secondary server using the zone transfer process.

▶ **Primary Server**—Designates the primary server for the domain by its FQDN. If you need to change the primary server for any reason, you can either browse to locate a suitable server or type its name here. If zone transfers are failing, check this name for accuracy, because if it is incorrect, zone transfers cannot take place.

▶ **Responsible Person**—Names the designated administrator by his/her Simple Mail Transfer Protocol (SMTP) email address. Even though email addresses generally use the @ symbol to separate the name from the domain, you need to use a period in this address. If zone transfers are not working properly, you can send a message to this email address.

▶ **Refresh Interval**—Specifies the interval at which the secondary server queries the master server to see if the zone data has changed. A low value enables the secondary DNS server to be more up to date, but at the expense of increased network traffic.

▶ **Retry Interval**—Specifies how much time will elapse before the secondary server tries again to contact the master server, in the event that the master server does not respond to the initial refresh attempt.

▶ **Expires After**—Specifies the length of time that a secondary server will resolve queries using the current information when it has been unable to contact the master server for an update. When this interval has been reached, the secondary server stops resolving queries until it is again able to contact the master server.

CAUTION

Try not to confuse the refresh and retry intervals. The refresh interval determines how often other DNS servers hosting the zone will attempt to renew the zone data. It is 15 minutes by default. The retry interval determines how often other DNS servers retry a request for updating the zone every time the refresh interval occurs. It is 10 minutes by default.

Zone Scavenging

Strange situations can occur in which resource records are not automatically removed from the DNS database. This can happen if a client such as a remote access client disconnects improperly from the network. In this case, the A resource record that is left behind is known as a *stale* resource record. These records take up space on a DNS server and might be used in attempts to resolve queries, resulting in errors and reduced DNS server performance.

For locating and removing these stale resource records, you can use a process known as *scavenging*. In this process, the DNS server searches for and deletes aged resource records. You can control the scavenging process by specifying which servers can scavenge the records, which zones are to be checked, and which records are to be scavenged if they become stale. By default, scavenging is disabled. To enable scavenging, access the General tab of the zone's Properties dialog box and click the Aging command button. This brings up the Zone Aging/Scavenging Properties dialog box shown in Figure 2.9. To enable scavenging, select the Scavenge Stale Resource Records check box and then specify values for the no-refresh and refresh intervals as described in the figure.

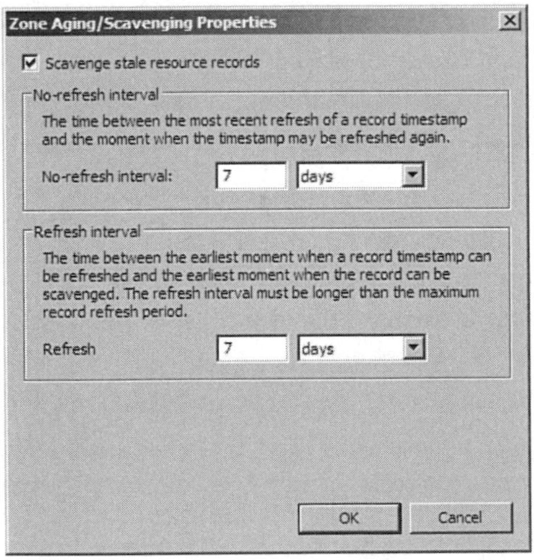

FIGURE 2.9 You can configure scavenging properties from the Zone Aging/Scavenging Properties dialog box.

TIP

You can also perform an immediate scavenging of all stale resource records on a DNS server without first configuring scavenging properties. To do so, right-click the DNS server in the console tree of DNS Manager and choose Scavenge Stale Resource Records. Then click Yes in the message box that displays.

Configuring DNS Server Settings

Every DNS server has a Properties dialog box associated with it, from which you can configure a comprehensive range of server properties. Right-click the DNS server and choose Properties to display the dialog box shown in Figure 2.10. The more important properties are discussed in this section.

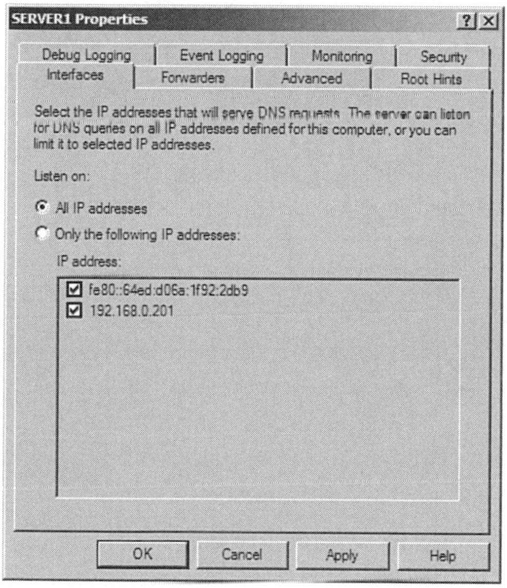

FIGURE 2.10 The DNS server's Properties dialog box enables you to configure many DNS server properties.

Forwarding

The act of *forwarding* refers to the relaying of a DNS request from one server to another one, when the first server is unable to process the request. This is especially useful in resolving Internet names to their associated IP addresses. By using a forwarder, the internal DNS server passes off the act of locating an external resource, thereby reducing its processing load and network bandwidth. The use of forwarding is also helpful for protecting internal DNS servers from access by unauthorized Internet users. It works in the following manner:

1. A client issues a request for a FQDN on a zone for which its preferred DNS server is not authoritative (for example, an Internet domain such as www.google.com).

2. The local DNS server receives this request but has zone information only for the internal local domain and checks its list of forwarders.

3. Finding the IP address of an external DNS server (such as one hosted by the company's ISP), the local DNS server forwards the request to the external server (forwarder).

4. The forwarder attempts to resolve the required FQDN and returns the result to the internal DNS server, which then returns the result to the requesting client.

You can specify forwarders from the Forwarders tab of the DNS server's Properties dialog box, as shown in Figure 2.11. Click Edit to specify the IP address of a forwarder. The server will resolve this IP address to its FQDN and display these in the Forwarders tab.

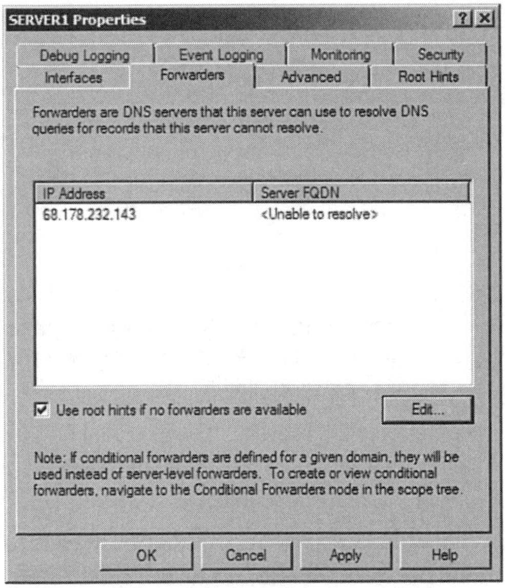

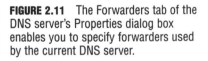

FIGURE 2.11   The Forwarders tab of the DNS server's Properties dialog box enables you to specify forwarders used by the current DNS server.

Conditional Forwarders

You can configure a DNS server as a conditional forwarder. This is a DNS server that handles name resolution for specified domains only. In other words, the local DNS server will forward all the queries that it receives for names ending with a specific domain name to the conditional forwarder.

The DNS snap-in provides a Conditional Forwarders node where you can specify forwarding information. Right-click this node and choose New Conditional Forwarder to display the dialog box shown in Figure 2.12.

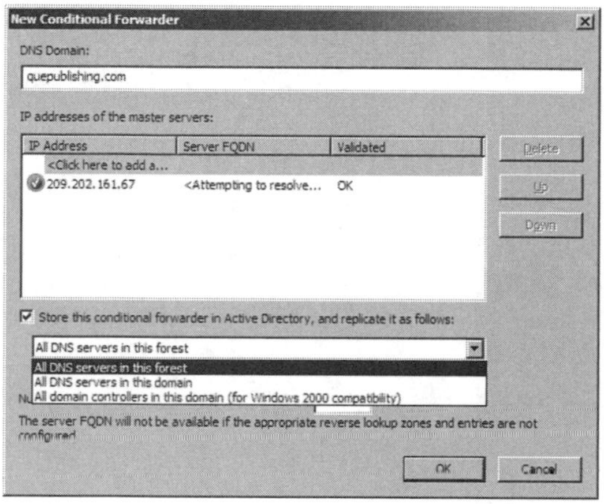

FIGURE 2.12 Creating a new conditional forwarder.

Type the DNS domain that the conditional forwarder will resolve and the IP address of the server that will handle queries for the specified domain. If you want to store the conditional forwarder information in AD DS, select the check box provided and choose an option in the drop-down list shown in Figure 2.12 that specifies the DNS servers in your domain or forest that will receive the conditional forwarder information. Then click OK. Information for the conditional forwarder that you have configured is added beneath the Conditional Forwarders node in the DNS Manager snap-in. Name queries for the specified DNS domain will now be forwarded directly to this server.

EXAM ALERT

The All DNS Servers in This Forest and All DNS Servers in This Domain options will replicate conditional forwarder information to DNS servers running Windows Server 2003 or 2008 only. If you have DNS servers running Windows 2000 that are to receive the conditional forwarder information, you must select the All Domain Controllers in This Domain option. An exam question might test your knowledge of this fact.

Root Hints

Whenever a DNS server is unable to resolve a name directly from its own database or with the aid of a forwarder, it sends the query to a server that is authoritative for the DNS root zone. The server must have the names and addresses of these servers stored in its database to perform such a query. These names and addresses are known as *root hints*, and they are stored in the cache.dns file, which is found at %systemroot%\system32\dns. cache.dns is a text file that contains NS and A records for every available root server.

When you install DNS on a server that is connected to the Internet, it should automatically download the latest set of root hints. You can verify that this has occurred by checking the Root Hints tab of the server's Properties dialog box. You should see a series of FQDNs with their corresponding IP addresses, as shown in Figure 2.13.

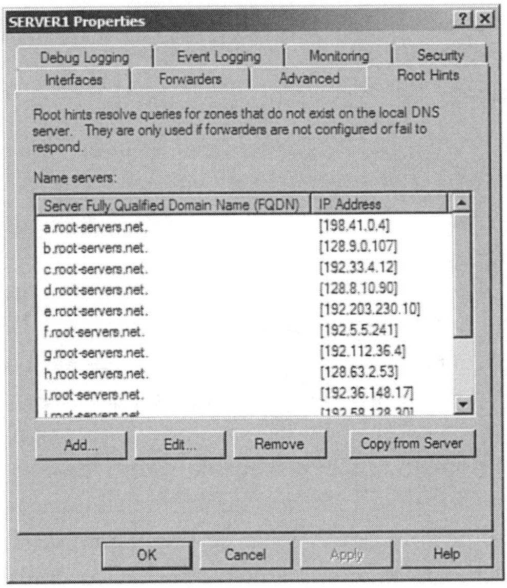

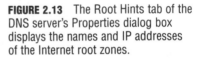

FIGURE 2.13 The Root Hints tab of the DNS server's Properties dialog box displays the names and IP addresses of the Internet root zones.

If your internal DNS server does not provide access to Internet name resolution, you can improve network security by configuring the root hints of the internal DNS servers to point to the DNS servers that host your root domain and not to Internet root domain DNS servers. To modify the configuration on this tab, perform one or more of the following actions:

- ▶ Select Add to manually type the FQDN and IP addresses of one or more authoritative name servers.

- ▶ Select an entry and click Edit to modify it or add an additional IP address to an existing record.

- ▶ Select an entry and click Delete to remove a record.

- ▶ Select Copy from Server to copy a list of root hints from another DNS server. This action is useful if your server was not connected to the Internet at the time DNS was installed.

Configuring Zone Delegation

As you have seen, you can divide your DNS namespace into a series of zones. You can delegate management of these zones to another location or work group within your company by delegating the management of the respective zone. Configuring *zone delegation* involves creating delegation records in other zones that point to the authoritative DNS servers for the zone being delegated.

You can use the New Delegation Wizard to create a zone delegation. The wizard uses the information you supplied to create name server (NS) and host (A or AAAA) resource records for the delegated subdomain. Perform the following procedure:

1. Right-click the parent zone in the console tree of DNS Manager and choose New Delegation. This starts the New Delegation Wizard.

2. Click Next and then enter the name of the delegated subdomain.

3. As shown in Figure 2.14, the wizard appends the parent zone name to form the FQDN of the domain being delegated. Click Next, and then click Add.

4. In the New Name Server Record, type the FQDN and IP address of the DNS server that is authoritative for the subdomain, and then click OK. Repeat if necessary to add additional authoritative DNS servers.

5. When finished, click Next and then click Finish.

The wizard uses the information you supplied to create NS and host (A or AAAA) resource records for the delegated subdomain.

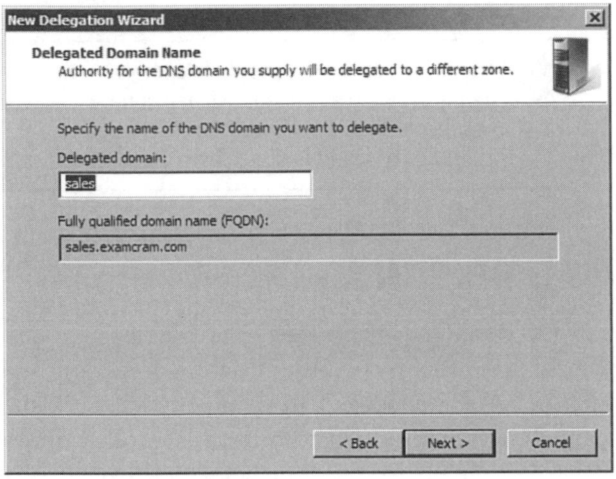

FIGURE 2.14 Creating a zone delegation.

Debug Logging

The DNS server also supports debug logging of packets sent to and from the DNS server to a text file named `dns.log`. This file is stored in the %systemroot%\system32\dns folder. To configure logging, right-click the server in the DNS Manager snap-in and choose Properties. Click the Debug Logging tab to see the dialog box shown in Figure 2.15.

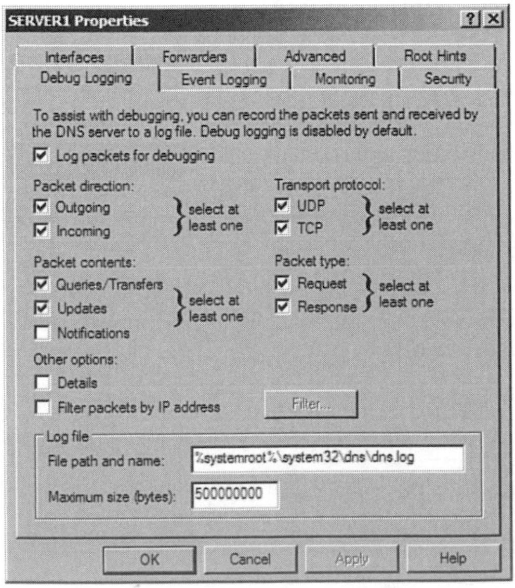

FIGURE 2.15 Configuring debug logging.

By default, no logging is configured. Select the Log Packets for Debugging check box, which makes all other check boxes available. Table 2.2 describes the available logging options.

TABLE 2.2   DNS Debug Logging Options

Option	Description
Packet Direction	Determines the direction of packets logged, incoming or outgoing or both.
Transport Protocol	Select UDP to log the number of DNS requests received over a UDP port, and select TCP to log the number of DNS requests received over a TCP port.
Packet Contents	Select at least one of the available options to determine the types of packets logged by the server: ▶ Queries/Transfers—Logs packets containing standard queries, according to RFC 1034. ▶ Updates—Logs packets containing dynamic updates, according to RFC 2136. ▶ Notifications—Logs packets containing notifications, according to RFC 1996.
Packet Type	Determines whether the request or response packets are logged, or both.
Other Options	Select Details to enable logging of detailed information.
	Select Filter to limit the packets that are logged according to IP address. This logs packets sent from specific IP addresses to the DNS server, or from the DNS server to these specific IP addresses (according to the incoming or outgoing choice).
Log File	Enables you to change the default file path, name, and maximum size. If the maximum size is exceeded, the DNS server overwrites the oldest logged data.

CAUTION

Configure debug logging only when absolutely necessary, only on required DNS servers, and only on a temporary basis. Its use is highly resource intensive. This is why debug logging is disabled by default.

To view the DNS log, first stop the DNS service by right-clicking the DNS server in DNS Manager and choosing All Tasks, Stop. Then open the log in either Notepad or WordPad. When you are finished, restart the DNS service by right-clicking the DNS server and choosing All Tasks, Start.

Event Logging

The Event Logging tab of the DNS server's Properties dialog box enables you to control how much information is logged to the DNS log, which appears in Event Viewer. You can choose from one of the following options:

▶ **No Events**—Suppresses all event logging (not recommended).

▶ **Errors Only**—Logs error events only.

▶ **Errors and Warnings**—Logs errors and warnings only.

▶ **All Events**—Logs informational events, errors, and warnings. This is the default.

Choosing either the Errors Only or Errors and Warnings option might be useful to reduce the amount of information recorded to the DNS event log.

Advanced Server Options

The Advanced tab of the DNS server's Properties dialog box shown in Figure 2.16 contains a series of options with which you should be familiar.

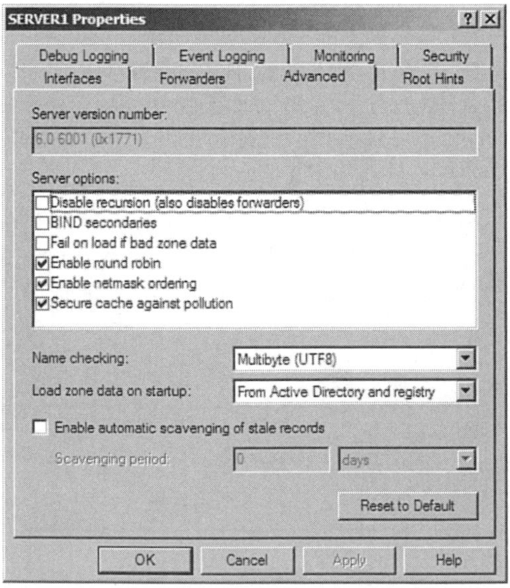

FIGURE 2.16 The Advanced tab of the DNS server's Properties dialog box.

Server Options

The Server Options section of the Advanced Server Options dialog box contains the following six options, the last three of which are selected by default:

- **Disable Recursion**—Prevents the DNS server from forwarding queries to other DNS servers. Select this check box on a DNS server that only provides resolution services to other DNS servers, because unauthorized users can use recursion to overload a DNS server's resources and thereby deny the DNS Server service to legitimate users.

- **BIND Secondaries**—During zone transfer, DNS servers normally utilize a fast transfer method that involves compression. If UNIX servers running a version of Berkeley Internet Name Domain (BIND) prior to 4.9.4 are present, zone transfers will not work. These servers use a slower uncompressed data transfer method. To enable zone transfer to these servers, select this check box.

- **Fail on Load if Bad Zone Data**—When selected, DNS servers will not load zone data that contains certain types of errors. The DNS service checks name data using the method selected in the Name Checking drop-down list on this tab.

- **Enable Round Robin**—*Round robin* is a load-balancing mechanism used by DNS servers to distribute name resolution activity among all available DNS servers. If multiple A or AAAA resource records are found in a DNS query (for example, on a multihomed computer), round robin sequences these resource records in repeated queries for the same computer.

- **Enable Netmask Ordering**—Prioritizes local subnets so that when a client queries for a host name mapped to multiple IP addresses, the DNS server preferentially returns an IP address located on the same subnet as the requesting client.

- **Secure Cache Against Pollution**—Cache pollution takes place when DNS query responses contain malicious items received from nonauthoritative servers. This option prevents attackers from adding such resource records to the DNS cache. The DNS servers ignore resource records for domain names outside the domain to which the query was originally directed. For example, if you sent a query for examcram.com and a referral provided a name such as examprep.com, the latter name would not be cached when this option was enabled.

Name Checking

The Name Checking setting enables you to configure the DNS server to permit names that contain characters that are not allowed by normal DNS standards outlined in RFC 1123. You can select the following options:

▶ **Strict RFC (ANSI)**—Uses strict name checking according to RFC 1123 host naming specifications. Noncompliant DNS names generate error messages.

▶ **Non RFC (ANSI)**—Permits nonstandard names that do not conform to RFC 1123 host naming specifications. ASCII characters that are not compliant to RFC 1123 specifications are accepted.

▶ **Multibyte (UTFB)**—The default setting, which enables the transformation and recoding of multibyte non-ASCII characters according to Unicode Transformation Format (UTF-8) specifications.

▶ **All Names**—Permits names containing any types of characters.

If you receive an error with ID 4006, indicating that the DNS server was unable to load the records in the specified name found in the Active Directory–integrated zone, the DNS name contains unsupported characters. You can resolve this problem by selecting the All Names option and restarting the DNS service, which enables the DNS names to be loaded. If the names are improper, you can delete them and then reset the Name Checking setting.

Loading Zone Data

When a DNS server containing an Active Directory–integrated zone starts up, it normally uses information stored in this zone and in the Registry to initialize the service and load its zone data. This option enables you to specify that the DNS server starts from the Registry only, or from a file named Boot located in the %systemroot%\System32\Dns folder. This optional file is similar in format to that used by BIND servers.

Server Scavenging

When DHCP registers A and PTR resource records automatically, these records remain in the DNS zone data indefinitely. If computers are frequently added to or removed from the network (for example, when many portable computers are in use), many stale resource records can accumulate. As mentioned earlier in this chapter, these records can degrade the DNS server's performance. By selecting the Enable Automatic Scavenging of Stale Records check box, the DNS server checks the age of each dynamically assigned record and removes records that are older than the scavenging period that you specify in this option (7 days by default). Note that Windows computers send a request to the DNS server to update their records every 24 hours; consequently, DNS records from active computers never become stale even if their TCP/IP configuration does not change.

Scavenging is disabled by default. You should enable scavenging if computers are frequently added to or removed from the network to ensure continued optimum performance of DNS servers.

NOTE

You can also set server scavenging properties by right-clicking the server in the console tree of DNS Manager and choosing Set Aging/Scavenging for All Zones. The Server Aging/Scavenging Properties dialog box that displays offers the same options previously shown in Figure 2.9 for zone scavenging; however, these settings are applied to all zones hosted by this server.

TIP

If you have improperly configured options on this tab and want to return to the default options, click the Reset to Default command button at the bottom of this tab, and then click Apply to apply this change without closing the dialog box or OK to apply the changes and close the dialog box.

Monitoring DNS

DNS Manager includes a testing capability that enables you to perform test queries that verify the proper installation and operation of the DNS server. In the console tree of the DNS snap-in, right-click the DNS server name and choose Properties to open the server's Properties page. Shown in Figure 2.17, the Monitoring tab enables you to perform two types of test queries:

▶ **Simple query**—The DNS client software performs a local query to a zone stored in the DNS server (including Active Directory–integrated zones).

▶ **Recursive query**—A recursive query is forwarded to another DNS server for resolution.

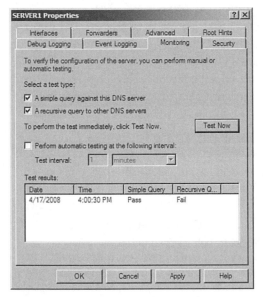

FIGURE 2.17   The Monitoring tab enables you to perform simple and recursive test queries against the DNS server.

To perform these queries, select the appropriate check boxes, as illustrated in Figure 2.17, and click the Test Now command button. The result is displayed in the field directly below. You can also schedule the test to occur automatically at preconfigured intervals.

A `Pass` result for the simple test confirms that DNS has been correctly installed on this server. If the simple test fails, you should ensure that the local server contains the zone `1.0.0.127.in-addr.arpa`. If the recursive test fails, check the connectivity to the remote server as well as the presence and correctness of the root hints file (`cache.dns`).

DNS also adds a log to the Event Viewer and several objects and counters to the Performance Monitor. In addition, you can use the `Nslookup` utility to verify the accuracy of resource records. Refer to "`Nslookup`" in Appendix A, "Need to Know More?" and *MCSA/MCSE Managing and Maintaining a Windows Server 2003 Environment Exam Cram 2 (Exam Cram 70-292)* (ISBN: 0789730111) for additional details on these monitoring tools.

Command-Line DNS Server Administration

You can perform most of the DNS administrative tasks outlined here from the command line by using the *dnscmd.exe* utility provided with Windows Server 2008 DNS. This is especially useful for scripting repetitive tasks and is the only method available for configuring DNS locally on a Server Core computer. (You can also connect to a Server Core computer from a remote computer running the DNS Manager snap-in.) Using this command, you can display and modify the properties of DNS servers, zones, and resource records. You can also force replication between DNS server physical memory and DNS databases or data files.

To use this utility, open a command prompt and type the following:

Dnscmd <server_name> command {parameters}

In this command, <server_name> is the name or IP address of the DNS server against which the command is to be executed (if omitted, the local server is used), *command* represents the dnscmd subcommand to be executed, and *parameters* represents additional parameters required by the subcommand being executed. Table 2.3 summarizes many of the more useful dnscmd subcommands.

TABLE 2.3 Useful Dnscmd Subcommands

Subcommand	Description
Clearcache	Clears resource records from the DNS cache memory.
Config	Enables the user to modify a range of configuration values stored in the Registry and individual zones.
Enumzones	Displays a complete list of zones configured for the server.
Info	Displays DNS server configuration information as stored in the server's Registry. You can specify which setting for which information will be returned.
Statistics	Displays or clears statistical data for the specified server. You can specify which statistics are to be displayed according to ID numbers.
Zoneadd *zone_name*	Adds a zone to the DNS server.
Zonedelete *zone_name*	Deletes the specified zone from the DNS server.
Zoneexport *zone_name*	Exports all resource records in the specified DNS zone to a text file.
Zoneinfo *zone_name*	Displays Registry-based configuration information for the specified DNS zone.

For a complete list and description of available dnscmd commands including parameters used with the dnscmd config command, refer to "Dnscmd syntax" in Appendix A.

Configuring Zone Transfers and Replication

When changes are made to zone data on the master DNS server, they must be replicated to all DNS servers that are authoritative for the zone. This is essential so that the data will be available for answering queries. If only a single DNS server is available and it fails to respond, the query will fail.

The following two methods of DNS replication are available in Windows Server 2008 DNS:

▶ Active Directory replication, which is used for replicating Active Directory–integrated zones.

▶ Zone transfer, which can be used by all types of DNS zones. Active Directory–integrated zones also use zone transfer to replicate data to a standard secondary zone located on another DNS server operated for purposes of fault tolerance, load balancing, and reduction of DNS network traffic.

Replication Scope

The replication scope of an Active Directory–integrated DNS zone refers to the subset of DNS servers or domain controllers that actively participate in replication of the specific zone. DNS in Windows Server 2008 makes available the replication scopes described in Table 2.4.

TABLE 2.4 Available DNS Replication Scopes

Replication Scope	Description
All DNS servers in the forest hosted on domain controllers running Windows Server 2003 or 2008	Replicates zone data to all Windows Server 2003 or 2008 domain controllers running DNS in the AD DS forest. Replicating zone data to the ForestDNSZones application directory partition provides the broadest replication scope.

TABLE 2.4 *Continued*

Replication Scope	Description
All DNS servers in the domain hosted on domain controllers running Windows Server 2003 or 2008	Replicates zone data to all Windows Server 2003 or 2008 domain controllers running DNS in the AD DS domain by replicating zone data to the DomainDNSZones application directory partition. This is the default replication scope.
All domain controllers in the AD DS domain	Replicates zone data to all domain controllers in the AD DS domain. This scope is required if you want Windows 2000 DNS servers to be included in the scope of an Active Directory–integrated zone. When this scope is used, zone data is stored in the domain directory partition.
All domain controllers hosting a specified application directory partition	Replicates zone data according to the replication scope of the specified application directory scope. Enables the replication of zone data to domain controllers in multiple domains without replicating the data to the entire AD DS forest.

To change the replication scope of an Active Directory–integrated zone, right-click the zone in DNS Manager and choose Properties. On the General tab of the zone's Properties dialog box, click Change next to Replication. From the dialog box shown in Figure 2.18, select the desired option, and then click OK.

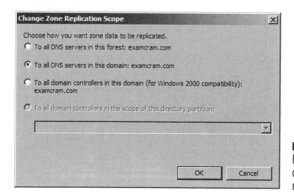

FIGURE 2.18 The Change Zone Replication Scope dialog box offers options for configuring a zone's replication scope.

Note that replication scope is not available for DNS zones that are not integrated with Active Directory. These zones use the zone transfer method only for replication.

EXAM ALERT

If you have Windows 2000 DNS servers, you must select the To All Domain Controllers in This Domain option in Figure 2.18. If you upgrade all Windows 2000 DNS servers to Windows Server 2003 or 2008, you can change the replication scope to any of the other available options.

Types of Zone Transfers

Every version of DNS since Windows 2000 has supported two types of zone transfer: *full zone transfer (AXFR)* and *incremental zone transfer (IXFR)*.

Full Zone Transfer

The original specifications for DNS supported only the full zone transfer process, in which the master server transmits the entire zone database to that zone's secondary servers. When a new secondary DNS server is added to the network, it uses AXFR to obtain a full copy of the zone's resource records. AXFR was the only zone transfer process supported by Windows NT 4.0 DNS.

Incremental Zone Transfer

The process of incremental zone transfer, as specified in RFC 1995, replicates only the modified portion of each zone file. It is, therefore, more efficient and uses less bandwidth than the full zone transfer process.

The DNS servers involved in the IXFR process use the following sequential procedure:

1. The secondary DNS server sends an IXFR request to the primary server. This request contains a serial number for the secondary server's current zone database, which is found in its SOA resource record. This serial number is incremented each time the zone information changes. The SOA record also contains a number called the refresh interval, which is 15 minutes by default and determines how often the server sends the IXFR request.

2. The master server checks the secondary server's serial number against the current one.

3. If the two serial numbers are equal, the master server determines that no zone transfer is needed at the current time, and the process ends.

4. If the primary server's serial number is higher, a zone transfer is required.

5. This server checks its history file that indicates which portions of the zone have been modified at what time. It uses this file to determine the updates that must be sent in response to the IXFR request.

6. When the secondary server receives the incremental zone transfer, it creates a new version of the zone file and replaces the updated records with the new ones, beginning with the oldest one.

7. When the secondary server has updated all the records, it replaces the old version of the zone with the newest version of the zone.

A full zone transfer may still take place rather than an incremental zone transfer under the following conditions:

▶ If the master DNS server does not support incremental zone transfers

▶ If the bandwidth required for sending an incremental zone transfer is greater than that required for sending a full zone transfer

▶ If the master DNS server does not possess all the data required for the incremental zone transfer, such as an accurate history file

DNS servers that load zone data from Active Directory use a similar process, in which they poll the directory at an interval determined by the refresh interval in the SOA record for updating and refreshing their zone.

Configuring Zone Transfers

The Zone Transfers tab of a zone's Properties dialog box enables you to configure the scope of zone transfers. Right-click the zone in DNS Manager, choose Properties, and then select the Zone Transfers tab. You can select any of the options displayed in Figure 2.19 to specify the scope of zone transfers.

By selecting the Only to Servers Listed on the Name Servers Tab, you enable zone transfers to all DNS servers for which NS records are specified in the zone data. The Name Servers tab and its configuration are discussed later in this section. By specifying the Only to the Following Servers option, you can specify DNS servers that are to receive zone transfers according to IP address or FQDN.

NOTE

If you are using Active Directory–integrated zones, zone data is automatically replicated to all other domain controllers in the domain. Consequently, you cannot limit zone transfers for Active Directory–integrated zones.

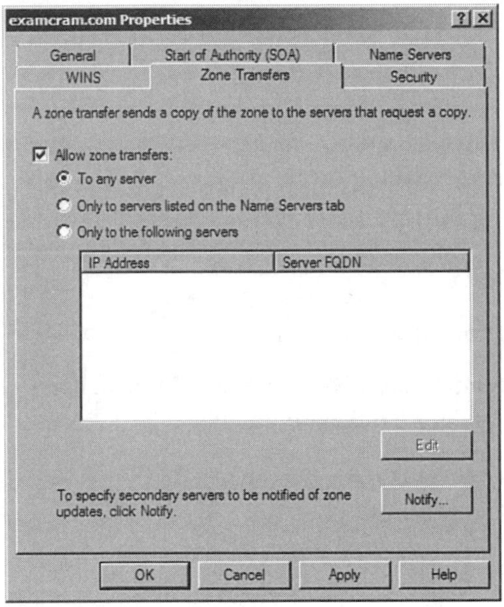

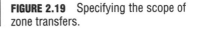

FIGURE 2.19 Specifying the scope of zone transfers.

Configuring DNS Notify

DNS Notify is a process in which the master DNS server for a zone notifies secondary servers of changes to the zone; that way, the secondary servers can determine whether they need to initiate a zone transfer. You can configure the DNS server for DNS Notify by specifying the list of IP addresses to which notifications are to be sent. Configuring the notify list also helps you to prevent attempts by unknown DNS servers to request zone updates from your server.

To configure the notify list, access the Zone Transfers tab of the zone's Properties dialog box previously shown in Figure 2.19 and click the Notify command button. In the Notify dialog box shown in Figure 2.20, ensure that Automatically Notify is selected. Then select Servers Listed on the Name Servers Tab to use the list of DNS servers for which NS records are configured (as discussed later in this section), or select The Following Servers to specify the desired servers by IP address. When finished, click OK to close the Notify dialog box and click OK again to close the zone's Properties dialog box.

NOTE

The notify list is required only for servers that operate as secondary DNS servers for zones that are not integrated with AD DS. You do not need to configure DNS Notify for Active Directory–integrated zones.

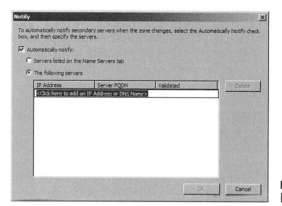

Secure Zone Transfers

If you are using DNS servers running BIND 9 or higher, you can specify that zone transfers be digitally signed. This feature enables secondary DNS servers to verify that zone transfers are being received from a trusted source.

As already discussed, you cannot limit the scope of zone transfer when using Active Directory–integrated zones. If you are concerned about zone data passing through an unsecured network segment, you can use a security mechanism such as IP Security (IPSec) to provide secure zone transfer.

Configuring Name Servers

The Name Servers tab of the zone's Properties dialog box shown in Figure 2.21 enables you to configure secondary name servers that are authoritative for the zone, which are DNS servers that receive zone updates for zones that are not integrated with AD DS. To add a name server to this list, click Add, and in the New Name Server Record dialog box shown in Figure 2.22, type the server FQDN and IP address. Click Resolve to validate the name and IP address combination, and then click OK. The FQDN and IP address are added to the list in the Name Servers tab. By selecting the zone name in the console tree of the DNS Manager snap-in, you can see the NS record that has been added to the list.

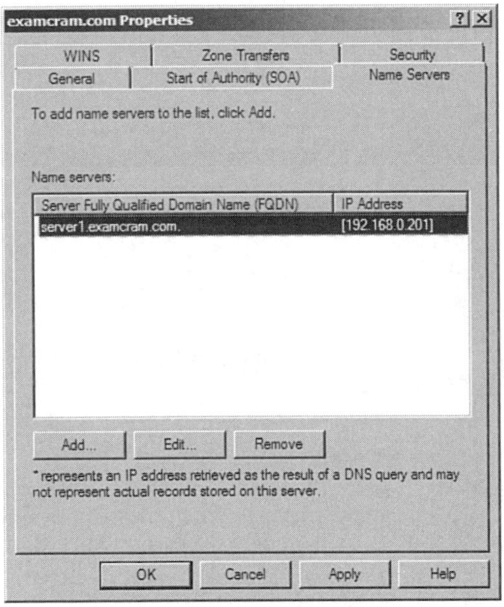

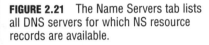

FIGURE 2.21 The Name Servers tab lists all DNS servers for which NS resource records are available.

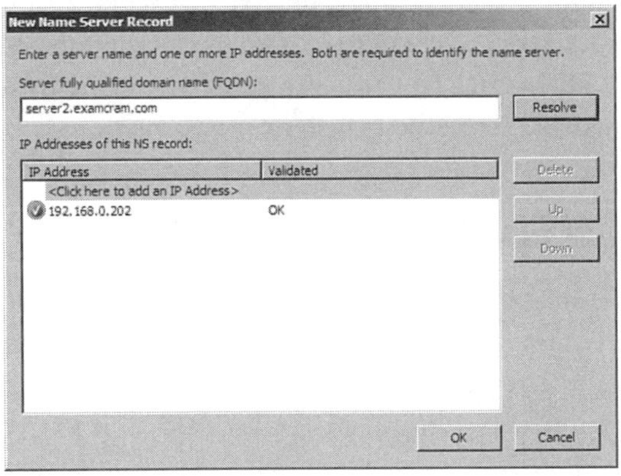

FIGURE 2.22 The New Name Server Record dialog box enables you to add a new name server to the list in the Name Servers tab of the zone's Properties dialog box.

To edit an entry in the Name Servers tab, select it and click Edit. The Edit Name Server Record dialog box, which is similar to the New Name Server Record dialog box, enables you to add additional IP addresses or modify the name of the server. You can prioritize the IP addresses on the IP address list by using the Up and Down buttons or delete an IP address by selecting it and using the Delete button. You can also delete an entry from the Name Servers tab by selecting it and clicking Remove.

Application Directory Partitions

Introduced in Windows Server 2003, an *application directory partition* (also simply called an *application partition*) contains application-specific data that needs to be replicated only to specific domain controllers in one or more domains of the Active Directory forest. DNS stores its Active Directory–integrated zone data in the following application directory partitions, which are automatically created when you install DNS during creation of your domain:

▶ **ForestDnsZones**—Contains forestwide DNS zone data, one partition per forest

▶ **DomainDnsZones**—Contains domainwide DNS zone data, one partition for each domain in the forest

By utilizing application directory partitions, Active Directory replicates its DNS data to other domain controllers in the forest. A benefit of application directory partitions is that their data can be replicated only to specific domain controllers, as opposed to domain partitions, which are replicated to all domain controllers in the domain. Consequently, replication traffic is reduced. For example, DNS application directory partitions are replicated only to those domain controllers that are running DNS. The same application directory partition can replicate to domain controllers in more than one domain in the forest.

Installing and Configuring Application Directory Partitions

An application directory partition is identified by its LDAP distinguished name (DN). For example, you can create an application partition named `app` on the examcram.com domain by using the DN `dc=app,dc=examcram,dc=com`. You can use the `ntdsutil` utility previously introduced in Chapter 1 for creating an application directory partition, as follows:

1. Log on to a domain controller or member server as a member of the Domain Admins or Enterprise Admins group.

2. Open a command prompt and type **ntdsutil**.

3. At the `ntdsutil` prompt, type **domain management**.

4. At the `domain management` prompt, type **connection**.

5. At the `connection` prompt, type **connect to server <server>**, where *<server>* is the name of the domain controller to which you want to connect.

6. Type **quit** to return to the `domain management` prompt.

7. At this prompt, type **create nc** *<application_directory_partition>*
   <domain_controller>, where *<application_directory_partition>* is
   the DN of the application directory partition you want to create, and
   <domain_controller> is the name of the domain controller on which
   you want to create the partition. Type **null** to create the application
   directory partition on the current domain controller. For example, to
   create an application directory partition named App1 on Server1, type
   create nc App1 Server1.

8. You receive a prompt informing you that the object was added to the
   directory. Type **quit** twice to exit the ntdsutil utility.

You can also use ntdsutil to delete application directory partitions that are no
longer required. At step 7 of this procedure, type **delete nc** *<application_*
directory_partition> <domain_controller>.

Creating Application Directory Partition Replicas

The previous procedure creates an application partition on the indicated
domain controller only. To replicate the partition to other domain controllers in
the domain or forest, you need to create an *application directory partition replica*.
In this manner, you can control the set of domain controllers among which the
partition is replicated.

The procedure for creating a replica is the same as that for creating the application directory partition as outlined in the previous section, except that at step 7,
you need to type **add nc replica** *<application_directory_partition>*
<domain_controller>. The DN you specify should be the same as that of the
partition you have created, and *<domain_controller>* is the name of the
domain controller where the replica is to be placed. For example, to add a replica
of the App1 application directory partition to server Server2, type **add nc**
replica App1 Server2.

Should you no longer require a replica on a given domain controller, you can
follow this procedure, using the remove nc replica command in place of the
add nc replica command.

Application Directory Partition Reference Domains

The *application directory partition reference domain* is the parent domain of the application directory partition; in other words, it is the domain name as included in the partition's DN. It is also known as the *security descriptor reference domain*.

You can change an application directory partition's reference domain by using the `ntdsutil` utility. Follow the procedure previously described for installing an application directory partition, and in step 7, type **set nc reference domain** *<application_directory_partition>* *<reference_domain>*, where *<reference_domain>* is the DN of the desired reference domain.

Exam Cram Questions

1. Chloe is responsible for administering DNS for a company that operates an AD DS network consisting of a single domain. Currently, two member servers are configured as the network's only DNS servers.

   Chloe would like to provide fault tolerance for the DNS zones so that if a single DNS server fails, updates can still be made to the DNS zones. In addition, she would like to ensure that only computers that are authorized by a domain controller can update the DNS resource record information.

   Which of the following must Chloe do to satisfy these requirements? (Choose all that apply.)

   - ○ **A.** Install DNS on at least two domain controllers.

   - ○ **B.** Create a stub zone.

   - ○ **C.** Create an Active Directory–integrated zone.

   - ○ **D.** Select the Secure Only Dynamic Updates option.

   - ○ **E.** Select the Secure and Nonsecure Dynamic Updates option.

2. Sharon is responsible for administering DNS on her company's AD DS network, which includes a single domain. All domain controllers on the network are configured as DNS servers with an Active Directory–integrated zone. When checking the configuration of one of the DNS servers, Sharon notices that the zone includes resource records for computers that were removed from the network several weeks ago. She decides she wants to remove these resource records immediately. What should she do?

   - ○ **A.** In DNS Manager, right-click the DNS server and choose Scavenge Stale Resource Records.

   - ○ **B.** From the Zone Aging/Scavenging Properties dialog box, select the Scavenge Stale Resource Records check box.

   - ○ **C.** From the Advanced tab of the DNS server's Properties dialog box, select Enable Automatic Scavenging of Stale Records.

   - ○ **D.** In DNS Manager, select the DNS zone, and then delete the stale resource records from the list that appears in the Details pane.

3. Duane administers the network for his company. His network consists of five server computers running Windows Server 2008 and 20 client computers running Windows XP Professional and Windows Vista Business. In the process of switching ISPs, it has been determined that the new ISP's DNS servers are all that is required to resolve names on the Internet for clients on Duane's network. Duane's primary DNS server will need to resolve names only for those clients located on his internal network. Currently,

it performs name resolution for both external and internal names. Duane needs to configure his DNS server so that it will no longer perform external name resolution for clients on his internal network.

Duane opens the DNS Manager console, right-clicks his DNS server, and chooses Properties. Which tabs of the Properties dialog box will Duane need to access to configure his DNS server to resolve internal names only? (Choose all that apply.)

- ○ **A.** Debug Logging
- ○ **B.** Event Logging
- ○ **C.** Monitoring
- ○ **D.** Security
- ○ **E.** Interfaces
- ○ **F.** Forwarders
- ○ **G.** Advanced
- ○ **H.** Root Hints

4. Mark is network administrator for Acme Construction Ltd. The company's network consists of a single AD DS domain called acmeconstr.com. Servers in the domain run either Windows Server 2003 or Windows Server 2008, and client computers run either Windows XP Professional or Windows Vista Business. Two Windows Server 2008 computers named NS01 and NS02 host DNS zones for the acmeconstr.com domain; NS01 hosts a standard primary zone, and NS02 hosts a standard secondary DNS zone. Queries that cannot be resolved by these servers are forwarded to Acme Construction's ISP.

Because Acme Construction has put a number of jobs out for tender in the past few months, its DNS servers are receiving an exceptionally high number of requests and are becoming bogged down as a result. Mark decides to create a new zone called bids.acmeconstr.com to handle the traffic. He decides to configure a new Windows Server 2008 DNS server called NS03 and dedicate it exclusively to servicing DNS requests for the bids.acmeconstr.com zone, where all future bids will be directed. To do this, he needs to delegate control of the bids.acmeconstr.com zone to the NS03 server. How should Mark proceed?

- ○ **A.** Manually create an A record for the NS03 server computer.
- ○ **B.** Use the New Delegation Wizard in the DNS console to delegate control of the new zone.
- ○ **C.** Manually create an A record and an NS record for the NS03 server computer.
- ○ **D.** Add the appropriate IP address for NS03 to the Forwarders tab on the NS01 and NS02 server computers.

5. Stuart is responsible for administering the DNS servers in his company's AD DS network, which contains an Active Directory–integrated zone. A DNS server named Server7 does not appear to be receiving accurate zone transfer information.

Stuart decides to capture information that relates to DNS update data that should be sent and received at Server7, so he enables every debugging option available on the Debug Logging tab of the server's Properties dialog box, as shown in the exhibit. The next day, after noticing that the log has collected a large quantity of data, he realizes that he does not need detailed information and that he should clear certain options. Which of the following options should Stuart clear? (Choose all that apply.)

- ○ **A.** Log Packets for Debugging
- ○ **B.** Queries/Transfers
- ○ **C.** Updates
- ○ **D.** Notifications
- ○ **E.** Details
- ○ **F.** Filter Packets by IP Address

6. Nancy is a systems administrator for her company, which has just purchased a new computer running Windows Server 2008. She has installed this computer as a DNS server on the internal network and has assigned it a static IP address of 172.22.1.3. She accesses the Monitoring tab of the server's properties dialog box on the DNS snap-in, selects the simple and recursive query test type, and runs these tests. However, she receives a Fail response in both test columns.

What should Nancy try first to troubleshoot this failure?

- ○ **A.** Determine whether the root hints are correct.
- ○ **B.** Restart the DNS server service.
- ○ **C.** Access the Debug Logging tab and specify logging of incoming and outgoing packets with the Queries/Transfers option.
- ○ **D.** Determine whether the server contains the `1.0.0.127.in-addr.arpa` zone.

7. Heidi is the network administrator for a financial company that operates an AD DS network consisting of a single domain. Servers on the network run a mix of Windows Server 2003 and Windows Server 2008. Heidi will be upgrading Windows Server 2003 DNS servers to Windows Server 2008 and needs to obtain information about the configuration of the DNS zones. Which of the following commands should she run?

- ○ **A.** `Dnscmd /enumzones`
- ○ **B.** `Dnscmd /statistics`
- ○ **C.** `Dnscmd /zoneinfo`
- ○ **D.** `Dnscmd /info`

8. Bill is responsible for administering DNS on his company's AD DS network, which includes a single domain configured with an Active Directory–integrated zone. The domain contains two Windows Server 2008 domain controllers that host the DNS zone and one Windows 2000 domain controller. He installs DNS on the Windows 2000 domain controller and adds the Active Directory–integrated zone to take some of the heavy name resolution load away from the two Windows Server 2008 domain controllers that are currently configured to host DNS on the network.

A week after setting up DNS on this server, Bill starts to receive reports from users who have been directed to incorrect servers or have been unable to reach some of the servers. He checks the Windows 2000 DNS server and notices that the zone data on this computer has not been properly updated. What should he do to resolve this problem?

- ○ **A.** Change the zone replication scope to the All DNS Servers in This Domain option.
- ○ **B.** Change the zone replication scope to the All Domain Controllers in This Domain option.
- ○ **C.** Add the Windows 2000 Server computer to the list on the Name Servers tab of the zone's Properties dialog box.
- ○ **D.** On the Zone Transfers tab of the zone's Properties dialog box, select the To Any Server option.

9. Donna administers a single AD DS domain called examcram.com. She has decided against configuring examcram.com as an Active Directory–integrated zone. Donna has designated her domain controllers as Pegasus01 and Pegasus02. Her DNS servers are called Hercules01, Hercules02, and Hercules03. Hercules01 is the master DNS server. Hercules02 and Hercules03 are secondary DNS servers.

   Donna would like only Hercules01 and Hercules02 to be authoritative for the examcram.com zone, so she specifies these two servers on the Name Servers tab of the examcram.com Properties dialog box. She accesses the Zone Transfers tab and clicks Notify to open the Notify dialog box. How should she configure the options in this dialog box so that all DNS servers are notified of any DNS zone updates? (Each correct answer represents part of the solution. Choose two answers.)

   ○ **A.** Select the Automatically Notify check box.

   ○ **B.** Clear the Automatically Notify check box.

   ○ **C.** Select the Servers Listed on the Name Servers Tab option.

   ○ **D.** Select the option labeled The Following Servers and specify IP address information for Hercules01, Hercules02, and Hercules03.

   ○ **E.** Select the option labeled The Following Servers and specify IP address information for Hercules01, Pegasus01, and Pegasus02.

   ○ **F.** Select the option labeled The Following Servers and specify IP address information for Hercules02 and Hercules03.

10. Julian has created an application directory partition named APP1 on a domain controller in the examprep.com domain to store data from a custom engineering package and replicate it to domain controllers named Server4 and Server5. Server5 is located in a child domain named design.examprep.com. What should Julian do to enable the partition to replicate to these domain controllers?

    ○ **A.** Specify design.examprep.com as the application directory partition reference domain.

    ○ **B.** Create new application directory partitions on both Server4 and Server5.

    ○ **C.** Create application directory partition replicas on both Server4 and Server5.

    ○ **D.** He does not need to do anything. AD DS replication will automatically replicate the partition to these domain controllers.

Answers to *Exam Cram* Questions

1. **A, C, D.** To meet these requirements, Chloe needs to configure the DNS zones as Active Directory–integrated zones. To have Active Directory–integrated zones, she needs to have DNS running on at least one domain controller, thereby enabling DNS to be replicated along with the remainder of Active Directory. She also needs to configure the drop-down list labeled Dynamic Updates to Secure only. A stub zone contains source information about authoritative name servers for its zone only. It does not promote fault tolerance, so answer B is incorrect. Choosing to allow secure and nonsecure updates permits any computer, regardless of whether it is authorized, to perform dynamic updates to the DNS zones, so answer E is incorrect.

2. **A.** Sharon should right-click the DNS server in DNS Manager and choose Scavenge Stale Resource Records. This action performs an immediate scavenging of all stale resource records without the need to configure scavenging properties first. If she were to select the Scavenge Stale Resource Records check box, it would not enable immediate scavenging of stale resource records, so answer B is incorrect. Selecting Enable Automatic Scavenging of Stale Records also does not enable immediate scavenging, so answer C is incorrect. Sharon could delete the stale resource records from the Details pane of the DNS Manager snap-in, but these records would be re-created by replication from the other DNS server, so answer D is incorrect.

3. **F, H.** Duane must access the Forwarders tab and the Root Hints tab. On the Forwarders tab, Duane needs to specify that an external server (namely, the ISP's server) will perform name resolution on behalf of his internal server. Then the local DNS server sends all queries for external names to the ISP's server. From the Roots Hints tab, Duane should clear all the root hints as found in the `cache.dns` file. He can optionally specify a local DNS server or the ISP's server in this file. The Debug Logging tab enables him to configure logging of packets sent to or from the DNS server. The Event Logging tab enables him to specify the level of events recorded by the DNS server, for performance analysis purposes. The Monitoring tab enables him to perform simple and recursive test queries for verifying DNS server functionality. The Security tab enables him to configure groups or users with administrative permissions on the server. The Interfaces tab allows him to specify the IP addresses that the server will listen to queries on. The Advanced tab enables him to configure options such as disabling recursion, BIND secondaries, round robin, netmask ordering, and so on. Duane does not need to configure any of these tabs for this scenario, so answers A, B, C, D, E, and G are incorrect.

4. **B.** Mark should use the New Delegation Wizard in the DNS console to delegate control of the new zone to the NS03 server computer. The wizard automatically creates the A and NS resource records required by the NS03 server. Manually creating and configuring these records would require an excessive amount of administrative effort, so answers A and C are incorrect. Aside from the fact that delegation takes precedence over forwarding if Mark added the appropriate IP address for NS03 to the Forwarders tab on the NS01 and NS02 server computers, those computers would still need to handle queries for the new zone in some fashion. Therefore, answer D is incorrect.

5. **B, D, E, F.** The Queries/Transfers option is not needed for this scenario, so Stuart can clear this check box. The Notifications option is not needed either, because he is attempting to troubleshoot an update problem, not a notification one. He should clear the Filter Packets by IP Address check box, because there is no need here to filter by IP address. Stuart has realized that he doesn't need detailed information, so he should clear the Details check box. If he were to clear the Log Packets for Debugging check box, no information would be collected, so answer A is incorrect. He needs to keep Updates selected because this is the type of data required according to the scenario, so answer C is incorrect.

6. **D.** Nancy should determine whether the server contains the `1.0.0.127.in-addr.arpa` zone. If this zone is absent, the simple test query will fail. In the DNS snap-in, Nancy should expand the entries for the server, select Reverse Lookup Zones, and verify that this zone is present. If it is not present, she should add it and retest. The root hints assist servers that are authoritative at low levels of the domain name-space in locating root DNS servers. If the root hints are not present, the recursive test will fail but the simple test will pass. Therefore, answer A is incorrect. If they are correct, Nancy should then stop and restart the DNS server service. This is not the first step she should try, so answer B is incorrect. Collecting debug logging data might help if all other troubleshooting steps fail, but it is also not the first step, so answer C is incorrect.

7. **C.** Heidi should run the `dnscmd /zoneinfo` command. This command displays Registry-based configuration information for the specified DNS zone. She would include the zone name as a parameter in this command and repeat the command as required to obtain information on additional zones. The `dnscmd /enumzones` command displays a list of zones configured on the server. The `dnscmd /statistics` command displays or clears statistical data for the server. The `dnscmd /info` command displays Registry-based server configuration information. None of these commands provide zone configuration information, so answers A, B, and D are incorrect.

8. **B.** Bill should change the zone replication scope to the All Domain Controllers In This Domain option. This option stores data for Active Directory–integrated zones in the domain directory partition so that zone data can be replicated properly to the Windows 2000 DNS server. The All DNS Servers in the Domain option replicates zone data to Windows Server 2003 and 2008 DNS servers only, so answer A is incorrect. Adding the Windows 2000 Server computer to the list on the Name Servers tab enables Bill to specify secondary name servers but does not solve the zone replication problem, so answer C is incorrect. Allowing zone transfers to any server also does not solve the problem as long as zone data is being stored in an application directory partition, so answer D is incorrect.

9. **A, F.** Donna should select the Automatically Notify check box. She should also select The Following Servers and specify IP address information for Hercules02 and Hercules03. This enables these two servers to be kept up to date regarding the status of the DNS zone. Clearing the Automatically Notify check box eliminates the other options found in the dialog box from further consideration, so answer B is incorrect. Specifying the Servers Listed on the Name Servers Tab option would not enable Hercules03 to be notified of updates, so answer C is incorrect. Hercules01 is the master DNS server, and as such, should not be specified in the Notify list, so answer D is incorrect. In this scenario, the domain controllers Pegasus01 and Pegasus02 are not running DNS, so answer E is incorrect.

10. **C.** Julian can use the application directory partition replica to create replicas of this partition on the domain controllers for which he wants the data replicated. Specifying a reference domain merely changes which domain is the parent of the application directory partition, so answer A is incorrect. Creating additional application directory partitions creates separate partitions without any link to the partition Julian has already created, so answer B is incorrect. Application directory partitions have their own separate replication topology, which Julian must configure to ensure the proper replication, so answer D is incorrect.

C H A P T E R 3

Active Directory Sites and Replication

Terms You'll Need to Understand

✓ Bridgehead server
✓ Connection object
✓ Distributed File System (DFS)
✓ Event Viewer
✓ Intersite Topology Generator (ISTG)
✓ Knowledge Consistency Checker (KCC)
✓ Repadmin
✓ Replication
✓ Replmon
✓ Site links
✓ Site link bridge
✓ Site link cost

Concepts/Techniques You'll Need to Master

✓ Creating Active Directory sites
✓ Assigning domain controllers to sites
✓ Configuring subnets
✓ Configuring site links
✓ Configuring preferred bridgehead servers
✓ Configuring site link costs
✓ Configuring intersite replication
✓ Monitoring intersite replication

You have learned how to install Active Directory forests, trees, and domains and perform the basic configuration actions related to these components. You have also learned how to configure the Domain Name System (DNS) to work properly with Active Directory installations of various sizes. Now you will turn your attention to configuring Active Directory to work properly in today's large organizations that are spread across multiple geographic locations, both local and international.

The Need for Active Directory Sites

Nowadays, most companies do business from multiple office locations, which might be spread across a single metropolitan area, or encompass an entire state, country, or even multiple international locations. Active Directory includes the concept of sites, which are groupings of computers and other objects that are connected by a high-speed local area network (LAN) connection.

An individual site includes computers that are on one or more Internet Protocol (IP) subnets. It can encompass one building or several adjacent buildings in a campus setting. Figure 3.1 shows an example with two sites, one located in Los Angeles and the other in Dallas. Sites are connected by slower wide area network (WAN) connections that might not always be available and are always configured with separate IP subnets. It is important to configure diverse locations connected by WAN links as separate sites to optimize the use of the WAN link, especially if your company needs to pay for the link according to the length of time it is active or the amount of data it sends.

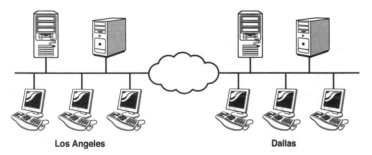

Los Angeles   Dallas

FIGURE 3.1 A site is a group of resources in one physical location.

The following are several benefits that you achieve by creating sites:

▶ **Configurable replication**—You can configure replication between sites to take place at specified intervals and only during specified times of the day. Doing so enables you to optimize bandwidth usage so that other network traffic between sites can proceed without delay.

▶ **Isolation of poorly connected network segments**—You can place network segments connected by less reliable connections such as dial-up links in their own site and bridge these sites according to network connectivity.

▶ **Site-based policies**—If certain locations such as branch offices need policies that should not be applied elsewhere on the network, you can configure site-based Group Policy to apply these policies. Chapter 6, "Configuring and Troubleshooting Group Policy," discusses this use of sites.

You should take into account the following factors when planning the site structure of your organization:

▶ **Physical environment**—Assess the geographic locations of your company's business operations, together with the nature of their internal and external links. It might be possible to include multiple locations—for example, on a campus, in a single site—if they are connected by a reliable high-speed link such as a T3 line.

▶ **Data replication versus available bandwidth**—A location that needs the most up-to-date Active Directory information and is connected with a high-speed link can be on the same site as the head office location. When properly configured, the network's site structure should optimize the process of Active Directory replication.

▶ **Site links and site link bridges**—Assess the type, speed, availability, and utilization of each physical link. Active Directory provides site links and site link bridges so that you can group sites for optimized intersite replication. These concepts are discussed later in this chapter.

NOTE

The site and domain structures are independent. Sites represent the physical structure of the network, and domains represent its logical structure. A single site can include portions of several domains, and each domain can be spread over multiple sites.

Configuring Sites and Subnets

Active Directory provides the Active Directory Sites and Services snap-in, which enables you to perform all configuration activities pertinent to sites. When you first open this snap-in, you will notice folders named Subnets and Inter-Site Transports, as well as a site named Default-First-Site-Name. By default, the new domain controller is placed in this site when you install Active Directory. You can rename this site to whatever you wish just as you can rename a file or folder. This section shows you how to create sites, add domain controllers to sites, and associate IP subnets with specific sites.

NOTE

You can also use Active Directory Sites and Services to manage Active Directory Lightweight Directory Services (AD LDS) instances. AD LDS is discussed in more detail in Chapter 4, "Configuring Additional Active Directory Roles."

TIP

You can use the Find command in Active Directory Sites and Services (the farthest right icon in the toolbar) to determine the site where an object such as a domain controller is located.

Creating Sites

You can create additional sites by using the Active Directory Sites and Services snap-in, as described by the following procedure:

1. Click Start, Administrative Tools, Active Directory Sites and Services.

2. Right-click Sites, and choose New Site.

3. In the New Object–Site dialog box shown in Figure 3.2, type the name of the site. Select a site link object from the list provided, and then click OK.

4. Windows informs you that the site has been created and reminds you of several other tasks that you should perform, including linking the site to other sites with appropriate site links, adding subnets, and installing or moving domain controllers to the site. Click OK.

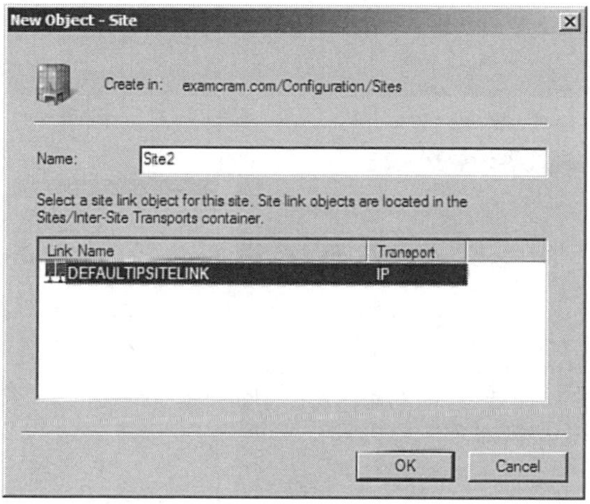

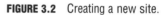

FIGURE 3.2 Creating a new site.

After you have created the new site, it appears in the console tree of Active Directory Sites and Services. The new site includes a default Servers folder that includes all domain controllers assigned to the site, as well as an NTDS Site Settings container that is described in a later section.

Adding Domain Controllers

The first task you should undertake is to add one or more domain controllers to your new site. To do this, proceed as follows:

1. Open Active Directory Sites and Services and expand the site that currently holds the domain controller that you want to move to the new site.

2. Select the Servers folder to display the domain controllers currently located in this site in the Details pane.

3. Right-click the server you want to move, and choose Move.

4. In the Move Server dialog box shown in Figure 3.3, select the site where you want to move the server, and then click OK.

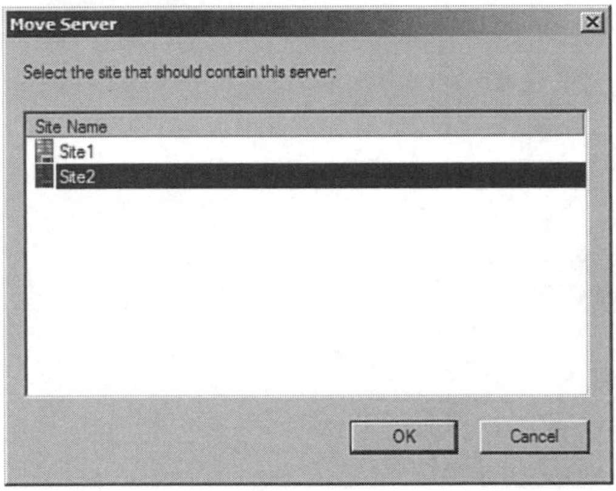

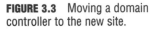

FIGURE 3.3 Moving a domain controller to the new site.

Creating and Using Subnets

Recall that the purpose of using sites is to control Active Directory replication across slow links between different physical locations. By default, Active Directory does not know anything about the physical topology of its network. You must configure Active Directory according to this topology by specifying the IP subnets that belong to each site you have created. Use the following procedure to assign subnets to each site:

1. In the console tree of Active Directory Sites and Services, right-click the Subnets folder and choose New Subnet.

2. In the New Object–Subnet dialog box shown in Figure 3.4, enter the IPv4 or IPv6 subnet address prefix being configured.

3. Select the site for this network prefix from the sites listed, and then click OK. The subnet you have added appears in the console tree under the Subnets folder.

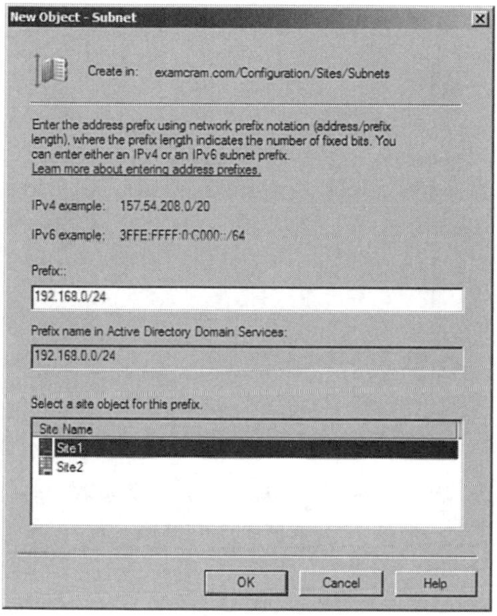

FIGURE 3.4 Creating a subnet.

You can view and edit a limited number of properties for each subnet in Active Directory Sites and Services. Right-click the subnet and choose Properties. The Properties dialog box shown in Figure 3.5 enables you to do the following:

> ▶ Provide a description of the site and its location. These items are for information purposes and help you document the purpose of the site for others who might be administering the site later.

> ▶ Change the site to which the subnet is assigned.

> ▶ View the site's Active Directory canonical name (CN) and its update sequence number (USN), and protect it from accidental deletion.

> ▶ Modify security permissions assigned to the object.

> ▶ View and edit attributes set by Active Directory for the site.

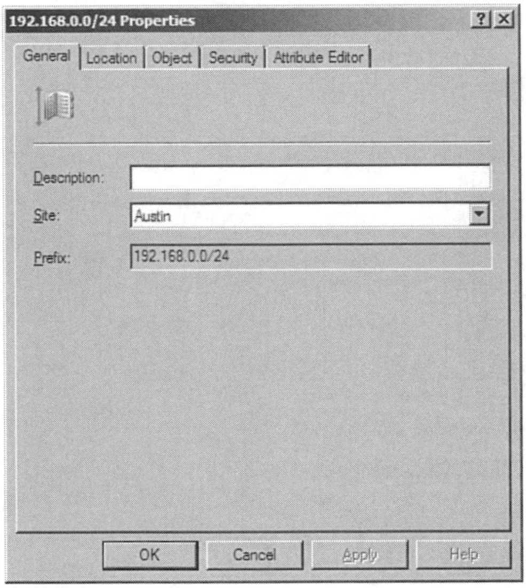

FIGURE 3.5 You can configure a subnet's properties from its Properties dialog box.

TIP

After you have configured your sites and their associated subnets, you can install a new domain controller directly to its desired site. The Active Directory Installation Wizard offers a Select a Site page that lists all sites you have configured for the domain to which you are installing a new domain controller. Refer to Chapter 1, "Getting Started with Windows Server 2008 Active Directory," for more information.

EXAM ALERT

Microsoft expects you to be familiar with IPv6 for the new generation of exams, including those for Vista and Windows Server 2008. You might see questions that assume you know about IPv6 networks or subnets on this or another Microsoft exam. For more information, refer to "IPv6" in Appendix A, "Need to Know More?" or to *Exam Cram* books on Exams 70-620 or 70-642.

Site Links, Site Link Bridges, and Bridgehead Servers

As has already been stated, one of the prime purposes of sites is to control Active Directory replication across slow links. Microsoft has created several additional types of objects in Active Directory that enable you to manage your network's physical topology and replication processes. In this section, you will learn about site links, site link bridges, and bridgehead servers.

The Need for Site Links and Site Link Bridges

A *site link* is an object used by Active Directory to replicate information between sites. This includes Active Directory information and other data such as shared folders. Each site link represents a WAN connection between two or more sites. You can use site links to optimize intersite replication according to the reliability, availability, and bandwidth of the available WAN links. Site links use either of the two following protocols for intersite data replication:

▶ **Remote Procedure Call (RPC) over IP**—This is the default replication protocol and the only one that supports replication within a domain. It enables low-speed, synchronous replication of all Active Directory Domain Services (AD DS) partitions using RPCs.

▶ **Simple Mail Transfer Protocol (SMTP)**—This is an asynchronous email-based protocol that can be used to replicate the schema and configuration partitions of the AD DS forest structure and the global catalog between domains. This protocol is useful for interdomain replication across unreliable links. To use this protocol, you must install an enterprise certification authority (CA) to sign the SMTP messages sent across the link. You also need to install SMTP on the domain controllers using this site link.

A *site link bridge* is a grouping of one or more site links that enable any two domain controllers to communicate directly with each other, whether or not they are directly linked by means of a site link. By default, Active Directory bridges all site links. You will see how you can modify the default configuration of site links and site link bridges in this section.

Configuring Site Links

By default, Active Directory creates a default site link object named DEFAULTIPSITELINK (refer to Figure 3.2) when you install it. You can create additional site links by completing the following procedure:

1. In the console tree of Active Directory Sites and Services, expand the Inter-Site Transports folder to reveal the IP and SMTP subfolders.

2. Right-click the folder corresponding to the desired transport protocol, and choose New Site Link.

3. In the New Object–Site Link dialog box shown in Figure 3.6, type a name for the site link. Ensure that at least two sites are included in the site link, and then click OK.

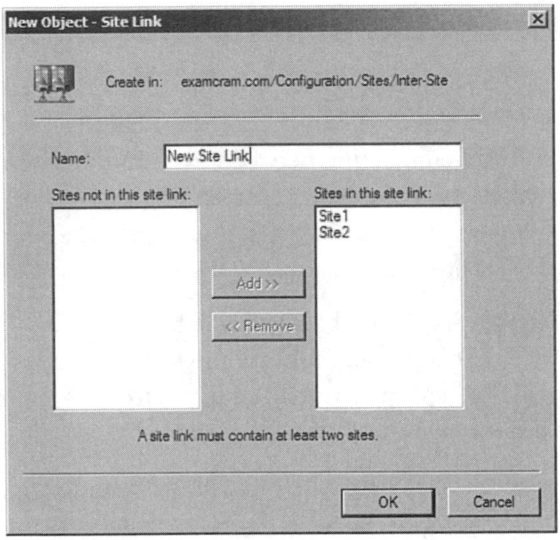

FIGURE 3.6   Creating a site link.

Site Link Bridges

By default, Active Directory creates site link bridges for all site links you have configured. Each site link bridge is a chain of site links that enables any two domain controllers to communicate directly with each other, whether or not they are directly connected with a site link. To begin, all site links for a single transport protocol (IP or SMTP) are included in one site link bridge for that protocol. This is known as *automatic site link bridging* or *transitive site links*.

In some cases such as the following, you might need to disable automatic site link bridging and create your own site link bridges:

▶ Your network is not completely routed. In other words, not all domain controllers can directly communicate with each other.

▶ A security policy prevents direct communication between all domain controllers.

▶ A large enterprise might contain many sites that are not well connected.

To disable automatic site link bridging and create your own site link bridges, proceed as follows:

1. In the console tree of Active Directory Sites and Services, expand the Inter-Site Transports folder to reveal the IP and SMTP subfolders.

2. Right-click the appropriate protocol (IP or SMTP), and choose Properties.

3. In the General tab of the protocol's Properties dialog box, clear the Bridge All Site Links check box. This disables automatic site link bridging.

4. Right-click the protocol again, and choose New Site Link Bridge.

5. In the New Object–Site Link Bridge dialog box shown in Figure 3.7, type a name for the site link bridge you are creating. Ensure that at least two site links are in the bridge, and then click OK.

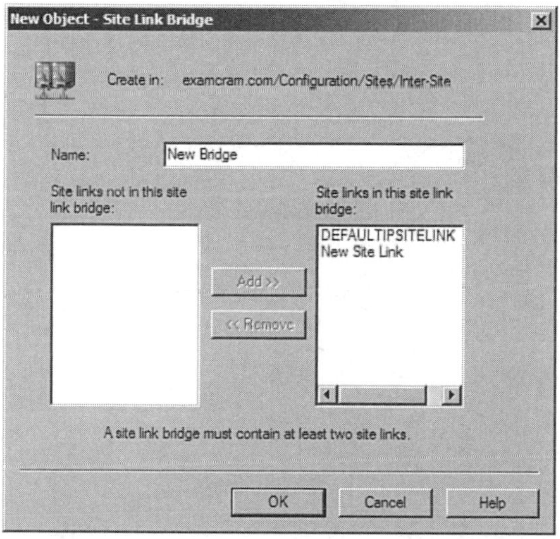

FIGURE 3.7 Creating a site link bridge.

EXAM ALERT

You might encounter a question containing a scenario in which multiple sites are linked by different bandwidth links and considerable intersite traffic is clogging a slow link when faster links crossing three or more sites are available. In such a case, you should create a site link bridge that encompasses the faster links. Such a bridge directs intersite replication traffic across the fast links.

Site Link Costs

Some networks consist of multiple sites with more than one physical link. For example, you might have a head office and branch office that are connected by a dedicated T1 link. Having experienced occasional downtime with the T1 link, you decide to install a dial-up link that uses regular phone lines as a backup connection between the two offices. In such a case, you would want replication to always utilize the T1 link when it is available. Active Directory enables you to handle such a scenario by means of a parameter called the *site link cost*.

By default, Active Directory sets the cost of each site link to 100. You should set the costs of various site links so that the cost of a faster, more reliable link is lower than that of a slower, less reliable link. In the example outlined here, you might set the cost of the dial-up link to 200, while leaving the T1 link at its default of 100.

You can extend this example to cover more complicated networks. Consider the network shown in Figure 3.8. In this example, domain controllers in each site are linked with two replication paths. As shown in the figure, you should configure site link costs according to bandwidth, availability, and reliability.

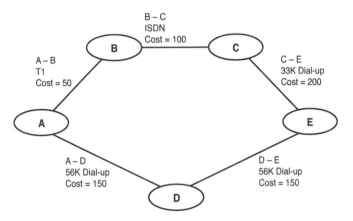

FIGURE 3.8   An example of site links and site link costs.

The total site link cost between two sites that are not directly linked is always the sum of the costs of all links crossed in making the connection. For example, Figure 3.8 shows two paths between sites A and E. Going by way of sites B and C, the cost is (50+100+200)=350. While going by way of site D, the cost is (150+150)=300. Therefore, the desired replication path is by way of site D. If this is not the appropriate replication path, you should adjust the costs so that the path that uses two dedicated plus one dial-up link becomes the preferred one. In doing so, you can adjust the costs so that replication traffic utilizes the fastest link.

Use the following procedure to configure site link costs:

1. In the console tree of Active Directory Sites and Services, select the folder (IP or SMTP) that contains the link whose cost you want to modify. The Details pane displays all site links and site link bridges associated with this protocol.

2. Right-click the desired site link, and choose Properties.

3. In the General tab of the dialog box shown in Figure 3.9, type the appropriate cost, or use the up/down arrows to select the desired value. Then click OK.

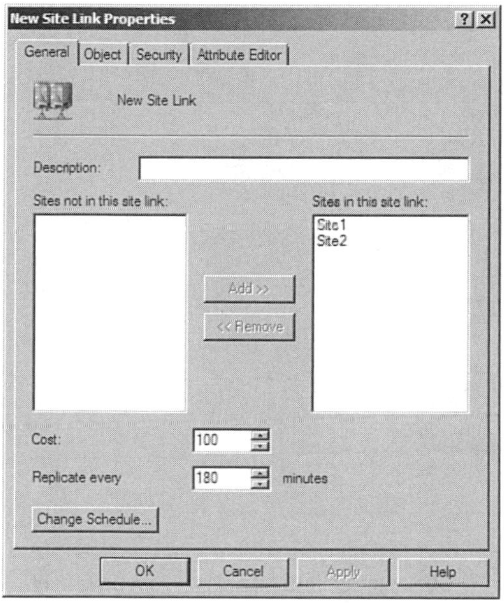

FIGURE 3.9 The Site Link Properties dialog box enables you to configure site link costs and replication schedules.

NOTE

The cost of a site link bridge is the sum of the costs of all links contained within the site link bridge. However, you must ensure that each site link in the bridge has at least one site in common with another site link in the bridge; otherwise, you cannot compute costs for the site link bridge, and such a bridge serves no real purpose.

Bridgehead Servers

A *bridgehead server* is the domain controller designated by each site's *Knowledge Consistency Checker (KCC)* to take control of intersite replication. The bridgehead server receives information replicated from other sites and replicates it to its site's other domain controllers. It ensures that the greatest portion of replication occurs within sites rather than between them.

In most cases, the KCC automatically decides which domain controller acts as the bridgehead server. However, you can use Active Directory Sites and Services to specify which domain controller will be the preferred bridgehead server. Simply open the General tab of the desired domain controller's Properties dialog box, as shown in Figure 3.10. From the list labeled Transports Available for Inter-Site Data Transfer, select the protocol(s) for which you want to designate this server as a preferred bridgehead server, and then click Add. As shown for the IP transport protocol in Figure 3.10, the protocol you have configured appears in the list on the right side of the dialog box.

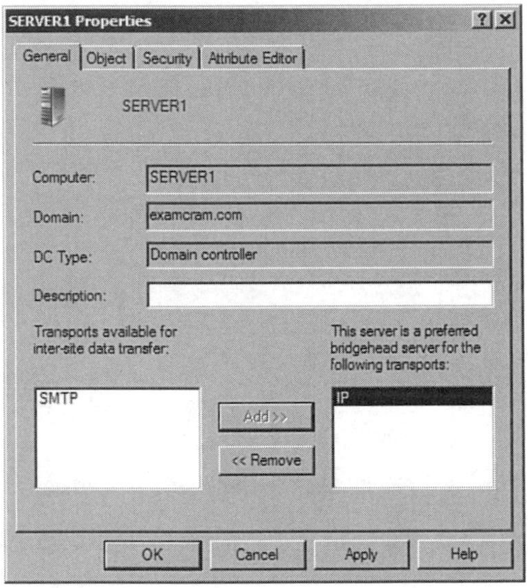

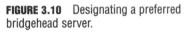

FIGURE 3.10 Designating a preferred bridgehead server.

Sites Infrastructure

Active Directory includes several sites infrastructure components that you must understand to properly manage your network's sites. This includes the KCC and the *Intersite Topology Generator (ISTG)*.

Knowledge Consistency Checker

The KCC is a process that runs automatically on every domain controller and creates intrasite and intersite Active Directory replication topologies. It creates optimum topologies every 15 minutes that take into account the currently existing conditions, including the addition of new sites and domain controllers. The KCC generates a bidirectional ring topology that provides for fault tolerance of replication paths, with at least two paths with no more than three hops between any two domain controllers on the network.

The KCC normally runs in the background without requiring configuration. If you need to force the KCC to run at any time, you can use one of the Active Directory replication monitoring tools: replmon or repadmin. These tools are discussed later in this chapter. Repadmin is installed by default in Windows Server 2008, and you can install replmon from the Active Directory management tools.

Intersite Topology Generator

The ISTG is a single domain controller in each site that the KCC uses to build its intersite replication topology. It considers the cost of intersite connections and checks whether any domain controllers have been added to or removed from each site. Using this information, the KCC then adds or removes *connection objects* to optimize replication as needed. If the forest is operating at either the Windows Server 2003 or Windows Server 2008 native forest functional level, the KCC uses an improved randomized process to determine the bridgehead servers used by each site for intersite replication.

The dcdiag tool, installed by default in Windows Server 2008, enables you to identify the ISTG computer in each site.

Configuring Active Directory Replication

In general, the process of replication refers to the copying of data from one server to another. This can include both the AD DS database and other data, such as files and folders. In particular, Active Directory replicates the following components or partitions of the database to other domain controllers:

- ▶ **Domain partition**—This contains all domain-specific information, such as user, computer, and group accounts. This partition is replicated to all domain controllers in its domain but is not replicated to other domains in the forest.

- ▶ **Configuration partition**—This contains forestwide configuration information. This partition is replicated to all domain controllers in the forest.

- ▶ **Schema partition**—Contains all schema objects and attributes. This partition is replicated from the schema master to all other domain controllers in the forest.

- ▶ **Application directory partitions**—As introduced in Chapter 2, "Active Directory and DNS," these partitions contain application-specific (such as DNS) information that is replicated to specific domain controllers in the forest.

> ▸ **Global catalog**—As introduced in Chapter 1, the global catalog contains partial information on all objects in each domain that is replicated to all global catalog servers in the forest.

Active Directory replicates all data in these partitions to the specified domain controllers in the domain so that every domain controller has an up-to-date copy of this information. By default, any domain controller can replicate data to any other domain controller; this process is known as *multimaster replication*. A read-only domain controller (RODC) can receive updated information from another domain controller (inbound replication), but it cannot replicate information to other servers. If your domain is spread across more than one site, a single domain controller in each site known as a *bridgehead server* replicates information to bridgehead servers in other sites; other domain controllers in each site replicate information to domain controllers in their own site only.

> **NOTE**
>
> An RODC can receive updates to the schema, configuration, and application directory partitions and the global catalog from any Windows Server 2003 or 2008 domain controller in its domain; however, it can receive updates to the domain partition from domain controllers running Windows Server 2008 only.

The process of replication is vital to the proper performance of Active Directory. If replication fails, the domain will not function properly. For this reason, Microsoft expects you to understand how replication works and how to configure and troubleshoot it for Exam 70-640.

For a further introduction to Active Directory replication, along with several example scenarios, refer to "Active Directory Replication Considerations" in Appendix A.

Intersite and Intrasite Replication

Most of the discussion in this chapter centers around the topic of intersite replication, because this is the type of replication that you will need to configure and troubleshoot. However, keep in mind that replication also occurs between domain controllers on the same site—in other words, *intrasite replication*. The KCC automatically configures intrasite replication so that each domain controller replicates with at least two others. In this way, should one replication partner become temporarily unavailable, no domain controller will miss an update. The KCC uses a default bidirectional ring topology, with additional connections as required to limit the number of hops between replication partners to three or less.

Table 3.1 compares several characteristics of intrasite and intersite replication.

TABLE 3.1   Comparison of Intrasite and Intersite Replication

Characteristic	Intrasite	Intersite
Compression	Uncompressed	Compressed
Interval	Frequent, automatic	Scheduled, configured
Connection type	Between all domain controllers in ring topology	According to site link cost
Transport protocol	RPC over IP	SMTP, RPC over IP

Intrasite replication is automatic and requires no additional configuration after you have established your site topology. You can modify intrasite replication if required; configuration of replication intervals, both intersite and intrasite, is discussed later in this chapter.

Distributed File System

Introduced in Windows Server 2003 R2, *Distributed File System (DFS)* replication improves on File Replication Service (FRS) replication previously used in Windows 2000 and the initial version of Windows Server 2003. New to Windows Server 2008, Active Directory uses DFS replication to replicate the SYSVOL shared folder, provided that the domain is operating at the Windows Server 2008 domain functional level. DFS replication uses an improved compression algorithm so that data is transmitted across limited bandwidth links more efficiently; in addition, it replicates only the changes to updated data. Windows Server 2008 still uses FRS replication to replicate other components of the AD DS database.

DFS facilitates access to information across the network, including files, load sharing, and the AD DS database. DFS includes the following two components:

- **DFS Namespaces**—Enables you to create logical groupings of shared folders on different servers that facilitate the access to data by users on the network. It is optimized to connect users to data within the same site wherever possible.

- **DFS Replication**—An efficient multimaster replication component that synchronizes data between servers with limited bandwidth network links. It is used for replicating AD DS including the SYSVOL folder in domains operating at the Windows Server 2008 domain functional level.

To use DFS replication, you must first install DFS on all domain controllers that will use DFS for replication. Open Server Manager and select Roles from the console tree. In the Details pane, scroll to Role Services under Files Services, and then select DFS Namespace and DFS Replication. Click Next, select Do Not Build a Namespace Now, click Next, and then click Install. Wait while the services are being installed, and then click Close when you are informed that installation was successfully completed.

After you have installed DFS, you can access the DFS Management snap-in from the Administrative Tools folder. This snap-in enables you to configure and manage DFS namespaces and replication groups. For further information on configuring and using DFS replication, refer to "Step-by-Step Guide for Distributed File Systems in Windows Server 2008" in Appendix A or to *MCTS 70-642 Exam Cram: Windows Server 2008 Network Infrastructure, Configuring* (ISBN: 078973818X).

> **NOTE**
>
> You can use DFS replication and DFS Namespaces either separately or together; each does not require the presence of the other. You can also use DFS replication to replicate standalone DFS namespaces.

One-Way Replication

An RODC supports inbound replication of Active Directory, including the SYSVOL folder only. This type of replication is referred to as *one-way replication*. It is what makes an RODC suitable for a location such as a branch office, where physical security can become an issue. In one-way replication, changes to the AD DS database are replicated to the RODC, but outbound replication does not occur; consequently, any changes to the database configured at the RODC are not saved in the database. You can prevent certain attributes from replicating to the RODC.

You can also configure one-way replication connections between other domain controllers. However, this is not recommended, because several problems can occur, such as health check topology errors, staging issues, and problems with the DFS replication database. Microsoft recommends that administrators make changes only at servers that are designated as primary servers. You can also configure share permissions on the destination servers so that normal users have only Read permissions. Then it is not possible to replicate changes backward from the destination servers and you have, in effect, a one-way replication scheme.

Replication Protocols

The IP and SMTP replication protocols used by Active Directory to replicate the AD DS database between sites have already been introduced. Table 3.2 provides additional comparative details on the two replication protocols.

TABLE 3.2   Comparison of Replication Protocols

Characteristic	RPC over IP	SMTP
Data replicated	All AD DS partitions	Configuration and schema partitions only
Where used	Intersite and intrasite	Intersite only
Certification authority required	No	Yes
Scheduling	Can be scheduled (synchronous)	Cannot be scheduled (asynchronous)

If you use SMTP replication, the data is replicated according to times you have configured for transmitting email messages. You must install and configure an enterprise CA and SMTP on all domain controllers that use the SMTP site link for data replication. The CA signs the SMTP messages exchanged between domain controllers, verifying the authenticity of AD DS updates. SMTP replication utilizes 56-bit encryption.

EXAM ALERT

Remember the difference between the IP and SMTP intersite transport protocols. SMTP replicates only the schema and configuration partitions of AD DS between domains and requires a certification authority and SMTP installed on the replicating domain controllers. It is useful for interdomain replication across unreliable links. An exam question might ask you to select an appropriate transport protocol for a given scenario.

Ports Used for Intersite Replication

The default ports used by ISTG for RPC-based intersite replication are the Transmission Control Protocol (TCP) and User Datagram Protocol (UDP) ports 135. LDAP over Secure Sockets Layer (SSL) employs TCP and UDP ports 636, Kerberos employs TCP and UDP ports 88, Server Message Block (SMB) over IP uses TCP and UDP ports 445, and DNS uses TCP and UDP ports 53. Global catalog servers also utilize TCP ports 3268 and 3269. You can modify the default ports for RPC-based replication by editing the following Registry key:

`HKEY_LOCAL_MACHINE\SYSTEM\CurrentControlSet\Services\NTDS\Parameters`

Add a `REG_DWORD` value named `TCP/IP Port`, and specify the desired port number. In addition, edit the following Registry key:

`HKEY_LOCAL_MACHINE\SYSTEM\CurrentControlSet\Services\NTFRS\Parameters`

Add a `REG_DWORD` value named `RPC TCP/IP Port Assignment`, and specify the same port number. Configure these changes at every domain controller, and make sure that you have configured all firewalls to pass traffic on the chosen port. For additional information on port numbers that you should open, refer to "Active Directory Replication over Firewalls" in Appendix A. Note that you can also secure RPC-based replication by using IP Security (IPSec) and configuring the firewalls to pass IPSec traffic. Refer to the same reference for more details.

Replication Scheduling

Active Directory permits you to schedule replication so that you can control the amount of bandwidth consumed. This is important because bandwidth affects the efficiency of replication. The frequency of replication is a trade-off between bandwidth consumption and maintaining the AD DS database in an up-to-date condition.

Although you mainly will be concerned with modifying the schedule of intersite replication, this section also takes a brief look at scheduling intrasite replication.

Intersite Replication Scheduling

By default, intersite replication takes place every three hours (180 minutes) and occurs 24 hours a day, 7 days a week. You can modify both the interval and frequency of replication, as described here.

To configure intersite replication scheduling, proceed as follows:

1. In Active Directory Sites and Services, expand the Inter-Site Transports folder.

2. Click the transport (normally IP) containing the site link whose schedule you want to modify. The Details pane displays all site links and site link bridges you have configured.

3. Right-click the appropriate site link and choose Properties. This displays the dialog box previously shown in Figure 3.9.

4. To limit the time intervals in which replication can take place, click Change Schedule.

5. Select the time block for which you want to deny replication, as shown in Figure 3.11. Then click OK.

6. In the text box labeled Replicate Every, use the up/down arrows to specify the desired replication interval, or type the replication interval. Then click OK or Apply.

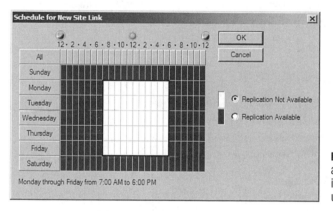

FIGURE 3.11 Configuring a time block in which intersite replication is unavailable.

If you were dealing with a limited-bandwidth link, you would want replication to take place only during times of low bandwidth utilization, such as at night (for example, replication is not available on weekdays between 7 a.m. and 6 p.m., as seen in Figure 3.11). On the other hand, if you were using a link that was available only at certain times of the day, you would schedule replication to take place only when the link was available.

You might have to ignore the replication schedule so that replication can occur at any time of day or night. This is useful if you want to ensure that new changes are replicated in a timely manner. To do so, right-click the transport protocol in the console tree of Active Directory Sites and Services, and choose Properties. On the General tab of the protocol's Properties dialog box, select the Ignore Schedules check box, and then click OK.

Intrasite Replication Scheduling

By default, intrasite replication takes place once per hour. You can change this schedule to twice or four times per hour according to specific time blocks and specific connection objects. To configure intersite replication scheduling, proceed as follows:

1. In Active Directory Sites and Services, expand the site of the connection you want to schedule.

2. Expand one of the servers included in the intersite replication to reveal the NTDS Settings folder.

3. Right-click this folder and choose Properties.

4. On the General tab of the connection's Properties dialog box, click Change Schedule.

5. On the Schedule For dialog box shown in Figure 3.12, select the desired time block and replication interval (once, twice, or four times per hour), and then click OK.

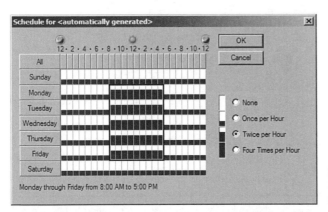

FIGURE 3.12 Modifying intrasite replication schedules.

Forcing Intersite Replication

If you have performed necessary actions such as adding new users or groups for a branch office, you might want Active Directory replication to occur immediately. In such a case, you can force replication from Active Directory Sites and Services by using the following procedure:

1. In the console tree of Active Directory Sites and Services, expand the server to which you want to force replication.

2. Select the NTDS Settings folder to display the connection objects in the Details pane.

3. Right-click the desired connection object, and choose Replicate Now, as shown in Figure 3.13.

FIGURE 3.13 Active Directory Sites and Services enables you to force immediate replication.

NOTE

When you force replication using this procedure, the replication is one way only, toward the selected domain controller. To ensure immediate replication, perform this action on both sides of the link. Use the Connect To option to connect to the other domain controller and manually force replication in the other direction.

TIP

You can also use the Connect To option to connect to the branch office domain controller and perform actions such as creating users or groups directly at this server. Doing so makes these objects immediately available at its site without waiting for intersite replication to occur.

Monitoring and Troubleshooting Replication

Proper replication of Active Directory is essential to its proper operation, and many things can and do go wrong. Microsoft provides the following tools that assist you in troubleshooting Active Directory replication problems:

▶ Event Viewer

▶ Active Directory Replication Monitor (`replmon`)

▶ Active Directory Replication Administrator (`repadmin`)

Event Viewer

Event Viewer, found as a component of Server Manager and as a separate MMC console in the Administrative Tools folder, enables you to view logs of events generated by Windows and its applications.

To access the Event Viewer logs from Server Manager, expand Diagnostics, then Event Viewer and Windows Logs. As shown in Figure 3.14, a series of logs is available. Select the desired log to view event information in the central pane, and select an event to view information, as shown in Figure 3.14. You can also double-click an event to obtain additional details on the event selected.

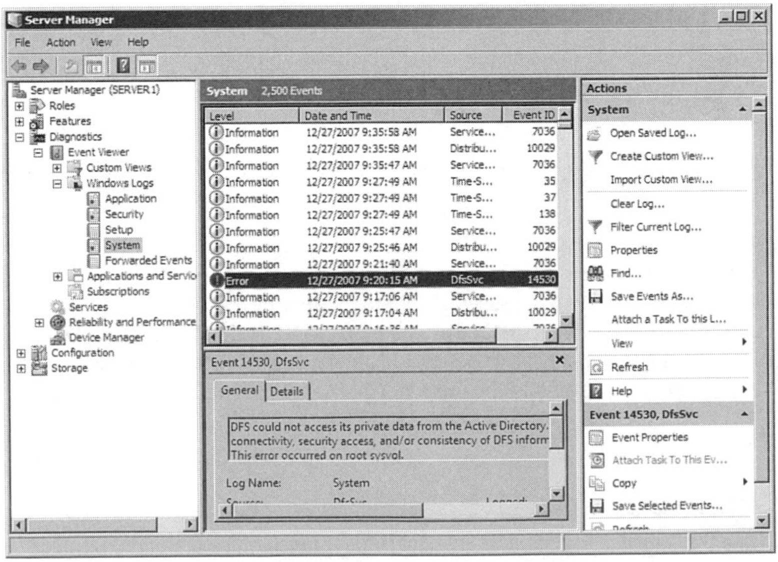

FIGURE 3.14 Event Viewer enables you to obtain information on several types of events occurring on your domain controller.

Replmon

Replmon is a GUI-based tool available from the Windows Server 2003 Support Tools folder. Navigate to the Support\Tools folder on the Windows Server 2003 CD-ROM and double-click `Suptools.msi`. You will receive a compatibility warning, but proceed to install the tools anyway.

You can start `replmon` from the Run command. When it starts, you need to add the servers you want to monitor. Right-click Monitored Servers and choose Add Monitored Server; then follow the instructions in the Add Monitored Server Wizard. Repeat this step to add all required domain controllers. The monitored servers and their available AD DS partitions are displayed in the console tree, as shown in Figure 3.15. So that `replmon` updates its information automatically, click Update Automatically, and then type the number of minutes to wait between monitoring intervals.

FIGURE 3.15 `Replmon` lists domain controllers according to the sites where they are located.

Some of the more important actions you can perform using `replmon` are as follows:

- ▶ **Obtain additional information about the status of replication at a selected server**—Right-click the desired server and select from the options shown in Figure 3.16.

- ▶ **Create status reports for servers**—Select Generate Status Report from the options shown in Figure 3.16 to create a replication status report, and then type a name for the file to be created. After that, select the type of data that you want to record from the Report Options dialog box that appears.

▶ **Display pending replication changes**—Changes made to any component of Active Directory are considered pending until replication has propagated them to all other domain controllers. To view pending replication changes, expand the desired directory partition from the left pane, as shown in Figure 3.15, to display the direct replication partners for this partition. Then right-click the desired replication partner, and choose Check Current USN and Un-Replicated Objects. Click OK to accept the default of Use Credentials Already Supplied for Server. The Un-Replicated Objects dialog box then displays a list of pending replication changes.

▶ **Perform manual synchronization of directory partitions**—If a domain controller or its network connection has been down for a period of time, you might want to synchronize its data manually. To do so, right-click the desired partition, and select Synchronize This Directory Partition with All Servers.

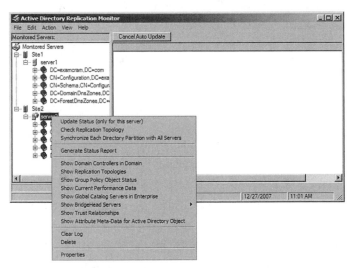

FIGURE 3.16 `Replmon` enables you to obtain extensive information about replication at each configured domain controller.

Repadmin

Repadmin is a command-line tool that is installed by default when you install AD DS. It provides most of the same functions as `replmon`. To obtain information about its available parameters, open a command prompt and type **repadmin /?**.

The following are several of the more important options you should be familiar with:

▶ **/options**—Informs you whether the current domain controller is a global catalog server.

▶ **/bridgeheads**—Displays information about the current replication topology from the current domain controller.

▶ **/replicate**—Forces replication between two replication partners. Specifies the fully qualified domain names (FQDN) of the replication partners and the naming context (the distinguished name of the director partition to be replicated).

▶ **/showmeta**—Displays a list of updated attributes in the AD DS database, together with their USNs.

▶ **/showreps**—Displays the replication partners for each AD DS partition being replicated, including information on the most recent replication attempt.

▶ **/add**—Manually creates a replication link between domain controllers for the AD DS partition that you specify. Specify servers using their Globally Unique Identifier (GUID) or FQDN.

▶ **/replsum**—Displays a summary report of the most recent replication events along with any problems that might have occurred.

EXAM ALERT

Ensure that you know these parameters of `repadmin` and how you would use them. Practice using them, and note the output that they produce. Also know how you would perform these tasks using either `replmon` or `repadmin`. The exam might ask you for two ways of performing a task.

Exam Cram Questions

1. Tom is the administrator for a company whose Active Directory domain spans four sites: Pittsburgh, Cincinnati, Detroit, and Chicago. He has configured site links to reflect the geography so that replication traffic takes the shortest routes. To that end, Tom configures the site link cost between shorter paths to 200 and the cost between longer paths to 100.

   The following week, Tom notices that replication is inconsistent and seems to take longer than it should. What should he check first in troubleshooting this problem?

   - ○ **A.** Tom should use the SMTP transport protocol rather than the IP protocol.

   - ○ **B.** Tom should change bridgehead servers at each site to the most powerful servers available to accommodate the increased traffic burden.

   - ○ **C.** Tom should configure site link bridges to bridge the links on the longer paths.

   - ● **D.** Tom should reverse the site link costs.

2. Your company, which has an office in Nashville, has just taken over a smaller company located in Memphis. You have set up a dedicated ISDN line to connect the two offices and added all users and computers in the Memphis office to your company's domain. You have created sites for both locations and assigned the domain controllers to their respective sites while working from the Nashville location.

   A few days later, users in Memphis start complaining about slow logon and resource access. What should you do to speed up access?

   - ● **A.** Assign the subnet containing computers located in Memphis to the Memphis site.

   - ○ **B.** Add an explicit UPN suffix for the users in the Memphis site.

   - ○ **C.** Configure replication between Nashville and Memphis to take place only at off-peak times.

   - ○ **D.** Obtain approval from management to upgrade the ISDN line to a T1 line.

3. Charles has consolidated resources in three domains into a single domain that encompasses 800 users and their computers in his company. The previous domains represented offices that are connected by ISDN links.

   Charles sets up three sites, one for each office, and configures site links to use SMTP for replicating between the offices. However, the domain controllers in the three offices are unable to replicate with each other. What should Charles do?

   - ○ **A.** Install an enterprise certification authority (CA).

   - ● **B.** Configure the links to use IP replication rather than SMTP replication.

○ **C.** Configure a site link bridge that encompasses all three site links.

○ **D.** Install a faster link, such as a T1.

4. Shelley is a network administrator for a company that operates a single domain Active Directory network. There are three sites that represent offices located in St. Louis, Detroit, and Chicago. These offices are connected with two T1 links: from St. Louis to Chicago and from Chicago to Detroit. No direct physical connection exists between St. Louis and Detroit. The site links are configured as described in the following table.

Site Link	Replication Schedule	Replication Interval	Site Link Cost
St. Louis to Chicago	2:00 a.m. to 7:00 a.m.	30 minutes	300
Chicago to Detroit	7:00 p.m. to 2:00 a.m.	45 minutes	100

Shelley works in the St. Louis office and configures most of the changes to Active Directory from that office. Users in Detroit complain that changes to Active Directory take more than a day to appear in their office. What should Shelley do to ensure that changes made in St. Louis appear in Detroit by the start of the following business day?

○ **A.** Reduce the replication interval of the Chicago to Detroit site link to 30 minutes.

○ **B.** Reduce the cost of the St. Louis to Chicago site link to 100.

● **C.** Modify the replication schedule of the St. Louis to Chicago site link to 10:00 p.m. to 4:00 a.m.

○ **D.** Create a site link bridge that bridges the two site links from St. Louis to Detroit.

5. Brent is a systems administrator for a company that operates a single domain Active Directory network. As a result of corporate expansion, the company is opening a new branch office in a neighboring city. Brent installs a new domain controller and several client computers in the new office, and he sets up a 56Kbps WAN link between the two offices. He needs to make sure that all changes to Active Directory that are configured on head office domain controllers are replicated to the new office domain controller as soon as possible. He also needs to make sure that network traffic over the WAN is kept minimal and that users in the branch office always authenticate to the domain controller in that office.

What should Brent do to meet these objectives?

○ **A.** Create a new OU for the branch office, and add all computer accounts for clients and the branch office domain controller to this OU.

○ **B.** Designate the branch office as a new Active Directory site. Configure the subnet that includes the computers in this office as belonging to that site, and specify the site link cost to be 1.

● **C.** Designate the branch office as a new Active Directory site. Configure the subnet that includes the computers in this office as belonging to that site, and specify a 15-minute intersite replication interval.

○ **D.** Designate the branch office as a new Active Directory site. Configure the subnet that includes the computers in this office as belonging to that site, and specify the replication interval to be 0.

6. Connie works for a company that has just opened a branch office in a neighboring city that is connected to the head office with an ISDN link. Her manager has requested that replication occur at least once daily during the daytime. However, the line is expected to be close to 90% utilized during the day but only about 30% utilized during night hours.

   Connie needs to make sure that replication does not use excessive bandwidth during the day but that at night it will provide adequate bandwidth to complete any synchronization. What should she do to complete this request with the least amount of effort?

   ○ **A.** Create one site link, available only at night with the default cost and replication interval. Once a day, force replication manually.

   ● **B.** Create one site link with the default cost and replication interval. Configure this link to be available from noon to 1 p.m. and during the nighttime hours.

   ○ **C.** Create two site links, one available only at night with the default cost and replication interval and one available only during the day with a site link cost of 500.

   ○ **D.** Create two site links, one available only at night with the default replication interval and the other available only from noon to 1 p.m. also with the default replication interval.

   ○ **E.** Create two site links, one available only at night with the default replication interval and the other available only during the day with a replication interval of four hours.

7. George is a network administrator for a company that operates an Active Directory domain with three sites representing the company's offices in Toronto, Ottawa, and Montreal. Each site has three domain controllers, one of which is designated as a preferred bridgehead server. There are direct T1 links from Toronto to Ottawa and from Ottawa to Montreal, each of which is configured as an Active Directory site link. The network is not fully routed, and the default bridging of site links is disabled.

   George needs to ensure that changes in Active Directory are properly replicated to all three sites even if any one domain controller in every site fails. What should he do?

   ○ **A.** Create a site link between the Toronto and Montreal sites.

○ **B.** Designate two of the three domain controllers in the Ottawa site as preferred bridgehead servers.

○ **C.** Bridge the two site links.

● **D.** Remove the preferred bridgehead server designations at all three sites.

8. Kathy is the network administrator for a company that operates an Active Directory network consisting of a single domain and five sites that represent the head office and four branch offices. The branch offices are connected to the head office with ISDN links.

Users at the branch offices inform Kathy that they are experiencing difficulties in locating Active Directory resources that should be available to them. Kathy discovers that replication is configured and working within the head office site, but it is not occurring between sites. There have been no recent outages affecting any of the ISDN links.

Which of the following might be the problem? (Choose two answers.)

○ **A.** The replication schedule and interval overlap.

● **B.** The replication schedule and interval do not overlap.

○ **C.** Site link costs are too high.

○ **D.** Kathy should reconfigure intersite replication to use the SMTP transport protocol rather than IP.

● **E.** The replication schedule is too short.

9. Phil is a systems administrator for a company whose Active Directory network contains two domains and five sites. Concerned that updates to the AD DS database are not reaching all remote sites in a timely fashion, he uses `replmon` to check the replication parameters and decides that he needs to modify the intersite replication schedules. More specifically, Phil needs to ensure that replication to one remote office connected to the rest of the network with a low bandwidth link takes place only during nonbusiness hours.

Which of the following should Phil do? (Each answer represents part of the solution. Choose two.)

● **A.** In the Details pane of the Active Directory Sites and Services snap-in, right-click the site link whose schedule needs to be modified, and choose Properties.

○ **B.** In the Details pane of the Active Directory Sites and Services snap-in, right-click the site whose schedule needs to be modified, and choose Properties.

○ **C.** In the Details pane of the Active Directory Sites and Services snap-in, right-click the Inter-Site Transports folder, and choose Properties.

○ **D.** Expand the Inter-Site Transports folder, right-click the transport protocol (IP or SMTP) that needs to be modified, and choose Properties.

    ●   **E.** Click Change Schedule, select the time block that represents normal office hours, and then select the Replication Not Available option.

    ○   **F.** Click Change Schedule, and then in the Replicate Every text box, enter **1440** (the number of minutes in one day) as the time interval between replication events.

10. Julia is a systems administrator for a large financial company that operates a single-domain network with 75 domain controllers and 20 sites. Although the network has run efficiently since being upgraded from Windows NT 4.0 to Windows Server 2003 several years ago and more recently to Windows Server 2008, Julia has recently noticed that several offices have not received updates to the AD DS database in a timely fashion.

   Julia monitors replication and notices that replication takes much longer, as much as 72 hours, to update changes at these sites. Which of the following tools should Julia use to determine the problem? (Choose all that apply.)

       ○   **A.** Active Directory Sites and Services

       ●   **B.** `repadmin`

       ●   **C.** `replmon`

       ○   **D.** `netdiag`

       ●   **E.** Event Viewer

Answers to *Exam Cram* Questions

1. **D.** Tom should reverse the site link costs. He has configured the longer paths with the shortest costs. Because the shortest cost links are preferred, he has created a topology in which the longer paths are used in preference. Tom should use SMTP only when there is unreliable communication across site links; further, SMTP is used only for replicating the schema and configuration partitions between domains, so answer A is incorrect. The ISTG and KCC look after selecting the most appropriate bridgehead server, so answer B is incorrect. The KCC also looks after bridging site links, so answer C is incorrect.

2. **A.** You should assign the subnet containing computers located in Memphis to the Memphis site. When you added the objects from Memphis to your domain, initially all objects in the directory from both locations were assigned to the default site. When you created a site for the Memphis location, by default no subnets were assigned to it; consequently, client computers and member servers in Memphis thought they were in the Nashville site, and all authentication and resource access traffic went across the ISDN link to Nashville. By assigning the Memphis subnet to its site, all traffic is handled locally for resources in its site instead of crossing the ISDN link. Explicit UPN suffixes are used to simplify logon procedures in a multidomain forest. They are not needed in

a single-domain operation, so answer B is incorrect. This is not a replication issue, so answer C is incorrect. Because this is an issue of traffic unnecessarily routed across the slow link, there is no need for a faster link such as a T1, so answer D is incorrect.

3. **B.** Charles should configure the links to use IP replication rather than SMTP replication. The problem here is that SMTP cannot be used to replicate the domain partition between domain controllers in the same domain, only the schema configuration and application partitions. RPC over IP can be used to replicate all partitions in the AD DS database. It is true that SMTP replication requires an enterprise CA at each location to work; however, just installing the CA would not enable replication of the domain partition. Therefore, answer A is incorrect. Active Directory bridges all site links by default. Charles does not need to create a site link bridge, so answer C is incorrect. Installing a faster link such as a T1 will not help, so answer D is incorrect.

4. **C.** As the site links are configured, replication cannot complete across both site links during one night. Consequently, changes made in St. Louis replicate to Chicago one day later and to Detroit on the second day. Shelley needs to modify the replication schedule to include a common time period so that replication crosses the entire network nightly. Modification of the replication interval or the site link cost will not help in this scenario, so answers A and B are incorrect. Because Active Directory bridges all site links automatically, Shelley does not need to create a site link bridge, so answer D is incorrect.

5. **C.** Active Directory uses the concept of sites to include physically distinct portions of a network that are well connected internally but separated from other portions of the network by a slow link such as a WAN connection. By designating the branch office as an Active Directory site, Brent can ensure that users in that office authenticate to the domain controller in the same office. He can also configure the intersite replication interval to balance the conservation of bandwidth with the rapid availability of Active Directory changes between the two offices. Creating an OU for the branch office does not cause users to always authenticate to the branch office domain controller, nor does it regulate replication traffic between the two offices; therefore, answer A is incorrect. In a scenario like this one where only one site link exists, the site link cost is immaterial, so answer B is incorrect. It is not possible to specify a zero replication interval; this number is processed as the nearest multiple of 15 minutes from 15 to 10,080 minutes (one week); therefore, answer D is incorrect.

6. **B.** Connie needs to configure one site link only. She should specify that replication be available from noon to 1 p.m. and during the nighttime hours. This enables her to meet the requirement of one replication during the day as well as the need for complete overnight synchronization. By allowing the daytime link to replicate between noon and 1 p.m. only, she has selected a time when traffic would likely be lower. Connie could manually force replication once a day; however, doing so takes daily effort, so answer A is incorrect. Site link costs do not influence the replication interval; they only enable the KCC to select the best link, so answer C is incorrect. Connie could configure two site links with two distinct replication schedules. However, this would take more effort than creating a single link, so answer D is incorrect. If Connie were to set a four-hour

daytime replication interval, replication would occur several times during the day. However, she needs only one replication during the day, so answer E is incorrect.

7. **D.** George should remove the preferred bridgehead server designations at all three sites. In constructing the intersite replication topology, the KCC automatically assigns one or more bridgehead servers at each site through which replication traffic will pass to other sites. In most cases, this designation is adequate. If a domain controller that the KCC has designated as a bridgehead server goes down, the KCC automatically assigns this role to another domain controller. In this case, George has manually desig- nated preferred bridgehead servers. If a manually designated bridgehead server goes down, the KCC does not reassign this role, and intersite replication can fail. George should not create a site link between two sites that are not directly connected, so answer A is incorrect. Designating more than one domain controller as a preferred bridgehead server will not help should both these servers go down, so answer B is incorrect. Modifying the automatic site link bridging will not help in this scenario, so answer C is incorrect.

8. **B, E.** If the replication interval and schedule do not overlap, replication will never occur. If the replication schedule is too short, sufficient time might not be available for replication to occur, especially over a slow link. The replication interval and schedule must overlap, so answer A is incorrect. Site link costs are immaterial in this scenario, so answer C is incorrect. Kathy would use SMTP mainly when there is irregular or inconsistent network connectivity. The situation states that a reliable link exists between the sites, so IP transport is appropriate and answer D is incorrect.

9. **A, E.** Phil can define the replication schedule on a site link basis. This setting is found in the Properties dialog box of the site link whose schedule needs to be modified. By clicking Change Schedule, he receives a Schedule for [site link] dialog box, which allows him to define the days and times that replication is allowed or not allowed. In this case, Phil should select normal office hours and then click the Replication Not Available radio button. This setting is not found in the site properties or in the Inter-Site Transports folder or Transport Protocol Properties dialog box locations, so answers B, C, and D are incorrect. The Replicate Every text box allows Phil to specify the number of minutes between replication events. Entering **1440** in this text box would result in replication taking place once every 24 hours, but it would not specify that this should occur outside office hours; therefore, answer F is incorrect.

10. **B, C, E.** Julia can use `replmon` and `repadmin` to monitor replication and check for problems. She can also use Event Viewer to locate errors in the various Windows logs. Active Directory Sites and Services does not provide replication-related data, so answer A is incorrect. `Netdiag` diagnoses network connectivity problems but not replication problems, so answer D is incorrect.

CHAPTER FOUR

Configuring Additional Active Directory Roles

Terms You'll Need to Understand

- ✓ Account partner
- ✓ Active Directory Federation Services (AD FS)
- ✓ Active Directory Lightweight Directory Services (AD LDS)
- ✓ Active Directory Rights Management Services (AD RMS)
- ✓ AD LDS instances
- ✓ ADSI Edit
- ✓ Application directory partition
- ✓ BitLocker
- ✓ Claim mapping

- ✓ Claims
- ✓ Credential caching
- ✓ Federation trust
- ✓ Federated application
- ✓ Hyper-V
- ✓ Ldp.exe
- ✓ Resource partner
- ✓ Single sign-on
- ✓ syskey
- ✓ Windows Server virtualization

Concepts/Techniques You'll Need to Master

- ✓ Configuring AD LDS
- ✓ Configuring AD RMS
- ✓ Configuring a read-only domain controller (RODC)
- ✓ Configuring AD FS

Now that you have learned how to configure Active Directory sites and replication, you'll learn about new roles and features included with Windows Server 2008 that are important to working with Active Directory. Several of these were introduced with Windows Server 2003 R2, and others are new to Windows Server 2008.

New Server Roles and Features

Chapter 1, "Getting Started with Windows Server 2008 Active Directory," introduced the concept of *server roles*, which are specific functions that a server can perform on the network, including Active Directory Domain Services (AD DS). Active Directory in Windows Server 2008 includes the following additional server roles, which we introduce here and provide additional details for later in this chapter:

▸ **Active Directory Lightweight Directory Services (AD LDS)**— Provides a storage location for directory-enabled application data. AD LDS is an upgrade to the Active Directory Application Mode (ADAM) introduced in Windows Server 2003 and enhanced in the R2 release. Essentially, it is a stripped-down version of AD DS without the overhead of domains and forests.

▸ **Active Directory Rights Management Services (AD RMS)**—Uses a certification base to confirm the identity of users or information on the network, thereby protecting the information from unauthorized access. AD RMS also provides a licensing service that confirms the privileges of users accessing information and a logging service for monitoring and troubleshooting purposes.

▸ **Active Directory Federation Services (AD FS)**—Provides a *single sign-on* capability for authenticating users to multiple web-based applications. AD FS security shares credentials across enterprise boundaries. Consequently, users needing access to these applications are not required to have additional user accounts.

▸ **Active Directory Certificate Services (AD CS)**—Provides a centralized certification authority (CA) for creating, managing, revoking, and working with digital certificates that verify the identity of individuals and applications within and beyond the domain environment. Active Directory Certificate Services are discussed in Chapter 9, "Active Directory Certificate Services."

In addition to these Active Directory–related server roles, Windows Server 2008 provides many additional server roles that are beyond the scope of this book. For information on these services, refer to *Exam Cram* books for Exams 70-642, 70-643, 70-646, and 70-647.

Many server roles also include *role services*, which are components that provide additional functionality to roles. The Active Directory domain controller is considered a role service in support of the AD DS role.

Furthermore, Windows Server 2008 includes components known as features, which provide additional functionality to roles or the server. While most features are optional, certain roles automatically install required features when you install the role. For example, AD DS automatically installs the Group Policy Management Console and a subset of the remote server administration tools.

You can install roles and features from either the GUI-based or command-line versions of Server Manager. From the GUI, right-click the Roles or Features node in the console tree and select Add Roles or Add Features, as required. Either of these starts a wizard that enables you to select the desired roles or features, similar to Figure 1.3 in Chapter 1. You can also remove roles and features from the same location by selecting Remove Roles or Remove Features. From the command-line version, type the following command to add a role:

```
Servermanagercmd -install <role>
```

In this command, `<role>` is the role you want to install (for example, `adlds` for installing AD LDS). To remove a role, type the following:

```
Servermanagercmd -remove <role>
```

In either case, you are informed of the success or failure after the installation or removal has finished.

Note that you can obtain help for the command-line version of Server Manager by typing **servermanagercmd /?**.

NOTE

You cannot remove the AD DS role from a domain controller using the Remove Roles Wizard. You must first run `dcpromo.exe` to demote the domain controller (as discussed in Chapter 1) and then use the wizard to remove AD DS.

Active Directory Lightweight Directory Services (AD LDS)

Built on the Lightweight Directory Access Protocol (LDAP) also used by AD DS, *AD LDS* provides additional directory services for Windows networks and applications without deploying additional domains or domain controllers. These include multimaster replication, support for application directory partitions and the Active Directory Service Interfaces (ADSI) application-programming interface (API), and LDAP over Secure Sockets Layer (SSL). As already mentioned, AD LDS is an upgrade to ADAM and provides data storage for directory-enabled applications that do not require the features of AD DS. You can configure multiple instances of AD LDS on one server, and each instance can have its own schema. Furthermore, you can run AD LDS without the need for a domain controller or DNS server.

Directory-based applications managed by AD LDS store their data in a directory in addition to or in place of ordinary flies or databases. Examples of directory-based applications include global address book, consumer relationship management (CRM), and human resources (HR) applications.

Similar to AD DS, each AD LDS instance includes a configuration partition and a schema partition. Each instance also includes one or more *application directory partitions* (in which application data is stored), but AD LDS instances do not include domain partitions.

> **NOTE**
>
> If you have deployed applications on your network that use ADAM in Windows Server 2003, these applications work with AD LDS without additional modification or configuration.

For more introductory information on AD LDS, refer to "Active Directory Lightweight Directory Services Overview" in Appendix A, "Need to Know More?"

Installing AD LDS

Installing AD LDS involves completion of the following two steps:

1. Installing the AD LDS role

2. Installing one or more AD LDS instances

This section looks at these two actions in more detail.

Installing the AD LDS Role

When you install AD LDS using the Add Roles Wizard, you receive the page shown in Figure 4.1 that provides links to additional information on this role. Review the information from the Help and Support Center referenced here for additional details.

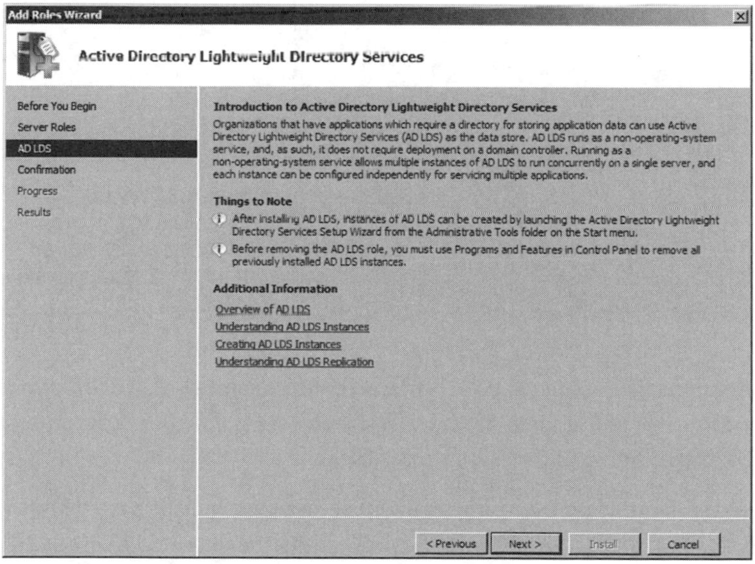

FIGURE 4.1 When you install AD LDS, you can access further information on this role.

To complete installing AD LDS, click Next, read the informational messages provided, and then click Install. You might need to reboot the server to complete the installation.

Installing AD LDS Instances

After you have installed AD LDS, you must create a new *AD LDS instance*, which simply represents a single running copy of the AD LDS directory service. Each instance includes a separate directory data store, a unique service name, and a unique service description. AD LDS provides the Active Directory Lightweight Directory Services Setup Wizard that guides you through this process. Proceed as follows to create a new AD LDS instance:

1. Click Start, Administrative Tools, Lightweight Directory Services Setup Wizard.

2. Click Next to bypass the welcome page.

3. On the Setup Options page shown in Figure 4.2, select A Unique Instance, and then click Next.

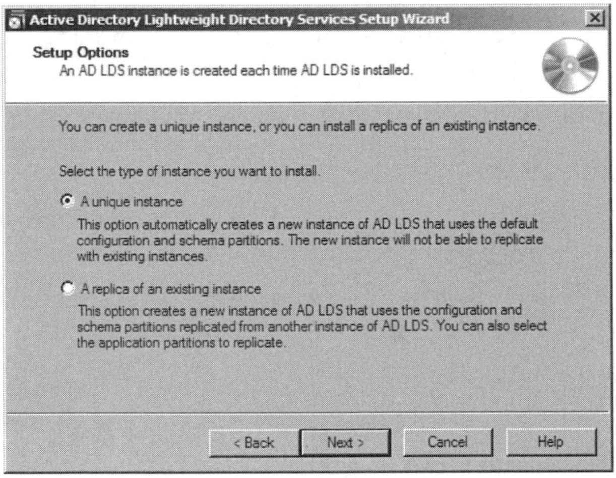

FIGURE 4.2 AD LDS enables you to create a new (unique) instance or use a replica of an existing instance.

4. On the Instance Name page, type a name for the instance that will help you identify its purpose later. Users will see this name at their computers when accessing the instance. Then click Next.

5. On the Ports page shown in Figure 4.3, accept the default ports of 389 and 636 used by AD LDS for communicating by means of LDAP and Secure Sockets Layer (SSL) from a server that is not a domain controller or 50000 and 50001 from a domain controller. If you want to use alternate port numbers, type these instead. Then click Next.

CAUTION

If you are installing AD LDS on a server where you intend to install AD DS later, you should not use the default ports as noted in Figure 4.3. Use ports 50000 and 500001 instead.

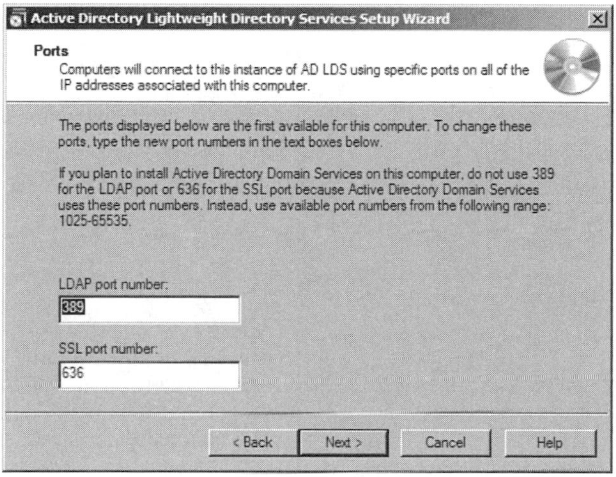

FIGURE 4.3 You can specify which ports are used by client computers in connecting to AD LDS.

6. On the Application Directory Partition page, select Yes, Create an Application Directory Partition to create an application partition now, or No, Do Not Create an Application Directory Partition if the application you are using creates its own application partition. If you select the Yes option, type an X.500 or DNS-style name for the application partition. Then click Next.

7. On the File Locations page, accept the file locations provided or type or browse to a different location if desired, and then click Next.

8. On the Service Account Selection page, select Network Service Account to configure AD LDS to perform its operations with the permissions of the default Windows service account, or select This Account and then type or browse to the user account under which the AD LDS service is to be run. Then click Next.

9. On the AD LDS Administrators page, select the required user or group that is to have administrative permissions for this AD LDS instance, and then click Next.

10. On the Importing LDIF Files page shown in Figure 4.4, select one or more of the provided types of LDIF files to be imported into the AD LDS application directory partition, and then click Next.

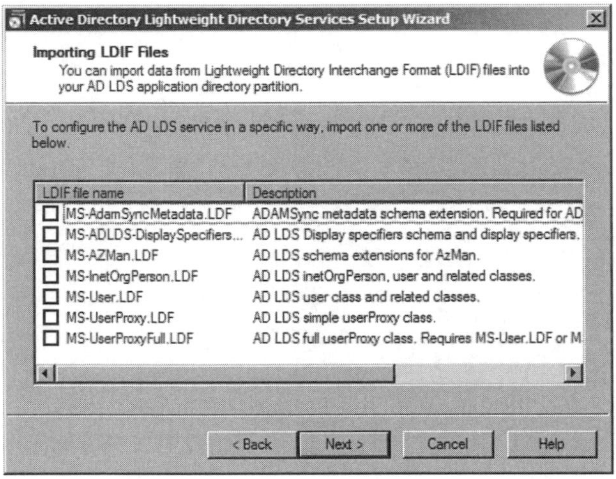

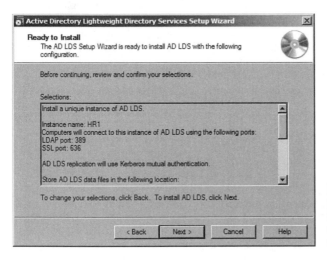

FIGURE 4.4 The wizard enables you to select from several types of LDIF files to be imported into the AD LDS application directory partition.

11. The Ready to Install page shown in Figure 4.5 provides a summary of the parameters you have specified for the instance you are creating. Review this information, and then click Next to continue or Back to change any of these parameters.

FIGURE 4.5 The wizard provides a summary of the installation configuration and allows you to make changes if required.

12. The Installing AD LDS page tracks the progress of installing the instance you have configured. When you see the completion page, click Finish.

TIP

You can also use an answer file to perform an unattended installation of a new AD LDS instance. For information on how to perform an unattended installation, refer to "Step-by-Step Guide for Getting Started with Active Directory Lightweight Directory Services" in Appendix A, and select the link labeled Step 2: Practice Working with AD LDS Instances.

Configuring Data Within AD LDS

After you have installed an AD LDS instance using the procedure described in the previous section, you can manage it by means of any of the following tools:

- The Active Directory Services Interface (ADSI) snap-in

- The `Ldp.exe` administrative tool

- The Active Directory Schema snap-in

- The Active Directory Sites and Services snap-in

Using the ADSI Edit Snap-In

ADSI Edit is used for viewing, creating, modifying, and deleting any AD LDS object. It is installed automatically to the Administrative Tools folder when you install either AD LDS or AD DS.

To use this tool, click Start, Administrative Tools, ADSI Edit. Then right-click the root node and choose Connect To. In the Connection Settings dialog box, type the distinguished name of the AD LDS instance you created (see Figure 4.6), and then click OK.

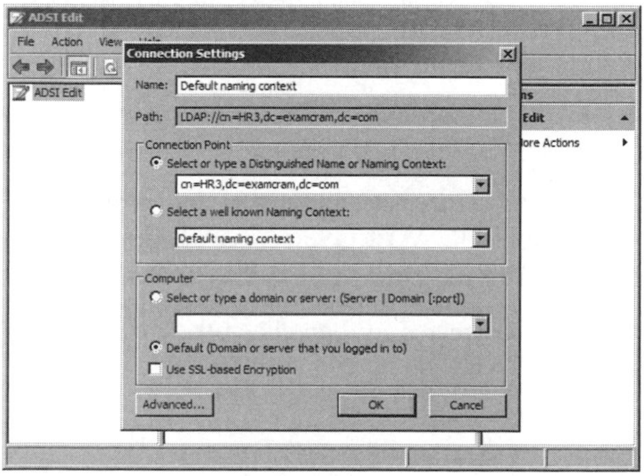

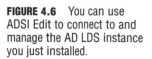

FIGURE 4.6 You can use ADSI Edit to connect to and manage the AD LDS instance you just installed.

Using Ldp.exe

This utility enables you to perform general administrative actions on any LDAP directory service, including AD DS and AD LDS. Its use involves connecting and binding to the instance to be managed and then displaying the hierarchy (tree) of a distinguished name of the instance to be managed.

Follow these steps to use Ldp.exe:

1. Open Server Manager and expand the Roles node in the console tree.

2. Select Active Directory Lightweight Directory Services to display information about AD LDS in the Details pane (see Figure 4.7).

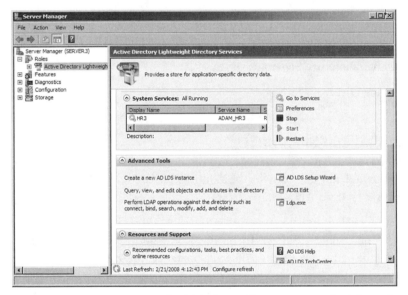

FIGURE 4.7 When you access AD LDS in Server Manager, you receive information about this role and its instances that are running on your computer.

3. Under Advanced Tools (you might need to scroll the information to locate this section), select Ldp.exe.

4. From the Connection menu, click Connect and type the name or IP address of the computer on which the AD LDS instance is installed. (You can type **localhost** if the AD LDS instance is on the local computer.)

5. Ensure that the port number is correct, and then click OK.

6. Return to the Connection menu, and click Bind to select the user account to be used for administering the AD LDS instance.

7. Select one of the options shown in Figure 4.8 and supply the required credentials, and then click OK.

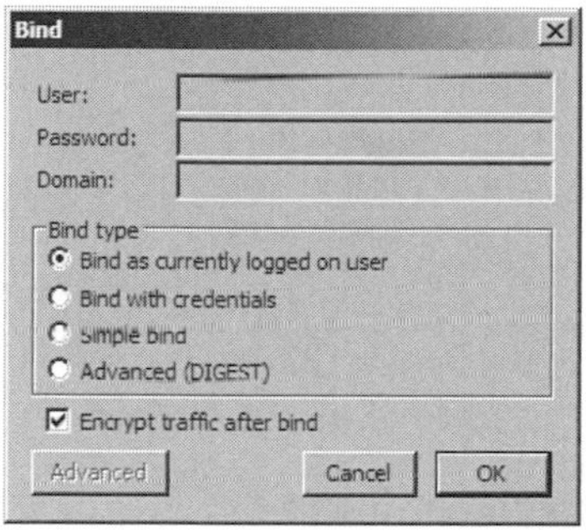

FIGURE 4.8   You have several options for binding a user account to the `ldp.exe` interface.

After you have completed these actions, you can display information about any LDAP objects in this instance by expanding the list in the console tree and selecting the desired object. `Ldp.exe` then provides comprehensive information about the selected object in its right-hand pane.

Using the Active Directory Schema Snap-In

The Active Directory Schema snap-in also enables you to view and manage objects in the schema associated with an AD LDS instance. Before you use this tool, you must register the snap-in and then install it. You learned about these actions in Chapter 1.

After you have installed the Active Directory Schema snap-in, open it, right-click Active Directory Schema in the console tree, and then click Change Active Directory Domain Controller. In the Change Directory Server dialog box shown in Figure 4.9, type the name or IP address of the server with the port specified when you created the AD LDS instance in the format *servername:port*, click OK, and then click Yes to confirm this connection. For the local server, type **localhost:389**.

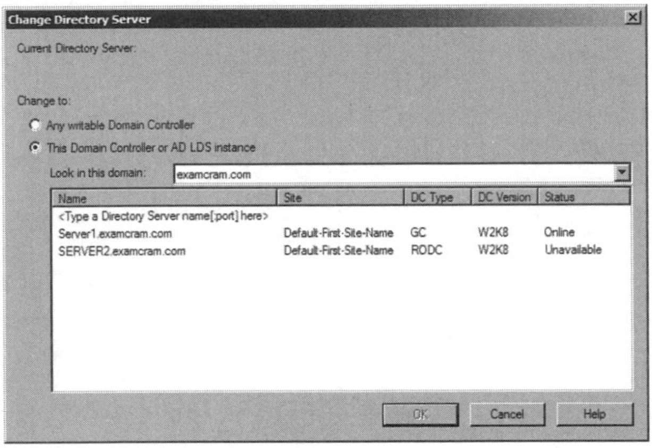

FIGURE 4.9 The Change Directory Server dialog box enables you to connect to the server hosting the AD LDS instance you are interested in.

Using the Active Directory Sites and Services Snap-In

The Active Directory Sites and Services snap-in enables you to connect to an AD LDS instance and administer directory data replication among all sites in an AD LDS configuration set. Open this snap-in from the Administrative Tools folder, right-click Active Directory Sites and Services at the top of the console tree, and then select Change Active Directory Domain Controller. Perform the same action in the Change Directory Server dialog box already shown in Figure 4.9 to connect to and manage replication within your AD LDS instance.

Migration to AD LDS

AD LDS enables you to import legacy X.500 directory-based applications and their data or migrate them directly to AD DS. Further, you can use a metadirectory server such as Microsoft Identity Integration Server (MIIS) to automatically synchronize the data during the migration procedure.

You can use the `ldifde` command from an administrative command prompt to import data from a legacy application or file. Open a command prompt and type the following:

```
Ldifde -I -f <filename> -s <servername>:<port> -a <username> <domain>
<password>
```

The parameters are described in Table 4.1.

TABLE 4.1 `Ldifde` **Parameters Used for Importing Data to AD LDS**

Parameter	Meaning
`-i`	Imports the specified file. Use `-e` to export data to the specified file.
`-f <filename>`	Specifies the file to be imported.
`-s <servername> <port>`	Specifies the name and port number used to connect to the AD LDS instance. If omitted, the current server is assumed.
`-a <username> <domain> <password>`	Specifies the username, its domain, and its password of the account used for binding to the specified directory service. If omitted, the currently logged on user is used.

You can also use `ldifde` to export data from an AD LDS instance. Simply use this command with the parameter `-e` in place of `-i`. This utility has additional parameters used with other situations. For a complete list of parameters, type **ldifde /?** at a command prompt, or refer to "Step-by-Step Guide for Getting Started with Active Directory Lightweight Directory Services" in Appendix A, and select the link labeled Step 2: Practice Working with AD LDS Instances.

Configuring an Authentication Server

Users requesting directory data from AD LDS instances must be authenticated before they can receive access. In general, these users run a directory-enabled application that makes an LDAP request to AD LDS. AD LDS must successfully authenticate users to the directory, a process also known as *binding*.

Users can bind to the AD LDS instance in several ways:

▶ Through a user account that resides directly in AD LDS (an AD LDS security principal)

▶ Through a local or domain user account

▶ Through an AD LDS proxy object

AD LDS User Accounts and Groups

You can use ADSI Edit to create user accounts, groups, and organizational units (OU) that reside directly in AD LDS. To do so, proceed as follows:

1. Open ADSI Edit and connect to the instance where you want to create the object, as previously described and shown in Figure 4.5.

2. Right-click the desired instance and choose New, Object to display the Create Object dialog box shown in Figure 4.10.

3. Select the appropriate class (for example, group, organizationalUnit, or user), and then click Next.

4. Provide values for the common name and SAM-Account Name attributes of the object to be created, and then click Finish. If you want to specify additional attributes such as group membership for a user, click More Attributes.

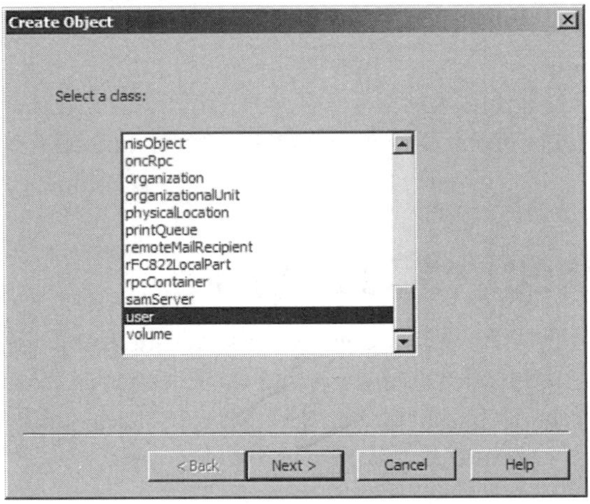

FIGURE 4.10 You can create objects such as users, groups, and OUs in an AD LDS instance by means of the Create Object dialog box.

You can add users to groups from the Properties dialog box of the appropriate group using the following procedure.

1. In ADSI Edit, right-click the group and choose Properties.

2. In the Attribute Editor tab of the group's Properties dialog box, scroll to select the Member attribute, and click Edit.

3. In the dialog box that appears (see Figure 4.11), click Add DN. Type the distinguished name for the user to be added, and then click OK three times.

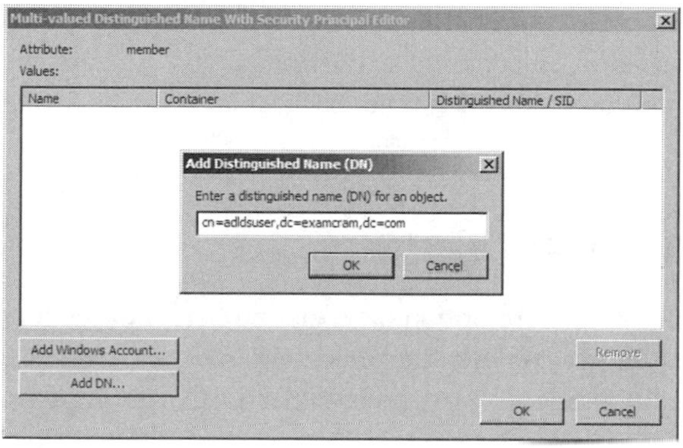

FIGURE 4.11 Adding an AD LDS user to a group.

You can also add a user account or group from AD DS to the AD LDS group. In the dialog box shown in Figure 4.11, select Add Windows Account, and then type or browse to the appropriate account in the Select Users, Computers, or Groups dialog box that displays.

NOTE

You can also use the dsadd.exe utility to create users, groups, and OUs in AD LDS. This utility is discussed in Chapter 5, "Active Directory Objects and Trusts."

EXAM ALERT

If a user requires access to applications or data stored in AD LDS but not to the network in general, it is a good practice to provide him with an AD LDS user account, also known as an AD LDS security principal. An exam question might give you choices of creating other types of user accounts.

Binding to an AD LDS Instance with an AD LDS User

You can use an AD LDS user (security principal) you have already created to bind to an AD LDS instance from the Ldp.exe routine. Proceed as follows:

1. From Server Manager, access Ldp.exe (refer to Figure 4.7).

2. From the Connection menu, click Connect, and specify the server and port associated with the required AD LDS instance.

3. Return to the Connection menu and click Bind. In the Bind dialog box (refer to Figure 4.8), select Simple Bind.

4. Type the distinguished name of the user in the User field and its password in the Password field, and then click OK.

You can also use an Active Directory user account to bind to the AD LDS instance. From the Bind dialog box, select Bind with Credentials. Specify the username, password, and domain of the Active Directory user account, and then click OK.

Use of AD LDS on Server Core

As discussed in Chapter 1, the Server Core option of Windows Server 2008 does not display a GUI; it displays only a command prompt window. You must use command syntax to perform administrative activities on a Server Core computer.

To install the AD LDS role, type the following command:

```
start /w ocsetup DirectoryServices-ADAM-ServerCore
```

Note that the /w option prevents the command prompt from returning until the installation is completed.

To install an AD LDS instance, you must have a text-based answer file that you can create in Notepad. Figure 4.12 shows a sample answer file. Type the following command:

```
%systemroot%\ADAM\adaminstall.exe /answer:<path_to_answer_file>
```

FIGURE 4.12 A sample answer file used for installing AD LDS on Server Core.

In this command, *path_to_answer_file* represents the complete path to the text-based answer file. You receive a series of informative messages that track the progress of creating the AD LDS instance and its directory partitions and objects, followed by a message that informs you that the Setup Wizard has completed successfully.

You can use the same ldifde command described earlier in this section to import data into your AD LDS instance running on a Server Core computer.

Active Directory Rights Management Services (AD RMS)

First introduced in Windows Server 2003 as Windows Rights Management Services, *AD RMS* enables you to create and work with rights-protected files and folders and ensures that only authorized users have access to these types of data. AD RMS includes a certification service that identifies authorized users, a licensing service that provides these users with access to protected documents, and a logging service that assists administrators in monitoring and troubleshooting AD RMS. The following are several benefits of AD RMS:

▶ **Protection of sensitive data**—You can enable AD RMS for applications such as word processors, email clients, and line-of-business applications to help protect sensitive information. AD RMS enables users to define who can perform actions on protected files, such as opening, editing, and printing them.

▶ **Enhanced protection**—AD RMS works together with current security actions such as firewalls and access control lists (ACL) to embed usage rights directly within each document. Its protection remains with the file even after its recipient has opened it.

▶ **Flexibility and customizability**—You can enable any application or server to work with AD RMS for safeguarding sensitive data. Information protection can be integrated into server-based solutions, including automated workflows, email gateways and information archival, document and records management, and content inspection.

The following are several enhancements to AD RMS introduced in Windows Server 2008:

▶ You can create an information protection solution that works with any AD RMS-enabled application to enforce usage access policies that protect sensitive data.

▶ AD RMS is integrated with Active Directory Federation Services (AD FS). AD FS is discussed later in this chapter.

▶ You can create right-protected files and templates and license right-protected data to trusted entities.

► Self-enrollment of AD RMS servers is supported.

► You can delegate administration using new AD RMS administrative roles.

CAUTION

You must have a rights-enabled application such as Microsoft Office 2007 to create content that AD RMS can protect.

Installing AD RMS

You can install AD RMS on any member server running Windows Server 2008 in the domain where the users will be accessing the rights-protected content. You must meet the following requirements before installing AD RMS. (For additional information, refer to "Pre-Installation Information for Active Directory Rights Management Servers" in Windows Server 2008 Help and Support.)

► Ensure that the domain and forest functional levels are set to Windows Server 2003 or higher.

► Create a user account that is a member of the Domain Users group only. This will be used as the AD RMS service account.

► Reserve a URL for the AD RMS cluster that will be used by the AD RMS installation. This URL must be different from the name of the AD RMS server.

► If you are installing a database server, use a separate server for this installation to optimize performance. Also, ensure that the user account that will install AD RMS has the right to create new databases on this server. The database server should run Microsoft SQL Server 2005 or later.

► Use a Secure Sockets Layer (SSL) certificate from a trusted root certification authority when installing the AD RMS cluster. Use self-signed certificates for testing purposes only.

► Install the AD RMS client software on all Windows 2000 or XP client computers that will be accessing a rights-protected client. Windows 2000 computers must have Service Pack 4 or later installed, and Windows Vista computers must have Service Pack 2 or later installed. Windows Vista computers have this software installed by default.

To install AD RMS, use an account with Domain Admin privileges that is different from the AD RMS service account already mentioned. You can use the Add Roles Wizard from Server Manager to install the AD RMS role. The wizard will ask you to install the following additional role services and features required by AD RMS:

▶ Internet Information Services (IIS): Web Server and Management Tools

▶ Windows Process Activation Service

▶ Message Queuing Services

Click Add Required Role Services and then click Next. You should read the information provided on the Introduction to Active Directory Rights Management Services page, including the links provided. Click Next, and follow the remaining steps provided by the wizard to complete the installation of AD RMS. Ensure that you specify a strong password, and keep a careful record of this password when prompted to specify the AD RMS cluster key password. This password is used to add additional AD RMS servers to the cluster that is automatically created and to restore the cluster from backup. You should also read the information provided on the Introduction to Web Server (IIS) page. When presented with the Confirm Installation Selections page, read the information provided, and then click Install to perform the installation. When the installation completes, review the Installation Results page for errors and warnings.

After you have completed this procedure, you must log off and log back on, or reboot the server. Once you have done this, you can access AD RMS from the Administrative Tools folder. It opens to the MMC snap-in shown in Figure 4.13.

TIP

Similar to AD RMS, many roles and features require the presence of certain additional roles and role services to function properly. The Add Roles Wizard asks you to install these components if they are not present. Refer to "Role, Role Service, and Feature Dependencies in Server Manager" in the Windows Server 2008 Help and Support Center for more information.

For additional information on working with AD RMS, refer to "Active Directory Rights Management Services Overview" and "Windows Server Active Directory Rights Management Services Step-by-Step Guide" in Appendix A.

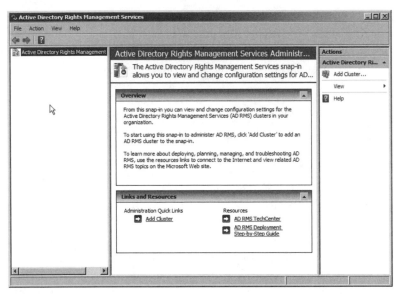

FIGURE 4.13   You can manage AD RMS from the AD RMS MMC snap-in.

Certificate Request and Installation

AD RMS uses a system of rights account certificates to identify users who are empowered to access and work with protected information from an AD RMS-enabled application. A user with such a certificate can assign usage rights and conditions to any data files she creates with a rights-enabled application. Another user attempting to access such a data file causes a request to be sent to the AD RMS licensing service within the AD RMS cluster. (Note that the AD RMS cluster can be a single server or a group of servers in a load-balancing configuration.) The service then issues a usage license that provides access according to the permitted uses assigned by the creator of the file. Usage rights remain with the document and stay with it regardless of its distribution within and outside the organization.

Users wanting to view right-protected documents must have a rights account certificate. When these users attempt to access the documents, their RMS-enabled application sends a request to the AD RMS server for access to the material. The server then issues a certificate that includes the usage license that interprets the conditions applied to the document and grants the permitted level of access.

Self-Enrollments

An AD RMS cluster is automatically enrolled without the need to connect to the Microsoft Enrollment Service. The enrollment process takes place by means of a server self-enrollment certificate. Previous Rights Management Server versions required that a server licensor certificate be signed by the Microsoft Enrollment Service by means of an Internet connection to this service.

Windows Server 2008 AD RMS includes a server self-enrollment certificate. This certificate signs the server's server licensor certificate. Consequently, you can run AD RMS on a network that is completely isolated from the Internet.

Delegation

AD RMS in Windows Server 2008 includes the ability to delegate responsibility using new AD RMS administrative roles. The following administrative roles are included with AD RMS:

▸ **AD RMS Enterprise Administrators**—Members of this group can manage all AD RMS policies and settings. When you install AD RMS, the user account used for installation and the local Administrators group are added to this group. Best practices stipulate that you should limit membership in this group to those users who need full AD RMS administrative control only.

▸ **AD RMS Template Administrators**—Members of this group can manage rights policy templates. This includes reading cluster information, listing rights policy templates, creating new templates or modifying existing ones, and exporting templates.

▸ **AD RMS Auditors**—Members of this group can manage audit logs and reports. They have read-only access to cluster information, logging settings, and available reports on the AD RMS cluster.

Use of these roles enables you to delegate management tasks without granting complete administrative control over the entire AD RMS cluster.

Active Directory Metadirectory Services (AD MDS)

First introduced in Windows Server 2003 as Identity Integration Feature Pack (IIFP), Active Directory Metadirectory Services provides a consistent, enterprise-wide view of user information in the AD DS directory database with application directories. AD MDS coordinates user information across AD DS along with other components including AD LDS and Microsoft Exchange Server. AD MDS enables you to combine identity information for users and resources into a single, logical view. AD MDS also automates the processing of new and updated identity information, thereby reducing the time spent in manually processing these types of data.

Read-Only Domain Controllers

As previously mentioned in Chapter 1, a read-only domain controller (RODC) contains a read-only copy of the AD DS database. It is most useful in situations such as a branch office where physical security of the domain controller might be of concern.

Installing a Read-Only Domain Controller

Before installing an RODC, you should perform the following preparatory actions:

- ▶ Raise the forest functional level to Windows Server 2003 or higher.

- ▶ Ensure that the PDC emulator role is hosted on a domain controller running Windows Server 2008.

- ▶ Run the `Adprep /rodcprep` utility. This utility updates the permissions on all the DNS application directory partitions in the forest so that they can be replicated properly. Run this utility on the schema master of the forest where you want to install an RODC. If all domain controllers in the domain run Windows Server 2008, it is not necessary to run this utility.

- ▶ Ensure that a writable domain controller that runs Windows Server 2008 is available and has network connectivity to the proposed RODC.

You can install an RODC using the same basic procedure outlined in Chapter 1 for installing additional domain controllers in the same domain. Note that the RODC cannot be the first domain controller in a new domain. When you receive the Additional Domain Controller Options page (see Figure 4.14), simply select the Read-Only Domain Controller option and complete the remainder of the installation procedure.

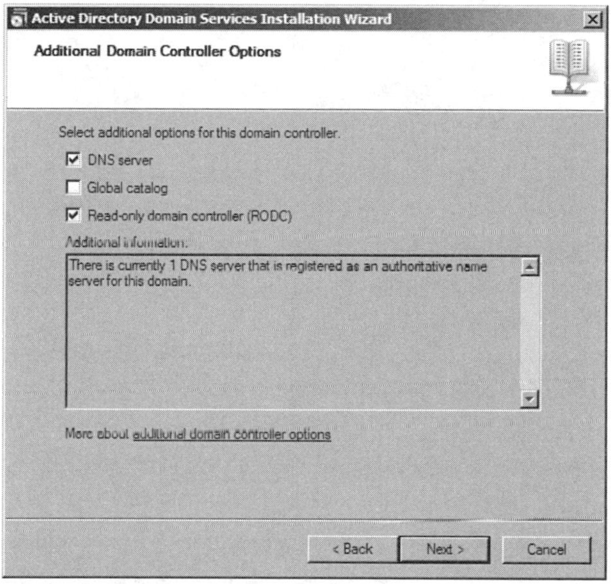

FIGURE 4.14 Installing an RODC.

<table>
<tr><td>**CAUTION**</td></tr>
</table>

Microsoft recommends that you install the DNS Server service on an RODC, so that clients in the branch office can perform name resolution even if the connection to the head office is unavailable.

The AD DS Installation Wizard also asks you to specify a group that is permitted to administer the RODC (see Figure 4.15). You should specify a group whose users are local to the office where the RODC is situated.

<table>
<tr><td>**TIP**</td></tr>
</table>

You can also install an RODC on a Server Core computer by using the appropriate answer file. For a sample answer file, refer to "Step-by-Step Guide for Read-Only Domain Controllers" in Appendix A, and select the "Steps for Deploying an RODC" link. The same reference also includes procedures for delegation of RODC installation and installation of an RODC from media.

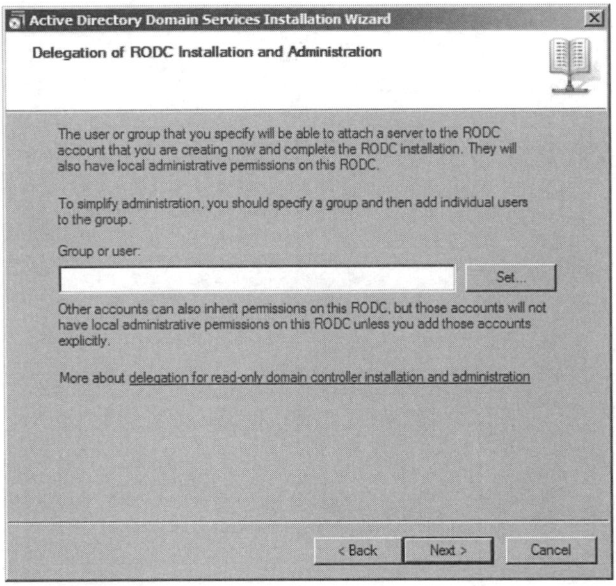

FIGURE 4.15 You can delegate administration of the RODC to a group during installation.

EXAM ALERT

Remember that before you install an RODC, you must ensure that the forest functional level is at least Windows Server 2003 and that the PDC emulator is running Windows Server 2008. Also remember that you must run the `Adprep /rodcprep` utility on the schema master unless all domain controllers in the domain are running Windows Server 2008. An exam question might trick you into other alternatives such as having the forest functional level at Windows Server 2008.

Unidirectional Replication

By default, an RODC does not perform outbound replication. In other words, all replication is unidirectional, from any writable domain controller to the RODC. This enhances the security provided by the RODC, in that even if an unauthorized user were somehow able to change the AD DS database on the RODC, these changes would not be replicated to other domain controllers. In addition, WAN bandwidth usage is reduced because the RODC does not send changes to servers in other sites.

You should note that all replication to an RODC is unidirectional. This includes any DFS replication, as well as replication of DNS zones, which is discussed later in this section.

Administrator Role Separation

You can configure a local user with administrative rights to the RODC without designating this user as a member of the Domain Admins group. This user is included in the RODC's local Administrators group stored on the Security Accounts Manager (SAM) on the RODC and has administrative rights to that server only. This is in contrast to writable domain controllers, at which local administrators are automatically members of the Domain Admins group and have administrative rights to all domain controllers in the domain. Consequently, you can designate a junior employee such as a desktop support technician as a local administrator with the authority to perform routine tasks such as administering file and print services, reconfiguring disks, monitoring and troubleshooting systems, and so on.

As you have seen, you define a user or group with administrative access to the RODC during the installation process. You can also add a user or group with administrative access at any time using the dsmgmt utility. Proceed as follows:

1. Open a command prompt and type **dsmgmt**.

2. At the dsmgmt prompt, type **local roles**.

3. At the local roles prompt, type **add** *domain\user* **administrators**, where *domain* is the domain name and *user* is the username or group name to be added. (For example, type **add examcram\user1 administrators** to add the examcram domain user named user1 to the administrative access group.)

4. Type **quit** twice to return to the command prompt.

To remove a user or group, perform the same procedure, substituting the keyword remove for add. For further available keywords, type **?** at the local roles prompt.

EXAM ALERT

Keep in mind that this is a simple means of extending administrative access to a local user without granting him the ability to manage other domain controllers in the domain.

Read-Only DNS

As you have seen, Microsoft recommends that you install DNS on the RODC during installation. As discussed in Chapter 2, "Active Directory and DNS," DNS in Windows Server 2008 includes all its zone data in application directory partitions. If you have configured DNS on another domain controller to host an Active Directory–integrated zone, the zone file on the RODC is always a read-only copy. Active Directory replicates all application directory partitions, including those associated with DNS in a unidirectional fashion.

A client computer that is updating its TCP/IP configuration must be referred to a writable DNS server that hosts a primary or Active Directory–integrated copy of the zone file. To do so, the RODC refers the client to a writable DNS server by checking the name server (NS) resource records that it has to locate the NS resource record of an appropriate DNS server.

> **CAUTION**
>
> If a branch office has only a single DNS server and RODC, you should configure client computers to point to a hub site DNS server, in case the local DNS server becomes unavailable. You can do this by specifying the IP address of the hub site DNS server in the Alternate DNS Server field of the client's TCP/IP Properties dialog box or by configuring the DHCP server to set the primary DNS server to the branch office server and the alternate DNS server to the hub site DNS server.

BitLocker

First introduced with Windows Vista, *BitLocker* is a hardware-enabled data encryption feature that serves to protect data on a computer that might become exposed to unauthorized access or theft. In the typical environment of a branch office hosting an RODC, you can use BitLocker to encrypt all the data on the server's hard disk.

To use BitLocker on any server including an RODC, you must prepare the computer prior to installing Windows Server 2008. The computer's hard disk must have two partitions—a smaller partition that remains unencrypted and is designated as the system partition, and a large partition to hold the Windows Server 2008 operating system files, applications, and data. After installing Windows Server 2008, you can install BitLocker from the Initial Configuration Tasks window that is displayed at the first logon or from the Add Features Wizard accessed from Server Manager. For detailed information, refer to "Windows BitLocker Drive Encryption" in Appendix A.

Replication of Passwords

Each RODC is partnered with a writable domain controller for password replication purposes. When you deploy an RODC, you must configure the password replication policy on its replication partner. When an RODC's replication partner sends AD DS database information to the RODC, user account information is replicated without password information. You can configure which user account passwords are replicated. This reduces the number of passwords that can be compromised if the RODC is breached.

The password replication policy acts as an access control list (ACL), indicating which user accounts can be permitted to store their passwords on the RODC. If a user account's password is stored on the RODC, this user can log on to the domain from the RODC without having to contact the writable domain controller, after the user has logged on once to the RODC. On the first logon, the RODC must contact the writable domain controller to verify the user's password; when the user changes her password, the RODC must contact the writable domain controller again so that the changed password can be recorded in the AD DS database.

TIP

You can specify the users whose passwords can be replicated, either to a single RODC or to all RODCs in the domain. For example, users who work at a single branch office can have their passwords replicated to that office's RODC. Traveling users who need to access the network from any branch office can have their passwords replicated to all RODCs in the domain.

Each RODC holds the following two lists of user accounts:

- ▶ **Allowed list**—Lists the user accounts whose passwords are allowed to be cached. By default, no users are included in this list. You can manually configure a different Allowed list for each RODC in the domain. Typically, this list includes those users who work at the branch office where the RODC is located.

- ▶ **Denied list**—Lists the user accounts whose passwords cannot be cached. By default, high-security user accounts such as members of the Domain Admins, Enterprise Admins, and Schema Admins groups are included in this list.

When a user attempts to log on to an RODC, the RODC checks its Allowed and Denied list to determine whether the password can be cached. It first checks the Denied list and denies the request if the user account is listed here. Then it checks the Allowed list and allows the request if the account is listed. If the account is not listed in either list, the request is denied. Note that this behavior is similar to the Allowed and Denied security permissions on NTFS files and folders.

Configuring a Password Replication Policy

To configure a password replication policy, you must be a member of the Domain Admins group and work from the writable domain controller that is partnered to the RODC. Proceed as follows:

1. Click Start, Administrative Tools, Active Directory Users and Computers.

2. In the console tree, select the Domain Controllers OU.

3. In the Details pane, right-click the required RODC and choose Properties.

4. Select the Password Replication Policy tab to view the list of accounts that are included in the Allowed and Denied lists by default.

5. To add a user or group to either list, click Add, and in the Add Groups, Users and Computers dialog box that appears, choose the appropriate option as shown in Figure 4.16, and then click OK.

6. Type the name of the desired user or group in the Select Users, Computers, or Groups dialog box, and then click OK. The user or group is added to the list.

7. Click OK to close the server's Properties dialog box.

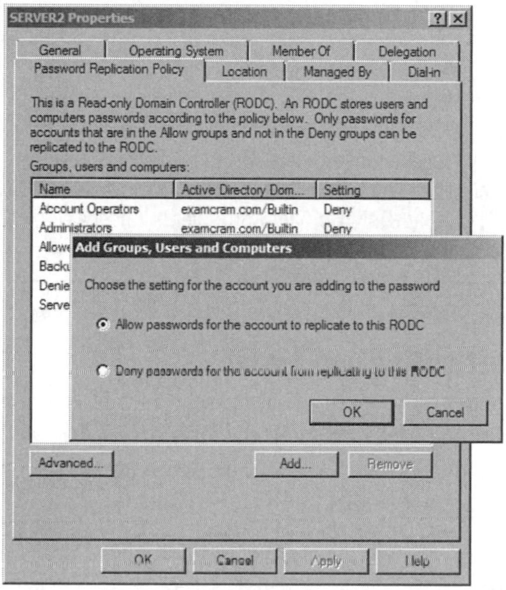

FIGURE 4.16 You can configure the password replication policy to allow or deny caching of passwords for users or groups.

Credential Caching

The RODC provides a feature known as *configurable credential caching*. In other words, you can specify which users have passwords cached on each RODC. By default, the password cache in the RODC does not include any passwords. Users logging on to the RODC for the first time must authenticate to the partnered writable domain controller across the WAN.

You can prepopulate the password cache so that passwords are available on the RODC to users without the need to cross the WAN, thereby enabling users to log on even if the WAN is unavailable. To do so, proceed as follows:

1. At the partnered writable domain controller, access the Password Replication Policy tab of the RODC's Properties dialog box, as previously shown in Figure 4.16.

2. Click Advanced, and then click Prepopulate Passwords.

3. On the Select Users or Computers dialog box that displays, type the usernames whose passwords you want to prepopulate, and then click OK.

TIP

If you suspect that the RODC's password cache has been compromised, you can reset its password cache. While logged on at the partnered writable domain controller as a member of the Domain Admins group, access the RODC's computer account in Active Directory Users and Computers, right-click the account, and choose Delete. On the Deleting Active Directory Domain Controller dialog box, select the check box labeled Reset All Passwords for User Accounts That Were Cached on This Read-Only Domain Controller. All users with cached passwords must obtain a new password after you perform this action.

Administering the RODC's Authentication Lists

You should take a look at the lists of cached credentials and users who have been authenticated by the RODC from time to time, to keep the lists up to date and remove any passwords that are not required. Such steps improve security at the RODC. To perform these actions, proceed as follows:

1. At the partnered writable domain controller, access the Password Replication Policy tab of the RODC's Properties dialog box, as previously shown in Figure 4.16.

2. Click Advanced to display the Advanced Password Replication Policy dialog box shown in Figure 4.17.

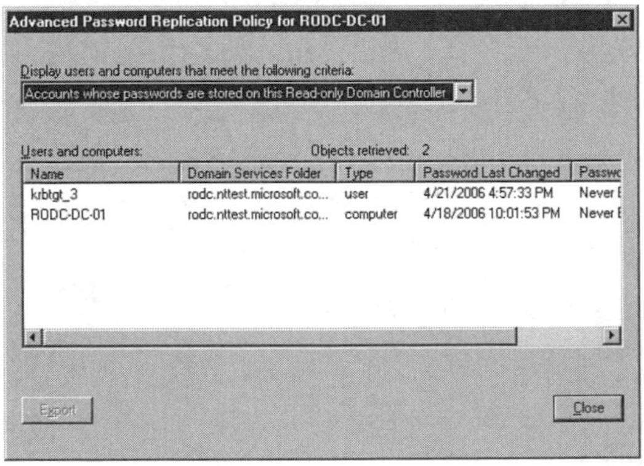

FIGURE 4.17 The Advanced Password Replication Policy dialog box enables you to perform two additional actions.

3. On the drop-down list labeled Display Users and Computers that Meet the Following Criteria, select one of the following options:

   ▶ **Accounts Whose Passwords Are Stored on This Read-Only Domain Controller**—Displays user, computer, and group accounts whose passwords have been cached according to the credential caching policy.

▶ **Accounts That Have Been Authenticated to This Read-Only Domain Controller**—Displays user, computer, and group accounts that the RODC has authenticated.

syskey

Windows 2000 and later computers encrypt the SAM database with a locally stored system key. For security purposes, Windows requires that password hashes be encrypted, thereby preventing the usage of stored, unencrypted password hashes. This system key is required for Windows to start.

By default, the system key is stored locally. For additional security, you can configure Windows to store the startup key on a floppy disk, or you can specify a password to be entered manually at startup. To do so, open a command prompt and type **syskey**. A dialog box displays and informs you that encryption of the accounts database (SAM) is enabled, and this encryption cannot be disabled. To configure further, click Update to display the Startup Key dialog box shown in Figure 4.18. To specify a manually entered password, click Password Startup and type and confirm the required password. To store a startup key on a floppy disk, insert a disk and select Store Startup Key on Floppy Disk. Then click OK.

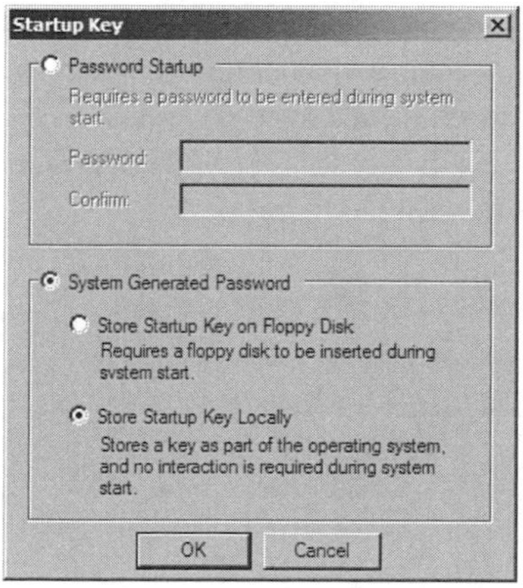

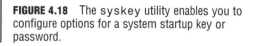

FIGURE 4.18 The syskey utility enables you to configure options for a system startup key or password.

By storing this floppy disk in a secured location away from the server, such as a locked cabinet, you can prevent an intruder who steals your RODC from starting it elsewhere and reading your AD DS database.

Active Directory Federation Services (AD FS)

Introduced with Windows Server 2003 R2, *AD FS* provides a single sign-on capability for authentication of users to multiple web-based applications within a single session. It enables companies and business partners to collaborate with each other without the need to establish trust relationships and without the need for users in these companies to remember multiple usernames and passwords. Windows Server 2008 enhances AD FS with improved installation and administration capabilities as well as integration with AD RMS and Microsoft Office SharePoint Services 2007.

To provide a simple example, refer to Figure 4.19. Let's assume that Examcram.com is hosting a web application to which users in its own company and partner company Quepublishing.com need access. Each company operates its own Active Directory forest, but neither IT director wants to set up a trust relationship similar to those discussed in Chapter 5. So both companies set up a server running Windows Server 2008 with AD FS that enables users in Quepublishing.com to authenticate to the web server operated by Examcram.com with their regular usernames and passwords. The Examcram.com AD FS server authenticates a user from Quepublishing.com and grants access to the web application. The company hosting the web application is known as the *resource partner*, and the company being trusted for access is known as the *account partner*. Web applications involved are known as *federated applications*. As you can see from Figure 4.19, this constitutes a type of trust between the AD FS servers *without* an external or forest trust between the two forests.

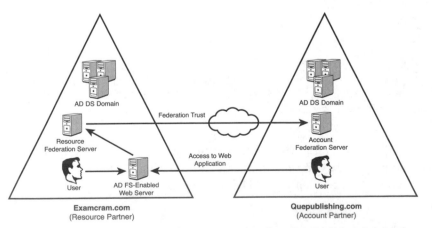

FIGURE 4.19 AD FS enables users from one company to authenticate to a federated application in a second company without the need for a separate username and password.

AD FS includes the following role services that can be configured for enabling of web-based single sign-on, federation of web-based resources, access customization, and authorization of users:

- **Federation Service**—Comprises one or more federation servers sharing a common trust policy. These servers handle authentication requests from external or Internet-based user accounts. The servers running this service in the resource and account partners are known as the *resource federation server* and *account federation server*, respectively.

- **Federation Service Proxy**—Serves as a proxy to the Federation Service on a perimeter network or demilitarized zone. This service uses WS-Federation Passive Requestor Profile (WS-FPRP) protocols to obtain user credentials from browser clients, and it forwards this information to the Federation Service on their behalf. The servers running this service in the resource and account partners are known as the *resource federation proxy* and *account federation proxy*, respectively. This service cannot be installed on the same server that runs the Federation Service.

- **Claims-aware agent**—Uses a claims-aware application to enable the querying of AD FS security token claims. This is a Microsoft ASP.NET application that uses claims that are present in an AD FS security token to perform authorization decisions and personalize applications. It includes the `default.aspx`, `web.config`, and `default.aspx.cs` files.

- **Windows token-based agent**—Used on a web server that hosts a Windows NT token-based application to support conversion from an AD FS security token to a Windows NT access token by means of Windows-based authorization mechanisms.

> **NOTE**
>
> A server running the Federation Service role can act as a proxy to another server running Federation Service, such as a server in the AD DS forest of a partner company. You do not need to install a separate federation proxy server.

The claims-aware agent and token-based agent are also known as AD FS web agents. For more information on AD FS role services, see "Understanding AD FS Role Services" in Windows Server 2008 Help and Support or "Active Directory Federation Services Role" in Appendix A.

EXAM ALERT

Understand the differences between the AD FS role services. An exam question might ask you to make a choice between these services.

Installing the AD FS Server Role

Similar to other server roles discussed in this chapter, you can install AD FS from the Add Roles Wizard in Server Manager. The server must be running IIS with the Microsoft ASP.NET 2.0 and Microsoft .NET Framework 2.0 add-ons; the wizard asks you to install these if they are not present. Perform the following steps to install the AD FS server role:

1. From the Roles node of Server Manager, select Add Roles, and bypass the Initial Configuration Steps page if this is presented.

2. On the Select Server Roles page, select Active Directory Federation Services, and then click Next.

3. The Introduction to AD FS page provides links to additional information from the Help and Support Center. Select these links to view additional information. You can return to the Add Roles Wizard at any time to continue the installation procedure.

4. On the Select Role Services page shown in Figure 4.20, select the role services you want to install on this computer. Then click Next.

5. If IIS and the Windows Process Activation Service are not installed on the server, the wizard displays a dialog box that asks you to install these services. Click Add Required Roles Services to proceed.

6. On the Choose a Server Authentication Certificate for SSL Encryption page, select an existing certificate if you have one. (This is the most secure option.) For learning purposes, it is sufficient to select the Create a Self-Signed Certificate for SSL Encryption option. Then click Next.

7. The Choose a Token-Signing Certificate page presents the same options as the previous one. Make your selection, and then click Next.

8. On the Specify Federation Server page, type the fully qualified domain name (FQDN) of your server, and then click Next. If you are installing the Federation Service role service, this is the name of the server you are working on; if you are installing the Federation Proxy role service or one of the web agent role services, this is the name of the Federation Service server.

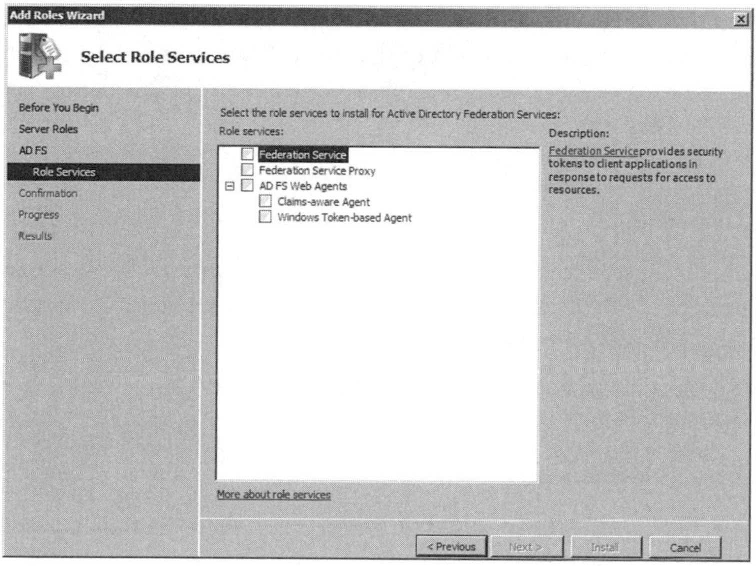

FIGURE 4.20 The Add Roles Wizard enables you to install any or all of the role services used by AD FS.

9. On the Select Trust Policy page, accept the default of Create a New Trust Policy unless you have an existing trust policy that you want to use. Then click Next.

10. If you are also installing the Web Server (IIS) role, you receive the Introduction to Web Server (IIS) page. Click links on this page to obtain additional information about this role, and then click Next.

11. Leave the default IIS role services selected, and then click Next.

12. On the Confirm Installation Selections page, review the information to ensure that you've made the correct selections. If you need to make changes, click Previous. When ready, click Install.

13. The wizard charts the progress of installation and displays a Results page when finished. Click Close.

NOTE

You must have a server running Windows Server 2008 Enterprise or Datacenter Edition to install AD FS with either the Federation Service or Federation Proxy Service role services. Further, to install Federation Service, your server must be joined to an AD DS domain. A server running Windows Server 2008 Standard Edition can only act as one of the AD FS web agent roles and must be able to connect to a server running the Federation Service or Federation Proxy Service.

After installing AD FS, you can access the AD FS snap-in from the Administrative Tools folder. This snap-in enables you to perform configuration activities for the Federation Service or federation server farm and manage other AD FS activities such as trust policies.

Trust Policies

Trust policies enable users to share documents protected in AD RMS across internal or external AD DS forests. You use the AD FS snap-in to configure trust policies, including the following tasks:

▶ Administer account stores in AD DS or AD LDS.

▶ Manage partners that will trust your company, including account partners and resource partners.

▶ Manage claims and certificates used by federation servers, as well as web applications protected by AD FS.

To configure an AD FS trust policy, open the AD FS snap-in and expand the node in the console tree to display the Trust Policy subnode. Right-click Trust Policy and choose Properties. In the General tab of the Trust Policy Properties dialog box shown in Figure 4.21, type the appropriate Federation Service uniform resource identifier (URI) (points to the federation server at the account partner organization). Then select the Display Name tab, type the name of the partner organization in the Display Name for this Trust Policy field, and then click OK.

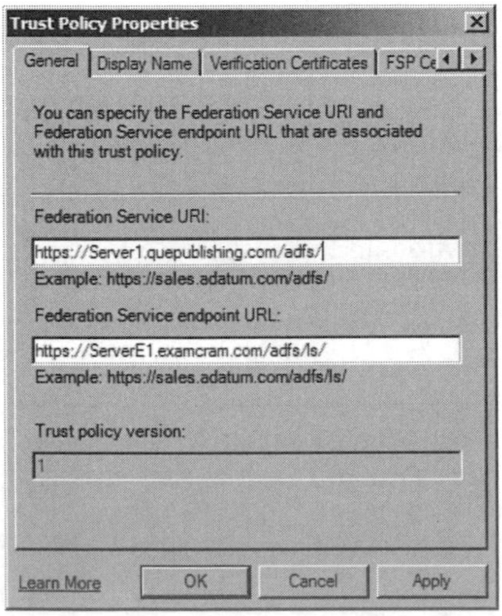

FIGURE 4.21 Configuring a trust policy.

For more information on using AD FS and AD RMS together, refer to "Using Identity Federation with Active Directory Rights Management Services Step-by-Step Guide" in Appendix A.

User and Group Claim Mapping

A *claim* is a statement made by a server about a client, such as its name, identity, key, group, privilege, or capability. Web applications use these claims to perform authorization decisions. The AD FS Federation Service negotiates trusts among disparate entities. It allows exchange of claims containing specified values, thereby allowing parties such as resource partners to use these claims in deciding whether to authorize access to its federated applications.

The following are several types of claims that you can enable when configuring the account partner:

- ▶ **UPN**—Specify a list of user principal name (UPN) domains and suffixes to be accepted from the account partner. Unknown UPN identities will be rejected.

- ▶ **Email**—Specify a list of email domains and suffixes to be accepted. Unknown email identities will be rejected.

- ▶ **Common name**—Specify whether common name claims can be accepted. This type of claim cannot be mapped; it is simply passed through if enabled.

- ▶ **Group**—Specify a set of incoming group claims to be accepted from the account partner. These incoming groups are associated with an organizational group claim, thereby creating a group mapping. Incoming groups that have no mapping are rejected.

- ▶ **Custom**—Specify custom information about users, such as ID numbers.

The first three types of claims are collectively known as organization or identity claims.

Claim mapping refers to the process of passing incoming claims to the federation partner, which in turn maps these claims into organization claims sent to the resource application by the resource federation service. In this process, claims proceed through the federation service from the account store to the account federation service to the resource partner or application, or from the account partner to the resource federation service to the resource application. This process is shown schematically in Figure 4.22.

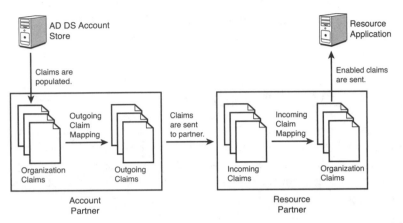

FIGURE 4.22 The exchange of claims between federation partners is known as claim mapping.

This process can be different for each federation partner. Defining this process is important for the configuration of the federation.

For more information on claims and claim mapping, refer to "Understanding Claims" in Windows Server 2008 Help and Support.

Configuring Federation Trusts

The AD FS snap-in enables you to perform the activities associated with configuring *federation trusts*. The console tree of this snap-in includes nodes for the federation service and trust policies between the organization in which the AD FS server is located ("My Organization") and partner organizations. This section looks at the following activities in terms of a resource partner that has one or more federated applications to be accessed by users in one or more account partners:

- ▶ Creating claims
- ▶ Creating account stores
- ▶ Enabling federated applications
- ▶ Creating federation trusts

Creating Claims

As already mentioned, a claim is a statement made by a server about a client. Perform the following procedure to create a new claim:

1. In the console tree of the AD FS snap-in, expand the Trust Policy node to reveal nodes for My Organization and Partner Organizations.

2. Expand My Organization, right-click Organization Claims, and select New, Organization Claim.

3. In the Create a New Organization Claim dialog box, type the desired claim name (note that this name is case sensitive), select the claim type (group claim or custom claim, as previously defined), and then click OK.

Creating Account Stores

An account store stores user accounts that AD FS must authenticate for using your organization's federated applications. To enable users from the account partner to authenticate, you must add an account store.

1. In the console tree of the AD FS snap-in, right-click the Account Stores subnode and choose New, Account Store.

2. Click Next to bypass the introductory page of the Account Store Wizard.

3. On the Account Store Type page, select the type of account store (AD DS or AD LDS), and then click Next.

4. On the AD LDS Store Details page, type a display name and URI for the account store, and then click Next.

5. On the AD LDS Server Settings page, specify the server's name or IP address, the port number, the LDAP search base distinguished name, and the username LDAP attribute, and then click Next.

6. On the Identity Claims page, select one or more identity claim types (UPN, email, or common name), specify their LDAP attributes, and then click Next.

7. On the Enable This Account Store page, ensure that the check box is selected, click Next, and then click Finish.

Enabling Applications

Applications that you want to make available to users in the account partner must be enabled (federated). AD FS provides the Add Applications Wizard to assist you in performing this task. To enable your federated application, perform the following steps:

1. In the console tree of the AD FS snap-in, right-click the Applications subnode and choose New, Application.

2. Click Next to bypass the welcome page of this wizard.

3. On the Application Type page, select the application type (in most cases, this is Claims-Aware Application), and then click Next.

4. On the Application Details page, provide a display name and the URL that points to the application, and then click Next.

5. On the Accepted Identity Claims page, select the type(s) of identity claims to be accepted by the application, and then click Next.

6. On the Enable This Application page, ensure that the application is enabled, and then click Next.

7. Click Finish.

Creating Federation Trusts

The federation trust is the relationship between your organization and the account partner. This relationship must be enabled in both directions so that their users in the account partner can access your applications. AD FS provides the Add Account Partner Wizard to facilitate this action, as follows:

1. Under the Partner Organizations node, right-click Account Partners and choose New, Account Partner.

2. Click Next to bypass the welcome page of this wizard.

3. If the account partner has provided a policy file, select Yes and provide the path to the policy file. Otherwise, click No and then click Next.

4. Provide the required information about the account partner on the Account Partner Details page, and then click Next.

5. Type or browse to the location of the verification certificate, and then click Next.

6. On the Federation Scenario page, if you do not have a forest trust relationship with the other company, select the Federated Web SSO option, and then click Next.

7. On the Account Partner Identity Claims page, select the appropriate claim types to be accepted, and then click Next.

8. Type the UPN suffixes to be accepted from the account partner, click Add after each one, and then click Next.

9. Type the email suffixes to be accepted from the account partner, click Add after each one, and then click Next.

10. Ensure that the Enable This Account Partner check box is selected, click Next, and then click Finish.

The account partner must complete the other side of this trust relationship from his server running AD FS. He should right-click Resource Partners and choose New, Resource Partner. The Add Resource Partner Wizard contains steps similar to those outlined here for adding an account partner.

For additional practice with configuring AD FS, refer to "Step-by-Step Guide for AD FS in Windows Server 2008" in Appendix A.

Windows Server 2008 Virtualization

New to the 64-bit editions of Windows Server 2008 is built-in virtualization (also known as *Hyper-V*), which enables you to run multiple instances of operating systems on a single server. It presents a robust, scalable virtualization platform with capabilities to run both 32- and 64-bit guest operating systems, as well as non-Windows operating systems, such as Linux. Previous editions of Windows Server required that you use an add-on product such as Microsoft Virtual Server 2005. Unlike such add-on products, Hyper-V acts as a true hypervisor, sitting directly above the hardware in the server architecture design. Consequently, Hyper-V machines should run much faster than previous virtualization designs.

The following are some of the advantages of Hyper-V in Windows Server 2008:

▶ It simplifies the procedures involved in setting up test labs. A test lab is useful for procedures such as validating patches, testing new software applications, and so on. You can set up a complete test lab including several servers and client computers on one or two machines.

▶ You can reduce the number of physical servers that must be deployed in the server room, thereby saving space and power requirements. Consequently, you reduce operational costs and improve utilization of server hardware.

▶ If a single virtual server crashes, it does not affect other virtual servers running on the same machine. Consequently, server availability is improved.

▶ Hyper-V also leverages other server components such as failover clustering to improve server availability.

▶ Security is improved because server virtualization reduces exposure of virtual servers that contain sensitive information. The host operating system is also protected from compromise by guest operating systems running on the host.

▶ Network-based security features such as Windows Firewall, Network Address Translation (NAT), and Network Access Protection (NAP) further enhance the security of virtual servers.

> **NOTE**
>
> Hyper-V runs on 64-bit editions of Windows Server 2008 only. You cannot run Hyper-V on 32-bit editions; you must run an add-on product such as Virtual Server 2005 or Virtual PC 2007 on these computers.

To install Hyper-V, start the Select Server Roles Wizard from Server Manager. On the Create Virtual Networks page, select any network adapters whose connections you want to make available to virtual machines. Then confirm your selections and click Install. When installation is completed, click Close and then restart your computer. When the computer has restarted, the Hyper-V Manager utility is available from the Administrative Tools folder. You can use this utility to create virtual machines, including specifying their name and location, memory usage, networking, and the location of the virtual hard disk(s). You can then install an operating system on the virtual machine from a CD-ROM, DVD-ROM, network location, or image (.iso) file.

In the context of this chapter, you can use Hyper-V to create networked environments that include any or all of AD LDS, AD FS, or AD RMS. The environment can include additional servers such as a database server, as well as client computers. You can also include a regular (writable) domain controller with an RODC and examine how replication works between the various machines. The major limitation is that you need plenty of memory—enough to enable all virtual computers that you will be running concurrently.

For additional information on Windows Server 2008 virtualization, refer to the *Exam Cram* book on Exam 70-643. Also refer to "Windows Server 2008 Hyper-V" in Appendix A.

Exam Cram Questions

1. Alex has installed AD LDS on a Windows Server 2008 computer and created an instance that he plans to use for data storage with two directory-enabled applications that he will deploy on his company's network. Which of the following tools can he use to manage the AD LDS instance he has created? (Choose all that apply.)

   ○ **A.** Active Directory Users and Computers

   ● **B.** Active Directory Sites and Services

   ○ **C.** Active Directory Domains and Trusts

   ● **D.** Active Directory Schema

   ● **E.** Active Directory Services Interface (ADSI)

   ● **F.** Ldp.exe

2. You are the administrator of your company's network. You have installed several AD LDS instances to enable connections to directory-enabled applications that run on your Windows Server 2008 network. A contractor named Alex requires access to one of these applications from his laptop computer running Windows Vista Business, but he should not have access to shared resources in Active Directory. What should you do to enable this access?

   ● **A.** Configure an AD LDS security principal for Alex.

   ○ **B.** Configure a domain user account for Alex.

   ○ **C.** Add Alex's local user account to the Domain Users group in Active Directory.

   ○ **D.** You do not need to do anything. Alex can access the applications simply by plugging his laptop into the network and using his local user account.

3. John is responsible for administering his company's servers that run AD RMS. Anna, a junior administrator, will help him by managing the server's AD RMS policies and settings. Which of the following roles should John delegate to Anna so that she can perform this task without the ability to perform additional tasks?

   ○ **A.** AD RMS Auditors

   ○ **B.** AD RMS Template Administrators

   ● **C.** AD RMS Enterprise Administrators

   ○ **D.** AD RMS Server Operators

4. Wendy is the network administrator for a company that operates an AD DS network consisting of a single domain that is operating at the Windows Server 2003 domain and forest functional level. Servers run either Windows Server 2003 or Windows Server 2008, and client computers run either Windows XP Professional or Windows Vista Business or Ultimate. Wendy is planning the deployment of AD RMS on the network to provide a rights-protected information system.

Which of the following should Wendy do to complete the deployment of AD RMS with the least amount of administrative effort and capital expenditure? (Each correct answer represents a partial solution. Choose two answers.)

○ **A.** Upgrade all Windows XP client computers to Windows Vista Business.

○ **B.** Upgrade all Windows XP client computers to Windows Vista Ultimate.

● **C.** Ensure that all Windows XP client computers have Service Pack 2 or later, and install the RMS client on these computers.

○ **D.** Upgrade domain controllers to Windows Server 2008, and set the domain and forest functional levels to Windows Server 2008.

● **E.** Obtain and install an SSL certificate from a trusted root certification authority.

5. Heather is an administrator for a company that operates an AD DS network consisting of a single domain that runs at the Windows 2000 domain functional level. There are three sites corresponding to the company's head office and two small branch offices. Domain controllers on the network run either Windows 2000 Server or Windows Server 2003, but the company plans to introduce domain controllers running Windows Server 2008 to the network.

Heather has read about all the advantages of using RODCs to authenticate users in her company's branch offices and is planning to set up an RODC in each of the branch offices. Which of the following does she need to do before setting up the RODCs? (Each correct answer represents part of the solution. Choose four answers.)

● **A.** Upgrade all Windows 2000 Server domain controllers to either Windows Server 2003 or Windows Server 2008.

○ **B.** Upgrade all Windows 2000 Server and Windows Server 2003 domain controllers to Windows Server 2008.

● **C.** Raise the domain and forest functional levels to Windows Server 2003.

○ **D.** Raise the domain and forest functional levels to Windows Server 2008.

○ **E.** Upgrade the PDC emulator to Windows Server 2003.

● **F.** Upgrade the PDC emulator to Windows Server 2008.

● **G.** Run the Adprep /rodcprep utility on the schema master.

○ **H.** Run the Adprep /rodcprep utility on the infrastructure master.

6. You are the network administrator for your company, which runs an AD DS domain. The company's head office is located in Dallas, and a branch office is located in Waco. You have installed an RODC in the Waco office to enable users in that office to authenticate to the domain without creating heavy WAN traffic.

   Nobody in the Waco office is highly skilled in network administration, but an employee named Fred has demonstrated the ability to perform hardware upgrades and minor configuration changes, so you would like him to have the ability to perform these actions on the RODC. What should you do to grant him this capability without giving him excessive domain administrative privileges?

   ○ **A.** Add his user account to the Domain Admins group.

   ● **B.** Add his user account to the local Administrators group on the RODC.

   ○ **C.** Add his user account to the Server Operators group.

   ○ **D.** Add his user account to the Power Users group.

7. Jim is a domain administrator for a company that operates an AD DS domain with three sites that represent the cities where his company does business. One of these three sites is a small office where he has installed an RODC. This office is connected to the head office with an ISDN line. Jim has configured the RODC to cache passwords for all users in the branch office.

   One weekend, contractors excavating for a new addition to the building holding the branch office accidentally severed the ISDN line. Repairs will take a day or two. On Monday morning, a user named Margaret reports that she is unable to log on. Which of the following is the most likely reason why she was unable to log on?

   ● **A.** Her user account is also listed in the Denied list on the RODC's password replication policy.

   ○ **B.** She changed her password on the previous Friday.

   ○ **C.** Her user account is included in the password cache that Jim has configured on the partnered writable domain controller.

   ○ **D.** Her user account is not included in the list of users contained in the RODC's SAM.

8. Susan is the administrator of a state government agency responsible for construction and maintenance of roads and highways. The agency operates a single domain within the government's AD DS forest. The functional level of the domain is Windows Server 2003, and all servers that hold data accessible to outside parties are located on a perimeter network.

   The agency frequently contracts road work to private consultants, who need access to a web-based application that holds specifications and other data required for the work projects. All private consultants operate AD DS networks with either Windows 2000 or Windows Server 2003 domain controllers.

Susan is required to provide access for consultant employees without creating or managing user accounts for these employees, and she must keep the internal network secure from external access. Which of the following should she do? (Each correct answer represents part of the solution. Choose all that apply.)

- ○ **A.** Install an AD RMS server and configure rights-protected documents.
- ● **B.** Install AD FS on an internal server and create a federated trust.
- ● **C.** Install an AD FS proxy server in the perimeter network.
- ● **D.** Install an AD FS web agent.
- ○ **E.** Install a domain controller on the perimeter network to simplify the authentication of consultant employees.
- ○ **F.** Install an AD LDS server on the perimeter network to simplify the authentication of consultant employees.

9. Gary is responsible for implementing AD FS on his company's Active Directory domain, which has a mix of domain controllers running Windows Server 2003 and Windows Server 2008. Users from several partner companies need to authenticate to a web application on a server that is located in the company's perimeter network. Which of the following role services should Gary install on this server?

- ○ **A.** Federation Service
- ● **B.** Federation Service Proxy
- ○ **C.** Claims-aware agent
- ○ **D.** Windows token-based agent

10. You are the network administrator for Examcram.com, which operates an Active Directory network with Windows Server 2008 domain controllers. Servers on your network are configured with both AD FS and AD RMS. You have set up a federation trust with a partner company named Quepublishing.com so that users can share documents protected in AD RMS across the boundary between the two forests. Which of the following do you need to configure to enable users to share these protected documents?

- ○ **A.** A group claim
- ○ **B.** A custom claim
- ○ **C.** An account store
- ● **D.** A trust policy

Answers to *Exam Cram* Questions

1. **B, D, E, F.** Alex can use any of Active Directory Sites and Services, Active Directory Schema, Active Directory Services Interface, and `Ldp.exe` to manage his AD LDS instance. All these tools perform various types of administrative activities in AD LDS. Neither Active Directory Users and Computers nor Active Directory Domains and Trusts performs AD LDS administrative actions, so answers A and C are incorrect.

2. **A.** You should configure an AD LDS security principal for Alex. This is a user account that resides directly in AD LDS and enables authentication of Alex to use the directory-enabled applications without granting him access to resources on the network. You should neither configure a domain user account for Alex nor add his local user account to the Domain Users group because these actions would give him more access than needed, so answers B and C are incorrect. Alex must be authenticated before he can receive access to directory-enabled applications, so answer D is incorrect.

3. **C.** John should delegate the AD RMS Enterprise Administrators role to Anna. This role enables her to manage all AD RMS policies and settings. The AD RMS Auditors role enables the ability to manage audit logs and reports. The AD RMS Template Administrators role enables the ability to manage rights policy templates. Neither of these roles enables the ability to manage polices and settings, so answers A and B are incorrect. There is no such role as AD RMS Server Operators. (The Server Operators group in AD DS enables members to perform several administrative functions on domain controllers but does not extend capabilities to AD RMS administration.) Therefore, answer D is incorrect.

4. **C, E.** Wendy should ensure that all Windows XP computers have Service Pack 2 or later installed and Install the AD RMS client on these computers. She should also obtain and install an SSL certificate from a trusted authority. Although this requires some capital expenditure, it increases the security of the AD RMS installation compared to that achieved with a self-signed certificate. She does not need to upgrade Windows XP computers to Windows Vista. This requires more administrative action and capital expenditure, so answers A and B are incorrect. She also does not need to upgrade domain controllers to Windows Server 2008, so answer E is incorrect.

5. **A, C, F, G.** Heather needs to upgrade all Windows 2000 domain controllers to either Windows Server 2003 or Windows Server 2008, and then raise the domain and forest functional levels to Windows Server 2003. She also needs to upgrade the PDC emula-tor to Windows Server 2008 and run the `Adprep /rodcprep` utility on the schema master. However, note that if all domain controllers are running Windows Server 2008, it is not necessary to run the `Adprep /domainprep` utility. It is not necessary to upgrade all the domain controllers to Windows Server 2008 or to raise the functional levels to Windows Server 2008, so answers B and D are incorrect. However, it is nec-essary to upgrade the PDC emulator to Windows Server 2008; upgrading this server to Windows Server 2003 is insufficient, so answer E is incorrect. Heather must run the `Adprep /rodcprep` utility on the schema master and not the infrastructure master, so answer H is incorrect.

6. **B.** You should add Fred's user account to the local Administrators group on the RODC. This group is stored in the local SAM of the RODC and grants him the capability of performing administrative tasks on that server only. Adding his user account to the Domain Admins group would grant him excessive privileges, so answer A is incorrect. Adding his user account to the Server Operators group would also grant him excessive privileges, so answer C is incorrect. The Power Users group was used in older Windows versions to grant users limited administrative capabilities. It does not grant specific capabilities in Windows Server 2008 and is only present for backward compatibility with certain applications, so answer D is incorrect.

7. **A.** If Jim has included Margaret's user account in both the Allowed and Denied lists in the RODC's password replication policy, the Denied list takes precedence, and she will be unable to log on if the WAN link is unavailable. If Margaret changed her password the previous Friday, the WAN link was still available at that time, and the new password would be propagated to the partner domain controller and included in the RODC's Allowed list; therefore, she would have been able to log on, so answer B is incorrect. If Margaret's user account is in the password cache (credential caching), she would be able to log on, so answer C is incorrect. The RODC's SAM includes users with local administrative capability on the RODC. Margaret does not need to be on this list to log on to the domain, so answer D is incorrect.

8. **B, C, D.** Susan should install AD FS on an internal server and create a federated trust. She should also install an AD FS proxy on the perimeter network, as well as an AD FS web agent. The proxy enables external users to access the web application, and the web agent authenticates these users, managing the security tokens and authentication cookies required by the web server. This scenario does not require rights-protected documents, so Susan does not need to install an AD RMS server; therefore, answer A is incorrect. Use of either an AD LDS server or a domain controller on the perimeter network would require that Susan administer user accounts for the external users. Use of AD FS eliminates this need, so answers E and F are incorrect.

9. **B.** Gary should install the Federation Service Proxy role service on this server. This service acts as a proxy to the Federation Service on a perimeter network or demilitarized zone. Servers running the Federation Service are installed within the main network, so answer A is incorrect. The claims-aware agent uses a claims-aware application to enable the querying of AD FS security token claims. It does not authenticate users, so answer C is incorrect. The Windows token-based agent runs on a web server that hosts a Windows NT token-based application. It also does not authenticate users, so answer D is incorrect.

10. **D.** You need to set up a trust policy. This enables users to share documents protected in AD RMS across internal or external AD DS forests. You can perform this task from the AD FS snap-in. A group claim specifies a set of incoming group claims to be accepted from the account partner (Quepublishing.com in this case), and a custom claim contains custom information about users. Claims are statements made by a

server about a client in the process of negotiating trusts. They are not applicable here, so answers A and B are incorrect. An account store stores user accounts that AD FS must authenticate to use your company's federated applications. While required, the account store does not enable users to share protected documents, so answer C is incorrect.

CHAPTER FIVE

Active Directory Objects and Trusts

Terms You'll Need to Understand

- ✓ AGDLP
- ✓ AGUDLP
- ✓ Built-in account
- ✓ Csvde
- ✓ Domain local group
- ✓ Domain user account
- ✓ Dsadd
- ✓ External trust
- ✓ Forest trust
- ✓ Global group
- ✓ Ldifde

- ✓ Local user account
- ✓ Nesting
- ✓ Protected Admin
- ✓ Realm trust
- ✓ Security identifier (SID)
- ✓ Shortcut trust
- ✓ SID filtering
- ✓ Template account
- ✓ Transitive trust
- ✓ Universal group
- ✓ User logon name

Concepts/Techniques You'll Need to Master

- ✓ Using command-line tools to create user, group, and computer accounts
- ✓ Adding and removing UPN suffixes
- ✓ Moving objects in Active Directory
- ✓ Configuring group membership
- ✓ Resetting user accounts
- ✓ Nesting groups
- ✓ Delegating administrative control to users and groups
- ✓ Creating and managing trust relationships

The heart and soul of any Active Directory implementation are the users who must access the network on a daily basis. A company must be able to ensure that its employees are able to access all the resources on the network that they require so that they can perform the activities associated with their jobs but not be able to access other resources that might contain confidential information. Further, companies work together with other companies in partnered or client-based arrangements that require access to each other's networks on a temporary or ongoing basis.

This chapter turns its attention to the nuts and bolts of Active Directory that enable all these activities to take place in a controlled manner. It shows you how to create user accounts for all these various employees and manage them in terms of groups. It then takes you through all the account management tasks before concluding with the various types of trust relationships that enable companies to work with each other in a properly administered fashion.

Creating User and Group Accounts

If a user is unable to log on to an Active Directory Domain Services (AD DS) network, he cannot gain access to the data and resources, such as files, folders, printers, and so on, that are stored on the network. Further, in most organizations numerous employees have similar work functions and requirements. Providing such employees access to resources individually would be a tedious and error-prone job were it not for the ability to group these users.

Introducing User Accounts

User accounts allow users to log on to computers and domains. User accounts embody specific information pertinent to a user, such as username, password, and specific logon limitations. User accounts can either be built-in accounts or self-generated. Each user account has a comprehensive set of configurable properties associated with it. Among these are group memberships, logon scripts, logon hours, account expiration, user profile, and dial-in permission.

The following three types of user accounts are present in an AD DS network:

> ▶ **Domain user accounts**—This account is used to provide access to an AD DS domain and all its associated resources. It is the most common account type on the network. You can give permission to an account from one AD DS domain to access resources in other domains.

> ▶ **Local user accounts**—This account exists on a standalone or member server, or a Windows XP Professional or Vista Business, Enterprise, or

Ultimate computer. It enables a user to log on to the computer with which it is associated and gain access to resources on that computer only. A local user account cannot gain access to domain-based resources.

▶ **Built-in user accounts**—These accounts exist for specific administrative or system tasks to ease the burdens of administration. Special accounts are defined up front that have permissions to various resources and components of the AD DS forest.

Introducing Group Accounts

Common networks have hundreds to thousands of users and large numbers of network resources such as files, folders, computers, and printers. Granting access to these resources based solely on user accounts would be time consuming, error prone, and highly repetitive. That's why there are groups. Simply put, you can create a group within AD DS and grant or deny access to this single entity. Then you can add user accounts as members of the group. Belonging to the group, the user accounts inherit the permissions assigned to the group. It is much simpler to modify the permissions once on a group object than many times on the users. Further, you can build a hierarchy of groups and assign different permissions to each level, an activity known as *nesting*. You achieve this by nesting the groups. Nesting groups further simplifies your security model.

Group Types

Windows Server 2008 provides two group types:

▶ **Security groups**—You can use these groups for assigning rights and permissions to users. You can also use them for distribution purposes, such as email lists. These group types have security information, such as unique *security identifiers (SID)*, assigned to them.

▶ **Distribution groups**—You can use these groups for distribution purposes, such as email lists. These groups do not possess SIDs and cannot be assigned permission to resources.

Group Scopes

Within each group type, Windows Server 2008 provides three group scopes:

▶ **Global**—These groups can include users, computers, and other global groups from the same domain. You can use them to organize users who have similar functions and therefore similar requirements on the network. For example, you might include all sales staff in one global group, all engineering staff in another global group, and so on.

▶ **Domain local**—These groups can include users, computers, and groups from any domain in the forest. They are most often utilized to grant permissions for resources and may be used to provide access to any resource in the domain in which they are located. It is thus logical for a domain local group to include global groups that contain all users with a common need for a given resource.

▶ **Universal**—These groups can include users and groups from any domain in the AD DS forest and can be employed to grant permissions to any resource in the forest. A universal group can include users, computers, and global groups from any domain in the forest.

Creating User, Computer, and Group Accounts

Before discussing the automation of AD DS account creation, this chapter takes a quick look at manual creation of accounts. This basic administrative task is done through the Active Directory Users and Computers console. When you open this console, you can navigate through the list of containers in the domain, as shown in the console tree. User accounts are typically located in the Users container, though they can be created in other folders as well.

Perform the following procedure to create a new user account:

1. Right-click the desired container and choose New, User.

2. In the New Object—User dialog box shown in Figure 5.1, type the user's first and last name, and assign a *user logon name*. When you type the user logon name, a pre-Windows 2000–compatible logon name is automatically created. This creates a NetBIOS-type name of the type used on older Windows NT networks.

3. Click Next, enter a password for the user, and confirm this password.

4. Configure additional account settings as required, including requiring the user to change the password at next logon and specifying whether users can change their own password, whether the password should never expire, and whether the account should be disabled.

5. Click Next and then click Finish to finish creating the account.

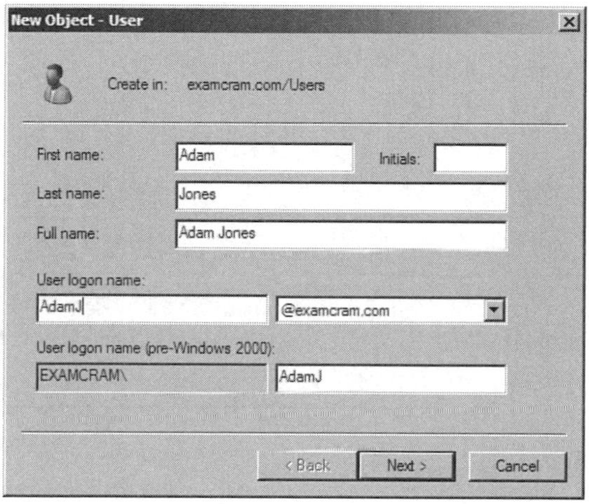

FIGURE 5.1   Creating a new user account.

Creating a new group is similar. Right-click the desired container (such as the domain, any OU, or the Users container) and select New, Group. In the New Object—Group dialog box, type the group name, and provide a group scope and type from the options already discussed. Then click OK.

Creating a computer account enables you to prepare for joining a client computer to the domain. Right-click the desired container and select New, Computer. In the New Object—Computer dialog box, type the computer name and, if necessary, click Change to assign the privilege of joining the computer to the domain to a different user or group. As for users, a NetBIOS-compatible name is automatically created for both groups and computers.

Use of Template Accounts

A *template account* is a special account that is used only for copying as needed when you have to create a large number of user accounts. You should configure it to hold the various properties that are required for each user, so that you need only enter individual information such as usernames.

Access the New Object—User dialog box in the appropriate AD DS container, and specify the following properties:

- ▶ Last name: template
- ▶ User logon name: _TEMPLATE
- ▶ Password: (blank)
- ▶ Account is disabled: (selected)

Note that using an underscore as the first character of the username causes this account to be listed at or close to the top of the list of user accounts. You can also use a name that is descriptive of the type of user being created, such as _SALESPERSON. Specifying that the account be disabled ensures that no one can log on using this account.

> **NOTE**
>
> By default, any user account that you create from a template remains disabled by default; you must manually enable these accounts before they can be used. This is a built-in security feature.

After completing this procedure, right-click the account and select Properties to configure common account properties such as the following:

- On the Account tab, specify any additional account options that may be required, such as requiring a smart card for interactive logon or the use of one of several types of encryption.

- On the Profile tab, specify a profile path to a share on a file server that will hold the user's documents and other settings—for example, \\server1\docs\%username%. By using the %username% variable, a subfolder for each employee is automatically created and given the same name as the employee's username. You can also specify a local path in the same location.

- On the Member Of tab, specify one or more groups that each user should be made a member of.

- Add any additional common properties that apply to all users, such as address and organizational information, and Terminal Services and remote access settings.

To use the template account, right-click it in the Details pane of Active Directory Users and Computers, and choose Copy. You receive the Copy Object—User dialog box, which is similar to the New Object—User dialog box shown in Figure 5.1. After you have provided name and password information, an account is created with all the properties you have provided for the template account.

Using Bulk Import to Automate Account Creation

While use of a template account can expedite the creation of a series of user accounts with similar properties, the creation of a large number of accounts in an enterprise environment can quickly become time consuming. If you need to create hundreds, or even thousands, of new user or group accounts, you can use one of several tools provided by Microsoft for automating the creation of new accounts, as follows:

- ▶ **Csvde**—The Comma Separated Value Data Exchange (`Csvde`) tool enables you to import data to AD DS from files containing information in the comma-separated variable (CSV) format. You can also export AD DS data to CSV-formatted files.

- ▶ **Ldifde**—The LDAP Data Interchange Format Data Exchange (`Ldifde`) tool enables you to create, modify, and delete directory objects. You can also extend the schema, export AD DS user and group information, and add data to AD DS from other directory sources. Note that `csvde` and `ldifde` do not allow you to export passwords.

- ▶ **Dsadd**—This enables you to add object types such as computers, contacts, groups, users, organizational units (OU), and quotas to AD DS.

- ▶ Scripts—You can use scripts and batch files with tools such as `Dsadd` to automate the creation of large numbers of accounts. You can also use Windows Script Host to automate account creation.

Csvde

This tool works with comma-separated text files with a `.csv` extension—in other words, values are separated from one another by commas. This is a format supported by many other applications such as Exchange Server and Microsoft Excel. Because Excel supports this format, it is a convenient tool for creating the `.csv` file.

The first line of the `.csv` file is known as the attribute line. It defines the format of the following lines according to attributes defined in the schema. The attributes are separated by commas and define the order of the attributes on each data line.

Following the attribute line, each line includes one set of user data to be included in the bulk import. The data must conform to the following rules:

- ▶ The sequence of the source values must be the same as that specified in the attribute line.

- ▶ A value containing commas must be enclosed in quotation marks.

- ▶ If a user object does not have entries for all the values included in the attribute line, you can leave the field blank; however, you must include the commas.

The following are examples of code lines conforming to these rules:

```
Dn,cn,objectClass,sAMAccountName,userPrincipalName,teletphoneNumber

"cn=Bob Wilson,OU=engineering,dc=examcram,dc=com", Bob Wilson,user,
➥BobW,BobW@examcram.com,555-678-9876
"cn=Clara Perkins,OU=sales,dc=examcram,dc=com", Clara Perkins,user,
➥ClaraP,ClaraP@examcram.com,555-678-4321

"cn=Vista1,OU=engineering,dc=examcram,dc=com",Vista1,computer,Vista1,,,
```

The last entry is an example of a computer object (`objectClass=computer`), with no values defined for `userPrincipalName` or `telephoneNumber`. You would normally import this object to the default Computers container; however, you can import it to any desired container.

To import the `.csv` file to AD DS, run the following command from the command prompt:

```
Csvde -I -f filename.csv
```

In this command, `-I` specifies import mode (the default is export mode), and `-f` `filename.csv` specifies the name of the file to be imported. After you press Enter, the command provides status information, including any errors that might occur. Once the command has completed, you should check some of the user accounts to confirm the command's proper completion.

EXAM ALERT

Csvde is a convenient tool for importing user and group account information provided in an Excel spreadsheet file, because Excel offers a convenient means for exporting data to a comma-separated text file. An exam question might take advantage of this fact.

Ldifde

The `Ldifde` tool works in a similar manner to `Csvde` except that it uses the LDIF file format, which is a line-separated format. In other words, each record is separated by a blank line. A record is a distinct collection of data to be added to AD DS or to modify existing data, such as a username or computer name.

Each line describes a singe attribute and specifies the name of the attribute (as defined by the schema) followed by its value. A line beginning with # is a comment line. The following example uses the text from one of the CSVs used in the previous section. This should facilitate your comparing the two formats:

```
# These are the attributes for Bob Wilson.
DN: cn=Bob Wilson,OU=engineering,dc=examcram,dc=com
CN: Bob Wilson
DisplayName: Bob Wilson
GivenName: Bob
Sn: Wilson
ObjectClass: user
SAMAccountName: BobW
UserPrincipalName: BobW@examcram.com
TelephoneNumber: 555-678-4321
PhysicalDeliveryOfficeName: 7th Floor, SE Corner
```

To use `Ldifde`, run the following command from the command prompt:

```
Ldifde -I -f filename.ldf
```

The usage and parameters of `Ldifde` are identical to those used with `Csvde`. Table 5.1 describes several more common parameters used by these commands. You can also use `Ldifde` to modify or delete accounts, extend the schema, export AD DS data to other applications or services, and import information from other directory services to AD DS.

TABLE 5.1 Common Parameters Used by Csvde and Ldifde

Parameter	Description
-I	Specifies import mode. If not specified, the default is export mode.
-f filename	Specifies the import or export filename.
-s servername	Specifies the domain controller to be used during import or export.
-c string1 string2	Replaces occurrences of string1 with string2. This is useful if you have to import data from one domain to another and need to modify the distinguished names accordingly.

(continues)

TABLE 5.1   *Continued*

Parameter	Description
-j *directory path*	Specifies the path to the log file. By default, this is the current directory path.
-b *username domain password*	Allows you to run the command using the credentials of another user account. Specify the username, domain, and password of the required account.

Dsadd

The dsadd command-line tool enables you to add objects, including users, groups, computers, OUs, contacts, and quotas to the AD DS database. To add a user, execute the following command:

```
Dsadd user UserDN –fn FirstName –le LastName –display DisplayName
➥-pwd {password ¦ *} –samid SAMName -tel PhoneNumber -disabled {yes ¦ no}
```

In this command, *userDN* refers to the distinguished name of the user you are adding, *FirstName* and *LastName* are the user's first and last names, *DisplayName* is the display name, *password* is the password (if you specify *, the user is prompted for the password), *SAMName* is the unique SAM account name, *PhoneNumber* is the user's telephone number, and disabled is the enabled/disabled status. (If you specify Yes, the account is disabled; if you specify No, the account is enabled.)

To add a group, execute the following command:

```
Dsadd group GroupDN –fn FirstName –secgrp {yes ¦ no} –scope {l ¦g ¦u}
➥-samid SAMName –memberof Group … -members member …
```

In this command, *GroupDN* refers to the distinguished name of the group you are adding, secgrp specifies whether the group is a security group (yes) or distribution group (no), scope refers to the group scope (l for domain local, g for global, u for universal), memberof specifies the groups to which the new group is to be added, and members specifies the members to add to the new group. By default, Windows creates a new group as a global security group.

Many additional parameters are available. For additional information, execute this command followed by /? or consult the Windows Server 2008 Help and Support Center.

Additional Command-Line Tools

AD DS provides the following additional command-line tools, the functionality of which is similar in nature to that of dsadd. To obtain information about the parameters associated with each tool, type the command name followed by /?.

▶ **dsmod**—Modifies objects

▶ **dsrm**—Removes objects

▶ **dsmove**—Moves objects to another container within the domain

▶ **dsget**—Provides information about objects

▶ **dsquery**—Displays objects matching search criteria

For more information on all the command-line tools discussed in this section, refer to "11 Essential Tools for Managing Active Directory" in Appendix A, "Need to Know More?"

Scripts

By creating scripts, you can fully utilize the power of these commands in automating the creation, modification, or deletion of multiple AD DS objects. You can choose from the following three scripting environments:

▶ **Batch files**—You can include commands such as dsadd, dsmod, or dsrm in a batch file, which enables the rapid processing of command-line tools for managing multiple AD DS objects.

▶ **Windows Script Host (WSH)**—This is a powerful scripting environment that enables you to run files containing commands written in the Microsoft Visual Basic Scripting Edition (VBScript) or JavaScript (JScript) languages.

▶ **Windows PowerShell**—This is a new, powerful, command-line shell and scripting language that works with existing scripting and command-line tools to provide a high level of productivity and system control. Windows PowerShell includes an extensive list of subcommands known as *CmdLets* with a comprehensive tutorial and help system to get you started. This is included by default with Windows Server 2008 and available as an add-on for Windows XP, Vista, and Server 2003.

Configuring the UPN

A user principal name (UPN) is a logon name formatted in a manner similar to that of an email address, such as user1@examcram.com. The first part uniquely identifies the user, and the second part, by default, identifies the domain to which she belongs. The UPN is especially convenient when logging on to a domain from a computer located in another domain in the forest or a trusted forest.

UPN Suffixes

Introduced in Windows Server 2003 is the concept of the UPN suffix. This is the portion of the UPN to the right of the at (@) character. By default, the UPN suffix is the DNS name of the domain to which the user belongs. You can provide an additional UPN suffix to simplify administrative and logon procedures. Doing so provides the following advantages:

▶ Using a common UPN suffix throughout a multidomain forest simplifies logon procedures for all users. This is especially true in the case of long child domain names. For example, a user with a default UPN of James@east.marketing.examcram.com could be provided with a simpler UPN, such as James@examcram.

▶ Using a common UPN suffix enables you to hide the true domain structure from users in external forests. It also simplifies configuring remote access servers for visitor access.

▶ You can use the UPN suffix to match the email domain name in cases where the company has more than one division with different email domain names but a common AD DS domain. Using the additional UPN suffix enables users to log on using their email addresses.

▶ A common UPN suffix is useful in enabling users to log on to a domain in an existing forest. However, if more than one forest uses the same UPN suffix, you can log on to a domain in the same forest only; furthermore, if you are using explicit UPNs and external trusts, you can use the UPN to log on to a domain in the same forest only.

Adding or Removing UPN Suffixes

You can create alternative UPN suffixes by opening the Active Directory Domains and Trusts console. In the console tree, right-click Active Directory Domains and Trusts and choose Properties to bring up the dialog box shown in Figure 5.2. Simply type the desired UPN suffix, click Add, and then click OK.

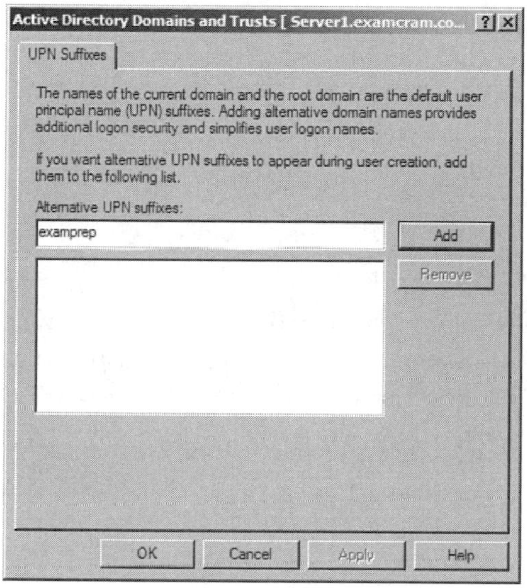

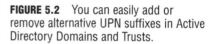

FIGURE 5.2 You can easily add or remove alternative UPN suffixes in Active Directory Domains and Trusts.

You can use the added UPN suffix in Active Directory Users and Computers to configure new or existing users. When adding a new user, the alternative UPN suffix is available from the drop-down list in the New Object—User dialog box (refer to Figure 5.1). You can also configure an existing user with the alternative UPN suffix from the Account tab of the user's Properties dialog box. As shown in Figure 5.3, the alternative UPN suffix is available in the drop-down list of the Account tab of the user's Properties dialog box.

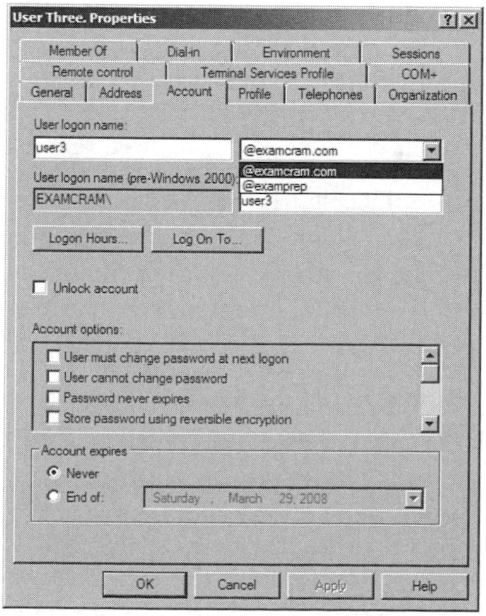

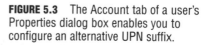

FIGURE 5.3 The Account tab of a user's Properties dialog box enables you to configure an alternative UPN suffix.

To remove an alternative UPN suffix, access the same dialog box shown in Figure 5.2, select the UPN suffix, and click Remove. Then accept the warning that users who use this UPN suffix can no longer log on to the network. You should then open Active Directory Users and Computers, select any user accounts that refer to this suffix, and change it to one that is still in use.

Configuring Contacts

A contact is simply a collection of information about an individual or organization. AD DS provides the Contacts folder, which you can use to store information such as the contact's name, email address, street address, and telephone number.

You can create a contact in the Users group or any OU in your domain's hierarchy. Right-click the container and choose New, Contact. This displays the dialog box shown in Figure 5.4.

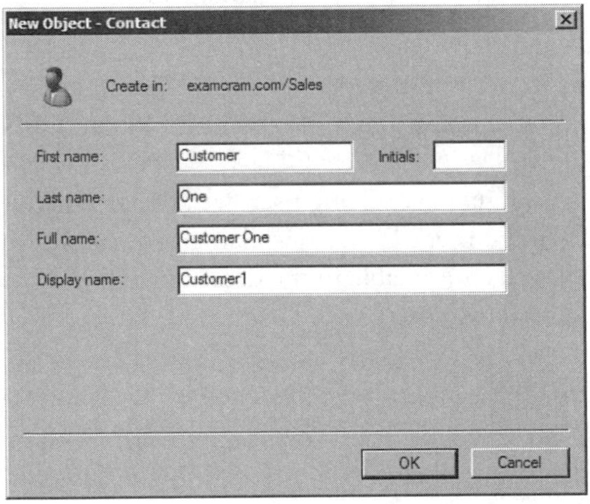

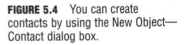

FIGURE 5.4 You can create contacts by using the New Object— Contact dialog box.

The contact you have created appears in the Details pane of Active Directory Users and Computers. Right-click the contact and choose Properties to configure a limited set of properties, including items like the address, telephone numbers, organization, and so on. You can also add the contact to groups for purposes such as creating distribution lists, which are discussed next.

You can automate the creation of contacts using any of the methods discussed in the previous section, and setting the `objectClass` value to `Contact`.

Creating Distribution Lists

Earlier in this chapter, the concept of distribution groups was introduced. The main purpose of a distribution group is to create a distribution list that is used with an email application such as Microsoft Exchange Server to send messages to a collection of users. When you send an email message to the group, it is automatically sent to all members of the group.

> **TIP**
>
> You can also use a security group for distribution purposes. This is useful when you need to be able to send messages to a group and provide the same group access to resources in AD DS.

Windows Server 2008 includes the Message Queuing feature, which provides guaranteed message delivery, efficient routing, security, and priority-based messaging between applications, including those that run on different operating systems. You can install Message Queuing from the Add Features Wizard in Server Manager.

Creating a distribution group is similar to creating other AD DS objects. Simply select the distribution group type from the New Object—Group dialog box discussed earlier. Then right-click the new group, choose Properties, and add the required users and groups from the Select Users, Contacts, Computers, or Groups dialog box (see Figure 5.5). Use semicolons to separate multiple names from each other.

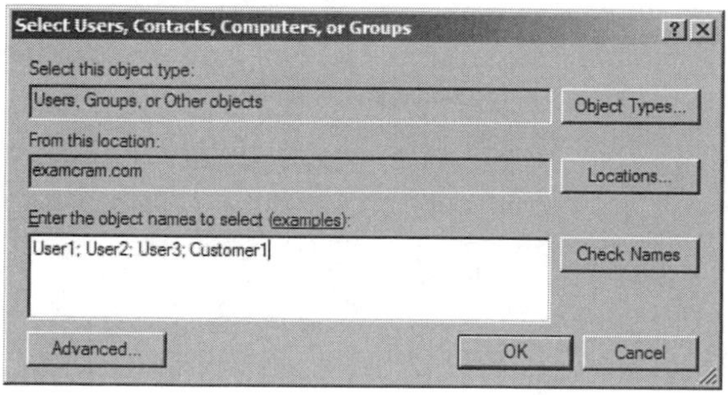

FIGURE 5.5 The Select Users, Contacts, Computers, or Groups dialog box enables you to add these types of objects to your distribution list.

To add contacts or computers to the list, click Object Types to display the Object Types dialog box shown in Figure 5.6 and select one or more of these object types.

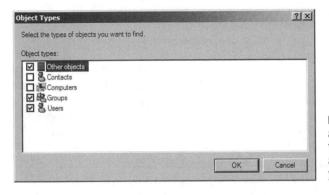

FIGURE 5.6 Select the appropriate object types from the Object Types dialog box to add these types of objects to your distribution list.

To send an email message to all members of a distribution list, simply right-click the list and choose Send Mail. The default email application opens and displays a blank outgoing message with the email addresses of all members automatically filled in. You can do the same thing by selecting New Message from your email application and filling in the group name in the To field.

Managing and Maintaining Accounts

After you have created user and group accounts that encompass all the employees in your organization's AD DS structure, you must be able to work with and manage all these accounts. Account management is a large part of an administrator's everyday actions. The following aspects of account management are discussed in this section:

- ▶ Creating and managing OUs
- ▶ Configuring group membership
- ▶ Nesting groups
- ▶ Resetting accounts
- ▶ Denying privileges
- ▶ Protected Admin
- ▶ Local and domain local groups
- ▶ Deprovisioning accounts
- ▶ Disabling and deleting accounts
- ▶ Delegating administrative control

The following sections briefly introduce each of these concepts.

Creating Organizational Units

Chapter 1, "Getting Started with Windows Server 2008 Active Directory," introduced the concept of OUs as logical subgroups in Active Directory that you can employ to locate resources used by a single work group, section, or department in a company and apply policies that apply to only these resources. Creating OUs is similar to creating other object types in Active Directory. Simply right-click the domain or other container where you want to create an OU, and choose New, Organizational Unit. In the New Object—Organizational Unit dialog box, type a name for the OU, and then click OK. You can also use the dsadd command-line tool.

You can create new OUs in the domain or any other OU that you have previously created, thereby generating a hierarchical structure. The following are several criteria you might want to use in designing an OU hierarchy:

- **Corporate organizational charts**—Create an OU hierarchy that mirrors the company's organizational layout, including departments, branches, sections, work units, and so on. Such a hierarchy facilitates the administration of the network, including assigning permissions, group policies, and so on.

- **Administrative control**—Create an OU hierarchy that enables you to assign junior administrators the ability to perform actions on certain parts of the domain only. Delegation of administrative control is discussed later in this chapter.

- **Geographical layout**—Create an OU hierarchy that mirrors the geographical arrangement of your company's operations. This can include multiple levels reflecting countries, states or provinces, or counties or cities. This enables you to design location-specific policies or administrative actions.

After you have created new OUs, it is easy to move objects such as users, computers, and groups to the new OU. Simply drag the required objects in Active Directory Users and Computers to the appropriate location. You can also right-click an object and choose Move. Select the desired destination in the Move dialog box, and then click OK. Furthermore, you can use the dsmove utility to move a series of objects at the same time.

TIP

Try to keep the OU hierarchy of your organization simple, with no more than two or three levels of OU nesting, if possible. Complex structures can result in unexpected application of Group Policy or difficulty in locating and administering objects.

Configuring Group Membership

A group is of no use until you have added members to it. As already stated, groups are used to collect a set of users who need to share a particular set of permissions to a resource, such as a file, folder, or printer. However, the available membership depends on the group scope. Table 5.2 outlines group membership and access considerations for the three group scopes.

TABLE 5.2 Comparison of Groups

	Global	Domain Local	Universal
Member List	User and group accounts from the same domain	User accounts and domain local groups from the same domain, global groups, and universal groups from any domain in the forest	User accounts, global groups, and other universal groups in any domain in the forest
Nesting	Universal and domain local groups in any domain and global groups in the same domain	Domain local groups in the same domain	Local and universal groups in any domain
Scope	Can be used in its own domain and any trusted domains	Can be used only in its own domain	Can be used in any domain in the forest
Permissions	Resources in all domains in the forest	Resources in the domain in which the group exists only	Resources in any domain in the forest

> **NOTE**
>
> If you have only a single domain in your forest, it is not necessary to use universal groups.

Using Active Directory Users and Computers, you can configure group membership in any of the following ways:

▶ **Add a series of users or groups to the group**—Right-click the group and choose Properties. On the Members tab, select Add, and then enter the desired account names in the Select Users, Contacts, Computers, or Groups dialog box (previously shown in Figure 5.5).

▶ **Add a user to one or more groups**—Right-click the user and choose Add to a Group. Then enter the desired groups in the Select Groups dialog box and click OK. Alternatively, select Properties, select the Member Of tab, and click Add. You can also use this procedure to add one group to another within the limits described in Table 5.2.

▶ **Use the dsadd utility**—This utility enables you to add any allowable combinations of users and groups and to script these actions.

You can also remove a user or group from another group if required. From the Members tab of the user or group's Properties dialog box, select the required entry and click Remove, or use the dsrm utility.

> **NOTE**
>
> Unlike previous versions of Windows, the allowable levels of group nesting do not depend on domain functional level. This is because Windows Server 2008 no longer supports Windows NT domain controllers and the Windows 2000 mixed functional level, which severely limited the extent of group nesting.

AGDLP/AGUDLP

Microsoft continues to recommend the same strategy for nesting groups that it has supported since Windows NT 4.0. The following list outlines the strategy:

1. Place accounts (A) into global groups (G).

2. Add the global groups to domain local groups (DL).

3. Finally, assign permissions (P) to the domain local groups.

In short, this strategy is known as *AGDLP*, Accounts to Global groups to Domain Local groups to Permissions.

You can use the same strategy in multidomain environments. Add users from each child domain to a global group in the same domain. Then add these global groups to a domain local group in the parent domain and grant permissions to this group. Figure 5.7 shows this strategy in graphical form.

You can extend this strategy to *AGUDLP* by using universal groups (U), as shown schematically in Figure 5.8. The two child domains, west.examcram.com and east.examcram.com, contain users who require access to developmental applications located in the examcram.com domain. By employing a universal group, you can grant access to these applications to users in both domains by employing just a single group (the universal group). Although you can grant access directly to the universal group, Microsoft recommends that you secure access to these resources by creating a domain local group in the domain where they are located and adding the universal group to this domain local group. Then grant the appropriate permissions to the domain local group.

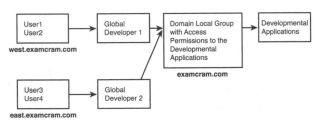

FIGURE 5.7 You can use the AGDLP strategy in multiple-domain situations.

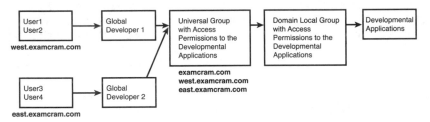

FIGURE 5.8 You can use a universal group to grant access to resources in more than one domain.

The following are several suggestions for using universal groups:

▶ Use universal groups sparingly, and use them only when their membership is relatively static. If universal group membership changes frequently, these changes result in a high level of network traffic between domain controllers in different domains, because any membership changes must be propagated to all global catalog servers in the forest.

▶ Use universal groups when you need to assign permissions to resources located in several domains. Simply follow the strategy illustrated in Figure 5.8, and grant the appropriate permissions to the domain local groups. Use of this strategy simplifies the allocation of permissions and reduces the amount of interdomain replication traffic.

▶ In a single-domain forest, you do not need to use universal groups. Use the AGDLP strategy only.

EXAM ALERT

You might receive a question that offers a choice of several methods for nesting groups. The correct answer is always according to the Microsoft-recommended AGDLP or AGUDLP strategies. Also remember the group nesting limitations summarized in Table 5.2.

Resetting Accounts and Passwords

A common task that network administrators and desktop or help desk personnel must perform is the resetting of passwords for users who have forgotten them. Related to this is the task of unlocking user accounts that have been locked out because of too many attempts at entering an incorrect password.

To reset a password, open Active Directory Users and Computers and select the container or OU of the account from the console tree listing. In the Details pane, right-click the user account and choose Reset Password. On the Reset Password dialog box shown in Figure 5.9, type and confirm a new password. By default, the user is required to change this password at next logon, thereby enabling him to select a password of his choice. He must select a password that is within the limits of the password complexity policy, which is discussed in Chapter 7, "Group Policy and Active Directory Security." If the account is locked out, select the check box labeled Unlock the User's Account.

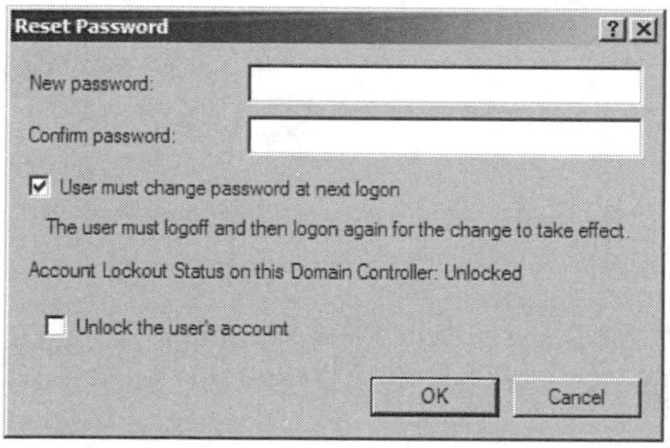

FIGURE 5.9 The Reset Password dialog box enables you to reset the password for a user who has forgotten his password.

NOTE

A Microsoft Gold Certified Partner, Lieberman Software, has produced an Account Reset Console that enables users to reset forgotten or expired passwords without the help of an administrator. Like other third-party add-on solutions, this product is beyond the scope of Exam 70-640.

Denying Privileges

You have learned about the assigning of permissions using the AGDLP and AGUDLP strategies. In both cases, you assign permissions to domain local groups for resources in the domain of the group. You can use the same strategy for denying access to domain local groups.

As was the case in all previous Windows versions, when you explicitly deny access to a user or group, members of that group are denied access to the resource, regardless of any permissions they might receive directly or by means of membership in other groups. To deny access, proceed as follows:

1. Right-click the resource (file, folder, printer, and so on) and choose Properties.

2. Select the Security tab of the resource's Properties dialog box, and click Edit.

3. On the Permissions dialog box that appears, click Add to add the required group, and then type the group name in the Select Users, Computer, or Groups dialog box that appears. Click OK.

4. Select the appropriate entry in the Deny column, as shown in Figure 5.10, and then click OK.

5. You receive a Windows Security message box that warns you that Deny entries take precedence over Allow entries. Click Yes to accept this warning, and then click OK to close the resource's Properties dialog box.

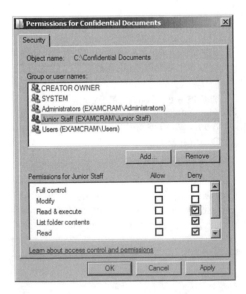

FIGURE 5.10 You can deny access to a resource from its Permissions dialog box.

Protected Admin

Previous versions of Windows Server limited the ability to perform tasks when using a nonadministrative user account, with the result that many users used an administrative account, whether they needed it or not. This practice often left the servers open to many types of attack by malware programs, such as viruses, Trojan horses, and spyware. Starting with Windows Vista and continued in Windows Server 2008, a new feature called User Account Control (UAC) requires users performing administrative tasks to confirm that they actually initiated the task. This includes all administrative accounts except the default Administrator account created when you install Windows Server 2008 or the default account created when you create the first domain controller in a new forest.

Microsoft recommends that you not use this default administrative account and instead create a different administrative account for everyday domain administration activities. In doing so, you are working with what Microsoft calls a *Protected Admin* account. This account works with standard user privileges, thereby preventing many types of attack. When you need to perform an administrative task, Windows displays a UAC prompt, as shown in Figure 5.11. Click Continue to perform the activity, or Cancel to quit. If a malicious program attempts to run, Windows displays the UAC prompt that includes the program name, alerting you to what program is asking for your permission. Thereby, you can cancel such an unexpected prompt and be protected from whatever damage could otherwise occur.

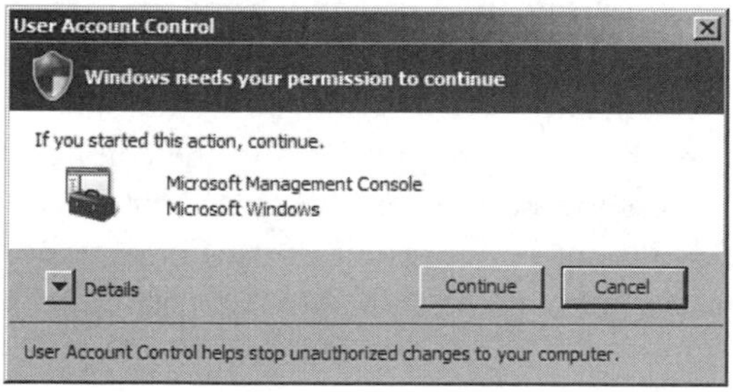

FIGURE 5.11 User Account Control displays this prompt to ask for approval of an administrative task.

If you are logged on as a user who is not a member of the Domain Admins group, you receive a slightly different UAC prompt, as shown in Figure 5.12. This prompt asks you to specify the username and password of an administrative account to proceed with your desired task.

FIGURE 5.12 User Account Control displays this prompt to ask for approval of an administrative task when logged on as a nonadministrative user.

> **CAUTION**
>
> When you receive a UAC prompt, always ensure that the action indicated is the one you want to perform. This is especially true if a UAC prompt appears unexpectedly, which might indicate a malware program attempting to run. Should this happen, click Cancel. The program cannot run. You should then scan your computer with one or more malware detection programs.

Local Versus Domain Groups

Similar to previous Windows versions, Windows Vista and Windows Server 2008 enable you to create local groups on any computer that is not configured as a domain controller. This group is similar in usage and membership capabilities to a domain local group. However, a local group is local to the computer on which it is created and grants access to resources on this computer only. It exists on the local computer's SAM and not in Active Directory. For access to resources located on more than one computer in the domain, always use domain local groups.

To create a local group in Windows Vista or Windows Server 2008, proceed as follows:

1. Open Server Manager, and then expand the Configuration node in the console tree to reveal the Local Users and Groups folder.

2. Expand this folder, right-click Groups, and choose New Group.

3. In the New Group dialog box shown in Figure 5.13, type a name and optional description for the group, and click Add to add members to this group.

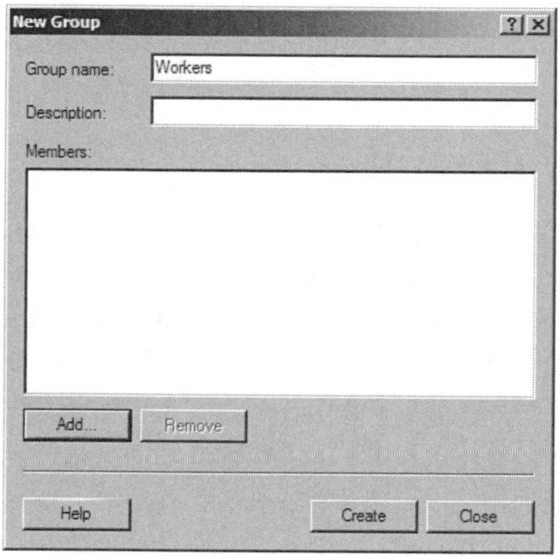

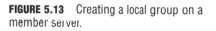

FIGURE 5.13 Creating a local group on a member server.

4. Type the usernames or group names in the Select Users, Computers, or Groups dialog box, and then click OK.

5. If you receive a Windows Security dialog box, type the name and password of an appropriate domain account (member of Domain Admins, Account Operators, or another user who has been delegated this permission).

6. Click Create to create the group.

On a Windows XP or Windows Vista computer, click Start, right-click My Computer or Computer, and choose Manage. If you receive a UAC prompt in Vista, click Continue. From the Computer Management console, expand the Local Users and Groups node, right-click Groups, choose New Group, and then proceed from step 3 in the previous list.

You can also use the net local group command from the command line to create and populate local groups. This command works on any member server or client computer, including Server Core machines. Type this command followed by /? to obtain information about its syntax.

Deprovisioning Accounts

What should you do if a user quits, is fired, or goes on some type of extended leave? You need to deprovision the user's account to prevent unauthorized access—in other words, prevent someone from logging on using this account. The next section looks at two choices for deprovisioning an account: disabling or deleting the account.

If you need to deprovision a group account, simply delete it. There is no means of disabling a group.

Disabling or Deleting Accounts

When a user leaves your company, you have several choices. If a replacement has been hired, you can simply rename the user account for the replacement. Otherwise, you can simply delete it. However, if there is a possibility that a replacement will be hired in the future, you have an additional choice: disabling the account. Disabling an account rather than deleting it provides several advantages:

▶ When an account is disabled, nobody can log on using that account. In this way, a disgruntled employee who has resigned or been fired cannot log on and delete or steal important data.

▶ Security is improved in the case of an employee taking an extended sabbatical or disability leave.

▶ The disabled account retains all group memberships, rights, and permissions assigned to it. When you hire a replacement, you can re-enable and rename the account. You do not need to create everything from scratch.

To disable an account, right-click it in Active Directory Users and Computers and choose Disable Account. You receive a message that the object has been disabled. To re-enable the account, right-click it and choose Enable Account. To delete an account, right-click it and choose Delete, or simply press the Delete key. You are asked whether you are sure you want to delete this account. Click Yes to confirm or No to cancel.

Delegating Administrative Control of Active Directory Objects

One of the major benefits of Active Directory is that you can split up administrative tasks among different individuals. You can assign different sets of administrative responsibility to different users, which can include segments of the directory structure such as OUs or sites. The following are several benefits of delegating administrative control:

▶ You can assign subsets of administrative tasks to users and groups.

▶ You can assign responsibility of a limited portion of the domain, such as OUs or sites, to users or groups.

▸ You can use a nested hierarchy of OUs for even more granular control over which users can perform certain administrative tasks.

▸ You can enhance network security by placing more restrictive limits on the membership of powerful groups, such as Domain Admins, Enterprise Admins, and Schema Admins.

Windows Server 2008 provides the Delegation of Control Wizard to facilitate the task of delegating administrative control. Proceed as follows:

1. In Active Directory Users and Computers, right-click the desired OU and choose Delegate Control. To delegate control over a site, right-click the desired site in Active Directory Sites and Services and choose Delegate Control.

2. Click Next to bypass the introductory page of the Delegation of Control Wizard.

3. On the Users or Groups page, click Add and type the name of the required user or group in the Select Users, Computers, or Groups dialog box. Click OK and then click Next.

4. On the Tasks to Delegate page shown in Figure 5.14, select the task or tasks you want to delegate. If you want to delegate a task that is not shown in the list provided, select the Create a Custom Task to Delegate option. Then click Next.

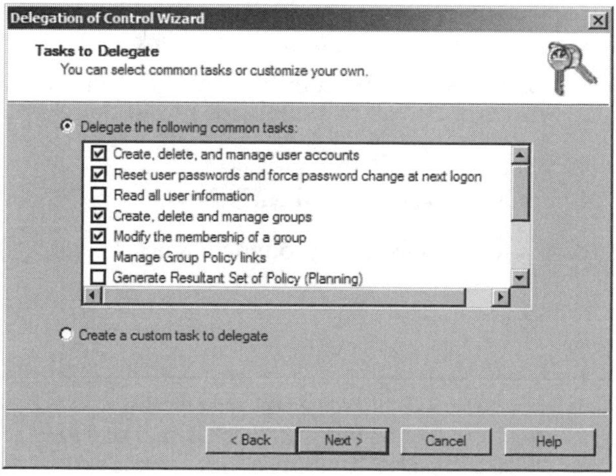

FIGURE 5.14 Using the Delegation of Control Wizard to delegate administrative tasks.

5. If you have chosen the Create a Custom Task to Delegate option, the Active Directory Object Type page enables you to delegate control over a large range of subfolders in the AD DS namespace. Click Next to choose whether to provide the ability to create or delete selected objects in the folder. You can choose from an extensive range of permissions. When finished, click Next.

6. Review the information presented on the completion page. If you need to make any changes, click Back. When done, click Finish.

EXAM ALERT

You should know when and how to use the Delegation of Control Wizard. The exam might present a scenario requiring a limited set of control over a given list of objects. You should also be aware that if you run the Delegation of Control Wizard multiple times, permissions granted are cumulative rather than having the wizard replace prior permissions each time you run it.

To view, modify, or delete permissions granted using this wizard, right-click the OU or site and choose Properties. Select the Security tab, and then click Advanced to display the Advanced Security Settings for (container) dialog box shown in Figure 5.15. This enables you to do the following:

▶ To add an additional user or group with permission to perform a listed task, select the permission entry and click Add. Then type the required user or group in the Select Users, Computers, or Groups dialog box.

▶ To modify the scope of a permissions entry, select it and click Edit. From the Permission Entry dialog box that appears, select the appropriate permissions. You can also explicitly deny permissions from this dialog box.

▶ To remove a delegated permission, select it and click Remove.

▶ To remove all delegated permissions from the container, click Restore Defaults.

TIP

To view the effective permissions granted to a user or group, click the Effective Permissions tab, and then select the required user or group. This tab displays a long list of permissions, with check marks beside the granted permissions. This includes all permissions inherited through membership in other groups.

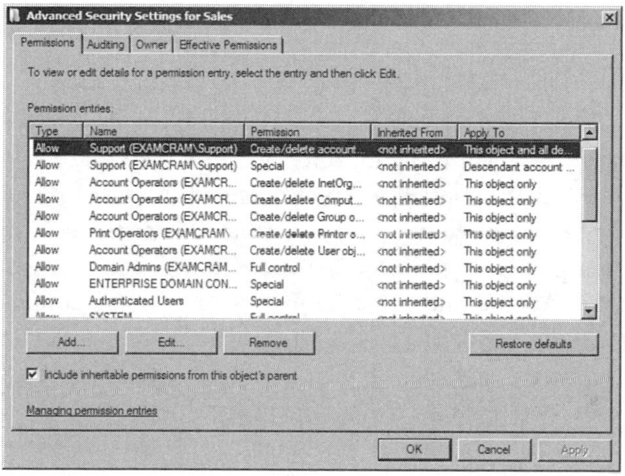

FIGURE 5.15 The Advanced Security Settings dialog box enables you to view and modify granular permissions.

Configuring Active Directory Trust Relationships

Business in the twenty-first century is rapidly becoming more globalized, with a growing number of companies doing business on an international scale with multiforest network enterprise structures. Such structures demand a level of trust among domains in the same and multiple forests. Active Directory has enabled several types of trust relationships to accommodate these needs.

Simply stated, a trust relationship is a configured link that enables a domain to access resources in another domain or a forest to access resources in another forest. A trust relationship provides such access to users without the need to create additional user accounts in the other forest or domain. Consequently, administrators do not need to configure multiple user accounts, and users do not need to remember multiple usernames and passwords.

This section examines the following types of trust relationships:

▶ Transitive trusts

▶ Forest trusts

▶ External trusts

▶ Realm trusts

▶ Shortcut trusts

Transitive Trusts

Microsoft introduced the concept of *transitive trusts* in Windows 2000. This represented a considerable improvement over the previous Windows NT trusts that required explicitly defining each trust relationship, a requirement that could become unwieldy in a large enterprise network. To understand the principle of transitive trusts, look at Figure 5.16. In a nontransitive trust, as was the case in Windows NT 4.0, if you configured Domain A to trust Domain B and Domain B to trust Domain C, Domain A would not trust Domain C unless you configured a separate trust relationship. Furthermore, the trust relationship worked in one direction only (as shown by the arrows in Figure 5.16); for a two-way trust relationship, you had to create two separate trusts, one in each direction.

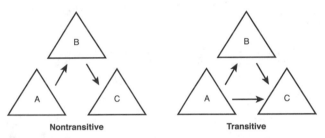

FIGURE 5.16 A transitive trust relationship enables trusts to "flow through" one domain to the next one, whereas in a nontransitive trust relationship, this does not occur.

In all versions of Active Directory back to Windows 2000, the default behavior is that all domains in the forest trust each other with two-way transitive trust relationships. Whenever you add a new child domain or a new domain tree to an existing forest, new trust relationships are automatically created with each of the other domains in the forest. These trusts do not require administrative intervention. The other types of trust relationships, discussed next, require manual configuration by the administrator.

Forest Trust Relationships

A *forest trust* is used to share resources between forests. This type of trust relationship consists of transitive trusts between every domain in each forest. The trust relationship is created manually and can be either one-way or two-way. The following are several benefits of forest trusts:

▶ They provide simple management of resource sharing by reducing the number of external trusts required in multidomain forests.

▶ They enable a wider scope of UPN authentication across all domains in the trusting forests.

▶ They provide increased administrative flexibility by allowing administrators to collaborate on task delegation across forest boundaries.

▶ Each forest remains isolated in certain aspects, such as directory replication, schema modification, and adding domains, all of which affect only the forest to which they apply.

▶ They improve the trustworthiness of authorization data. You can use both the Kerberos and NTLM authentication protocols when authenticating across forests.

It is important to remember that you can establish a forest trust relationship only when both forests are operating at the Windows Server 2003 or higher forest functional level. You can use the New Trust Wizard to create a forest trust. Perform the following procedure:

1. From one of the domains that will be participating in the trust relationship, open Active Directory Domains and Trusts.

2. In the console tree, right-click the domain and choose Properties.

3. Select the Trusts tab to display the dialog box shown in Figure 5.17.

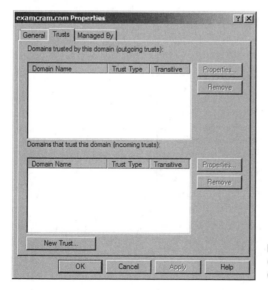

FIGURE 5.17 You can manage all types of trusts from the Trusts tab of the domain's Properties dialog box.

4. Click New Trust to start the New Trust Wizard with a Welcome page.

5. Click Next, and on the Trust Name page shown in Figure 5.18, type the name of the forest with which you want to create the trust relationship. Then click Next again.

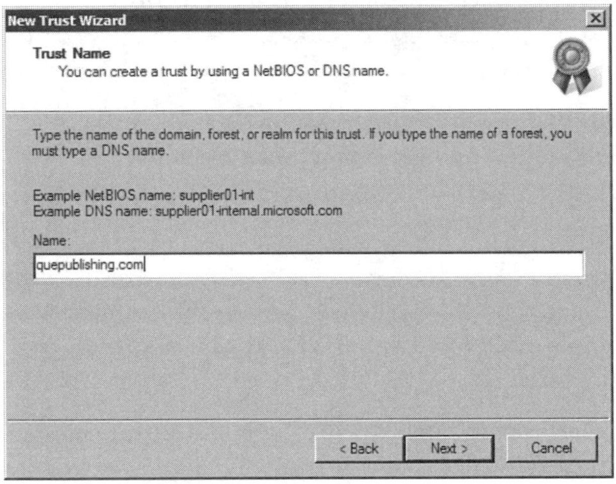

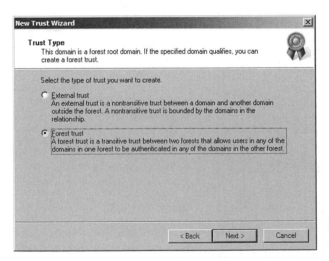

FIGURE 5.18 Use the Trust Name page to specify the name of the domain or forest with which you are creating the trust.

6. The Trust Type page shown in Figure 5.19 offers you a choice between an external trust and a forest trust. Select Forest Trust and then click Next.

FIGURE 5.19 Use the Trust Type page to select the type of trust you want to create.

7. On the Direction of Trust page shown in Figure 5.20, make a choice between the following types of trusts, and then click Next.

  ▸ **Two-way**—Creates a two-way trust, in which users in both domains can be authenticated in each other's domain.

  ▸ **One-way: Incoming**—Creates a one-way trust in which users in your (trusted) domain can be authenticated in the other (trusting) domain. Users in the other domain cannot be authenticated in your domain.

  ▸ **One-way: Outgoing**—Creates a one-way trust in which users in the other (trusting) domain can be authenticated in your (trusted) domain. Users in your domain cannot be authenticated in the other domain.

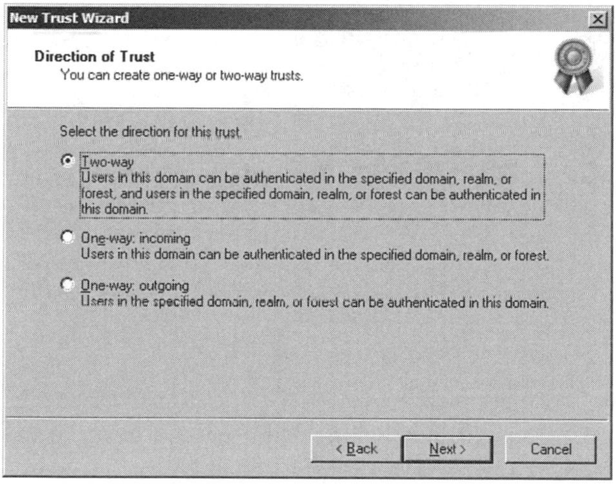

FIGURE 5.20 The Direction of Trust page provides choices for creating one-way or two-way trusts.

8. On the Sides of Trust page, select Both This Domain and the Specified Domain if you have the appropriate permission to create the trust in both domains. Otherwise, select This Domain Only. Then click Next.

9. The next step depends on your answer to the Sides of Trust page, as follows:

  ▸ If you selected This Domain Only, the Trust Password page asks you to specify a password that conforms to security guidelines. The administrator in the other forest is required to type the same password when completing the other side of the trust. Type and confirm a password, and then click Next.

▶ If you selected Both This Domain and the Specified Domain, the Outgoing Trust Authentication Level—Local Forest page shown in Figure 5.21 asks you to specify either Forest-Wide Authentication, which authenticates users from the trusted forest for all resources in the local forest, or Selective Authentication, which does not create default authentication. This choice of authentication scopes is discussed later in this chapter. Make a choice, and then click Next.

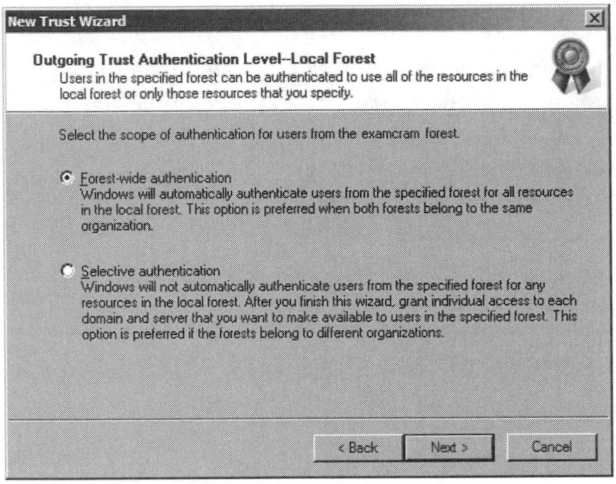

FIGURE 5.21 The Outgoing Trust Authentication Level—Local Forest page provides two choices of authentication scope for users in the trusted forest.

10. The Trust Selections Complete page summarizes the options you have selected. Review these selections, and click Back if necessary to make any required changes. To create the trust relationship, click Next.

11. The Trust Creation Complete page informs you that the trust relationship was successfully created. Click Next to finish the process.

12. The Confirm Incoming Trust page asks whether you want to confirm the incoming trust. To confirm the incoming trust, enter a username and password for the administrator account in the other domain.

13. When the Completing the New Trust Wizard page confirms the creation of the trust from the other side, click Finish.

After completing the New Trust Wizard, the name of the domain, with the trust type, appears in the Trusts tab of the domain's Properties dialog box.

EXAM ALERT

Remember the prerequisites for creating a forest trust. All domains involved must be at the Windows Server 2003 or higher domain functional level, and the forests must be at the Windows Server 2003 or higher forest functional level. Also remember that a forest trust is the simplest way to connect forests when access to resources in multiple domains is needed and when Kerberos authentication across the forest boundary is required.

External Trust Relationships

External trust relationships are one-way individual trust relationships that you can set up between two domains in different forests. They are nontransitive, which means you use them explicitly to define a one-to-one relationship between domains. You can use them to create trust relationships with AD DS domains operating at the Windows 2000 domain functional level or with Windows NT 4.0 domains. Furthermore, you can use an external trust if you need to create a trust relationship that involves only specific domains within two different forests.

You can use the New Trust Wizard in much the same way as described in the previous section to create an external trust relationship. Simply select External Trust on the Trust Type page previously shown in Figure 5.19. You receive the same options shown in Figure 5.20 for configuring one-way or two-way trusts, and you receive the authentication choices shown in Figure 5.21, except that they refer to the two domains involved in the trust relationship. After you complete the wizard, the Trusts tab of the domain's Properties dialog box shows the trust type and transitivity of the trusts you have created.

Realm Trust Relationships

You can use a *realm trust* to share information between an AD DS domain and any non-Windows realm that supports Kerberos V5, such as UNIX. A realm trust supports UNIX identity management to allow users in UNIX realms to seamlessly access Active Directory resources by means of password synchronization with Windows Server 2008's Server for Network Information Service (NIS) feature. Password synchronization enables users with accounts in UNIX realms in AD DS to synchronize password changes across both the AD DS domain and the UNIX realm. Furthermore, an AD DS domain controller can act as a master NIS server for the UNIX realm.

When you specify the name of a UNIX realm in the New Trust Wizard, the Trust Type page offers an option to set up a realm trust. You also receive the choice of transitivity as well as whether to make the trust one-way or two-way.

Shortcut Trust Relationships

Unlike the previously discussed trusts, a *shortcut trust* relationship exists within a single forest. It is an additional trust relationship between two child domains, which optimizes the authentication process when a large number of users require access to resources in another domain. It is especially useful if the normal authentication path must cross several domains. Figure 5.22 shows an example of such a situation.

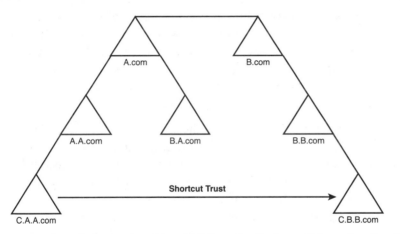

FIGURE 5.22 A shortcut trust is useful if the authentication path to another domain in the forest must cross several domain boundaries.

Suppose that users in the C.A.A.com domain require access to the C.B.B.com domain, which is located in another tree of the same forest. The authentication path must cross five domain boundaries to access the C.B.B.com domain. If an administrator sets up a shortcut trust between these two domains, the logon process speeds up considerably. This is also true for other possible authentication paths, such as B.A.com to B.B.com or even C.A.A.com to B.A.com. When you enter the name of a domain in the same forest, the New Trust Wizard automatically recognizes that you want to create a shortcut trust and provides similar options to those already discussed.

A Separate Research Forest

A major aircraft manufacturer landed a contract with NASA to design one module of a prototype spacecraft for a manned Mars mission. Realizing that the research necessary to complete this project successfully required a high level of security, management asked the senior network administrator to set up a separate forest in the organization's Windows Server 2008 AD DS design.

For the project to succeed, researchers needed access to certain data stored in the organization's existing forest. Their user accounts would be in the new forest. Users in the existing forest did not require access to the research forest. The administrator had to choose a trust model that would enable the appropriate levels of access.

With these needs in mind, the administrator decided to set up a one-way external trust relationship in which the existing forest trusted the research forest. This enabled him to place the researchers who needed access into a group with access to the appropriate resources in the existing forest. Because the trust relationship was one way, no access in the opposite direction was possible.

Authentication Scope

As you have already seen in Figure 5.21, the New Trust Wizard offers a choice between two authentication scopes: selective authentication and domain-wide or forest-wide authentication.

▶ **Domain-wide authentication**—Available in the case of external trusts, this option permits unrestricted access by any users in the trusted domain to all available shared resources in the trusting domain, according to sharing and security permissions attached to the resources. It is the default option for external trusts.

▶ **Forest-wide authentication**—Available in the case of forest trusts, this option permits unrestricted access by any users in the trusted forest to all available shared resources in any domain of the trusting forest, according to sharing and security permissions attached to the resources. It is the default option for forest trusts. Microsoft recommends the domain-wide and forest-wide options for trusts within the same organization only.

▶ **Selective authentication**—This option does not create any default authentication. It enables you to specify the users and groups from a trusted forest who are permitted to authenticate to servers containing resources in the trusting forest. Microsoft recommends this option for trusts that involve separate organizations, such as contractor relationships. It improves security by limiting the quantity of authentication requests that can pass through the trust.

You can change the authentication scope of a trust relationship after creating it from the trust's Properties dialog box. In the Trusts tab of the domain's Properties dialog box in Active Directory Domains and Trusts, select the domain name that you want to configure, and then click the Properties button. Next, select the Authentication tab of the trust's Properties dialog box, and select from the options shown in Figure 5.23.

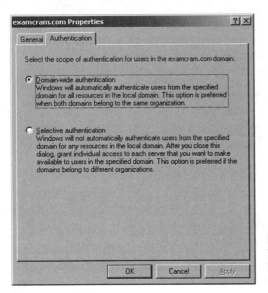

FIGURE 5.23 The Authentication tab of the trust's Properties dialog box enables you to change the trust's authentication scope.

NOTE

This procedure displays only the authentication settings for the outgoing trust. To obtain the current authentication settings for the incoming side of a two-way forest trust, connect to the other forest (right-click Active Directory Domains and Trusts and choose the Change Forest option), and then view the authentication settings for this side of the trust.

SID Filtering

SID filtering is another mechanism that enhances the security of communications between forests in a trust relationship. When a user from a trusted domain attempts to authenticate to a trusting domain, SID filtering validates the SIDs within the user's authentication ticket by verifying that the incoming authentication request contains only SIDs of security principals in the trusted domain. If SIDs from domains other than the trusted domain are present, they are filtered out, thereby denying the authentication request.

You can use the `netdom` command-line tool to configure SID filtering. By default, SID filtering is enabled on external trusts but not on domain trusts. To disable SID filtering, type the following command:

```
Netdom trust <trusting_domain> /domain:<trusted domain> /quarantine:No
```

In this command, *trusting_domain* and *trusted_domain* are the names of the trusting and trusted domains, respectively. You must be a member of the Domain Admins or Enterprise Admins group or specify the username and password of an appropriate account using the `/usero:` and `/passwordo:` keywords, respectively. To re-enable SID filtering, type this command with the keyword `/quarantine:Yes`.

For additional details and other usage scenarios on the `netdom trust` command, type **netdom trust /?** at a command line. For more information on authentication scopes and SID filtering, refer to "Security Considerations for Trusts" in Appendix A.

Exam Cram Questions

1. Peter works for a company that has an AD DS forest that consists of a forest root domain plus five domains. He needs to create a group containing 70 users who require access to resources in all six domains. All the user accounts are located in the forest root domain. Which group scope should he use?

   ○ **A.** Local

   ○ **B.** Domain local

   ○ **C.** Global

   ● **D.** Universal

2. Kathy is the network administrator for `Examcram.com`. The network consists of a single AD DS forest consisting of eight domains. Seven of the domains contain Windows Server 2008 domain controllers. The functional level of all the domains is Windows Server 2003. The network includes a Microsoft Exchange Server 2007 network.

   Kathy needs to create groups that are to be used solely as email distribution lists for sending messages within the organization. She wants to accomplish this goal with the minimum quantity of replication traffic and minimizing the size of the AD DS database. How should she proceed?

   ○ **A.** She should create universal distribution groups and make the appropriate users from each domain members of a universal distribution group.

   ○ **B.** She should create universal security groups and make the appropriate users from each domain members of a universal security group.

   ● **C.** She should create global distribution groups in each domain and make the appropriate users from each domain members of the global distribution group in the respective domain. She should then create universal distribution groups and make the global distribution groups in each domain members of the universal distribution groups.

   ○ **D.** She should create global security groups in each domain and make the appropriate users from each domain members of the global security group in the respective domain. She should then create universal security groups and make the global security groups in each domain members of the universal security groups.

3. Jennifer is responsible for maintaining the user and group accounts databases in her company's AD DS domain. The company is expanding its operations and will be hiring several hundred new university graduates as soon as they have finished their exams. These graduates will work in several departments of the company and require access to numerous shared resources in various components of the network.

Human Resources (HR) has prepared an Excel spreadsheet containing all required information on the new hires, such as names, addresses, work departments, locations, and so on. Jennifer must create new user and group accounts for these new hires. What should she do to create the accounts with the least amount of administrative effort?

- ● **A.** Export the Excel spreadsheet to a comma-separated text file and use `Csvde` to create the required accounts.

- ○ **B.** Export the Excel spreadsheet to an LDIF-formatted file and use `Ldifde` to create the required accounts.

- ○ **C.** Use the `dsadd` command to add the required accounts to the database.

- ○ **D.** Use the New Object—User and New Object—Group Wizards to create the required accounts.

4. Michael is a systems administrator for Examcram.com, which has just merged with a former competitor named Widgets.com. Customers and business partners of the second company have communicated with the company's employees using their email addresses of the format user@widgets.com. This is a well-established relationship that has existed for a number of years. Managers in both companies want to retain these email addresses.

   Michael is merging the networks of the two companies under the Examcram.com AD DS domain, which operates at the Windows Server 2008 domain and forest functional level. Users in the company use their email addresses to log on. Michael needs to incorporate the new users from Widgets.com into the network while retaining their existing email address and using these addresses to log on to the Examcram.com domain.

   What should Michael do to accomplish this objective with the least amount of administrative effort?

   - ○ **A.** Create a new Active Directory forest named widgets.com, and create user accounts for the new users in that forest.

   - ○ **B.** Create a new domain as a separate domain tree named widgets.com, and create user accounts for the new users in that domain.

   - ○ **C.** Create user accounts for the new users in the existing domain, and assign them user logon names in the format of user@widgets.com.

   - ● **D.** In Active Directory Domains and Trusts, specify an alternative UPN suffix of examcram.com. Then create user accounts for the new users in the existing domain, and specify the use of this UPN suffix.

5. You are the systems administrator for a company that operates a single domain AD DS network. A user named Steven has created a group named Designers on his computer, which runs Windows Vista Ultimate. He has added the domain user accounts of several colleagues in his work unit to the Designers group and now wants to assign permissions to a shared folder on the work unit's file server to the group. However, when he accesses the shared folder, he is unable to add the Designers group to the folder's ACL.

   Steven approaches you for help. What should you do?

   ○ **A.** Create a domain local group named Work Unit and add the domain user accounts of the colleagues to this group. Then create a global group named Designers, add the Work Unit group to this group, and add the Designers domain local group to the folder's ACL.

   ● **B.** Create a global group named Work Unit and add the domain user accounts of the colleagues to this group. Then create a domain local group named Designers, add the Work Unit group to this group, and add the Designers domain local group to the folder's ACL.

   ○ **C.** Ask Steven to create local user accounts for each of the work colleagues on the file server and add these accounts to the Designers group.

   ○ **D.** Ask Steven to check the network connectivity between his computer and the file server. His action should work if the connectivity is not a problem.

6. Sharon is the systems administrator for an engineering company whose head office is in Columbus, with branch offices located in six Ohio cities. Sharon's manager wants the head office to maintain centralized control of corporate resources, while an individual in each branch office is to have control over user accounts, passwords, shared folders, and printers in his respective office only.

   How should Sharon design her company's AD DS structure to enable this requirement?

   ○ **A.** Create two forests, one for the head office and another for the branch offices. Within the branch office forest, create a domain for each office. Link the forests by means of a forest trust. Make the branch office individuals members of the domain's Domain Admins group.

   ○ **B.** Create a separate domain in its own tree for each branch office, and then make the branch office individuals members of the domain's Domain Admins group.

   ○ **C.** Create a separate child domain for each branch office, and then make the branch office individuals members of the domain's Domain Admins group.

   ○ **D.** Create a separate OU for each branch office, and then delegate the appropriate level of control to the branch office individuals.

   ● **E.** Sharon does not need to create additional AD DS containers because she can delegate control of each branch office site to the appropriate individuals.

7. David is the manager of the IT staff for a company that operates an AD DS network consisting of a single domain with separate OUs for each of the company's seven departments. As a result of company growth, the task of administering the network has become increasingly difficult. To improve the efficiency of network administration, David needs to assign individual members of the IT staff group to administer single OUs only.

   In which of the following ways should David distribute the administrative tasks among individual IT staff members without granting them excessive privileges? (Each correct answer represents a complete solution to the problem. Choose two answers.)

   ○ **A.** Add the individual IT staff members to the Domain Admins global group.

   ● **B.** Use the Delegation of Control Wizard to delegate Full Control of each OU to the individual IT staff member.

   ○ **C.** Grant the individual IT staff members Full Control permission for the Domain Controllers OU.

   ● **D.** Add the individual IT staff member to the access control list (ACL) for a different single OU with Full Control permission.

8. Sandra is the senior administrator of a Windows Server 2003 forest that consists of a single domain, and Ralph is a UNIX administrator who works alongside. The company's CIO has asked Sandra and Ralph to reduce the total cost of ownership of the two networks by improving the efficiency of user access from one network to the other and reducing the current duplication of resources existing in the Windows and UNIX networks.

   Which of the following should Sandra and Ralph do? (Each correct answer represents part of the solution. Choose two answers.)

   ○ **A.** Create an external trust between the Windows domain and the UNIX realm.

   ○ **B.** Create a forest trust between the Windows forest and the UNIX realm.

   ● **C.** Create a realm trust between the Windows domain and the UNIX realm.

   ● **D.** Upgrade the Windows network to Windows Server 2008.

   ○ **E.** Migrate the UNIX network to Windows Server 2008 AD DS.

9. Mark's company has just merged operations with a former competitor. Mark's company operates an AD DS forest with four domains in a single tree and running at the Windows Server 2008 functional level. The other company operates a forest with three domains in a single tree and running at the Windows Server 2003 functional level.

   Managers at the other company want to keep their operations as separate as possible; however, employees whose user accounts are in various domains of both forests require access to resources in all domains. What should Mark do to enable access to the other forest with the least amount of effort?

   ○ **A.** He should create an external trust between child domains of the two forests.

   ○ **B.** He should create a shortcut trust between child domains of the two forests.

   ● **C.** He should create a forest trust between the two forests.

   ○ **D.** He should inform his manager that the other company's forest should be reconfigured as a second tree in his company's forest.

10. You are the network administrator for a financial company. A junior administrator named Karla has just created a new one-way outgoing trust relationship between your company's domain and a contractor's domain. The purpose of this trust is to enable engineers in your company to send detailed design charts and specifications to the contractor without having to fax them. However, engineers report that they are unable to access the contractor's domain. What should you do to enable access, while keeping resources in your company's domain secure?

   ○ **A.** In the trust's Properties dialog box, change the direction of the trust from outgoing to incoming.

   ○ **B.** In the trust's Properties dialog box, change the authentication scope of the trust from selective authentication to domainwide.

   ○ **C.** Remove the trust relationship and create a new two-way trust relationship.

   ● **D.** Remove the trust relationship and create a new one-way incoming trust relationship.

Answers to *Exam Cram* Questions

1. **C.** Peter should use a global group. All 70 users belong to a single domain, so a global group is most appropriate in this situation. He would create a local group on a member server or client computer for access to resources on that computer only, so answer A is incorrect. He would use a domain local group for access to resources in a single domain only. Because the users need access to resources in all six domains, answer B is incorrect. (Note, however, that Peter can and should add the global group to domain local groups in each domain for access to the resources.) Peter does not need a universal group because all users are located in a single domain, so answer D is incorrect.

2. **C.** Kathy should create global distribution groups in each domain and make the appropriate users from each domain members of the global distribution group in the respective domain. She should then create universal distribution groups and make the global distribution groups in each domain members of the universal distribution groups. To ensure that replication traffic is kept down, she should create global groups and place these groups into universal groups—the AGUDLP practice. For this reason, she should not place the users directly into universal groups, so answer A is incorrect. The given scenario requires creation of email distribution lists and does not state that permissions are to be granted to these groups, so Kathy should not use security groups. Consequently, answers B and D are incorrect.

3. **A.** Jennifer should export the Excel spreadsheet to a comma-separated text file and use Csvde to create the required accounts. She can automate the creation of hundreds or even thousands of user, group, or computer accounts in this manner. Excel cannot export to an LDIF-formatted file, so answer B is incorrect. Jennifer might be able to use dsadd to script the creation of the accounts, but the procedure would not be as simple as using Csvde, so answer C is incorrect. It would take far more effort than required to use the New Object—User and New Object—Group dialog boxes to complete this task, so answer D is incorrect.

4. **D.** Michael should specify an alternative UPN suffix of examcram.com, create user accounts for the new users in the existing domain, and specify the use of this UPN suffix. The UPN is a logon name specified in the format of an email address, and the UPN suffix is the part of the logon name after the @ character. By default, the UPN suffix is the DNS domain name of the domain where the user account is located (in this case, examcram.com). Michael can specify widgets.com as an alternative UPN suffix and then use it when creating user accounts for the new users in Active Directory Users and Computers. Creating a new forest or domain tree named widgets.com would require additional ongoing administrative effort, so answers A and B are incorrect. It is not possible to simply assign the user logon names in the format of user@widgets.com without first specifying the alternative UPN suffix, so answer C is incorrect.

5. **B.** The problem here is that Steven attempted to assign permissions for a resource on one machine to a local group configured on a different machine. In contrast to a domain local group, a local group can be used to configure permissions on resources on its computer only. So Steven needs to use a domain local group, and the recommended solution follows the AGDLP strategy. You cannot add a domain local group to a global group, so answer A is incorrect. Creating local user accounts for each user on the file server is not the recommended strategy, so answer C is incorrect. Network connectivity is the problem; Steven cannot use a local group from one computer on another one, so answer D is incorrect.

6. **E.** Sharon does not need to add additional containers to the AD DS design because she can delegate control of each site to the appropriate individuals. The Delegation of Control Wizard enables Sharon to delegate control of each site to these individuals, thereby granting them authority over items in their site but not those in other sites.

There is no need to create separate forests, trees, or domains and add these users to the Domain Admins groups because Active Directory provides for delegation of control, so answers A, B, and C are incorrect. Because Sharon can run the Delegation of Control Wizard on a site, she does not need to create OUs, so answer D is incorrect.

7. **B, D.** David can either use the Delegation of Control Wizard or assign Full Control permission to the respective OU in order to grant the individual members of the IT staff group the capability to administer single OUs only. If he were to add the individual IT staff members to the Domain Admins group, these users would receive administrative capabilities across the entire domain, so answer A is incorrect. Granting the individual IT staff members Full Control permission for the Domain Controllers OU would not accomplish the proper task, so answer C is incorrect.

8. **C, D.** Sandra and Ralph should create a realm trust between the Active Directory network and the UNIX realm. They should also upgrade the Active Directory network to Windows Server 2008. The trust enables them to reduce the duplication of resources across the networks. In addition, Windows Server 2008 features enhanced UNIX interoperability, including automatic password synchronization (first introduced in Windows Server 2003 R2). Sandra and Ralph should not create an external trust because this type of trust can only be created between two Active Directory domains or an Active Directory and a Windows NT domain, so answer A is incorrect. They should not create a forest trust because this type of trust can only be created between two Active Directory forests, so answer B is incorrect. It is not necessary, and might not be feasible, to migrate the UNIX realm to Active Directory, so answer E is incorrect.

9. **C.** By creating a forest trust, Mark can enable transitive trust relationships between all domains of the forests involved. In this scenario, the forest trust is the best option because users require access to more than one domain in the other company's forest. Mark could create external trusts between various child domains. This would take more administrative effort, so answer A is incorrect. A shortcut trust is a shortened path between two child domains in the same forest and not between two different forests, so answer B is incorrect. No need exists for reconfiguring the other company's forest as a second tree in Mark's company's forest, so answer D is incorrect.

10. **D.** You should remove the trust relationship and create a new one-way incoming trust relationship. Karla has created the trust relationship in the wrong direction. It is not possible to reverse the direction of the trust from the trust's Properties dialog box, so answer A is incorrect. Changing the authentication scope of the trust does not solve the problem, so answer B is incorrect. Creating a two-way trust is not necessary; doing so reduces security because employees of the contractor company could then access your domain. Therefore answer C is incorrect.

CHAPTER SIX

Configuring and Troubleshooting Group Policy

Terms You'll Need to Understand

- ✓ ADMX Central Store
- ✓ Assigned applications
- ✓ Block inheritance
- ✓ Enforced
- ✓ Filtering
- ✓ Group Policy Modeling
- ✓ Group Policy object (GPO)
- ✓ Group Policy Results
- ✓ Inheritance
- ✓ Linked policy
- ✓ Loopback processing
- ✓ Published applications
- ✓ Resultant Set of Policy (RSoP)
- ✓ Starter GPOs
- ✓ Windows Installer
- ✓ Windows Management Instrumentation (WMI)

Concepts/Techniques You'll Need to Master

- ✓ Creating a GPO
- ✓ Linking an existing GPO
- ✓ Modifying Group Policy
- ✓ Delegating administrative control of Group Policy
- ✓ Specifying a domain controller for managing GPOs
- ✓ Modifying Group Policy inheritance
- ✓ Using loopback processing
- ✓ Filtering Group Policy settings
- ✓ Using Starter GPOs to create new GPOs
- ✓ Controlling use environments by using administrative templates
- ✓ Deploying software by using Group Policy
- ✓ Maintaining software by using Group Policy
- ✓ Troubleshooting Group Policy using the Resultant Set of Policy snap-in
- ✓ Troubleshooting Group Policy using the Group Policy Modeling Wizard
- ✓ Troubleshooting Group Policy using gpresult.exe

Users are naturally curious beings. It is human nature to explore your computer and see what you can do, what Control Panel is all about, and so on. Invariably, problems result, users make changes and cannot back out of them, and they call the help desk for assistance. For a business network to function properly, it is mandatory that a secure means of limiting what users can do be in place. Microsoft has recognized this fact ever since the days of Windows NT and its System Policy.

Beginning with Windows 2000, Group Policy has enabled administrators to exert more control over users' environments and reduce the extent of user-originated problems. Successive iterations of Windows have added additional components to the list of available policies. Windows Server 2008 is no exception.

Overview of Group Policy

Group Policy lies at the heart of every Active Directory implementation. It does far more than just define what users can and cannot do with their computers. It is a series of configuration settings that you can apply to an object or series of objects in Active Directory to control a user's environment in numerous contexts, including the following:

- ▶ **Network access**—Enables you to control access to network devices, including terminal servers and wireless access.

- ▶ **Folder redirection**—Enables you to use Group Policy settings to redirect users' local folders to network shares.

- ▶ **Logon/logoff/startup/shutdown scripts**—Enables you to assign scripts on a user or computer basis for such events as logon, logoff, startup, or shutdown.

- ▶ **Application deployment**—Enables you to administer applications on your network, including their assignment, publication, updating, repair, and removal.

- ▶ **Security options of all types**—Enables you to use Group Policy security settings to enforce restrictions and control access on user or computer properties.

Group Policy can be applied to server and client computers running Windows 2000 and up and includes both computer and user settings. As the names suggest, computer policies are computer specific and are applied when the computer starts up; user policies are user specific and are applied when the user logs on to the computer.

Group Policy in Windows Server 2008 provides several new features, including the following:

- **Additional policy settings**—Microsoft has considerably expanded the areas that you can manage in Group Policy. Some categories you can now manage include blocking device installation, power settings management, and control of access to external devices. Settings on many additional categories have been enhanced, such as security settings, Internet Explorer settings, and location-based printer assignment.

- **Exclusive use of the Group Policy Management Console (GPMC)**—You can no longer access Group Policy from a container's Properties dialog box, as was the case in previous Windows versions. GPMC is included by default in Windows Server 2008 and is the sole location of Group Policy management actions.

- **Comments for Group Policy settings**—Large organizations have many individuals responsible for policy administration. This feature enables you to document the purpose of policies and their settings for the benefit of others.

- **Use of ADMX format**—ADMX refers to Extensible Markup Language (XML)–based files. This is a new format that stores all configuration objects and allows for language-neutral and language-specific resources. For example, you can configure Group Policy in the United States, and a colleague in Germany can review your settings in German.

- **Network Location Awareness (NLA)**—This improves the ability of Group Policy to respond to changes in network conditions. It provides more efficient startup times while a computer is waiting to access a domain controller and the capability to reapply a policy when a wireless network connection is created after the user has already logged on. It also improves the efficiency of deploying policy changes to mobile users across virtual private networks (VPN).

For additional details on new Group Policy features in Windows Server 2008, refer to "Group Policy" in Appendix A, "Need to Know More?"

Group Policy Objects

A *GPO* is a series of settings that can be applied to a local computer, site, domain, or organizational unit (OU). Each GPO is identified by its Globally Unique Identifier (GUID), which is a 128-bit number assigned when the GPO is created. This identifier is unique to the forest and is stored as an attribute used to identify it within the Active Directory hierarchy.

The content of GPOs is stored in the following two containers:

▸ **Group Policy containers (GPC)**—These are AD DS objects that store the properties of GPOs, including attributes and version information. Included are subcontainers for user and computer Group Policy data.

▸ **Group Policy templates (GPT)**—A GPT is a folder hierarchy that contains all the information for its GPO and is stored in the shared folder %systemroot%\SYSVOL\sysvol\<domain_name>\Policies. Within this folder are subfolders that are defined by the GUID for each respective GPO that contain all the policy information. Also included are a file named Gpt.ini, which includes a version number that is incremented each time the policy is modified, and a parameter that determines whether the GPO is enabled or disabled.

NOTE

Besides the GPOs stored in Active Directory, every computer has its own local GPO, which is stored on the local hard drive in the \windows\system32\GroupPolicy folder. Settings in this GPO apply only to the computer on which it is configured and are always overridden by policy settings applied in AD DS. It is recommended that you not use these settings within a domain environment, except for standalone machines that do not belong to a domain or specific settings that are required by one or two machines only.

Creating and Applying GPOs

You perform all Group Policy administrative activities, including creating, editing, and applying GPOs from the GPMC. First available for download with Windows Server 2003 R2, GPMC is included by default with Windows Server 2008 and is the sole location for managing all aspects of Group Policy. This section looks at the GPMC and goes through a sample procedure showing how to create and link a new GPO:

1. Click Start, Administrative Tools, Group Policy Management. This opens the GPMC, which shows a node for your forest in the console tree that you can expand to reveal subnodes for every domain with entries for each OU as well as a Group Policy Objects node.

2. In the console tree, expand the Group Policy Objects node. You will notice two default GPOs: the Default Domain Policy and the Default Domain Controllers Policy. These are installed automatically when you

create your domain. Policy settings that you define here are automatically applied to the entire domain and to the domain controllers, respectively.

3. Select one of these policies. As shown in Figure 6.1, the Details pane displays GPO properties and configuration options. Information includes the following tabs:

> ▶ **Scope**—Enables you to display GPO link information and configure security group filtering and WMI filtering.

> ▶ **Details**—Displays information on the owner, dates created and modified, version numbers, GUID value, and enabled status. The enabled status is the only configurable option on this tab.

> ▶ **Settings**—Enables you to display policy settings, as shown in Figure 6.2. You can expand and collapse nodes to locate information on any policy setting. Note that the settings shown here are configured for the Default Domain Policy GPO by default when you install AD DS.

> ▶ **Delegation**—Enables you to view and modify GPO permissions.

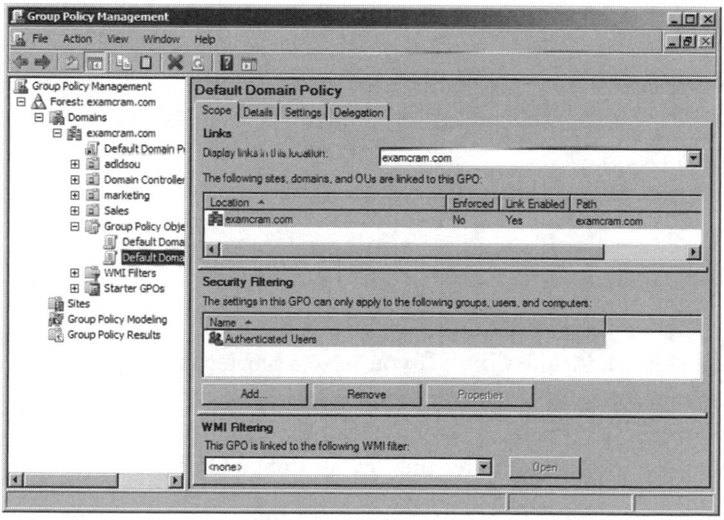

FIGURE 6.1 You perform all Group Policy management activities from the GPMC.

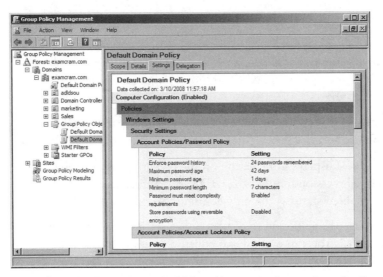

FIGURE 6.2   The Settings tab of a GPO enables you to view configured policy settings.

4. To create and link a GPO to an OU, right-click the desired OU and select Create a GPO in This Domain and Link It Here. This displays the New GPO dialog box, as shown in Figure 6.3.

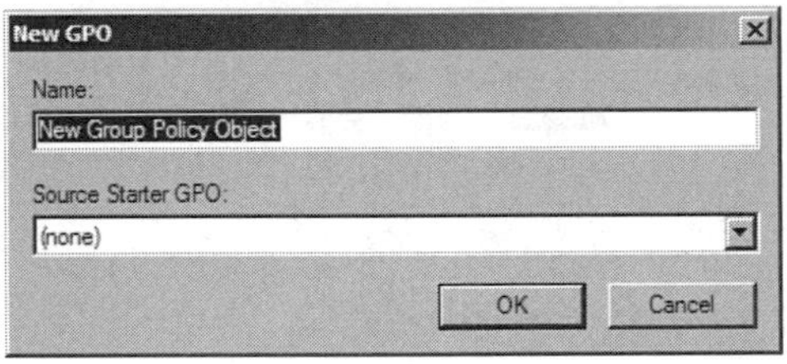

FIGURE 6.3   The New GPO dialog box enables you to create and name a new GPO.

5. Type a suitable name for the GPO. If you have a Starter GPO that includes settings you want to include in the new GPO, type its name in the Source Starter GPO field, and then click OK. The new GPO is added to the list in the console tree under the Group Policy Objects node.

6. To define policy settings for the new GPO, right-click it and choose Edit. This brings up the Group Policy Management Editor console, as shown in Figure 6.4. The rest of this chapter and Chapter 7, "Group Policy and Active Directory Security," discuss the more significant policy settings with which you should be familiar.

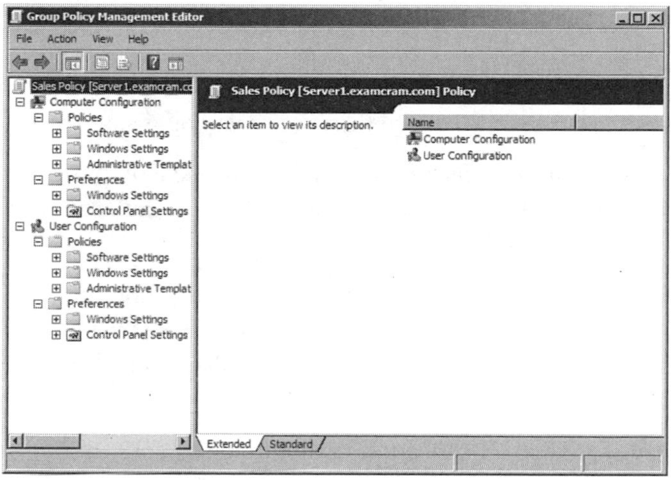

FIGURE 6.4 You can configure all policies associated with a GPO from the Group Policy Management Editor snap-in.

TIP

You can also access the GPMC directly from Server Manager under the Features node. In this case, the GPMC opens as a component snap-in within the Server Manager console.

The Group Policy Management Editor (formerly known as the Group Policy Object Editor) is where you perform all policy configuration actions for your GPO. Now is a good time to take a brief look at this tool; many of the configuration activities are covered later in this chapter and in Chapter 7. This tool has the following container structure:

▶ **Root Container**—Defines the focus of the Group Policy Management Editor by showing the GPO that is being edited plus the fully qualified domain name (FQDN) of the domain controller from which you are working.

▶ **Computer Configuration**—Contains all computer-specific policy settings. Remember that these settings are processed when the computer starts up and before the user logs on.

▶ **User Configuration**—Contains all user-specific policy settings. Remember that these settings are processed after the user logs on.

▶ **Policies**—Includes classic and new Group Policy settings for Software Settings, Windows Settings, and Administrative Templates.

- ▶ **Preferences**—Include new Group Policy extensions that expand the range of configurable policy settings. Included are items such as folder options, mapped drives, printers, local users and groups, scheduled tasks, services, and Start menu settings. You can manage these items without using scripts.

- ▶ **Software Settings**—A subcontainer found under both the Computer and User Configuration Policies containers that holds software installation settings for computers and users.

- ▶ **Windows Settings**—A subcontainer found under both the Computer and User Configuration Policies and Preferences containers that holds script and security settings, plus other policy settings that affect the behavior of the Windows environment.

- ▶ **Administrative Templates**—A subcontainer found under both the Computer and User Configuration Policies containers that holds most of the settings that control the appearance of the desktop environment. New to Windows Server 2008 is an All Settings subnode that provides a comprehensive list of all policy settings that you can sort according to name, state, comment, or path, or filter according to several criteria.

- ▶ **Control Panel Settings**—A subcontainer found under both the Computer and User Configuration Preferences containers that holds most of the preferences settings related to Control Panel applets.

NOTE

When you create a new GPO or edit an existing one, users affected by the GPO must log off and log back on again to receive the new settings in the User Configuration node. If you have configured new settings in the Computer Configuration node, users must reboot their computers to receive the new settings.

Managing GPOs

You have seen how to create a GPO. Now it's time to turn your attention to several additional activities that you should be aware of, including the following:

- ▶ Linking GPOs

- ▶ Managing GPO links

- ▶ Deleting a GPO

- ▶ Delegating control of GPOs

- ▶ Specifying a domain controller

Chapter 8, "Monitoring and Maintaining the Active Directory Environment," covers the backing up and restoring of GPOs.

Linking GPOs

The GPMC also enables you to create unlinked GPOs and *link* any GPO to other Active Directory containers. To create an unlinked GPO, right-click Group Policy Objects and choose New. You receive the same dialog box previously shown in Figure 6.3. The resulting GPO is not linked to any container.

To link this (or any other) GPO to a domain or OU, right-click the domain or OU in the console tree of the GPMC and choose Link an Existing GPO. From the dialog box shown in Figure 6.5, choose the GPO that you want to link in this location, and then click OK.

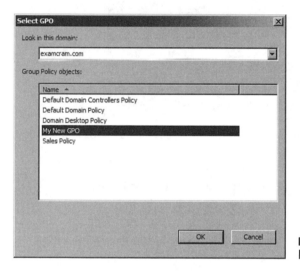

FIGURE 6.5 Selecting a GPO for linking to a domain.

Linking a GPO to a site is similar. However, the Sites node in the GPMC does not show any sites by default. To include the available sites, right-click Sites and choose Show Sites. Then select the desired site and click OK. Once you have done this, you can right-click the desired site and choose Link an Existing GPO to display the same dialog box previously shown in Figure 6.5.

Managing GPO Links

When you perform the procedure outlined in the previous section, you can link GPOs to multiple AD DS containers. This is perfectly acceptable; however, you might need to view the existing GPO links to keep track of them. You can do so by selecting the desired GPO under the Group Policy Objects node of the GPMC. As shown in Figure 6.6, the Links section of the GPO's properties shows the available links. In a multiple-domain environment, simply select the required domain from the drop-down list. To view links to sites, select All Sites from the drop-down list; to view links to all sites and domains in the forest, select Entire Forest from this list.

FIGURE 6.6 The Links section enables you to locate all sites, domains, and OUs to which a GPO is linked.

Should you need to delete a GPO link to test its effects or because the GPO is linked to the wrong AD DS container, you can delete the link. Expand the container from which you want to delete the link, right-click the desired GPO, and choose Delete (or press the Delete key). Click OK in the dialog box shown in Figure 6.7 to confirm its deletion.

FIGURE 6.7 Deleting a GPO link.

Deleting a GPO

You might want to delete a GPO completely if you no longer need its settings. To do so, select it from the Group Policy Objects node and press the Delete key. Then click Yes in the dialog box shown in Figure 6.8 to confirm its deletion.

FIGURE 6.8 Deleting a GPO.

CAUTION

Be sure you will never need the GPO again before you delete it! There is no way to recover a deleted GPO. If you need it back, you must re-create it and all the policy settings contained within it. If you might want the GPO back, it is better to disable it or remove the links.

Delegating Control of GPOs

Chapter 5, "Active Directory Objects and Trusts," showed you how to delegate control of Active Directory objects to users and groups to enable partial administrative control and ease the overall burden of administration. By default, only members of the Domain Admins and Group Policy Creator Owners groups have permissions to create GPOs. You can extend this concept to the administration of GPOs. Several methods for performing this task are available. First, you can add the required user or group to the Group Policy Creator Owners Group. This group has the right to create GPOs in any container by default.

To delegate the creation of GPOs to additional users or groups, select the Group Policy Object node from the console tree of GPMC. As shown in Figure 6.9, this tab displays a list of groups and users with permission to create GPOs in the domain.

To add a user or group to this list, click Add and add the required user or group from the Select User, Computer, or Group dialog box that appears. To remove a user or group, select it and click Remove, and then click OK in the message box that appears.

You can also delegate control of specific GPOs to users or groups. Select the required GPO from the list in the Group Policy Object node of GPMC, and click the Delegation tab. Click Add and add the required user or group from the Select User, Computer, or Group dialog box. Then select the required permissions from the list shown in the dialog box in Figure 6.10, and click OK. You can then modify the permissions or configure advanced permissions by clicking Advanced and specifying the required permissions from the Security Settings dialog box that is displayed.

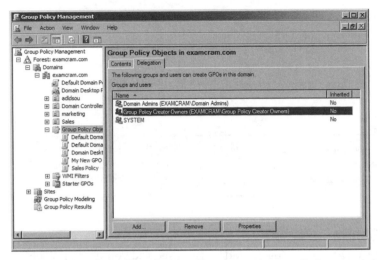

FIGURE 6.9   The Delegation tab shows the users and groups that are granted permission to create GPOs.

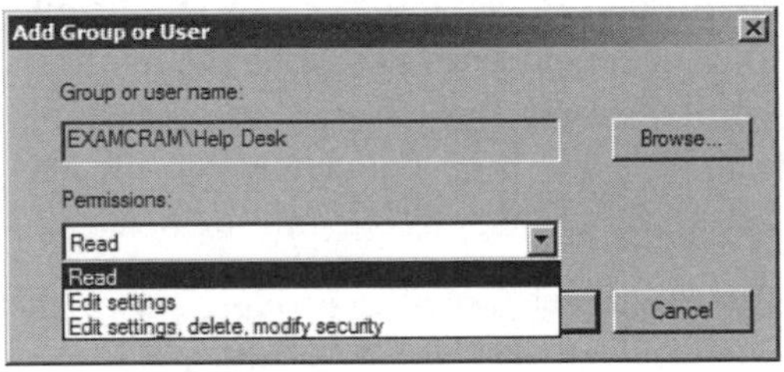

FIGURE 6.10   You have a choice of three permissions when adding a user or group to the administrative delegation list of a GPO.

NOTE

You can also use the Delegation of Control Wizard to delegate the task of managing Group Policy links for a site, domain, or OU. This enables the user to create or delete links to existing GPOs but not the ability to create new GPOs or edit existing ones. You can also delegate the control of Group Policy Container objects from the list of custom tasks. This wizard was introduced in Chapter 5.

Specifying a Domain Controller

It is possible to edit a GPO from any writable domain controller or even to connect to a writable domain controller from a client computer running Windows XP or Vista. You might want to specify which domain controller you are working against for any of the following reasons:

▶ If multiple administrators are working on the same GPO from multiple machines, conflicting changes will be overwritten and lost.

▶ If you are working against a domain controller at a remote site, you might encounter slow performance, which can become frustrating. You can select a local domain controller to avoid this problem.

▶ If you are editing a GPO that is to be applied to users or computers at the remote site, it might be advantageous to work against the domain controller in the same site so that changes take effect immediately rather than waiting for replication to occur.

▶ It ensures that you are working against the PDC emulator. By default, AD DS defaults to this domain controller. However, you might want to change this if the PDC emulator is not readily available.

To select a domain controller, right-click your domain in GPMC and choose Change Domain Controller. Select an appropriate option from those provided in the Change Domain Controller dialog box shown in Figure 6.11. The selected domain controller saves your changes and replicates them to other domain controllers in the next AD DS replication.

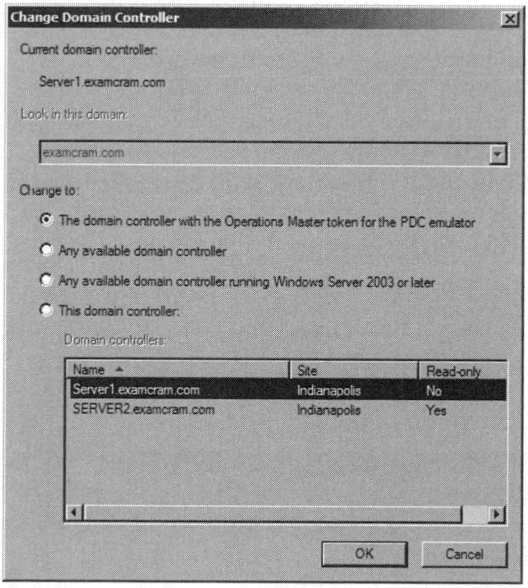

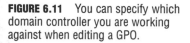

FIGURE 6.11 You can specify which domain controller you are working against when editing a GPO.

Configuring GPO Hierarchy and Processing Priority

All GPOs except the local GPO are associated with, or linked to, some AD DS container, such as sites, domains, and OUs. While it is possible to create an unlinked GPO, it is not applied until you link it to an AD DS container.

As already mentioned, each GPO contains both computer-specific and user-specific settings. Computer-specific settings are applied when the computer starts up and before the user logs on; user-specific settings are applied after the user logs on. Consequently, if any user-specific settings conflict with computer-specific settings, the user-specific settings override the computer-specific settings.

By default, all GPOs are applied in the following well-defined order:

1. The local (L) GPO is applied first.

2. Site-based (S) GPOs are applied next, overriding any conflicting local policy settings.

3. Domain-based (D) GPOs are applied next, overriding any conflicting local or site-based settings.

4. OU-based (OU) GPOs are applied last, overriding any conflicting local, site, or domain-based settings.

This sequence can be abbreviated as LSDOU. It is important to remember this sequence because it determines how GPOs with conflicting policy settings apply to both the user and the computer. Furthermore, because all computer-specific settings are applied before user logon and user-specific settings are applied after logon, any user-specific setting, even a local one, overrides a conflicting computer-specific setting applied at any level.

> **EXAM ALERT**
>
> Know the group policy processing order. An exam question might present a sequence of conflicting policies and ask you which one is applicable in a given scenario. It is important that you remember the LSDOU sequence as well as the computer, then user, sequence.

OU Hierarchy

As you saw in Chapter 5, you can create a nested hierarchy of OUs. When more than one level of OU is present, policies linked to the parent OU are applied first, followed by child OUs in order. Consequently, the lowest level OU policy becomes the determining factor should conflicts in the various GPOs arise.

Microsoft provides several controls that you can use to modify the default sequence of GPO application. These include the following:

▶ **Enforced**—Enforces the application of policy settings, regardless of settings defined in lower-level GPOs.

▶ **Block Inheritance**—Prevents the application of policy settings from containers higher in the LSDOU hierarchy.

▶ **Modifying the sequence of a GPO application**—Enables you to specify in which sequence multiple GPOs linked to the same AD DS container will be applied.

▶ **Disabling user objects**—Allows you to selectively disable GPOs or portions of GPOs.

Enforced

Known as *No Override* prior to use of the GPMC, the *Enforced* setting is a method of altering the default policy *inheritance* behavior in Windows Server 2008. Specifying this option prevents policies contained in the Enforced GPO from being overwritten by other GPOs that are processed later. For example, if you want to set up a domain desktop policy that applies to all domain users and do not want conflicting settings at the OU level to apply, you can configure this option from the Scope tab of a policy's properties, as displayed in the Details pane of the GPMC.

To specify the Enforced option, select the desired GPO in the console tree. Within the Scope tab of the GPO's Properties, right-click the container where you want to enforce the policy, and select Enforced, as shown in Figure 6.12. The word Yes under Enforced informs you that this policy is now enforced.

Note that you can specify the Enforced option for individual GPOs. This is useful when you want to include critical corporate-wide policies in a domain-based GPO that is to apply to all domain users, regardless of OU-based policies. You should link such a GPO high in the hierarchy, such as at a site or domain.

NOTE

Note that the Enforced option applies to the link and not to the GPO. If the same GPO is linked to more than one AD DS container, it is possible for the GPO to be enforced on one link but not on another one.

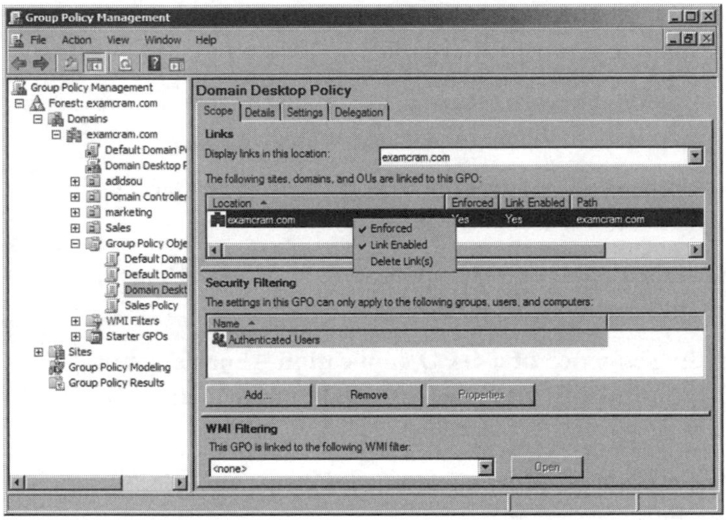

268

Chapter 6: Configuring and Troubleshooting Group Policy

FIGURE 6.12 An enforced policy is labeled Yes in the Enforced column within the Links section of the Scope tab of the GPO's Properties in the Details pane of GPMC.

Block Inheritance

Known as *Block Policy Inheritance* prior to use of the GPMC, the *Block Inheritance* setting enables you to prevent GPOs that are linked to parent containers to be applied at the lower level. A situation in which this might be useful is when the administrator of an OU wants to control all GPOs that apply to computers or users in the OU without inheriting settings from the site or parent domain.

To configure the Block Inheritance option, right-click the domain or OU in the console tree of GPMC where you want to apply this setting, and select Block Inheritance, as shown in Figure 6.13. This displays a blue exclamation point icon against this container in the console tree.

What happens if you have configured both the Block Inheritance and Enforced options at the same time? If a parent GPO is configured with the Enforced option, it overrides the application of Block Inheritance at a lower level. For example, if you have configured the Domain Desktop Policy GPO shown previously in Figure 6.12 with the Enforced option and then configure the Sales OU with Block Inheritance as shown in Figure 6.13, settings in the Domain Desktop Policy GPO still apply to users in the Sales OU.

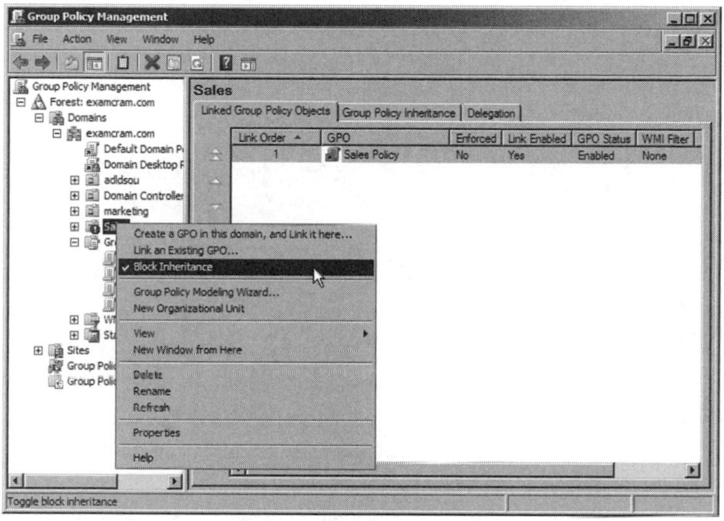

FIGURE 6.13   Configuring the Block Inheritance option.

TIP

Try to use the Enforced and Block Inheritance options sparingly. Their extensive use can make it extremely complex to troubleshoot policy application–related problems, especially as the size of your domain and the number of GPOs grow. The use of Group Policy results to determine policy application is discussed later in this chapter.

Modifying the Sequence of a GPO Application

You have already seen the default LSDOU sequence that applies when processing GPOs linked to different types of Active Directory containers. But what happens if more than one GPO is linked to the same container? Consider the situation for the Sales OU, as shown in Figure 6.14. The GPOs are applied in reverse order—bottom to top. Therefore, if settings conflict, those in the GPO highest in the order will prevail. In this example, it would be the Sales Policy. You can modify the sequence of policy application. Simply select the desired GPO and use the Up or Down buttons as needed.

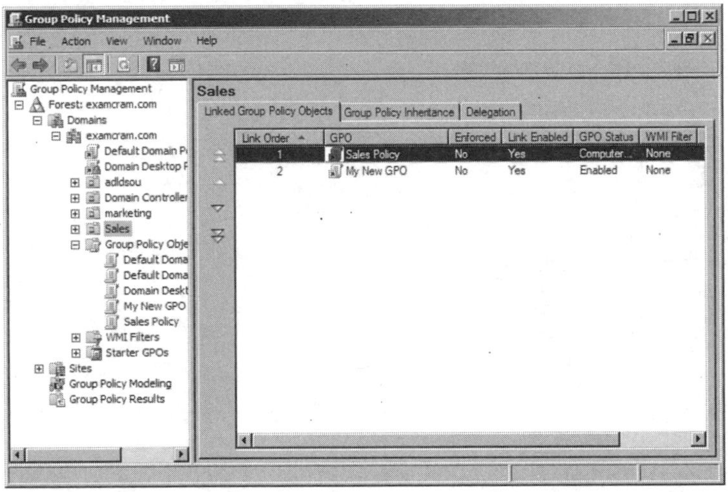

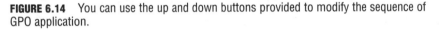

FIGURE 6.14   You can use the up and down buttons provided to modify the sequence of GPO application.

Disabling User Objects

When troubleshooting Group Policy problems, you might want to disable portions of a GPO. The Details tab of the GPO's properties in the Details pane of the GPMC enables you to disable the entire GPO or the computer or user configuration settings. Select the desired option from the GPO Status drop-down list, as shown in Figure 6.15. After you have completed policy troubleshooting, you can re-enable the GPO from the same location.

TIP

If a given GPO has no settings configured in one of the Computer Configuration or User Configuration branches, you can speed up policy processing by disabling that branch from this location.

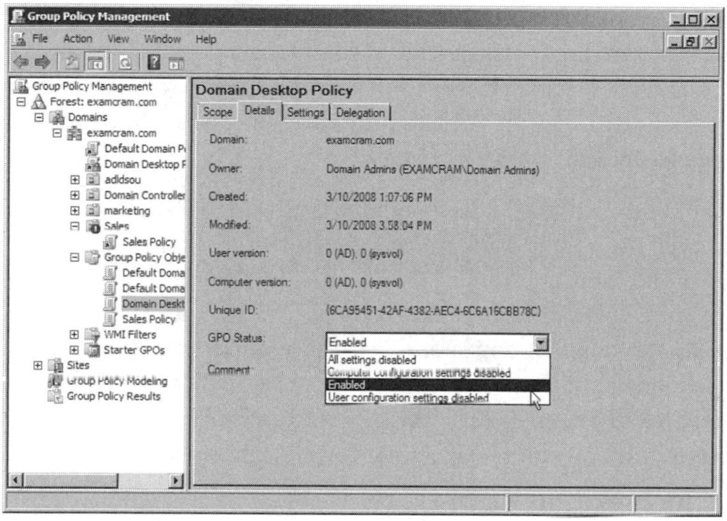

FIGURE 6.15 You can disable either the computer or user configuration portion of a GPO, or the entire GPO from its Details tab.

Group Policy Filtering

The settings already discussed provide you with powerful options for restricting the range of GPO applications according to the logical makeup of your AD DS forest. But what if you wanted to do more—for example, lock down the desktop settings of ordinary workers but at the same time provide the full range of applications and controls to others such as IT workers? Microsoft has provided the following two options for *filtering* the effect of Group Policy application:

▶ **Security Filtering**—Enables you to filter the application of a GPO according to a user or computer's membership in a security group.

▶ **Windows Management Instrumentation (WMI)**—Enables you to modify the scope of a GPO according to the attributes of destination computers.

Security Filtering of GPOs

The Security Filtering section of the Scope tab of a GPO's Properties displays the users, groups, and computers to which the GPO settings apply. These users, groups, and computers automatically have the Apply Group Policy permission granted to them.

To filter the application of a GPO, select it in the console tree of GPMC and select the Delegation tab from its properties in the Details pane. This tab lists all users and groups with specified permissions on the GPO. You can add or remove users or groups by using the Add and Remove buttons in the same way as described for the Scope tab.

This location enables you to explicitly deny application of a GPO to certain groups. For example, you might want to lock down the desktops of all users except members of the Domain Admins group. To do this, you would deny the Apply Group Policy permission to this group. Click Advanced, and on the Security Settings dialog box that appears, select the required group and deny the Apply Group Policy permission, as shown in Figure 6.16. Then click OK. You are reminded that the Deny entry takes precedence over Allow entries. Click Yes to accept this warning. The entry for this group under Allowed Permissions in the Delegation tab now states Custom to inform you that you have set a customized permission.

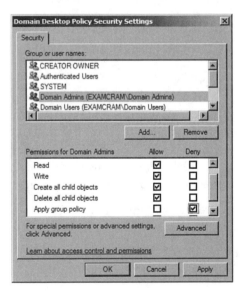

FIGURE 6.16 You can deny the application of a GPO to a given group by selecting the Deny entry for the Apply Group Policy permission.

Windows Management Instrumentation (WMI)

Introduced with Windows XP and Windows Server 2003 and continued with Windows Vista and Windows Server 2008, WMI filters enable an administrator to modify the scope of a GPO according to the attributes of destination computers.

WMI in Windows Server 2008 provides several new features, including the following:

- ► **Improved tracing and logging**—WMI uses Event Tracing for Windows, which enables the logging of WMI events available in Event Viewer.

- ► **Connection with User Account Control**—UAC now affects what WMI data is returned, remote access to WMI, and how WMI runs scripts.

- ► **Enhanced WMI namespace security and auditing**—You can now secure WMI namespace security in the Managed Object Format file. Further, WMI audits system access control lists (SACL) and reports events to the Security event log.

The WMI Filters node in GPMC enables you to configure WMI filters. You can create new WMI filters and import filters from external locations at this location. These WMI filters are then available to any GPO in your forest. Use the Scope tab of a GPO's Properties in GPMC to apply a WMI filter to the GPO.

EXAM ALERT

You do not need to know how to write WMI filter queries for Exam 70-640. However, you do need to know that WMI filters can query destination computers for hardware and other attributes. Also remember that Windows 2000 computers do not support WMI and always apply GPOs to the WMI filters that are linked.

Group Policy Loopback Processing

As has already been stated, the normal behavior of Group Policy is to apply computer settings when the computer starts up, followed by user settings when the user logs on. In certain cases, it might be undesirable for the settings to be applied when the user is logging on to a particular computer. For example, your organization might have a kiosk computer located in its lobby for public access. If users occasionally log on to these computers, it would be undesirable for certain user settings to be applied that are used when users log on to their corporate workstations. Likewise, administrators might receive certain settings, such as assigned software, that are appropriate to their workstations but not appropriate when they log on to a domain controller.

Microsoft provides the *loopback processing* mode to handle situations of this kind. This setting causes affected computers to apply only the set of computer-based

GPOs to any user who logs on to these computers. You have the choice of the following two modes of loopback processing:

▶ **Merge**—Combines user-specific and computer-specific settings but allows computer-specific settings to override user-specific ones. For example, if a user in the Sales OU logs on to a computer in the Kiosk OU, the settings for the two OUs are merged. If a conflict occurs, the settings for the computer-specific policy (in this case, the Kiosk OU) prevail.

▶ **Replace**—Replaces user-specific policy settings with the list already obtained for the computer (for example, the Kiosk OU policy settings). Here, the user-based settings that would normally apply to the user (in this case, the Sales OU) are disregarded.

To enable loopback processing, open the Group Policy Management Editor focused on the required GPO. Navigate to the Computer Configuration\ Policies\Administrative Templates\System\Group Policy node, right-click the User Group Policy Loopback Processing Mode policy, and choose Properties. Select Enabled from the Properties dialog box shown in Figure 6.17, select either Replace or Merge from the drop-down list, and then click OK.

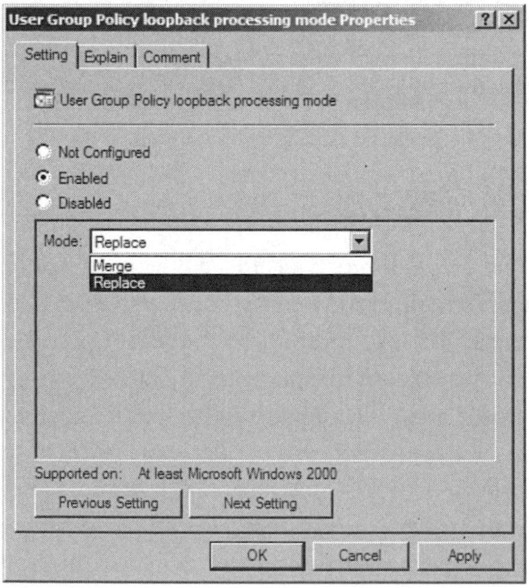

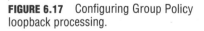

FIGURE 6.17 Configuring Group Policy loopback processing.

Configuring GPO Templates

Microsoft has completely reworked the Administrative Template format for Windows Server 2008, replacing the previous ADM format with a new XML-based ADMX format. This format provides several new advantages, including the following:

▶ You can create a central ADMX store to hold these files; this store is accessible to anyone with the privilege of editing GPOs.

▶ Because the ADMX files are stored in this location, they are no longer duplicated in individual GPOs as they were with the old ADM format, thereby reducing the size of the SYSVOL folder.

▶ The ADMX files support multiple languages in the descriptive text associated with a GPO.

▶ The ADMX files are backward compatible with the older ADM files, so organizations with a large number of ADM files do not need to convert them to ADMX.

You can work with either the older ADM files or ADMX in Windows Server 2008 Group Policy. However, ADMX files work with Windows Vista and Windows Server 2008 only and can be managed from computers running these operating systems only.

User Rights

User rights are defined as a default set of capabilities assigned to built-in domain local groups that define what members of these groups can and cannot do on the network. They consist of Privileges and Logon Rights.

You can manage these predefined user rights from the Computer Configuration\Policies\Windows Settings\Security Settings\Local Policies\User Rights Assignment node in the Group Policy Management Editor. When focused on the Default Domain Controllers Policy GPO, you can view the default rights assignments, as shown in Figure 6.18. To modify the assignment of any right, right-click it and choose Properties. In the Properties dialog box, click Add User or Group, and in the Add User or Group dialog box, type or browse to the required user or group. Then click OK.

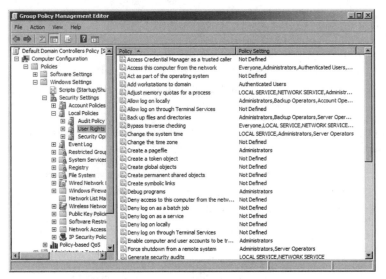

FIGURE 6.18 The Default Domain Controllers Policy GPO includes an extensive set of predefined user rights assignments.

You can also create a new GPO and configure a series of settings in this node to be applied to a specific group. Then you can link the GPO to an appropriate OU and grant the required group the Read and Apply Group Policy permissions. This is an easy way to grant user rights over a subset of the domain to a junior group of employees, such as help desk technicians.

ADMX Central Store

When you are administering domain-based GPOs, you can use the new *ADMX central store*, which is the new storage location that considerably reduces the quantity of storage space required for GPO maintenance, especially in a large domain with many OUs and many linked GPOs.

The central store is not available by default; you must create it so that the GPOs you are working with can access the same set of ADMX files. It is a folder structure within the SYSVOL folder on the domain controllers in each domain of your forest. It contains a root-level folder with all language-neutral ADMX files plus subfolders that contain the language-specific ADML resource files.

To create the central store and populate it with ADMX files, perform the following steps:

1. In Windows Explorer, navigate to %systemroot%\sysvol\domain\ Policies and create a subfolder named PolicyDefinitions.

2. Create a subfolder within PolicyDefinitions for each language used in your organization, such as EN-US for U.S.-based English, FR-CA for Canadian French, or ES for Spanish.

3. Copy language-neutral ADMX files from %systemroot%\ PolicyDefinitions to the subfolder you created in step 1.

4. Copy language-specific ADML files from the appropriate subfolder in the same location to the language-specific subfolder.

After you have performed this procedure, the Group Policy Management Editor automatically reads all ADMX files from the central store of the domain in which the GPO was created. You only need to perform this procedure once for each domain; Active Directory replication automatically propagates the central store and its contents to all other domain controllers.

TIP

Microsoft provides the downloadable ADMX Migrator tool that enables you to convert existing ADM files to ADMX or to edit existing ADMX files. This tool is available from http://www.microsoft.com/downloads/details.aspx?FamilyId=0F1EEC3D-10C4-4B5F-9625-97C2F731090C&displaylang=en.

For more information on language-neutral ADMX and language-specific ADML files, refer to "ADMX Technology Review" in Appendix A.

Administrative Templates

Administrative templates (both the older ADM files and the newer ADMX files) provide the principal means of administering the user environment and controlling the end-user interface. You can use administrative templates to deny access to certain functions of the operating system (for example, the capability to install or remove software) or to define settings that affect a user's computing experience (for example, desktop wallpaper or screen savers). These become a part of the GPO in which you configure them, and they are automatically applied to all computers and users within the scope of influence of this GPO.

You can configure Administrative Templates sections within either the Computer Configuration or User Configuration sections of the GPO. Some policy settings are available in both sections; the section you choose when applying them determines whether they apply to the computer regardless of who is logged on, or to the user regardless of which computer he is logged on to.

Table 6.1 summarizes the types of settings available in the Administrative Templates nodes of Computer Configuration and User Configuration.

TABLE 6.1 Groups of Administrative Template Settings

Setting	What You Can Control	Applied To
Control Panel	Part or all of the Control Panel settings. This capability is useful in the corporate environment, where many help desk calls come from users who have experimented with settings in the Control Panel. You can restrict or prevent users from installing unauthorized or pirated software and limit the extent to which users can modify the display appearance, including wallpaper, screen saver, and so on. You can also show or hide specified applets; control the users' ability to add, delete, and search for printers; and restrict the language selection used for Windows menus and dialog boxes.	Computers and Users
Desktop	What is seen or not seen on the user's desktop. These items include many of the ones that are configurable in the Start menu and taskbar, such as Documents and Network Locations. You can also configure options that pertain to the Active Desktop enhancements and options that pertain to the size and refinement of Active Directory searches.	Users
Network	Behavior of offline files, network connections, and several other networking parameters. Network connection settings specify how Windows Firewall functions, including allowed actions in domain and standard profiles. Different settings are available in the Computer Configuration and User Configuration containers.	Computers and Users
Printers	The publication of printers in Active Directory, including web-based printing. You can prevent users from adding or deleting printers. You can also control the directory pruning service, which checks the operational status of printers on the network.	Computers
Shared Folders	Whether users can publish shared folders and Distributed File System (DFS) roots.	Users

TABLE 6.1 *Continued*

Setting	What You Can Control	Applied To
Start Menu and Taskbar	What is seen or not seen on the user's Start menu and taskbar. You can hide items that you do not want users to have available, such as the Search command; the Run command; the Documents, Pictures, Music, and Network icons; and so on. You can also remove submenus from the Start menu and gray out unavailable Windows Installer Start menu shortcuts.	Users
System	A large range of system functions, including Group Policy itself. Logon policies determine how scripts are processed, the effect of slow links, and so on. You can control the installation of external devices and their drivers by users and control read and write access to removable storage devices. You can control how power management and sleep mode settings are specified on computers. You can restrict access to specified Windows applications and disable users' ability to run Registry editing tools such as `Regedit`.	Computers and Users
Windows Components	Components such as NetMeeting, Internet Explorer, Windows Explorer, Microsoft Management Console, BitLocker Drive Encryption, Task Scheduler, Terminal Services, Windows Installer, Windows Messenger, Windows Media Player, and Windows Update. You can control the behavior of these programs—from what functionality is available to the user to configuring an application's features.	Computers and Users

Although settings in these nodes keep inexperienced users from poking around in places you would rather not have them access, users can access these items by other means. If the users can access a command prompt, they can run many of these components. However, by hiding items such as the Network and Sharing Center and its associated tasks such as View Computers and Devices, you can make it difficult for users to explore servers just for the fun of seeing what they can find.

To configure a policy in the Administrative Templates folder, right-click it and choose Properties. From the Setting tab of the policy's Properties dialog box, select one of the following three options:

> ▶ **Not Configured**—Does not modify the Registry. It permits any other setting from a higher-level GPO to remain applied.

▶ **Enabled**—Modifies the Registry to specify that the setting is enabled.

▶ **Disabled**—Modifies the Registry to specify that the setting is disabled.

Each policy settings' Properties dialog box contains two additional tabs:

▶ **Explain**—Provides a description that assists you in selecting the policies to be applied, as shown in Figure 6.19.

▶ **Comment**—Enables you to type a descriptive comment of your choice. From here you can inform other administrators of facts, such as when and why you enabled this policy.

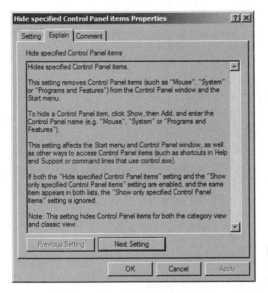

FIGURE 6.19 The Explain tab of the Hide Specific Control Items Properties dialog box.

A Typical Policy Application Scenario

Suppose that you are the network administrator for a large retail department store chain. You are setting up a system of computers that customers can use to search the store's large online catalog and order merchandise. Credit cards are processed and merchandise is shipped directly to the customers.

In such an environment, customers would be accessing your network, and you would not want them to alter the operating system or the user environment. So you would lock down components such as the Start menu and taskbar, the desktop, and the Control Panel from their User Configuration subnodes to prevent changes from being made. You would disable the Control Panel, remove the Run line from the Start menu, hide all

(continues)

(continued)

desktop icons, and prevent users from saving changes upon exiting. In addition, you would use settings under the System node in both Computer Configuration and User Configuration to disable Registry editing so that a savvy customer couldn't circumvent your policy settings by disabling them in the Registry. You would also disable the command prompt so a customer couldn't execute programs from this location.

By configuring all these settings and others, you can essentially lock down the user environment, which is what you would want in this type of scenario.

Restricted Groups

The Restricted Groups node, available under Computer Configuration\
Policies\Windows Settings\Security Settings, enables you to specify who (user or group) can be a member of a group and which groups each group can belong to. Such groups can include local groups on member servers or client computers, such as the local Administrators group. For example, you can specify which users or groups can be members of the local Administrators group on all member servers and client computers affected by the GPO so that local users cannot make themselves administrators of their computers. If any other members have been specified for a restricted group, they are removed when the policy applies. It is reapplied each time Group Policy is refreshed, which is every five minutes for domain controllers and every 90 minutes for member servers and client computers.

To specify a restricted group, navigate to the Computer Configuration\
Policies\Windows Settings\Security Settings node, right-click Restricted Groups, and choose Add Group. Specify the group to be restricted, and click OK. In the dialog box shown in Figure 6.20, click Add under Members of This Group, and specify the members to be added as shown, separating multiple entries with semicolons. To specify a group that the restricted group can belong to, click Add under This Group Is a Member Of, and type the name of the required group. After clicking OK, the restricted group name and its membership appear in the Details pane of the Group Policy Management Editor.

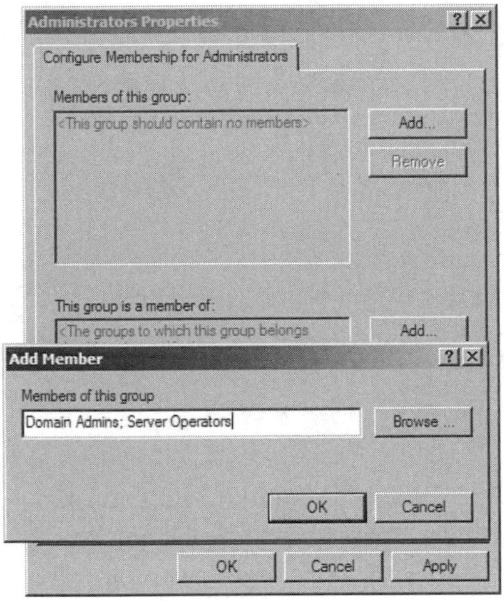

FIGURE 6.20 Restricting the membership of the local Administrators group.

Starter GPOs

Another new feature in Windows Server 2008 Group Policy is the ability to create *Starter GPOs*. These are sets of preconfigured Administrative Template policy settings, including comments, which you can use for ease of creating new GPOs. When you use a Starter GPO to create a new GPO, the new GPO includes all settings, their values, comments, and delegation as defined in the Starter GPO. It also enables you to import and export it to other environments, such as additional domains in the forest or a trusted forest.

To create a Starter GPO, right-click the Starter GPOs folder and choose New. In the New Starter GPO dialog box, type a name and optional comment, and then click OK. This adds the Starter GPO to this folder, as shown in Figure 6.21.

To configure settings in this Starter GPO, right-click it and choose Edit to open the Group Policy Starter GPO Editor snap-in. This tool works the same way as the Group Policy Management Editor, except that only the Administrative Templates folder is available under both Computer Configuration and User Configuration. The settings and their comments that you configure here are incorporated into all GPOs that you create later from this Starter GPO.

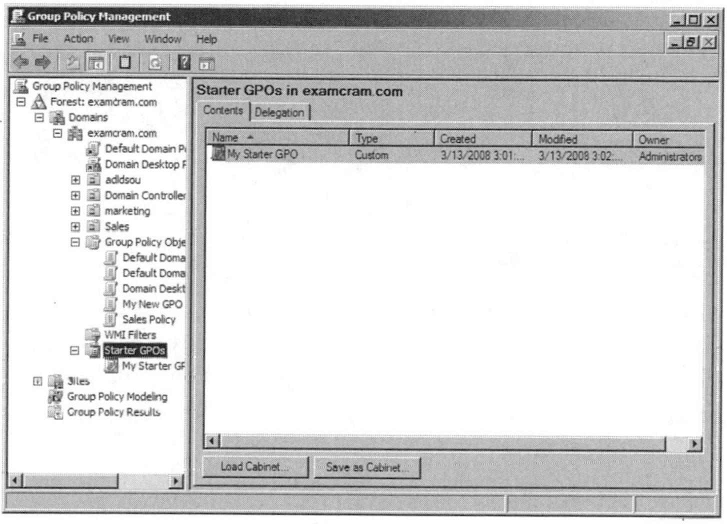

FIGURE 6.21 Starter GPOs are stored in the Starter GPOs folder and are available for use in creating new GPOs.

You can also perform the following tasks with Starter GPOs:

▸ **Delegate the action of creating Starter GPOs**—Select the Delegation tab. Then click Add to add a user or group with the ability to create additional Starter GPOs in the domain.

▸ **Export for use elsewhere in the forest or another forest**—Click Save as Cabinet and specify a location to save the set of Starter GPOs.

▸ **Import GPOs from another forest**—Click Load Cabinet, and in the Load Starter GPO dialog box that appears, click Browse for CAB to locate and import the desired file.

After you have created a Starter GPO, you can use this GPO to create new GPOs. To do so, right-click the required site, domain, or OU and choose Create a GPO in This Domain, and Link It Here, or right-click the Group Policy Objects container and choose New. In the New GPO dialog box previously shown in Figure 6.3, select the starter GPO from the Source Starter GPO drop-down list and click OK. You can now use the Group Policy Management Editor on this GPO to add any additional required settings.

EXAM ALERT

Remember the proper method of applying a Starter GPO. You can create another GPO that is linked to an AD DS object, but you cannot directly link a Starter GPO to an AD DS object, as an exam answer choice might suggest.

Shell Access Policies

The shell can be thought of as the command interpreter that passes commands to the operating system. It is a separate software program that works from the nongraphical command prompt interface. Using this, a knowledgeable user can often circumvent restrictive policy settings by entering the corresponding command from the command prompt.

To prevent users from accessing the command prompt, open an appropriate GPO in the Group Policy Management Editor and navigate to the User Configuration\Policies\Administrative Templates\System node, right-click Prevent Access to the Command Prompt, and choose Properties. Enable this setting, and select an appropriate option for Disable the Command Prompt Script Processing Also.

- ▶ If you select Yes, no scripts can be run. This prevents the user from running batch files, but it also prevents any logon, logoff, startup, or shutdown scripts from running even if these have been configured in Group Policy to run.

- ▶ If you select No, logon, logoff, startup, or shutdown scripts can run, but the user might be able to execute script files from within a program window.

Using Group Policy to Deploy Software

Prior to Windows 2000, no simple means of software deployment existed. You had to take the installation disks to each computer and manually install the application or update. Beginning with Windows 2000, Microsoft included the Software Installation and Maintenance feature, which enables administrators to deploy software so that it is always available to users and repairs itself if needed.

Users benefit from Group Policy software deployment in several ways:

▶ Should a user's computer fail, a support technician needs only to provide a replacement computer with Windows XP or Vista installed. The user logs on, and her assigned set of software is automatically installed.

▶ A user who needs access to the network from multiple computers always has her assigned set of software available.

▶ A user who changes job responsibilities within the organization can automatically receive new software required by her new position.

▶ Assigned software is *resilient*—that is, if a user deletes files or folders required by the software package, the files are automatically replaced the next time the user attempts to run the program. This saves trips to computers by support people to repair problems.

▶ You can specify that software that is no longer required is automatically removed, including all required files and Registry entries, while any shared files (such as .dll files used by other programs) are retained.

Software Installation and Maintenance enables you to manage the following steps in the software life cycle:

▶ **Software installation**—You can deploy almost any type of software application, including custom in-house applications. You can use Microsoft Software Installer (.msi) files to specify the software installation conditions, including the available components and options. You can also use transform (.mst) files to specify installation options, such as languages.

▶ **Software upgrades and patches**—You can use patch (.msp) files to add hotfixes and other patches as required. You can also deploy service packs as they become available and upgrade software to new versions—for example, Office 2003 to Office 2007.

▶ **Software removal**—When a program is no longer used or supported by the IT department, you can remove it from users' computers. You can specify an option to provide users with an option to retain obsolete software or remove it automatically without a user option.

Assigning and Publishing Software

Software Installation and Maintenance provides three methods of software deployment. The method you employ depends on which users require access to the software package and its urgency. You can either assign the package to users or computers or publish it to users. No option exists for publishing software to computers.

Assigning Software to Users

When you assign a software package to users, the software follows them around to whatever computer they log on to. Consequently, the software is always available to them. When users log on to the computer after the application has been assigned, the application appears in the Start menu and, if specified, an icon on the desktop. When users invoke the application from either of these points, it is automatically installed.

Assigning Software to Computers

When you assign software to computers, it is available to all authenticated users of the computer, regardless of their group membership or privileges. The software package is installed when the computer is next restarted after the package has been assigned. For example, suppose that you have a design application that should be available on all computers in the Engineering OU but not to computers elsewhere on your network. You would assign this application to computers in a GPO linked to the Engineering OU.

Publishing Software to Users

When you publish software to users, it is not advertised in the same manner as when you assign it. It does not appear in the Start, All Programs menu, and no icons appear on the desktop. To install it, users need to go to the Add or Remove Programs (XP) or Programs and Features (Vista) applet in the Control Panel. Users can also install it by double-clicking a file whose extension is associated with the application (document activation). If the users double-click a file of unknown file extension, a query is sent to Active Directory to determine whether an application is available for that file type (and the users have the proper permissions to that application). If so, the application is installed.

NOTE

Software deployed using Group Policy is resilient only if you have assigned it to the users or computers that require the software. Published software is not resilient; users need to return to the Control Panel Add or Remove Programs to reinstall a damaged published software program.

EXAM ALERT

An exam question might give you choices that include publishing software to computers. Remember that you cannot publish software to computers. This is true because users must manually commence the installation of published software.

Deploying Software Using Group Policy

Before you deploy a new software package, you must copy the installation files to a distribution point, which is a shared folder accessible to both the server and all client computers requiring the package. You can then use any existing GPO or create a new GPO for deploying the package. The following steps outline the general procedure:

1. Open the Group Policy Management Editor focused on the required GPO.

2. Navigate to the appropriate node for software deployment, as follows:

   ▶ To assign or publish an application to users, navigate to User Configuration\Policies\Software Settings\Software Installation.

   ▶ To assign an application to computers, navigate to Computer Configuration\Policies\Software Settings\Software Installation.

3. Right-click this node and choose New, Package.

4. In the Open dialog box that appears, navigate to the shared folder where the .msi file is located, select it, and click Open.

5. In the Deploy Software dialog box shown in Figure 6.22, select the option with which you want to deploy the software package, and then click OK. You would select Advanced to include transforms or modifications to the software packages.

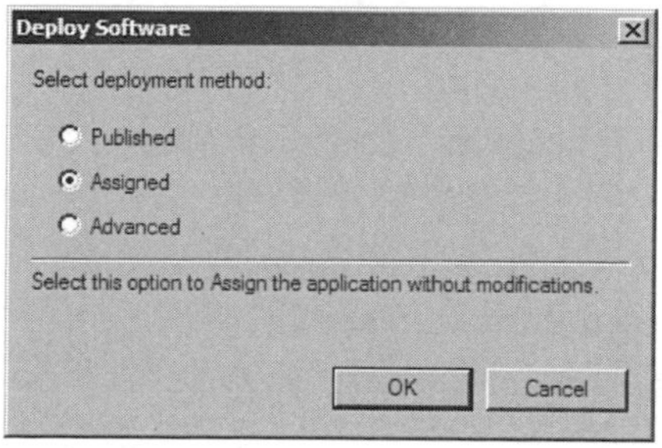

Deploy Software ☒

Select deployment method:

○ Published
⦿ Assigned
○ Advanced

Select this option to Assign the application without modifications.

OK   Cancel

FIGURE 6.22 Selecting the method of software deployment.

When you finish this procedure, the deployed package appears in the Details pane of the Group Policy Management Editor with its version, deployment state (published or assigned), and path to source files.

> **NOTE**
>
> You should select a network share by means of its Universal Naming Convention (UNC) path in step 4 of this procedure; otherwise, users will be unable to locate the package. If you do not select a UNC path, a warning message will alert you to this fact.

Software Installation Properties

You can configure global properties of all software installation packages deployed to either users or computers, as well as properties of individual software packages.

To assign global properties, right-click the appropriate Software Installation node and choose Properties to bring up the Software Installation Properties dialog box shown in Figure 6.23.

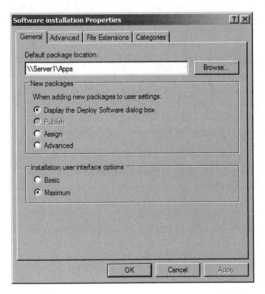

FIGURE 6.23 Configuring global software installation properties.

The General tab allows you to configure the following items:

▶ **Default Package Location**—The UNC path to the shared folder containing the installation files.

- ▶ **New Packages**—Specify the deployment type. The default option is Display the Display Software dialog box, which displays the dialog box previously shown in Figure 6.22 so that you can select the deployment method individually for each software package.

- ▶ **Installation User Interface Options**—Determines what the user sees during application installation. Select Basic to provide only progress bars and error messages. The Maximum option provides additional information, including all installation messages and dialog boxes displayed during installation.

Select the Advanced tab to configure the following additional options:

- ▶ **Uninstall the Applications When They Fall Out of the Scope of Management**—Automatically removes the software if the GPO that installed it is no longer applied to the user or computer. For example, suppose that a user in the Sales OU has a sales application installed from a GPO linked to this OU. His job responsibilities change, and he is moved to the Marketing OU; consequently, he no longer needs this application, and it is removed from his computer.

- ▶ **Include OLE Information When Deploying Applications**—The Object Linking and Embedding (OLE) option allows you to specify whether information about Component Object Model (COM) components included with a package are deployed so that these components can be installed as required in a manner similar to file extension activation.

- ▶ **Make 32-Bit X86 Windows Installer Applications Available to Win64 Machines** and **Make 32-Bit X86 Down-Level (ZAP) Applications Available to Win64 Machines**—Specify whether 32-bit applications of the indicated type will be made available to 64-bit computers.

The File Extensions tab enables you to specify the order of precedence for applications that are capable of opening a file with a given extension. Type the required extension, and the available applications display automatically. Then select these applications and use the Up and Down buttons to order them in the appropriate sequence.

The Categories tab enables you to group published applications into categories, which are informational only. They are displayed to users who access programs from the Control Panel Add or Remove Programs (XP) or Programs and Features (Vista) applet. They assist users in locating the appropriate applications.

Software Package Properties

You can configure individual software package properties from its Properties dialog box. Right-click the package in the Details pane of the Group Policy Management Editor snap-in and choose Properties to display this dialog box, which has the following six tabs:

▶ **General**—Includes product information, such as the name and version number. You can include contact information and a friendly name for users.

▶ **Deployment**—As shown in Figure 6.24, you can define or change the deployment type (published or assigned). You can also specify publication options, including whether the package should be uninstalled if it falls out of the scope of management, whether it is displayed in the Control Panel Add or Remove Programs applet, and whether an assigned program is installed at logon. You also have the same installation user interface options previously seen in the General tab of Figure 6.24. Advanced options determine whether the language setting should be ignored when installing the software and whether 32-bit applications are made available to 64-bit computers.

▶ **Upgrades**—Defines the applications that are to be upgraded by this package as well as packages that can upgrade this package. You can also choose whether to make this package a required upgrade for existing packages.

▶ **Categories**—Enables you to specify the category into which a program is displayed in the Control Panel Add or Remove Programs (XP) or Programs and Features (Vista) applet.

▶ **Modifications**—Enables you to apply modifications or transforms to the package to customize the deployment. For example, suppose your company operates in different countries that require localized language dictionaries in Microsoft Word. You can deploy transforms (.mst files) that include the required language files.

▶ **Security**—Determines the level of access users have to the package. You can make applications available to specified users, computers, or groups only. Administrators and others who manage software installation should receive the Full Control permission, and users installing the software should receive the Read permission.

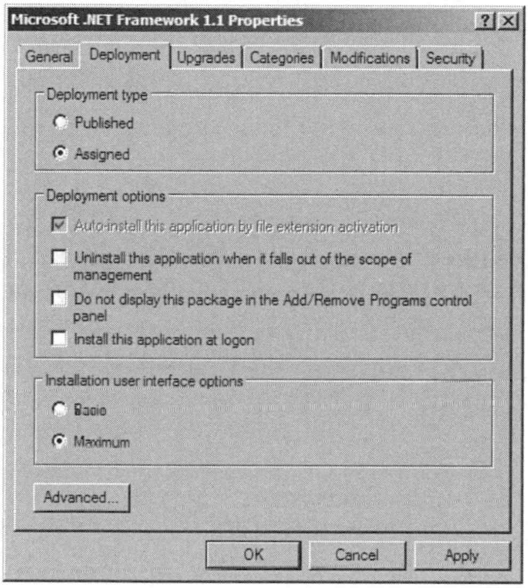

FIGURE 6.24 You can configure several advanced settings for an application after you have deployed it.

Software Redeployment

When you modify any of a software package's properties as described in the previous section, you must redeploy the software package so that users receive the modifications. To redeploy the package, right-click it in the Details pane of Group Policy Management Editor, and choose All Tasks, Redeploy. You are warned that redeploying the application will reinstall it wherever it is installed. Click Yes to proceed.

EXAM ALERT

An exam question might present a scenario asking whether you would assign or publish an application. If it specifies that it is mandatory that the application should be installed, you should assign it. Assign the application to computers if all computers in the scope of the GPO require it, regardless of the user who is logged on; assign it to users if all users in the scope of the GPO require it, regardless of the computer to which they are logged on. If the application is not mandatory but the users will have an option to install it, you should publish it. Again, don't forget that you cannot publish an application to computers.

Upgrading Software

As new versions of applications are released, it might be desirable to upgrade the current packages to take advantage of the new features that are generally offered with the upgraded version.

Group Policy makes it simple for you to deploy an upgraded software package. Simply follow the steps already outlined in this chapter to deploy the upgraded package, usually in the same GPO that holds the package to be upgraded. After you have deployed it, right-click the new package and choose Properties to display the dialog box previously shown in Figure 6.24 and select the Upgrades tab. Click Add to display the Add Upgrade Package dialog box shown in Figure 6.25, and configure the following options:

- **Choose a Package From**—If the original software package was deployed from a different GPO, select A Specific GPO and click Browse to locate the appropriate GPO from the Browse for a Group Policy Object dialog box that appears. Otherwise, leave the default option selected.

- **Package to Upgrade**—Select the package to be upgraded.

- **Uninstall the Existing Package, Then Install the Upgrade Package**—Select this option if you are replacing the application with a completely different one, such as from a new vendor. You might have to use this option for some applications that cannot be installed over current installations.

- **Package Can Upgrade over the Existing Package**—Use this option when upgrading to a newer version of the same product. It retains the user's application preferences, document type associations, and so on.

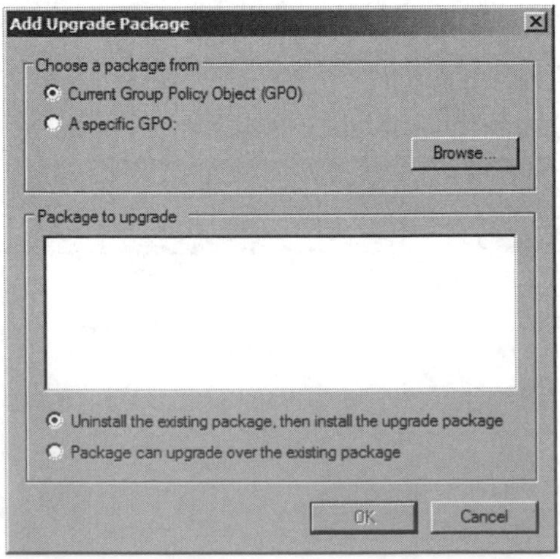

FIGURE 6.25 The Add Upgrade Package dialog box.

When you deploy an upgrade package, you can designate the upgrade as either optional or mandatory.

▶ **Mandatory upgrade**—Automatically upgrades the current version of the software the next time the computer is started or the user logs on. To configure this option, select the Required Upgrade for Existing Packages check box on the Upgrades tab of the package's Properties dialog box.

▶ **Optional upgrade**—The user can either upgrade the application or continue to use the current version. The user can even have both versions installed and access either one as he chooses. To configure this option, leave the above check box cleared.

Removal of Software

When software that was deployed using Group Policy and Windows Installer becomes outdated or is no longer useful to your company, you can use a GPO to remove the software. Software removal can be either mandatory, which automatically removes it from the affected computers, or optional, which allows users to continue to use it but no longer supports it or makes it available for reinstallation.

To remove deployed software, open the GPO from which it was deployed, navigate to the appropriate Software Installation node, right-click the application, and choose All Tasks, Remove. You see the Remove Software dialog box shown in Figure 6.26, which provides the following two choices:

▶ **Immediately Uninstall the Software from Users and Computers**— Automatically removes the software the next time the affected computer is rebooted or the user logs on. The user does not get the option to keep the software.

▶ **Allow Users to Continue to Use the Software, But Prevent New Installations**—The software is not automatically removed, and the user can continue to use it. However, users who remove the software and others who do not have it can no longer install it.

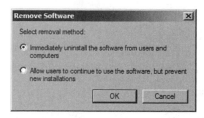

FIGURE 6.26 Software removal can be either mandatory or optional.

Troubleshooting the Application of Group Policy Objects

As you have seen in this chapter, Group Policy is an all-encompassing, powerful tool that enables you to configure a large number of settings that affect users and computers in your network. Although you might be able to keep up with what Group Policy is doing in a small organization, the application of policy settings tends to quickly become more complicated as the organization grows and multiple administrators configure additional policy settings.

Complicated implementations of Group Policy often generate unexpected results. Back in the days of Windows 2000, troubleshooting problems frequently meant printing out settings applied at the various levels, disabling certain GPOs or portions of them, and performing a long series of tests. Since Windows Server 2003, Microsoft has included tools that help you troubleshoot, test, and plan. These include the Resultant Set of Policy snap-in, the Group Policy Modeling Wizard, and Group Policy Results.

Resultant Set of Policy

First introduced with Windows Server 2003, *Resultant Set of Policy* (RSoP) is a powerful tool that queries computers running Windows XP/Vista/Server 2003/Server 2008 and informs you of which policies have been applied and in what order. You can run RSoP in either planning mode or logging mode:

▶ **Planning mode**—Allows you to perform a what-if scenario that predicts the effects of a proposed series of policies on a specified user/computer combination. This mode is also known as *Group Policy Modeling*.

▶ **Logging mode**—Allows you to analyze a specific user/computer combination to obtain information on policy application for this combination. This mode is also known as *Group Policy Results*.

Planning Mode/Group Policy Modeling

Planning mode provides the opportunity to apply GPO settings to an object, such as a user or computer, to see the net effect a new policy will have. In other words, it performs a what-if analysis and reports of the policy settings you would have if you configured the settings you have specified while running RSoP. The following are several situations in which this is useful:

▶ Simulating the effect of a series of policy settings on a computer or user according to the site, domain, or OU where the computer or user is located

▶ After creating a new user or group account in AD DS or making changes to security group membership

▶ Predicting the effect of moving a computer or user to a different site or OU

▶ Simulating the effect of a slow network connection

▶ Simulating a loopback condition

You can run RSoP planning mode from any of the following locations:

▶ **From Active Directory Users and Computers**—Enables you to simulate the effect of policies applied to a domain or OU. Right-click the required domain or OU and choose All Tasks, Resultant Set of Policy (Planning).

▶ **From Active Directory Sites and Services**—Enables you to simulate the effect of policies applied to a site. Right-click the required site and choose All Tasks, Resultant Set of Policy (Planning).

▶ **From Group Policy Management Console**—GPMC includes a Group Policy Modeling node that enables you to simulate the effect of policies applied to a site, domain, or OU. Right-click this node and choose Group Policy Modeling Wizard.

▶ **From its own console**—Enables you to create a customized MMC console that includes the RSoP snap-in. Add the snap-in to an empty console by clicking File, Add/Remove Snap-In, and then adding Resultant Set of Policy from the list of available snap-ins. After you have done this, you can right-click the Resultant Set of Policy node and choose Generate RSoP Data to start the Resultant Set of Policy Wizard.

Whether the wizard launched is called the Group Policy Modeling Wizard (as it is when started from GPMC) or the Resultant Set of Policy Wizard (as it is when started from any of the other locations), the options provided and the procedure followed are similar, as outlined here:

1. If you start from the RSoP snap-in, select Planning mode and click Next.

2. On the User and Computer Selection page shown in Figure 6.27, select a specific user and/or computer to test a planning scenario, or accept the information supplied according to the AD DS object you started at. If you started from the Group Policy Planning node of GPMC or from a custom console, you need to enter information on this page. Make a selection, and then click Next.

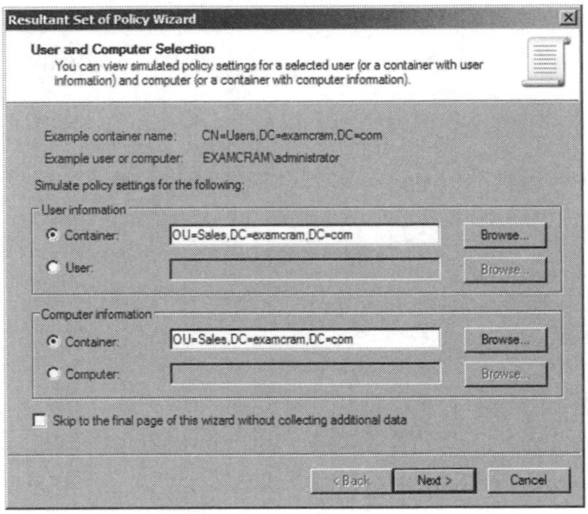

FIGURE 6.27 Entering user and computer information into the Resultant Set of Policy Wizard.

TIP

At most of the pages in this wizard, you can speed up the wizard by selecting the check box labeled Skip to the Final Page of This Wizard Without Collecting Additional Data, if you do not have additional information that you want to enter. This takes you directly to the Summary page.

---

3. On the Advanced Simulation Options page, select any of the following as required. Then click Next:

   ▶ **Slow Network Connection**—Ignores any policies configured not to apply across a slow connection.

   ▶ **Loopback Processing**—Invokes the loopback processing mode described earlier in this chapter, including the Replace and Merge options.

   ▶ **Site**—Enables you to select a site whose policies are to be applied, or (None) to not include sites.

4. On the User Security Groups page, specify any required changes to the selected user's security groups, and then click Next.

5. On the Computer Security Groups page, specify any required changes to the selected computer's security groups, and then click Next.

6. On the WMI Filters for Users page, include any required filters, and then click Next. Then repeat for computers on the WMI Filters for Computers page.

7. Review your selections on the Summary of Selections page, and then click Next to perform the simulation.

8. When the completion page appears, click Finish. The wizard displays a Resultant Set of Policy snap-in that looks similar to the Group Policy Management Editor snap-in.

9. To view the effect of applied GPOs, expand the desired node in the console tree. As shown in Figure 6.28, only the subnodes for which policies have been configured appear.

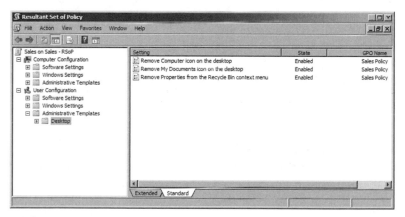

FIGURE 6.28   The RSoP snap-in displays only those policies for which GPOs are configured.

10. To view the hierarchy of any configured policy, right-click it and choose Properties. From the Properties dialog box that appears, select the Precedence tab to display the GPOs for which this policy has been configured. As shown in Figure 6.29, these GPOs appear with the priorities ascending from bottom to top. The top policy setting is the one that will apply.

NOTE

If you run RSoP from GPMC, the Details pane displays its results with the Settings tab displaying a hierarchical series of applied policy settings similar in appearance to that of Figure 6.2 shown previously.

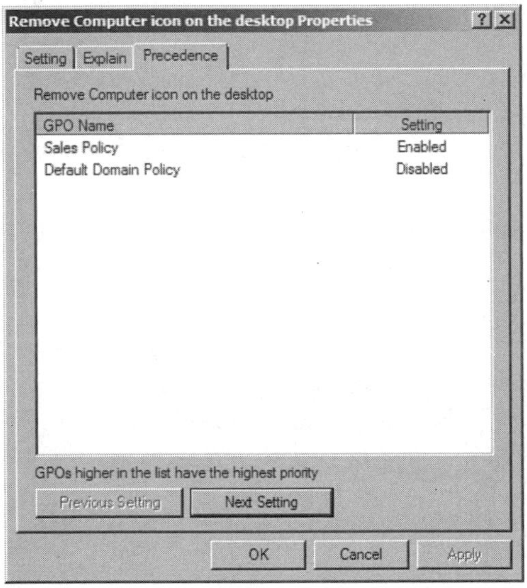

FIGURE 6.29 The Precedence tab displays GPOs for which the policy is configured, with the highest priority setting at the top.

Logging Mode/Group Policy Results

First Logging mode provides the ability to determine which policies are currently being applied to an object. In this mode, you can create a report and determine what each of the policies is doing to an object. This is useful for troubleshooting Group Policy problems. You can run logging mode using any of the following methods:

▶ **From the Run dialog box**—Log on to the computer where you want to run RSoP as the appropriate user, click Start, Run, type `rsop.msc`, and then press Enter. This displays the RSoP snap-in containing only those nodes for which a policy is configured.

▶ **From Active Directory Users and Computers**—Navigate to the OU or container where the appropriate user account is located, right-click the account, and choose All Tasks, Resultant Set of Policy (Logging). This starts the Resultant Set of Policy Wizard.

▶ **From Group Policy Management Console**—GPMC includes a Group Policy Results node that enables you to select the required user and computer. Right-click this node and choose Group Policy Results Wizard.

▶ **From its own console**—Enables you to create a customized MMC console that includes the RSoP snap-in, as already described, which enables you to start the Resultant Set of Policy Wizard.

CAUTION

For Group Policy Results to work properly, the selected user must have logged on to the selected computer since the applicable GPOs were last configured.

Running this wizard is similar to running the wizard in planning mode, except that you only have choices for specifying the required computer and user. When run from GPMC, you receive a hierarchical view of the results, and when run from the other locations, you receive the RSoP snap-in, both of which display information similar to that displayed in Figures 6.28 and 6.29 for planning mode. You can receive the RSoP snap-in view from GPMC by right-clicking the subnode under Group Policy Results and choosing Advanced View.

EXAM ALERT

The user in question must log on to the computer in question before RSoP works in logging mode. You might be asked to choose between planning mode and logging mode for a user who has not logged on to that specific computer or to troubleshoot the reasons why RSoP in logging mode does not work for a specific user.

Using the Delegation of Control Wizard

In Chapter 5, the Delegation of Control Wizard was introduced and explained regarding its use for delegating partial administrative control to domains, sites, and OUs. You can also use the Delegation of Control Wizard to delegate the ability to perform the following tasks within Group Policy:

▶ **Manage Group Policy links**—Enables the ability to apply GPOs to the site, domain, or OU where the task is delegated but does not enable the ability to create new GPOs or edit existing ones.

▶ **Generate Resultant Set of Policy (Planning)**—Enables the ability to run the Group Policy Modeling Wizard on the site, domain, or OU where the task is delegated.

▶ **Generate Resultant Set of Policy (Logging)**— Enables the ability to run the Group Policy Results Wizard on the site, domain, or OU where the task is delegated.

Gpresult

Gpresult is a command-line version of RSoP that you can use to display logging mode information or create batch files. It is also useful for collecting RSoP data on a Server Core computer. Figure 6.30 shows a sample of the results obtained by running this tool against the local computer.

FIGURE 6.30 The results of running gpresult.exe against the local computer.

For more information on gpresult, refer to "Gpresult" in Appendix A.

Gpupdate

Introduced in Windows Server 2003, Gpupdate is a tool that refreshes Group Policy settings. Its syntax is as follows:

```
Gpupdate [/target:{computer | user}] [/force] /[wait:value] [/logoff]
➡[/boot]
```

Table 6.2 describes the options available with this command.

TABLE 6.2   Options Available with the Gpupdate Command

Option	Description
/target {computer | user}	Enables only the computer or user settings to be processed when specified. Otherwise, both computer and user settings are processed.
/force	Forces the reapplication of all settings.

TABLE 6.2 *Continued*

Option	Description
/wait:*value*	Specifies the number of seconds that policy processing waits to finish. By default, this is 600 seconds. 0 means "no wait" and −1 means "wait indefinitely."
/logoff	Logs off after completion of refresh to enable processing of client-side extensions such as software installation and folder redirection that require the user to log off and back on.
/boot	Restarts the computer when the refresh completes to enable processing of client-side extensions such as computer-based software installation policies that require the computer to be rebooted.

TIP

It is helpful to use the Gpupdate /force command immediately after creating or editing a GPO so that its settings take effect immediately rather than waiting until the next policy refresh time.

Exam Cram Questions

1. Harry is responsible for configuring Group Policy on a network that includes a single AD DS domain with four sites: San Antonio, Denver, Charlotte, and Montreal.

   Harry has created a GPO named Restrictions that limits access to several desktop components. These restrictions are to be applied to all employees with the following exceptions: On the network, administrators need to have access to everything on their desktops. In addition, managers and supervisors require access to all components on their desktops and laptops. The domain has OUs as follows: Employees, which is located at the top of the OU tree; and Supervisors, Managers, Administrators, Research, Financial, Legal, Sales, and Marketing OUs configured as children of the Employees OU. Which two of the following are some of the Active Directory containers to which Harry should link the Restrictions GPO?

   - ○ **A.** The Charlotte site
   - ○ **B.** The domain
   - ● **C.** The Legal OU
   - ○ **D.** The Employees OU
   - ● **E.** The Marketing OU

2. Debbie is the systems administrator for a company that operates an AD DS forest containing three domains. There are six sites, each of which represents a city where the company does business. Each site contains at least two domains and several OUs within each domain, and each site is configured with a proxy server that all users are expected to access the Internet through.

   Debbie has created GPOs that set the proxy configuration for all computers in the forest, including portable computers that traveling users carry to different offices in the course of their job duties. How should she configure this GPO to ensure that users always access the Internet by means of the proxy server in the office where they are located?

   - ● **A.** She should link each GPO to its site and specify the Enforced option.
   - ○ **B.** She should link each GPO to its site and do nothing else.
   - ○ **C.** She should link each GPO to the OUs located in its site and specify the Block Inheritance option.
   - ○ **D.** She should link each GPO to the domains located in its site and specify the Block Inheritance option.
   - ○ **E.** She should link each GPO to the domains located in its site and do nothing else.

3. Ryan is the network administrator for a retail camera outlet, which has stores in six locations across the Chicago metropolitan area. Each store has computers that are available to customers for ordering digital prints. The camera outlet operates a single AD DS domain with sites representing each store and five OUs: Administration, Operations, Sales, Support, and Executive. All computers that are accessible to customers are located in the Operations OU.

Ryan has configured the following settings in several GPOs:

▶ The domain GPO specifies that the wallpaper should be blue. This GPO is configured with the <u>Enforce option.</u>

▶ The Downtown site specifies that the wallpaper should be red.

▶ The Sales OU specifies that the wallpaper should be purple.

▶ The Operations OU specifies that the wallpaper should be green. The OU is configured with the Block Inheritance option.

When a user logs on to a computer in the Downtown site to order prints, what color will the wallpaper be?

● **A.** Blue

○ **B.** Red

○ **C.** Purple

○ **D.** Green

4. Greg is responsible for administering GPOs in a company that operates a single domain AD DS network. All servers run Windows Server 2008, and all client computers run either Windows XP Professional or Windows Vista Business. The company employs 75 data entry clerks and 6 data entry supervisors whose user accounts are located in the Data Entry OU. The data entry clerks must receive restricted desktops that allow them to perform only the functions that are necessary to do their jobs. Greg configures a GPO that contains the required restrictions and links it to the Data Entry OU. There are also several companywide policy settings configured in the Default Domain Policy GPO that all users in the company must receive.

Later, the data entry supervisors complain that the restricted desktops prevent them from performing several critical job functions that are not required of the data entry clerks. What should Greg do to ensure that the data entry supervisors do not receive the restricted desktops, with the least amount of administrative effort?

○ **A.** In the Data Entry OU, create a child OU, and move the supervisor's user accounts there. Then configure the child OU with the Block Inheritance option.

○ **B.** In the Data Entry OU, create a child OU, and move the supervisor's user accounts there. Configure another GPO linked to the child OU, in which all desktop restriction policies applied to the data entry clerks are set to Not Configured, and specify Enforced for this GPO.

● **C.** In the Data Entry OU, create a global security group named Supervisors and add the supervisors' user accounts to this group. Then assign the Supervisors group the Deny—Apply Group Policy permission to the GPO that restricts the data entry clerks' desktops.

○ **D.** In the Data Entry OU, create a global security group named Supervisors, and add the supervisors' user accounts to this group. Configure another GPO in which all desktop restriction policies are set to Not Configured, and assign the Supervisors group the Allow—Apply Group Policy permission to the second GPO.

5. You are the network administrator for a municipal library system, which operates a single domain AD DS network. Each branch library has a series of computers that library patrons use for locating books and other information. All client computer accounts for the domain are located in a single OU, including those in staff offices.

Occasionally, a staff member uses one of these computers to access protected information from her domain user account. You must ensure that the computer settings for these computers take precedence over the user settings specified in Group Policy. However, when applying Group Policy, you notice that the user settings override the computer settings. What should you do?

○ **A.** Enable the loopback processing mode with the merge option.

● **B.** Enable the loopback processing mode with the replace option.

○ **C.** Disable the computer settings for the affected GPO.

○ **D.** Disable the user settings for the affected GPO.

6. Maria is the domain administrator for a company that operates an AD DS domain with sites that span 20 cities in the United States, Canada, and Mexico. All client computers run either Windows Vista Business or Windows Vista Ultimate. Maria has created ADMX files that define Registry-based policy settings that are to be applied to client computers in all sites of the domain.

Maria needs to create custom ADMX files that support French and Spanish language users in offices where these languages are used. She also needs to ensure that the custom ADMX files are available to all administrators in the domain. What should she do?

○ **A.** Create ADMX files and copy them to the %systemroot%\sysvol\ domain\policies\PolicyDefinitions folder on the domain controller.

○ **B.** Create ADMX files and copy them to the %systemroot%\sysvol\ domain\policies\PolicyDefinitions folder on each client computer.

● **C.** Create ADML files and copy them to the %systemroot%\sysvol\
domain\policies\PolicyDefinitions*[MUIculture]* folder on the domain
controller.

○ **D.** Create ADML files and copy them to the %systemroot%\sysvol\
domain\policies\PolicyDefinitions*[MUIculture]* folder on each client computer.

7. George is responsible for creating and managing GPOs for a company that operates
an AD DS forest with three domains, each of which has 10 or more OUs representing
different work groups in the company. All servers run Windows Server 2008, and client
computers run either Windows XP or Windows Vista. The functional level of the forest
is Windows Server 2008.

George needs to create a series of similar GPOs that will be linked to various OUs in
the forest. What should he do to accomplish this task with the least amount of
administrative effort?

○ **A.** Create a Starter GPO and link it to the required OUs. Then edit this GPO to
introduce OU-specific settings.

● **B.** Create a Starter GPO and copy it to each domain. Then use the Starter
GPO to create GPOs in the required OUs, and edit these GPOs to introduce
OU-specific settings.

○ **C.** Create one GPO and link it to all OUs that require its settings. Then edit the
GPO in each OU to introduce OU-specific settings.

○ **D.** Create a new GPO in each OU that contains the required settings for its OU.

8. Tricia is a junior administrator for a large enterprise corporation whose Active Directory
network contains two domains, seven sites, and 11 OUs, each of which represents a
different company department. The IT manager has assigned Tricia the responsibility
of administering the Design OU and has provided her with Full Control permission for
this OU.

Tricia needs to configure a GPO for deployment of a specialized design application to
all employees in the Design department of each of the company's offices. These
employees should have access to the application at all times, regardless of which
department they are accessing the application from. The application is not to be available to employees of other departments, even if they are working from computers
located in the Design department.

Which of the following steps should Tricia take to deploy this application?

● **A.** She should create a GPO that is linked to the Design OU. In this GPO, she
should add a Windows Installer package for the application under the User
Configuration\Policies\Software Settings\ Software Installation node. On the
Deploy Software dialog box, she should select Assigned.

○ **B.** She should create a GPO that is linked to the Design OU. In this GPO, she should add a Windows Installer package for the application under the Computer Configuration\Policies\Software Settings\Software Installation node. On the Deploy Software dialog box, she should select Assigned.

○ **C.** She should create a GPO that is linked to the Design OU. In this GPO, she should add a Windows Installer package for the application under the User Configuration\Policies\Software Settings\ Software Installation node. On the Deploy Software dialog box, she should select Published.

○ **D.** She should create a GPO that is linked to the Design OU. In this GPO, she should add a Windows Installer package for the application under the Computer Configuration\Policies\Software Settings\Software Installation node. On the Deploy Software dialog box, she should select Published.

9. David is responsible for software deployment throughout his company, which operates an AD DS domain with eight OUs that represent administrative divisions in the company. Employees frequently are moved between administrative divisions, and their work responsibilities and software needs change when this happens. Furthermore, they should not have access to software that they no longer need after a move.

When employees move, David must ensure that these requirements are met. What should he do?

○ **A.** In the Upgrades tab of the Software Installation Properties dialog box, select the Required Upgrade for Existing Packages check box.

○ **B.** In the General tab of the Software Installation Properties dialog box, select the Display the Deploy Software dialog box.

● **C.** In the Advanced tab of the Software Installation Properties dialog box, select the Uninstall the Applications When They Fall Out of the Scope of Management check box.

○ **D.** In the Delegation tab of the Properties for the associated GPOs, ensure that the Apply Group Policy permission is granted only to those security groups that require access to the applications.

10. Arlene is responsible for managing GPOs in a company that operates an AD DS network consisting of a single domain. Member servers in the domain have computer accounts in an OU named Member Servers. Client computers have computer accounts in 12 OUs organized according to departments. Users have user accounts in an OU named CorpUsers.

Company policy states that all users are to have Microsoft Word available on their computers, but that Word is not to be installed on domain controllers or member servers. What should Arlene do to accomplish this requirement without affecting any other policies or settings?

○ **A.** Create a GPO configured with Word listed in the User Configuration\ Policies\Software Settings node. Link this GPO to the domain, and configure the Domain Controllers OU and the Member Servers OU with the Block Inheritance option.

○ **B.** Create a GPO configured with Word listed in the User Configuration\ Policies\Software Settings node. Link this GPO to the domain, and configure the Deny—Apply Group Policy setting for all member server and domain controller computer accounts.

○ **C.** Create a GPO configured with Word listed in the Computer Configuration\ Policies\Software Settings node. Link this GPO to the domain, and configure the Domain Controllers OU and the Member Servers OU with the Block Inheritance option.

● **D.** Create a GPO configured with Word listed in the Computer Configuration\ Policies\Software Settings node. Link this GPO to the domain, and configure the Deny—Apply Group Policy setting for all member server and domain controller computer accounts.

11. Bob is responsible for software deployment and maintenance for his company, which operates an AD DS network consisting of a single domain. The company is planning to upgrade all users from Microsoft Office 2003 to Office 2007, and Bob must ensure that employees are unable to use Office 2003. In addition, he must ensure that users retain their user files such as customized spell check dictionaries after the upgrade.

What should Bob do to accomplish these objectives? (Each correct answer represents part of the solution. Choose two answers.)

○ **A.** Select the Advanced Deployment option from the Deploy Software dialog box.

● **B.** Select the Required Upgrade for Existing Package option from the Add Upgrade Package dialog box.

○ **C.** Select the Uninstall the Existing Package, Then Install the Upgrade Package option from the Add Upgrade Package dialog box.

● **D.** Select the Package Can Upgrade over the Existing Package option from the Add Upgrade Package dialog box.

○ **E.** Select the Immediately Uninstall the Software from Users and Computers option from the Remove Software dialog box.

12. Ellen is responsible for configuring and maintaining Group Policy in her company's AD DS domain. The domain contains computers running Windows XP Professional, Windows Vista Business, Windows Server 2003, and Windows Server 2008. There are eight OUs representing company departments, all of which have multiple GPOs linked to them.

    Because of an organizational change, Ellen needs to move the Design OU under the Engineering OU. She needs to find out which objects in the Design OU are adversely affected by GPOs linked to the Engineering OU. She must achieve this goal without disruption to users. Which of the following should she do?

    ○ **A.** Use the Group Policy Modeling Wizard for the Engineering OU. Choose the Design OU to simulate policy settings.

    ○ **B.** Use the Group Policy Results Wizard for the Engineering OU. Choose the Design OU to simulate policy settings.

    ○ **C.** Use the Group Policy Modeling Wizard for the Design OU. Choose the Engineering OU to simulate policy settings.

    ○ **D.** Use the Group Policy Results Wizard for the Design OU. Choose the Engineering OU to simulate policy settings.

Answers to *Exam Cram* Questions

1. **C, E.** Harry should link the Restrictions GPO to the Research, Financial, Legal, Sales, and Marketing OUs to accomplish the objectives of this question. These OUs include the accounts of all employees who should receive the restrictions. If Harry were to link the GPO to the Charlotte site, all users at that site would receive the policy, including administrators, managers, and supervisors who are located at that site. Users at other sites would not receive the policy. Therefore, answer A is incorrect. Harry should not link the GPO to either the domain or the Employees OU because all employees, including administrators, managers, and supervisors, would receive the restrictions. Therefore, answers B and D are incorrect.

2. **A.** Debbie should link each GPO to its site and specify the Enforced option. Linking the GPOs to their sites ensures that they always apply to computers located in that site. She must specify the Enforced option, or GPOs linked to domains or OUs could apply conflicting settings that are not desirable; consequently, answer B is incorrect. Linking the GPOs to any other container would produce mixed results because the scenario specifies that every site includes two or more domains and several OUs, so answers C, D, and E are incorrect.

3. **A.** In this case, the wallpaper will be blue. The normal sequence of processing GPOs is local, site, domain, OU (LSDOU), which means that without further configuration, the OU-based policy would prevail. By specifying the Enforced option in the domain-based GPO, conflicting policies applied at the OU level will not apply; consequently, the

wallpaper will be blue. Site-based policies are overwritten by domain- and OU-based policies unless they are enforced, so the wallpaper will not be red; therefore, answer B is incorrect. The computer does not belong to the Sales OU, so the wallpaper will never be purple; therefore, answer C is incorrect. When both Block Inheritance and Enforced are applied at the same time, the Enforced setting takes precedence, so answer D is incorrect.

4. **C.** By assigning the Supervisors group the Deny—Apply Group Policy permission to the GPO that restricts the data entry clerks' desktops, Greg can prevent the data entry supervisors from receiving the restricted desktop settings while ensuring that the data entry clerks still receive these settings and that the supervisors receive the settings in the Default Domain Policy GPO. If Greg were to place the supervisors in a child OU and enable the Block Inheritance option, the supervisors would not receive the restricted desktop settings, but they also would not receive the settings in the Default Domain Policy GPO, so answer A is incorrect. If he were to configure a second GPO linked to the child OU, in which all desktop restriction policies applied to the data entry clerks were set to Not Configured, and he specified Enforced for this GPO, the supervisors would still receive the restricted desktops, so answer B is incorrect. If he were to have configured the desktop restriction policies set to Disabled in the second GPO, this would accomplish the objective of this scenario, but such a solution takes more administrative effort and is more subject to error than the recommended solution of filtering the first GPO. Therefore, answer D is incorrect.

5. **B.** You should enable the loopback processing mode with the replace option. This option ensures that the user-based settings that would normally be applied are disregarded. If you were to use the merge option, this would merge both the user and computer settings, resulting in a combined set of policies, so answer A is incorrect. Disabling the computer settings would enable library patrons to access restricted information, so answer C is incorrect. Disabling the user settings would affect not just the public computers but also those in the staff offices, so answer D is incorrect.

6. **C.** Maria should create ADML files and copy them to the %systemroot%\sysvol\ domain\policies\PolicyDefinitions*[MUIculture]* folder on the domain controller. ADML files are language-specific policy definition files that enable administrators to apply the policies in the localized languages. In this case, *[MUIculture]* would be FR-CA for French-language files and ES for Spanish-language files. Maria would not use ADMX files because these are not language-specific, so answer A is incorrect. She does not need to copy these files to every client computer that requires them, because they are distributed from domain controllers, so answers B and D are incorrect.

7. **B.** George can use a Starter GPO to create the similar GPOs required by this scenario. This is a set of preconfigured Administrative Template policy settings, including comments, which he can use for ease of creating new GPOs. He would then right-click each OU in turn and choose New GPO, and in the New GPO dialog box, he would specify the Starter GPO as a starting point for creating the required GPO. He cannot link the Starter GPO to the required OUs, so answer A is incorrect. Creating one GPO

and linking it to all OUs would result in the same GPO being applied to each OU, so answer C is incorrect. George could create a new GPO in each OU that contains the required settings for its OU, but this would take more administrative effort, so answer D is incorrect.

8. **A.** Tricia needs to assign the software package to users in the Design OU because of the requirement for it to be available to all employees in this department, regardless of the computer to which they log on, and because it is not to be available to employees of other departments, even if they log on to computers in the Design department. If Tricia were to assign or publish the software package to computers, it would not be available to Design employees if they logged on to computers in other departments, and it would be available to users logging on to computers in the Design department. Therefore, answers B and C are incorrect. It is not possible to publish software to computers, so answer D is incorrect.

9. **C.** By selecting the Uninstall the Applications When They Fall Out of the Scope of Management check box, David can ensure that applications are removed when a user is moved from one administrative division (OU) to another. This check box is found on the Advanced tab of the Software Installation Properties dialog box for all software, and also on the Deployment tab of an individual application's Properties dialog box. The Required Upgrade for Existing Packages check box is used to ensure that users receive an upgrade of an older software package; it does not remove packages that are no longer required, so answer A is incorrect. The Display the Deploy Software dialog box option enables David to select the assigned or published option for individual applications when adding new software packages; it does not remove applications that are no longer required, so answer B is incorrect. The Apply Group Policy permission ensures that GPOs are properly applied but does not remove applications that are no longer required; therefore, answer D is incorrect.

10. **D.** Because the domain includes a large number of OUs, it makes more sense to apply the policy at the domain level rather than linking it to the individual OUs. Arlene can ensure that the GPO does not apply to domain controllers and member servers by denying access to the GPO for their computer accounts. If she were to configure the policy in the User Configuration section, it would not stop Word from being installed on the servers because all users require Word, including administrative users who log on to these servers; therefore, answers A and B are incorrect. If Arlene were to use the Block Inheritance option, other policy settings could be affected, so answers A and C are incorrect.

11. **B, D.** By selecting the Required Upgrade for Existing Packages check box on the Upgrades tab of the package's Properties dialog box, Bob ensures that the upgrade is mandatory; in other words, Office 2003 is automatically upgraded to Office 2007 without the users having an option. By selecting the Package Can Upgrade over the Existing Package option, Bob ensures that the user's application preferences, document type associations, and so on are retained. The Advanced Deployment option is used for adding modifications to existing packages, not for configuring upgrades, so answer A is incorrect. The Uninstall the Existing Package, Then Install the Upgrade

Package option totally removes all references to the previous version, including components such as spell check dictionaries, so answer C is incorrect. The Immediately Uninstall the Software from Users and Computers option would also remove components such as spell check dictionaries, so answer E is incorrect.

12. **C.** Ellen should use the Group Policy Modeling Wizard for the Design OU. She should choose the Engineering OU to simulate policy settings. This wizard processes an RSoP planning mode query, which tests potential policy settings prior to actually putting them into production. Ellen needs to test the settings for the Design OU, not the Engineering OU, so answer A is incorrect. She would use the Group Policy Results Wizard to perform an RSoP logging mode query, which tests the application of current policy settings, not to test policy settings that have not yet been applied. Therefore, answers B and D are incorrect.

CHAPTER 7

Group Policy and Active Directory Security

Terms You'll Need to Understand

- ✓ Account lockout
- ✓ Account policies
- ✓ Auditing
- ✓ Auditpol.exe
- ✓ Fine-grained password policies
- ✓ Password settings objects (PSO)

Concepts/Techniques You'll Need to Master

- ✓ Managing security configurations
- ✓ Configuring account policies
- ✓ Configuring fine-grained password policies
- ✓ Using Group Policy to configure auditing policies
- ✓ Using Auditpol.exe to configure auditing policies

You have seen how Group Policy works and how to set up Group Policy objects (GPO) to configure various aspects of the Windows computing environment. You have also learned about Group Policy succession and how you can modify the sequence in which GPOs are applied and its effect when policy settings conflict with one another. You have also read about the use of Group Policy to maintain a consistent software environment, where users and computers receive a well-regulated set of software applications that can be modified and upgraded as required, as well as the removal of outdated software. This chapter focuses on the use of Group Policy to create and enforce a secure computing environment that protects your computers and data from whatever the bad guys might attempt to throw at you.

Use of Group Policy to Configure Security

You can use Group Policy to manage security settings quite effectively on a Windows Server 2008 network. An enhanced range of security options is available, with settings designed for both user and computer configuration. Microsoft continues to expand the available range of security policies, compared to those included with previous versions of Windows Server. The most significant addition to security settings in Windows Server 2008 is that of fine-grained password policies, which enable you to set different password policies for different portions of your AD DS domain.

Group Policy in Windows Server 2008 includes a large range of security options designed for both user and computer configuration. As you can see in Figure 7.1, most of these security settings are applied to the Computer Configuration section in the Group Policy Management Editor. This section is mainly concerned with account policies.

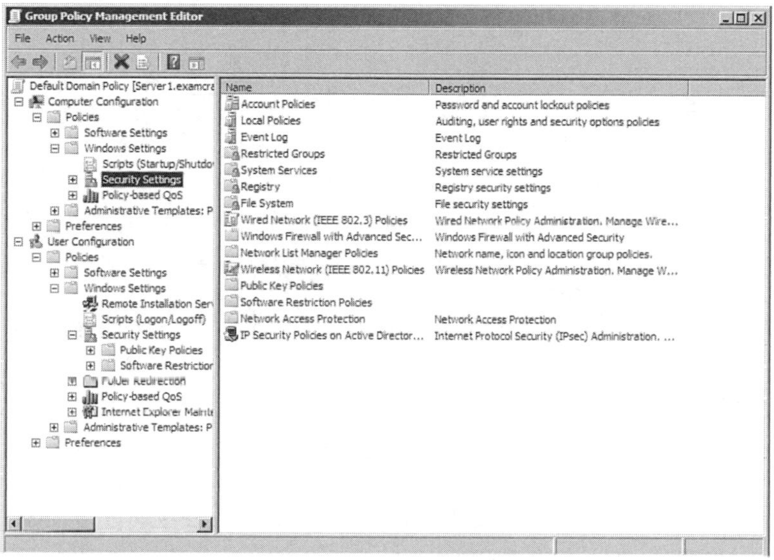

FIGURE 7.1 Group Policy includes both computer- and user-based security settings.

Configuring Account Policies

The *Account Policies* node contains settings related to user accounts, including the password policy, account lockout policy, and Kerberos policy. Before looking at the new Windows Server 2008 feature of fine-grained password policies, this section examines these policies and how to configure them, in general. It briefly introduces each of these concepts in the following sections.

Domain Password Policies

You can use domain-based Group Policy to configure password policy settings that help to protect users of Windows 2000/XP/Vista client computers. The options available in Windows Server 2008 are similar to those introduced in Windows 2000 and continued in Windows Server 2003. Password policies are generally intended to make passwords more difficult for intruders to discover. Figure 7.2 shows the available password policies and their default settings.

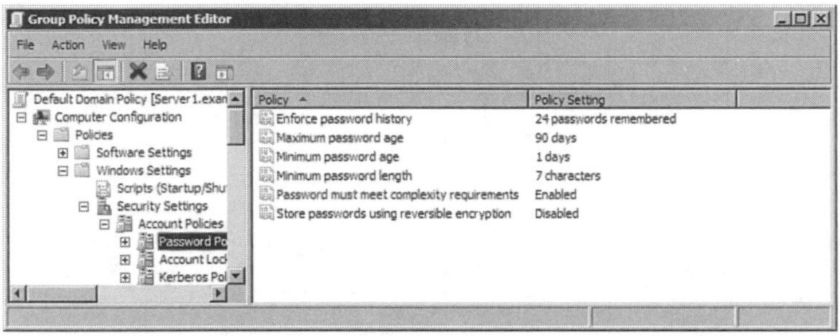

FIGURE 7.2 Windows Server 2008 provides default values for the available password policies.

The following password policy settings are available:

▶ **Enforce Password History**—Determines the number of passwords remembered by AD DS for each user. Values range from 0 to 24. A user cannot reuse a password retained in the history list. A value of 0 means that no password history is retained and a user can reuse passwords at will. Windows Server 2008 continues with the default of 24 established with Windows Server 2003 SP1.

▶ **Maximum Password Age**—Determines the number of days that a user can use a password before being required to specify a new one. Values range from 0 to 999. A value of 0 means that a user is never required to change his password. The default is 90 days.

▶ **Minimum Password Age**—Determines the minimum number of days a password must be used before it can be changed. Values range from 0 to 999 days and must be less than the maximum password age. A value of 0 allows the user to immediately change a new password. This value would allow a user to cycle through an entire history list of passwords in a short time—in other words, repeatedly changing a password so he could reuse his old password. This obviously defeats the purpose of enforcing password history. The default is 1 day.

▶ **Minimum Password Length**—Determines the minimum number of characters that can make up a password. Values range from 0 to 14. A value of 0 permits a blank password. Use a setting of 10 or higher for increased security. The default is 7 characters.

▶ **Password Must Meet Complexity Requirements**—Stipulates that a password must meet complexity criteria, as follows: The password cannot contain the user account name or full name, or parts of the name that exceed two consecutive characters. It must contain at least three of the following four items:

- ▶ English lowercase letters

- ▶ English uppercase letters

- ▶ Numerals

- ▶ Nonalphanumeric characters, such as $; [ ] { } ! .

▶ **Store Passwords Using Reversible Encryption**—Determines the level of encryption used by Windows Server 2008 for storing passwords. Enabling this option reduces security because it stores passwords in a format that is essentially the same as plain text. This option is disabled by default. You should enable this policy only if needed for clients who cannot use normal encryption, such as those using Challenge Handshake Authentication Protocol (CHAP) authentication or Internet Information Services (IIS) Digest Authentication.

To configure these policies, expand the Computer Configuration node of the appropriate GPO, as shown in Figure 7.2. Right-click the desired policy and choose Properties. Then configure the appropriate value and click OK. Each policy setting also has an Explain tab that provides additional information on the policy setting and its purpose.

> **EXAM ALERT**
>
> Password policies are unique in that they apply only when configured in a domain-based GPO. Although they appear in other GPOs, any configuration in GPOs linked to other containers is ignored.

Account Lockout

A cracked user account password jeopardizes the security of the entire network. The *account lockout* policy is designed to lock an account out of the computer if a user (or intruder attempting to crack the network) enters an incorrect password a specified number of times, thereby limiting the effectiveness of dictionary-based password crackers. The account lockout policy contains the following settings:

▶ **Account Lockout Duration**—Specifies the number of minutes that an account remains locked out. Every account except for the default Administrator account can be locked out in this manner. You can set this value from 0 to 99999 minutes, or about 69.4 days. A value of 0 means that accounts that have exceeded the specified number of failed logon attempts are locked out indefinitely until an administrator unlocks the account.

▶ **Account Lockout Threshold**—Specifies the number of failed logon attempts that can occur before the account is locked out. You can set this value from 0 to 999 failed attempts. A value of 0 means that the account will never be locked out. Best practices recommend that you should never configure a setting of 0 here.

▶ **Reset Account Lockout Counter After**—Specifies the number of minutes to wait after which the account lockout counter is reset to 0. You can set this value from 1 to 99999.

When you configure this policy, Windows Server 2008 sets default values for the account lockout settings. To configure an account lockout policy, right-click any of the three values and choose Properties, and then accept the default provided or specify a value of your choice. As shown in Figure 7.3, Windows suggests default values for the other two policy settings. Click OK to define the policy settings and set these defaults. If you want to change the other settings, right-click the appropriate settings and choose Properties, and then enter the desired value.

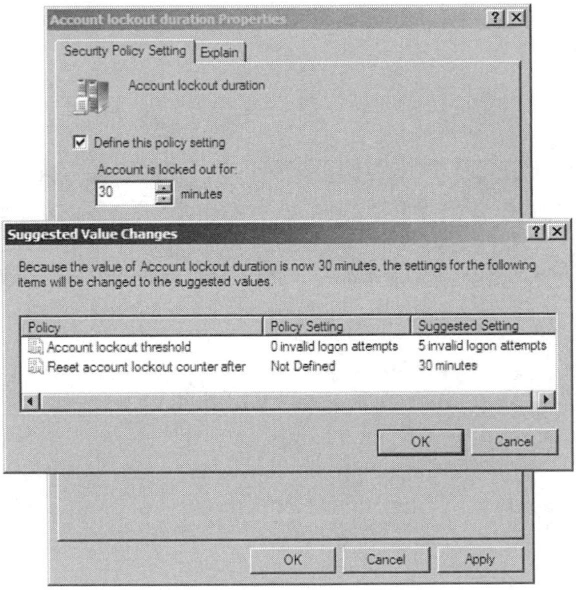

FIGURE 7.3 When you define an account lockout policy, Windows suggests defaults for the other two lockout policy settings.

Unlocking an Account

When a user account is locked out because of too many incorrect attempts at entering a password, it is simple for an administrator or user who is delegated the task to unlock it. Right-click the user account in Active Directory Users and

Computers and choose Properties. On the Account tab of the user's Properties dialog box, the Unlock Account check box should display a message stating `This account is currently locked out on this Active Directory Domain Controller`. Select the check box, and then click OK or Apply.

Kerberos Policy

The Kerberos Policy subnode contains settings that enforce use logon restrictions according to validation requests made to the Kerberos Key Distribution Center (KDC) against the user rights policy of the user account. By default, the policies in this section are enabled. They define the maximum lifetime for user and service tickets as well as the maximum tolerance for computer clock synchronization.

> **CAUTION**
>
> Kerberos policies generally do not appear on Exam 70-640. However, you should be aware of the Maximum Tolerance for Computer Clock Synchronization policy setting. This setting specifies the maximum time difference in minutes between the domain controller clock and that on a client computer attempting authentication. If the clocks differ by more than the specified amount (five minutes by default), authentication fails.

Fine-Grained Password Policies

Active Directory domains in Windows 2000 and Windows Server 2003 permitted only a single password and account lockout policy, defined at the domain level. If an organization wanted different password policy settings for a specified group of users, an administrator had to create a new domain or use a third-party custom password filter. Windows Server 2008 introduces the concept of *fine-grained password policies*, which enable you to apply granular password and account lockout policy settings to different sets of users within the same domain. For example, you can apply stricter policy settings to accounts associated with users who have access to classified or restricted information, such as legal and product research departments. At the same time, you can maintain more relaxed settings for accounts of other users where these types of information are not available.

To configure a fine-grained password policy, you must be a member of the Domain Admins group, and the domain functional level must be set to Windows Server 2008. You can also delegate control of the task to other users if required.

Fine-grained password policies are stored in AD DS by means of two new object classes that are defined in the schema:

▶ **Password Settings Container**—Created by default under the domain's System container, the Password Settings Container stores the *password settings objects (PSO)* for the domain.

▶ **Password Settings Object**—Holds attributes for all the password policy and account lockout policy settings, as defined earlier in this section. It also contains a multivalued link attribute that links the PSO to users or groups, and an integer precedence value that resolves conflicts if multiple PSOs are applied to the same user or group.

You can link a PSO to a user, global security group, or InetOrgPerson object that is in the same domain. Note that if you link a PSO to a distribution group or a group with a different scope, the PSO is ignored. If multiple PSOs are linked to a single user or group because of membership in multiple groups, only one PSO can be applied; settings cannot be merged between PSOs.

> **EXAM ALERT**
>
> Remember the prerequisites for configuring and applying fine-grained password policies. You must be a member of the Domain Admins group, the domain functional level must be set to Windows Server 2008, and the policies must be applied to the users or global security groups that need them.

Password Settings Precedence

If more than one PSO is linked to a user or group, the PSO that applies is determined by the precedence attribute, which is associated with each PSO and has an integer value of 1 or greater. The lower the precedence attribute, the higher the priority of a given PSO; for example, a PSO with a precedence value of 3 overrides another PSO with a precedence value of 5.

The following rules determine the resultant PSO that is applied to a user or group when multiple PSOs are present:

▶ If a PSO is directly linked to the user object, it prevails. Should more than one PSO be linked directly to the user, the PSO with the lowest precedence value prevails, and a warning message is logged to the event log.

▶ If no PSO is linked directly to the user object, all PSOs applied to the user according to membership in global security groups are evaluated, and the PSO with the lowest precedence value prevails. If more than one PSO with the same precedence value is present, the PSO that is obtained first is used.

> ► If no PSO is linked to either the user object or any global security groups it is a member of, the settings in the Default Domain Policy GPO are applied.

NOTE

You cannot apply a PSO directly to an organizational unit (OU). If you want to apply consistent password settings to all users in an OU, you should add these users to a global security group and apply the PSO to this group. If you move a user from one OU to another with different password security needs, you must update this user's group membership to reflect the change.

TIP

It is recommended that you specify a unique precedence value for each PSO. This simplifies troubleshooting of password precedence settings problems. But remember that setting a PSO for a user means this PSO takes precedence over PSOs linked to groups, regardless of their precedence setting.

Configuring Fine-Grained Password Policies

As already stated, you must be a member of the Domain Admins group to create and manage PSOs. You can use the ADSI Edit utility to configure a fine-grained password policy. This involves specifying values for all the Password Policy and Account Lockout Policy settings described earlier in this chapter. This tool was introduced in Chapter 4, "Configuring Additional Active Directory Roles." Perform the following steps:

1. Click Start, Run, type **adsiedit.msc**, and then press Enter.

2. If the domain name is not visible in the console tree, right-click ADSI Edit and choose Connect To. If Default Naming Context and your domain name are visible in the Connection Settings dialog box, accept them. Otherwise, type the fully qualified domain name (FQDN) of your domain. Then click OK.

3. Expand your domain name to locate the CN=System container, and then expand this container to locate the CN=Password Settings Container object.

4. Select this container to display any PSOs that are configured in the domain in the Details pane.

5. Right-click this container and choose New, Object. This starts a wizard that enables you to define your PSO.

6. In the Create Object dialog box, the `msDS-PasswordSettings` object class is the only available class. Ensure that it is selected, and then click Next.

7. Provide a descriptive value for your PSO, as shown in Figure 7.4, and then click Next.

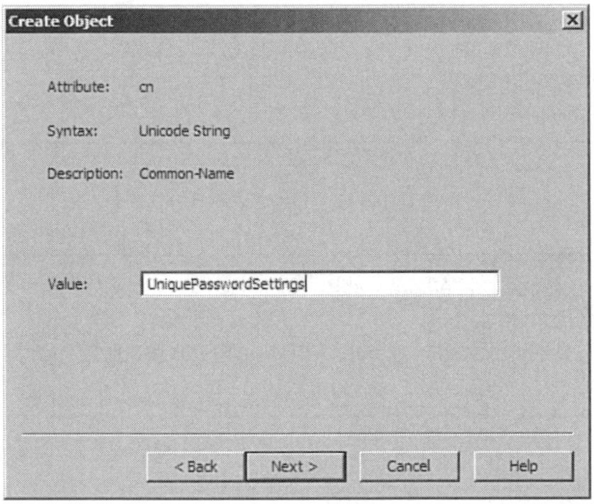

FIGURE 7.4 Provide a descriptive value that helps you to identify the PSO later.

8. Type a value for the Password Settings Precedence, and then click Next.

9. For Password Reversible Encryption Status for User Accounts, type **False** unless you need reversible encryption, and then click Next.

10. Type a value for the password history length, and then click Next.

11. To require password complexity, type **True**, and then click Next.

12. Specify a minimum password length, and then click Next.

13. For the Minimum Password Age for User Accounts value, type a value in the format *days:hours:minutes:seconds* (for example, **1:00:00:00**), and then click Next.

14. Type a value for Maximum Password Age for User Accounts in the same format, and then click Next.

15. Type a value for the lockout threshold (number of incorrect passwords before account locks out), and then click Next.

16. Type a value for the lockout observation window (time for resetting lockout counter) in the same format as already described (for example, **00:00:30:00** for 30 minutes), and then click Next.

17. Type a value for the lockout duration in the same format, and then click Next.

18. If you want to define additional optional attributes, click More Attributes. Otherwise, click Finish to complete the creation of the PSO.

To apply the PSO to a user or group, proceed as follows:

1. Open Active Directory Users and Computers and select Advanced Features under the View menu.

2. In the console tree, expand System, and then select Password Settings Container. This displays the PSO in the Details pane.

3. Right-click the PSO and choose Properties.

4. Select the Attribute Editor tab. As shown in Figure 7.5, this tab displays the values of all attributes that have been configured for the PSO, including those set when you created the PSO.

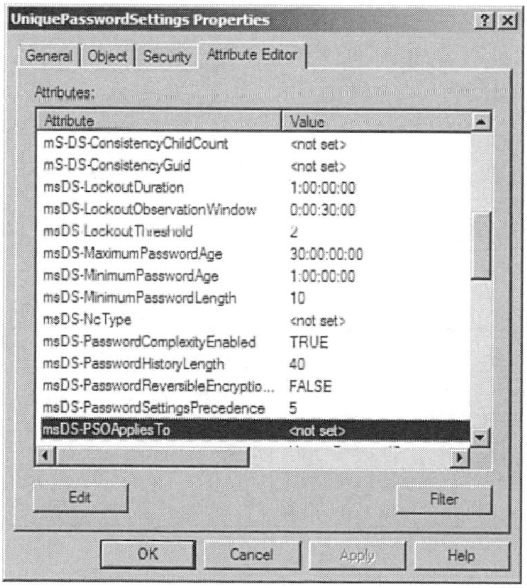

FIGURE 7.5 The Attribute Editor tab of the PSO's Properties dialog box includes the values of the password and lockout attributes that you configured.

5. Scroll to select the msDS-PSOAppliesTo attribute, and then click Edit.

6. On the Multi-valued Distinguished Name With Security Principal Editor dialog box that displays, click Add Windows Account, type the user or group name, and then click OK. As shown in Figure 7.6, the name you added is displayed in this dialog box. You can also add a user or group with its LDAP distinguished name (DN) by clicking the Add DN button.

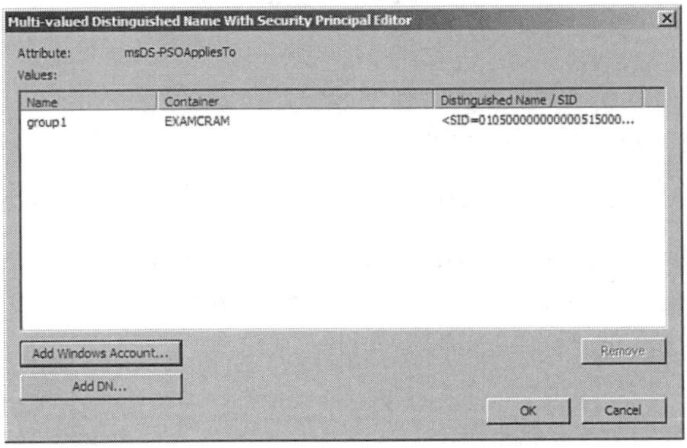

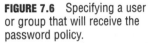

FIGURE 7.6 Specifying a user or group that will receive the password policy.

7. Click OK. The security identifier (SID) of the user or group appears in the Value column of the Attribute Editor tab. You can repeat this process as many times as needed to link the PSO to additional users or groups.

8. Click OK to close the PSO's Properties dialog box.

NOTE

You can also use the ldifde utility to create a PSO and specify users or groups to which the PSO can apply. Chapter 5, "Active Directory Objects and Trusts," introduced this utility. Refer to "Step-by-Step Guide for Fine-Grained Password and Account Lockout Policy Configuration" in Appendix A, "Need to Know More?" and select the links provided for steps 1 and 2 for additional details.

Managing Fine-Grained Password Policies

You can perform several additional managerial tasks on your PSO, as follows:

▶ **Editing policy settings**—As described in the previous section, access the Attribute Editor tab of the PSO's Properties dialog box. Select the policy setting to be edited and click Edit. Then specify the desired value in the Editor dialog box that appears.

▶ **Modify the PSO's precedence value**—In the Attribute Editor tab of the PSO's Properties dialog box, select the `msDS-PasswordSettingsPrecedence` value, click Edit, and then specify the desired value in the Integer Attribute Editor dialog box that appears.

▶ **Delete the PSO**—If you no longer need the PSO, select it in the Details pane of Active Directory Users and Computers and press the Delete key (or right-click it and choose Delete). Click Yes in the confirmation message box that appears. The policy settings for any users or groups employing this PSO revert to the settings in a lower-priority PSO or to the Default Domain Policy GPO if no other PSO exists.

Viewing the Resultant PSO

As already stated, a PSO configured for the user takes priority over one that is configured for a group to which the user belongs, and group-based PSOs are applied according to the precedence value. If you have configured a large number of PSOs, troubleshooting their application can become problematic. To facilitate this process, you can view which PSO is applying to a user or group. Proceed as follows:

1. In Active Directory Users and Computers, ensure that Advanced Features is selected.

2. Select the Users container or the OU of the desired user account to display the user account in the Details pane.

3. Right-click the user account and choose Properties.

4. Select the Attribute Editor tab, and then click Filter. In the options list that appears, ensure that Show Attributes/Optional and Show Read-Only Attributes/System-Only are checked.

5. Scroll the attribute list to locate `msDS-ResultantPSO`. The value of this attribute displays the DN of the effective PSO, as shown in Figure 7.7. If it displays `<not set>`, the password settings in the Default Domain Policy GPO are in effect for this account. Click View to see the complete DN.

For additional information on fine-grained password policies, including some recommended scenarios for applying these policies, refer to "Step-by-Step Guide for Fine-Grained Password and Account Lockout Policy Configuration" in Appendix A. Links in this appendix also provide additional information on the available attributes and their permitted values.

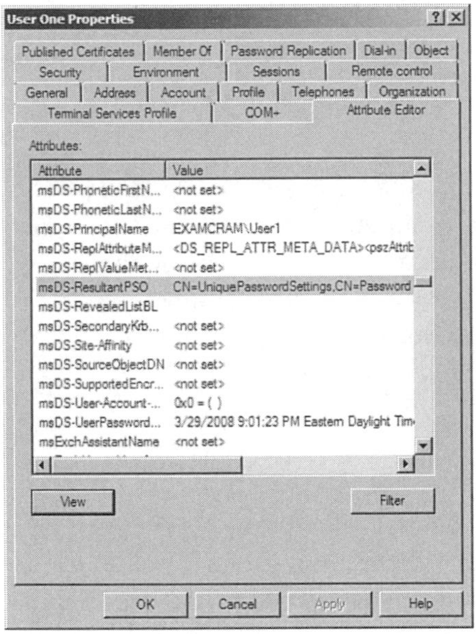

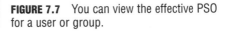

FIGURE 7.7 You can view the effective PSO for a user or group.

Security Options

Besides account policies, the Security Settings subnode of Computer Configuration includes a large range of additional security-related policy settings. These settings are summarized here:

▶ **Local Policies**—Includes audit policies, discussed later in this chapter, and user rights assignment, discussed in Chapter 6, "Configuring and Troubleshooting Group Policy." The Security Options subnode within this node includes a large set of policy options, as shown in Figure 7.8, that are important in controlling security aspects of the computers to which the GPO applies. Several of the more important options that you should be familiar with are as follows:

  ▸ **Accounts: Rename Administrator Account**—This option renames the default administrator account to a value you specify. Intruders cannot simply look for "Administrator" when attempting to crack your network.

  ▸ **Interactive Logon: Do Not Display Last User Name**—Enable this option to prevent the username of the last logged-on user from appearing in the Logon dialog box, thus preventing another individual from seeing a username. This can also reduce lockouts.

▶ **Interactive Logon: Do Not Require CTRL+ALT+DEL**—When enabled, a user is not required to press Ctrl+Alt+Delete to obtain the Logon dialog box. Disable this policy in a secure environment to require the use of this key combination. Its use prevents rogue programs such as Trojan horses from capturing usernames and passwords.

▶ **Interactive Logon: Require Smart Card**—When enabled, users must employ a smart card to log on to the computer.

▶ **User Account Control**—Several policy settings determine the behavior of the UAC prompt for administrative and nonadministrative users, including behavior by applications that are in secure locations on the computer, such as %ProgramFiles% or %Windir%.

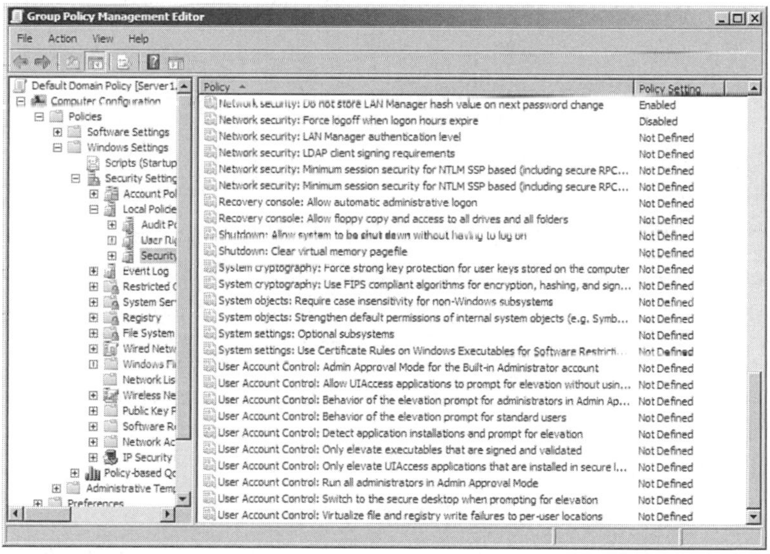

FIGURE 7.8 You can configure numerous local security policy settings with Group Policy in Windows Server 2008.

For more information on the policy settings in this node, refer to "Domain Controller and Member Server Policy Settings" in Appendix A.

▶ **Event Log**—Configuration options for the Event Viewer logs, including log sizes and action taken when an event log is full.

▶ **Restricted Groups**—Determines who can belong to certain groups, as discussed in Chapter 6.

- ▶ **System Services**—Enables you to configure system services properties, such as startup type, and restrict users from modifying these settings.

- ▶ **Registry**—Enables you to control the permissions that govern who can access and edit portions of the Registry.

- ▶ **File System**—Enables you to configure permissions on folders and files and prevent their modification.

- ▶ **Wired Network (IEEE 802.3) Policies**—Enables you to specify the use of IEEE 802.1X authentication for network access by Windows Vista computers, including the protocol to be used for network authentication.

- ▶ **Windows Firewall with Advanced Security**—Enables you to configure properties of Windows Firewall for domain, private, and public profiles. You can specify inbound and outbound connection rules as well as monitoring settings.

- ▶ **Network List Manager Policies**—Enables you to control the networks that computers can access and their location types, such as public and private (which automatically specifies the appropriate firewall settings according to location type). You can also specify which networks a user is allowed to connect to.

- ▶ **Wireless Network (IEEE 802.11) Policies**—Enables you to specify wireless settings, such as enabling 802.1X authentication and the preferred wireless networks that users can access.

- ▶ **Public Key Policies**—Enables you to configure public key infrastructure (PKI) settings. Chapter 9, "Active Directory Certificate Services," discusses several of these policies.

- ▶ **Software Restriction Policies**—Enables you to specify which software programs users can run on network computers, which programs users on multiuser computers can run, and the execution of email attachments. You can also specify whether software restriction policies apply to certain groups such as administrators.

- ▶ **Network Access Protection**—Network Access Protection (NAP) is a new Windows Server 2008 feature that enables you to define client health policies that restrict access to your network by computers that lack appropriate security configurations. The NAP policies enable you to specify settings for client user interface items, trusted servers, and servers used for enforcement of client computer security health status.

▶ **IP Security Policies on Active Directory**—Controls the implementation of IP Security (IPSec) as used by the computer for encrypting communications over the network.

You can obtain additional information on many of these policy settings in the Windows Server 2008 Help and Support and from "Security Settings Overview for GPMC" in Appendix A.

Additional Security Configuration Tools

Windows Server 2008 includes the following additional tools that are useful in configuring and maintaining the security of your AD DS network:

▶ **Security Configuration Wizard**—This wizard assists you in maintaining the security of your servers and checks for vulnerabilities that might appear as server configurations change over time. It is particularly useful in maintaining the security of servers hosting roles that are not installed using Server Manager, such as SQL Server and Exchange Server, as well as servers that host non-Microsoft applications. Microsoft also includes a command-line version, scwcmd.exe, which is useful in configuring Server Core computers.

▶ **Security Templates snap-in**—From this snap-in, you can save a custom security policy that includes settings from the various subnodes of the Security Settings node of Computer Configuration discussed in the preceding settings. It is most useful in defining a security configuration for standalone servers that are not members of a domain.

▶ **Security Configuration and Analysis snap-in**—This snap-in enables you to analyze and configure local computer security. You can compare security settings on the computer to those in a database created from the Security Templates snap-in and view any differences that you find. You can then use this database to configure the computer's security so that it matches the database settings.

NOTE

Unlike previous versions of Windows Server, Windows Server 2008 does not include pre-defined security templates, such as the Compatible, Secure Server, and High Secure Server templates included with Windows Server 2003. However, you can use the Security Templates snap-in to create a custom template that you can use for configuring security settings on standalone servers or servers in another forest.

These security tools are most useful in situations involving standalone computers and servers running custom applications and are not emphasized on Exam 70-640. For more information on these tools, refer to "Server Security Policy Management in Windows Server 2008" in Appendix A.

Auditing of Active Directory Services

Auditing enables you to track actions performed by users across the domain, such as logging on and off or accessing files and folders. When you create and apply an auditing policy, auditable events are recorded in the Security log of the computer where they happen. You can then use Event Viewer to view any computer's Security log by connecting to the required computer.

New Features of Active Directory Auditing

Windows Server 2008 introduces a new command-line tool, `auditpol.exe`, as well as subcategories in the Audit Directory Service Access category. In previous versions of Windows Server, a single Directory Service Access category controlled the auditing of all directory service events. In Windows Server 2008, four subcategories of directory service access are available:

- **Directory Service Access**—Tracks all attempts at accessing AD DS objects whose system access control lists (SACL) have been configured for auditing. This includes deletion of objects.

- **Directory Service Changes**—Tracks modifications to AD DS objects whose SACLs have been configured for auditing. The following actions are included:

  - When an attribute of an object has been modified, the old and new values of the attribute are recorded in the Security log.

  - When a new object is created, values of their attributes including new attribute values are recorded in the Security log. This includes objects moved from another domain.

  - When objects are moved from one container to another, the distinguished names of the old and new locations are recorded in the Security log.

  - When objects are undeleted, the location in which they are placed is recorded in the Security log. Any added, modified, or deleted attributes are recorded also.

> ▶ **Directory Service Replication**—Tracks the beginning and end of the synchronization of a replica of an Active Directory naming context.

> ▶ **Detailed Directory Service Replication**—Tracks additional AD DS replication events, including the establishment, removal, or modification of an Active Directory replica source naming context, replication of attributes for an AD DS object, or removal of a lingering object from a replica.

The `auditpol.exe` tool enables you to configure auditing from the command line. You must use this tool to enable the auditing of the new directory service access subcategories outlined here. We discuss this tool later in this section.

> **NOTE**
>
> These new auditing categories also apply to auditing of Active Directory Lightweight Directory Services (AD LDS).

Use of GPOs to Configure Auditing

Group Policy enables you to configure success or failure for several types of actions. In other words, you can choose to record successful actions, failed attempts at performing these actions, or both. For example, if you are concerned about intruders who might be attempting to access your network, you can log failed logon events. You can also track successful logon events, which is useful if the intruders succeed in accessing your network.

You can use Group Policy to enable auditing at domain controllers, member servers, and client computers. Be aware that all auditing takes place only at the local computer where the events take place, and that these events are recorded on that computer's Security log. To enable auditing on all domain controllers, configure the auditing settings in the Default Domain Controllers Policy GPO; to enable auditing on other domain computers, configure the auditing settings in the Default Domain Policy GPO or in another GPO as required.

Available Auditing Categories

Windows Server 2008 enables you to audit the following types of events:

> ▶ **Account logon**—Logon or logoff by a domain user account at a domain controller. You should track both success and failure.

▶ **Account management**—Creation, modification, or deletion of computer, user, or group accounts. Also included are enabling and disabling of accounts and changing or resetting of passwords. You should track both success and failure.

▶ **Directory service access**—Access to an AD DS object as specified by the object's SACL. This category includes the four subcategories mentioned earlier in this section; enabling directory service access from the Group Policy Management Editor enables all four subcategories. Enable this category for failures. (If you record success, a large number of events will be logged.)

▶ **Logon events**—Logon or logoff by a user at a member server or client computer. You should track both success and failure. (Success logging can record an unauthorized access that succeeded.)

▶ **Object access**—Access by a user to an object such as a file, folder, or printer. You need to configure auditing in each object's SACL to track access to that object. Track success and failure to access important resources on your network.

▶ **Policy change**—Modification of policies, including user rights assignment, trust, and audit policies. This category is not normally needed unless unusual events are occurring.

▶ **Privilege use**—Use of a user right, such as changing the system time. Track failure events for this category.

▶ **Process tracking**—Actions performed by an application. This category is primarily for application developers and does not need to be enabled in most cases.

▶ **System events**—Events taking place on a computer, such as an improper shutdown or a disk with little free space remaining. Track success and failure events.

NOTE

Note the difference between Logon and Account Logon events. Logon events refer to authentication of a local user at a workstation or member server, while Account Logon events refer to the authentication of a domain user account at a domain controller.

EXAM ALERT

Know which types of actions to audit for different scenarios. For example, the exam might present a drag-and-drop interface where you must select success and failure actions to achieve a given objective.

Configuring Auditing

To configure auditing policies, access the Group Policy Management Editor focused on the desired GPO. For auditing actions on domain controllers, this will generally be the Default Domain Controllers Policy GPO. Navigate to the Computer Configuration\Policies\Windows Settings\Security Settings\Local Policies\Audit Policy node and click this node to display the available policies in the Details pane.

To enable auditing of any of these event types, right-click it and choose Properties. On the Properties dialog box shown in Figure 7.9, select Define These Policy Settings, select Success and/or Failure as required, and then click OK. New to Windows Server 2008, the Explain tab of each policy's Properties dialog box provides more information on what the setting does.

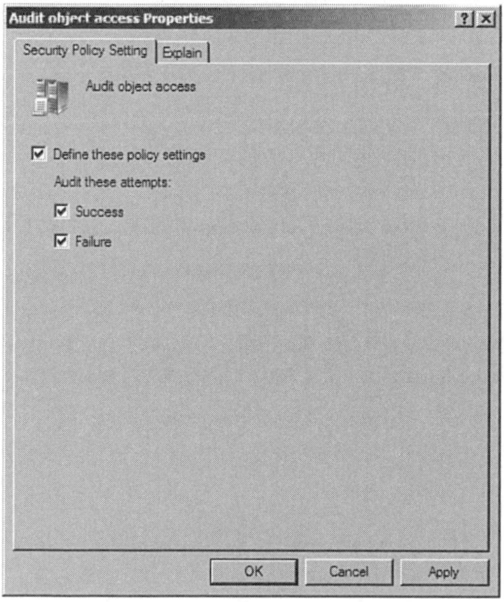

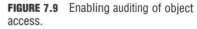

FIGURE 7.9 Enabling auditing of object access.

To track object access or directory service access, you must configure the SACL for each required object. In Windows Explorer, right-click the required file, folder, or printer, and choose Properties. On the Properties dialog box, click Advanced to open the Advanced Security Settings dialog box, and then select the Auditing tab. To add users or groups to this tab, click Edit and then click Add. Type the required users or groups in the Select User, Computer, or Group dialog box, and then click OK. On the Auditing Entry dialog box that appears (see Figure 7.10), select the types of actions you want to track, and then click OK. The completed auditing entries appear in the Advanced Security Settings dialog box, as shown in Figure 7.11. Click OK twice to close these dialog boxes.

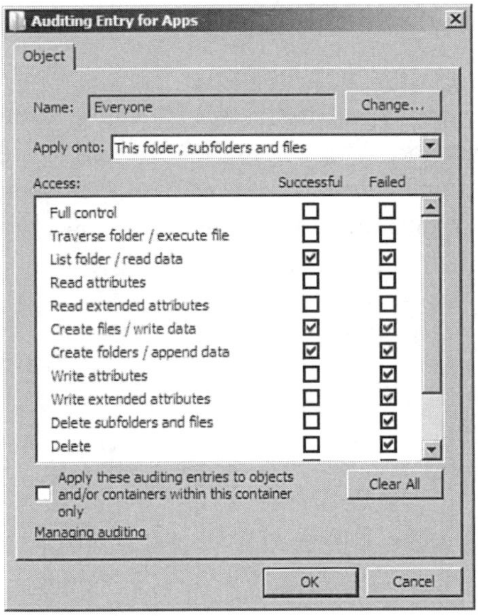

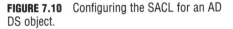

FIGURE 7.10 Configuring the SACL for an AD DS object.

After you have configured object access auditing, attempts to access audited objects appear in the Security log, which you can view from Event Viewer either in Server Manager, as shown in Figure 7.12, or in its own snap-in from the Administrative Tools folder. For more information on any audited event, right-click the event and choose Event Properties.

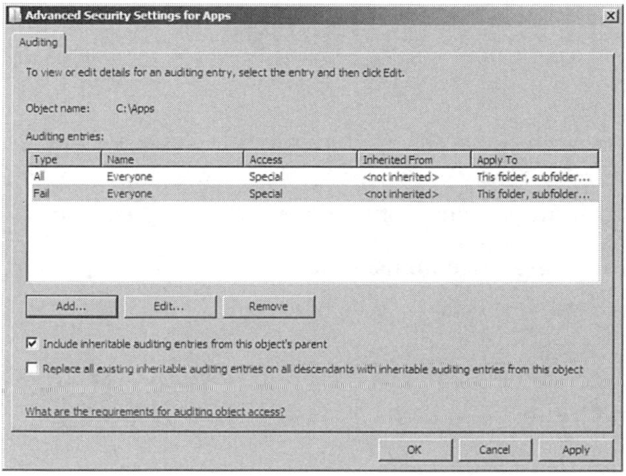

FIGURE 7.11 The Advanced Security Settings dialog box displays information on the types of object auditing actions that have been specified.

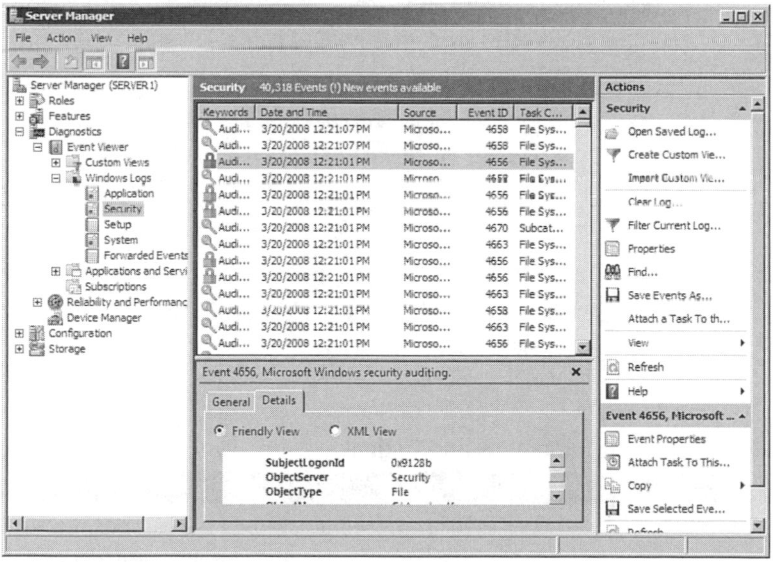

FIGURE 7.12 Event Viewer displays failed attempts at accessing an object with a lock icon.

TIP

Ensure that the Security log has adequate space to audit the events that you configure for auditing, because the log can fill rapidly. The recommended size is at least 128MB. You should also periodically save the existing log to a file and clear all past events. If the log becomes full, the oldest events are overwritten (and therefore lost) by default. You can also configure the log to archive when full and not to overwrite events, but new events are not recorded. Loss of recorded events can be serious in the case of high-security installations.

Use of `Auditpol.exe` to Configure Auditing

The `Auditpol.exe` tool performs audit policy configuration actions from the command line. This is the only tool you can use to configure auditing on a Server Core computer or to configure directory service auditing subcategories.

To use this tool, type the following at a command line:

```
Auditpol command [<sub-command><options>]
```

Table 7.1 describes the available commands, and Table 7.2 describes several of the more important subcommands and options that you should be aware of.

TABLE 7.1   `Auditpol` Commands

Command	Meaning
/get	Displays the current auditing policy
/set	Sets the audit policy
/list	Displays audit policy categories and subcategories, or lists users for whom a per-user audit policy is defined
/backup	Saves the audit policy to a specified file
/restore	Retrieves the audit policy from a specified file
/clear	Clears the audit policy
/remove	Removes per-user audit policy settings and disables system audit policy settings

TABLE 7.2   `Auditpol` Subcommands and Options

Option	Meaning
/user:<username>	Specifies the security principal for a per-user audit. Specify the username by security identifier (SID) or by name. Requires either the /category or /subcategory subcommand when used with the /set command.
/category:<name>	One or more auditing categories separated by | and specified by name or Globally Unique Identifier (GUID).
/subcategory:<name>	One or more auditing subcategories separated by | and specified by name or GUID.
/success:enable	Enables success auditing when using the /set command.

TABLE 7.2 *Continued*

Option	Meaning
/success:disable	Disables success auditing when using the /set command.
/failure:enable	Enables failure auditing when using the /set command.
/failure:disable	Disables failure auditing when using the /set command.
/file	Specifies the file to which an audit policy is to be backed up, or from which an audit policy is to be restored.

For example, to configure auditing for directory service changes, you type the following:

```
Auditpol /set /subcategory:"directory service changes" /success:enable
```

Additional subcommands and options are available with most of the auditpol commands discussed here. For information on the available subcommands and options available for a specified command, type **auditpol /command /?**.

Exam Cram Questions

1. Evan is responsible for configuring Group Policy in his company's domain. The domain functional level is set to Windows Server 2003. Evan's manager has requested that he implement an account policy that specifies that all user accounts will be locked out if an incorrect password is entered five times within a one-quarter hour period. The account is to remain locked out until a support technician unlocks it.

   How should Evan configure the account policy? (Each correct answer represents part of the solution. Choose three answers.)

   ○ **A.** Set the account lockout threshold to 0.

   ○ **B.** Set the account lockout threshold to 1.

   ● **C.** Set the account lockout threshold to 4.

   ● **D.** Set the account lockout duration to 0.

   ○ **E.** Set the account lockout duration to 1.

   ○ **F.** Set the reset account lockout counter value to 0.25.

   ● **G.** Set the reset lockout counter to 15.

   ○ **H.** Set the reset lockout counter to 900.

2. Laura is the systems administrator for a company that operates an AD DS domain. The domain and forest functional level are set to Windows Server 2008. She has configured a password policy for users in her company's domain that specifies that passwords must be at least seven characters long. The CIO has informed her that users in the legal department should have highly secure passwords. She configures a password policy in a GPO linked to the Legal OU that specifies that passwords be at least 12 characters long.

   A few days later, she receives a call from the CIO asking her why she has not yet implemented the stricter password policy. What must Laura do to implement the policy with the least amount of administrative effort?

   ○ **A.** She needs to create a global security group, add the required users to this group, and ensure that the group has the Allow–Apply Group Policy permission applied to it.

   ○ **B.** She needs to create a new domain, place the legal users and their computers in this domain, and then reapply the password policy to this domain.

   ○ **C.** She needs to create a password settings object containing the required password settings and apply this object to the Legal OU.

● **D.** She needs to create a global security group and add the required users to this group. She then needs to create a password settings object containing the required password settings and apply this object to the group containing these users.

3. You are excited about the new capability of configuring fine-grained password policies and want to try it out. To which of the following groups should your user account belong so that you can configure a fine-grained password policy?

   ○ **A.** Account Operators

   ● **B.** Domain Admins

   ○ **C.** Enterprise Admins

   ○ **D.** Schema Admins

4. Dennis is responsible for configuring security settings on a Windows Server 2008 computer. This computer runs specialized software and is configured as a standalone server that is not a member of his company's AD DS domain. He needs to configure security settings that are similar to those applied to member servers in the domain.

   What should Dennis do to accomplish this task with the least amount of administrative effort?

   ● **A.** He should use the Security Templates snap-in to create a security database of the settings on a member server. He should then use the Security Configuration and Analysis snap-in to configure the standalone server with the settings contained in the database.

   ○ **B.** He should use the Security Configuration and Analysis snap-in to analyze the security settings on the member server and then use this snap-in to configure the standalone server with the settings contained in the database.

   ○ **C.** He should use the Security Templates snap-in to configure the security settings on the standalone server with settings contained in the Securews.inf security template.

   ○ **D.** He should copy the settings on the member server and configure these settings manually on the standalone server.

5. You are the administrator of a company that operates an AD DS network that contains two domains. Both domains operate at the Windows Server 2003 domain and forest functional levels. You have installed a new Windows Server 2008 computer and promoted this server to be an additional domain controller in your domain.

Having heard about the new capability of configuring fine-grained password policies, you decide to give it a try and configure a PSO that specifies a minimum of 10 characters. You then associate this PSO with your user account and attempt to change your password to a new one that is 8 characters long.

When this attempt succeeds, you wonder why the new PSO was not applied to your account. Which of the following is the reason you were able to specify an 8-character password?

- ○ **A.** You need to associate the PSO with a global security group to which your user account belongs before it is applied.

- ○ **B.** You need to associate the PSO with an OU to which your user account belongs before it is applied.

- ● **C.** You need to upgrade all domain controllers in the domain to Windows Server 2008 and set the domain functional level to Windows Server 2008 before the PSO is effective.

- ○ **D.** You need to upgrade all domain controllers in both domains of the forest to Windows Server 2008 and set the domain and forest functional levels to Windows Server 2008 before the PSO is effective.

6. Ruth is the administrator of an AD DS network that operates at the Windows Server 2008 domain and forest functional level. Her manager has asked her to implement success and failure auditing of directory service changes on the domain controller. The manager does not want success auditing of directory service access to be implemented because problems have occurred with events being overwritten in security logs before Ruth has had time to check them.

Which of the following tools should Ruth use to configure auditing as requested?

- ● **A.** `Auditpol.exe`

- ○ **B.** `ADSIEdit.exe`

- ○ **C.** `Ntdsutil.exe`

- ○ **D.** Group Policy Management Editor

7. Barry is the network administrator for Examcram.com, which operates an AD DS network. The network includes servers running Windows Server 2003 and Windows Server 2008 and client computers running Windows XP Professional and Windows Vista Business. His manager has requested that he implement auditing of the following:

- ▶ Attempts to log on to any local computer

- ▶ Creation of a user account or group or changing of a user account password

What auditing components should Barry configure? (Each correct answer represents part of the solution. Choose two answers.)

● **A.** Audit account management, success

○ **B.** Audit account logon events, success and failure

○ **C.** Audit object access, success

● **D.** Audit logon events, success and failure

8. Veronica is responsible for configuring Group Policy on her company's AD DS network. She has deployed a new software package to all computers in the Financial OU. Users in this OU report that their computers are restarting spontaneously at frequent intervals.

Veronica wants to enable an auditing policy in a GPO in an attempt to troubleshoot this problem. Which type of events should she audit?

○ **A.** Logon events

○ **B.** Process tracking events

● **C.** System events

○ **D.** Privilege use events

○ **E.** Policy change events

Answers to *Exam Cram* Questions

1. **C, D, G.** Evan should specify an account lockout threshold of 4 passwords, and account lockout duration of 0, and a reset account lockout counter value of 15 minutes. The account lockout threshold specifies the number of incorrect passwords that can be entered before the account locks out. It can be set from 0 to 999, and a value of 0 means that the account never locks out. The account lockout duration can be set from 0 to 99,999 minutes, and a value of 0 means that the account remains locked out until unlocked by an administrator or individual who has been delegated this responsibility. The reset account lockout counter value specifies the number of minutes to wait until the lockout counter resets itself to 0. It can be set to any value between 0 and 99999; a value of 0 means that this counter is never reset. If Evan set an account lockout threshold to 0, the accounts would never lock out, and if he set it to 1, the accounts would lock out after one incorrect password, so answers A and B are incorrect. If Evan set the account lockout duration to 1, the accounts would lock out for one minute only, so answer E is incorrect. If he set the reset account lockout counter value to 0, the account lockout counter would never reset, so answer F is incorrect. If he set the reset account lockout counter to 900, the counter would not reset until 15 hours had elapsed. (The value of this counter is specified in minutes, not seconds.) Therefore, answer H is incorrect.

2. **D.** Laura needs to create a global security group and add the required users to this group. She then needs to create a password settings object containing the required

password settings and apply this object to the group containing these users. The new fine-grained password policy in Windows Server 2008 enables her to create a password policy that applies only to specified users or groups. Laura cannot link a GPO to a group, so answer A is incorrect. Laura could create a new domain and apply the policy in this manner. This was the method she would have needed to do before Windows Server 2008; however, application of a fine-grained password policy takes far less administrative effort and expense, so answer B is incorrect. It is not possible to apply a fine-grained password policy to an OU, so answer C is incorrect.

3. **B.** Your user account must belong to the Domain Admins global group before you can create a fine-grained password policy. Membership in the Account Operators group is insufficient, so answer A is incorrect. Membership in either the Enterprise Admins or Schema Admins group is not required for creating a fine-grained password policy, so answers C and D are incorrect.

4. **A.** Dennis should use the Security Templates snap-in to create a security database of the settings on a member server. He should then use the Security Configuration and Analysis snap-in to configure the standalone server with the settings contained in the database. This procedure copies the security settings that he has already configured to the standalone server; he can subsequently configure any additional settings that might be needed manually. The Security Configuration and Analysis snap-in does not create a database of settings, it compares existing settings to those in the database and configures the server to these settings; therefore, answer B is incorrect. The `Securews.inf` security template was used in Windows 2000 and Windows Server 2003 to configure security settings on member servers and workstations. It is no longer available in Windows Server 2008, so answer C is incorrect. Dennis could manually configure settings, but this would take far more administrative effort, so answer D is incorrect.

5. **C.** To have a PSO apply properly, the domain functional level must be at the Windows Server 2008 functional level. To achieve this functional level, you must upgrade all domain controllers to Windows Server 2008. You can associate a PSO with a user account, so answer A is incorrect. It is not possible to associate a PSO with an OU, so answer B is incorrect. It is not necessary to upgrade other domains in the forest to Windows Server 2008 if no PSO is being applied in these domains, so answer D is incorrect.

6. **A.** Ruth should use the `Auditpol.exe` command-line tool to configure auditing of directory service changes. This is a new auditing category that is included in the Directory Service Access category but must be configured from `Auditpol.exe` to be implemented on its own. Ruth would use `ADSIEdit.exe` to perform low-level editing of AD DS objects, including the implementation of fine-grained password policies. She would use `Ntdsutil.exe` to perform several AD DS management actions, including the seizure of operations masters roles. Neither of these tools can be used to configure auditing, so answers B and C are incorrect. Ruth could implement auditing of the Directory Service Access category from the Group Policy Management Console, but this would not fulfill the requirements of this scenario, so answer D is incorrect.

7. **A, D.** The audit account management event includes creation, modification, or deletion of user accounts or groups, renaming or disabling of user accounts, or configuring and changing of passwords; and the audit logon events tracks logons at local computers. Audit account logon events are logon and logoff activity at member servers and client computers, so answer B is incorrect. Audit object access tracks when a user accesses an object such as a file, folder, Registry key, or printer that has its own SACL specified, so answer C is incorrect.

8. **C.** Veronica should implement success auditing of system events to identify the cause of the problems that are being experienced. This tracks actions taking place on a computer, such as improper shutdowns or restarts. Logon events track logon and logoff activity at member servers and client computers, but they do not track the causes of improper shutdowns as experienced here, so answer A is incorrect. Process tracking events track actions performed by an application, but not improper shutdowns, so answer B is incorrect. Privilege use events track the use of system rights, so answer D is incorrect. Policy change events track the modification of policies including user rights assignment, trust, and audit policies. This also is not required here, so answer E is incorrect.

CHAPTER 8

Monitoring and Maintaining the Active Directory Environment

Terms You'll Need to Understand

- ✓ Active Directory log files
- ✓ Authoritative restore
- ✓ Directory Services Restore Mode (DSRM)
- ✓ Defragmentation
- ✓ Linked value replication
- ✓ Network Monitor
- ✓ Nonauthoritative restore
- ✓ Ntds.dit
- ✓ Reliability and Performance Monitor
- ✓ Server Performance Advisor
- ✓ System state data
- ✓ Task Manager
- ✓ Wbadmin.exe
- ✓ Windows System Resource Manager (WSRM)

Concepts/Techniques You'll Need to Master

- ✓ Backing up Active Directory
- ✓ Performing primary, normal, and authoritative restores of AD DS
- ✓ Using removable media to perform backups and restores
- ✓ Backing up, restoring, exporting, and importing GPOs
- ✓ Performing offline defragmentation and compaction of AD DS
- ✓ Using Windows Server 2008 monitoring tools to monitor AD DS

In previous chapters, you learned how Active Directory Domain Services (AD DS) replicates its database across the entire forest. You learned about the structure of AD DS, how to delegate authority to various components of AD DS, and how to use Group Policy to configure and secure the network environment.

Now it's time to turn your attention to monitoring and troubleshooting of AD DS. Things can and do go wrong, often in subtle ways. You need to know how to restore Active Directory from a backup, which is often the fastest way to recover from these problems. Further, you need to know how to back up Active Directory before you can restore it. You also need to know how to monitor your servers and use the information obtained to locate and repair problems before they become disruptive to your entire network's operations.

Backing Up and Recovering Active Directory

All computers fail sooner or later. And people (maybe even you) accidentally delete valuable data. A good backup and recovery strategy is vital to an organization's continued well-being. Without it, your organization's existence could be threatened. Backup and recovery is just as important for your AD DS database as it is for your critical production files.

Windows Server 2008 includes a new backup application called Windows Server Backup. This application works somewhat differently from the older backup application included with Windows 2000 and Windows Server 2003. The following are some of the more significant differences:

- ▶ Windows Server Backup works by backing up critical volumes. These are the volumes that are required for recovering AD DS and include the SYSVOL volume, the system and boot volumes, and the volumes that host the *Ntds.dit* database file and the *Active Directory log files*.

- ▶ The composition of the *system state data* depends on the server roles installed on the server and the volumes that host the critical operating system and role files. System state consists of at least the following items and can include more depending on the installed server roles:

  - ▶ Registry
  - ▶ COM+ Class Registration database
  - ▶ System and boot files
  - ▶ AD DS and Active Directory Certificate Services (AD CS) databases

- ▶ SYSVOL folder

- ▶ Cluster service information

- ▶ Internet Information Services (IIS) metadirectory

- ▶ System files that are under Windows Resource Protection

▶ Windows Server Backup enables you to choose between three recovery modes: full server recovery, system state recovery, and file/folder recovery.

▶ You can use Windows Server Backup to perform a manual backup, or you can schedule automated backups to a dedicated backup volume on the server.

▶ In addition to local and network-based hard disk volumes, you can use CDs or DVDs as backup media. Magnetic tape volumes are no longer supported.

▶ Windows Server Backup does not enable you to back up individual files or folders. You must back up the entire volume that hosts the files or folders to be backed up.

> **NOTE**
>
> Members of the Backup Operators group can perform manual backups but cannot schedule backups by default. You must possess administrative credentials to schedule backups, and you cannot delegate this privilege.

Use of Windows Server Backup

Windows Server Backup enables you to protect against all types of data loss for reasons ranging from hardware or storage media failure to accidental deletion of objects or the entire AD DS database. This section looks at installing Windows Server Backup, using it to back up to different types of media and scheduling backups.

Installing Windows Server Backup

Unlike previous versions of Windows, Windows Server Backup is not installed by default; you must install it as a server feature from Server Manager. Use the following procedure to install Windows Server Backup:

1. Open Server Manager, and select the Features node.

2. In the Details pane, click Add Features.

3. Scroll the features list to select Windows Server Backup Features. If you also want command-line tools for performing backups, expand Windows Server Backup Features and select this option.

4. If you receive a message asking to install required features, click Add Required Features. Then click Next.

5. Review the information provided by the Confirm Installation Selections page, and then click Install.

6. When you're informed that installation has completed, click Close.

EXAM ALERT

Be aware of the new backup utilities in Windows Server 2008 and the need to install them before use. Windows Server 2008 no longer supports the `ntbackup.exe` utility or the Automated System Recovery (ASR) tool, as an exam question might attempt to trick you on.

Backing Up Critical Volumes of a Domain Controller

Windows Server Backup enables you to back up your domain controller to different types of media, including a fixed or removable hard disk volume installed on the server, a network share, or removable media such as CDs or DVDs. To perform this type of backup, you must be a member of the Administrators or Backup Operators group, and an appropriate backup volume must be available. To perform a single backup of critical volumes, proceed as follows:

1. Click Start, Administrative Tools, Windows Server Backup. You can also open Server Manager, expand Storage, and then select Windows Server Backup from this location.

2. From the Action menu, select Backup Once. This starts the Backup Once Wizard with a Backup Options page, as shown in Figure 8.1.

3. If you have previously scheduled a backup on this server, you can use the option The Same Options That You Used in the Backup Schedule Wizard for Scheduled Backups to perform this backup. Otherwise, click Different Options, and then click Next.

4. On the Select Backup Configuration page, select Custom, and then click Next.

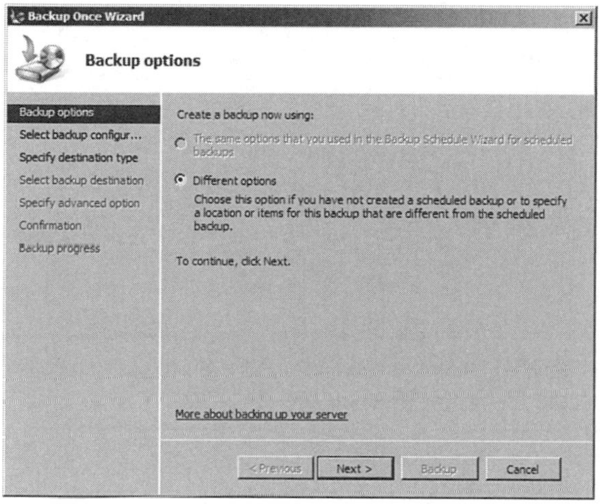

FIGURE 8.1 The Backup Options page provides options for using previous options if available and configuring different options.

5. On the Select Backup Items page, ensure that the Enable System Recovery option is selected, and then click Next. This ensures that all critical volumes are backed up.

6. On the Specify Destination Type page, select either Local Drives or Remote Shared Folder as required, and then click Next.

7. If you choose the Remote Shared Folder option, type the path to the shared folder on the Specify Remote Folder page. If you select the Local Drives option, select a suitable volume. Then click Next.

8. Choose the type of Volume Shadow Copy Service (VSS) backup you want from the options shown in Figure 8.2, and then click Next.

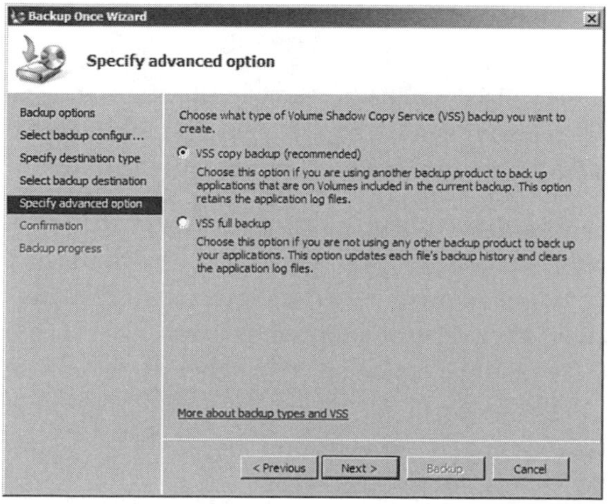

FIGURE 8.2 The Specify Advanced Option page presents two options for performing a VSS backup.

9. Review the options presented by the Confirmation page, and then click Backup to perform the backup.

10. The Backup Progress page charts the status of the backup operation. When you are informed that the backup is complete, click Close. Windows Server Backup displays this backup and its results in the main portion of the application window.

TIP

You can use a similar procedure to back up the entire server. From the Select Backup Configuration page at step 4, select the Full Server (Recommended) option.

The Wbadmin Command

You can perform backups from the command line with the new *wbadmin.exe* utility, which is installed with the Add Features Wizard when you select the option described earlier to add command-line tools. This tool supports subcommands that enable or disable scheduled backups, run one-time backups, list details of available backups as well as items included in the backups, provide the status of a currently running backup, and perform system state backups and recoveries. The use of this command in running system state recoveries is discussed later in this section.

To obtain information on the available subcommands, type **wbadmin /?** at a command prompt. For example, to back up the system state, you would run the wbadmin start systemstatebackup command. To obtain information on this and other available subcommands, type **wbadmin subcommand /?**, where *subcommand* is the subcommand you want to obtain information for.

Scheduling a Backup

You can schedule a backup to take place when the server utilization is minimized, such as during the night. Scheduling a backup also ensues that the backup will be performed on a regular basis without administrator intervention.

The procedure for scheduling a backup is similar to that described in the previous section. From the Windows Server Backup application, click Backup Schedule to start the Backup Schedule Wizard. After selecting an option from the Select Backup Configuration page, you are presented with the Specify Backup Time page shown in Figure 8.3. Select one or more times a day for the backup to take place. Then select a destination disk and accept the warning that the selected disk will be reformatted. After the disk is formatted, note the warning on the Summary page of the wizard and click Close. Windows Server Backup provides information on the regularly scheduled backup in its main application window.

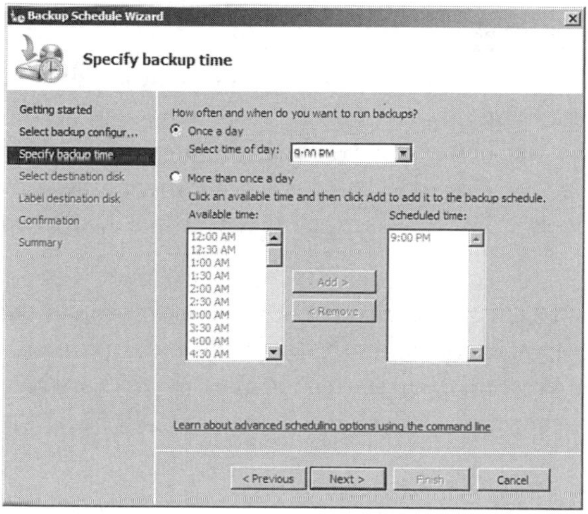

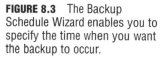

FIGURE 8.3 The Backup Schedule Wizard enables you to specify the time when you want the backup to occur.

After you have scheduled a backup, the option previously shown in Figure 8.1 becomes available so that you can use the options you specified in running the Backup Schedule Wizard to perform an unscheduled backup at any time.

Use of Removable Media

You can also perform backups to removable media, including recordable CDs, DVDs, or external hard drives. This is especially convenient for creating an additional backup copy for offsite storage purposes or for preparing to install a new domain controller using the Install from Media option. The procedure is similar to that described in the previous section. Windows Server Backup will ask for additional media as required.

TIP

Windows Server Backup stores backups in Virtual Hard Disk (VHD) format. You can use Microsoft Virtual PC or Virtual Server to mount a backup image as a disk drive on a virtual machine and browse its contents as if it were a normal disk drive.

Recovering Active Directory

The whole idea behind planning, organizing, and undertaking a backup job is that data will be easy to recover if a disaster occurs. Windows Server Backup provides three options for restoring data: Nonauthoritative restore, authoritative restore, and full server recovery.

Directory Services Restore Mode

Directory Services Restore Mode (DSRM) is a special version of Safe Mode that takes the domain controller offline and makes it function as a standalone server, unable to service requests of any kind across the network. This mode is used for all AD DS recovery operations. You also must log on as a local administrator using the Directory Services Restore Mode password that you specified when you installed the domain controller.

DSRM exposes the domain controller to security risks. Anyone who knows the DSRM password can start the domain controller in this mode and copy, modify, or delete data. As with other passwords, you should change this password regularly. The ntdsutil utility enables you to change this password. Perform the following procedure:

1. Click Start, Run, type **ntdsutil**, and press Enter.

2. At the ntdsutil prompt, type **set dsrm password**.

3. At the Reset DSRM Administrator Password prompt, type **reset password on server null**.

4. Type and confirm a new password. Note that the password is not displayed on the screen.

5. Type **quit** twice to exit ntdsutil.

TIP

You can reset the DSRM password on a remote server using this procedure. At step 3, replace the keyword null with the server name.

CAUTION

When you boot the server into DSRM, there is no AD DS security. Anyone who uses this mode is free to do whatever she wishes. You cannot prevent this except by ensuring the physical security of the domain controller. Furthermore, any administrator can reset the DSRM password by following the preceding procedure when logged into the domain controller running in normal mode; you do not need to know the current password to perform this procedure. Only give domain administrator privileges to individuals you trust.

Nonauthoritative Restore

Also called a normal restore, the *nonauthoritative restore* is the simplest form of restore from backup media. Because the data will probably be out of date (presumably, some changes have been made to AD DS since the previous backup), normal replication processes will ensure that the database is properly updated. This type of restore is called nonauthoritative because the restored data is subordinate to the "live" AD DS data. In other words, this type of restore results in the restoration of data from other functional domain controller(s) that is in turn overwritten or updated through replication by the "authoritative" data already live from AD DS. Naturally, you need to have at least one other functioning domain controller to perform this type of restore.

To perform this type of restore, you can use either a backup of critical volumes created as described earlier in this section or a full server backup. Perform the following procedure:

1. Restart your computer and press F8 as the server begins to boot.

2. After a few seconds, the Advanced Boot Options screen should appear. (If it does not, you might need to shut down the computer completely and then restart it.) From this screen, use the down arrow to select Directory Services Restore Mode, as shown in Figure 8.4, and then press Enter.

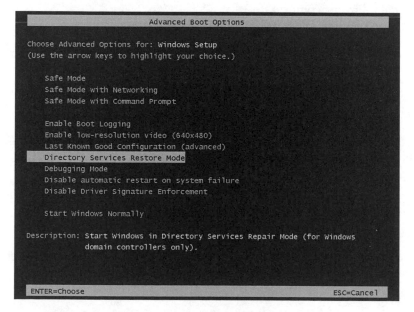

FIGURE 8.4 Selecting Directory Services Restore Mode.

3. If you have previously scheduled a backup on this server, you can use the previous options to perform this backup. Otherwise, click Different Options, and then click Next.

4. Windows checks the file system on the boot volume. This may take several minutes. When the Install Windows dialog box appears, log on using your domain administrative credentials.

5. The desktop appears, indicating that you are running in Safe Mode. This occurs because DSRM is a type of Safe Mode in which AD DS is not running and the server is acting as a standalone server.

6. Click Start, Switch User, and then click Other User.

7. Type .\administrator. Then type the DSRM password. This logs you on as the local administrator.

8. Open a command prompt, and type the following command:

```
wbadmin get versions -backuptarget:<target_drive>:
➥-machine:<backup_server_name>
```

In this command, `<target_drive>` is the location of the backup to be restored, and `<backup_server_name>` is the name of the server to be restored. This command returns information on the available backup target that you use for the next command.

9. Type the following command:

```
wbadmin start systemstaterecovery -version:<MM/DD/YYYY-HH:MM>
➥ -backuptarget:<target_drive>: -machine:<backup_server_name> -quiet
```

In this command, `<MM/DD/YYYY-HH:MM>` is the version of the backup to be restored, -quiet runs the command without user prompts, and the other items are as in the previous command.

10. When you are informed that the restore has completed, restart your computer. If you receive a message that other people are logged on to the computer, click Yes.

11. When the computer restarts, if the logon security context displays the DSRM administrator account, click Switch User to log on with a domain account.

Authoritative Restore

An *authoritative restore* is a special type of restore that does not replicate changes made to the AD DS database since the last backup. This is useful if an object such as a user, group, or OU has been deleted by mistake. If an administrator has made such an error, the deletion is replicated to other domain controllers.

If you were to simply restore the deleted objects according to the procedure outlined in the previous section, you would get the deleted objects back—but only temporarily. AD DS replication would replicate the most recent copy to the restored server, and the restored information would be lost. When you perform an authoritative restore, the update sequence number (USN) of the restored object is incremented by 100,000, making it more current than any other version. This version is then replicated to other domain controllers.

You can perform an authoritative restore by using the ntdsutil command immediately after performing a nonauthoritative restore while the server is still running in DSRM. Proceed as follows:

1. Complete steps 1 to 9 of the previous procedure to perform a nonauthoritative restore, but do not restart your computer.

2. At a command prompt, type **ntdsutil** and press Enter.

3. At the ntdsutil prompt, type **authoritative restore** and press Enter.

4. At the authoritative restore prompt, type **restore subtree <DN>**, where *<DN>* is the distinguished name of the object you want to restore (for example, ou=legal,dc=examcram,dc=com).

5. Click Yes on the message box that asks whether you are sure you want to perform the authoritative restore.

6. When the authoritative restore is completed, you should see the message Authoritative Restore completed successfully. Type **quit** to exit the authoritative restore prompt, and type **quit** again to exit ntdsutil.

7. Restart the server in normal mode. AD DS replication propagates the restored objects to the other domain controllers.

> **CAUTION**
>
> Be careful when performing an authoritative restore. You will lose all updates to the restored subtree since the time the backup was performed. If you do not specify the subtree properly, you could also lose additional updates to AD DS.

Recovering Back-Links of Authoritatively Restored Objects

In Chapter 5, "Active Directory Objects and Trusts," you learned how users and groups in one domain can be made members of groups in other domains of the same forest. When this is done, the accounts have what is termed *back-links* in the groups in the second domain. If you have performed an authoritative restore of groups that have these back-links, you must use the ntdsutil utility on a domain controller in other domains to recover them. To do this, you must perform the following procedure:

1. Copy the .txt file created by ntdsutil during the authoritative restore in the first domain to a domain controller in the second domain.

2. Restart this domain controller in Directory Services Restore Mode, log on as the DSRM local administrator, and restore it from backup media.

3. While running the second domain controller in Directory Services Restore Mode, type **ntdsutil** and press Enter.

4. Type **authoritative restore** and press Enter.

5. Type **create ldif files from <*text_path*>**, where <*text_path*> is the path and filename of the .txt file created by ntdsutil during the first authoritative restore procedure.

6. Exit ntdsutil as previously described, and then restart this domain controller normally.

Refer to "Create an LDIF File for Recovering Back-Links for Authoritatively Restored Objects" in Appendix A, "Need to Know More?" for more information.

Performing a Full Server Recovery of a Domain Controller

If you have a full server backup available, you can perform a full server recovery of your domain controller. This backup can be located on a separate internal hard drive or on an external hard drive, DVD, or network share. You must also have the Windows Server 2008 installation DVD. The full server recovery procedure restores the operating system, AD DS, and all applications and data from all volumes of the original domain controller.

Use the following procedure to perform a full server recovery:

1. Insert the Windows Server 2008 DVD-ROM, and start your computer.

2. When prompted, press a key to boot the server from the DVD.

3. From the Install Windows screen, click Next, and then click Repair Your Computer.

4. Ensure that your operating system is highlighted on the System Recovery Options dialog box, and then click Next.

5. On the System Recovery Options dialog box shown in Figure 8.5, select Windows Complete PC Restore.

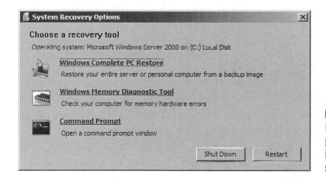

FIGURE 8.5 The System Recovery Options dialog box presents options for recovering a computer that will not start normally.

6. After a few seconds, the Restore Your Entire Computer from a Backup dialog box appears. In most cases, you should leave the default of Use the Latest Available Backup (Recommended) selected. Click Next.

7. The Choose How to Restore the Backup page shown in Figure 8.6 provides additional options. Select any of these that you need, click Next, and then click Finish.

8. You are warned that Windows Complete PC Restore will erase all data on the selected disks. Select the check box provided, and click OK to proceed.

9. When the restore has completed, you are informed, and your computer is restarted automatically. Click Restart Now to restart immediately, or click Don't Restart to restart your computer later.

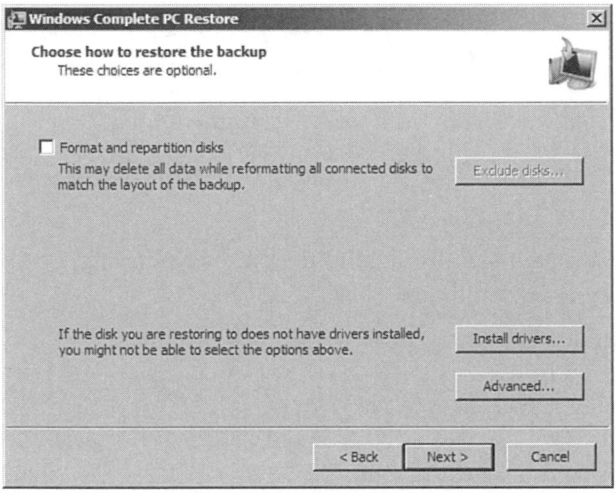

FIGURE 8.6 You can select from these additional recovery options.

Linked Value Replication

Linked value replication is a feature that enables you to replicate changes in group membership more efficiently. This feature replicates only the changes rather than replicating the whole membership when a change occurs. Available when the forest functional level is Windows Server 2003 or higher, this feature improves replication consistency by requiring less network bandwidth and processor usage during replication. It also prevents the loss of updates when administrators are modifying group membership simultaneously at different domain controllers. It is especially useful if you have large groups that contain hundreds, or even thousands, of members. Read-only domain controllers (RODC) depend on linked value replication to operate properly; this is why you cannot deploy an RODC in a domain where the functional level is Windows 2000.

Backing Up and Restoring GPOs

Group Policy Management Console (GPMC) provides the capability of backing up and restoring Group Policy objects (GPO). This procedure copies all data in the GPO to the file system. Included are its Globally Unique Identifier (GUID) and domain, its settings, its discretionary access control list (DACL), links to Windows Management Instrumentation (WMI) filters and IP security settings (but not the filters or settings themselves), a date and time stamp, and a user-supplied description.

Backing Up GPOs

You can back up a single GPO or all GPOs in a domain from GPMC. Use the following procedure:

1. Open the GPMC and expand the console tree to locate the required GPO in the Group Policy Objects node.

2. Right-click the GPO to be backed up and select Back Up. Or to back up all GPOs in the domain, right-click the Group Policy Objects node and select Back Up All.

3. On the Back Up Group Policy Object dialog box shown in Figure 8.7, type or browse to the folder where you want to store the backup. Type an optional description for the backup, and then click Back Up.

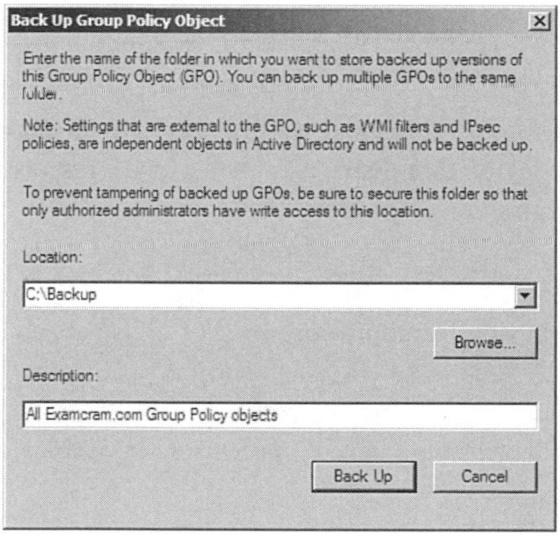

Back Up Group Policy Object

Enter the name of the folder in which you want to store backed up versions of this Group Policy Object (GPO). You can back up multiple GPOs to the same folder.

Note: Settings that are external to the GPO, such as WMI filters and IPsec policies, are independent objects in Active Directory and will not be backed up.

To prevent tampering of backed up GPOs, be sure to secure this folder so that only authorized administrators have write access to this location.

Location:

`C:\Backup`

Browse...

Description:

`All Examcram.com Group Policy objects`

Back Up   Cancel

FIGURE 8.7 Backing up a GPO.

4. A Backup dialog box charts the progress of the backup. When the back-up is complete, click OK.

Restoring GPOs

If you have deleted a GPO by mistake and want it back, or if you have edited it in an undesirable fashion or it has become corrupted, you can easily restore the GPO from the GPMC. Right-click the Group Policy Objects folder in the console tree of GPMC and choose Manage Backups. The Manage Backups dialog box shown in Figure 8.8 displays available backups and enables you to perform restores.

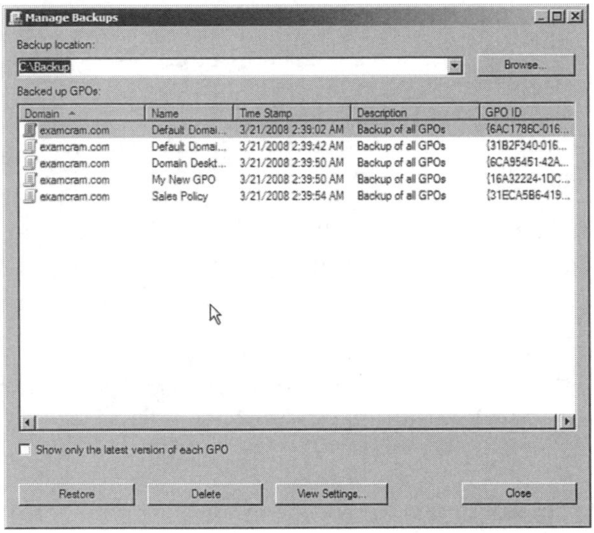

FIGURE 8.8 The Manage Backups dialog box enables you to view, restore, and import GPOs.

To restore a GPO from this dialog box, select the desired GPO and click Restore. Then click OK in the message box that displays to perform the restore. When informed that the restore is complete, click OK.

Importing GPOs

From GPMC, you can export GPOs to other domains or import GPOs that you have exported from other domains. To export a GPO, you simply back it up as already described. The import operation is similar to a restore, except that it is done to a different domain. The Import Settings Wizard assists you in performing the import, as follows:

1. In the console tree of GPMC, right-click the GPO to be imported and choose Import Settings.

2. The Import Settings Wizard displays a welcome page describing this action. Click Next.

3. The Backup GPO page warns you that importing settings permanently deletes existing settings. If you want to back up these settings, click Backup, or click Next to import the GPO without performing a backup.

4. On the Backup Location page, type or browse to the backup folder, and then click Next.

5. On the Source GPO page, select the desired GPO and click Next.

6. The wizard scans the settings to determine if any security principals or UNC paths need to be transformed. When finished, click Next.

7. The completion page displays a summary of the settings to be imported. Click Finish to perform the import.

8. An Import dialog box tracks the progress of the import action. When informed that the import is complete, click OK.

Use of Scripts for Group Policy Backup and Restore

GPMC also provides several Windows Script Host (WSH) script files that assist you in performing deployments of Group Policy at the enterprise level or in configuring Group Policy from a Server Core machine. These scripts also assist you in creating what Microsoft refers to as a *staging environment* for testing the application of GPOs and then porting them to the production environment once you are assured that they will work properly with no adverse effects. You can find them in the Scripts folder of GPMC.

Useful WSH scripts that you should know about include the following:

▶ **BackupGPO.wsf** and **BackupAllGPOS.wsf**—Back up GPOs.

▶ **RestoreGPO.wsf** and **RestoreAllGPOs.wsf**—Restore GPOs.

▶ **CopyGPO.wsf** and **CopyAllGPOs.wsf**—Copy a GPO from one domain to another. You can use these when copying from a staging domain to a production one, or between two domains in the same forest or different forests.

▶ **CreateGPO.wsf**—Creates a GPO with the specified name, in the specified domain.

▶ **ImportGPO.wsf**—Imports a backup GPO into any domain.

For more information on these scripts, refer to "Group Policy Management Console Scripting Examples" in Appendix A.

EXAM ALERT

You do not need to know the command syntax used by Group Policy scripts for Exam 70-640, but you should be aware of which script is used for which operation. An exam question could test this fact.

Offline Maintenance of Active Directory

Active Directory requires that certain maintenance operations be performed while AD DS is offline. This book has already discussed restoring AD DS when the server is running in DSRM. This section looks at additional maintenance operations that you will be required to perform from time to time. This includes offline *defragmentation* and compaction of the AD DS database and database storage allocation.

Restartable Active Directory

New in Windows Server 2008 is the ability to stop or restart AD DS from Microsoft Management Console snap-ins or the Net.exe command-line tool. This feature enables you to perform tasks such as offline defragmentation of the AD DS database without the need to restart the domain controller in DSRM. In addition, it reduces the time required to perform these actions.

A domain controller can operate in any of three possible modes:

> ▶ **AD DS Started**—This is the normal mode, in which the domain controller can perform authentication requests and all other actions normally performed by a domain controller.

> ▶ **AD DS Stopped**—The domain controller acts much like a member server. It cannot service requests for directory services, but other services that might be running on the domain controller (for example, DHCP or file services) can run normally. Any services that depend on AD DS are stopped, such as DNS, File Replication Service (FRS), Kerberos Key Distribution Center (KDC), and Intersite Messaging. You can perform many types of maintenance actions in this status.

> ▶ **DSRM**—The domain controller is completely offline, acting as a stand-alone server. It does not service external requests. As already discussed, you use this mode to perform all types of AD DS restore actions.

You can stop AD DS from the Server Manager MMC snap-in. In the console tree, expand Configuration and select Services to display the list of services in the Details pane. Right-click Active Directory Domain Services and select Stop. The Stop Other Services dialog box shown in Figure 8.9 displays, informing you of the other services that will also stop. Click Yes to stop AD DS and these services. A message box that follows the progress of stopping these services displays.

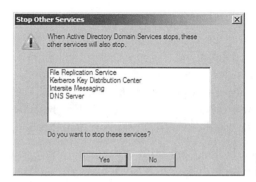

FIGURE 8.9 Stopping AD DS also stops these other services.

To restart AD DS, simply right-click Active Directory Domain Services and choose Start. This restarts the other services automatically as well.

You can also stop and restart AD DS from the command line. Type **net stop ntds** to stop AD DS, and type **net start ntds** to restart AD DS. Confirm your action when requested.

For additional information on Restartable AD DS, refer to "Windows Server 2008 Restartable AD DS Step-by-Step Guide" in Appendix A.

Offline Defragmentation and Compaction

As you work with the AD DS database, performing actions such as creating, modifying, and deleting objects, the database file (`ntds.dit`) can become fragmented just like any other file. Data becomes fragmented and read/write operations take longer to process because the disk head must move back and forth.

AD DS defragmentation can occur in two modes: online and offline. The following sections provide information about these modes.

Online Defragmentation

Online defragmentation takes place automatically while the server is online and able to process directory requests. AD DS performs an online defragmentation every 12 hours on an ongoing basis; however, recovered space is retained within the database and not released to the file system. This process can fully defragment the AD DS database file, but it can never reduce the `ntds.dit` file's size. Even if the quantity of data in the database has reduced (for example, after deleting numerous objects), the empty space remains within the database. You must perform a manual, offline defragmentation to recover this space.

Offline Defragmentation

Offline defragmentation enables you to reduce the `ntds.dit` file size, but it requires that the domain controller be taken offline. Because this process is more vulnerable to corruption by means of issues such as power failures or hardware problems, an offline defragmentation never takes place on the live database file. Instead, a copy of this file is made, and this copy is defragmented. When the defragmentation is complete, you must copy the new file into its original location.

Unlike previous versions of Windows Server, you do not need to restart the server in DSRM. Perform the following procedure to stop AD DS and defragment the database:

1. Open a command prompt, type **net stop ntds** to stop AD DS, and press Enter. You can also use Server Manager as previously described.

2. Type **ntdsutil** and press Enter.

3. At the `ntdsutil` prompt, type **activate instance ntds** and press Enter.

4. At the `ntdsutil` prompt, type **files** and press Enter.

5. At the `file maintenance` prompt, type **info** and press Enter. Note the current path and size of the AD DS database and log files.

6. At the `file maintenance` prompt, type **compact to <drive:\folder>**, where *<drive:\folder>* is the path to the location where the compacted file will be stored. Press Enter. When this process is complete, you are informed of the path to the new `ntds.dit` file.

7. Type **quit** twice to exit `ntdsutil`.

8. As instructed at the end of the compaction process, delete the log files in the log folder, copy the old `ntds.dit` file to an archival location, and then copy the new `ntds.dit` file over the old version.

9. To verify the integrity of the new database file, repeat steps 2 to 4 to return to the `ntdsutil file maintenance` prompt. Then type **integrity** and press Enter.

10. Type **quit** twice to exit `ntdsutil`.

11. Type **net start ntds** to restart AD DS.

TIP

You can also use this procedure to defragment the AD LDS database. This involves stopping and restarting the AD LDS instance being defragmented. AD LDS instances were discussed in Chapter 4, "Configuring Additional Active Directory Roles."

EXAM ALERT

Ensure that you have adequate free disk space available before defragmenting the AD DS database. You must have free space on the current drive that holds at least 15% of the current database size. This space is used for temporary storage during the compaction process.

For more information on the offline defragmentation process, refer to "Compact the Directory Database File (Offline Defragmentation)" in Appendix A.

Active Directory Database Storage Allocation

As your organization's AD DS structure grows, you might find that available disk space drops to an undesirably low value. If the operating system files and the AD DS database and log files are on the same physical disk, the disk might become overburdened with requests, resulting in slow performance. Other conditions might also require upgrades or maintenance of the physical disk holding the database or log files.

Any of these situations might require that you move the database or log files to a new disk. You must stop AD DS and use the ntdsutil utility to perform these tasks. This ensures that the Registry is updated with the new path to these files. Simply copying the files to a new location does not update the Registry and would require that you use the regedit.exe command to perform this task.

To move these files to a new location, you should first determine their size and ensure that you have a disk volume of adequate size to accommodate future growth. By default, these files are stored at %systemroot%\ntds. Use the dir command to determine the current size of the files. Microsoft recommends that the new volume be at least 20% larger than the current size of the files or 500MB each for the database and log files (minimum total of 1GB), but best practices suggest that the volume should be considerably larger than this value.

After you have installed a volume of appropriate size, back up the system state using the procedure described earlier in this chapter. This ensures that you can recover should problems occur during the move process. Then perform the following steps:

1. Open a command prompt, type **net stop ntds** to stop AD DS, and press Enter. You can also use Server Manager as previously described.

2. Type **ntdsutil** and press Enter.

3. At the ntdsutil prompt, type **activate instance ntds** and press Enter.

4. At the ntdsutil prompt, type **files** and press Enter.

5. At the file maintenance prompt, type **move db to *<drive:\folder>*,** where *<drive:\folder>* is the path to the new database location. Then type **move logs to *<drive:\folder>*,** where *<drive:\folder>* is the path to the location of the new log files.

6. Type **quit** twice to exit ntdsutil.

7. Type **net start ntds** to restart AD DS.

Monitoring Active Directory

You have seen how to back up and restore AD DS. Even with the tools provided, restoring AD DS can be a harrowing experience. Operating a consistent program of monitoring your domain controllers can provide insight into impending failures and other problems and reduce the need for restorative actions. Monitoring can achieve two goals: First, it can help you to maintain consistent performance over time, and second, it can help you to investigate problems such as sudden failures of hardware components.

Microsoft provides a wealth of support tools to assist you in managing and monitoring AD DS. Previous chapters have looked at several of these tools. Chapter 3, "Active Directory Sites and Replication," looked at the use of replmon, repadmin, and Event Viewer for monitoring AD DS replication, and Chapter 6, "Configuring and Troubleshooting Group Policy," looked at the use of Resultant Set of Policy (RSoP) for troubleshooting Group Policy. This section looks at the following additional tools for monitoring and troubleshooting AD DS:

▶ Network Monitor

▶ Task Manager

- ▶ Event Viewer

- ▶ Reliability and Performance Monitor

- ▶ Windows System Resource Manager

- ▶ Server Performance Advisor

Many of these tools are accessible from the new Server Manager console which, as you have learned, provides a centralized location for accessing many of the server functions. Additional monitoring and troubleshooting tools that are available here and covered on other Windows Server 2008 exams include Device Manager, Windows Firewall with Advanced Security (including IP Security [IPSec] monitoring), and Task Scheduler.

Network Monitor

Network Monitor enables you to capture, view, and analyze frames (packets) as they are transmitted over a network to all network adapter cards on your computer. By analyzing these frames, you can troubleshoot network problems, such as when users cannot log on because they are unable to communicate with domain controllers, DNS servers, or other servers. Network Monitor can perform security-related actions, such as the following:

- ▶ Detection of intrusion attempts and successes

- ▶ Detection of unauthorized users and tracing of their activity on the network

- ▶ Logs of captures, which provide information on network actions including source and destination addresses, protocols, and data transferred, thereby maintaining a record of actions that can include unauthorized ones

You can filter Network Monitor to capture or display only frames that meet certain criteria, thereby shortening the long list of frames included in the Frame Summary pane and facilitating the location of a certain frame type. Some of the more common filter criteria are the following:

- ▶ Frames captured by a specified network adapter

- ▶ Frames using a specified protocol

- ▶ Frames with a specified property, such as those originating from a specified IP address

Network Monitor is not included with Windows Server 2008 by default. You need to access http://go.Microsoft.com/fwlink/?LinkID=92844 to download Network Monitor 3.1 as a Microsoft Installer (.msi) file. Double-click the file and click Run on the Open File–Security Warning dialog box that appears. Follow the instructions in the setup wizard, selecting the Typical setup type to install the most common program features. After installation has completed, click Start, All Programs, Microsoft Network Monitor 3.1 to start the program. Network Monitor starts and displays the interface shown in Figure 8.10, which includes a summary of new features as well as several how-to tips.

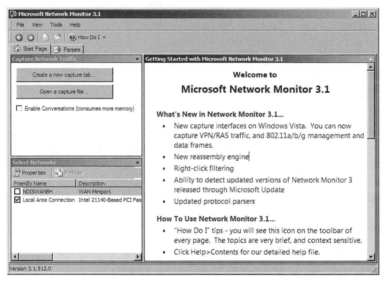

FIGURE 8.10   When you start Network Monitor, you see a summary of new features.

To capture network traffic, click Create a New Capture Tab. By default, a tab named Capture1 is added to the top of the window that displays a multipane arrangement within which captured data will be displayed. Click Start from the Capture menu to capture network traffic across the network adapter card of your server. As shown in Figure 8.11, each frame captured creates one line within the Frame Summary pane, including such details as source and destination computers (name or IP address), protocol name, and description. The time offset is the number of seconds elapsed since the capture was started. To display information about a particular frame, select it. The Frame Details pane provides information on the selected frame, and the Hex Details pane provides a hexadecimal rendering of the bits contained within the frame. You can also view this information in its own window by using Ctrl or Shift to select multiple frames, right-clicking, and choosing View Selected Frame(s) in a New Window. You can obtain additional information within the Frame Details pane by clicking any of the "+" squares visible at the beginning of lines. Network Monitor continues to capture frames until you click Stop from the Capture menu.

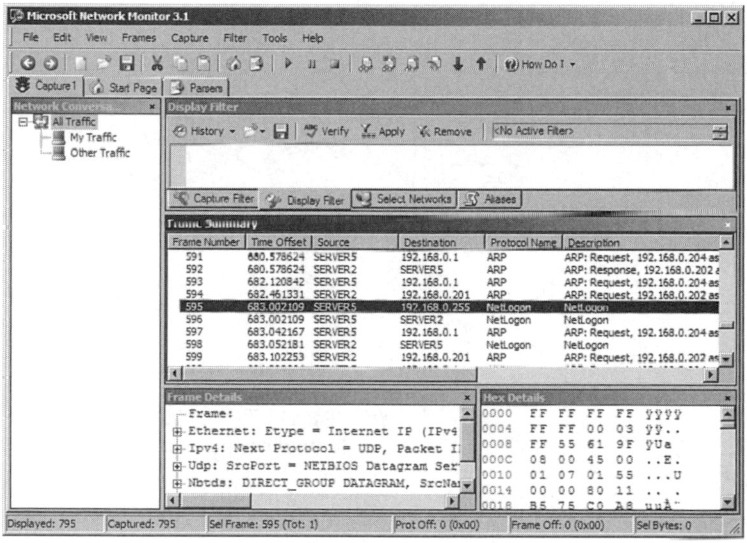

FIGURE 8.11 Network Monitor provides information on all frames that it captures.

Details of using Network Monitor are beyond the scope of Exam 70-640 and will not be elaborated on here. For additional information on Network Monitor, consult *MCTS 70-642 Exam Cram: Windows Server 2008 Network Infrastructure, Configuring* (ISBN: 078973818X) and the Help files that are installed on your computer when you install Network Monitor.

Task Manager

Task Manager provides information about currently running processes, including their CPU and memory usage, and enables you to modify their property or terminate misbehaving applications.

You can use any of the following methods to start Task Manager:

▶ Press Ctrl+Shift+Esc.

▶ Press Ctrl+Alt+Delete, and then select Task Manager from the list that appears.

▶ Right-click a blank area of the taskbar, and then select Task Manager.

▶ Click Start, Run, type **taskmgr**, and then press Enter.

As shown in Figure 8.12, Task Manager has six tabs that perform the following actions:

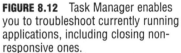

FIGURE 8.12 Task Manager enables you to troubleshoot currently running applications, including closing non-responsive ones.

▶ **Applications**—This tab displays all applications running on the computer. To terminate an ill-behaved program, select it and click End Task.

▶ **Processes**—This tab provides information on all processes running on the computer. New to Windows Vista and Windows Server 2008 is the Description column, which provides a detailed description of each process. You can modify the property of a running process or terminate an ill-behaved one. You can also display additional information by clicking View, Select Columns. The Select Process Page Columns dialog box that appears enables you to choose from a large number of variables associated with each process.

▶ **Services**—New to Windows Vista and Windows Server 2008, this tab provides information on services installed on the computer, including their status, the service group to which they belong, and descriptive information. You can start a stopped service or stop a started one by right-clicking it and choosing the appropriate command. You can access the Services snap-in by clicking the Services command button, which enables you to configure more properties such as startup type and recovery options should a service fail.

▶ **Performance**—This tab provides a limited performance monitoring function that includes processor and physical memory usage statistics.

The memory graph now displays actual memory usage rather than the page file usage displayed in Windows Server 2003. If your server is equipped with dual processors or a dual-core processor, the CPU usage history graph is split to show the activity of both processors or cores.

▶ **Networking**—This tab provides information on network utilization across the local network adaptors.

▶ **Users**—This tab displays the users who have sessions, active or disconnected, running on the local server. You can disconnect or log users off, or you can send them messages.

The menu bar of Task Manager enables you to access additional options. From the File menu, you can start a new process. This action is equivalent to using the Run dialog box and is useful should the Explorer process become terminated or misbehave. From the Options menu, you can keep the Task Manager window always visible on the desktop. From the View menu, you can adjust the refresh rate of the graphs on the Performance and Networking tabs.

Event Viewer

Event Viewer was introduced in Chapter 3 with regard to its use in monitoring and troubleshooting AD DS replication, and in Chapter 7, "Group Policy and Active Directory Security," with regard to viewing audited events. As mentioned in these chapters, you can access Event Viewer from the Diagnostics folder of Server Manager or from its own console in the Administrative Tools folder. Event Viewer contains two folders of logs: Windows Logs, which contains five logs common to all servers, and Applications and Services Logs, which contains a series of logs dependent on the roles and role services installed on the server.

The following Windows Logs are present on all servers:

▶ **Application**—Displays events recorded by system applications, as well as applications written to Microsoft standards, such as many antivirus programs.

▶ **Security**—Displays results of audited actions as configured in Group Policy. Auditing was discussed in Chapter 7.

▶ **Setup**—Records information related to the installation of applications and features on the server.

▶ **System**—Displays events logged by Windows kernel and device drivers, including reasons for the failure of services to start and the cause of stop (blue screen) errors. This log also records errors related to directory access problems.

▶ **Forwarded Events**—Saves events collected from remote computers. To enable this log, you must create an *event subscription*, which describes the events that will be collected and where they will be collected from.

Logs included in the Applications and Services node record events related to the particular application or service included as a subnode. Included here are several that are found on all servers, such as Hardware Events, Internet Explorer, and Key Management Service. The AD DS server role adds additional logs such as Directory Service (see Figure 8.13), File Replication Service, and DNS Server (if DNS is installed). You will also find a log related to each instance of AD LDS here. The Microsoft subnode includes a large number of subfolders that are too numerous to mention here; two items of interest to Active Directory administrators are Group Policy and Backup.

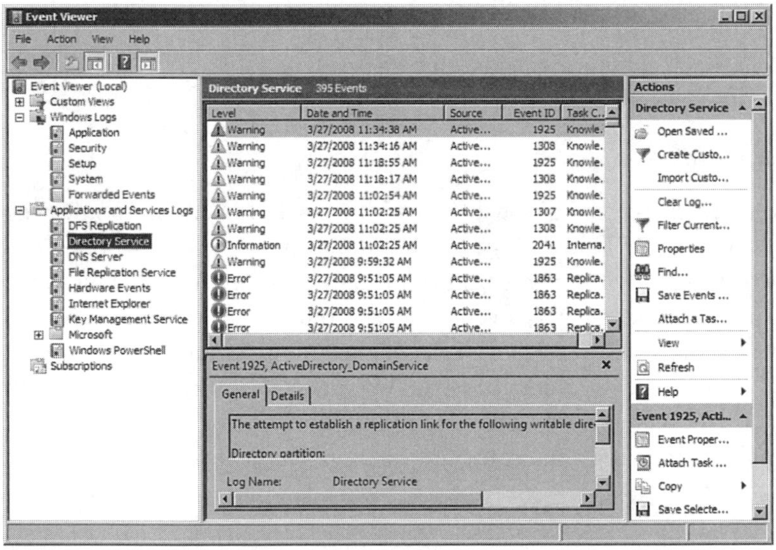

FIGURE 8.13 The Directory Service log records events related to AD DS.

Customizing Event Viewer

With the large number of logs present in Windows Server 2008, you might think that keeping track of these logs would be a major undertaking. Microsoft has added the Custom Views folder at the top of Event Viewer to gather logs from various locations. Appearing at the top of the console tree as shown in Figure 8.13, this folder includes an Administrative Events node as well as nodes for each of the server roles installed on the computer. The Administrative Events node includes critical, error, and warning events from all logs gathered in a single location, which facilitates your ability to find events that require attention. Each log under Server Roles gathers events at all levels from the various Windows Logs and Applications and Services Logs that relate to that particular server role, again facilitating your ability to locate these events rapidly. You can also create your own custom views in this area; simply right-click Custom Views and choose Create Custom View to create a new custom view or Import Custom View to import one created on another computer. As shown in Figure 8.14, you can create customized logs according to the following criteria:

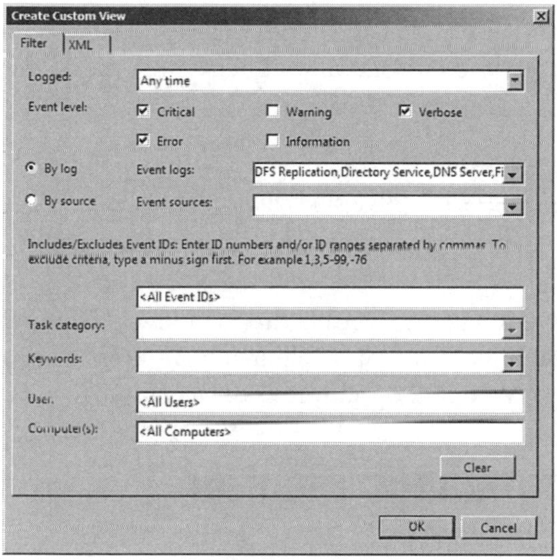

FIGURE 8.14 The Create Custom View dialog box enables you to create your own customized event log.

▶ **Logged**—Supply a time interval ranging from Last Hour to Last 30 Days, or choose Any Time or a customized range of dates and times.

▶ **Event Level**—Choose one or more of the event levels: Critical, Error, Warning, or Information. Choose Verbose to provide additional detail on the logged events. (In previous Windows versions, you had to perform a Registry edit to obtain additional detail.)

▶ **By Log**—This enables you to select the logs from which you want to display events.

▶ **By Source**—This enables you to select from the service, program, or driver that logged the event. You can select only one of these options: By Log or By Source.

▶ **Event IDs**—These are numbers that uniquely define each type of event. You can select the event ID numbers to be displayed (or leave the default of All Event IDs selected).

▶ **Task Category**—This enables you to select task categories to be displayed.

▶ **Keywords**—This enables you to select keywords such as Audit Success and Audit Failure.

▶ **User**—This enables you to select the user account(s) associated with an event. Separate multiple usernames with commas.

▶ **Computer(s)**—This enables you to select the computer(s) associated with an event. Separate multiple computer names with commas.

After you have created your custom view and clicked OK, you are asked to type a name and optional description for the custom view. Then select the folder where you want to store the view.

You can also customize the level of detail shown by any of the default logs. Right-click a log and choose Filter Current Log. The Filter Current Log dialog box enables you to choose from most of the same categories already described for creating a custom log. The By Log and By Source options are not available.

For additional information on Event Viewer, consult the Windows Help and Support Center by choosing Help Topics from the Help menu. You can also go online by selecting the TechCenter Web Site option from this location.

Reliability and Performance Monitor

The Windows Server 2008 *Reliability and Performance Monitor* console replaces and updates the Performance Console tool used with Windows 2000 and Windows Server 2003. It is included as a component of the Diagnostics section of Server Monitor and is accessible as a standalone MMC console from the Administrative Tools folder. As shown in Figure 8.15, it includes the following monitoring tools:

▶ **Performance Monitor**—Provides a real-time graph of server performance, either in the present time or as logged historical data.

▶ **Reliability Monitor**—Performs an overall reliability analysis of computer stability with time.

▶ **Data Collector Sets**—Records server performance data into log files. Data collectors are separated into groups that you can use for monitoring performance under different conditions. This feature was previously known as Performance Logs and Alerts.

▶ **Reports**—Produces performance report data. This feature was included as the Report function of the System Monitor console in previous Windows versions.

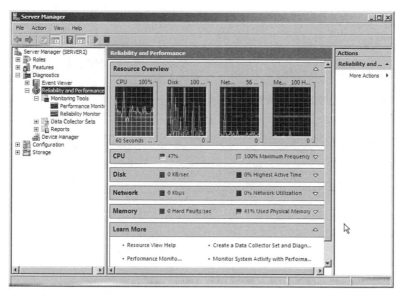

FIGURE 8.15 You can monitor and log your server's performance from the Reliability and Performance Monitor console.

For additional information on Reliability and Performance Monitor and its various components, refer to "Step-by-Step Guide for Performance and Reliability Monitoring in Windows Server 2008" in Appendix A.

Resource Overview

New to Windows Server 2008 is the Resource Overview panel, which appears as a default window when you start Reliability and Performance Monitor (see Figure 8.15). This panel provides a summary of processor, disk, network, and memory performance statistics, including minigraphs of recent performance for these components. Click the triangle at the right side of each of these components to display additional information. This information includes the application whose resource usage is being monitored (referred to as the image) and the process identifier number (PID) of the application instance, as well as several statistical measures that pertain to each of the components.

Performance Monitor

As shown in Figure 8.16, Performance Monitor provides a configurable real-time graph of computer performance and enables you to perform tasks such as the following:

▸ Identify performance problems such as bottlenecks

▸ Monitor resource usage

▸ Establish trends of server performance with time

▸ Monitor the effects of changes in server configuration

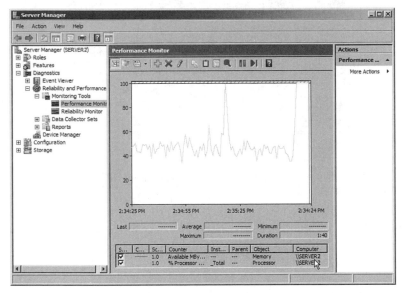

FIGURE 8.16 Performance Monitor displays a real-time graph of activity for selected objects and counters.

Performance Monitor records information on a series of hardware or software components known as *objects*. These can be any components that possess a series of measurable properties. These measurable properties are known as *counters*. Objects that have multiple occurrences (for example, processors on a dual-processor machine) possess *instances*, which relate to the performance of each processor, in this case. You can select which objects and counters you want to monitor in any given situation.

Reliability Monitor

Reliability Monitor is a new tool that utilizes the built-in Reliability Analysis Component (RAC) to provide a trend analysis of your server's stability over

time. It provides the System Stability Chart shown in Figure 8.17, which corre-
lates the trend of your computer's stability against events that might destabilize
the computer. It tracks the following types of events:

▶ **Software (Un)installs**—Installation or removal of programs, including
Windows updates and drivers. Information provided includes the name
of the program, Windows update name, or driver name; its version; the
activity (install or uninstall); its success or failure; and the date the event
occurred.

▶ **Application Failures**—Software programs that hang or crash.
Information provided includes the program name, its version number,
the type of failure, and the date.

▶ **Hardware Failures**—Failure of components such as disks or memory.
Information provided includes the failed device, the failure type, and the
date.

▶ **Windows Failures**—Problems such as operating system crashes or boot
failures. Information provided includes the type of failure, the Stop code
or detected problem, and the date.

▶ **Miscellaneous Failures**—Other types of failures, such as improper
shutdowns. Information includes the failure type, details, and date.

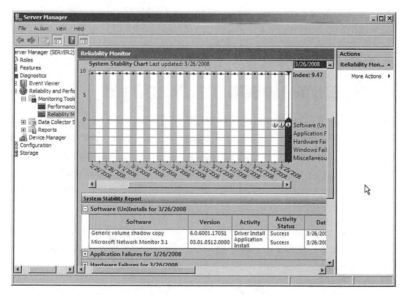

FIGURE 8.17 The System Stability Chart and System Stability Report provide a trend analysis
of your server's stability.

Data Collector Sets

Data collector sets are series of performance objects and counters that enable you to log server performance over time for later viewing and analysis in the Performance Monitor snap-in. Previously known as Performance Logs and Alerts, this feature enables you to do the following:

▶ Establish a performance baseline for each server, which is a log of server performance that you can save for later comparison with future performance and tracking of any changes that might have occurred over time.

▶ Identify potential bottlenecks in server performance so that you can take corrective action.

▶ Monitor the effectiveness of any changes you make to the server's configuration.

▶ Alert you to events of unusual server performance, such as a consistently high percentage of processor utilization or low available memory. These might indicate hardware or software problems or the need to upgrade some system component. These alerts are displayed in the Application log in Event Viewer.

To create a data collector set, expand the Data Collector Sets node in Reliability and Performance Monitor, as shown in Figure 8.16, and select User Defined. Then right-click a blank area in the Details pane and select New, Data Collector Set. After that, follow the steps provided by the Create New Data Collector Set Wizard.

Windows System Resource Manager

Windows System Resource Manager (WSRM) is an administrative feature that enables you to control how processor and memory resources are allocated to applications, services, and processes running on the server. Managing resource allocation reduces the risk of these items competing for processor and memory resources, thereby improving the efficiency and performance of the computer. It is especially useful on servers that are running Terminal Services.

To install WSRM, access the Features node of Server Manager and click Add Features. In the Select Features page of the Add Features Wizard, scroll down to select Windows System Resource Manager. The wizard asks you to install Windows Internal Database. Accept this request, click Next, and then click Install.

After you have installed WSRM, you can access it from the Administrative Tools folder. You can monitor the computer where you have installed it, or you can connect to another computer. WSRM opens in its own snap-in, which has nodes for the following items in the console tree:

▶ **Resource Allocation Policies**—WSRM uses this to determine how computer resources such as processor and memory are allocated to processes running on the server. WSRM provides four built-in resource allocation policies, or you can create a custom resource allocation policy according to your network's need.

▶ **Process Matching Criteria**—WSRM uses this to match processes running on the server and aggregate the matched processes into groups, which you can then manage in resource allocation policies. Two built-in process-matching criteria are included, or you can create your own custom criteria.

▶ **Conditions**—You can have up to six preconfigured events, which represent conditions under which WSRM can automatically switch to a different matching policy.

▶ **Calendar**—This enables you to schedule resource management. You can create a one-time event or recurring events with which you can associate a resource allocation policy. You can also schedule when a resource allocation policy will take effect or end. Multiple schedules are supported.

▶ **Resource Monitor**—This uses Performance Monitor to display a custom set of counters that assist you in understanding how resource management works and how often your policies change the usage of server resources. See Figure 8.18.

▶ **Accounting**—You can log accounting data about applications. This includes information about applications that exceeded their allocated resources and changes made by the management policy. This data is stored in an accounting database on the local computer, on another computer running WSRM, or on a SQL Server database.

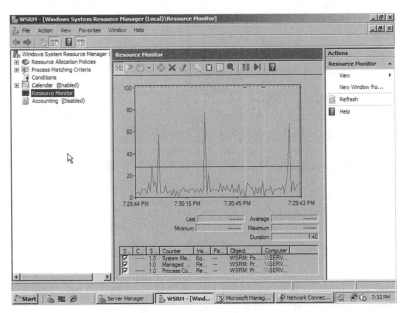

FIGURE 8.18 The Resource Monitor component of WSRM provides a snapshot of your server's performance.

For additional information on WSRM, consult *MCTS 70-643 Exam Cram: Windows Server 2008 Applications Infrastructure, Configuring* (ISBN 0789738198) or "Microsoft Windows Server Code Name 'Longhorn' Windows System Resource Manager Step-by-Step Guide" in Appendix A.

Server Performance Advisor

Server Performance Advisor was introduced in Windows Server 2003 as a tool that gathers information from a series of sources, including performance counters, Registry keys, and Event Tracing for Windows. It provides an in-depth view of current server performance and provides suggestions for making improvements. You can configure Server Performance Advisor to repeat the process of gathering information on a regular basis to obtain trend information that assists in identifying trouble spots.

Server Performance Advisor automatically detects the server roles you have configured and installs data collector groups that are pertinent to these roles. You can also create custom data collector groups. Each data collector group is defined in an XML-based configuration template that includes the appropriate performance counters, event traces, and Registry keys for the server role in question. It also provides reports that enable you to present the data in formats appropriate for different individuals or groups.

In Windows Server 2008, the functionality of Server Performance Advisor is integrated into Reliability and Performance Monitor. The Reports feature of this tool includes four predefined server diagnostics: Active Directory Diagnostics, LAN Diagnostics, System Diagnostics, and System Performance. Each of these includes a specific set of performance objects and counters suited for monitoring these aspects of server performance. Also included is a User Defined subnode that you can use to configure your own custom report.

Exam Cram Questions

1. Lynn is the systems administrator for a company that operates an AD DS network consisting of a single domain. She needs to perform a system state backup of the network's domain controllers to ensure that she can restore AD DS should a catastrophic
   failure occur. Which of the following tools should she use?

   ○ **A.** Ntbackup.exe

   ● **B.** Wbadmin.exe

   ○ **C.** Ntdsutil.exe

   ○ **D.** Windows Server Backup

2. Working at one of the six domain controllers in his company's network, Brendan accidentally deleted his company's Executive OU. Realizing that none of the executives
   would be able to log on the next morning, Brendan knew he must restore this OU as
   rapidly as possible. Fortunately, a backup of the system state of the domain controller
   had been created the day before.

   Which of the following actions does Brendan need to perform? (Each correct answer
   represents part of the solution. Choose two answers.)

   ○ **A.** Use the net stop ntds and the wbadmin start
   systemstaterecovery commands to restore system state
   from backup.

   ○ **B.** Start the domain controller in Safe Mode, and then use the wbadmin
   start systemstaterecovery command to restore system state
   from backup.

   ● **C.** Start the domain controller in Directory Services Restore Mode, and then
   use the wbadmin start systemstaterecovery command to
   restore system state from backup.

   ○ **D.** Select the Repair Your Computer option.

   ● **E.** Use the ntdsutil program to mark the restored Executive OU as authoritative by specifying the LDAP DN of the Executive OU.

   ○ **F.** Select the Format and Repartition Disks option.

3. Rebecca is the network administrator for a clothing manufacturer. The company's network
   is configured as a single AD DS domain. All domain controllers run Windows Server
   2008, and the domain and forest functional levels are set to Windows Server 2008.

   The company buys out a competitor that operates a single domain AD DS network running
   at the Windows Server 2008 domain and forest functional levels. Rebecca wants to
   export the settings of a GPO from her company and import them into the second company. How can she perform this task with the least amount of administrative effort?

○ **A.** Use the `BackupGPO.wsf` script to back up the settings in her domain, and then use the `RestoreGPO.wsf` script to import them into the second domain.

● **B.** Use the `BackupGPO.wsf` script to back up the settings in her domain, and then use the `ImportGPO.wsf` script to import them into the second domain.

○ **C.** Use the `Wbadmin` command to back up the settings in her domain, and then use the `Wbadmin` command to restore them to the second domain.

○ **D.** Create a forest trust between the two companies, and then access the required GPO from the Group Policy Management Console and copy it to the second company.

4. Trevor is a network administrator for a company that operates an AD DS forest containing two domains in separate trees named quepublishing.com and examcram.com. A junior administrator has accidentally deleted the Financial OU from the quepublishing.com domain. This domain contains some security groups that have back-links of groups in the examcram.com domain as members.

   Trevor authoritatively restores the Financial OU, but users in this OU report that they are unable to access objects in the examcram.com domain. He realizes that he should create an LDIF file for recovering the back-links of these groups in the examcram.com domain for the authoritatively restored objects in the Financial OU. Which utility should he use to perform this operation?

   ● **A.** Ntdsutil.exe

   ○ **B.** Esentutl.exe

   ○ **C.** Ldifde.exe

   ○ **D.** Wbadmin.exe

5. Melissa is the network administrator for an accounting company based in Pittsburgh. During a standard review of the AD DS files on one of the domain controllers, she notices that the hard drive containing the `ntds.dit` file is running out of space. However, there is plenty of space available on another hard drive in the same server. She decides to move the `ntds.dit` file to this hard drive. What should she do to accomplish this task with the least amount of administrative effort?

   ○ **A.** Restart the server in Directory Services Restore Mode and use the `ntdsutil` utility to move the `ntds.dit` file.

   ○ **B.** Restart the server in Directory Services Restore Mode and use Windows Explorer to move the `ntds.dit` file.

   ● **C.** Use the `net stop ntds` command to stop AD DS and then use the `ntdsutil` utility to move the `ntds.dit` file.

○ **D.** Use the `net stop ntds` command to stop AD DS and then use Windows Explorer to move the `ntds.dit` file.

6. You are really counting your blessings because the company you work for has gone through a major downsizing in which almost one-quarter of all jobs have been eliminated, mostly through layoffs. As a result, you have been cleaning up your company's AD DS network by clearing out a lot of user and group accounts that are no longer needed.

   You have been monitoring the `ntds.dit` file and have been expecting it to reduce because it now holds much less data. However, you have seen nothing yet. What should you do?

   ○ **A.** You must wait for 24 hours for the deletions to be propagated to other domain controllers.

   ○ **B.** You must wait for 60 days because objects that are deleted from AD DS are assigned a tombstone of 60 days and are not immediately deleted. The file will not reduce until after this tombstone period has expired.

   ○ **C.** You should back up and restore the database to compress the file.

   ● **D.** You must perform an offline defragmentation of the database, because the space that was consumed by the deleted objects remains empty within the `ntds.dit` file until you do this.

7. You would like to display a real-time graph of processor and memory usage on your Windows Server 2008 computer so that you can decide whether you need some type of hardware upgrade. Which of the following tools can you use for this purpose? (Choose all that apply.)

   ○ **A.** Network Monitor

   ● **B.** Task Manager

   ○ **C.** Event Viewer

   ● **D.** Reliability and Performance Monitor

   ● **E.** Windows System Resource Manager

   ○ **F.** Server Performance Advisor

8. Andy is the network administrator for a company that runs an AD DS network with a single domain. One of the domain controllers has been running slowly during much of the day, and Andy suspects that he might need to upgrade the processor. He has added additional RAM to the computer, but he wants to be informed of potential processor bottlenecks.

Andy decides he wants to have the domain controller inform him when the processor utilization exceeds 85%. What should he do? (Each correct answer represents part of the solution. Choose two answers.)

○ **A.** Configure Windows System Resource Manager to generate an alert when the Processor\%Processor Time counter exceeds 85%.

○ **B.** Configure Performance Monitor to generate an alert when the Processor\%Processor Time counter exceeds 85%.

● **C.** Configure a data collector set to generate an alert when the Processor\%Processor Time counter exceeds 85%.

○ **D.** In Server Manager, he should ensure that the Alerter service is configured to start automatically and send a message to his computer. He will then receive a message box on his computer when an alert is created.

● **E.** View the Application log in Event Viewer to determine whether any alerts have been generated.

○ **F.** View the System log in Event Viewer to determine whether any alerts have been generated.

9. Amanda has configured the Performance Monitor snap-in in the Reliability and Performance Monitor console to track several NTDS performance objects on her domain controller so that she can have a performance baseline against which she can compare future domain controller performance. After viewing the graph for several minutes, she realizes she needs to save the data logged in the graph for future reference. What should she do to save all monitoring data, including the points that are no longer visible?

○ **A.** She needs to right-click the graph and choose Save Image As. In the dialog box that appears, she needs to specify the name of a comma-delimited file to which Performance Monitor will save all data.

○ **B.** She needs to choose the File, Export command. In the dialog box that appears, she needs to specify the name of a comma-delimited file to which Performance Monitor will save all data.

● **C.** She has used the wrong tool. She needs to use the data collector sets to configure logging so that she can save the performance data.

○ **D.** She has used the wrong tool. She needs to use the Windows System Resource Manager tool and select Resource Manager logging so that she can save the performance data. .

10. Ian has just installed Windows System Resource Manager on a server in his company's test network and wants to try it out before deploying it to servers on the company's production network. Which of the following are actions that this tool can perform for him? (Choose all that apply.)

   - ● **A.** Display a real-time performance graph for his server.

   - ○ **B.** Alert him to performance problems on the server.

   - ● **C.** Create and use a policy that determines how computer resources such as processor and memory are allocated to processes running on his server.

   - ● **D.** Gather information about applications that exceeded their allocated resources and changes that the management policy made.

   - ○ **E.** Perform a trend analysis of his server's stability over time.

Answers to *Exam Cram* Questions

1. **B.** Lynn should use the Wbadmin.exe tool to back up the system state on her domain controllers. More specifically, she should type **wbadmin start systemstatebackup**. The Ntbackup.exe tool was used to perform backups on older Windows versions. It is no longer included with Windows Server 2008, so answer A is incorrect. The Ntdsutil.exe tool is used to perform numerous Active Directory maintenance operations, including authoritative restores. It is not used to perform backups, so answer C is incorrect. The Windows Server Backup tool enables Lynn to perform a full backup or a critical-volume backup. It does not enable a system state backup, so answer D is incorrect.

2. **C, E.** To restore the Executive OU properly, Brendan needs to do an authoritative restore. First, he needs to start the domain controller in Directory Services Restore Mode and restore the system state data from backup. Then he needs to mark the restore of the Executive OU as authoritative, which he can do with the ntdsutil command. While stopping AD DS enables Brendan to do several other directory management actions such as defragmenting the database, he cannot perform a restore using this method, so answer A is incorrect. He also cannot do a restore using Safe Mode, so answer B is incorrect. The Repair Your Computer and Format and Repartition Disks options are part of performing a Windows Complete PC Restore option and not part of the authoritative restore, so answers D and F are incorrect.

3. **B.** Rebecca should use the BackupGPO.wsf script to back up the settings in her domain, and then use the ImportGPO.wsf script to import them into the second domain. The RestoreGPO.wsf script is used to restore backed-up GPOs in the same domain, so answer A is incorrect. Rebecca cannot use Wbadmin to back up and restore GPOs, so answer C is incorrect. It is not necessary to establish a forest trust between the two domains for the purpose of exporting and importing a GPO, so answer D is incorrect.

4. **A.** Trevor should use the `ntdsutil.exe` utility to perform this task. If an object with back-links in another domain has been authoritatively restored, he needs to run the `create ldif files from <file_path>` command on a domain controller in the other domain (examcram.com in this instance). He can run this command from the `authoritative restore` prompt within `ntdsutil`. Before Trevor runs this command, he must copy the `.txt` file created by `ntdsutil` during the authoritative restore to a location on the domain controller in the examcram.com domain or an accessible shared folder location and then restore this domain controller from backup. The `Esentutl` tool provides utility functions for the Extensible Storage Engine for Windows. It does not restore back-links, so answer B is incorrect. The `Ldifde` tool enables Trevor to perform several operations on LDIF files but not restoring back-links, so answer C is incorrect. The `Wbadmin` tool enables him to perform backups and restores but does not allow the restoration of back-links, so answer D is incorrect.

5. **C.** Melissa should use the `net stop ntds` command to stop AD DS and then use the `ntdsutil` utility to move the `ntds.dit` file. To move the file, she must use this utility to make sure that the appropriate Registry settings are also modified. She could restart the server in Directory Services Restore mode and then use `ntdsutil` to move the file. This was the method she would have needed in older Windows versions. It is still valid but takes more administrative effort than simply stopping AD DS; therefore, answer A is incorrect. Melissa cannot use Windows Explorer to move the file because this method would not automatically modify the Registry; therefore, answers B and D are incorrect.

6. **D.** You must perform an offline defragmentation of the database to recover the space once used by the deleted objects. Waiting for another 24 hours does not help, so answer A is incorrect. Although tombstoning exists as described, this process does not affect the space used by the database file, so answer B is incorrect. Backing up and restoring data will not change the overall file size, so answer C is incorrect.

7. **B, D, E.** Task Manager, Reliability and Performance Monitor, and Windows System Resource Manager can display graphs of processor and memory usage. Network Monitor displays information about data frames transmitted across the network. Event Viewer displays information about events taking place on the computer, applications running on the computer, or successful or failed accesses to resources. Server Performance Advisor was used in Windows Server 2003 as a tool that gathers information from a series of sources, including performance counters, Registry keys, and Event Tracing for Windows. None of the latter three tools display performance graphs, so answers A, C, and F are incorrect.

8. **C, E.** Andy needs to create a manually configured data collector set and access the Performance Counter Alert option. When he does this, he can view alerts in the Application log in Event Viewer. Note that he can connect to the domain controller from his desktop computer to view these alerts. (Right-click Event Viewer, choose Connect to Another Computer, and type the name of the required server.) Both WSRM and Performance Monitor enable Andy to view performance data in real time; however, neither one can create alerts, so answers A and B are incorrect. He cannot configure the

Alerter service to display alerts to his desktop, so answer D is incorrect. He needs to look in the Application log and not the System log to find alerts, so answer F is incorrect.

9. **C.** Amanda needs to use data collector sets to log data over time so she can obtain a performance baseline for the domain controller. The Save Image As option saves an image of the currently visible data but does not save data that is no longer visible, so answer A is incorrect. Performance Monitor does not have an Export option for saving performance data, so answer B is incorrect. The Resource Manager option in WSRM enables Amanda to view performance data but not save it, so answer D is incorrect.

10. **A, C, D.** Using WSRM, Ian can display a real-time performance graph for his server. He can also create and use a policy that determines how computer resources such as processor and memory are allocated to processes running on the server. In addition, he can gather information about applications that have exceeded their allocated resources and changes made by the management policy. He would need to use a data collector set in Reliability and Performance Monitor to alert him to performance problems on the server, so answer B is incorrect. He would need to use the Reliability Monitor feature in Reliability and Performance Monitor to perform a trend analysis of his server's stability over time, so answer E is incorrect.

9

Active Directory Certificate Services

Terms You'll Need to Understand

- ✓ Authority Information Access (AIA)
- ✓ Autoenrollment
- ✓ Certificate enrollment
- ✓ Certificate revocation list (CRL)
- ✓ Certificate template
- ✓ Certification Authority (CA)
- ✓ CRL distribution point (CDP)
- ✓ Delta CRL
- ✓ Enrollment agents
- ✓ Enterprise CA
- ✓ Intermediate CA
- ✓ Issuing CA
- ✓ Key recovery agent (KRA)
- ✓ Online Certificate Status Protocol (OCSP)
- ✓ Online responder
- ✓ Public key infrastructure (PKI)
- ✓ Root CA
- ✓ Smart cards
- ✓ Standalone CA
- ✓ Subordinate CA
- ✓ Versions 1, 2, and 3 templates

Concepts/Techniques You'll Need to Master

- ✓ Planning, installing, and managing CA hierarchies
- ✓ Understanding the difference between enterprise and standalone CAs
- ✓ Configuring certificate templates
- ✓ Configuring certificate autoenrollment and Web-based enrollment
- ✓ Managing archival and recovery of keys
- ✓ Managing certificate stores
- ✓ Backing up and restoring the CA database
- ✓ Understanding the various certificate templates and their use
- ✓ Managing certificate enrollment
- ✓ Configuring certificate autoenrollment
- ✓ Creating and restricting enrollment agents
- ✓ Understanding certificate revocation
- ✓ Managing CRLs and delta CRLs
- ✓ Configuring online responders

Internet commerce is a burgeoning activity these days, with more and more companies engaging in online selling. At the same time, the bad guys are trying to rip people off with ever-changing tactics. An important line of defense against their actions is that of certifying your websites so that users coming to them are assured that they are legitimate and not imposters that are attempting to steal their identities and more. Windows Server 2008 continues the trend of recent server versions in offering its own certificate service that is integrated with Active Directory. This chapter shows you how to install and configure a *public key infrastructure (PKI)*, including various aspects of configuring and managing *certification authorities (CA)*, certificates, *certificate templates*, and keys. It looks at various aspects of configuring CA servers, including backup, restore, and archival of certificates and keys; use of certificate templates; various methods of certificate enrollments; and certificate revocation.

What's New with Certificate Services in Windows Server 2008?

Active Directory Certificate Services (AD CS) in Windows Server 2008 is included as a server role that enables you to perform all certificate management activities without the need for add-on software programs. Included with AD CS are the following role services:

▶ **Certification Authority**—Enables you to perform all types of certificate management, including the creation, configuration, and revocation of digital certificates for computers, users, and organizations. You can link multiple CAs to form a PKI.

▶ **Certification Authority Web Enrollment**—Enables you to configure web-based certificate enrollment, including autoenrollment. You can also perform smart card enrollment and create enrollment agents that clients can use to request certificates.

▶ **Online Certificate Status Protocol (OCSP)**—Enables clients to use OCSP as a means of determining certificate revocation status.

▶ **Microsoft Simple Certificate Enrollment Protocol**—Allows routers and other network devices to obtain certificates.

391

What's New with Certificate Services in Windows Server 2008?

The following are several of the more important new or changed capabilities in Windows Server 2008 Certificate Services:

▶ Windows Server 2008 introduces a new *version 3 (V3) certificate template* that supports issuing suite b-compliant certificates, which provide enhanced security without sacrificing performance. Support for the older versions 1 and 2 templates is continued. V3 certificate templates can use the latest cryptographic algorithms and ensure the security of communications between clients and CAs.

▶ Windows Server 2008 replaces the previous ActiveX enrollment control with a new Component Object Model (COM)–based enrollment control. This provides enhanced support for web-based enrollment pages for enrolling certificates on Windows Vista and Windows Server 2008 client computers, while providing backward compatibility within limits for Windows 2000/XP/Server 2003 machines. These older clients cannot use web-based enrollment with version 3 certificate templates; however, they can with version 1 or 2 templates.

▶ Group Policy certificate settings enable you to manage certificate settings on all domain computers from a central location. Some examples include management of certificate revocation and renewal of expired certificates. You can also manage several types of certificate stores.

▶ You can use Group Policy to distribute certificates by placing them in the appropriate certificate stores. Certificate types include trusted root CA certificates, enterprise trust certificates, intermediate CA certificates, trusted publisher certificates, untrusted certificates, and peer trust certificates.

▶ You can regulate the users' ability to manage their own trusted root certificates and peer trust certificates. You can also specify whether domain users can trust both enterprise root CAs and non-Microsoft CAs, or only enterprise root CAs.

▶ New methods of managing *certificate revocation lists (CRL)* have been added, including the publication of CRLs and delta CRLs in several locations that enhance the ability of clients to access these lists. You can also use OCSP for checking certificate revocation status. OCSP uses computers configured with the *Online Responder* service to provide revocation status information for certificates issued by one or more CAs within your PKI hierarchy. New Group Policy settings also enhance the management of CRLs and OCSP data.

▶ Enterprise PKI (PKIView) is a new MMC snap-in included with Windows Server 2008 that facilitates the monitoring and troubleshooting of multiple CAs within your PKI hierarchy. It indicates the status of various CAs at a glance.

▶ Network Device Enrollment Service (NDES) enables software on network devices such as routers and switches to enroll for X.509 certificates from a server running AD CS.

This chapter introduces you to the most important procedures for configuring AD CS that you need to know for Exam 70-640. If you want to perform additional procedures, including an advanced lab setup that simulates real-world situations more realistically, refer to the procedures in "Windows Server 2008 Step-by-Step Guides," in Appendix A, "Need to Know More?" In this URL, scroll to `Windows Server 2008 Active Directory Certificate Services Step-By-Step Guide.doc` and click the Download button to obtain this document.

Installing Active Directory Certificate Services

You can install AD CS as a server role from the Add Roles Wizard in Server Manager. Before covering the installation procedure, this chapter introduces the concepts of certificate authority roles and hierarchies. You should not use a single CA but rather a hierarchy of two or more CAs. This provides load balancing and fault tolerance, and it enables you to create an offline root CA so that you can ensure the security of the entire hierarchy.

Certificate Authority Types and Hierarchies

Windows Server 2008 makes available the following two types of CAs:

▶ *Enterprise CA*—This type of CA is integrated with Active Directory Domain Services (AD DS). It is installed on a domain controller running Windows Server 2008, Enterprise Edition, and stores its certificates within AD DS.

▶ *Standalone CA*—This type of CA maintains a separate certificate database that is not integrated with AD DS. It is installed on a member server or standalone server.

A PKI can consist of a two-tier or three-tier hierarchy or CA servers. Within this hierarchy, you can have up to three distinct CA roles:

- ▶ *Root CA*—This CA is located at the top of every CA hierarchy. It may exist in the form of a root CA operated by your organization, or it could be a CA owned and operated by a third-party issuing authority. In the latter case, you would install the certificate issued by the third-party company on an intermediate or issuing CA server in your own organization.

- ▶ *Intermediate CA*—Within a three-tier hierarchy, this CA is directly subordinate to the root CA and issues certificates that validate the issuing CAs. Organizations commonly situate intermediate CA servers in different geographical locations, such as cities where offices are located. Intermediate CAs do not exist in a two-tier CA hierarchy.

- ▶ *Issuing CA*—At the bottom of a two- or three-tier hierarchy, the issuing CA issues certificates to users and client computers as needed. Companies often dedicate different issuing CA servers to specific certificate types, such as smart cards and Encrypting File System (EFS).

TIP

When you set up a CA hierarchy, you should use a standalone root CA with enterprise intermediate and issuing CAs. Doing so enables you to keep the standalone CA offline and physically protected in a locked vault. You would bring this CA online only when needed for issuing certificates to CA servers lower in the hierarchy, thereby protecting your PKI from compromise. You should not use an offline enterprise CA because it cannot maintain its integration with AD DS when offline. Consequently, it would never be up to date.

Installing Root CAs

The procedure for installing a CA depends on its position in the hierarchy. You begin installing a hierarchy with the root CA, then intermediate CAs if required, and finally the issuing CAs. Installation of these various types of CAs is similar and proceeds as follows from the Add Roles Wizard in Server Manager:

1. Ensure that you are logged on as a member of the local Administrators group to install a standalone CA or as a member of the Domain Admins group to install an enterprise CA.

2. In the Roles node of Server Manager, click Add Roles.

3. On the Select Server Roles page of the Add Roles Wizard, select Active Directory Certificate Services, and then click Next.

4. The Introduction to Active Directory Certificate Services provides links to additional information from the server Help and Support files. It is useful to select these links and read the information provided for further understanding of AD CS and its actions. When finished, return to the wizard and click Next.

5. The Select Role Services page shown in Figure 9.1 enables you to install additional role services. Select the required services and then click Next. To add the Certification Authority Web Enrollment and Online Responder services, you must add Internet Information Services (IIS) if it is not already installed on the server. Click Add Requested Role Services.

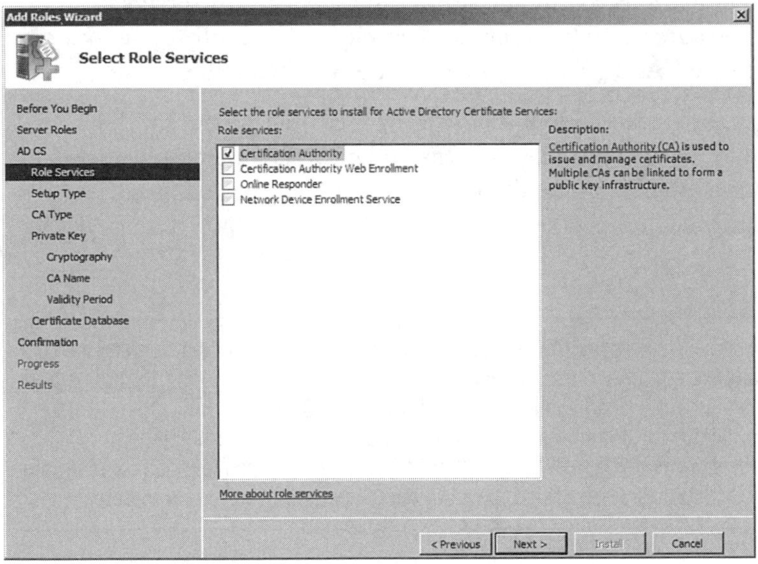

FIGURE 9.1 You can install additional role services from the Select Role Services page when you are installing AD CS.

NOTE

You cannot add the Network Device Enrollment Service role service until you have installed and configured AD CS.

6. On the Specify Setup Type page, select the required type, as shown in Figure 9.2. If you're installing on a server that is not a domain controller, only the Standalone type will be available. Click Next.

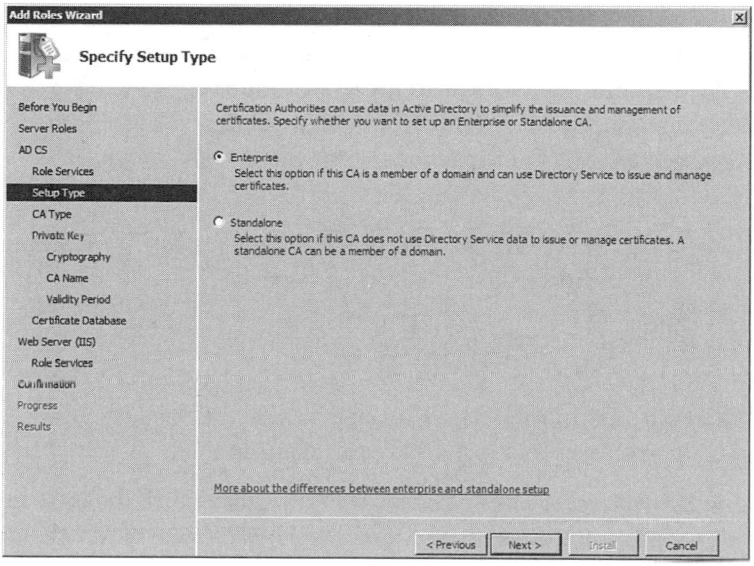

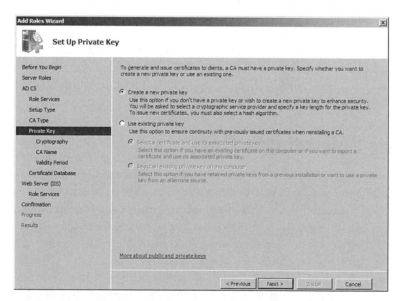

FIGURE 9.2 The wizard asks if you want to install an enterprise or standalone CA.

7. On the Specify CA Type page, select Root CA for the first CA. When adding CAs to an existing hierarchy, select Subordinate CA. Then click Next.

8. The Set Up Private Key page shown in Figure 9.3 provides options for creating a private key. Select an appropriate option, and then click Next.

FIGURE 9.3 You must have a private key to set up a CA. This page provides options for creating a new key or using an existing one.

9. If you are using an existing private key, the wizard asks you to select and import the certificate with which the private key is associated. If you are creating a new private key, the wizard presents options for selecting a cryptographic service provider (CSP), hash algorithm, and key length. For learning purposes, it is adequate to accept the defaults provided. Click Next.

10. On the Configure CA Name page, accept the common name provided or type a name of your choosing, and then click Next.

11. On the Set Validity Period, accept the default of 5 years or type a different period if desired. Then click Next.

12. On the Configure Certificate Database page, accept the default folder locations or type **Browse** to select an alternate location. Then click Next.

13. If installing IIS, you receive the Web Server (IIS) page. Click the links to additional information if desired, and then click Next. Click Next again to accept the IIS role services to be installed.

14. On the Confirm Installation Selections page, review the information provided. If you need to change settings, click Previous to return to the appropriate wizard page. When finished, click Install to install AD CS with the indicated settings.

15. The Installation Progress page tracks the installation of the roles and role services being installed. When informed that the installation is complete, click Close.

When you complete the CA installation, a Certification Authority MMC console is added to the Administrative Tools folder. Tools included in this console are discussed in later sections of this chapter. IIS also adds an Internet Information Services (IIS) Manager console to the same folder.

Installing Subordinate CAs

As already mentioned, *subordinate CAs* can include intermediate CAs in a three-tier PKI hierarchy and issuing CAs in either a two- or three-tier hierarchy. After you have installed the root CA, you can install intermediate CAs if required, and then you can install issuing CAs. The procedure for installing these CAs is similar to that described in the previous section. When installing a subordinate CA on a domain controller, you can select the Enterprise option on the Specify Setup Type page shown in Figure 9.2 and the Subordinate CA option in the Specify CA Type page described in step 7 of the preceding procedure. You receive the Request Certificate from a Parent CA page shown in Figure 9.4, from which you must browse for the parent CA or save a certificate request file to be sent later to the parent CA. To locate a standalone root CA server, select the Computer Name option and then type the name of the root CA server in the Select Computer dialog box that appears. After you have been authenticated to the root CA server, the installation wizard completes in the same manner as the root CA installation.

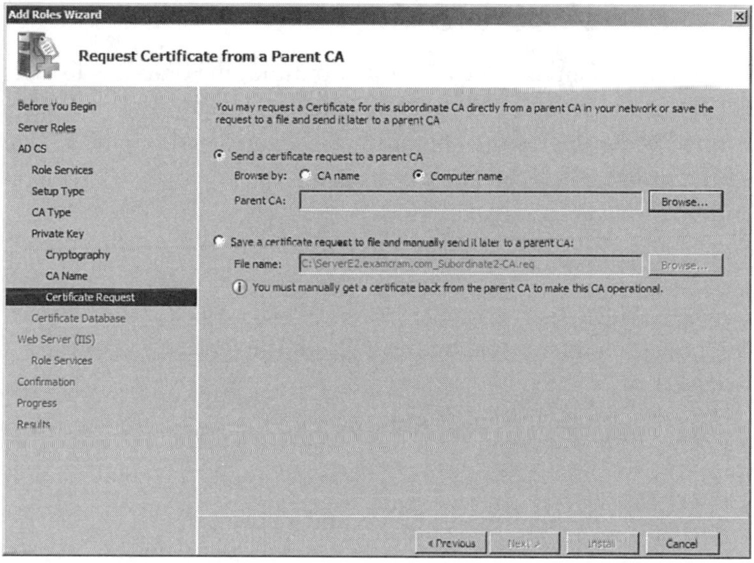

FIGURE 9.4   When setting up a subordinate CA, you must have a certificate issued by the parent CA.

Certificate Requests

As with previous Windows Server versions, Windows Server 2008 provides web-based *certificate enrollment*. It enables you to issue and renew certificates for the following:

- ▶ Domain-based users and computers
- ▶ Users and computers outside your domain
- ▶ Users and computers that are not directly connected to your network
- ▶ Users with non-Microsoft computers
- ▶ Downloading of certificate trust lists

AD CS enables users to request certificates by means of the Certificate Services web pages, which are automatically installed when you install AD CS. You can also configure *autoenrollment* of certificates, which enables users and computers to automatically receive certificates and renew expired certificates when required.

Various types of certificate enrollments are discussed later in this chapter.

Certificate Practice Statements

A certificate practice statement is a document that outlines the practices IT uses to manage the certificates it issues. It describes how the company's certificate policy is interpreted according to the operating procedures and organizational architecture of the company. Included in the certificate practice statement is information of the following types:

▶ Identifying information for the CA, including its name, server name, and DNS address

▶ Certificate policies implemented by the CA and the types of certificates that it issues

▶ Policies, procedures, and processes for issuing, renewing, and recovering certificates

▶ Available cryptographic algorithms, CSPs, and key lengths

▶ CA security, including physical, network, and procedural components

▶ Certificate revocation policies, including conditions under which certificates are revoked, in addition to CRL distribution points and publication intervals

▶ The lifetime of each certificate that the CA issues with a policy for renewing certificates before they expire

Microsoft includes an outline that assists you in creating a certificate practice statement, available for download at http://go.microsoft.com/fwlink/?LinkID=9554. On this page, click the Download button opposite the name Job_Aids_Designing_and_Deploying_Directory_and_Security_Services. zip. On the File Download page that appears, click either Open or Save, and then on the folder contents that are downloaded, select the DSSPKI_2.doc document. Create a certificate practice statement for each CA in your PKI. This statement can include multiple certificate policies. Note that the certificate practice statement for a subordinate CA can reference common or general information found in the parent CA's certificate practice statement.

Managing Certificate Templates

A certificate template is a file that defines the format and content of certificates that the CA issues. It specifies properties such as the users and computers allowed to enroll for certificates covered by the template, and it defines the enrollment types permitted. Each certificate template includes a discretionary access control list (DACL) that defines those users and groups that are permitted to perform actions such as reading and configuring the template, as well as enrolling or autoenrolling certificates based on the template. An enterprise CA stores its certificate templates and their permissions in Active Directory on a forestwide basis.

AD CS includes a Certificate Templates snap-in that enables you to configure and manage all types of available certificate templates. Later sections discuss actions you can perform from this snap-in.

Certificate Template Types

Windows Server 2008 supports three types of certificate templates:

- **Version 1 templates**—These are the original templates introduced in Windows 2000. They are read-only and do not support autoenrollment.

- **Version 2 templates**—Introduced in Windows Server 2003, these templates are supported only on computers running Windows XP, Server 2003, or later. They are editable and support autoenrollment. Only servers running Windows Server 2003 or 2008 Enterprise or Datacenter edition can issue certificates based on these templates.

- **Version 3 templates**—These templates are new to Windows Server 2008 and are supported only on computers running Windows Vista and Windows Server 2008. They support new features available with Windows Server 2008, including Cryptography API: Next Generation and suite b-compliant certificates, which support new cryptographic algorithms such as Elliptic Curve Cryptography.

Configuring Certificate Templates

AD CS provides the Certificate Templates snap-in (`Certtmpl.msc`), which offers the following capabilities:

▶ Creating additional templates by duplicating and modifying existing templates

▶ Modifying template properties such as validity and renewal periods, CSP, key size, and key archival

▶ Configuring policies applied to certificate enrollment, issuing, and application

▶ Allowing the autoenrollment of certificates based on versions 2 and 3 templates

▶ Configuring access control lists (ACL) on certificate templates

To access the Certificate Templates snap-in, type **certtmpl.msc** in the Run dialog box. You can also access this snap-in from the Certification Authority snap-in by right-clicking Certificate Templates in the console tree and clicking Manage. The Details pane lists all available certificate templates. You can configure the properties of any certificate template by right-clicking it and choosing Properties. From the Properties dialog box, you can configure the following properties:

▶ **General tab**—This enables you to specify validity and renewal periods and publish certificates in Active Directory.

▶ **Request Handling tab**—As shown in Figure 9.5, this enables you to configure the following certificate template properties for versions 2 and 3 certificate templates:

▶ **Purpose**—This enables you to specify one or more purposes of the template, including encryption, signature, or signature and encryption. You can also enable the inclusion of symmetric algorithms allowed by the subject and the archival of the private encryption key, as well as the deletion of revoked or expired certificates.

▶ **Add Read Permissions to Network Service on the Private Key**—Available for version 3 computer templates only, this option grants the Read permission on the private key to Network Service on the computer to which the certificate is issued.

▶ **Do the Following When the Subject Is Enrolled and When the Private Key Associated with This Certificate Is Used**—This provides options for the amount of user input required. The default is Enroll Subject Without Requiring Any User Input. For example, you can request that a user enter his PIN when enrolling for a smart card certificate.

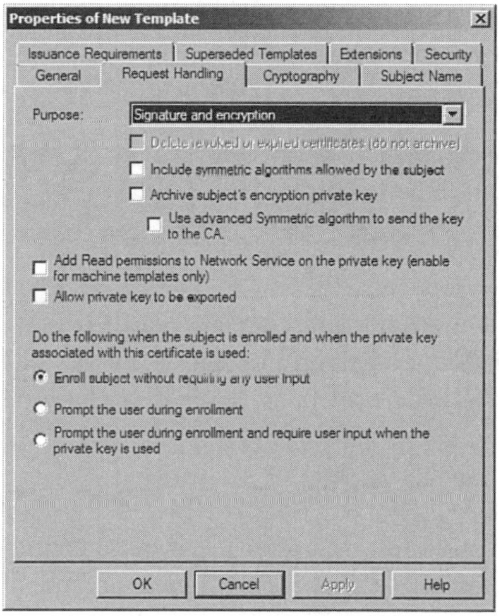

FIGURE 9.5 The Request Handling tab of a version 3 certificate template properties dialog box.

▶ **Cryptography tab**—Available on version 3 templates only, this tab enables you to define the encryption and hash algorithms and minimum key sizes used. The minimum key size can range from 512 to 16384 bits and is 2048 bits by default. Longer key sizes provide greater security but consume more processing power. You can also choose which cryptographic providers to use. On version 2 templates, the minimum key size and CSP provider are specified on the Request Handling tab.

▶ **Subject Name tab**—This enables you to define the subject name of a certificate template. You can choose to supply the name in the request or build it from several types of AD DS information.

▶ **Issuance Requirements tab**—This enables you to specify default issuance criteria, including the CA certificate manager approval and the number of authorized signatures required.

▶ **Superseded Templates tab**—This enables you to specify any templates that are superseded by the current template.

▶ **Extensions tab**—This enables you to define the properties of extensions, such as application policies, certificate template information, issuance policies, and key usage.

▶ **Security tab**—This enables you to define permissions for users and groups on the certificate template. These permissions are discussed in the next section.

EXAM ALERT

Know the options on the Request Handling tab well. An exam question might present a live version of this tab that requires you to configure multiple options.

The Properties dialog box of a version 1 template contains only five tabs: General, Request Handling, Subject Name, Extensions, and Security. The available options on most of these tabs are considerably fewer than those on the versions 2 and 3 templates.

Securing Template Permissions

The Security tab of a template's Permissions dialog box enables you to configure the template's ACL and define the security rights for enrollment and use of certificates. The following five permissions are defined from this tab:

▶ **Full Control**—Grants or denies the other four permissions.

▶ **Read**—Enables the user or computer to enumerate the templates.

▶ **Write**—Enables you to modify the template's properties or duplicate the template.

▶ **Enroll**—Enables users and computers to enroll certificates based on the template.

▶ **Autoenroll**—Enables autoenrollment of user and computer certificates. Not available on version 1 templates.

A user or computer must have both the Read and Enroll permissions to enroll a certificate from a selected certificate template. The enterprise CA enforces the Enroll permission when the user requests a certificate using the template. By default, members of the Domain Admins and Enterprise Admins groups have the Read, Write, and Enroll permissions.

To configure a certificate template for autoenrollment, open the Security tab of the template's Properties dialog box. Add the required group if it's not already present, and select the Read, Enroll, and Autoenroll permissions under the Allow column (see Figure 9.6). Also select the appropriate option on the Request Handling tab (previously shown in Figure 9.5) from the following:

▶ **Enroll Subject Without Requiring Any User Input**—Allows "silent" certificate autoenrollment without the need for users to be aware of the certificate usage

▶ **Prompt the User During Enrollment**—Sends a message to the user during enrollment, such as to request that a user enter her PIN for a smart card

▶ **Prompt the User During Enrollment and Require User Input When the Private Key Is Used**—Prompts the user during both enrollment and use of the private key

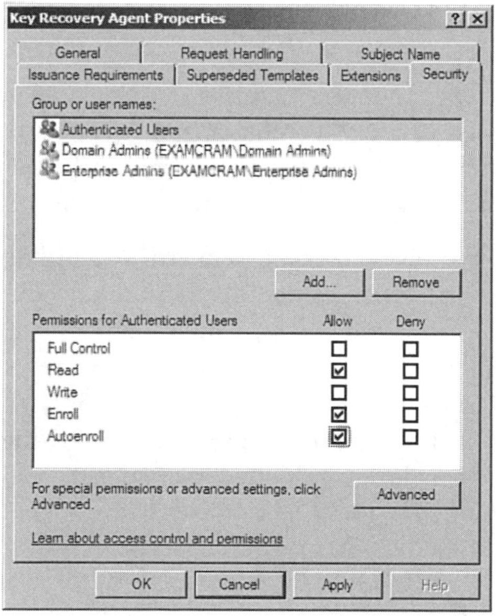

FIGURE 9.6 Configuring permissions for autoenrollment.

Enabling the Use of Templates

By default, AD CS allows certificates to be enrolled from only a limited number of templates. In the Certification Authority snap-in, select Certificate Templates from the console tree to display the list of available templates. To enable the use of a template, add it to this list. Right-click the Certificate Templates node and choose New, Certificate Template to Issue. From the list in the Enable

Certificate Templates, select one or more templates to be enabled, and then click OK. To disable the use of a template in the list, right-click it and choose Delete (or select it and press the Delete key). Then click Yes in the Disable Certificate Templates message box that appears.

Managing Different Certificate Template Versions

As already stated, certificate templates come in three versions: 1, 2, and 3. You can tell which version a template is configured for by default, by noting the entry in the Minimum Supported CAs column in the Details pane of the Certificate Templates snap-in:

- ▶ **Version 1 templates**—Windows 2000
- ▶ **Version 2 templates**—Windows Server 2003, Enterprise edition
- ▶ **Version 3 templates**—Windows Server 2008

The extent of configurable properties depends on the template version: Version 1 templates have few available properties, whereas versions 2 and 3 templates have far more properties, as already described. However, you can create versions 2 or 3 templates from version 1 templates by duplicating them.

Duplicating a template also enables you to customize their properties according to the tabs in the template's Properties dialog box, as described in the previous section. To duplicate a template, right-click it and choose Duplicate Template. In the Duplicate Template dialog box shown in Figure 9.7, select the server type for the duplicated template (Windows 2003 Server for version 2 and Windows Server 2008 for version 3), and then click OK. Type a display name for the new template in the General tab of the Properties dialog box that appears, and configure any other desired properties on the various tabs of this dialog box.

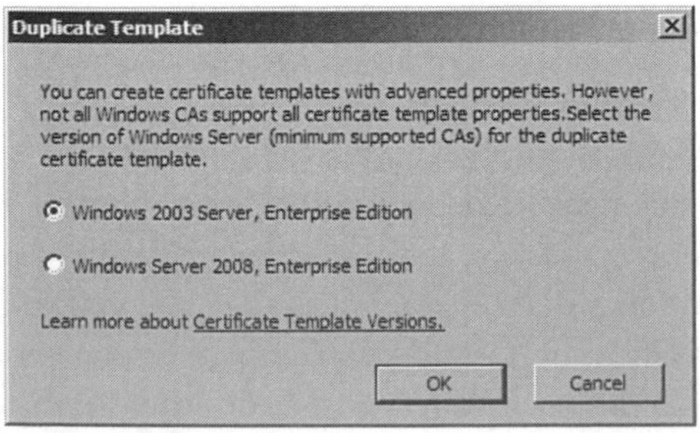

FIGURE 9.7 When you duplicate a certificate template, you can choose which server the new template is compatible with.

EXAM ALERT

Remember the differences between template versions. An exam question might present a scenario in which the autoenrollment options are not available in the template's Properties dialog box. Such a template is version 1. The solution is to duplicate the template and create a version 2 or 3 copy.

Key Archival

You can archive the private key of specific certificates when they are issued. Doing so enables you to recover the key if it becomes lost by corruption or accidental deletion. An archived key is stored in the CA's database until it is needed for key recovery.

You can create a certificate template that allows key archiving from the Certificate Templates snap-in by performing the following steps:

1. Right-click an appropriate certificate template (for example, the Users template) and choose Duplicate Template. Then select an appropriate option in the Duplicate Template dialog box previously shown in Figure 9.7.

2. Provide a name such as **Archived User** for this template.

3. Select the Request Handling tab, and then select the Archive Subject's Encryption Private Key option (refer to Figure 9.5). Then click OK.

4. To enable this template for certificate enrollment, right-click the Certificate Templates node in the Certification Authority snap-in and choose New, Certificate Template to Issue, select the new template from the Enable Certificate Templates dialog box, and then click OK.

By default, members of the Domain Users group have the Enroll permission for this template. If autoenrollment is required, select the Autoenroll permission from the Security tab for the appropriate users or groups. Autoenrollment is discussed later in this chapter.

Key Recovery Agents

After you have configured a certificate template for archival, certificates created from this template are archived in the CA's database. If a key is lost or corrupted, you can recover the key of a particular subject so that you can access data protected by that key. AD CS provides the *key recovery agent* (KRA) for recovering private keys archived by the CA.

To configure the enrollment of users or groups as key recovery agents, proceed as follows:

1. Open the Security Templates snap-in, right-click the Key Recovery Agent Properties template, and choose Properties.

2. Access the Security tab as described previously and shown in Figure 9.6, and add the required user or group with the Read and Enroll permissions.

3. From the Issuance Requirements tab of the same dialog box, clear the check box labeled CA Certificate Manager Approval, and then click OK.

4. Go to the Certification Authority snap-in and enable the Key Recovery Agent template in the Certificate Templates node of this snap-in, as described earlier in this section.

5. Create a new MMC console and add the Certificates snap-in, specifying My User Account when requested. The console tree of the new console contains a Certificates–Current User node.

6. Double-click the Certificates–Current User node to expand it and display a series of folders in the Details pane.

7. Right-click the Personal folder and choose All Tasks, Request New Certificate. This starts the Certificate Enrollment Wizard.

8. Read the notices in the introductory page, and then click Next.

9. On the Request Certificates page shown in Figure 9.8, select Key Recovery Agent, and then click Enroll.

10. The wizard displays a page while the certificate is created and then informs you that the certificate has been enrolled and installed on the computer. Click Finish.

11. Save the console to a convenient location as Certificates.msc. Then close it.

12. Back in the console tree of the Certification Authority snap-in, right-click your server name and choose Properties.

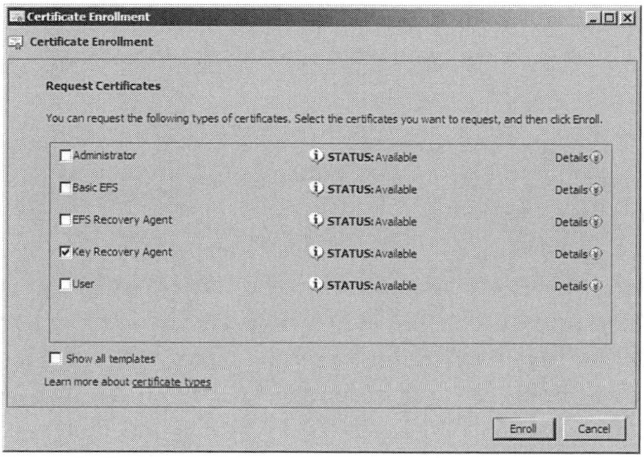

FIGURE 9.8 Requesting a key recovery agent certificate.

13. Select the Recovery Agents tab of the CA's Properties dialog box and click Add. Then select your certificate from the Key Recovery Agent Selection dialog box and click OK. As shown in Figure 9.9, the key recovery agent certificate is listed in the Recovery Agents tab.

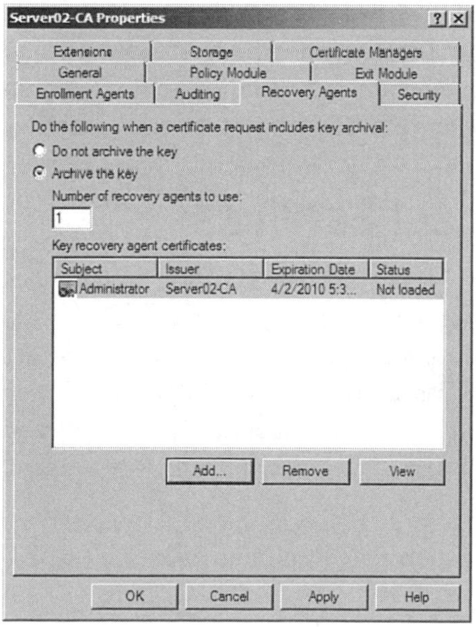

FIGURE 9.9 The key recovery agent certificate is listed in the Recovery Agents tab of the CA's Properties dialog box.

14. Click OK, and then click Yes to restart AD CS as prompted.

15. Repeat step 5 to create another MMC console and add the Certificates snap-in. However, this time, select Computer account and then select Local Computer.

16. In the console tree of this snap-in, expand Certificates (Local Computer), expand KRA, and select Certificates. The key recovery agent certificate should appear in the Details pane.

After you perform this procedure, the user account you employed becomes configured to act as a key recovery agent. Any user who is configured as a key recovery agent can use the `Certutil.exe` utility to recover archived keys. This procedure requires that you know the 20-digit hexadecimal serial number of the archived key. For additional details on key recovery agents and their use, including detailed procedures for archiving and recovering keys, refer to "Active Directory Certificate Server Enhancements in Windows Server Code Name 'Longhorn'" and "Key Archival and Recovery" in Appendix A.

Managing Certificate Enrollments

As already mentioned, Windows Server 2008 introduces the new server role feature of Certification Authority Web Enrollment, which enables you to configure web-based certificate enrollment including autoenrollment. Users can obtain new or renewed certificates across an Internet or intranet connection.

Network Device Enrollment Services

As introduced earlier in this chapter, NDES is an AD CS role service that enables software on network devices such as routers and switches to enroll for X.509 certificates from a server running AD CS. NDES is Microsoft's implementation of the Simple Certificate Enrollment Protocol (SCEP), which enables software on network devices that do not have accounts in AD DS—and therefore cannot otherwise be authenticated to the network—to enroll for certificates.

NDES utilizes an Internet Server Application Programming Interface (ISAPI) filter on IIS that performs the following actions:

▶ Creates one-time enrollment passwords that are provided to administrators

▶ Receives and processes SCEP enrollment requests for network device software

▶ Recovers pending requests from the CA

NDES is especially valuable for organizations that are using IPSec with network devices such as switches and routers and want to ensure the security of their communications across such devices.

You cannot install NDES at the same time you install the other AD CS role services. To install NDES, open Server Manager, expand the Roles node, and select Active Directory Certificate Services. Then scroll the Details pane to locate the Role Services section, and click Add Role Services, as shown in Figure 9.10. The Add Role Services Wizard will ask you to select a user account for NDES to use when authorizing certificate requests. You must add this user account to the IIS_IUSRS group before running the Add Role Services Wizard. Follow the remaining steps in the wizard, and click Install when the Summary page appears.

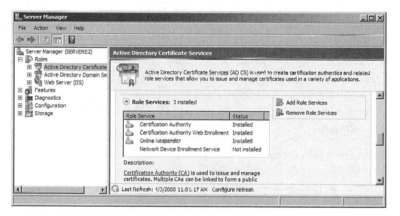

FIGURE 9.10 You can install NDES on a server running AD CS from its section in Server Manager.

For additional information on NDES, refer to "AD CS: Network Device Enrollment Service" in Appendix A.

EXAM ALERT

An exam question might refer to either the Microsoft Simple Certificate Enrollment Protocol or NDES. Although NDES is a service and MCSEP is a protocol, the exam might use these terms interchangeably.

Certificate Autoenrollment

The entire purpose of establishing a PKI is to provide users and computers with confidentiality when sending and receiving data across the network. PKI also provides authentication and integrity services. To perform these services, PKI uses a system of certificates that give clients and servers the ability to exchange cipher keys that encryption algorithms use. You do not need to know the intricacies of these keys and algorithms for Exam 70-640, but you do need to be familiar with the process of automatically enrolling users and computers to receive their certificates.

The process of autoenrollment handles all aspects of obtaining and renewing certificates for users and computers. It streamlines the process involved and greatly reduces administrative effort required for these actions. Users need not be aware of these actions unless you explicitly configure certificate templates for user interaction.

Autoenrollment requires an enterprise CA running on Windows Server 2008 Enterprise or Datacenter edition. Client computers must be running Windows XP or higher and be members of the domain. In addition, you must use certificates based on version 2 or 3 certificate templates. Perform the following steps to enable autoenrollment:

1. Right-click the required template in the Certificate Templates snap-in and choose Properties. If the template is version 1, right-click it and choose Duplicate Template. In the Duplicate Template dialog box previously shown in Figure 9.7, select Windows 2003 Server, Enterprise Edition, or Windows Server 2008, Enterprise Edition as required.

2. In the Properties of New Template dialog box that appears, provide an appropriate name.

3. Access the Security tab of the template's Properties dialog box and grant the required user or group with the Read, Enroll, and Autoenroll permissions, as previously shown in Figure 9.6.

4. From the Request Handling tab, specify the appropriate option for prompting the user during autoenrollment, as previously shown in Figure 9.5.

5. Go to the Certification Authority snap-in and enable this template in the Certificate Templates node of this snap-in, as described earlier in this chapter.

6. Configure a Group Policy object (GPO) linked to the appropriate AD DS container to enroll certificates automatically. To do so, navigate to the Computer Configuration\Policies\Windows Settings\Security Settings\Public Key Policies node. Right-click Certificate Services Client–Auto-Enrollment and choose Properties. This displays the dialog box shown in Figure 9.11, which enables you to configure the appropriate settings.

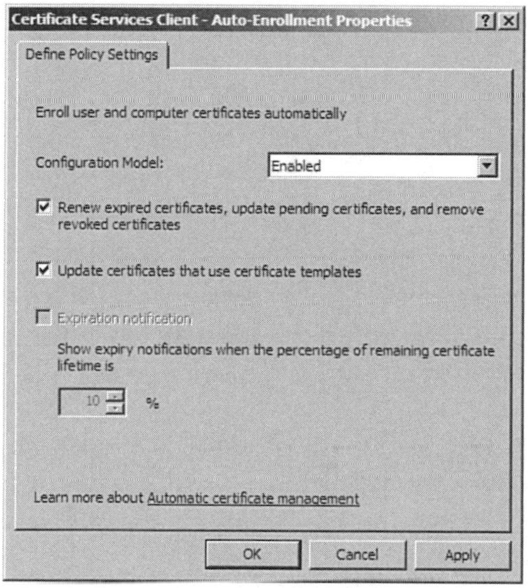

FIGURE 9.11 Configuring autoenrollment settings in Group Policy.

Web Enrollment

The Certification Authority Web enrollment role service, which was installed with the CA installation procedure outlined in the previous section, enables users to request and obtain new and renewed certificates across the Internet or a local intranet. This role service provides web pages that walk users through several tasks associated with certificate requests.

To request a certificate, proceed as follows:

1. Open Internet Explorer and type **http://<CA_servername>/certsrv**. In this command, *<CA_servername>* is the name or IP address of the certificate server (not the CA name).

2. The Microsoft Active Directory Certificate Services Welcome web page appears, as shown in Figure 9.12. Click Request a Certificate.

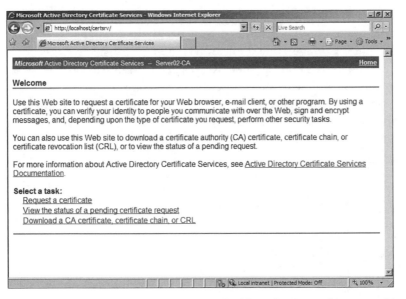

FIGURE 9.12 The Microsoft Active Directory Certificate Services web pages enable you to request certificates and perform other certificate management activities.

3. On the Select Server Roles page of the Add Roles Wizard, select Active Directory Certificate Services, and then click Next.

4. On the Request a Certificate page, select User Certificate to obtain a user certificate, or Advanced Certificate Request to obtain other types of certificates.

5. If you are requesting a user certificate, no further information is required. Click Submit to complete the certificate request. If you select Advanced Certificate Request, you receive the options shown in Figure 9.13. Select the option Create and Submit a Request to This CA to submit a certificate request, or select the second option if you have saved a previously created base 64–encoded CMC or PKCS#10 certificate request file.

6. If you select the Create and Submit a Request to This CA option, you receive the Advanced Certificate Request page shown in Figure 9.14. This page enables you to select the required certificate template, key options, and additional options according to the properties of the template specified. Complete these options and click Submit.

7. If you receive a Web Access Confirmation message box, click Yes to proceed.

8. When informed that the certificate was issued, click Install This Certificate. You will be informed when the new certificate is installed.

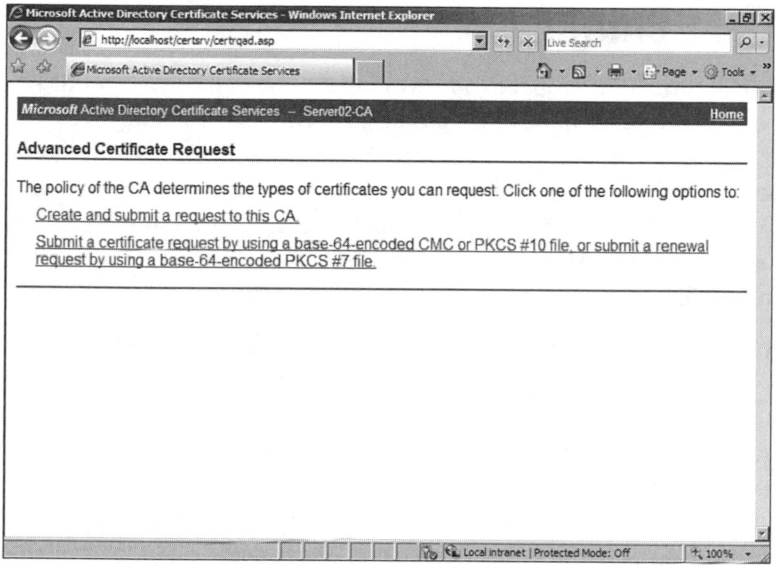

FIGURE 9.13   You can create other certificate requests, or you can submit a previously created certificate request file.

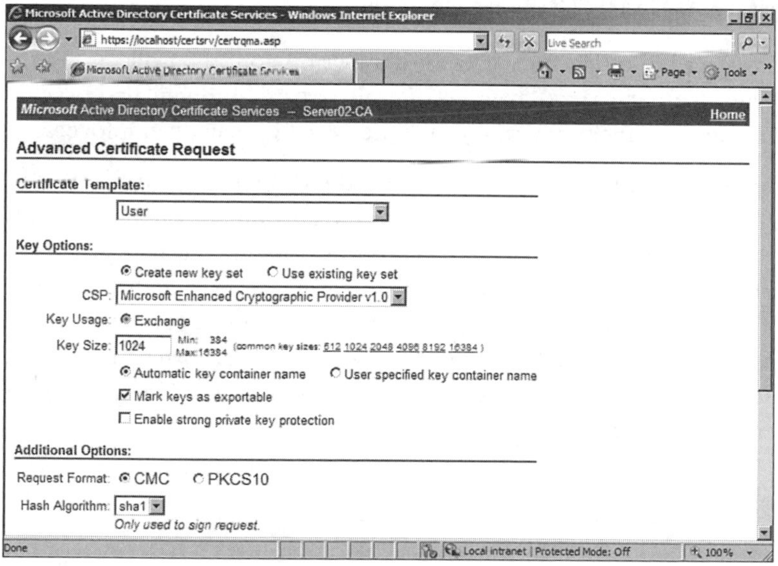

FIGURE 9.14   The Advanced Certificate Request page enables you to specify additional options related to the desired certificate.

Smart Card Enrollment

To improve the security of user logons and avoid the hassle of password problems, organizations are turning toward more advanced forms of user authentication. Windows Server 2008 continues the support of *smart cards*, introduced in Windows Server 2003. A smart card is a credit card–sized electronic device that stores public and private keys, thereby providing for secure, tamperproof identification and authentication. You can use it for secure authentication of clients logging on to an AD DS domain as well as remote access logons.

This system of authentication uses a smart card reader that attaches to a standard peripheral interface such as a USB port. Many manufacturers produce plug-and-play smart card readers that Microsoft has certified for use on computers running Windows XP/Vista/Server 2003/Server 2008. Many of the newest portable computers even feature built-in smart card readers. You will also need one or more smart card writers for use during the enrollment process. More information on supported smart cards, readers, and writers is available from the Windows Vista or Windows Server 2008 Help and Support Center.

Creating Enrollment Agents

An *enrollment agent* is a user who is granted the permission to enroll for certificates on behalf of other users. They are typically trusted individuals in secure environments, possibly including senior help desk or IT security employees.

Windows Server 2008 introduces a new restricted enrollment agent functionality that enables limiting the permissions granted to enrollment agents for smart card certificate enrollment so that they can enroll for only certain groups of smart card holders. Previously, enrollment agents were unrestricted—there was no means of limiting the enrollment agent to enrolling only a certain group of users. The new functionality allows the use of an enrollment agent for one or many certificate templates. You can choose which users or security groups the enrollment agent can enroll on behalf of.

> **CAUTION**
>
> Always ensure that only trusted employees are granted enrollment agent privileges. Use a security group for designating users as enrollment agents. For additional security, use the Restricted Groups feature in Group Policy to limit the membership of this group. Any user with an Enrollment Agent certificate can enroll for a certificate and generate a smart card on behalf of other users according to the enrollment policy. A malicious user could use the resulting smart card to log on to the network and impersonate the actual user.

To configure restricted enrollment agents, ensure that you are logged on as a CA administrator. First create security groups for the enrollment agents and for the users whom the agents will be permitted to enroll. Then proceed as follows:

1. Open the Certification Authority snap-in.

2. Right-click your CA server at the top of the console tree and choose Properties.

3. On the Enrollment Agents tab of the server's Properties dialog box, select Restrict Enrollment Agents.

4. An Enrollment Agents message box warns you that restrictions on delegated enrollment agents are only enforced on Windows Server 2008 CAs or higher. It also reminds you to ensure that your enrollment agent policy is appropriate. Click OK to proceed.

5. In the Enrollment Agents list box, Everyone is added by default. You must add the group containing the user accounts of the enrollment agents before removing this group. Click Add.

6. In the Select User, Computer, or Group dialog box, type the name of the group where the enrollment agents are located and click OK.

7. The group you added appears in the Enrollment Agents list box. Select Everyone and click Remove.

8. In the Certificate Templates list box, permission is granted for all templates by default. You must add one or more templates before removing this entry. Click Add.

9. In the Enable Certificate Templates dialog box, select one or more templates, and then click OK.

10. The templates you added appear in the Certificate Templates list box. Select <All> and click Remove.

11. In the Permissions list box, Everyone is granted Allow access by default. You must add the required group here before removing this group. Click Add.

12. In the Select User, Computer, or Group dialog box, type the name of the group where the smart card users are located, and click OK.

13. The group you added appears in the Permissions list box. Select Everyone and click Remove.

14. Click OK or Apply to apply your selections. The completed Enrollment Agents tab will appear, similar to that shown in Figure 9.15.

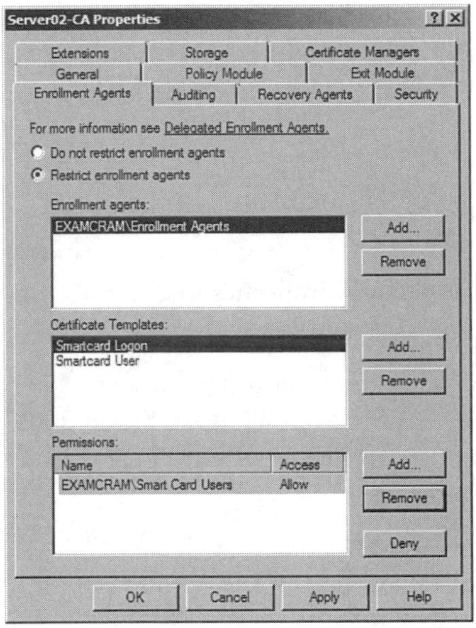

FIGURE 9.15 Configuring restricted enrollment agents policy.

TIP

You can add only one entry in any of the three list boxes in the Enrollment Agents tab at a time. To add additional entries, simply click Add again.

The enrollment agents must possess an Enrollment Agent certificate so that they can enroll users with certificates according to the permissions you have granted them in the restricted enrollment agent policy. You can autoenroll these agents for an Enrollment Agent certificate by following the procedure outlined earlier in this chapter. When you create the GPO that contains the autoenrollment settings, grant the group containing the agents the Read and Apply Group Policy permissions, and remove any other groups from the GPO's Delegation tab as described in Chapter 6, "Configuring and Troubleshooting Group Policy."

CAUTION

You cannot limit the users whom an enrollment agent can enroll for by means of Active Directory containers such as OUs; you must use security groups for this purpose. Also note that you must use a CA based on Windows Server 2008 Enterprise or Datacenter edition; you cannot use Windows Server 2008 Standard edition.

For more information on restricted enrollment agents, refer to "Active Directory Certificate Server Enhancements in Windows Server Code Name 'Longhorn'" in Appendix A.

Configuring Certificate Authority Server Settings

Several additional settings are available from the Certification Authority console that you should be aware of. Besides key archival, which has already been discussed, this includes the configuration of certificate stores, the backup and restore of the certificate database, and the assignment of administrative roles for your certificate server.

Certificate Stores

Certificates are stored in *certificate stores*, which are located in a protected area of the registry on all server and client computers. A series of certificate stores can exist for each user, computer, and service. Table 9.1 describes several certificate stores that you can access from the Certificates snap-in.

TABLE 9.1   Certificate Stores

Certificate Store	What It Contains
Personal	User and computer certificates associated with private keys accessible to the user or computer
Trusted Root Certification Authorities	Certificates for implicitly trusted root CAs, including certificates in the Third-Party store and root certificates from your company and Microsoft
Enterprise Trust	Certificate Trust Lists (CTL)
Intermediate Certification Authorities	Certificates for subordinate CAs
Trusted Publishers	Certificates from CAs that are trusted by software restriction policies
Untrusted Publishers	Certificates from CAs that are not implicitly trusted
Third-Party Root Certification Authorities	Certificates from commercial CAs such as Equifax and VeriSign
Trusted People	Certificates issued to explicitly trusted people or entities
Certificate Enrollment Requests	Pending or rejected certificate requests

You can use Group Policy to distribute certificates to most of the stores listed in this table but not to the Third-Party Root Certification Authorities store. For more details on certificate stores and their purposes, refer to "Display Certificate Stores" in Windows Server 2008 Help and Support.

Backing Up Certificates and Keys

You can use the Certificate Export Wizard to back up certificates with their associated private keys. You should do this to ensure that they are available for recovery or to move them to a different computer. Follow this procedure to back up certificates:

1. In the Certificates console for a user, service, or computer account, right-click the certificate to be exported and choose All Tasks, Export.

2. Click Next to bypass the welcome page of the Certificate Export Wizard.

3. If a private key is associated with the certificate being exported, the Export Private Key page asks you if you want to export this key. Click Yes or No as appropriate, and then click Next.

4. On the Export File Format page, choose a file format from the selections listed as follows. Then click Next.

   ▶ **DER encoded binary X.509 (CER)**—A platform-independent method for encoding certificates for transfer between computers or other devices

   ▶ **Base-64 encoded X.509 (CER)**—For encoding of certificates into ASCII text format for transfer to other computers

   ▶ **Cryptographic Message Syntax Standard–PKCS #7 Certificates (.P7B)**—For transfer of certificates without private keys between computers or to removable media

   ▶ **Personal Information Exchange–PKCS #12 (.PFX)**—For transfer of certificates with private keys from one computer to another or to removable media

5. Specify a filename for the exported file. The file will be saved to the desktop by default; click Browse to specify another location.

6. If exporting the private key, type and confirm a password for the key.

7. Click Finish to export the certificate.

Restoring Certificates and Keys

You can use the Certificate Import Wizard to restore backed-up certificates or import them to other computers. Follow this procedure to import certificates with their private keys:

1. In the Certificates console for a user, service, or computer account, right-click the appropriate certificate store and choose All Tasks, Import.

2. The Certificate Import Wizard starts. Click Next.

3. On the File to Import page, type or browse to the desired file, and then click Next.

4. If importing a private key, type the password. Also select the following check boxes as appropriate:

   ▶ **Enable Strong Private Key Protection**—This requires prompting before the private key is used. Do not select if a service account or computer uses the key because no means for confirmation exists, and the key will fail.

   ▶ **Mark This Key as Exportable**—You should generally select this option so that you can export the key again later.

   ▶ **Include All Extended Properties**—Selected by default, this option ensures that all extended properties of the certificate are imported.

5. On the Certificate Store page, ensure that the certificate is imported to the correct store. Click Next and then click Finish to import the certificate.

Using Group Policy to Import Certificates

You can use Group Policy to make certificates and their associated keys available to all computers covered by a GPO. To do this, open the Group Policy Management Editor focused on this GPO and navigate to the Computer Configuration\Policies\Windows Settings\Security Settings\Public Key Policies node. As shown in Figure 9.16, you can import certificates to several certificate stores from this node. Right-click the appropriate node and choose Import. Then follow the steps already outlined in the Certificate Import Wizard to complete the import.

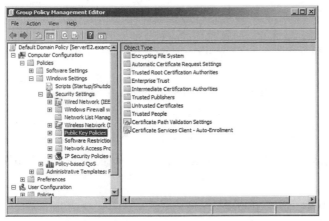

FIGURE 9.16 Group Policy enables you to import certificates to several certificate stores.

Certificate Server Permissions

The Security tab of the CA server's Properties dialog box enables you to configure four permissions. Normally you do not need to modify these permissions, but you should be aware of their existence:

▶ **Read**—Enables users to read records from the CA's database. This permission is not required for users to obtain certificates; it is normally granted only to those who administer CA servers.

▶ **Issue and Manage Certificates**—Enables users to approve requests for granting and revoking certificates. Users granted this permission receive the Certificate Manager role.

▶ **Manage CA**—Enables users to configure and maintain the CA. Users granted this permission receive the PKI Administrator role.

▶ **Request Certificates**—Enables users to request certificates. This is the only permission required for users to request certificates. It is granted to the Authenticated Users group by default.

EXAM ALERT

You might encounter a scenario on an exam question where you must limit the users who can enroll for certificates. To do this, remove the Authenticated Users group from the permissions list and add a group containing the required users with the Request Certificates permission.

Certificate Database Backup and Restore

Backing up the certificate database is as important as any other backup chore and enables you to recover it if any problems occur. You can use the Wbadmin command to back up system state data, as already described in Chapter 8, "Monitoring and Maintaining the Active Directory Environment," because the Certificate Services database is part of the system state. You can also use the Critical Volumes Backup procedure described in the same chapter.

In addition, Certificate Services enables you to back up its database by itself. To do so, perform the following steps:

1. In the Certification Authority snap-in, right-click the certificate server and choose All Tasks, Back Up CA.

2. Click Next to bypass the welcome page of the Certification Authority Backup Wizard.

3. On the Items to Back Up page of the Certification Authority Backup Wizard shown in Figure 9.17, select the items to be backed up (private key and CA certificate, and certificate database and certificate database log). Also, type or browse to an empty folder where you want to store the backup. Then click Next.

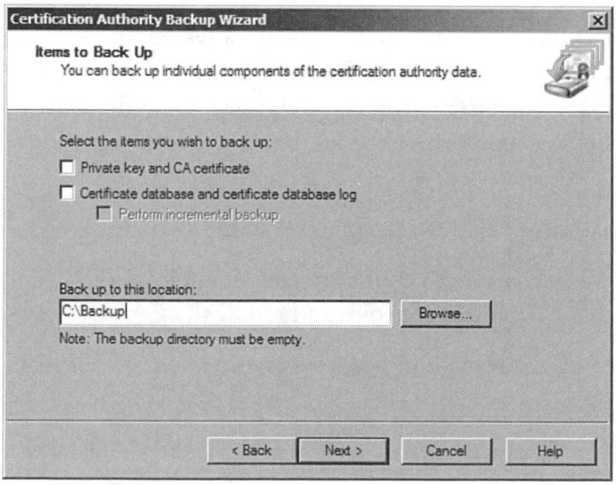

FIGURE 9.17 Backing up the certificate server.

4. Type and confirm a password for the private key, and then click Next.

5. Click Finish to perform the backup.

> **TIP**
>
> The folder where you store the backup must be empty. If you specify a nonexistent folder, the backup wizard will ask you if you want to create the folder.

You can restore the Certificate Services database by performing the following steps:

1. In the Certification Authority snap-in, right-click the certificate server and choose All Tasks, Restore CA.

2. You are informed that you must stop AD CS. Click OK.

3. Click Next on the Certification Authority Restore Wizard, select the items to be restored, and type or browse to the location of the backup files. Then click Next.

4. Type the password for the private key that you specified when you performed the backup, click Next, and then click Finish.

5. Click Yes to restart Certificate Services. If you have additional files to be restored, click No and repeat this procedure.

Assigning Administration Roles

AD CS in Windows Server 2008 enables you to implement a system of *role-based administration*, which allows you to assign predefined task-based roles to different individuals. You should divide these roles among several individuals to ensure that no single person can compromise your PKI. In addition, you can audit the actions of others.

The following PKI administrative roles are available:

▶ **PKI Administrator**—Enables you to configure and maintain the CA. You can also assign other CA administrative roles and renew the CA certificate.

▶ **Certificate Manager**—Enables you to approve certification enrollment and revocation requests.

▶ **Backup Operator**—Enables you to back up and recover the CA database, configuration, and database keys.

▶ **Audit Manager**—Enables you to configure auditing and view and maintain the audit logs.

▶ **Key Recovery Manager**—Enables you to request retrieval of private keys that the service stores.

Besides these roles, the Enrollee nonadministrative role enables users to request certificates from the CA.

By default, members of the local Administrators, Domain Admins, and Enterprise Admins groups are PKI administrators on enterprise CA servers. They are granted the authority to assign other users to the PKI administrative roles described here. On standalone CA servers, members of the local Administrators group (and the Domain Admins group if the server is a member of an AD DS domain) are PKI administrators.

You can assign these roles to the appropriate individuals by creating groups and then assigning these groups the appropriate user rights and permissions. Right-click the CA name in the Certification Authority snap-in and choose Properties, and then select the Security tab to assign permissions to groups. Refer to "Implement Role-Based Administration" in Windows Server 2008 Help and Support for the required rights and permissions.

Managing Certificate Revocation

You might need to revoke a certificate before its expiry date for various reasons, such as compromise of the certificate or termination of the user to whom the certificate was issued. When you revoke a certificate, the revoked certificate is published in the CRL. Applications requiring certificates check this CRL to ensure that certificates are still valid. Management and maintenance of certificate revocation is an important task in the day-to-day administration of your organization's PKI.

Prior to Windows Vista, the CRL was the only certificate revocation–checking mechanism supported by Microsoft. Introduced to Internet Explorer 7 in Windows Vista and Windows Server 2008 is the concept of the *Online Certificate Status Protocol (OCSP)* as a new method of certificate status checking. OCSP includes a client component on each Vista and Server 2008 computer, as well as the server component, which is the online responder. This section looks at the online responder as well as the traditional CRL.

To revoke a certificate, select the Issued Certificates node of the Certification Authority snap-in. Right-click the certificate to be revoked and select All Tasks, Revoke Certificate. Select a reason code from those displayed in the drop-down list of the Certificate Revocation dialog box (see Figure 9.18), and then click Yes. The certificate is removed from the Issued Certificates list and added to the Revoked Certificates list and the CRL.

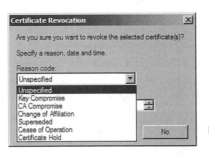

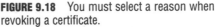

FIGURE 9.18 You must select a reason when revoking a certificate.

TIP

If you are unsure about the validity of a certificate, you should specify the "Certificate Hold" reason when revoking it. Specifying this reason gives you an option to unrevoke the certificate later.

Certificate Revocation Lists

As already mentioned, applications check the CRL to ensure that certificates are still valid. Because CRLs can become long, Windows Server 2008 includes the concept of a *delta CRL*, which is a list of certificates that have been revoked since the last publication of a full CRL. By using delta CRLs, you can publish CRL information more frequently with less replication traffic.

Delta CRLs are published on a differential basis—in other words, each delta CRL includes all revoked certificates since the previous full CRL was published. Figure 9.19 provides an example of CRL publishing. In this example, certificates C1 and C2 were revoked prior to publishing the first base CRL. Certificate C3 was then revoked and appeared in the delta CRL. Certificate C4 was revoked next, and the next delta CRL contained both certificates C3 and C4. Finally, a new base CRL was published that contains all revoked certificates. That's why an application that checks CRLs needs to check only the base CRL and the most recent delta CRL to obtain a complete list of revoked certificates.

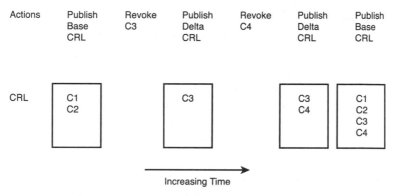

FIGURE 9.19 An example of base and delta CRL publication.

You can configure the publication intervals of CRLs and delta CRLs by following these steps:

1. In the Certification Authority console, right-click Revoked Certificates and choose Properties.

2. On the CRL Publishing Parameters tab of the Revoked Certificates Properties dialog box, specify the publication intervals for CRLs and delta CRLs.

3. To view current CRLs and delta CRLs, select the View CRLs tab and click the appropriate command button.

Before you begin to issue certificates from the CA hierarchy, you should place a copy of the root certificate and the CRL (which is empty to begin with) at the locations specified in the policy module. You can obtain copies of the CA certificate and CRLs (base and delta) from the Certificate Services web pages at `http://<server>/certsrv`, where `<server>` is the name of the certificate server (refer to Figure 9.12). On the home page, select the `Download a CA Certificate, Certificate Chain, or CRL` link, and then select the appropriate link on the page that appears. On the File Download page that appears, click Save and specify the appropriate location for the CRL in the Save As dialog box.

CAUTION

Revoking a CA certificate revokes all certificates issued by this CA. Any application that obtains a CRL showing that the parent certificate has been revoked will reject these certificates.

CRL Distribution Point (CDP)

A *CRL Distribution Point (CDP)* is a location on the network where applications can locate the most recent base and delta CRLs to check for certificate validity. The Extensions tab of the CA's Properties dialog box enables you to add, remove, or modify CDPs in issuing certificates. To do this, right-click the CA server's name in the Certification Authority snap-in and choose Properties. Select the Extensions tab to display the dialog box shown in Figure 9.20. You can perform the actions described in Table 9.2 from this location.

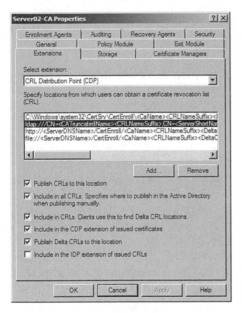

FIGURE 9.20 The Extensions tab of the CA server's Properties dialog box enables you to configure the CDP locations.

TABLE 9.2 Configuring a CDP

Available Action	Procedure to Follow
Add a CDP	Click Add, type the URL to the new CDP, and click OK.
Remove a CDP	Select the CDP, click Remove, and click Yes to confirm its removal.
Specify that a URL will be used as a CDP	Select the CDP and select the Publish CRLs to This Location check box.
Specify that a URL will be included in all CRLs and published in AD DS	Select the CDP and select the check box labeled Include in All CRLs. Specifies Where to Publish in the Active Directory When Publishing Manually.

TABLE 9.2 *Continued*

Available Action	Procedure to Follow
Specify that a URL will be published in CRLs to point clients to a delta CRL	Select the CDP and select the check box labeled Include in CRLs. Clients Use This to Find Delta CRL Locations.
Specify that a URL will be used as a delta CRL distribution point	Select the CDP and select the Publish Delta CRLs to This Location check box.

You can also specify that a URL will not be used for one of these actions by clearing the corresponding check box. After making changes to any of these items, you must stop and restart the Certificate Services service. Click Yes when requested.

For additional information on configuring CDPs, refer to "Specify Certificate Revocation List Distribution Points in Issued Certificates" in Appendix A.

Troubleshooting CRLs

Any application that checks CRLs must be able to locate the CRL before it can accept a certificate. If the application cannot locate the CRL, it fails and the certificate holder is not authenticated. When troubleshooting certificate problems, you need to determine whether or not the issue lies in the CRL. The following are several CRL-related problems that you might encounter:

▶ A CRL is valid for a period that is approximately the same as its publication period, which is one week by default. When changes occur to the CRL or delta CRL, they are not reflected in the context of the user or computer until expiry of a cached CRL or delta CRL. Consequently, information on revoked certificates may not be immediately available. Use a short delta CRL publication interval to alleviate this problem.

▶ Applications that check the CRL must be able to locate the current CRL and delta CRL. Ensure that copies of the CRLs are published to URLs or file locations that the applications can access.

▶ If you are changing the location of a CRL, information on this location is not added to certificates published prior to the change. Only change the location of a CRL when it is absolutely necessary.

▶ Applications that check the CRL must be able to access all CRLs in the CA hierarchy. If you are employing an offline root CA, you need to ensure that a copy of its CRL is made available at an online location. Configure this online location before any certificates are issued.

Configuring Online Responders

The online responder is an optional role service in AD CS that is new to Windows Server 2008. It is based on OCSP and provides signed responses to clients requesting revocation information for certificates issued by the CA that signed the OCSP signing certificate. Windows Server 2008 provides the OCSP Response Signing certificate template that is used to generate a certificate used by computers configured as online responders. The following are several types of certificates whose certificate validity is often checked using OCSP:

▶ Smart card logon

▶ Enterprise Secure Multipurpose Internet Mail Extensions (S/MIME)

▶ Secure Sockets Layer (SSL)/Transport Layer Security (TLS)

▶ Extensible Authentication Protocol (EAP)/TLS-based virtual private network (VPN)

The Online Responder role service is available on computers running either the Enterprise or Datacenter editions of Windows Server 2008. You can install this service at the same time that you install AD CS from the Add Roles Wizard in Server Manager, as described earlier in the chapter. You can also add this service later by using the Add Role Services Wizard in a similar manner to that described for NDES earlier in this chapter. After you have installed this role service, the Online Responder Management snap-in shown in Figure 9.21 is available from the Administrative Tools folder.

The next sections examine the online responder properties, revocation configuration, and array configuration. Additional information on the online responder role service, including troubleshooting hints, is available in "Online Responder Installation, Configuration, and Troubleshooting Guide" in Appendix A.

Configuring Responder Properties

Several configurable properties are available that are global to the online responder actions and services. To access them, right-click Online Responder in the console tree and choose Properties. This opens the Online Responder Properties dialog box shown in Figure 9.22.

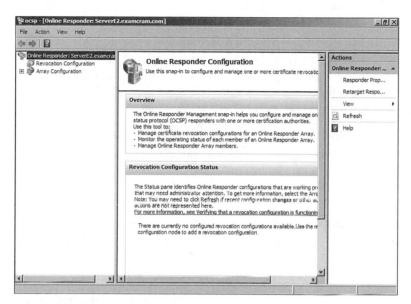

FIGURE 9.21 You can configure the online responder from the Online Responder Configuration snap-in.

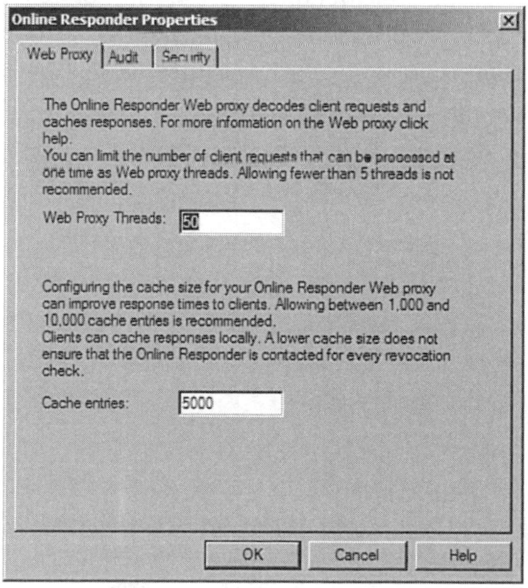

FIGURE 9.22 The Online Responder Properties dialog box.

You can manage the following properties from this dialog box:

▶ **Web Proxy tab**—Enables you to configure the numbers of web proxy threads and cache entries allowed. Increasing these numbers uses more of the server's memory, and reducing them reduces the number of clients that can be served.

▶ **Audit tab**—Enables you to specify that certain actions will be logged to the server's Security log. These include starting or stopping the online responder service, changing the online responder's configuration or security settings, and logging requests submitted to the online responder. Note that you must configure auditing of object access in Group Policy, as described in Chapter 8, for these events to be audited.

▶ **Security tab**—Enables you to configure permissions for submitting proxy requests for certificate revocation status and for managing the online responder service.

Revocation Configurations

A revocation configuration includes a series of definitions that enable the online responder to provide a signed OCSP response. Included are the CA certificate, the signing certificate, and the source of the revocation information.

To add a revocation configuration, right-click Revocation Configuration and choose Add Revocation Configuration. This starts the Add Revocation Configuration Wizard, which takes you through the steps outlined in Figure 9.23 to create your revocation configuration. For detailed information on each of these steps, refer to the previously mentioned "Online Responder Installation, Configuration, and Troubleshooting Guide" in Appendix A.

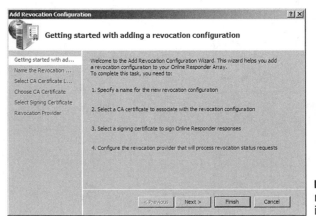

FIGURE 9.23 Creating a revocation configuration involves four steps.

CAUTION

Before running the Add Revocation Configuration Wizard, you should enable the CA server to issue a certificate based on the OCSP Response Signing certificate template from the Certification Authority snap-in, as described earlier in this chapter.

Array Configurations

An array is one or more computers on which the online responder service is installed and managed from the Online Responder snap-in. Each computer in an array uses the same global property set and the same revocation configurations. One of these servers is defined as the array controller and resolves any synchronization conflicts and ensures that updated revocation information is sent to all members of the array.

To add an array member, right-click the Array Configuration node and choose Add Array Member. Then type the distinguished name of the desired computer in the Select Computer dialog box or click Browse to locate the computer. Then click OK.

Authority Information Access

Authority Information Access (AIA) is an extension that can be applied to CA-issued certificates that points to URLs where you can retrieve an issuing CA's certificate. This extension is defined in Request for Comments (RFC) 3280 and states how to access CA information and services for the issuer of the certificate who uses this extension. More specifically, for the Online Responder service to work properly, you must include the URL for the online responder in the AIA extension of certificates issued by the CA.

Use the following steps to configure an AIA extension:

1. In the Certification Authority snap-in, right-click the server and choose Properties.

2. Select the Extensions tab (previously shown in Figure 9.20).

3. From the Select Extension drop-down list at the top of this tab, select Authority Information Access (AIA).

4. Select an HTTP-based URL in the Specify Locations from Which Users Can Obtain the Certificate for this CA list box. If you want to add a URL not shown in this list box, click Add.

5. Select the check boxes labeled Include in the AIA Extension of Issued Certificates and Include in the Online Certificate Status Protocol (OCSP) Extension, and then click OK.

6. You are informed that you must restart AD CS for the changes to take effect. Click Yes.

Exam Cram Questions

1. Dawn is planning a PKI for her company that will include a multiple-tier hierarchy of CA servers. Which of the following types of CA servers should she plan to keep offline as a safeguard against certificate compromise?

   ○ **A.** Standalone root

   ○ **B.** Enterprise root

   ○ **C.** Intermediate

   ○ **D.** Issuing

2. Kevin is installing a PKI for his company, which operates an AD DS domain in which all servers run Windows Server 2008. He has installed a root CA and is now at the computer that will host an enterprise subordinate CA. However, on the Specify Setup page, he discovers that the Enterprise CA option is grayed out and only the Standalone CA option is available. What must Kevin do to install an enterprise subordinate CA on this computer?

   ○ **A.** Log on to the server as a member of the Enterprise Admins group.

   ○ **B.** Log on to the server as a member of the Schema Admins group.

   ○ **C.** Use Server Manager to install AD DS on this server.

   ○ **D.** Run dcpromo.exe to promote the server to a domain controller.

   ○ **E.** Install a standalone CA on the server, and then use the Certification Authority console to promote the server to an enterprise CA.

3. Kim is the systems administrator of a manufacturing company that operates an AD DS network consisting of a single domain. All servers run Windows Server 2008, and client computers run either Windows XP Professional or Windows Vista Business.

   The CIO has requested that Kim set up a PKI that will automatically issue certificates to all users in the domain. The PKI must be configured so that it is as secure from compromise as possible. Which of the following must Kim configure? (Choose all that apply.)

   ○ **A.** An online enterprise root CA and an enterprise subordinate CA

   ○ **B.** An offline enterprise root CA and an enterprise subordinate CA

   ○ **C.** An offline standalone root CA and an enterprise subordinate CA

   ○ **D.** An offline standalone root CA and a standalone subordinate CA

   ○ **E.** An autoenrollment user template, and enabling this template on the subordinate CA

○ **F.** A web-based enrollment agent on the subordinate CA

○ **G.** A GPO linked to the domain that enables certificate autoenrollment in the User Configuration section of the GPO

○ **H.** A GPO linked to the domain that enables certificate autoenrollment in the Computer Configuration section of the GPO

4. Steve is responsible for establishing a smart card autoenrollment policy for users in his company that operates an AD DS network consisting of a single domain. He accesses the Security tab of the Smartcard User Properties dialog box in the Certificate Templates snap-in and discovers that the Autoenroll permission is not present.

   What should Steve do to enable autoenrollment from this template?

   ○ **A.** Obtain a certificate from a trusted third-party certification authority such as VeriSign and install this certificate on his computer.

   ○ **B.** Log off and log on as a member of the Enterprise Admins group.

   ○ **C.** Duplicate the template and configure the duplicate for autoenrollment.

   ○ **D.** Simply configure the template with the existing Read and Enroll permissions.

5. Mary is responsible for managing the PKI of a large company that operates an AD DS network consisting of five domains. The company is introducing a system of smart card logons to improve network security and circumvent the hassles involved with forgotten passwords.

   Mary needs to enable a group of trusted employees to enroll smart card user certificates on behalf of other employees in their work departments. She has placed the user accounts of these employees in a security group named Trusted. She must ensure that these trusted employees do not receive additional privileges. What should she do?

   ○ **A.** Configure the Trusted group as restricted enrollment agents.

   ○ **B.** Configure the Trusted group as Certificate Managers.

   ○ **C.** Configure the Trusted group as PKI Administrators.

   ○ **D.** Add the Trusted group to the Account Operators domain global group.

6. Brenda is the security administrator for a company that operates an AD DS network consisting of a single domain. All servers run Windows Server 2008, and client computers run either Windows XP Professional or Windows Vista Enterprise. The network includes an offline root CA and three enterprise-issuing CAs.

In addition to the locally issued certificates, Brenda needs to enable the use by domain clients of several certificates that have been issued by third-party CAs. What does she need to do to ensure that all domain clients will trust certificates issued by the third-party CAs?

- ○ **A.** Install the third-party CA certificates on her company's root CA and place this CA online for a sufficient time so the certificates can replicate to other network servers.

- ○ **B.** Install the third-party CA certificates on her company's issuing CAs.

- ○ **C.** Add a copy of each third-party CA certificates to the Trusted Root Certification Authorities node in the Default Domain Policy GPO.

- ○ **D.** Add a copy of each third-party CA certificates to the Trusted Root Certification Authorities certificate store on each client computer.

7. You want to create a backup of Certificate Services on your Windows Server 2008 computer, which you have configured as an enterprise subordinate CA. Which of the following procedures can you use? (Choose all that apply).

- ○ **A.** Use Wbadmin.exe to back up the Certificate Services folder.

- ○ **B.** Use Wbadmin.exe to perform a critical volumes backup.

- ○ **C.** Use Wbadmin.exe to perform a system state backup.

- ○ **D.** Use the Certificate Export Wizard to perform a backup.

- ○ **E.** In the Certification Authority snap-in, right-click the certificate server and choose All Tasks, Back up CA.

- ○ **F.** In the Certificate Templates snap-in, right-click the certificate server and choose All Tasks, Back Up CA.

8. Jackie is the domain administrator for her company, which operates an AD DS domain in which all servers run Windows Server 2008, and client computers run either Windows XP Professional or Windows Vista Business. One server is configured as an offline standalone root CA, and two servers are configured as online enterprise subordinate CAs. Another administrator named Len is responsible for all operations of the CA hierarchy. The CIO is concerned that operation of the CA hierarchy would be severely affected should Len's account be compromised.

What should Jackie do to reduce the possibility of this occurrence?

- ○ **A.** Create a special user account for Len that has a 20-character password, and limit the privileges of this account to administration of the CA servers.

- ○ **B.** Implement role-based administration in the CA hierarchy.

❍ **C.** Configure the subordinate CA servers so that certificate enrollment and renewal take place on different servers.

❍ **D.** Reconfigure the offline standalone root CA as an offline enterprise root CA.

❍ **E.** Reconfigure the offline standalone root CA as an online enterprise root CA.

9. Betsy is responsible for administering her company's PKI. The company has an offline root CA and four enterprise subordinate CAs, each of which issues certificates to users in a major division of the company.

   As a result of corporate downsizing and reorganization, one of the four major divisions is being disbanded. Betsy must ensure that resources on the network will not accept certificates from the subordinate CA located in the division that is being disbanded. Which of the following should she do? (Each correct answer represents part of the solution. Choose three answers.)

   ❍ **A.** At the disbanded division's subordinate CA, revoke all the certificates that it has issued.

   ❍ **B.** Uninstall the AD CS role from the disbanded division's subordinate CA.

   ❍ **C.** Bring the offline root CA online, revoke the disbanded division's subordinate CA's certificate, and then take the root CA back offline.

   ❍ **D.** Publish a new base CRL.

   ❍ **E.** Publish a new delta CRL.

   ❍ **F.** Copy the new CRL to the network's CRL distribution point.

   ❍ **G.** Add the AIA extension to all URLs where certificates issued by the disbanded division's subordinate CA can be retrieved.

10. Jim is responsible for administering AD CS within his company's AD DS domain. He has configured a PKI that consists of a standalone root CA and two enterprise subordinate CAs on servers running Windows Server 2008 Enterprise Edition. He wants to configure the subordinate CAs to support the Online Responder service for keeping track of revoked certificates. Which of the following tasks must Jim perform? (Each correct answer represents part of the solution. Choose two answers.)

    ❍ **A.** Enable the use of the OCSP Response Signing certificate template from the Certificate Templates snap-in.

    ❍ **B.** Configure the CA servers to publish delta CRLs.

    ❍ **C.** From the Extensions tab of the CA server's Properties dialog box, configure a CRL distribution point on the CA servers.

○ **D.** From the Extensions tab of the CA server's Properties dialog box, select the URL for the online responder, and select the check box labeled Include in the AIA Extension of Issued Certificates.

○ **E.** From the Extensions tab of the CA server's Properties dialog box, select the URL for the online responder, and select the check boxes labeled Include in the AIA Extension of Issued Certificates and Include in the Online Certificate Status Protocol (OCSP) Extension.

Answers to *Exam Cram* Questions

1. **A.** Dawn should keep a standalone root CA offline as a safeguard against compromise. She should bring this CA online only to issue certificates to CA servers lower in the CA hierarchy. She should not use an enterprise root CA for this purpose because it would become out of date with respect to other AD DS servers, so answer B is incorrect. Intermediate and issuing CAs are involved in active day-to-day issuing of certificates and must not be allowed to go offline, so answers C and D are incorrect.

2. **D.** Kevin must run `dcpromo.exe` to promote the server to a domain controller. An enterprise CA can run only on a domain controller, and if Kevin is at a member server, the Enterprise CA option will be unavailable. Kevin does not need to be a member of either the Enterprise Admins or Schema Admins group to install an enterprise CA, so answers A and B are incorrect. Merely using Server Manager to install AD DS without promoting the server to domain controller is insufficient, so answer C is incorrect. The Certification Authority console does not offer an option to promote a standalone CA to an enterprise CA, so answer E is incorrect.

3. **C, E, H.** Kim should set up an offline standalone root CA and an enterprise subordinate CA. She should then configure an autoenrollment user template, enable this template on the subordinate CA, and configure a GPO linked to the domain that enables certificate autoenrollment in the Computer Configuration section of the GPO. The combination of an offline standalone root CA and an enterprise subordinate CA provides a secure top-level PKI structure that minimizes the risk of compromise. If an online enterprise root CA were compromised, the entire PKI would have to be rebuilt and new certificates issued, so answer A is incorrect. An offline enterprise root CA would not remain up to date with respect to AD DS, so answer B is incorrect. A standalone subordinate CA would not maintain its database in AD DS. This is not the best idea, so answer D is incorrect. A web-based enrollment agent is not required for autoenrollment, so answer F is incorrect. The User Configuration section of the GPO does not enable certificate autoenrollment, so answer G is incorrect.

4. **C.** Steve should duplicate the template and configure the duplicate for autoenrollment. The Smartcard User template is a version 1 template that was originally supplied with Certificate Services in Windows 2000. It does not support autoenrollment. By duplicating this template, Steve can create either a version 2 or version 3 template, both of

which support autoenrollment. He does not need a certificate from a third-party certification authority, so answer A is incorrect. Logging on as a member of the Enterprise Admins group does not provide the Autoenroll permissions, so answer B is incorrect. The Autoenroll permission is required for certificate autoenrollment to be available, so answer D is incorrect.

5. **A.** Mary should configure the Trusted group as restricted enrollment agents. Certificate Services in Windows Server 2008 enables her to designate a security group as restricted enrollment agents, who are granted the permission to enroll for certificates on behalf of other users. The Certificate Manager administrative role enables role holders to approve certification enrollment and revocation requests, and the PKI Administrator role enables role holders to configure and maintain the CA. Both these roles grant the users more administrative authority than required for this scenario, so answers B and C are incorrect. The Account Operators group enables users to create and manage user and group accounts but does not enable the enrollment of certificates, so answer D is incorrect.

6. **C.** Brenda should add a copy of each third-party CA certificates to the Trusted Root Certification Authorities node in the Default Domain Policy GPO. This node is found under Computer Configuration\Policies\Windows Settings\Security Settings\Public Key Policies. It enables her to ensure that all domain computers receive a copy of the required certificates. Installing the certificates on the root or issuing-CA servers would enable these servers to trust the third-party certificates but would not allow client computers to trust these certificates, so answers A and B are incorrect. Manually placing a copy of each certificate in the Trusted Root Certification Authorities certificate store on each client computer would take far more administrative effort than using Group Policy to accomplish the same task, so answer D is incorrect.

7. **B, C, E.** Any of these procedures will back up Certificate Services. There is no specific Certificate Services folder, so answer A is incorrect. The Certificate Export Wizard allows you to back up a certificate but does not enable you to back up Certificate Services, so answer D is incorrect. The Certificate Templates snap-in does not provide an option for backing up Certificate Services, so answer F is incorrect.

8. **B.** Jackie should implement role-based administration in the CA hierarchy. This way she can assign different predefined task-based roles such as PKI Administrator, Certificate Manager, and Key Recovery Manager to different individuals. Doing so reduces the chance that the entire PKI would be compromised should one user account become compromised. Use of a special user account with a strong password and a Password Settings Object (PSO) to enforce a strong password might help to prevent the account's compromise, but it is still preferable to implement role-based administration, so answer A is incorrect. Configuring the subordinate CA servers so that certificate enrollment and renewal take place on different servers would not help here, so answer C is incorrect. Reconfiguring the offline standalone root CA as an offline enterprise root CA would prevent it from being up to date and is not recommended, so answer D is incorrect. Placing this machine online would increase the risk of compromising the entire CA hierarchy, so answer E is incorrect.

9. **C, D, F.** Betsy should revoke the certificate of the disbanded division's subordinate CA, publish a new base CRL, and copy this CRL to the network's CDP. Revoking the certificate of the disbanded division's subordinate CA automatically revokes all certificates that this CA issues, so she does not need to revoke certificates from this CA; therefore, answer A is incorrect. Betsy might want to uninstall AD CS from the disbanded division's subordinate CA, but this is not required by this scenario, so answer B is incorrect. She could publish a delta CRL, but it is more expedient to publish a new base CRL that ensures all applications and processes across the network are aware of the large number of certificates that have been revoked in this process; therefore, answer E is incorrect. The AIA extension is used to locate the URL of an online responder. Online responders are not being used in this scenario, so answer G is incorrect.

10. **A, E.** Jim should enable the use of the OCSP Response Signing certificate template. This enables the installation of an OCSP Response Signing certificate on the computer on which the online responder role service is installed. Jim also must select the URL for the online responder and select the check boxes labeled Include in the AIA Extension of Issued Certificates and Include in the Online Certificate Status Protocol (OCSP) Extension. He should also ensure that IIS is installed on the CA servers. The online responder clients use this URL to check certificates for revocation. The use of online responders replaces the use of CRLs, delta CRLs, and CRL distribution points, so answers B and C are incorrect. If Jim does not select the Include in the Online Certificate Status Protocol (OCSP) Extension check box, clients will be unable to locate the online responder server; therefore, answer D is incorrect.

CHAPTER 10

Practice Exam 1

Exam Cram Questions

1. Nolan is a network administrator for a company that operates an Active Directory Domain Services (AD DS) network consisting of two domains. The company has offices in Los Angeles and Tokyo, which are connected by a 128kbps WAN link. Each office is represented by a separate AD DS site, as well as its own domain.

   Nolan's company stores resource location information in AD DS so that users can perform searches to locate the appropriate resources using the Entire Directory option. However, users in the Tokyo office report that search times for resources are unacceptably slow.

   What can Nolan do to improve search times at the Tokyo office?

   - ○ **A.** Configure a global catalog server at the Tokyo office.
   - ○ **B.** Enable universal group caching at the Tokyo office.
   - ○ **C.** Configure a domain controller for the Los Angeles domain in the Tokyo office.
   - ○ **D.** Configure a domain controller for the Tokyo domain in the Los Angeles office.

2. Sam is a domain administrator for a company that operates a single domain AD DS network. All servers run Windows Server 2008. Sam needs to grant a junior administrator named Julie the ability to create child organizational units (OU) in the company's Employees OU. She needs to verify the existence of the OUs she creates, but she should not be able to perform other administrative tasks. Sam accesses the Delegation of Control Wizard and specifies Julie's user account. Which of the following should he do?

   O **A.** Select the Create a Custom Task to Delegate option, select Organizational Unit objects, and then grant Julie the Read and Write permissions.

   O **B.** Select the Create a Custom Task to Delegate option, and then select the option labeled This Folder, Existing Objects in This Folder, and Creation of New Objects in This Folder.

   O **C.** Select the Delegate the Following Common Tasks option, and then select Create, Delete, and Manage OUs.

   O **D.** Select the Create a Custom Task to Delegate option, select Organizational Unit objects, and then grant Julie the Read and Create All Child Objects permissions.

3. Evan is the systems administrator for a company that operates an AD DS network consisting of a single domain and five sites, which represent the head office and four branch offices. Each branch office is configured with a read-only domain controller (RODC).

   Evan receives a call from a branch office employee named Melissa, who is experiencing extremely long delays in logging on to the network. Evan wants to verify whether Melissa's credentials are cached at the RODC.

   What should Evan do? (Each correct answer represents part of the solution. Choose three answers.)

   O **A.** Access the Active Directory Sites and Services snap-in.

   O **B.** Access the Active Directory Users and Computers snap-in.

   O **C.** Access the Properties dialog box for Melissa's user account.

   O **D.** Access the Properties dialog box for the RODC in Melissa's branch office.

   O **E.** Click Advanced, and then select the Accounts Whose Passwords Are Stored on This Read-Only Domain Controller option from the drop-down list.

   O **F.** Click Advanced, and then select the Accounts That Have Been Authenticated to This Read-Only Domain Controller option from the drop-down list.

4. Shannon has installed a new 500GB hard disk on her Windows Server 2008 computer, which is a domain controller on her company's network. The present disk is almost full, and she wants to move the `ntds.dit` database file to the new disk, so she stops AD DS. Which of the following tools should she use to move the database file?

    ◯ **A.** Windows Explorer

    ◯ **B.** `wbadmin.exe`

    ◯ **C.** `ntdsutil.exe`

    ◯ **D.** `adsiedit.msc`

5. Sanjay administers the network for a company called Examprep Ltd. His company's website uses the Domain Name System (DNS) name www.examprep.com. A single web server has been hosting the site since Sanjay first began working for Examprep Ltd.

Recent system and network monitoring activities have indicated that the website is experiencing a tremendous surge in popularity. Sanjay obtains approval to add two additional server computers running Windows Server 2008 and Internet Information Services (IIS) to handle the increased traffic. Sanjay configures each of the three web server computers to use the name www.examprep.com. He also configures each server to use a different IP address. It is Sanjay's intent that external users should access the web servers equally.

In the Advanced tab of the DNS server's Properties dialog box, which item on the Server options list should Sanjay select to distribute user access equally among the web servers?

    ◯ **A.** Disable Recursion (Also Disables Forwarders)

    ◯ **B.** BIND Secondaries

    ◯ **C.** Fail on Load If Bad Zone Data

    ◯ **D.** Enable Round Robin

    ◯ **E.** Enable Netmask Ordering

    ◯ **F.** Secure Cache Against Pollution

6. Bill is the network administrator for Examcram Ltd., which operates an AD DS domain in which all servers run Windows Server 2008. He has configured an offline root enterprise certification authority (CA) and an online enterprise issuing CA.

Examcram Ltd. acquired a company named Que, which operates its own AD DS domain. Bill wants to set up a virtual private network (VPN) connection between the networks of the two companies that is secured with Layer 2 Transport Protocol/IP Security (L2TP/IPSec). He installs a VPN server on his network, including a certificate from the issuing CA; a network administrator at Que performs similar actions on his network.

Bill tests the connection and receives an error message stating that the certificate from Que is not trusted. What should he do to ensure that users can establish a secured VPN connection between the networks of the two companies?

○ **A.** Set up a forest trust relationship between the two domains.

○ **B.** Place a copy of the Que root CA's certificate in the Trusted Root Certification Authorities certificate store on his company's VPN server.

○ **C.** Place a copy of the Que root CA's certificate on the online enterprise issuing CA in Examcram Ltd.

○ **D.** Configure an online responder on his VPN server that includes a copy of the Que root CA's certificate.

7. Nellie is the network administrator for a financial company that operates a series of branch offices in major North American cities. The company operates an AD DS network consisting of a single domain, in which each office is configured as its own site. To improve the efficiency of intersite replication, Nellie has decided that she needs to create a site link bridge.

Which of the following steps should Nellie perform to accomplish this task? (Each correct answer represents part of the solution. Choose three answers.)

○ **A.** In the console tree of Active Directory Sites and Services, right-click the Inter-Site Transports folder and choose New Site Link Bridge.

○ **B.** In the console tree of Active Directory Sites and Services, right-click the Simple Mail Transport Protocol (SMTP) folder and choose New Site Link Bridge.

○ **C.** In the console tree of Active Directory Sites and Services, right-click the IP folder and choose New Site Link Bridge.

○ **D.** In the New Object–Site Link bridge dialog box, type a name for the site link bridge.

○ **E.** In the New Object–Site Link bridge dialog box, select at least two sites you want bridged, and then click Add.

○ **F.** In the New Object–Site Link bridge dialog box, select at least two site links you want bridged, and then click Add.

○ **G.** In the New Object–Site Link bridge dialog box, select the check box labeled Bridge All Site Links.

8. Teresa is a systems administrator for her company, which operates an AD DS network consisting of a single domain. Her boss has asked her to change the password for a user named Ken. She attempts to contact him to get his current password but has been unable to. The boss is worried that someone might have the password for this account. What is the best course of action for Teresa to take?

   ○ **A.** Teresa should disable the account. This will force Ken to call in with the information she needs.

   ○ **B.** Teresa should lock out the account. This will force Ken to call in with the information she needs.

   ○ **C.** Teresa should delete the user account and re-create it with the new password. Ken will call in as soon as he is unable to log on.

   ○ **D.** Because Teresa is an administrator, she can reset the password for Ken's account without needing the user's current password.

9. Marilyn administers the DNS servers in her company's AD DS domain. All domain controllers in the domain run Windows Server 2008. Users on the network have been reporting name resolution errors in recent days, so Marilyn decides to monitor DNS traffic, including individual name resolution queries. What should she do to accomplish this task with the least amount of administrative effort?

   ○ **A.** Access the Debug Logging tab of each DNS server's Properties dialog box and configure the logging options.

   ○ **B.** Enable Network Monitor to capture frames being transmitted to or from the DNS servers.

   ○ **C.** In Performance Monitor, configure a data collector set and capture information for DNS-related counters.

   ○ **D.** Access the Event Logging tab of each DNS server's Properties dialog box and select both errors and warnings.

10. Julio is the network administrator for a company that has deployed a new AD DS domain containing Windows Server 2008 domain controllers and member servers and Windows Vista Enterprise client computers.

    Julio's boss would like him to keep track of any attempts, authorized or otherwise, to modify the configuration of directory objects in the domain. Julio has configured the system access control lists (SACL) of these objects to enable auditing. What else must Julio do?

    ○ **A.** In a domain-based Group Policy object (GPO), enable auditing of object access attempts.

    ○ **B.** In a domain-based GPO, enable auditing of directory service access attempts.

○ **C.** In a domain-based GPO, enable auditing of directory service changes attempts.

○ **D.** Use the `auditpol.exe` tool to enable auditing of object access attempts.

○ **E.** Use the `auditpol.exe` tool to enable auditing of directory service access attempts.

○ **F.** Use the `auditpol.exe` tool to enable auditing of directory service changes attempts.

11. Melanie is the network administrator for a company that operates an AD DS network with a single domain and three domain controllers named DC1, DC2, and DC3. DC1 and DC2 host the company's DNS zone. Melanie has scheduled nightly full server back-ups for all three domain controllers.

A flood in the server room damages all three domain controllers. The insurance company purchases three new servers and delivers them rapidly to Melanie. She needs to restore AD DS and ensure that name resolution services are restored as rapidly as possible. How should she proceed? (Each correct answer represents part of the solution. Choose all that apply.)

○ **A.** Install Windows Server 2008 on all three servers.

○ **B.** Restart all three servers in Safe Mode.

○ **C.** Restart all three servers in Directory Services Restore Mode.

○ **D.** Restart all three servers from the Windows Server 2008 DVD and choose Repair Your Computer.

○ **E.** Run `dcpromo.exe` to promote all three servers to domain controllers.

○ **F.** Perform a nonauthoritative restore of system state on all three domain controllers.

○ **G.** Perform an authoritative restore of system state on all three domain controllers.

○ **H.** Perform a Windows Complete PC Restore procedure on all three domain controllers.

12. Betty's AD DS domain uses a standard DNS zone with a primary DNS server called Alpha and two secondary servers called Beta and Gamma. All three servers are listed as name servers on the Name Servers tab of the DNS zone's Properties dialog box. Their IP addresses are `192.168.1.61`, `192.168.1.62`, and `192.168.1.63`, respectively.

Betty has configured zone transfer to allow zone transfers only to servers listed on the Name Servers tab. Nevertheless, zone transfers are not taking place across the network in a timely fashion. Betty clicks the Notify button on the Zone Transfers tab and notices that the dialog box is configured as shown in the following figure. What should she do? (Each correct answer represents part of the solution. Choose all that apply).

- ○ **A.** Select the Automatically Notify check box.

- ○ **B.** Select The Following Servers option.

- ○ **C.** Add the IP address 192.168.1.63 to the list.

- ○ **D.** Remove the IP address 192.168.1.62 from the list.

- ○ **E.** Select the Servers Listed on the Name Servers Tab option.

13. You are responsible for configuring Group Policy in your company's AD DS domain. The domain contains OUs that mirror the company's departmental organization. Another administrator has applied a GPO to the Sales OU that limits user access to their computers. Your manager has noticed that this GPO has reduced the number of help desk calls generated by the users in this department, so he asks you to apply the same policies to the Marketing department. What is the best way to accomplish this task?

- ○ **A.** Create a new GPO containing the required settings, and link this GPO to the Marketing OU.

- ○ **B.** Use the GPO linked to the Sales OU as a Starter GPO to create a new GPO linked to the Marketing OU.

- ○ **C.** Add the group containing the Marketing team members to the Sales OU.

- ○ **D.** Simply link the current GPO to the Marketing OU.

14. Kent is the network administrator for a company that operates an AD DS network consisting of a single domain. The company has four domain controllers that run either Windows Server 2003 or Windows Server 2008.

Kent has obtained a new computer on which he plans to install Windows Server 2008 and promote to a domain controller. This computer will replace an older domain controller, which holds the RID master and PDC emulator roles and will be recommissioned as a backup file server.

Before demoting this domain controller to a member server, Kent must transfer these roles to another domain controller. Which of the following tools can he use for this purpose? (Each correct answer represents a complete solution to the problem. Choose two answers.)

- ○ **A.** Active Directory Domains and Trusts
- ○ **B.** Active Directory Sites and Services
- ○ **C.** Active Directory Users and Computers
- ○ **D.** Active Directory Schema
- ○ **E.** The `Ntdsutil` utility

15. Ruby suspects that an intruder has been attempting to obtain usernames and passwords from her company's Windows Server 2008 domain controller. She would like to capture data transmitted across the network adapter of the domain controller. Which tool should she use?

- ○ **A.** Network Monitor
- ○ **B.** Task Manager
- ○ **C.** Reliability and Performance Monitor
- ○ **D.** Event Viewer
- ○ **E.** Windows System Resource Manager (WSRM)

16. Stuart has successfully installed and configured an enterprise root CA for his company, which operates an AD DS network consisting of a single domain. Stuart has also configured a certificate template for autoenrollment.

What additional tasks must Stuart perform to enable autoenrollment of user certificates? (Each correct answer represents part of the solution. Choose two answers.)

- ○ **A.** Install Internet Information Services (IIS) 7.0 on the CA.
- ○ **B.** Install an enterprise subordinate CA.
- ○ **C.** Configure a Certificate Trust List (CTL).

○   **D.**   Configure the CA to issue certificates based on the template he has just configured.

○   **E.**   Configure a GPO linked to the domain to enroll certificates automatically.

17. Michelle administers a server named Server3 that has Active Directory Lightweight Directory Services (AD LDS) installed. She installs an instance of AD LDS with its associated application directory partition that will store data for a directory-enabled engineering design application.

    Michelle wants to create a new OU in the AD LDS application directory partition that will organize users that require access to the design application. Which of the following tools can she use for this purpose? (Each correct answer represents a complete solution to the problem. Choose two answers.)

    ○   **A.**   `Ldp.exe`

    ○   **B.**   `Ntdsutil.exe`

    ○   **C.**   `Dsadd.exe`

    ○   **D.**   `Adsiedit.msc`

    ○   **E.**   `Dssite.msc`

18. Allison is the network administrator for a company that operates an AD DS network consisting of a single domain. The network includes a standalone root CA and an enterprise subordinate issuing CA.

    Allison has configured an autoenrollment certificate template and a GPO that enables users to automatically receive certificates. She needs to provide certificates for routers and switches on the network. How should she proceed?

    ○   **A.**   Install the Simple Certificate Enrollment Protocol (SCEP) on the issuing CA server.

    ○   **B.**   Configure an online responder on the issuing CA server.

    ○   **C.**   Configure a certificate template that includes the Authority Information Access (AIA) extension.

    ○   **D.**   Create a security group that contains the machine accounts for the routers and switches, and then grant this group the Autoenroll permission for the required template.

19. Paul administers the network for a new company whose AD DS root domain will be named que.com. He installs Windows Server 2008 on a computer named DC01 and runs dcpromo.exe on this computer to create the first domain controller in the new forest. He accepts the option to create a new DNS server.

Paul also sets up a Windows Server 2008 member server running Internet Information Services (IIS) 7.0 and 12 client computers running Windows Vista Business. He configures all 13 of these computers with static IP addresses and specifies the IP address of DC01 as their preferred DNS server.

Which of the following steps must Paul take to ensure that both the address (A) and pointer (PTR) resource records of the client computers and the IIS server are recorded properly when he adds them to the que.com domain?

○ **A.** Create a forward lookup zone for the network and enable it to accept dynamic updates.

○ **B.** Create a reverse lookup zone for the network and enable it to accept dynamic updates.

○ **C.** Enable DC01 to accept dynamic updates.

○ **D.** Configure the client computers to send updates to DC01.

○ **E.** Enable the zones for que.com to accept dynamic updates.

20. Ted is the network administrator for Examprep Ltd. The company has a subsidiary named Que. The Examprep network consists of a single AD DS forest containing one domain named examprep.com. The domain and forest functional levels are Windows Server 2008. The Que network consists of a single Windows NT 4.0 domain named QUE. A file server named Server2 is a member of the examprep.com domain. All users in both domains need to save files on Server2 every day. Ted needs to ensure that the domain administrators of the QUE domain cannot grant users in the examprep.com domain permissions on servers in the QUE domain. What should Ted do to accomplish this objective?

○ **A.** Create a one-way external trust relationship in which the examprep.com domain trusts the QUE domain.

○ **B.** Create a one-way external trust relationship in which the QUE domain trusts the examprep.com domain.

○ **C.** Upgrade the QUE domain to Windows Server 2008 and make this domain the root domain of a second tree in the existing forest.

○ **D.** Upgrade the QUE domain to Windows Server 2008 and make this domain the root domain of a new forest. Create a two-way forest trust relationship.

21. Rob is a network administrator for a company that operates a single domain AD DS network. All servers run Windows Server 2008, and all client computers run Windows XP Professional. Both portable and desktop client computers are used on the network. The domain is organized into a series of organizational units (OU) that reflect the departmental structure of the company.

The CIO has requested that no unattended portable computer be left logged on to the network unless it's protected by a password. This requirement is to be enforced on portable computers only, because all desktop computers are located in areas that are protected by building security. Rob needs to configure a Group Policy object (GPO) in such a manner that this rule will be properly enforced for portable computers only. How should he accomplish this objective using the least amount of administrative effort and without modifying any other policy settings for these computers?

- ○ **A.** Create a GPO linked to the domain that specifies a password-protected screen saver. Use a Windows Management Instrumentation (WMI) filter to query for the hardware chassis type information so that this GPO applies only to portable computers.

- ○ **B.** Create a global security group and move all computer accounts of portable computers to this group. Create a GPO linked to the domain that specifies a password-protected screen saver. Filter the GPO so that only this group has the Allow–Read and Allow–Apply Group Policy permissions.

- ○ **C.** Create a child OU under each OU where portable computers are found, and move all portable computer accounts to this OU. Create a GPO that specifies a password-protected screen saver. Link this GPO to each child OU containing portable computers.

- ○ **D.** Create one OU, and move all portable computer accounts there. Create a GPO linked to this OU that specifies a password-protected screen saver.

22. Maggie is the network administrator for a company that operates an AD DS forest containing two geographically distinct domains: examcram.com located in Atlanta and west.examcram.com located in San Jose. Each domain has a single site named by its city and containing three domain controllers. The two sites are connected by an ISDN link.

Maggie is configuring the placement of global catalog servers to optimize user logon and resource access. Which of the following configurations should she use?

- ○ **A.** Place a single global catalog server at the Atlanta site only.

- ○ **B.** Place a single global catalog server at each site.

- ○ **C.** Place two global catalog servers at the Atlanta site only.

- ○ **D.** Place two global catalog servers at the San Jose site only.

- ○ **E.** Place two global catalog servers at each site.

23. Liz wants to audit access to files on the shared folder \\Server3\Docs to determine who has been attempting to perform unauthorized modifications.

Which of the following does she need to do to accomplish this task? (Each correct answer represents part of the solution. Choose two answers.)

○ **A.** Enable the Audit success and failure for directory service access setting.

○ **B.** Enable the Audit success and failure for account logon setting.

○ **C.** Enable the Audit success and failure for object access setting.

○ **D.** Configure the Server3 server for auditing.

○ **E.** Configure the Docs shared folder for auditing.

○ **F.** Configure each file in the Docs shared folder for auditing.

24. Which of the following characteristics properly describe how data is sent during inter-site replication? (Choose all that apply.)

○ **A.** Intersite replication of data is scheduled.

○ **B.** Intersite replication is frequent and processed automatically.

○ **C.** Intersite replication can use either RPC over IP or SMTP transport protocols.

○ **D.** Data is sent compressed.

○ **E.** Data is sent uncompressed.

○ **F.** All domain controllers in each site participate directly in intersite replication.

25. Dennis is responsible for monitoring the performance of all Windows Server 2008 computers in his company's AD DS domain. He needs to create a baseline record of server performance for each of the domain controllers and member servers. Which tool should he use for this purpose?

○ **A.** Windows System Resource Manager

○ **B.** Task Manager

○ **C.** The Reliability Monitor tool in the Reliability and Performance Monitor console

○ **D.** The Data Collector Sets tool in the Reliability and Performance Monitor console

○ **E.** The Performance Monitor tool in the Reliability and Performance Monitor console

26. Gerry is the network administrator for a company that operates an AD DS domain named examcram.com. Servers run a mix of Windows 2000 Server, Windows Server 2003, and Windows Server 2008. Client computers run either Windows XP Professional or Windows Vista Business. The company acquires another company named Prep Ltd. Gerry creates a new domain named prep.examcram.com to reflect the changes in corporate structure. He must now manage two DNS servers: dns1.examcram.com and dns2.prep.examcram.com.

Dns1.examcram.com is the Start of Authority (SOA) for examcram.com, and dns2.prep.examcram.com is the SOA for prep.examcram.com. Gerry has also configured an intranet server called trans.prep.examcram.com that employees from both companies can access for updates on issues relating to the two companies becoming one corporate concern.

A user of a client computer in examcram.com called vista25.examcram.com reports that she cannot access the intranet server. Gerry discovers that he cannot ping this server by name from the client computer. What can he do to correct this problem? (Each correct answer represents a complete solution to the problem. Choose two answers.)

- ○ **A.** Add a stub zone for examcram.com on dns2.prep.examcram.com.

- ○ **B.** Add a stub zone for prep.examcram.com on dns1.examcram.com.

- ○ **C.** Add an A resource record for dns2.prep.examcram.com on dns1.examcram.com.

- ○ **D.** Add an A resource record for dns1.examcram.com on dns2.prep.examcram.com.

- ○ **E.** Configure zone delegation for prep.examcram.com on dns1.examcram.com.

- ○ **F.** Add a PTR record for prep.examcram.com on dns1.examcram.com.

27. Stephanie has installed a standalone root CA and an enterprise subordinate issuing CA for her company's domain. Which of the following additional tasks should she perform before issuing certificates to users on the network? (Each correct answer represents part of the solution. Choose three answers.)

- ○ **A.** Configure certificate templates.

- ○ **B.** Configure the Certificate Services web pages.

- ○ **C.** Configure certificate revocation lists (CRL) or online responders.

- ○ **D.** Configure key archival and recovery.

28. Karen is a network manager for a global musical instrument company that operates a complicated AD DS forest consisting of five domain trees and a total of 32 individual domains. The domain structure includes the following tree root domains:

mm-corp.us, asiamusical.com, willywilly.com.au, worldwideguitars.com, and virtual-realm.com

Users in development.california.mm-corp.us often need to collaborate with their Australian counterparts in development.willywilly.com.au, and users in both domains complain that it takes an extremely long time for shared folders to open even though there is excellent connectivity between physical locations.

Which of the following should Karen do to improve this situation?

- ○ **A.** Karen should purchase additional bandwidth to reduce the delay in accessing shared resources.

- ○ **B.** Karen can create a forest trust between the california.mm-corp.us and willywilly.com.au domain trees.

- ○ **C.** Karen should create a shortcut trust between development.california.mm-corp.us and development.willywilly.com.au.

- ○ **D.** Karen should move the users from the two domains into a common domain.

29. Rick is responsible for planning operations master role placements in his company's AD DS forest, which consists of a forest root domain and three child domains. Four domain controllers in the forest root domain are called Server1, Server2, Server3, and Server4, as shown in the figure. He needs to determine on which server to place the infrastructure master role. Which of the following represents the best placement of the infrastructure master in the forest root domain?

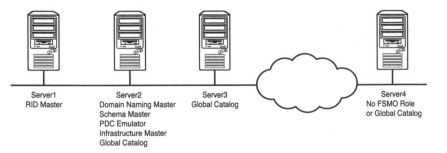

Server1	Server2	Server3		Server4
RID Master	Domain Naming Master	Global Catalog		No FSMO Role
	Schema Master			or Global Catalog
	PDC Emulator			
	Infrastructure Master			
	Global Catalog			

- ○ **A.** On Server1, which hosts the RID master but not the global catalog. This server has a direct connection to Server2 and Server3.

- ○ **B.** On Server2, which hosts all four other operations master roles plus the global catalog.

○ **C.** On Server3, which does not host other operations master roles but does host the global catalog.

○ **D.** On Server4, which is located across a WAN connection from Server1 and does not host other operations master roles.

30. Roy is responsible for maintaining DNS on his company's AD DS network, which consists of a single domain in which all servers run Windows Server 2008. The company operates an office in downtown Denver and a suburban office in Littleton.

After upgrading a member server in the company's suburban office to a domain controller, users at that office report that logon to the domain is slow. Upon investigating the problem, Roy notices that the service (SRV) resource records for the new domain controller are not registered in the DNS zone for the suburban office. What should he do to reregister these SRV resource records as quickly as possible?

○ **A.** Restart the DNS Server service.

○ **B.** Restart the DNS Client service.

○ **C.** Restart the Netlogon service.

○ **D.** Reboot the domain controller.

31. Brian is responsible for maintaining AD DS replication on his company's network, which consists of three domains and nine sites. When he uses `replmon` to check the automatically configured replication topology, he notices that connection paths are not established in what he thinks is the optimum manner.

What can Brian do to manually change the topology?

○ **A.** Edit the Registry to indicate the appropriate paths.

○ **B.** Use Active Directory Sites and Services to manually create a site link object connecting the required servers.

○ **C.** Force the Knowledge Consistency Checker (KCC) to update the replication topology.

○ **D.** Brian cannot modify the replication paths. The KCC does not permit this type of configuration.

32. Carol is the network administrator for a company that operates an AD DS network consisting of a single domain. Company executives have signed a long-term partnership agreement with another company that also operates an AD DS network. Users in Carol's company will require access to rights-protected confidential information that is stored on web servers located on the second company's network. Users in the second company will not require access to documents on Carol's network.

Which two of the following should Carol configure on her network? (Each correct answer represents part of the solution. Choose two answers.)

○ **A.** Active Directory Lightweight Directory Services (AD LDS)

○ **B.** Active Directory Rights Management Services (AD RMS)

○ **C.** Active Directory Federation Services (AD FS)

○ **D.** Active Directory Certificate Services (AD CS)

○ **E.** A one-way external trust relationship

33. Alfredo is the network administrator for a company that operates an AD DS network consisting of a single domain. Servers run Windows Server 2008, and client computers run Windows Vista Enterprise. The domain contains OUs that are structured according to the departmental structure of the company, and all OUs have multiple GPOs linked to them.

As a result of departmental reorganization, the Design OU needs to be moved under the Engineering OU. Alfredo needs to determine which objects in the Design OU are adversely affected by GPOs linked to the Engineering OU. What should Alfredo do to achieve this goal without disruption to users?

○ **A.** Use the Group Policy Modeling Wizard for the Design OU. Choose the Engineering OU to simulate policy settings.

○ **B.** Use the Group Policy Modeling Wizard for the Engineering OU. Choose the Design OU to simulate policy settings.

○ **C.** Use the Group Policy Results Wizard for the Design OU. Review the policy results for users in the OU.

○ **D.** Use the Group Policy Results Wizard for the Engineering OU. Review the policy results for users in the OU.

34. Darcy's company operates an AD DS forest consisting of a single tree with an empty root domain and five child domains that represent operational divisions. Darcy is responsible for maintaining the FSMO roles. In total, how many FSMO roles are present in this tree?

○ **A.** One schema master, one domain naming master, six RID masters, six PDC emulators, and six infrastructure masters

○ **B.** One schema master, one domain naming master, five RID masters, five PDC emulators, and five infrastructure masters

○ **C.** Six schema masters, six domain naming masters, six RID masters, six PDC emulators, and six infrastructure masters

○ **D.** One schema master, one domain naming master, one RID master, one PDC emulator, and one infrastructure master

35. You administer the network for a catering company called Thoughtful Food. Your firm operates a single domain AD DS network that includes three Windows Server 2008 computers and a mix of Windows XP Professional and Windows Vista Business clients. Management has notified you that a competitor known as Engorge & Devour has taken a keen interest in your pumpkin soup recipe. Two employees of Thoughtful Food have recently resigned and taken up positions with Engorge & Devour, and management is afraid that they will attempt to steal proprietary formulas and recipes belonging to Thoughtful Food by breaking into your network. You are tasked with improving logon security on Thoughtful Food's network by limiting the number of failed logon attempts for all users on the network and by establishing an audit policy for tracking failed logon attempts.

    Which of the following tasks should you undertake to complete this task? (Each correct answer represents part of the solution. Choose two answers.)

    ○ **A.** Edit the Default Domain Policy GPO to enable auditing and account lockout.

    ○ **B.** Monitor the security log for failed account management attempts on each domain controller.

    ○ **C.** Monitor the security log for failed logon attempts on each domain controller.

    ○ **D.** Configure a local security policy on each computer in the domain.

36. Ryan is the senior network administrator for his company. The CIO has asked him to create an OU structure that enables the Research department to administer its own user accounts so that the IT department staff other than Ryan don't have permissions to this OU. Ryan is the only member of the Enterprise Admins group, other than the domain's default administrator account, whose password is known only by Ryan and the CIO.

    Ryan creates a Research Admins security group and Research OU, delegates administrative permissions to the Research Admins group, and removes the IT department security group from the permissions list.

    A few days later, Ryan discovers that another administrator has been resetting user accounts for Research employees. What has he missed?

    ○ **A.** Ryan needs to create a separate Research domain to isolate it from the corporate domain.

    ○ **B.** Ryan needs to change the password on the domain administrator account because the other administrator must be using that account.

    ○ **C.** Ryan needs to remove the Enterprise Admins group from the permissions list.

    ○ **D.** Ryan needs to remove the Domain Admins group from the permissions list.

37. Edward has accidentally deleted the Management OU from a domain controller in his company's AD DS network. The deletion has propagated to other domain controllers, and Edward urgently needs to get this OU back before he receives complaints from managers who are unable to log on. He has a system state backup that was created the previous evening. Which of the following steps must he perform to get this OU back? (Each correct answer represents part of the solution. Choose all that apply, and arrange these steps in the order in which Edward must perform them.)

- ○ **A.** At a command prompt, type the `wbadmin get versions` command.
- ○ **B.** Restart the domain controller normally.
- ○ **C.** At a command prompt, type the `net stop ntds` command.
- ○ **D.** Use the `ntdsutil` utility to mark the restored OU as authoritative.
- ○ **E.** Restart the domain controller using the Windows Server 2008 DVD, and select the Repair Your Computer option.
- ○ **F.** Restart the domain controller in Directory Services Restore Mode.
- ○ **G.** At a command prompt, type the `wbadmin start recovery` command.
- ○ **H.** At a command prompt, type the `wbadmin start systemstaterecovery` command.
- ○ **I.** At a command prompt, type the `net start ntds` command.

38. Karla is the network administrator for a company that operates an AD DS network consisting of a parent domain and two child domains. All DNS servers run Windows Server 2008, and all DNS zones are configured as Active Directory–integrated zones hosted on domain controllers.

Karla notices that the zone data for one of the child domains contains several entries for unknown computers that are not domain members. What should she do to prevent this from occurring in the future?

- ○ **A.** Select the Secure Only option on the General tab of the zone's Properties dialog box.
- ○ **B.** Change the zone replication scope to the All DNS Servers in This Domain option.
- ○ **C.** On the Zone Aging/Scavenging Properties dialog box, select the Scavenge Stale Resource Records option.
- ○ **D.** Right-click the server in the console tree of DNS Manager and choose Scavenge Stale Resource Records.

39. Jane is the network administrator for a company whose AD DS forest includes a domain tree called que.org with child domains named calif.que.org, ariz.que.org, and texas.que.org. In the California domain, there is an OU named Sales. This OU contains a user named Don Smith. Jane has implemented several GPOs within the domain, including the following:

▶**Site Group Policy**—The wallpaper is set to Green. Task Manager is disabled.

▶**Domain Group Policy**—The Display Properties tab is disabled. (Enforced setting is selected.) Task Manager is not disabled.

▶**OU1 Policy**—The wallpaper is set to Red. The Display Properties tab is enabled. (Block Inheritance is set to On.)

▶**OU2 Policy**—The wallpaper is set to Blue.

The OU policies are set in the order of OU1 being on top and OU2 being on the bottom of the application order list. What is the resultant set of policies?

- ○ **A.** Don logs on and his wallpaper is red. Task Manager is not disabled. Display Properties is disabled.

- ○ **B.** Don logs on and his wallpaper is green. Task Manager is disabled. Display Properties is enabled.

- ○ **C.** Don logs on and his wallpaper is blue. Task Manager is not disabled. Display Properties is disabled.

- ○ **D.** Don logs on and his wallpaper is green. Task Manager is disabled.

40. You are responsible for maintaining the CRLs in your company. A new user named Brigitte has been hired to work in the Accounting department, and you issue a certificate to her. You receive an email from Human Resources informing you that Brigitte has failed a preliminary security evaluation and might be unsuitable for this job, so you revoke her certificate.

The next morning, Human Resources informs you that the security evaluation has proven to be successful, and Brigitte needs her certificate back. So you attempt to unrevoke the certificate but receive an error message stating that this attempt failed. Which of the following is the most likely reason you were unable to unrevoke her certificate?

- ○ **A.** You should delete the delta CRL containing the revoked certificate before you can unrevoke it.

- ○ **B.** You should restore the CRL to the day before you revoked the certificate.

- ○ **C.** You specified the Unspecified reason code when you revoked the certificate. You should have used the Certificate Hold reason code.

- ○ **D.** You should have unrevoked the certificate before it was published to the latest base CRL. Once a revoked certificate is published in the base CRL, you cannot unrevoke it.

41. While performing some standard maintenance on his domain controller, Frank accidentally deleted an OU containing 350 user accounts, 50 printers, and several groups. Now Frank realizes his mistake and wants to restore all the deleted items in the most efficient way possible. Fortunately for Frank, he does have the backup of the server's system state from the previous evening. Frank restores from the backup; however, the next morning he discovers that the OU is once again deleted.

How can Frank restore the deleted OU without having it automatically delete again during the next replication cycle?

- ○ **A.** Frank needs to perform an authoritative restore of AD DS while running the server in Directory Services Restore Mode.

- ○ **B.** Frank needs to stop AD DS from a command prompt, perform an authoritative restore of AD DS, and then restart AD DS from the command prompt.

- ○ **C.** Frank needs to perform an authoritative restore of AD DS while running the server in Safe Mode.

- ○ **D.** Frank needs to perform an authoritative restore of AD DS while AD DS is running normally.

42. Maria is the administrator responsible for maintaining her company's intersite replication topology. The company operates an AD DS network consisting of a single domain with sites representing all cities where the company does business. The head office is in Chicago, and large regional offices are located in San Francisco, Atlanta, and Toronto. These regional offices are connected to the head office with T3 lines.

Each region also has three or four smaller branch offices, each of which is connected to its regional office with an ISDN line. Branch offices in St. Louis, Indianapolis, and Milwaukee are also connected to the Chicago head office with ISDN lines. For fault tolerance and load balancing purposes, each office has its own Windows Server 2008 domain controller. All site links have been created.

Maria wants to create a replication topology that allows only the regional offices to communicate with the head office. She must ensure that each branch office communicates only with the closest regional office. What should she do?

- ○ **A.** Manually create connection objects between the domain controllers in the head office and the regional offices, and between each branch office and its regional office. Use IP as the transport protocol.

- ○ **B.** Manually create connection objects between the domain controllers in the head office and the regional offices, and between each branch office and its regional office. Use SMTP as the transport protocol.

○ **C.** Manually create connection objects between the domain controllers in the head office and the regional offices. Allow KCC to automatically create the connection objects between the branch offices and the regional offices.

○ **D.** Allow KCC to automatically create the connection objects between the main office and all other offices.

43. Jonathan is the systems administrator for his company, which runs a large AD DS network that consists of several domains contained within two tree structures. The company has operations in both North America and Asia. Jonathan works in the Los Angeles head office, where the root domain is located, including the domain controllers that hold the roles of domain naming master and schema master. One weekend, the domain naming master crashed, and the hardware techs discovered that it requires several new parts, including a new SCSI hard drive, and that the parts will take at least ten days to be delivered and installed. However, Jonathan urgently needs to create two new domains that will encompass the company's new ventures into Australia. Without a functioning domain naming master, he is unable to create the new domains. He realizes that it is necessary to have another domain controller seize the role of domain naming master.

Which of the following does Jonathan need to do to accomplish this task?

○ **A.** Use Active Directory Users and Computers.

○ **B.** Use Active Directory Domains and Trusts.

○ **C.** Use the `ntdsutil` command-line utility.

○ **D.** Install another new computer with Windows Server 2008. Use `dcpromo.exe` to promote it to a domain controller and specify that it is to be a domain naming master.

44. Mary is a network administrator for a pharmaceutical company that operates a single-domain AD DS network. After a successful breach of a password belonging to a top scientist in the company's Research department, her boss asked her to implement a password policy that requires a minimum length of 12 characters, a minimum age of 7 days, a maximum age of 30 days, and complexity requirements. Users in other departments are to be subject to the current policy, which requires a minimum length of 7 characters, a minimum age of 2 days, a maximum age of 60 days, and complexity requirements. Which of the following does Mary need to do to implement these password policies?

○ **A.** Create a separate OU for the Research department. Then create a GPO linked to this OU that specifies these policies.

○ **B.** Create a separate domain for the Research department. Then create a GPO linked to this domain that specifies these policies.

○ **C.** Create a global security group for the members of the Research department, and filter the settings in a GPO so that they apply only to members of this department.

○ **D.** Create a global security group for the members of the Research department, and use `adsiedit.exe` to create a policy that applies the required password settings to this group.

45. You have configured an AD FS server on your network so that users in a partner company can access data by means of a web-based application. You are creating a claims-aware agent that will use a claims-aware application to enable the querying of AD FS security token claims. Which of the following files must you ensure are present for the claims-aware agent to be properly configured? (Each correct answer represents part of the solution. Choose three answers.)

○ **A.** `Web.config`

○ **B.** `Metabase.xml`

○ **C.** `Default.aspx`

○ **D.** `Default.aspx.cs`

○ **E.** `MS-AdamSyncConf.XML`

○ **F.** `ntds.dit`

46. Phil is the network administrator for a company that operates an AD DS network consisting of a single domain. DNS is running as an Active Directory–integrated zone on two domain controllers named Server1 and Server2. One morning, several users inform him that they were unable to access a resource by name. In attempting to troubleshoot this problem, Phil notices that the event logs at Server2 contain several errors with ID 4006 and contain a message that the DNS server was unable to load the records in the specified name found in the Active Directory–integrated zone.

What should Phil do to enable proper name resolution and prevent these errors from occurring in the future?

○ **A.** Access the Debug Logging tab of the server's Properties dialog box, and enable logging of incoming and outgoing packets for queries and transfers.

○ **B.** Access the Monitoring tab of the server's Properties dialog box, and perform a simple and recursive test; then check that the `cache.dns` file is present and configured properly.

○ **C.** Access the Advanced tab of the server's Properties dialog box, and select the All Names option in the Name Checking section of this tab.

○ **D.** Access the Advanced tab of the server's Properties dialog box, and select the Strict RFC (ANSI) option in the Name Checking section of this tab.

47. George has been asked to deploy software to computers in his company's AD DS domain. The software should be available on the client machines but not necessarily installed. The idea is that users can access the Control Panel Add or Remove Programs applet and install the applications they need as they want them. At a managers' meeting, George announces that he intends to publish applications to the computers using Group Policy. Is this a good decision?

    ○ **A.** Yes, but George could have assigned or published the software because the end result when targeting computers is the same.

    ○ **B.** Yes, the difference between assigning and publishing is that an assigned application appears on the Start menu, even if the application is not installed. Published applications do not. They simply appear in the Add or Remove Programs applet.

    ○ **C.** No, this is not the best solution. George should assign the software to the computers. Published packages appear on the Start menu.

    ○ **D.** No, this simply does not work. George cannot publish software to a computer. He can only assign software to computers. However, both options are available to users.

48. Christina is the network administrator for a company that operates an AD DS network consisting of a single domain. Her company has just acquired a firm whose network used an older version of Novell NetWare. The acquired company's network needs to be integrated into your company's network environment. All the company's hardware and software have been auctioned off. The NetWare administrator has provided his user account information to Christina in comma-separated file format.

Which of the following tools should Christina use to import these user accounts into her company's domain?

    ○ **A.** Microsoft Excel

    ○ **B.** Active Directory Users and Computers

    ○ **C.** Csvde

    ○ **D.** Ldifde

    ○ **E.** Dsadd

49. Oliver is a systems administrator for a company that operates an Active Directory forest with two domains and eight sites. All servers run Windows Server 2008, and all client computers run either Windows XP Professional or Windows Vista Business. Administrators at remote sites have informed Oliver that intersite replication is slow at times, and he needs to investigate the source of this problem. How should he obtain information regarding the possible causes of this problem? (Choose all that apply.)

○ **A.** Use Event Viewer to check for errors and warnings that relate to replication problems.

○ **B.** Use Reliability and Performance Monitor to monitor the counters in the NTDS object.

○ **C.** Use `ntdsutil` to obtain information about replication slowdowns and failures.

○ **D.** Use `repadmin` to obtain information about replication slowdowns and failures.

50. Sandra is the systems administrator for a company that operates an AD DS network consisting of a single domain. There are two sites connected by a 128kbps dial-up link, one representing the head office with 200 users and the second representing a suburban branch office with 30 users. The branch office has one domain controller and one file server.

    Users in the branch office report that access to resources in the head office is frequently slow. Upon investigating, Sandra notices that AD DS replication between the sites consumes much of the available bandwidth on the dial-up link. This replication is configured to use the Remote Procedure Call (RPC) over IP replication protocol. What should Sandra do to improve the usage of the available bandwidth?

    ○ **A.** Reduce the site link cost.

    ○ **B.** Replace the domain controller in the branch office with a read-only domain controller (RODC).

    ○ **C.** Replace the IP site link with an SMTP site link.

    ○ **D.** Configure intersite replication to take place during nonbusiness hours only.

51. Duncan has configured Certificate Services on his company's domain-based PKI to publish a base CRL every Friday at 8 p.m. and a delta CRL Monday to Thursday at 8 p.m. On Wednesday morning, an accounting application needs to check the CRL to ensure that a user's certificate is valid. Which of the following CRLs does the application check?

    ○ **A.** The base CRL and Tuesday's delta CRL.

    ○ **B.** The base CRL and Wednesday's delta CRL.

    ○ **C.** The base CRL and both Monday's and Tuesday's delta CRL.

    ○ **D.** The base CRL and all of Monday's, Tuesday's, and Wednesday's delta CRLs.

    ○ **E.** Tuesday's delta CRL only.

    ○ **F.** Wednesday's delta CRL only.

52. Judy is the systems administrator for a company that operates an AD DS network consisting of two domains in a single domain tree. The head office is located in Kansas City and includes five domain controllers running Windows Server 2008. The company also has a branch office located in Omaha that has a single domain controller running Windows Server 2003 and 30 client computers running Windows XP Professional. All users and computers in the branch office belong to the Omaha Users OU in the child domain. The two offices are connected by means of an ISDN line. Each office is configured as a separate site in AD DS.

Judy wants to ensure that domain logons are processed efficiently, with minimal traffic across the ISDN line, so she has decided to implement universal group membership caching.

On which AD DS object should she enable universal group membership caching?

- ○ **A.** Kansas City site
- ○ **B.** Omaha site
- ○ **C.** Child domain
- ○ **D.** Omaha Users OU

53. Lenny is the network administrator for a company that operates an AD DS network on which a PKI based on Active Directory Certificate Services (AD CS) has been installed. He has configured a certificate template that provides autoenrollment of user certificates.

One of the users in his office has a Macintosh computer and requires a certificate from the company's PKI. How should Lenny proceed?

- ○ **A.** Use the web enrollment service to issue this user a certificate.
- ○ **B.** Use the Simple Certificate Enrollment Protocol (SCEP) to issue this user a certificate.
- ○ **C.** Include the Authority Information Access (AIA) extension on the certificate template.
- ○ **D.** Include the Macintosh machine in a group that is granted the Autoenroll permission for the certificate template.

54. Erica is administrator of Acme Construction, which operates an AD DS network consisting of a single domain. Acme is headquartered in Toronto, with branch offices in Buffalo, Detroit, and Miami. The Acme companywide domain name will be acmeconstr.com. Initially, Erica plans to install a DNS server at headquarters and another in each of the three branch offices. She plans to have the DNS server in Toronto host her company's domain. Additionally, Erica intends to delegate responsibility for maintaining DNS systems and zone information to network administrators located at each of the branch offices.

Which of the following plans will achieve the desired results for Erica?

- ○ **A.** The DNS server in Toronto will host a standard primary zone for the acmeconstr.com domain. Each branch office will host a standard primary zone.

- ○ **B.** The DNS server in Toronto will host a standard primary zone for the acmeconstr.com domain. Branch offices will be configured as subdomains. Each branch office will host a standard secondary zone for its subdomain.

- ○ **C.** The DNS server in Toronto will host a standard primary zone for the acmeconstr.com domain. Branch offices will be configured as subdomains. Each branch office will host a standard primary zone for its subdomain.

- ○ **D.** The DNS server in Toronto will host a standard primary zone for the acmeconstr.com domain. Branch offices will be configured as subdomains. Each branch office will host a stub zone for its subdomain.

55. Brett is the systems administrator for a company that operates an AD DS domain with two sites corresponding to the head office and a suburban branch office. Servers run a mix of Windows Server 2003 R2 and Windows Server 2008, and client computers run a mix of Windows XP Professional and Windows Vista Business.

Brett deploys Active Directory Rights Management Services (AD RMS) on a server in the head office and sets up a rights-enabled application to enable users to create and work with rights-protected files and folders. Users of Windows XP Professional computers report that they are unable to create rights-protected files.

Brett must enable all users to create rights-protected files. What should he do to accomplish this objective with the least amount of administrative effort?

- ○ **A.** Install the AD RMS client software on all Windows XP client computers.

- ○ **B.** Upgrade all Windows XP client computers to Windows Vista.

- ○ **C.** Upgrade all domain controllers to Windows Server 2008.

- ○ **D.** Install Active Directory Metadirectory Services (AD MDS) on a Windows Server 2008 computer.

56. Matt is testing security and desktop settings policies for use on his company's AD DS domain, which has two Windows Server 2008 domain controllers. He has created these policies in a test lab and is planning to import them to the company domain after several users in the test lab have employed them for a few weeks. What should he do so that he can easily import these policies at a later time?

- ○ **A.** Take a domain controller from the company domain offline, and configure the policies on it. Bring it back online when the test period is completed.

❍ **B.** Take a domain controller from the test lab offline, and bring it online in the company's domain when the test period is completed.

❍ **C.** Use the Group Policy Management Console to back up the GPO containing these policies.

❍ **D.** Use Windows Server Backup to perform a critical volumes backup of a domain controller in the test lab.

57. Arlene is a network administrator for a company that operates a web server farm containing 40 web servers that belong to an AD DS domain. All domain controllers and web servers run Windows Server 2008. Arlene needs to configure the web servers with custom security settings that include password length and complexity policies, auditing of account logon and object access, and protection against spoofing and man-in-the-middle attacks. She needs to set up a procedure that enables her to deploy and refresh security settings as required and verify that the settings have been properly applied.

What should Arlene do?

❍ **A.** Create a custom server installation image, and use imaging software to deploy it to the various servers.

❍ **B.** Create a custom administrative template using the ADMX format.

❍ **C.** Use Group Policy to apply a custom IPSec policy.

❍ **D.** Use Group Policy to apply a custom security template.

58. Trevor is responsible for administering a single AD DS domain for a small university. At present, his only DNS server is a domain controller called Deecee01. Deecee01's zone is a primary one and is not stored in Active Directory. Because student's client computers need access to only the university's server computers, Trevor has added A records for these servers that have been added to the zone.

Enrollment is up, and a building expansion program promises to expand IT services. Trevor would like to streamline DNS administration by configuring dynamic updates. Dr. Hilliard, who sits on the IT planning committee, has expressed "profound concern" that dynamic updates will open the door to hacker/students using rogue PCs to register their records into the zone. This activity could mark the revival of a peer-to-peer file-sharing problem that has been brought under control.

How can Trevor assure Dr. Hilliard that dynamic updates are performed safely on his network? (Each correct answer is part of the solution. Choose all that apply.)

❍ **A.** Convert his standard primary zone to an Active Directory–integrated zone.

❍ **B.** In the General tab of the zone Properties dialog box, select Secure only at the Dynamic Updates list.

◯ **C.** In the General tab of the zone Properties dialog box, select Nonsecure and Secure at the Dynamic Updates list.

◯ **D.** Configure the DNS server to not support incremental zone transfers.

◯ **E.** Enable scavenging for the zone.

59. Jim is the systems administrator for a company that operates an AD DS network consisting of a single domain. He is configuring the properties of several GPOs, one of which is linked to the domain, and the others are linked to various OUs, including child OUs. At the domain level, Jim configures a Restricted Desktop GPO that removes the Network and Games folders from the Start menu. On the Scope tab for this policy in Group Policy Management Console (GPMC), he sets the Enforced option to Yes. Jim also configures another GPO that disables the removal of the Network folder, links it to the IT OU, and specifies Block Inheritance so that the IT staff will be able to use this folder. Later, a couple of IT staffers call to complain that they are unable to reach the Network folder.

What is the most likely reason that IT staffers are unable to reach the Network folder?

◯ **A.** Block Inheritance takes precedence over Enforced.

◯ **B.** Enforced takes precedence over Block Inheritance.

◯ **C.** When both these options are set, they cancel each other out.

◯ **D.** The policies that Jim configured at the OU level were ignored because these options can be set only at the site or domain level.

60. Lynda is responsible for planning an upgrade of her company's Windows Server 2008 Active Directory network to Windows Server 2008. Management has asked her how the upgrade will improve connectivity and functionality with the UNIX users in her company. Which of the following features should Lynda describe for management? (Each correct answer represents part of the solution. Choose three answers.)

◯ **A.** Forest trusts

◯ **B.** Realm trusts

◯ **C.** Shortcut trusts

◯ **D.** External trusts

◯ **E.** Server for NIS

◯ **F.** AD LDS

◯ **G.** AD RMS

◯ **H.** Password synchronization

CHAPTER 11

Answer Key to Practice Exam 1

Answers at a Glance

1. A	**21.** A	**41.** A
2. D	**22.** B	**42.** D
3. B, D, E	**23.** C, E	**43.** C
4. C	**24.** A, C, D	**44.** D
5. D	**25.** D	**45.** A, C, D
6. B	**26.** B, E	**46.** C
7. C, D, F	**27.** A, C, D	**47.** D
8. D	**28.** C	**48.** C
9. A	**29.** A	**49.** A, B, D
10. F	**30.** C	**50.** D
11. D, H	**31.** B	**51.** A
12. A, E	**32.** B, C	**52.** B
13. D	**33.** A	**53.** A
14. C, E	**34.** A	**54.** C
15. A	**35.** A, C	**55.** A
16. D, E	**36.** D	**56.** C
17. C, D	**37.** F, A, H, D, B	**57.** D
18. A	**38.** A	**58.** A, B
19. B	**39.** A	**59.** B
20. A	**40.** C	**60.** B, E, H

Answers to *Exam Cram* Questions

1. **A.** Nolan should configure a global catalog server at the Tokyo office. It contains directory information about all objects in the forest, including the location of resources in each domain of the forest. Universal group caching stores information about universal group membership in the domain controller where it is implemented but does not store information about resources in Active Directory Domain Services (AD DS), so answer B is incorrect. Replicating the entire contents of each domain between domain controllers in the two sites across the WAN link would overload the link and is unnecessary for solving this problem, so answers C and D are incorrect.

2. **D.** In the Delegation of Control Wizard, Sam needs to select the Create a Custom Task to Delegate option, select Organizational Unit objects, and then grant Julie the Read and Create All Child Objects permissions. This set of permissions provides Julie with adequate capability to perform the tasks required of her. Granting her the Read and Write permissions over the same task or granting her control of this folder, existing objects in this folder, and creation of new objects in this folder, would provide her with more capabilities than required to perform her tasks. Consequently, answers A and B are incorrect. The Delegate the Following Common Tasks option enables Sam to delegate several common tasks, including Create, Delete, and Manage User Accounts and Create, Delete, and Manage Groups. However, there is no Create, Delete, and Manage OUs option in this section of the Delegation of Control Wizard, so answer C is incorrect.

3. **B, D, E.** Evan should access the Active Directory Users and Computers snap-in. From the Domain Controllers OU, he should right-click the read-only domain controller's (RODC) computer account and choose Properties. He should then select the Password Replication Policy tab of the RODC's computer account Properties dialog box and select the Accounts Whose Passwords Are Stored on This Read-Only Domain Controller drop-down list entry. If Melissa's user account is included in the password replication policy, it will appear here. If it is not present, Evan can click Add and then add her user account. The Active Directory Sites and Services snap-in does not enable Evan to check the status of the password replication policy, so answer A is incorrect. Evan needs to check the properties of the RODC computer account and not Melissa's user account, so answer C is incorrect. The Accounts That Have Been Authenticated to This Read-Only Domain Controller option displays a

list of users who have been authenticated by the RODC, regardless of whether their passwords are cached at the RODC, so answer F is incorrect.

4. **C.** Shannon should use the `ntdsutil.exe` tool to move the `ntds.dit` database file to the new hard disk volume. This tool updates references to the database file in the Registry, ensuring that AD DS will locate the file so that it can function properly. If Shannon were to use Windows Explorer to move the file, references in the Registry would not be updated, and AD DS would be unable to locate it; therefore, answer A is incorrect. She would use `wbadmin.exe` to perform backups and restores. This tool does not move the database file as required in this scenario, so answer B is incorrect. `Adsiedit.msc` is used to perform low-level editing of AD DS objects, including the implementation of fine-grained password policies. It does not move the database file, so answer D is incorrect.

5. **D.** Round robin rotates the order of matching resource records in the response list for the web server addresses returned to Domain Name System (DNS) clients. This ensures that clients will access web servers equally. This is the most common approach for performing DNS load balancing and is selected by default on a Windows Server 2008 computer. Selecting Disable Recursions prevents a DNS server from querying other DNS servers for name resolution. The Bind Secondaries option enables zone transfers to older UNIX servers that run versions of BIND prior to version 4.9.4. The Fail on Load If Bad Zone Data option causes a DNS server to reject zone transfers if errors are discovered in the transfer. The Enable Netmask Ordering option causes the DNS server to reorder the A resource records based on local subnet priority if the request is for a multihomed computer. The Secure Cache Against Pollution option prevents unauthorized users from adding resource records from nonauthoritative servers to the DNS cache. None of these options provide the load balancing required by this scenario, so answers A, B, C, E, and F are all incorrect.

6. **B.** Bill should place a copy of the Que root certification authority's (CA) certificate in the Trusted Root Certification Authorities certificate store on his company's virtual private network (VPN) server. Doing so enables users connecting through the VPN link to receive a copy of the Que root CA's certificate and be properly authenticated to the VPN link. Use of the VPN connection does not require a forest trust relationship; further, this would not enable the certificate to be trusted, so answer A is incorrect. Placing a copy of the Que root CA's certificate on the Examcram online enterprise CA would allow this server but not the VPN server to trust the Que root CA, so answer C is incorrect. An online responder is used

to provide signed responses to clients requesting certificate revocation information. This scenario does not involve checking the Que root CA certificate for revocation, so answer D is incorrect.

7. **C, D, F.** Nellie needs to right-click the IP folder and choose New Site Link Bridge. In the New Object–Site Link bridge dialog box, she should type a name for the site link bridge, select at least two site links to be bridged, and then click Add. The Inter-Site Transports folder does not provide the option to create a site link bridge, so answer A is incorrect. The Simple Mail Transport Protocol (SMTP) transport protocol is used only for intersite replication of the configuration and schema partitions in multidomain forests, so answer B is incorrect. Nellie must select two site links and not two sites, so answer E is incorrect. The check box labeled Bridge All Site Links is not found in the New Object–Site Link Bridge dialog box; it is in the Properties dialog box for the intersite transport being configured. Furthermore, Nellie should clear this check box and not select it; therefore, answer G is incorrect.

8. **D.** Teresa simply needs to right-click the user account in Active Directory Users and Computers and choose Reset Password. She can enter and confirm a new password without having to enter the current password. By default, the user is required to change this password at next logon, thereby enabling the user to select a password of his choice. It is not necessary to disable the user account, so answer A is incorrect. Teresa cannot lock out the account; this occurs only if an account lockout policy has been configured and then only after the user has entered an incorrect password the specified number of times. So answer B is incorrect. Deleting and re-creating the user account would be a far greater administrative burden than required. This action would create an entirely different account with a new security identifier (SID) and require that Teresa re-create all group memberships and permissions associated with the account. Consequently, answer C is incorrect.

9. **A.** Marilyn should access the Debug Logging tab of each DNS server's Properties dialog box and configure the logging options. This enables the server to capture debug packet information, which is stored in the `Dns.log` file. She can then view this information from the DNS log in Event Viewer. Network Monitor would capture DNS frames among others, but Marilyn would need to search through a large amount of data to locate relevant information. This would take considerably more administrative effort, so answer B is incorrect. A data collector set analyzes overall server performance but does not record information related to individual name resolution queries, so answer C is incorrect. The Event Logging tab

provides possible information about problems on the DNS server but does not provide information on individual queries, so answer D is incorrect.

10. **F.** Julio should use the `auditpol.exe` tool to enable auditing of directory service changes attempts. Directory service changes is a new auditing category in Windows Server 2008 that tracks modifications to directory objects whose SACLs have been configured for auditing. This includes modification of an object's attribute, creation of new objects, moving of objects between AD DS containers, and deletion of objects. Object access auditing tracks access to or modification of system objects such as files, folders, or printers. This is not required by the present scenario, so answers A and D are incorrect. Auditing of directory service access tracks attempts at accessing directory objects but not modifying them, so answers B and E are incorrect. Julio can enable auditing of directory service changes by using `auditpol.exe` only; it is not possible to enable auditing of this category using a Group Policy object (GPO), so answer C is incorrect.

11. **D, H.** Melanie should use the Windows Server 2008 DVD to restart all three servers and choose the Repair Your Computer option. She should then perform the Windows Complete PC Restore procedure on the servers. This procedure restores the operating systems, AD DS, and all applications and data from all volumes of the original domain controller. Melanie does not need to first install Windows Server 2008 on the servers because the Windows Complete PC Restore procedure restores the operating system, so answer A is incorrect. She should not restart the servers in Safe Mode, so answer B is incorrect. She would use Directory Services Restore Mode if she were restoring from a system state backup, so answer C is incorrect. She does not need to run `dcpromo.exe` because the restore procedure restores AD DS, so answer E is incorrect. She does not need to perform either a nonauthoritative or an authoritative restore of system state because she is restoring from a full server backup, not a system state backup, so answers F and G are incorrect.

12. **A, E.** Betty should select the Automatically Notify check box. She should then select the Servers Listed on the Name Servers Tab option. The Notify dialog box enables her to configure secondary DNS servers to be automatically notified when changes occur to the zone data in the primary zone. Because all the secondary servers are listed on the Name Servers tab in this scenario, there is no need for Betty to select The Following Servers or to add or remove items in the list box. Therefore, answers, B, C, and D are incorrect.

13. **D.** Because the GPO already exists and it is possible to link the same GPO to more than one AD DS container, the simplest method to accomplish this task is to link the current GPO to the Marketing OU. You could create a new GPO linked to the Marketing OU, but this solution would take more administrative effort, so answer A is incorrect. You cannot use a GPO that is already linked to an OU as a Starter GPO, so answer B is incorrect. Adding the group containing the Marketing team members to the Sales OU might have unexpected results due to other policies being applied, so answer C is incorrect.

14. **C, E.** Kent can use either the Active Directory Users and Computers snap-in or the `Ntdsutil` utility to transfer these roles to the new domain controller. He would use the Active Directory Domains and Trusts utility to transfer the domain naming master role. This role is not involved here, so answer A is incorrect. The Active Directory Sites and Services snap-in is not used for transferring FSMO roles, so answer B is incorrect. He would use the Active Directory Schema snap-in to transfer the schema master role. This role is not involved here, so answer D is incorrect.

15. **A.** Network Monitor enables Ruby to capture, view, and analyze frames (packets) as they are transmitted over a network to all network adapter cards on the server. She can configure filters that limit the display to only those frames originating from specified sources or using specified protocols to more rapidly locate those that might indicate suspicious activity. Task Manager provides information about currently running processes and enables her to modify their property or terminate misbehaving applications. Reliability and Performance Monitor enables her to monitor the performance of her server, including the display of real-time performance graphs and logs of performance data. Event Viewer logs data about events occurring on the server, including errors, warnings, and informational events. Windows System Resource Manager (WSRM) enables her to control how processor and memory resources are allocated to applications, services, and processes running on the server. None of these other tools capture information about data transmitted across the network adapter cards, so answers B, C, D, and E are incorrect.

16. **D, E.** These two steps are the minimum necessary requirements for completing the procedure for enabling autoenrollment of user certificates. Stuart would need to install Internet Information Services (IIS) only if he needs to use the certificate enrollment web pages, which are not needed during autoenrollment, so answer A is incorrect. Although companies

should install an enterprise subordinate CA and take the root CA offline to prevent its compromise, installing the subordinate CA is not necessary, so answer B is incorrect. A Certificate Trust List (CTL) is a signed list of trusted root CA certificates considered as reputable for purposes such as client authentication or secure email. It is not needed for certificate autoenrollment, so answer C is incorrect.

17. **C, D.** Michelle can use `Dsadd.exe` or `Adsiedit.msc` to create an OU within an Active Directory Lightweight Directory Services (AD LDS) application directory partition. `Dsadd` is a command-line tool that enables her to add objects, including users, groups, computers, OUs, contacts, and quotas, to any directory-enabled database, including both AD DS and AD LDS. `Adsiedit.msc` is the Active Directory Services Interface (ADSI) snap-in, which enables her to view, create, modify, or delete any AD LDS object. `Ldp.exe` enables Michelle to perform general administrative actions on any Lightweight Directory Access Protocol (LDAP) directory service, including AD DS and AD LDS, but this does not include creating objects such as OUs, so answer A is incorrect. `Ntdsutil` enables her to perform many administrative actions, including transfer and seizure of operations master roles and authoritative restores, but it does not enable her to create objects in the database, so answer B is incorrect. `Dssite.msc` is the Active Directory Sites and Services snap-in, which enables her to connect to an AD LDS instance and administer directory data replication. It does not enable her to create objects, so answer E is incorrect.

18. **A.** Allison should install the Simple Certificate Enrollment Protocol (SCEP) on the issuing CA server. This protocol enables software on network devices that do not have accounts in AD DS—and therefore cannot otherwise be authenticated to the network—to enroll for certificates. Microsoft's implementation of this protocol is known as Network Device Enrollment Services (NDES) and is included as a role service in AD CS. An online responder is a role service that provides signed responses to clients requesting certificate revocation information; it is an alternate to the Certificate Revocation List (CRL). The Authority Information Access (AIA) extension points to URLs from which issuing CA's certificates can be retrieved. None of these options allow for network device certificate enrollment, so answers B and C are incorrect. While security groups can include computer accounts, routers and switches do not have machine accounts, and it is not possible to include these devices in a security group to be granted the Autoenroll permission, so answer D is incorrect.

19. **B.** Paul must create a reverse lookup zone for the network and enable it to accept dynamic updates. This action ensures that the pointer (PTR) resource records are recorded properly. By default, when Paul promoted DC01 to domain controller and installed DNS, the forward lookup zone was created but not reverse lookup zone, so Paul must create this zone. Because the forward lookup zone was created by default, answer A is incorrect. The zones are enabled to accept dynamic update; it is not necessary to enable the server, so answer C is incorrect. The client computers send their updates to DC01 automatically, so answer D is incorrect. Dynamic updates are enabled automatically for the new zone, so answer E is incorrect.

20. **A.** Ted should create a one-way external trust relationship in which the examprep.com domain trusts the QUE domain. In this scenario, permissions need to flow in only one direction, so Examprep needs to trust Que. If the trust is created such that the QUE domain trusts the examprep.com domain, this is the wrong direction, so answer B is incorrect. Because this problem can be solved using an external trust, there is no need to upgrade either domain, so answers C and D are incorrect.

21. **A.** Windows Management Instrumentation (WMI) filters enable Rob to specify a query that filters the effect of a GPO. Rob can configure the WMI filter on the WMI Filters node of the Group Policy Management Console (GPMC). Hardware chassis type information is a type of information that can be entered into the query. Creating a global group and moving the computer accounts of all portable computers to this group would take more administrative effort than using a WMI filter, so answer B is incorrect. Rob could accomplish the required task by means of creating child OUs in each department and linking the GPO to these OUs, but this would take far more administrative effort than using a WMI filter, so answer C is incorrect. If he were to create a single OU to hold the portable computer accounts and enforce the restriction on this OU, policies in other GPOs linked to departmental OUs would no longer apply, so answer D is incorrect.

22. **B.** By placing a single global catalog server at each site, Maggie can achieve the objectives of optimized response time for logon and resource access. If she were to place a single global catalog server at the Atlanta site only, users at the San Jose site would need to send requests over the slow WAN link because the domain controller would need to check universal group membership at the global catalog server on the Atlanta site, so answer A is incorrect. The same would be true if she placed two

global catalog servers at the Atlanta site, so answer C is incorrect. This would also be true for users in Atlanta if Maggie placed two global catalog servers in San Jose, so answer D is incorrect. Placing two global catalog servers at each site would achieve load-balancing and fault tolerance but would generate additional replication traffic across the WAN link, thereby reducing performance. Therefore, answer E is incorrect.

23. **C, E.** Auditing of files and folders is a two-step process. Liz needs to configure the auditing of object access, which she can do using Group Policy. Liz also needs to configure auditing of the folder that contains the files to be audited, which she can do from Computer or Windows Explorer. Auditing of directory service access tracks access of an object in AD DS that has a system access control list (SACL) specified but not a file or folder, so answer A is incorrect. Account logon tracks users logging on and off but does not track file and folder access, so answer B is incorrect. You cannot audit a server directly, so answer D is incorrect. You could specify auditing for each file in the Docs shared folder, but this takes extra administrative effort, so answer F is incorrect.

24. **A, C, D.** Intersite replication data is sent compressed and according to a schedule that you can configure. It can use either RPC over IP or SMTP transport protocols. Intrasite replication (as opposed to intersite replication) is frequent and processed automatically, and it is sent uncompressed; therefore, answers B and E are incorrect. Intersite replication originates from the preferred bridgehead server at each site and does not directly involve domain controllers that are not bridgehead servers; therefore, answer F is incorrect.

25. **D.** Dennis should use the Data Collector Sets tool in the Reliability and Performance Monitor console. This tool records server performance data into log files; he can later view this data using the Performance Monitor tool. Windows System Resource Manager performs several tasks related to how processor and memory resources are allocated on the server. It includes a Resource Monitor tool that displays performance counters; however, this tool does not create a baseline log as required here, so answer A is incorrect. Task Manager enables him to view performance data, but it does not create logs, so answer B is incorrect. Reliability Monitor provides an overall reliability analysis of computer stability with time but does not create performance logs, so answer C is incorrect. Dennis can use Performance Monitor to view previously logged performance data; however, this tool does not store logs for future use, so answer E is incorrect.

26. **B, E.** Gerry can solve this problem by adding a stub zone for prep.examcram.com on dns1.examcram.com or by configuring zone delegation for prep.examcram.com on dns1.examcram.com. A stub zone is a read-only copy of a zone that stores only those resource records necessary to identify the authoritative DNS servers for that zone. It enables the DNS server hosting a parent zone to be aware of the authoritative DNS servers for the child zone, thereby enabling clients to find the intranet server. Delegation of a zone to a child zone on another DNS server enables the parent to be aware of new authoritative DNS servers for the child zone, also solving this problem. Adding a stub zone for examcram.com on dns2.prep.examcram.com is the wrong direction for solving this problem, so answer A is incorrect. Simply adding A records to zone information doesn't let either DNS server know where the Start of Authority (SOA) for a particular zone resides, so answers C and D are incorrect. DNS uses PTR resource records to resolve IP addresses to their corresponding fully qualified domain names (FQDN); the scenario does not indicate a problem with this action, so answer F is incorrect.

27. **A, C, D.** Stephanie should configure certificate templates, CRLs or online responders, and key archival and recovery before she begins issuing certificates to users on her network. When she installs Certificate Services with IIS, the Certificate Services Web pages are automatically installed and configured. They need no further configuration, so answer B is incorrect.

28. **C.** The way that Kerberos authentication within complex forests works is that when users in a domain request access to resources in a different domain tree of the same forest, the authentication path passes upward to each successive parent domain in the tree and then down the other tree to the desired domain. Then the access token is passed back across the same path in reverse. A shortcut trust creates a direct authentication path between the two child domains, circumventing this roundabout path. Purchasing additional bandwidth would have minimal improvement and would be quite expensive, so answer A is incorrect. A forest trust is used between two forests and not between domain trees of the same forest, so answer B is incorrect. It is most likely that administrative and organizational reasons would prohibit merging domains in this scenario, so answer D is incorrect.

29. **A.** Rick should place the infrastructure master on a domain controller that does not host the global catalog but has a direct connection to a global catalog server. If he places the infrastructure master on a global catalog server, the infrastructure master would be unable to locate

outdated data; therefore, it would never update that data. Consequently, answers B and C are incorrect. For the infrastructure master to function properly, it should be located in the same site as a global catalog server, so answer D is incorrect.

30. **C.** Roy should restart the Netlogon service at the suburban office domain controller. Doing so reregisters the domain controller's SRV resource records. He can perform this action from the Services branch of Server Manager or by typing **net stop netlogon** and then **net start netlogon**. Neither the DNS Server service nor the DNS Client service is responsible for reregistering the service (SRV) resource records, so answers A and B are incorrect. Roy could reregister these records by rebooting the domain controller, but this would take more time, so answer D is incorrect.

31. **B.** Brian can use Active Directory Sites and Services to manually create a site link object connecting the required servers. He cannot perform this task by editing the Registry, so answer A is incorrect. The Knowledge Consistency Checker (KCC) would probably re-create the same replication topology and not the one that Brian thinks should be present, so answer C is incorrect. Because Brian can use Active Directory Sites and Services to modify the replication topology, answer D is incorrect.

32. **B, C.** Carol should configure Active Directory Rights Management Services (AD RMS) and Active Directory Federation Services (AD FS). AD RMS enables her to create and work with rights-protected files and folders and ensure that only authorized users have access to these types of data. AD FS provides a single sign-on capability for authenticating users to multiple web-based applications, such as those holding data on the other company's servers in this scenario. Active Directory Lightweight Directory Services (AD LDS) provides storage for directory-enabled application data without the need for a full directory service. Active Directory Certificate Services (AD CS) provides a centralized certification authority for working with digital certificates. Neither AD LDS nor AD CS is needed in this scenario, so answers A and D are incorrect. Carol can enable access for her users to the web-based data on the other company's network by means of AD FS, so it is not necessary to create a one-way external trust relationship; therefore, answer E is incorrect.

33. **A.** Alfredo should use the Group Policy Modeling Wizard for the Design OU. Choose the Engineering OU to simulate policy settings. This wizard performs a Resultant Set of Policy (RSoP) planning mode query,

which is a what-if analysis that reports the policy settings that he would have if he configured the settings he specified while running the query. Using the wizard for the Engineering OU and choosing the Design OU to simulate policy settings would simulate the effect of placing the Engineering OU under the Design OU, not the other way around, so answer B is incorrect. The Group Policy Results Wizard is used to troubleshoot the results of currently applied policy, not to simulate policy settings that have not yet been applied, so answers C and D are incorrect.

34. **A.** The schema master and domain naming master are forestwide roles, and the other three flexible single-master operations (FSMO) roles are domainwide roles. Consequently, there is one schema master and one domain naming master, plus six RID masters, six PDC emulators, and six infrastructure masters in this forest. Even though the root domain is configured as an empty root, it has one of each of the domainwide FSMO roles, so answer B is incorrect. Because the schema master and domain naming master are forestwide roles, only one of each is required, so answer C is incorrect. Every domain must have its own RID master, PDC emulator, and infrastructure master, so answer D is incorrect.

35. **A, C.** You should edit the Default Domain Policy GPO to specify auditing and account lockout parameters for the domain. You must also monitor each domain controller's security log for failed logon attempts. Auditing allows you to discover when and where any failed logon attempts occur. Account Management includes items such as the creation, changing, or deletion of a user or group account and the renaming, disabling, or enabling of a user account or change of password. Auditing and monitoring of these events would not meet the requirements of this scenario, so answer B is incorrect. Configuring local security policy on each computer would apply only to these computers and not to the domain controllers that authenticate users on the domain. Therefore, answer D is incorrect.

36. **D.** Ryan needs to remove the Domain Admins group from the permissions list. By default, the Domain Admins and Enterprise Admins groups have administrative authority over any OU in the domain. In this scenario, another administrator with membership in the Domain Admins group has been performing the account resets. It is not necessary to create a separate domain; an OU is better suited to the requirements of this scenario than a domain, so answer A is incorrect. The other administrator is not necessarily the default domain administrator; he could be any member of the Domain Admins group, so answer B is incorrect. The scenario states that only Ryan belongs to the Enterprise Admins group, so answer C is incorrect.

37. **F, A, H, D, B.** Edward must perform these steps in the specified sequence to perform an authoritative restore of the system state on the domain controller. He must restart the domain controller in Directory Services Restore Mode and log on as the local administrator (not the domain administrator). At a command prompt, he must first use the `wbadmin get versions` command to obtain information on the available backup target that he feeds into the `wbadmin start systemstaterecovery` command. When the restore is complete, he must use `ntdsutil` to mark the restore of the Management OU as authoritative, and then he just restart the domain controller normally. Note that the exam might present a question of this nature in which you must drag the required tasks to a work area and drop them in the correct sequence. The answer will be scored as incorrect if the tasks are not in the correct sequence even if the list contains all the correct tasks. Edward cannot perform this task by stopping and restarting AD DS; he must use Directory Services Restore Mode, so answers C and I are incorrect. He would use the Repair Your Computer option only if performing a full server recovery, which is not required here. Therefore, answer E is incorrect. He would use the `wbadmin start recovery` command to recover a specified set of volumes, files, or folders, but not to restore System State as required in this scenario. Therefore, answer G is incorrect.

38. **A.** Karla should select the Secure Only option on the General tab of the zone's Properties dialog box. This option prevents computers that are not domain members from registering resource records in DNS. The problem observed here is not caused by an improper zone replication scope, so answer B is incorrect. Scavenging removes resource records from computers that have been disconnected from the network, such as remote access computers that have improperly disconnected and have left behind invalid (stale) resource records. Scavenging would remove the improper resource records but would not prevent them from being added by nondomain computers in the future. Therefore, answers C and D are incorrect.

39. **A.** Policies are processed in the local, site, domain, organizational unit (LSDOU) sequence. Consequently, the policies in this scenario are applied in the Site, Domain, OU2, OU1 sequence. On top of this, the Enforced setting prevents policy settings at the domain level from being overwritten by conflicting polices in either the OU2 or OU1 policies. The Block Inheritance setting at OU1 prevents the site or domain GPO policies from applying, except that in this case the Enforced setting in the Domain policy overrides the Block Inheritance setting.

Consequently, the wallpaper is red (OU1 policy applies), Task Manager is not disabled (domain policy applies), and Display Properties is disabled (Domain policy). The wallpaper is not green because the lower-level settings override this setting, so answers B and D are incorrect. Display Properties is not enabled because the Enforced setting on the Domain policy overrides the Block Inheritance setting on the OU1 policy, so answer C is incorrect. The Domain policy causes Task Manager to not be disabled, so answer B is incorrect.

40. **C.** If there is a possibility you might want to unrevoke a certificate, you must specify the Certificate Hold reason when revoking it. Any certificate that has been revoked using a different reason cannot be unrevoked, and you must issue a new certificate in this circumstance. You cannot simply delete the delta CRL, so answer A is incorrect. It is not possible to restore a CRL to a previous day, so answer B is incorrect. The ability to unrevoke a certificate is not related to its publication in the base CRL, so answer D is incorrect.

41. **A.** Frank needs to perform an authoritative restore of AD DS while running the server in Directory Services Restore Mode. An authoritative restore will increment the version number by 100,000, ensuring that the restored OU is viewed by the other domain controllers as being the most recent. Although Frank can perform other maintenance actions after stopping AD DS from a command prompt, the authoritative restore is not one of these actions, so answer B is incorrect. It is also not possible to perform an authoritative restore while the server is running in Safe Mode or normally, so answers C and D are incorrect.

42. **D.** In a scenario such as this one, KCC will automatically create the connection objects between the main office and all other offices. The way this network is designed, with a star topology rather than a mesh, the KCC will naturally build a topology using the most efficient routes. Therefore, it is not necessary to manually create connection objects for any portion of this topology, so answers A and C are incorrect. Furthermore, the SMTP transport protocol replicates only the configuration and schema AD DS partitions and not the domain partition, so answer B is incorrect.

43. **C.** To seize the role of domain naming master, Jonathan needs to use the ntdsutil command-line utility. It is appropriate to seize this role in this scenario because the hard disk of the old server has failed, and it will have to be reinstalled after parts have arrived. Consequently, to AD DS, it will be an entirely new domain controller, and the old domain controller will never be online again. Role seizure is appropriate under these

circumstances. Active Directory Users and Computers can transfer any of the three domainwide operations master roles but cannot seize any of these roles, so answer A is incorrect. Using Active Directory Domains and Trusts, Jonathan can transfer the role of domain naming master to another domain controller but not seize this role, so answer B is incorrect. Jonathan cannot specify the role of domain naming master during the promotion of another server to domain controller, so answer D is incorrect.

44. **D.** Windows Server 2008 enables Mary to create a fine-grained password policy, in which password settings are contained in a Password Settings Object (PSO) that she can create using `adsiedit.exe`. She can then link the PSO to a global security group containing the members of the Research department who need these settings applied. Mary cannot create these settings in a GPO linked to an OU because they would be ignored, so answer A is incorrect. Prior to Windows Server 2008, Mary would have needed to create a separate domain for these users, but the ability to create a PSO in Windows Server 2008 renders this action unnecessary. Although she could still use this procedure, it requires considerably more administrative effort; therefore, answer B is incorrect. Mary cannot use a security group and filter the settings to accomplish this task, so answer C is incorrect.

45. **A, C, D.** The claims-aware agent includes the `web.config`, `default.aspx`, and `default.aspx.cs` files. All three of these files must be present for the agent to function. IIS uses `Metabase.xml` to hold configuration information. `MS-AdamSyncConf.xml` is a configuration file that AD LDS uses. `Ntds.dit` is the database file that AD DS or AD LDS uses. AD FS doesn't use any of these files, so answers B, E, and F are incorrect.

46. **C.** The 4006 error means that the DNS name contains characters that are not supported by the default Multibyte (UTFB) name checking setting. Selecting the All Names option enables the translation of DNS names containing any type of characters. Logging of incoming and outgoing packets would provide Phil with information concerning the type of data passing through the DNS server, but it would not prevent these errors, so answer A is incorrect. The `cache.dns` file is not at fault here, so answer B is incorrect. The Strict RFC (ANSI) option would use strict name checking and could actually make this situation worse and generate more 4006 errors than observed, so answer D is incorrect.

47. **D.** When using the Computer Configuration option in the Group Policy Management Console to distribute software, the Published option is unavailable (grayed out). Software can only be assigned to computers.

Because George cannot publish software to computers, answer A is incorrect. It is true that assigned applications appear on the Start menu, whereas published applications appear in the Add or Remove Programs applet; however, answer B does not differentiate between assigned and published applications and is therefore incorrect. Published applications do not appear on the Start menu, so answer C is incorrect.

48. **C.** Christina should use the `Csvde` utility to import these user accounts into her company's domain. This utility is designed to handle Active Directory information stored in comma-separated file format. Microsoft Excel can use the comma-separated file format but is unable to import the information into AD DS, so answer A is incorrect. Christina could use Active Directory Users and Computers for this task, but she would have to enter all the data manually. This is a much greater administrative burden, so answer B is incorrect. The `Ldifde` utility supports the Lightweight Directory Interchange File (LDIF) format but not the comma-separated format, so answer D is incorrect. She could use `Dsadd` to add users by means of a script, but this method would be more complicated than using `Csvde`, so answer E is incorrect.

49. **A, B, D.** Some of the tools Oliver can use include Event Viewer, Reliability and Performance Monitor, and `repadmin`. The Event Viewer logs enable him to view errors and warnings that might indicate the source of a replication problem. The NTDS object in Reliability and Performance Monitor contains a series of counters that monitor functionality within Active Directory, including the Directory Replication Agent. `Repadmin` provides information related to directory replication failures. In particular, its `/showreps` command displays the replication partners, both inbound and outbound, the time of the last replication attempt, and whether or not it was successful. The `/showconn` command displays the connection objects for the domain controller, the enabled state of the replication, and the transport protocol in use. Oliver can also use the `replmon` tool to monitor Active Directory replication. `Ntdsutil` is an administrative tool that enables Oliver to perform a range of actions including transfer and seizure of operations master roles, authoritative restores, and offline database defragmentation, but it does not provide information on replication problems. Therefore, answer C is incorrect.

50. **D.** Sandra should configure intersite replication to take place during non-business hours only. In a situation such as this one, intersite replication is taking up a large portion of the limited bandwidth. By default, intersite

replication takes place every three hours and occurs 24 hours a day, 7 days a week. Sandra can access the Properties dialog box of the site link and click Change Schedule. On the dialog box that appears, she can specify that replication is not available during business hours. Alternatively, she could solve the problem by decreasing the replication interval, but this would still result in slow response when replication is taking place. The site link cost has no effect in this situation, so answer A is incorrect. Replacing the domain controller with an RODC would still require unidirectional replication from the head office domain controllers to the RODC, so answer B is incorrect. An SMTP site link would not replicate the domain directory partition, so answer C is incorrect.

51. **A.** The application will check the base CRL and Tuesday's delta CRL. The application is performing its check before Wednesday's delta CRL has been issued, so answer B is incorrect. The delta CRL contains all certificates revoked since the publication of the most recent base CRL. It does not need to check previous delta CRLs, so answers C and D are incorrect. The application must check the base CRL as well as the latest delta CRL, so answers E and F are incorrect.

52. **B.** Judy should enable universal group membership caching (UGMC) at the Omaha site. Doing so improves the efficiency of user logons in the situation of a small branch office connected to the head office with a low-bandwidth WAN connection and low-end servers, where the replication load might place an undesirable load on either the server or the connection. Judy should not enable UGMC at the Kansas City site, because this should be done at the site where no global catalog servers exist, so answer A is incorrect. UGMC is never enabled at the domain or OU level, so answers C and D are incorrect.

53. **A.** Lenny should use the web enrollment service to issue this user a certificate. This service enables users on non-Microsoft computers who are not part of the domain to obtain certificates over the Internet or a local intranet. The Simple Certificate Enrollment Protocol (SCEP) enables certificates to be issued to network devices such as routers, which do not have machine accounts. It does not enable certificates to be issued to Macintosh computers, so answer B is incorrect. The Authority Information Access (AIA) extension points to URLs from which issuing CA's certificates can be retrieved. It does not enroll certificates for computers, so answer C is incorrect. It is not possible to add non-Microsoft computers to groups for certificate autoenrollment, so answer D is incorrect.

54. **C.** Erica should configure the branch offices as subdomains. Additionally, each branch office should host a standard primary zone for its subdomain. Because the scenario states that the administrators in the branch offices are to be responsible for their specific DNS information and that their DNS servers be configured to host standard primary zones, the branch offices must be configured as subdomains, because primary zones require their own domain. This is the only option that allows administrators to control the information stored in their respective DNS zones. If each branch office were to host a standard primary zone, it would not be possible for administrators in each branch office to administer that office's DNS configuration, so answer A is incorrect. Secondary zones are read-only and must receive their information from a primary standard zone; consequently, local administrators cannot control their zone data, so answer B is incorrect. A stub zone contains read-only copies of the SOA record plus NS and A records for authoritative names servers only. It does not allow local administrative control, so answer D is incorrect.

55. **A.** Brett should install the AD RMS client software on all Windows XP client computers. In addition, he should ensure that these computers have Service Pack 2 (SP2) or higher installed. This software is available for download from Microsoft and is required to enable users on Windows XP computers to create rights-protected content. Brett could upgrade these computers to Windows Vista, but this would require far more administrative effort and expense, so answer B is incorrect. It is not necessary to upgrade domain controllers to Windows Server 2008 or install AD MDS on a server; neither of these actions would enable users on Windows XP computers to create rights-protected content, so answers C and D are incorrect.

56. **C.** Matt should use the Group Policy Management Console to back up the GPO containing these policies. This procedure copies all data in the GPO to the file system, thereby creating a file that you can import to another domain, such as the production domain in this scenario. Taking a domain controller from the company domain offline would leave only one domain controller online in this scenario, removing any fault tolerance and load-balancing. Therefore, answer A is incorrect. Taking a domain controller from the test lab to the company domain would not accomplish anything because it would be unable to join the company domain without being demoted, so answer B is incorrect. It is not possible to restore just the GPO in question from a critical volumes backup, so answer D is incorrect.

57. **D.** Arlene needs to use Group Policy to apply a custom security template. She can create the security template using the Security Templates snap-in. After she has tested the template, she can save it to a shared folder location and apply it to all the web servers by placing the servers in an OU and importing the template to the Computer Configuration\Windows Settings\Security Settings node of a GPO linked to the OU. She can also use the `secedit` utility or the Security Configuration and Analysis snap-in to analyze the security settings. Imaging procedures will create servers with identical security identifiers (SID). This is not desirable, so answer A is incorrect. Custom ADMX templates or IPSec policies do not contain the security settings that are required by this scenario, so answers B and C are incorrect.

58. **A, B.** Trevor should convert his standard primary zone to an Active Directory–integrated zone and then specify secure dynamic updates. Only Active Directory–integrated zones can be configured for secure dynamic update. Configuring this option prevents unauthorized attempts at modifying zone data and enables him to control which computers are registered with DNS. Allowing both nonsecure and secure dynamic updates would open up possibilities for unauthorized computers modifying the zone, so answer C is incorrect. Removing support for incremental zone transfers won't tighten security, so answer D is incorrect. Enabling scavenging for the zone enables the deletion of stale resource records but does not improve security, so answer E is incorrect.

59. **B.** When both of these options have been set, Enforced takes precedence over Block Inheritance; the latter works only when Enforced has not been specified. Consequently, because Jim removed the Network folder at the domain level and specified the Enforced option, the OU-level policy that prevents hiding the Network folder is not able to take effect. Block Inheritance does not take precedence over Enforced; neither do the options cancel each other out, so answers A and C are incorrect. You can set these options at any level (site, domain, or OU), so answer D is incorrect.

60. **B, E, H.** A realm trust enables users to share information between an AD DS domain and any non-Windows realm that supports Kerberos V5, such as UNIX. A realm trust also supports UNIX identity management to allow users in UNIX realms to seamlessly access Active Directory resources by means of password synchronization with Windows Server 2008's Server for Network Information Service (NIS) feature. Password synchronization enables users with accounts in UNIX realms in AD DS to synchronize password changes across both the AD DS domain and the

UNIX realm. A forest trust enables information sharing between domains in two AD DS forests operating at the Windows Server 2003 or higher functional level. A shortcut trust shortens the authentication path between two child domains in an AD DS forest. An external trust connects two single domains in different forests. None of these three trust relationships offers a connection to UNIX networks, so answers A, C, and D are incorrect. AD LDS provides LDAP-based directory access to users without the need for a full-blown directory service. It does not offer service to UNIX users, so answer F is incorrect. AD RMS enables the creation of rights-protected documents on an AD DS network. UNIX users cannot access such information, so answer G is incorrect.

C H A P T E R 12

Practice Exam 2

Exam Cram Questions

1. Managers at Betty's company, which operates an AD DS network consisting of a single domain, have requested that she configure all computers used by data entry clerks so that they are unable to access the Internet. However, data entry supervisors need access to the Internet. All computers used by both data entry clerks and supervisors run either Windows XP Professional or Windows Vista Business.

   All members of the data entry team belong to the Data Entry security group, and data entry supervisors also belong to the Supervisors security group.

   Which of the following should Betty do to accomplish this objective?

   ○ **A.** Create two Group Policy objects (GPO): one to disable Internet access and the other to enable Internet access. Grant the Data Entry group the Read and Apply Group Policy permissions on the first GPO, and grant the Supervisors group the Read and Apply Group Policy permissions on the second GPO.

   ○ **B.** Create one GPO that disables Internet access, and grant the Data Entry group the Read and Apply Group Policy permissions.

   ○ **C.** Create one GPO that disables Internet access, and grant the Data Entry group the Read and Apply Group Policy permissions. Grant the Supervisors group the Read permission only on this GPO.

   ○ **D.** Create one GPO that disables Internet access, and grant the Data Entry group the Read and Apply Group Policy permissions. Also, deny the Supervisors group the Apply Group Policy permission on this GPO.

2. Julian is the network administrator for a company that has operated a UNIX-based network and is switching to a Windows Server 2008–based Active Directory Domain Services (AD DS) network. He installs Windows Server 2008 on a new computer and runs dcpromo.exe to promote this server to the first domain controller in the new domain.

   Julian wants to ensure that AD DS has been properly installed on the new domain controller. Which of the following should he do? (Each correct answer represents part of the solution. Choose three answers.)

   ○ **A.** Open Active Directory Users and Computers, and verify that an organizational unit (OU) named Users is present.

   ○ **B.** Open Active Directory Users and Computers, and verify that an OU named Domain Controllers is present.

   ○ **C.** In Windows Explorer, navigate to the %systemroot% folder, and verify the existence of the Active Directory database and shared system volume folders.

   ○ **D.** In Windows Explorer, navigate to the root of the system drive, and verify the existence of the Active Directory database and shared system volume folders.

   ○ **E.** Open the Domain Name System (DNS) Manager snap-in, and verify that two zones containing the domain name are present in the console tree. One of these should be prefixed with _msdcs.

   ○ **F.** Open the DNS Manager snap-in, and verify that a reverse lookup zone containing the domain name has been created and is visible in the console tree.

3. Kim is the network administrator for a company that operates an AD DS network consisting of one domain and four sites. She installs a new domain controller and a new member server in one of the sites, but she notices several days later that replication is not taking place properly. Investigating this problem, Kim discovers that these servers have been placed in the wrong site. What should she do to correct this problem? (Each correct answer represents part of the solution. Choose two answers.)

   ○ **A.** Use Active Directory Sites and Services to place the domain controller in the correct site.

   ○ **B.** Use Active Directory Sites and Services to place the member server in the correct site.

   ○ **C.** Use Active Directory Users and Computers to place the domain controller in the correct site.

   ○ **D.** Use Active Directory Users and Computers to place the member server in the correct site.

   ○ **E.** Reconfigure the domain controller with an IP address corresponding to the subnet specified for the correct site.

   ○ **F.** Reconfigure the member server with an IP address corresponding to the subnet specified for the correct site.

4. Peter has been given the responsibility of configuring Certificate Services for certificate autoenrollment. His company operates a public key infrastructure (PKI) that includes a standalone root certification authority (CA) and an enterprise subordinate CA. The PKI has recently been upgraded from Windows 2000 to Windows Server 2008. He wants to enable autoenrollment of certificates using a template that has been used in the past for web-based enrollment of certificates from the previous Windows 2000-based PKI. Which of the following steps should Peter perform? (Each correct answer represents part of the solution. Choose all that apply.)

   ○ **A.** Configure an additional Windows Server 2008 computer as an autoenrollment-based subordinate CA.

   ○ **B.** In the Certificate Templates snap-in, right-click the certificate template and choose Duplicate Template.

   ○ **C.** From the Request Handling tab of the template's Properties dialog box, specify an option for prompting the user during autoenrollment.

   ○ **D.** From the Security tab of the template's Properties dialog box, grant the required user or group the Read and Enroll permissions.

   ○ **E.** From the Security tab of the template's Properties dialog box, grant the required user or group the Read, Enroll, and Autoenroll permissions.

   ○ **F.** Enable the template from the Certificate Templates node of the Certification Authority snap-in.

   ○ **G.** Configure a GPO linked to the domain to enroll certificates automatically.

5. Paul is the network administrator for a company that operates an AD DS network consisting of a single domain. Servers run Windows Server 2008, and client computers run either Windows XP Professional or Windows Vista Business or Ultimate.

Paul wants to deploy Active Directory Rights Management Services (AD RMS) to provide rights-enabled protection for sensitive corporate documents. Which of the following additional role services and features must Paul install when he is installing AD RMS? (Each correct answer represents part of the solution. Choose all that apply.)

   ○ **A.** Internet Information Services (IIS)

   ○ **B.** Active Directory Certificate Services (AD CS)

   ○ **C.** Active Directory Metadirectory Services (AD MDS)

○ **C.** Debbie should place the users into local groups and then place the local groups into universal groups. After that, she should place the universal groups into global groups.

○ **D.** The universal groups are configured properly in this scenario; the traffic is being generated from other sources.

9. Hubert is the systems administrator for a clothing manufacturer based in San Francisco. During a standard review of the AD DS files on his domain controller, he notices that the hard drive containing the `ntds.dit` file is running out of space. However, plenty of space is available on the RAID-5 array attached to the server. He decides to move the file to the RAID-5 array. How should he perform this procedure using the least amount of administrative effort?

○ **A.** Restart the server in Directory Services Restore Mode and use Windows Explorer to move the file.

○ **B.** Restart the server in Directory Services Restore Mode and use the `ntdsutil` utility to move the file.

○ **C.** From a command prompt, stop AD DS, use the `ntdsutil` utility to move the file, and then restart AD DS.

○ **D.** From a command prompt, stop AD DS, use Windows Explorer to move the file, and then restart AD DS.

○ **E.** While the server is running, open a command prompt and use `ntdsutil` to move the file.

○ **F.** While the server is running, use Windows Explorer to move the file.

10. Kas is a systems engineer for a company that operates an AD DS domain with two Windows Server 2003 domain controllers and three Windows Server 2008 domain controllers. She is responsible for assigning the flexible single-master operations (FSMO) roles to specific domain controllers for optimum network functionality.

Kas needs to ensure proper synchronization of the system clocks on all computers on the network. To this end, she wants to have one of the Windows Server 2008 domain controllers look after this requirement. Which of the following roles should she assign to this domain controller?

○ **A.** Domain naming master

○ **B.** Schema master

○ **C.** Infrastructure master

○ **D.** PDC emulator

○ **E.** RID master

11. Alexander is the domain administrator for the examcram.com domain, which operates at the Windows Server 2008 functional level. He has configured AD CS on a server in the domain. Several users in the legal.examcram.com domain attempt to enroll for a user certificate but receive a message that the template was not found. What should Alexander do so that these users can locate this template?

   ○ **A.** Create a duplicate of the User certificate template and specify the Windows Server 2008 option. Then specify the Autoenroll permission for the Authenticated Users group.

   ○ **B.** Place the users in a security group and configure the Security tab of the template's Properties dialog box with the appropriate permissions to the template.

   ○ **C.** Configure the automatic certificate request policy in a GPO linked to the legal.examcram.com domain.

   ○ **D.** Configure the web enrollment pages to use basic authentication.

12. Rachel is responsible for ensuring that the servers on her company's Windows Server 2008 network can handle all requests sent by users on the network. She wants to display graphs of server performance data in real time and, at the same time, create resource allocation policies that determine how server resources such as processor and memory are allocated to processes running on the server. Furthermore, she wants the ability to configure events under which the server will automatically modify how server resources are allocated. Which of the following tools enables her to perform all these actions?

   ○ **A.** Network Monitor

   ○ **B.** Task Manager

   ○ **C.** Reliability and Performance Monitor

   ○ **D.** Event Viewer

   ○ **E.** Windows System Resource Manager (WSRM)

13. Jordan is the network administrator for a timeshare resort that provides wireless Internet access to guests using their portable computers. The network contains a Windows Server 2008 computer that runs Dynamic Host Configuration Protocol (DHCP) and provides guests with TCP/IP configuration, including the address of a DNS server that hosts an Active Directory–integrated zone.

   Jordan notices that resort employees are able to generate address (A) records, but both employees and guest computers are generating pointer (PTR) resource records. Jordan must prevent guest computers from generating PTR resource records without affecting employee network access. What should he do?

○ **A.** Configure the reverse lookup zone as a secondary zone, and disable dynamic updates.

○ **B.** Configure the reverse lookup zone as a secondary zone, and select the Secure Only dynamic updates option.

○ **C.** Configure the reverse lookup zone as an Active Directory–integrated zone, and disable dynamic updates.

○ **D.** Configure the reverse lookup zone as an Active Directory–integrated zone, and select the Secure Only dynamic updates option.

14. Roy is the network administrator for Examcram, which operates a single AD DS domain named examcram.com. Servers run Windows Server 2008, and client computers run a mix of Windows XP Professional and Windows Vista Enterprise. Examcram's main office is located in Buffalo, and there is a branch office in Rochester. Roy creates a GPO that redirects the Start menu for users in the Rochester office to a shared folder on a file server.

Users in Rochester report that many of the programs they normally use are missing from their Start menus, even though the programs were available on the Start menu the previous day. Logging on to one of the client computers, Roy notices that all the programs in question are present on the Start menu. Roy verifies that users can access the shared folder on the server. He needs to find out why the Start menu changed for the affected users. How can he accomplish this task? (Each correct answer represents a complete solution to the problem. Choose two answers.)

○ **A.** On one of the affected computers, run the `gpresult` command.

○ **B.** On one of the affected computers, run the `gpupdate` command.

○ **C.** In the Group Policy Management Console, right-click the Group Policy Results node and choose Group Policy Results Wizard.

○ **D.** In the Group Policy Management Console, right-click the Group Policy Modeling node and choose Group Policy Modeling Wizard.

○ **E.** In Active Directory Sites and Services, right-click the Rochester site and choose All Tasks, Resultant Set of Policy (Planning).

15. Christina is responsible for the implementation of her company's AD DS infrastructure. More specifically, she needs to ensure that the domain controllers holding the FSMO roles are readily available so that the tasks they perform are done without delay. Her company's domain has four domain controllers, one of which runs Windows Server 2008 Datacenter edition and is centrally located for availability to all sites on her company's network. Christina needs to configure this server to ensure the uniqueness of Active Directory object IDs on the network.

Which of the following FSMO roles should she place on this server?

- ○ **A.** Domain naming master
- ○ **B.** Schema master
- ○ **C.** Infrastructure master
- ○ **D.** PDC emulator
- ○ **E.** RID master

16. Steve is the systems administrator for a company that operates an AD DS network consisting of a single domain. He is planning the use of groups that will be employed for granting users access to a series of shared folders and printers. The foyer of the company head office also has several kiosks that visitors can use for accessing corporate information and ordering products.

    Steve needs to create an access control plan that addresses both of these concerns. Which of the following should he do to create a plan that is simple to administer?

    - ○ **A.** Because groups can contain user, group, and computer accounts, Steve can create a single group that includes both company users and kiosk-based computers.

    - ○ **B.** Because groups can contain only user accounts and other groups, Steve should create groups for his users and place a firewall between the kiosk computers and the company network.

    - ○ **C.** Steve should create a single logon for the kiosk computers. He should create a group for the users and assign them permissions, and then he should grant the kiosk-based user specific permissions to network resources.

    - ○ **D.** Steve should create groups for the company employees. For the kiosk computers, Steve can create another group with dedicated users, one per kiosk, and apply permissions to this group so that visitors can access the resources available to them.

17. Carolyn is the network administrator for a company that has offices in seven U.S. cities. The company operates an AD DS network with a single domain and sites representing the cities where offices are located. The offices are connected with WAN links of varying bandwidth, and Carolyn has configured site links in Active Directory for the various available links.

    Her company operates a small office located in Duluth, which connects to the company's Minneapolis office by a T1 link and to the company's Chicago office by a 56Kbps dial-up link. The Minneapolis and Chicago offices are also connected by a T1 link.

A junior administrator in Duluth calls Carolyn to inform her that every time administrators in Chicago issue updates to AD DS (which has occurred frequently in recent weeks), a domain controller in Duluth dials the 56Kbps link despite the rapid T1 link being available. What should Carolyn do to minimize the times the 56Kbps link is dialed?

- ○ **A.** Configure the 56Kbps link to use Simple Mail Transport Protocol (SMTP) replication rather than IP.

- ○ **B.** Configure the 56Kbps link to be available outside business hours only.

- ○ **C.** Create a site link bridge that encompasses the Duluth-to-Minneapolis and Minneapolis-to-Chicago site links, and then set the cost of the 56Kbps link to 300.

- ○ **D.** Create a site link bridge that encompasses the Duluth-to-Minneapolis and Minneapolis-to-Chicago site links, and then set the cost of the site link bridge to 50.

18. Which of the following are unique characteristics of a read-only domain controller (RODC) that are not found on an ordinary domain controller? (Choose all that apply.)

- ○ **A.** An RODC does not perform outbound replication of AD DS data.

- ○ **B.** You can configure local users with administrative rights to the RODC without adding them to the Domain Admins global group.

- ○ **C.** You can install a read-only copy of Active Directory–integrated zones on an RODC.

- ○ **D.** An RODC can update a user's password without referral to another domain controller.

- ○ **E.** An RODC can hold a database of preauthorized user credentials that enables these users to log on without contacting another domain controller.

19. Ursula is the network administrator for a company that operates an AD DS network consisting of a single domain. The network includes a certification authority (CA) server that issues certificates automatically to permanent employees of the company.

The company hires several dozen interns from nearby colleges every summer to provide vacation relief and perform other tasks. Company policy stipulates that interns are not to be granted certificates from the CA server. What should Ursula do to ensure that interns do not receive certificates?

- ○ **A.** Include the user accounts of the interns in a security group, and configure a Restricted Enrollment Agent policy that denies the right for this group to enroll for certificates.

- ○ **B.** Remove the Authenticated Users group from the access control list (ACL) on the Security tab of the CA server's Properties dialog box.

○ **C.** Include the user accounts of the interns in a security group, and grant this group the Deny–Request Certificates permission from the Security tab of the CA server's Properties dialog box.

○ **D.** Include the user accounts of the interns in a security group, and grant this group the Deny–Autoenroll permission on the security template that issues certificates to users in the domain.

20. Theodore is the network administrator for a company that operates an AD DS network consisting of a single domain. All servers run Windows Server 2008, and all client computers run either Windows XP Professional or Windows Vista Enterprise or Ultimate.

Users in the company's Legal OU handle a large quantity of extremely sensitive documents, and the CIO has asked Theodore to require these users to have 12-character passwords. What should Theodore do to implement this requirement? (Each correct answer represents part of the solution. Choose two answers.)

○ **A.** Ensure that the domain functional level is set to Windows Server 2003 or higher.

○ **B.** Ensure that the domain functional level is set to Windows Server 2008.

○ **C.** Create a GPO linked to the Legal OU, and then specify a 12-character length password setting in this GPO.

○ **D.** Create a new child domain for the Legal department, and then specify a 12-character length password setting in this domain's Default Domain Policy GPO.

○ **E.** Create a Password Settings Object (PSO) specifying a 12-character length password, and apply this PSO to a group containing the users in the Legal OU.

○ **F.** Create a PSO specifying a 12-character length password, and apply this PSO to the Legal OU.

○ **G.** Specify the Block Inheritance option for the Legal OU.

21. Leanne is responsible for maintaining the network configuration of her company's AD DS domain, which includes a DHCP server and a DNS server, both of which run Windows Server 2008. In recent weeks, she has removed numerous older computers that ran various operating systems from Windows 98 to Windows 2000 and replaced them with newer computers running Windows Vista and Windows Server 2008.

Leanne would like to receive a list of all DNS resource records so that she can compare these records with the IP addresses assigned by the DHCP server and check for static addresses that were used by the decommissioned computers. What should she do? (Each correct answer represents a complete solution to the problem. Choose two answers.)

○ **A.** In the DNS Manager snap-in, right-click the zone and choose Export List.

○ **B.** In the DNS Manager snap-in, right-click the server and choose Configure a DNS Server. Then select the Export List option.

○ **C.** In the DNS Manager snap-in, select the zone to display the list of resource records in the Details pane. Select the desired resource records, right-click, and choose Copy. Then open a blank document in Notepad and paste the records into this document.

○ **D.** Use the `Dnscmd /zoneinfo` command.

○ **E.** Use the `Dnscmd /info` command.

○ **F.** Use the `Dnscmd /zoneexport` command.

22. Richard is the network administrator for a company that operates an AD DS network consisting of a single domain. All users in the Finance department have user accounts in the Finance OU. Richard creates a GPO linked to the Finance OU and configures it to publish Microsoft Excel.

Some of the users in the department report that the application is not available from the Start menu, and other users report that Excel was installed successfully after they double-clicked an Excel spreadsheet. Richard needs to ensure that all users in the Finance OU can run Excel. What should he do?

○ **A.** Run the `gpresult` command on each client computer where a user reports a problem.

○ **B.** Run the `gpupdate` command on each client computer where a user reports a problem.

○ **C.** Access the Security tab of the software package's Properties dialog box. Grant the users in the Finance department the Full Control permission. Then instruct users who report a problem to log off and log back on.

○ **D.** Access the Deployment tab of the software package's Properties dialog box. Change the deployment type from Published to Assigned. Then instruct users who report a problem to log off and log back on.

23. Which of the following are valid domain functional levels for a domain containing Windows Server 2008 domain controllers? (Choose all that apply.)

○ **A.** Windows 2000 mixed

○ **B.** Windows 2000 native

○ **C.** Windows Server 2003 native

○ **D.** Windows Server 2008 interim

○ **E.** Windows Server 2008 native

24. Linda is the network administrator for a company whose AD DS network consists of two domains and five sites. Her boss, Ryan, has created a new object class in the forest's schema that he wants to have available to all domains and sites as soon as possible, so Linda decides to force replication to all other domain controllers in the forest.

Which of the following tools can Linda use for this purpose? (Each correct answer represents a complete solution to the problem. Choose two answers.)

- ○ **A.** Active Directory Domains and Trusts
- ○ **B.** Active Directory Sites and Services
- ○ **C.** Gpupdate /force
- ○ **D.** Replmon
- ○ **E.** Ntdsutil

25. Brandon is the systems administrator for a company that operates an AD DS network consisting of a single domain. The company hires a large number of interns and other temporary staff, after these individuals leave the company, their user accounts are deleted. Over a period of some months, the AD DS database has increased significantly in size, resulting in the available disk space becoming very low. Brandon would like to get some of the wasted space back, so he plans to perform an offline defragmentation of one of the domain controllers.

What is the minimum disk space Brandon should free up on the domain controller to ensure that the offline defragmentation proceeds properly?

- ○ **A.** 500MB
- ○ **B.** 10% of the current database size
- ○ **C.** 15% of the current database size
- ○ **D.** 25% of the current database size
- ○ **E.** There is no specific minimum, as long as some space is available to begin the defragmentation process.

26. Wilson is the network administrator for a company that operates an AD DS network consisting of a single domain and four sites representing the company's offices, which are located in Dallas, Austin, San Antonio, and Houston. Each site has at least one domain controller that runs DNS and hosts an Active Directory–integrated zone. Domain controllers in the company run a mix of Windows 2000 Server, Windows Server 2003, and Windows Server 2008.

Wilson's company places a contract with a second company in Houston to provide extensive educational materials for company employees. He configures a conditional forwarder on a Houston DNS server to point to a private web server at the second company's network, but employees in the Dallas, Austin, and San Antonio offices report that they are unable to access the private web server.

On contacting administrators in the Dallas, Austin, and San Antonio offices, Wilson discovers that the conditional forwarder setting does not appear in their DNS servers. What should he do?

- O **A.** Use Active Directory Sites and Services to force intersite replication.

- O **B.** Configure the conditional forwarder with the All Domain Controllers in This Domain option.

- O **C.** Configure the conditional forwarder with the All DNS Servers in This Domain option.

- O **D.** Configure a new zone delegation for each of the Dallas, Austin, and San Antonio sites.

27. Scott is responsible for maintaining AD CS on his company's AD DS network, which consists of a single domain. He has used the Certificate Services snap-in to configure a version 2 certificate template that will be used for archiving the subject's encryption private key. Certificates issued with this template will be used for signature purposes. However, Scott discovers that the private keys associated with these certificates are not being archived. What should he do?

- O **A.** On the template's Request Handling tab, select the Signature and Encryption option, and then select Archive Subject's Encryption Private Key.

- O **B.** On the template's Request Handling tab, select the Allow Private Key to Be Exported option.

- O **C.** Duplicate the template, and select the Windows Server 2008 option to create a version 3 certificate template.

- O **D.** On the template's Security tab, enable the Autoenroll permission.

28. Jennifer is a network administrator for a company that operates an AD DS network containing two domains in a single tree. One of the hard disks on a domain controller failed and had to be replaced. As a result, she had to restore the `ntds.dit` file from backup.

When Jennifer restarted the domain controller in Directory Services Restore Mode, she entered her administrator password but was denied access. Which of the following is most likely the reason why she was denied access to Directory Services Restore Mode?

    ○ **A.** Jennifer changed her password a few days ago. Because this domain controller had failed beforehand, AD DS did not replicate the password change. She needs to use her old password.

    ○ **B.** A domain-based Group Policy setting denies Jennifer the right to log on locally to the domain controller.

    ○ **C.** Jennifer is not a member of the Enterprise Administrators group. Only members of the Enterprise Administrators group are allowed access to the Directory Services Restore Mode in a forest that contains more than one domain.

    ○ **D.** Jennifer entered the password to the domain rather than the password she specified when installing AD DS.

29. Ian is the network administrator for a company that operates an AD DS network consisting of a single domain and three sites representing the Philadelphia head office and the Denver and Sacramento branch offices. The offices are connected with dedicated T1 lines, for which Ian has configured site link objects.

Users in the branch offices report that it takes a long time to log on to the domain. Ian monitors the network and notices that all authentication traffic is being sent to the Philadelphia domain controllers. What should he do to improve network performance?

    ○ **A.** Schedule intersite replication to take place less frequently.

    ○ **B.** Schedule intersite replication to take place more frequently.

    ○ **C.** Create a subnet for each office, associate the subnet with its site, and move each domain controller object to its site.

    ○ **D.** Create a subnet for each office, associate the subnet with the Philadelphia site, and move each domain controller object to the Philadelphia site.

30. Doug is the network administrator for a company that operates an AD DS forest consisting of four domains. The domain and forest functional levels are set to Windows Server 2008.

One department in one of the four domains recently moved to a new building. The move affected a total of 75 users. Doug must change the Address property in each of the 75 user accounts.

How should he accomplish this task with the least amount of administrative effort?

    ○ **A.** In Active Directory Users and Computers, click Action, Find, and then search on the Office Location field for all users with the old address. Export the information to a tab-delimited file, modify the addresses, and use the `Ldifde` utility to import the file into Active Directory.

○ **B.** In Active Directory Users and Computers, click Action, Find, and then search on the Office Location field for all users with the old address. Export the information to a comma-delimited file, modify the addresses, and use the `Csvde` utility to import the file into Active Directory.

○ **C.** In Active Directory Users and Computers, click Action, Find, and then search on the Office Location field for all users with the old address. Then simultaneously modify the address property in their accounts' Properties.

○ **D.** Use `Csvde` to export the 75 user accounts to a `.csv` file. Change the address, and then use `Csvde` to import the modified accounts.

31. Cindy is a systems administrator for a company that operates a single domain AD DS network. All servers run Windows Server 2008, and all client computers run Windows XP Professional. Cindy is setting up special user-based options for installation of a custom accounting application provided by a software vendor. She wants to configure the software options so that users can view the installation process as it takes place on their computers. She creates a GPO linked to the domain and in the Group Policy Management Editor; she creates a software installation policy that assigns the software in the User Configuration\Policies\Software Settings\Software Installation branch. Which of the following should she configure?

○ **A.** Under Installation User Interface Options on the Deployment tab of the package's Properties dialog box, select Basic.

○ **B.** Under Installation User Interface Options on the Deployment tab of the package's Properties dialog box, select Maximum.

○ **C.** Under Deployment Options on the Deployment tab of the package's Properties dialog box, select Do Not Display This Package in the Add/Remove Programs Control Panel option.

○ **D.** Under Deployment Options on the Deployment tab of the package's Properties dialog box, select Install This Application at Logon.

32. Ellen is the network administrator for a regional hospital complex that operates an AD DS forest containing a root domain and two child domains. All domain controllers in the root domain and one child domain run Windows Server 2003, and the domain controllers in the second child domain run Windows 2000 Server.

Ellen is planning an upgrade of the domain controllers in the root domain to Windows Server 2008. She is also planning to install a read-only domain controller (RODC) in this domain.

Which of the following configuration actions represent the minimum actions that Ellen must perform to upgrade the forest to accept Windows Server 2008 domain controllers, including the RODC? (Each correct answer represents part of the solution. Choose all that apply.)

○ **A.** Upgrade all domain controllers in the second child domain to Windows Server 2003 or 2008.

○ **B.** Upgrade all domain controllers in the forest to Windows Server 2008.

○ **C.** Upgrade the PDC emulator in the root domain to Windows Server 2008.

○ **D.** Raise the domain and forest functional levels to Windows Server 2003.

○ **E.** Raise the domain and forest functional levels to Windows Server 2008.

○ **F.** Run the `Adprep /forestprep` command at the schema master.

○ **G.** Run the `Adprep /forestprep` command at the domain naming master.

○ **H.** Run the `Adprep /domainprep` command at the RID master in the forest root domain.

○ **I.** Run the `Adprep /domainprep` command at the infrastructure master in the forest root domain.

○ **J.** Run the `Adprep /rodcprep` command at the infrastructure master in the forest root domain.

○ **K.** Run the `Adprep /rodcprep` command at the PDC emulator in the forest root domain.

33. Jose is a network administrator for a community college. He has installed DNS on a Windows Server 2008 computer called DNS1 that hosts a primary DNS zone for the college's domain. The college network is also home to a UNIX server that has been configured to host the secondary DNS zone. This server, named DNS2, runs BIND 2.4.1. The chief network architect has assigned Jose the task of ensuring that DNS2 can receive zone transfers from DNS1.

    Which of the following options should Jose enable to achieve this result?

    ○ **A.** Disable Recursion (Also Disables Forwarders)

    ○ **B.** BIND Secondaries

    ○ **C.** Fail on Load If Bad Zone Data

    ○ **D.** Enable Round Robin

    ○ **E.** Enable Netmask Ordering

    ○ **F.** Secure Cache Against Pollution

34. You are the senior network administrator for a company that operates an AD DS network consisting of a single domain with a series of OUs and child OUs that mirrors the company's organizational chart. A junior administrator named Heather has configured a GPO that contains policy settings that should be applied to a parent OU but not to a

child OU directly beneath it. She has configured the child OU with the Block Inheritance setting. However, after receiving some calls from members of the child OU, you realize that the settings in this GPO are being applied to the child OU despite the fact that Heather specified the Block Inheritance setting for the parent OU. What is the problem?

○ **A.** Heather misconfigured the Block Inheritance setting. She should have specified this setting on the parent OU.

○ **B.** Heather misconfigured the Block Inheritance setting. She should have specified this setting against the GPO and not on the child OU.

○ **C.** Heather has also specified the Enforced setting on the GPO.

○ **D.** To prevent the policy from applying in the child OU, Heather must specify the Enforced setting in the local policies of the client computers.

35. Janet is responsible for security on her company's network. While reviewing the security log one morning, she notices that a hacker has been using brute-force methods to attempt to crack passwords on the network.

Janet's company does not have the financial resources to implement a more secure authentication method such as smart cards at the present time, so she decides to create a policy to strengthen password security. Which of the following should she do? (Each correct answer is part of the solution. Choose all that apply.)

○ **A.** Enable the Password Must Meet Complexity Requirements setting.

○ **B.** Enable the Store Password Using Reversible Encryption setting.

○ **C.** Enable the Users Must Change Password at Next Logon setting.

○ **D.** Increase the Minimum Password Length setting.

○ **E.** Decrease the Maximum Password Age setting.

36. Carm is the senior network administrator for a large investment company that operates an AD DS forest consisting of nine domains in four domain trees. The forest functional level is Windows 2000.

In recent months, a vigorous server upgrade program has been in place throughout the company, and all domain controllers and most member servers have been upgraded to Windows Server 2008. Carm verifies that the domain functional level of each of the tree root domains has been set to Windows Server 2008 and is now proceeding to upgrade the forest functional level to Windows Server 2008. However, he is unable to select this functional level. What might be causing this problem? (Choose all that apply.)

○ **A.** Carm must log on using an account that is a member of the Schema Admins group.

○ **B.** Carm must log on using an account that is a member of the Enterprise Admins group.

○ **C.** Some of the child domains might still be at the Windows 2000 or 2003 domain functional level.

○ **D.** Carm must raise the forest functional level to Windows Server 2003 first and let this change propagate throughout the forest before he can raise the forest functional level to Windows Server 2008.

○ **E.** Two of the child domains are connected by a shortcut trust relationship. Carm must remove this trust before he can raise the forest functional level.

37. Veronica is in charge of Group Policy object (GPO) creation for her company, which operates an AD DS network consisting of six domains and 20 sites. Although Veronica is responsible for creating all GPOs, other administrators are responsible for applying the GPOs to the domains for which they are responsible. Veronica wants to grant these administrators permission to apply the GPOs but not to modify them.

How can Veronica maintain control over the creation of GPOs while permitting other administrators to determine where they will be applied?

○ **A.** Right-click the desired domain in the Group Policy Management Console and select Delegate Control. In the Delegation of Control Wizard, she should select the Manage Group Policy Links task.

○ **B.** Right-click the desired domain in the Group Policy Management Console and select Delegate Control. In the Delegation of Control Wizard, she should specify the required users or groups and then select the Manage Group Policy Links task.

○ **C.** Right-click the desired users or groups in Active Directory Users and Computers and select Delegate Control. In the Delegation of Control Wizard, she should select the Manage Group Policy Links task.

○ **D.** Right-click the desired domain in Active Directory Users and Computers and select Delegate Control. In the Delegation of Control Wizard, she should specify the required users or groups and then select the Manage Group Policy Links task.

38. Justin is configuring a certificate template that will enable autoenrollment of smart cards for users in his company's Windows Server 2008 domain. He needs to ensure that a user creating a new smart card is prompted to enter her PIN as part of the enrollment procedure. He opens the Request Handling tab of the certificate template. Which of the following options should he select?

○ **A.** Prompt the User During Enrollment

○ **B.** Prompt the User During Enrollment and Require User Input When the Private Key Is Used

○ **C.** Add Read Permissions to Network Service on the Private Key

○ **D.** Allow Private Key to Be Exported

39. Cassandra is in charge of monitoring and maintaining her company's domain controllers. She opens Event Viewer on a domain controller named Server1 and notices that several thousand events, many of which are related to updates delivered via Windows Update, are present. She wants to create a custom log to locate the most important events rapidly, so she opens the Create Custom View dialog box. Which of the following criteria can she use in creating the custom log? (Choose all that apply.)

○ **A.** Time interval during which the events were logged

○ **B.** Event level, such as critical, error, warning, and so on

○ **C.** The logs from which she wants to view data

○ **D.** Event ID numbers

○ **E.** Task categories

○ **F.** Users and computers associated with the event

40. David is responsible for maintaining DNS in his company, which operates an AD DS network consisting of a single domain. DNS is installed on two of the domain controllers so that the zone data can be stored in an Active Directory–integrated zone.

   Recently, performance of the domain controller has been sluggish, so David has started to investigate the cause. He first noticed that processor use was averaging around 90% and frequently reached 100%. He needs to monitor DNS queries that this server is receiving.

   Which utility should David use to obtain data related to this problem?

○ **A.** He should monitor the DNS-related counters in Reliability and Performance Monitor.

○ **B.** He should access the Monitoring tab of the server's Properties dialog box in DNS Manager.

○ **C.** He should access the Event Logging tab of the server's Properties dialog box in DNS Manager, and the DNS Server logs in Event Viewer.

○ **D.** He should access the Debug Logging tab of the server's Properties dialog box in DNS Manager.

41. Arlene is a junior network administrator for a company that operates an AD DS network consisting of four domains and seven sites, each representing a city where the company does business. The domains represent separate business divisions. Some users require access to resources in other domains at various sites, and recently access has been slow at busy times of the day.

Arlene decides that a need exists for several additional global catalog servers in each domain. Which tool should she use to create these global catalog servers?

- ○ **A.** Active Directory Domains and Trusts.

- ○ **B.** Active Directory Sites and Services.

- ○ **C.** The `ntdsutil` command-line utility.

- ○ **D.** It is not possible to create more than one global catalog server per domain.

42. John is responsible for configuring certificate autoenrollment for his Windows Server 2008 environment and would like to implement this feature as soon as possible. John is considering a third-party solution because he wants to have the most secure environment possible, and he wants to assign certificates to both users and computers. Which of the following most accurately describes Windows Server 2008's certificate autoenrollment capabilities?

- ○ **A.** Windows Server 2008 enables John to assign certificates to both users and computers. There is no need to use a third-party tool.

- ○ **B.** Windows Server 2008 offers autoenrollment to users but not to computers. Consequently, John should look for a third-party tool that assigns to computers only.

- ○ **C.** John's instincts are correct. Because Group Policy in Windows Server 2008 can assign certificates to computers only, he should find a third-party tool to do this task.

- ○ **D.** Certificates are more important for computers. Although in theory it is possible to utilize a third-party tool to assign certificates to users, assigning them to computers gives John better control and is actually more secure.

43. Stephanie is a network administrator for Examcram.com, which has just merged with a former competitor named Que.com. Customers and business partners of the second company have communicated with the company's employees using their email addresses of the format user@que.com. This is a well-established relationship that has existed for a number of years, and managers in both companies want to retain these email addresses.

Stephanie is merging the networks of the two companies under the examcram.com AD DS domain, which operates at the Windows Server 2008 domain and forest functional level. Users in the company use their email addresses to log on, and Stephanie needs to incorporate the new users from que.com into the network while retaining their existing email address and using these addresses to log on to the examcram.com domain.

What should Stephanie do to accomplish this objective with the least amount of administrative effort?

- ○ **A.** Create a new Active Directory forest named que.com, and create user accounts for the new users in that forest.

- ○ **B.** Create a new domain as a separate domain tree named que.com, and create user accounts for the new users in that domain.

- ○ **C.** Create user accounts for the new users in the existing domain, and assign them user logon names in the format of user@que.com.

- ○ **D.** Create user accounts for the new users in the existing domain, and specify an alternative UPN suffix of que.com.

44. Which of the following are true about intersite replication that uses the SMTP transport protocol? (Choose all that apply.)

- ○ **A.** SMTP can be used to replicate all partitions of AD DS data between all sites in forests containing one or more domains.

- ○ **B.** SMTP can be used to replicate the configuration and schema partitions of AD DS data and the global catalog between all sites in multidomain forests only.

- ○ **C.** SMTP requires the presence of an enterprise certification authority (CA) to sign the messages sent across intersite links.

- ○ **D.** SMTP replication cannot be scheduled because it is asynchronous.

- ○ **E.** SMTP replication can be used for both intersite and intrasite replication.

45. Gary is the network administrator for a company that has entered into a partnership relationship with a second company. He has set up an Active Directory Federation Services (AD FS) server to enable users in the second company to access web-based data by means of a single sign-on capability.

Gary wants to test which claims the Federation Service sends in AD FS security tokens. Which of the following should he configure?

- ○ **A.** A Windows token-based agent
- ○ **B.** A Federation Service proxy
- ○ **C.** A trust policy
- ○ **D.** A claims-aware application

46. Ester's company is expanding its North American operations to Asia. To accommodate these operations, she needs to add several objects and attributes to the schema. Her boss has added her user account to the Schema Admins group for this purpose.

Working from a branch office domain controller, Ester attempts to locate the Active Directory Schema snap-in. She calls the help desk and asks to be given the appropriate permission to access this snap-in, but she is told that this is not a permissions issue. What does Ester need to do to access this snap-in? (Each correct answer represents part of the solution. Choose two answers.)

- ○ **A.** She must first register the Schema snap-in by using the `regsvr32` command from the Run dialog box.
- ○ **B.** She needs to install the Active Directory Schema snap-in to a new MMC console.
- ○ **C.** She needs to go to the schema master computer to modify the schema. Because the domain controller she is working from does not have this snap-in, it must not be the schema master.
- ○ **D.** She should contact the help desk manager because she has received incorrect advice from the support technician. She needs to belong to both the Schema Admins and Enterprise Admins groups to access this snap-in.

47. Janet is the network administrator for a company that operates an AD DS network consisting of a single domain. The domain uses standard DNS with a primary master DNS server named NS01 located in Pittsburgh. NS02 and NS03 are secondary DNS servers located in Johnstown and Altoona, Pennsylvania, respectively. NS03 is initiating zone transfer with NS01 for no apparent reason. This activity is having an impact on the bandwidth available on the 236Kbps link between Pittsburgh and Altoona.

Janet decides that she should manually configure the wait time between zone transfer requests to 20 minutes, so she navigates to the Start of Authority (SOA) tab of the zone's Properties dialog box. Which of the following properties should she configure?

- ○ **A.** Refresh Interval
- ○ **B.** Retry Interval
- ○ **C.** Expires After
- ○ **D.** Minimum (Default) Time to Live (TTL)
- ○ **E.** TTL for This Record

48. Carol is a junior network administrator who has been given the responsibility of applying Group Policy settings to all Windows XP- and Vista-based computers on her company's AD DS network. To allow herself the greatest flexibility, she decides to apply GPOs to the security group level. A colleague tells her that she should not do this because it is too complex. Carol disagrees, saying that she prefers to use groups for this purpose because it minimizes administrative effort. Who is correct and why?

○ **A.** Carol is correct. There are alternative ways of doing this, but Carol's method is the least time consuming administratively.

○ **B.** The colleague is correct. Although it is possible, it is complex to manage.

○ **C.** The colleague is correct. However, the reason is much simpler—it is not possible to link GPOs to security groups.

○ **D.** The colleague is correct. However, the reason for this is not related to complexity; instead, it has to do with Active Directory and the overhead of creating unnecessary replication.

49. Merle is responsible for securing a new physical printer that her company has pur-chased especially for printing confidential documents. She installs the printer in a secure office and configures a logical printer for the device on a Windows Server 2008 computer. She also configures the appropriate permissions and enables auditing in a GPO for her company's domain.

After printing several documents to the new printer, Merle examines the print server's security logs and finds that no entries related to the printer have been recorded. What is the most likely cause for the lack of entries in the security log?

○ **A.** The security log does not record activity by an administrator.

○ **B.** Merle failed to enable auditing in the printer's Properties dialog box.

○ **C.** The events were recorded in a log on the domain controller.

○ **D.** The security log only records attempts by unauthorized users to access the printer.

50. Wayne is the network administrator for a medical office that operates an AD DS net-work consisting of a single domain. He suspects that unauthorized users have been attempting to access the DNS server, and he wants to log packets being sent to and received from a specific range of IP addresses at the DNS server. What should he do?

○ **A.** Access the Monitoring tab of the DNS server's Properties dialog box, and enable both simple and recursive queries.

○ **B.** Access the Event Logging tab of the DNS server's Properties dialog box, and enable the All Events option.

○ **C.** Access the Debug Logging tab of the DNS server's Properties dialog box, and enable Log Packets for Debugging and specify the Filter Packets by IP Address option.

○ **D.** Configure Network Monitor with a capture filter that enables the capture of frames originating from the required range of IP addresses.

51. Evelyn is planning a PKI for her company's AD DS network. She needs to install an enterprise root CA on a Windows Server 2008 computer on the network. Which of the following computers can she use for this purpose? (Choose all that apply.)

- ○ **A.** Windows Server 2008 Web edition
- ○ **B.** Windows Server 2008 Standard edition, configured as a member server
- ○ **C.** Windows Server 2008 Standard edition, configured as a domain controller
- ○ **D.** Windows Server 2008 Enterprise edition, configured as a member server
- ○ **E.** Windows Server 2008 Enterprise edition, configured as a domain controller
- ○ **F.** Windows Server 2008 Datacenter edition, configured as a member server
- ○ **G.** Windows Server 2008 Datacenter edition, configured as a domain controller

52. Hazel is responsible for monitoring Active Directory functionality on her company's network. She needs to know the update sequence number (USN) of the most recent changes to the AD DS database at a domain controller named DC3. What should she do?

- ○ **A.** Configure a data collector set in Reliability and Performance Monitor with counters for the NTDS performance object.
- ○ **B.** Use the Resource Monitor feature of Windows System Resource Manager.
- ○ **C.** In replmon, right-click DC3 and choose Update Status.
- ○ **D.** Use the repadmin utility with the /showmeta option.

53. Tom is a network administrator for a large automotive manufacturer that operates an AD DS network that includes five domains in a single tree. Because of poor sales and rising fuel prices, management has eliminated the production of one model and laid off several hundred workers. Tom deleted a considerable number of objects, including both user and computer accounts, as a result of this downsizing. Several months later, he checked the size of the AD DS database file on the child domain containing this work group and noticed that it had not decreased in size.

What is the most likely reason for the database file not decreasing in size?

- ○ **A.** Tom should have checked the size of the SYSVOL shared folder instead. Deleting these objects should result in a decrease in this folder's size.
- ○ **B.** Simply deleting these objects does not reduce the size of the database file. Tom needs to perform an offline defragmentation of the database for it to decrease in size.
- ○ **C.** Someone else has added other entries to the AD DS database since the time Tom deleted these user and computer accounts from the database.

○   **D.** Tom needs to wait longer for AD DS replication to remove all records pertaining to the deleted objects from every domain controller. At this time, Active Directory will automatically defragment the database.

54. Kathy is the senior administrator for a company that is expanding its operations. She is planning to work all weekend to create two new domains, but she receives word on Friday that the domain naming master has crashed. The hardware tech informs her that it will take a week to obtain the required parts to get it back up and running again.

Kathy knows she cannot create these domains and that the CIO needs her to complete this task as soon as possible, so she decides to seize the domain naming master role. Which tool will she use to perform this task?

○   **A.** Active Directory Domains and Trusts

○   **B.** Active Directory Sites and Services

○   **C.** The `ntdsutil` command-line utility

○   **D.** The `wbadmin` command-line utility

55. Dan is responsible for administering the DNS configuration for his company, which operates an AD DS network consisting of a single domain and sites corresponding to the New York boroughs where offices are located. The Manhattan office houses a primary standard DNS server named NS01 plus a secondary name server named NS02. The Brooklyn office houses two standard secondary name servers called NS03 and NS04. A facility in the Bronx houses two additional standard secondary DNS servers called NS05 and NS06.

Lately, the administrative overhead of looking after these servers and configuring zone transfers has taken up a lot of time. In addition, the zone transfers generate an excessive amount of network traffic. Dan needs to reduce both the administrative time and the network traffic, so he opens the DNS Manager snap-in at NS01 and accesses the Properties dialog box for his zone. From the General tab, he clicks the Change button opposite the zone type. Which options should he configure? (Each correct answer represents part of the solution. Choose two answers.)

○   **A.** He should select Primary Zone.

○   **B.** He should select Secondary Zone.

○   **C.** He should select Stub Zone.

○   **D.** He should select the Store the Zone in Active Directory option.

○   **E.** He should clear the Store the Zone in Active Directory option.

56. Mike is the systems administrator for a company that operates an AD DS network consisting of a single domain. The company operates a head office and three branch offices, each of which has been set up with a read-only domain controller (RODC) to handle employee authentication locally.

A technician named Christina regularly travels to the branch offices to ensure that the computer network in each office is working properly. Her job duties require that she perform administrative actions on each RODC, but she does not need to perform such actions on domain controllers located at the head office. She must be ensured that she can log on to each RODC with her domain user account even if the connection to the head office happens to be down.

Which of the following actions should Mike perform so that Christina can perform her duties, without granting her excessive administrative privileges? (Each correct answer represents part of the solution. Choose two answers.)

- ○ **A.** Configure each RODC with a password replication policy that includes Christina's user account in the Denied list.

- ○ **B.** Configure each RODC with a password replication policy that includes Christina's user account in the Allowed list.

- ○ **C.** Add Christina's user account to the Domain Admins global group.

- ○ **D.** Add Christina's user account to the Server Operators global group.

- ○ **E.** Add Christina's user account to each RODC's local Administrators group.

57. Joanne is the network administrator for a company that builds outdoor furniture. The company operates an AD DS network consisting of a single domain in which each department has its own OU. All servers run Windows Server 2008, and the domain and forest functional levels are set to Windows Server 2008.

Joanne's company purchases another company that manufactures camping and recreational equipment. All servers on this company's network run Windows Server 2003, and the domain and forest functional levels are set to Windows Server 2003. Executives in both companies have agreed that the acquired company network will remain as a separate forest. Joanne needs to create several similar GPOs in different OUs in her company's network. She also needs to take the settings from the Financial OU in her company's network and copy them to the Financial OU in the acquired company's domain. What should she do to accomplish these tasks with the least amount of administrative effort? (Each correct answer represents part of the solution. Choose two answers.)

- ○ **A.** In the outdoor furniture company's domain, create a Starter GPO, and link this GPO to the appropriate OUs. Then make any necessary changes for each OU.

Chapter 12

○ **B.** In the outdoor furniture company's domain, create a Starter GPO. Then create GPOs based on the Starter GPO, and link them to the appropriate OUs.

○ **C.** In the outdoor furniture company's domain, use Group Policy Management Console (GPMC) to back up the GPO linked to the Financial OU. Then import this GPO to the other company's network, and link it to the Financial OU in that domain.

○ **D.** In the outdoor furniture company's domain, use GPMC to back up the Starter GPO. Then import this GPO to the other company's network, and use it to create the appropriate GPO in this network's Financial OU.

58. You are the network administrator for a company that operates an AD DS network consisting of a single domain. The domain contains OUs that mirror the departmental structure of the company. A user named Jill, who is a member of the Marketing OU, has been delegated permission to reset passwords in that OU. Jill has been transferred to the Design OU and will no longer need the capability of resetting passwords in the Marketing OU.

How should you prevent Jill from resetting passwords in the Marketing OU, with the least amount of administrative effort?

○ **A.** Move Jill's user account from the Marketing OU to the Design OU. Her permissions will be reset automatically.

○ **B.** Run the Delegation of Control Wizard to revoke Jill's permissions to the Marketing OU.

○ **C.** Access the Security tab of the Marketing OU Properties dialog box, and remove Jill's permission to reset passwords.

○ **D.** Delete Jill's user account, and then re-create it in the Marketing OU.

59. Mark is the network administrator for a company that operates a network containing a single AD DS domain. Servers run a mix of Windows Server 2003 and Windows Server 2008, and client computers run a mix of Windows XP Professional and Windows Vista Enterprise. Certificate Services is installed on a Windows Server 2008 domain controller and configured as an Enterprise CA. The company's written security policy stipulates that employees must have user certificates that are to be issued by designated managers. These managers are to be the only individuals authorized to approve, issue, and revoke certificates. Their user accounts are included in the CertMgrs global security group.

What should Mark do to enable the authorized managers to perform these tasks without providing them with excess privileges?

○ **A.** Grant the CertMgrs group the Allow–Manage CA permission on the CA server.

○ **B.** Issue each member of the CertMgrs group the Enrollment Agent certificate.

◯   **C.** Grant the CertMgrs group the PKI Administrator administrative role.

◯   **D.** Grant the CertMgrs group the Certificate Manager administrative role.

60. Elaine is responsible for maintaining the user account database for a local school board located in a suburban area just outside a major city. The state has implemented new county school boards that abolish the local boards and join them to the county boards; Elaine must add several thousand new user accounts to the school board's AD DS domain.

Elaine uses a bulk import tool to import these user accounts, but the process stops after several hundred user accounts have been successfully imported. While troubleshooting the problem, the superintendent asks her to ensure that user accounts for school principals are added as soon as possible, so she opens Active Directory Users and Computers and attempts to create these user accounts. However, this attempt fails.

Which of the following is the most likely cause of this problem?

◯   **A.** The infrastructure master for the domain is unavailable.

◯   **B.** The RID master for the domain is unavailable.

◯   **C.** The `.csv` file Elaine is using is corrupted, so she must re-create this file.

◯   **D.** Elaine must wait until the user accounts she has added have replicated to all domain controllers in all sites of the domain before she can continue.

CHAPTER 13

Answer Key to Practice Exam 2

Answers at a Glance

1. D	**21.** A, F	**41.** B
2. B, C, F	**22.** D	**42.** A
3. A, F	**23.** B, C, E	**43.** D
4. B, C, E, F, G	**24.** B, D	**44.** B, C, D
5. A, D, E	**25.** C	**45.** D
6. B, C	**26.** B	**46.** A, B
7. D	**27.** A	**47.** A
8. B	**28.** D	**48.** C
9. C	**29.** C	**49.** B
10. D	**30.** C	**50.** C
11. B	**31.** B	**51.** E, G
12. E	**32.** A, C, D, F, I, K	**52.** D
13. D	**33.** B	**53.** B
14. A, C	**34.** C	**54.** C
15. E	**35.** A, D, E	**55.** A, D
16. A	**36.** B, C	**56.** B, E
17. C	**37.** D	**57.** B, C
18. A, B, C, E	**38.** B	**58.** C
19. C	**39.** A, B, C, D, E, F	**59.** C
20. B, E	**40.** A	**60.** B

Answers to *Exam Cram* Questions

1. **D.** In this scenario, the data entry supervisors are members of both the Data Entry and Supervisors groups. To enable the data entry supervisors to access the Internet, Betty needs to deny the Supervisors group the Apply Group Policy permission. It might be possible to accomplish this task by creating two Group Policy objects (GPO) if they are configured so that the supervisors' GPO is applied after the data entry GPO; however, this approach takes more administrative effort, so it is not the best solution. Consequently, answer A is incorrect. If Betty were to simply grant the Data Entry group the Read and Apply Group Policy permissions, the data entry supervisors would be unable to reach the Internet because of their membership in the Data Entry group, so answers B and C are incorrect.

2. **B, C, E.** When Julian created the first domain, an organizational unit (OU) named Domain Controllers was automatically created. In addition, Domain Name System (DNS) is installed and contains two zones with the domain name, one of which is prefixed with _msdcs. Further, the Active Directory database and shared system volume folders are created under the %systemroot% folder. Active Directory Users and Computers will contain a folder named Users. This is not an OU, so answer A is incorrect. The Active Directory database and shared system volume folders are created under the %systemroot% folder and not in the root of the system drive, so answer D is incorrect. A reverse lookup zone is not created in DNS by default, so answer F is incorrect.

3. **A, F.** Active Directory Sites and Services enables you to specify the site into which a domain controller should be placed. Each site contains a Servers object that contains the domain controllers located within the site. Kim can right-click the incorrectly placed server and choose Move, and then in the Move Server dialog box, select the correct site and click OK. She can use this procedure for domain controllers only and not member servers, so answer B is incorrect. For member servers, she must reconfigure the server with an IP address corresponding to the subnet specified for the correct site; this procedure automatically moves the server to the specified site. Kim cannot use Active Directory Users and Computers to move either the domain controller or the member server, so answers C and D are incorrect. She cannot move the domain controller by specifying an IP address corresponding to the subnet for the correct site, so answer E is incorrect.

4. **B, C, E, F, G.** Peter needs to perform all these steps to enable autoenrollment of certificates on his Windows Server 2008-based PKI. He must create a duplicate of the template previously used for enrollment in Windows 2000 because Windows 2000–based templates do not support autoenrollment. The option for prompting the user enables the user to provide any required input such as a PIN for a smart card. Users must have the Read, Enroll, and Autoenroll permissions for autoenrollment to succeed. Peter then needs to complete the task by enabling the template in the Certificate Templates node of the Certification Authority snap-in and configuring an appropriate GPO to enroll certificates automatically. Peter does not need to configure another Windows Server 2008 computer to enable autoenrollment, so answer A is incorrect. The Read and Enroll permissions are insufficient to enable autoenrollment; users must have the Autoenroll permission as well, so answer D is incorrect.

5. **A, D, E.** Paul must install IIS, Windows Process Activation Service, and Message Queuing Services when he installs Active Directory Rights Management Services (AD RMS). If these roles and services are not present, the installation wizard will ask him to install them. AD RMS uses a system of rights account certificates to identify users who are empowered to access and work with protected information from an AD RMS-enabled application, but Paul does not need to install Active Directory Certificate Services (AD CS) when he is installing AD RMS. Therefore, answer B is incorrect. Active Directory Metadirectory Services (AD MDS) provides a view of user information in the AD DS directory database and coordinates information across AD DS along with other components such as Active Directory Lightweight Directory Services (AD LDS) and Microsoft Exchange Server. AD RMS does not require Active Directory Metadirectory Services (AD MDS), so answer C is incorrect.

6. **B, C.** Diane should access the Zone Transfers tab of the same dialog box, click Notify, and then ensure that The Following Servers is selected and that the IP addresses of the perimeter zone secondary DNS servers are specified. Specifying this option on the Notify list ensures that only the authorized secondary DNS servers receive notifications of zone updates. Diane should also access the Start of Authority (SOA) tab of the zone's Properties dialog box and increase the value of the Refresh interval. An increase in the value of this interval reduces the bandwidth required for the zone transfer SOA requests sent by both perimeter network DNS servers. Specifying Servers Listed on the Name Servers Tab would cause additional zone transfers that involve the primary DNS servers in the

internal network, so answer A is incorrect. Decreasing the value of the Refresh interval would increase the amount of zone transfer traffic across the firewall server, so answer D is incorrect. The Retry interval specifies how much time will elapse before the secondary server tries again to contact the master server, in the event that the master server does not respond to the initial refresh attempt. Its value is immaterial to the problem specified in this scenario, so answers E and F are incorrect. Dynamic updates are used by the master DNS servers to maintain the Active Directory–integrated zone and are not utilized by the secondary servers on the perimeter zone. Diane should not modify this setting, so answer G is incorrect.

7. **D.** Stan should configure the password for the App user account to never expire. In this scenario, the App user account is governed by the policies configured in the Default Domain Policy GPO, which specifies a maximum password age of 30 days. After this time interval, the password associated with this account is no longer valid, and the account will no longer be able to log on; that's why the users could no longer access the application used by this account. Changing the maximum password age setting to its maximum of 999 would affect all domain users and thereby reduce the domain's security. Furthermore, the domain logon would still expire after this time interval (almost three years), and the problem would recur, so answer A is incorrect. Stan could configure a PSO with a 999-day password age, but this would take more administrative effort, and the problem would still recur as mentioned here, so answer B is incorrect. Changing the value of Enforce Password History to 0 would enable immediate reuse of a password, but the App user account password would still expire after 30 days. Furthermore, all domain users would be able to reuse their passwords immediately, thereby reducing domain security. Therefore, answer C is incorrect.

8. **B.** Debbie should place the users into global groups and then place the global groups into universal groups. After that, she should place the universal groups into domain local groups. Because of the manner in which universal group membership changes are replicated as she has configured them here, the user objects are being referenced and creating excess replication. Simply placing the universal groups into domain local groups while still adding the users directly to the universal groups does not reduce replication traffic, so answer A is incorrect. Local groups are local to the machine on which they are created and are not available to the domain, so answer C is incorrect. As already explained, the universal group configuration is creating this large quantity of replication traffic, so answer D is incorrect.

9. **C.** Hubert should open a command prompt, stop AD DS, use the ntdsutil utility to move the file, and then restart AD DS. To move this file, he must use this utility to ensure that the appropriate Registry settings are also modified. The use of Windows Explorer to move this file will not allow the Registry to be automatically modified, so answers A, D, and F are incorrect. Hubert could restart the server in Directory Services Restore mode and use the ntdsutil utility to move the file; this method would work and in fact was the required procedure before Windows Server 2008. However, it takes more administrative effort, so answer B is incorrect. Hubert cannot move this file while it's in use, so answers E and F are incorrect.

10. **D.** Besides acting as a primary domain controller for pre-Windows 2000 client computers, the PDC emulator acts as a time server for the domain and ensures that the system clocks on all other computers are synchronized. The PDC emulator connects to an Internet time server to ensure that it has the proper time setting. None of the other FSMO roles are involved in time synchronization, so answers A, B, C, and E are incorrect.

11. **B.** Alexander should place the users in a security group and configure the Security tab of the template's Properties dialog box with the appropriate permissions to the template. By default, only members of the Authenticated Users group in the parent domain have permissions on the templates. This scenario does not specify the need for certificate autoenrollment, so answer A is incorrect. Automatic certificate request polices are also used for autoenrollment, so answer C is incorrect. The users were able to authenticate to the web enrollment pages but not the required template, so web authentication was not a problem; therefore, answer D is incorrect.

12. **E.** Windows System Resource Manager (WSRM) is a new Windows Server 2008 tool that enables Rachel to control how processor and memory resources are allocated to applications, services, and processes running on the server. She can use this tool to set up resource allocation policies that determine how computer resources such as processor and memory are allocated to processes running on the server. She can specify process-matching criteria and conditions under which WSRM can switch to a different matching criterion. She can also use this tool to display performance counters in real time. Network Monitor captures network traffic across her server's network adapter card but does not perform any of the tasks required here, so answer A is incorrect. Both Task Manager and Reliability and Performance Monitor can display real-time server performance data, but they do not enable her to set up resource allocation policies and control how server resources are allocated, so answers B and

C are incorrect. Event Viewer logs data about events occurring on the server, including errors, warnings, and informational events. It does not perform any of the tasks required here, so answer D is incorrect.

13. **D.** Jordan should configure the reverse lookup zone as an Active Directory–integrated zone and select the Secure Only dynamic updates option. Configuring this option prevents any computers that are not domain members from creating pointer (PTR) resource records. This includes all computers operated by guests who are accessing the Internet from the resort's wireless access points. If Jordan were to disable dynamic updates to the reverse lookup zone, employees would be prevented from creating updated PTR resource records, so answers A and C are incorrect. It is not possible to configure the Secure Only dynamic updates option on a secondary zone, so answer B is incorrect.

14. **A, C.** In a situation such as this one, Roy needs to determine which policy settings are in effect for the users and computers in question. Roy needs to perform a Resultant Set of Policy (RSoP) logging mode analysis. He can do this by right-clicking the Group Policy Results node and choosing Group Policy Results Wizard or by running the `gpresult` command. The `gpupdate` command would refresh the application of Group Policy; however, in this scenario, the policy is already working unexpectedly the following day, and after users have logged off/on. Such an action causes Group Policy to refresh, and it is necessary to determine why it is not applying properly, so answer B is incorrect. Roy would use the Group Policy Modeling Wizard to test the effects of a proposed change affecting the application of Group Policy; this wizard performs an RSoP planning mode analysis. To check the cause of a policy change that has been implemented, Roy needs to use logging mode and not planning mode, so answers D and E are incorrect.

15. **E.** The RID master handles the assignment of security identifiers (SID) to objects being created in the domain. The RID master hands out a pool of several hundred relative identifiers (RID) to every domain controller in the domain so that they can create new objects with unique identifiers. The domain naming master ensures that the names of child domains are unique. The schema master updates the AD DS schema for the forest. The infrastructure master ensures that references to objects in other domains are current. The PDC emulator functions as a time server and as a primary domain controller to pre-Windows 2000 clients. None of these roles ensure that objects within the domain have unique names, so answers A, B, C, and D are incorrect.

16. **A.** Groups can contain any of user, group, or computer accounts, as proven by the title of the Select Users, Computers, or Groups dialog box that appears when populating a new group. Use of a firewall would be a considerable administrative burden, so answer B is incorrect. Use of additional groups or a single logon for the kiosk computers is possible, but these schemes would take more administrative effort than creating a single group containing both user and computer accounts. Consequently, answers C and D are incorrect.

17. **C.** Carolyn should create a site link bridge that encompasses the Duluth-to-Minneapolis and Minneapolis-to-Chicago site links, and then she should set the cost of the 56Kbps link to 300. The use of a site link bridge enables her to route AD DS replication across a pair of fast links rather than a single, much slower link. The cost of a site link bridge is the sum of the costs of the site links contained within it. In this case, it is 200. (When costs are not provided, you should assume that the cost of each site link is the default value of 100.) Consequently, Carolyn must set the cost of the 56Kbps link to a value greater than the cost of the site link bridge so that replication preferentially follows the two T1 links rather than the slower 56Kbps link. Simple Mail Transport Protocol (SMTP) replication replicates only the schema and configuration partitions between different domains, so answer A is incorrect. Configuring the 56Kbps link to be available outside business hours only would prevent daytime replication, but replication would still use this link at other times, so answer B is incorrect. It is not possible to specify a cost for a site link bridge, so answer D is incorrect.

18. **A, B, C, E.** All these items are characteristics of a read-only domain controller (RODC), which is a new feature of Windows Server 2008. When a user updates his password, the RODC must contact the writable domain controller with which it is partnered to complete the password change request, so answer D is incorrect.

19. **C.** Ursula should include the user accounts of the interns in a security group and grant this group the Deny–Request Certificates permission from the Security tab of the certification authority (CA) server's Properties dialog box. The Request Certificates permission is granted to members of the Authenticated Users group by default and enables these users to enroll for certificates. By denying this permission to the security group containing the interns, the Deny entry takes precedence over Allow entries and prevents the interns from receiving certificates. The Restricted Enrollment Agent policy limits permissions granted to enrollment agents. It does not affect which users can receive certificates, so

answer A is incorrect. If Ursula were to remove the Authenticated Users group from the access control list (ACL) in the Security tab, no users in the company would be able to receive certificates unless their groups are specifically added to this ACL, so answer B is incorrect. The Deny–Autoenroll permission would prevent the interns from autoenrolling for certificates but would not prevent them from obtaining certificates by another means such as web-based enrollment, so answer D is incorrect.

20. **B, E.** Theodore should ensure that the domain functional level is set to Windows Server 2008. He should then create a Password Settings Object (PSO) specifying a 12-character length password and apply this PSO to a group containing the users in the Legal OU. Fine-grained password policies are a new feature of AD DS in Windows Server 2008 that enables the ability to specify a different password or account lockout policy settings for a user or group. The domain functional level must be Windows Server 2008; a setting of Windows Server 2003 is inadequate for configuring fine-grained password policies, so answer A is incorrect. Password policy settings applied in a GPO linked to an OU are disregarded, so answer C is incorrect. Prior to Windows Server 2008, Theodore would have needed to create a child domain to apply a different password policy. Because he can apply a PSO, it is not necessary to do this, so answer D is incorrect. He must apply the PSO to a user or group, not directly to an OU, so answer F is incorrect. Specifying Block Inheritance for the Legal OU does not stop a domain-based password policy from applying, so answer G is incorrect.

21. **A, F.** Leanne can accomplish this objective by right-clicking the DNS zone and choosing Export List. She can also use the `Dnscmd /zoneexport` command. Either of these actions exports all resource records in the specified DNS zone to a text file. The Configure a DNS Server right-click option starts a wizard that enables her to create forward and reverse lookup zones, specify root hints, or specify forwarders. This wizard does not offer an option to export DNS resource records, so answer B is incorrect. There is no Copy option on the right-click menu accessed from the Details pane of DNS Manager, so answer C is incorrect. The `Dnscmd /info` command displays DNS server configuration information as stored in the server's Registry. The `Dnscmd /zoneinfo` command displays Registry-based configuration information for the specified DNS zone. Neither of these two commands enables the export of zone information to a text file, so answers D and E are incorrect.

22. **D.** The fact that users were able to run Excel after double-clicking on an Excel spreadsheet but that it was not available from the Start menu indicates that the software was published to the users rather than assigned. Richard can ensure that all users can run Excel by changing its deployment type from Published to Assigned, which he can do from the Deployment tab of the package's Properties dialog box. The gpresult command would show the policy settings that are being applied. However the problem here is not whether the policy settings were applied; rather, it was the deployment type that Richard had selected, so answer A is incorrect. The Gpupdate command refreshes the application of policy settings. Again, the problem is not the application of policy settings, so answer B is incorrect. Users do not require the Full Control permission to have the software available, so answer C is incorrect.

23. **B, C, E.** A domain containing Windows Server 2008 domain controllers can exist in any one of three domain functional levels: Windows 2000 native, Windows Server 2003 native, and Windows Server 2008 native. The Windows 2000 mixed functional level was available in Windows 2000 and Windows Server 2003 domains to support the existence of Windows NT 4.0 backup domain controllers. This functional level is not supported in Windows Server 2008, so answer A is incorrect. No Windows Server 2008 interim functional level exists (a Windows Server 2003 interim functional level did exist that supported Windows NT 4.0 and Windows Server 2003 domain controllers), so answer D is incorrect.

24. **B, D.** Linda can use Active Directory Sites and Services or the Replmon utility to force AD DS intersite replication. She can also use Repadmin to do the same task. Active Directory Domains and Trusts enables Linda to perform tasks such as raising the functional level or creating trust relationships, but it cannot force replication, so answer A is incorrect. The Gpupdate /force command forces Group Policy replication but not replication of AD DS objects, so answer C is incorrect. Linda can use ntdsutil to perform a variety of maintenance tasks, including transfer or seizure of FSMO roles or authoritative restores, but this tool does not force AD DS replication, so answer E is incorrect.

25. **C.** As a minimum, Brandon should free up an amount of disk space equivalent to 15% of the current database size so that the offline defragmentation process proceeds smoothly. This space is used for temporary storage during the defragmentation process. The amount of disk space depends on the size of the database and cannot be estimated at 500MB, so answer A is incorrect. Ten percent of the current size is insufficient, so answer B is incorrect. Although having 25% of the current size available

might improve the speed of the defragmentation process, this is more than the required minimum, so answer D is incorrect. Because there is a specified minimum, answer E is incorrect.

26. **B.** Wilson should configure the conditional forwarder with the All Domain Controllers in This Domain option. This option enables replication to all domain controllers, including those running Windows 2000. The problem in this scenario is not with a directory replication failure, so answer A is incorrect. The All DNS Servers in This Domain option replicates to Windows Server 2003 and Windows Server 2008 domain controllers only. Because Windows 2000 domain controllers are present on the network, conditional forwarding on this zone will not be established on these servers, so answer C is incorrect. Zone delegation is not an issue in this scenario, so answer D is incorrect.

27. **A.** Scott should access the template's Request Handling tab. He should select the Signature and Encryption option from the Purpose drop-down list, and then select Archive Subject's Encryption Private Key. This option is not available if he has selected Signature from the Purpose drop-down list because the Signature option requires that the key not be recoverable. The Allow Private Key to be Exported option only allows users to export keys for backup; it does not provide for key archival, so answer B is incorrect. Scott does not require a version 3 template to enable key archival, so answer C is incorrect. Key archival does not require the ability to autoenroll certificates, so answer D is incorrect.

28. **D.** When Jennifer first promoted the server to domain controller, she had to enter a Directory Services Restore Mode (DSRM) administrator password. This password is stored locally in the security accounts manager (SAM) and not in Active Directory. When she starts the computer in DSRM, it acts as a standalone server and is not connected to Active Directory. Consequently, domain user accounts and passwords are unavailable. Changes to a password on her domain account are irrelevant because she must use the DSRM password here, so answer A is incorrect. It is possible that a Group Policy setting would deny the Log on Locally right, but this would prevent an administrator from accessing the server, so answer B is incorrect. Jennifer does not need to belong to the Enterprise Administrators group to use DSRM. In fact, anyone with access to the DSRM password can access this mode. (This is why it is important to protect this password carefully so that an unauthorized user does not get at the database.) Consequently, answer C is incorrect.

29. **C.** After Ian has configured each site properly with its associated subnet and moved each domain controller object to its site, users logging on to client computers in each office will be authenticated by a domain controller located in their own office, rather than crossing the T1 links to the Philadelphia office. As the network is presently configured, the domain controllers think that they are all on the same network and replicate according to the highly frequent intrasite replication conditions. Consequently, scheduling intersite replication to take place either more or less frequently will not improve matters, so answers A and B are both incorrect. Ian should not move the domain controllers to the Philadelphia site; they need to remain on the sites associated with their physical locations, so answer D is incorrect.

30. **C.** By selecting Find from the Action menu in Active Directory Users and Computers, Doug can pull up the Find Users, Contacts, or Groups dialog box. From this location, he can select the Office Location field and enter the old address of the department being moved. This will return the user accounts of the 75 users. He can then right-click and select Properties to bring up the Properties of Multiple Users dialog box, and he can change the address in this dialog box. Ldifde does not export information to a tab-delimited file; it exports information to the LDAP directory interchange file (LDIF) file format. Consequently, answer A is incorrect. Doug could use Csvde to export the user accounts to a comma-delimited file and then edit this file. However, Csvde can be used to import new objects only; it cannot be used in modifying existing objects, so answers B and D are incorrect.

31. **B.** Cindy should select Maximum from the Installation User Interface Options on the Deployment tab of the package's Properties dialog box. This option provides the entire user interface that is supported by the application during installation. If she were to select the Basic option, users would see only progress bars and errors, so answer A is incorrect. The Do Not Display This Package in the Add/Remove Programs Control Panel option removes the package from this location so that users are less able to remove the application; it does not affect the amount of information users see during program installation, so answer C is incorrect. The Install This Application at Logon option fully installs the application using its default options; it also does not affect the amount of information users see during the installation, so answer D is incorrect.

32. **A, C, D, F, I, K.** To install an RODC in your AD DS forest, your forest must meet the following requirements:

   ▶ The domain and forest functional levels must be at least Windows Server 2003. Consequently, all domain controllers in all domains of the forest must run Windows Server 2003 or higher.

   ▶ You must run `Adprep /forestprep` on the schema master of the forest before introducing Windows Server 2008 domain controllers.

   ▶ You must run `Adprep /domainprep` at the infrastructure master of each domain where you plan to introduce Windows Server 2008 domain controllers.

   ▶ The PDC emulator must be running on a Windows Server 2008 computer in the domain where you plan to introduce an RODC—in this case, the forest root domain.

   ▶ You must run `Adprep /rodcprep` at the PDC emulator of the domain where you plan to introduce an RODC.

   All these steps are necessary and should be performed in the order given here before you can introduce an RODC. It is not necessary to upgrade all domain controllers in the forest to Windows Server 2008, nor to raise the domain and forest functional levels to Windows Server 2008, so answers B and E are incorrect. You must run the `Adprep /forestprep` command at the schema master and not the domain naming master, so answer G is incorrect. You must run the `Adprep /rodcprep` command at the infrastructure master and not the RID master, so answer H is incorrect. You must run the `Adprep /rodcprep` command at the PDC emulator and not the infrastructure master, so answer J is incorrect.

33. **B.** To ensure that DNS2 can receive zone transfers from DNS1, Jose should select the BIND Secondaries option on DNS1. Selection of this option prevents DNS1 from performing fast zone transfers to the secondary DNS server (DNS2). This is needed in this case because older UNIX servers, running versions of BIND earlier than version 4.9.4, cannot handle fast zone transfers. Selecting Disable Recursions prevents a DNS server from querying other DNS servers for name resolution. Round robin rotates the order of matching resource records in the response list for the web server addresses returned to DNS clients. The Fail on Load If Bad Zone Data option causes a DNS server to reject zone transfers if errors are discovered in the transfer. The Enable Netmask Ordering option causes the DNS server to reorder the A

resource records based on local subnet priority if the request is for a multihomed computer. The Secure Cache Against Pollution option prevents unauthorized users from adding resource records from nonauthoritative servers to the DNS cache. None of these options enable DNS2 to receive zone transfers as required for this scenario, so answers A, C, D, E, and F are incorrect.

34. **C.** If both the Block Inheritance and Enforced settings have been applied, the Enforced setting prevails. Consequently, if Heather specifies the Enforced setting, the policies in the GPO are applied to the child OU even if Block Inheritance has been specified on this OU. Setting the Block Inheritance option on the parent OU would block site- and domain-based GPOs from applying to both the parent and child OUs, so answer A is incorrect. The Block Inheritance setting is applied to an AD DS container and not to an individual GPO, so answer B is incorrect. It is not possible to specify Enforced at the local level, so answer D is incorrect.

35. **A, D, E.** Each of these settings helps to increase password security. The Password Must Meet Complexity Requirements setting requires that users employ three of the four character groups (uppercase letters, lowercase letters, numerals, and special characters). The Minimum Password Length setting specifies the minimum number of characters in the password, and the Maximum Password Age setting defines the maximum number of days a user can employ a password before being required to change it. Storing passwords using reversible encryption actually decreases password security, so answer B is incorrect. If a hacker gains a password, it does not matter whether he has to change it right away, so answer C is incorrect.

36. **B, C.** Carm must log on using an account that is a member of the Enterprise Admins group. He also must ensure that all domains in the forest, not just the tree root domains, are at the Windows Server 2008 domain functional level. He does not need to be a member of the Schema Admins group, so answer A is incorrect. He can raise the forest functional level from Windows 2000 to Windows Server 2008 in one step provided that all domains are at the Windows Server 2008 domain functional level, so answer D is incorrect. There is no need to remove external or shortcut trust relationships, so answer E is incorrect.

37. **D.** The Delegation of Control Wizard enables Veronica to delegate the task of managing Group Policy links, which provides the administrators in the other domains the ability to apply the GPOs but not modify them.

She has to do this once for each domain within which she wants to delegate control. The Group Policy Management Console does not offer the ability to delegate administrative control, so answers A and B are incorrect. It is not possible to delegate control of users or groups, only of sites, domains, or OUs, so answer C is incorrect.

38. **B.** Justin should select the Prompt the User During Enrollment and Require User Input When the Private Key Is Used option. This option causes a message box to be displayed asking the user to input her PIN. The Prompt the User During Enrollment option does not require that the PIN be entered, so answer A is incorrect. The Add Read Permissions to Network Service on the Private Key option grants the Read permission on the private key to Network Service on the computer to which the certificate is issued. This is not used for user-based certificates, so answer C is incorrect. Justin might need to select the Allow Private Key to Be Exported option to enable the export of private keys associated with the smart card certificates as a backup precaution. However, this option does not require input of the PIN, so answer D is incorrect.

39. **A, B, C, D, E, F.** All of these criteria are available from which Cassandra can create a custom log that displays the types of events that she wants to monitor. She can also select other criteria, such as the source of the event (services, programs, or drivers) and keywords associated with the event, such as Audit Success and Audit Failure.

40. **A.** The DNS counters found in the Reliability and Performance Monitor console enable David to obtain data related to a performance problem such as this one. When he installs DNS on a Windows Server 2008 computer, a comprehensive set of DNS counters is added to the Reliability and Performance Monitor console that he can view in a real-time graph, or he can use the Data Collector Sets tool to log information for later analysis. The Monitoring tab of the server's Properties dialog box enables David to perform simple and recursive test queries on the server but does not allow him to collect monitoring data, so answer B is incorrect. The DNS server log in Event Viewer records event messages, including any errors that the DNS server may have logged. He should look here to locate any problems that the server may be encountering, but he cannot obtain monitoring data here, so answer C is incorrect. The Debug Logging tab of the server's Properties dialog box enables him to monitor data being received from or sent to other computers by the DNS server. It does not provide monitoring data needed in this scenario, so answer D is incorrect.

41. **B.** Arlene can designate additional global catalog servers from the Active Directory Sites and Services snap-in by accessing the Properties dialog box for the NTDS Settings object. She cannot use the Active Directory Domains and Trusts tool or the `ntdsutil` utility for this purpose, so answers A and C are incorrect. Although you can have only one of each operations master roles in each domain, you can have as many global catalog servers as you want, so answer D is incorrect.

42. **A.** Windows Server 2008 provides the capability to assign certificates to both users and computers. Because John can assign certificates to both users and computers in Windows Server 2008, answers B and C are incorrect. Furthermore, in a fully secure environment, certificates should be assigned to both the computers and the users, so answer D is incorrect.

43. **D.** Stephanie should create user accounts for the new users in the existing domain and specify an alternative UPN suffix of que.com. She can specify this UPN suffix in Active Directory Domains and Trusts; then it will be available when she creates the user accounts in Active Directory Users and Computers. Creating a new forest or domain tree named que.com would require considerable additional administrative effort and is not required by this scenario, so answers A and B are incorrect. It is not possible to simply assign the user accounts user logon names in the format of user@que.com without first specifying que.com as an alternative UPN suffix, so answer C is incorrect.

44. **B, C, D.** SMTP replication can be used to replicate the configuration and schema partitions of AD DS data and the global catalog between all sites in multidomain forests only. It requires the presence of an enterprise CA, and cannot be scheduled because it is asynchronous. SMTP does not replicate the domain partition and cannot be used for replication within a domain, so answer A is incorrect. SMTP also cannot be used for intra-site replication, so answer E is incorrect.

45. **D.** Gary should configure a claims-aware application. This is a Microsoft Active Server Pages (ASP) .NET application that uses claims that are present in an Active Directory Federation Services (AD FS) security token to perform authorization decisions and personalize applications. The Windows token–based agent is used on a web server that hosts a Windows NT token-based application to support conversion from an AD FS security token to a Windows NT access token. A Federation Service proxy acts as a proxy to the Federation Service on a perimeter network or demilitarized zone. A trust policy enables users to share

documents protected in AD RMS across internal or external AD DS forests. None of these can test which claims the Federation Service sends in AD FS security tokens, so answers A, B, and C are incorrect.

46. A, B. By default, the Active Directory Schema snap-in is not present when a domain controller is installed, so Ester has to install it. First, she needs to register this snap-in by using the `regsvr32` command from the Run dialog box. She cannot install this snap-in until she performs this step. Ester does not need to be at the schema master because she can connect to it from another computer, so answer C is incorrect. She does not need to belong to the Enterprise Admins group to access the Schema snap-in, so answer D is incorrect.

47. A. Janet needs to increase the Refresh Interval to 20 minutes from its original value of 15 minutes. This will change the time that all secondary DNS servers wait before they request a zone transfer from their master server. Increasing this single parameter decreases the number of occasions through the day that secondary servers request zone transfers. This will, in turn, decrease the amount of traffic on the 256Kbps link between Pittsburgh and Altoona. The Retry Interval governs how long a secondary server waits to retry a failed zone transfer. This is not the problem here, so answer B is incorrect. The Expires After text box specifies the amount of time that a secondary DNS server considers records to be reliable for a zone when it is not in contact with the primary server for the zone. The Minimum (Default) Time to Live (TTL) text box controls the amount of time that a secondary server considers cached records to be valid. The TTL for This Record refers to the actual Start of Authority (SOA) record. None of these settings are relevant to this scenario, so answers C, D, and E are incorrect.

48. C. You cannot link GPOs to security groups. Instead, you must target sites, domains, or OUs. Because you cannot link GPOs to security groups, answer A is incorrect. Complexity is not a factor here, so answer B is incorrect. The act of configuring a GPO does not create a lot of replication, so answer D is incorrect.

49. B. Enabling auditing of any type of object access is a two-stage process. In this case, Merle only performed the first part, which was enabling auditing in a GPO applicable to the Active Directory container (site, domain, or OU) in question. She must also enable auditing of each specific object, which she can do from the object's Properties dialog box (in this case, the printer's Properties). The security log records activities performed by all users, administrators, authorized users, unauthorized uses, and so on, so answers A and D are incorrect. The events are recorded on the Security log of the computer where they occurred, so answer C is incorrect.

50. **C.** Wayne should access the Debug Logging tab of the DNS server's Properties dialog box, enable Log Packets for Debugging, and specify the Filter Packets by IP Address option. This option enables him to specify the range of IP addresses within which DNS will collect debug logging information. He would also select both the Incoming and Outgoing options under Packet Direction on this tab. The simple and recursive queries verify whether DNS can resolve zone data, but these queries do not log incoming or outgoing requests at the DNS server, so answer A is incorrect. The Event Logging option does not log individual queries sent to or from the DNS server, so answer B is incorrect. Wayne could specify a capture filter in Network Monitor, but this would capture much more traffic than that captured by debug logging, so answer D is incorrect.

51. **E, G.** Evelyn can install an enterprise root CA on a domain controller running either Windows Server 2008 Enterprise edition or Datacenter edition. It is not possible to install an enterprise root CA on a computer running either the Web edition or the Standard edition of Windows Server 2008, so answers A, B, and C are incorrect. The server must be configured as a domain controller and not as a member server, so answers D and F are incorrect.

52. **D.** The repadmin utility with the /showmeta option displays a list of updated attributes in the AD DS database, with their update sequence numbers (USN), thereby providing Hazel with the information she needs. Neither the NTDS performance object counters nor the Resource Monitor feature of Windows System Resource Manager provides this information, so answers A and B are incorrect. Hazel could use replmon, but she would have to right-click the server and choose Properties. The Update Status option simply updates the date and time of the most recent replication, so answer C is incorrect.

53. **B.** Simply deleting objects from AD DS does not reduce the size of the database file. AD DS marks deleted objects as being tombstoned to ensure their proper deletion from all replication partners. After the tombstone period has expired (60 days by default), AD DS removes these objects permanently. AD DS cannot defragment the database while it is active. Consequently, Tom needs to stop AD DS by using the net stop ntds command and then use ntdsutil to defragment the database. The

60. B. The RID master keeps track of all relative identifiers (RID) assigned within its domain and issues blocks of 500 RIDs to all other domain controllers in the domain so that administrators can create accounts. If this computer becomes unavailable, Elaine can create new user accounts until the available pool of RIDs is exhausted, after which new account creation will fail until the RID master can issue a new pool of RIDs. The infrastructure master is not involved in user account creation, so answer A is unavailable. If the `.csv` file had become corrupted, Elaine would have been able to manually add the principals' user accounts, so answer C is incorrect. It is not necessary to replicate the user accounts to other domain controllers before continuing to add additional accounts, so answer D is incorrect.

APPENDIX A

Need to Know More?

Chapter 1

Tulloch, Mitch. *Introducing Windows Server 2008*. Redmond, Washington: Microsoft Press, 2007.

Microsoft Corporation. "Server Management." Available on the web at http://www.microsoft.com/windowsserver2008/servermanagement.mspx.

Microsoft Corporation. "Windows Server 2008 Server Manager Technical Overview." Available on the web at http://technet2.microsoft.com/windowsserver2008/en/library/18dd1257-2cd1-48f0-91f1-3012cf0fcc831033.mspx?mfr=true.

Microsoft Corporation. "Steps for Installing AD DS." Available on the web at http://technet2.microsoft.com/windowsserver2008/en/library/6c141f6a-6c7b-462f-b2a8-a06c543022981033.mspx?mfr=true.

Microsoft Corporation. "Server Core Installation Option of Windows Server 2008 Step-by-Step Guide." Available on the web at http://technet2.microsoft.com/windowsserver2008/en/library/47a23a74-e13c-46de-8d30-ad0afb1eaffc1033.mspx?mfr=true.

Microsoft Corporation. "Performing an Unattended Installation of Active Directory." Available on the web at http://technet2.microsoft.com/windowsserver/en/library/fee4156e-b601-45e1-aeba-f3fa2f8c3e5e1033.mspx?mfr=true.

Microsoft Corporation. "Characteristics of Object Classes." Available on the web at http://msdn2.microsoft.com/en-us/library/ms675579.aspx.

Microsoft Corporation. "Characteristics of Attributes." Available on the web at http://msdn2.microsoft.com/en-us/library/ms675578.aspx.

Microsoft Corporation. "Configuring Operations Master Roles." Available on the web at http://technet2.microsoft.com/windowsserver2008/en/ library/7a585c8a-95af-43aa-bb96-d0e620118a161033.mspx?mfr=true.

Microsoft Corporation. "Configure the Windows Time Service." Available on the web at http://technet2.microsoft.com/windowsserver2008 /en/library/ 92a73b00-12b7-49d0-b6be-007e626f387d1033.mspx?mfr=true.

Microsoft Corporation. "Identifying Your Windows Server 2008 Functional Level Upgrade." Available on the web at http://technet2. microsoft.com/ windowsserver2008/en/library/4e703a77-d9ba-4a26-b756-eba5499f15581033. mspx?mfr=true.

Microsoft Corporation. "Understanding AD DS Functional Levels." Available on the web at http://technet2.microsoft.com/WindowsServer2008/en/ library/dbf0cdec-d72f-4ba3-bc7a-46410e02abb01033.mspx.

Microsoft Corporation. "Appendix of Unattended Installation Parameters." Available on the web at http://technet2.microsoft.com/windowsserver2008/en/ library/bcd89659-402d-46fb-8535-8da1feb8d4111033.mspx?mfr=true.

Chapter 2

Microsoft Corporation. "Configuring DNS for the Forest Root Domain." Available on the web at http://technet2.microsoft.com/windowsserver/en/ library/7e893f77-8b4a-492a-9a24-ec679dd422841033.mspx?mfr=true.

Microsoft Corporation. "Active Directory–Integrated DNS Zones." Available on the web at http://technet2.microsoft.com/windowsserver2008 /en/ library/9cea6817-e512-4a1d-80a1-ae312329c1061033.mspx?mfr=true.

Microsoft Corporation. "Step-by-Step Guide for DNS in Small Networks." Available on the web at http://download.microsoft.com/download/b/1/0/ b106fc39-936c-4857-a6ea-3fb9d1f37063/Windows%20Server%202008%20Step-by-Step%20Guide%20for%20DNS%20in%20 Small%20Networks.doc.

Microsoft Corporation. "Dnscmd Syntax." Available on the web at http://technet2.microsoft.com/windowsserver/en/library/d652a163-279f-4047-b3e0-0c468a4d69f31033.mspx?mfr=true.

Microsoft Corporation. "Nslookup." Available on the web at
http://technet2.microsoft.com/windowsserver2008/en/library/41516932-7833-
434a-aa92-b4cf0f9a7ef71033.mspx?mfr=true.

Chapter 3

Microsoft Corporation. "IPv6." Available on the web at
http://technet.microsoft.com/en-us/network/bb530961.aspx.

Microsoft Corporation. "Active Directory Replication over Firewalls."
Available on the web at http://technet.microsoft.com/en-us/library/
bb727063.aspx.

Microsoft Corporation. "Step-by-Step Guide for Distributed
File Systems in Windows Server 2008." Available on the web at
http://technet2.microsoft.com/windowsserver2008/en/library/cf810bb7-
51ed-4535-ab0d-86a7cd862e601033.mspx?mfr=true.

Hunter, Laura E. "A Guide to Active Directory Replication." Available on the
web at http://www.microsoft.com/technet/technetmag/issues/2007/
10/Replication/default.aspx.

Microsoft Corporation. "Active Directory Replication Considerations."
Available on the web at http://technet2.microsoft.com/
windowsserver2008/en/ library/e7caabff-3795-49fa-8338-
bbe56e49eae41033.mspx?mfr=true.

Anonymous. "Active Directory Replication Guide." Available
on the web at http://searchwinit.techtarget.com/general/0,295582,sid1_
gci1 263312,00.html?track=NL-458&ad=598055&asrc=EM_NLT_
1895671&uid=64259.

Olsen, Gary. "Case Study: How to Force Immediate Active
Directory Replication for All Core Sites." Available on the web at
http://searchwinit.techtarget.com/tip/0,289483,sid1_gci1255756,00.
html?track=NL-458&ad=592914&asrc=EM_NLT_1618462&uid=64259.

Chapter 4

Tulloch, Mitch. *Introducing Windows Server 2008*. Redmond, Washington:
Microsoft Press, 2007. Chapter 5, "Managing Server Roles," Chapter 6,
"Windows Server Core," and Chapter 7, "Active Directory Enhancements."

Microsoft Corporation. "Step-by-Step Guide for Getting Started with Active Directory Lightweight Directory Services." Available on the web at http://technet2.microsoft.com/windowsserver2008/en/library/141900a7-445c-4bd3-9ce3-5ff53d70d10a1033.mspx?mfr=true.

Microsoft Corporation. "Active Directory Lightweight Directory Services Overview." Available on the web at http://technet2.microsoft.com/windowsserver2008/en/library/6a3bedf7-9c5b-4ada-9a51-6b794adc9ab81033.mspx?mfr=true.

Microsoft Corporation. "Windows Server Active Directory Rights Management Services Step-by-Step Guide." Available on the web at http://technet2.microsoft.com/windowsserver2008/en/library/437d3040-89f0-40ac-a2af-c288a48714c41033.mspx?mfr=true.

Microsoft Corporation. "Active Directory Rights Management Services Overview." Available on the web at http://technet2.microsoft.com/windowsserver2008/en/library/74272acc-0f2d-4dc2-876f-15b156a0b4e01033.mspx?mfr=true.

Microsoft Corporation. "Server Core Installation Option of Windows Server 2008 Step-by-Step Guide." Available on the web at http://technet2.microsoft.com/windowsserver2008/en/library/47a23a74-e13c-46de-8d30-ad0afb1eaffc1033.mspx?mfr=true.

Microsoft Corporation. "Step-by-Step Guide for Read-Only Domain Controllers." Available on the web at http://technet2.microsoft.com/windowsserver2008/en/library/ea8d253e-0646-490c-93d3-b78c5e1d9db71033.mspx?mfr=true.

Microsoft Corporation. "Windows BitLocker Drive Encryption." Available on the web at http://technet2.microsoft.com/windowsserver2008/en/library/a2ba17e6-153b-4269-bc46-6866df4b253c1033.mspx?mfr=true.

Microsoft Corporation. "Active Directory Federation Services Role." Available on the web at http://technet2.microsoft.com/windowsserver2008/en/library/f5e12c1f-a3fa-453d-98ce-be29352afaca1033.mspx?mfr=true.

Microsoft Corporation. "Using Identity Federation with Active Directory Rights Management Services Step-by-Step Guide." Available on the web at http://technet2.microsoft.com/windowsserver2008/en/library/703206ee-638c-40c9-beb5-d474602b02af1033.mspx?mfr=true.

Microsoft Corporation. "Step-by-Step Guide for AD FS in Windows Server 2008." Available on the web at http://technet2.microsoft.com/windowsserver2008/en/library/a018ccfe-acb2-41f9-9f0a-102b80a3398c1033.mspx?mfr=true.

Microsoft Corporation. "Windows Server 2008 Hyper-V." Available on the web at http://www.microsoft.com/downloads/details.aspx?familyid=0FE4E411-8C88-48C2-8903-3FD9CBB10D05&displaylang=en.

Chapter 5

Tulloch, Mitch. *Introducing Windows Server 2008*. Redmond, Washington: Microsoft Press, 2007. Chapter 7, "Active Directory Enhancements."

Microsoft Corporation. "LDIFDE–Export/Import Data from Active Directory." Available on the web at http://support.microsoft.com/kb/555634.

Microsoft Corporation. "Create Distribution Lists." Available on the web at http://technet2.microsoft.com/WindowsServer2008/en/library/f61fac4a-f0de-4f8e-9d4f-c06bd43a8f791033.mspx.

Microsoft Corporation. "Domain and Forest Trust Tools and Settings." Available on the web at http://technet2.microsoft.com/windowsserver/en/library/108124dd-31b1-4c2c-9421-6adbc1ebceca1033.mspx?mfr=true.

Microsoft Corporation. "Trust Types." Available on the web at http://technet2.microsoft.com/WindowsServer/en/library/116d34e5-5615-4fb8-a8ef-47b94c294b581033.mspx.

Microsoft Corporation. "Security Considerations for Trusts." Available on the web at http://technet2.microsoft.com/windowsserver/en/library/1f33e9a1-c3c5-431c-a5cc-c3c2bd579ff11033.mspx?mfr=true.

Microsoft Corporation. "11 Essential Tools for Managing Active Directory." Available on the web at http://technet.microsoft.com/en-us/magazine/cc137799.aspx.

Chapter 6

Tulloch, Mitch, Tony Northrup, and Jerry Honeycutt. *Windows Vista Resource Kit, Second Edition*. Redmond, Washington: Microsoft Press, 2007. Chapter 13, "Managing the Desktop Environment," and Chapter 24, "Managing Software Updates." Redmond, Washington: Microsoft Press, 2008.

Tulloch, Mitch. *Introducing Windows Server 2008*. Redmond, Washington: Microsoft Press, 2007. Chapter 4, "Managing Windows Server 2008."

Microsoft Corporation. "Planning and Deploying Group Policy." Available on the web at http://www.microsoft.com/downloads/details.aspx?FamilyID= 73D96068-0AEA-450A-861B-E2C5413B0485&displaylang=en.

Microsoft Corporation. "Group Policy Frequently Asked Questions (FAQ)." Available on the web at http://technet2.microsoft.com/windowsserver/en/ technologies/featured/gp/faq.mspx.

Microsoft Corporation. "Thank You for Downloading Group Policy Preferences Overview." Available on the web at http://www.microsoft.com/ downloads/thankyou.aspx?familyId=42e30e3f-6f01-4610-9d6e-f6e0fb7a0790&displayLang=en.

Microsoft Corporation. "Group Policy." Available on the web at http:// technet2.microsoft.com/windowsserver2008/en/library/3b4568bc-9d3c-4477-807d-2ea149ff06491033.mspx?mfr=true.

Microsoft Corporation. "Managing Group Policy ADMX Files Step-by-Step Guide." Available on the web at http://technet2.microsoft.com/WindowsVista/ en/library/02633470-396c-4e34-971a-0c5b090dc 4fd1033.mspx?mfr=true.

Microsoft Corporation. "Gpresult." Available on the web at http:// technet2.microsoft.com/windowsserver2008/en/library/dfaa3adf-2c83-486c-86d6-23f93c5c883c1033.mspx?mfr=true.

Microsoft Corporation. "ADMX Technology Review." Available on the web at http://technet2.microsoft.com/WindowsVista/en/library/ef346453-eee8-4abe-ba6c-2160fee3be461033.mspx?mfr=true.

Chapter 7

Tulloch, Mitch, Tony Northrup, and Jerry Honeycutt. *Windows Vista Resource Kit, Second Edition*. Redmond, Washington: Microsoft Press, 2007. Chapter 13, "Managing the Desktop Environment." Redmond, Washington: Microsoft Press, 2008.

Tulloch, Mitch. *Introducing Windows Server 2008*. Redmond, Washington: Microsoft Press, 2007. Chapter 7, "Active Directory Enhancements."

Microsoft Corporation. "Windows Server 2008 Reviewers Guide." Available on the web at http://technet.microsoft.com/en-us/windowsserver/2008/bb414776.aspx.

Microsoft Corporation. "Step-by-Step Guide for Fine-Grained Password and Account Lockout Policy Configuration." Available on the web at http://technet2.microsoft.com/windowsserver2008/en/library/2199dcf7-68fd-4315-87cc-ade35f8978ea1033.mspx?mfr=true.

Microsoft Corporation. "Windows Server 2008 Security Guide Overview." Available on the web at http://technet.microsoft.com/en-us/library/cc264463.aspx.

Microsoft Corporation. "Domain Controller and Member Server Policy Settings." Available on the web at http://technet.microsoft.com/en-us/library/cc264462.aspx.

Microsoft Corporation. "Audit Policies and Subcategories." Available on the web at http://technet.microsoft.com/en-us/library/cc264465.aspx.

Microsoft Corporation. "Security Settings Overview for GPMC." Available on the web at http://technet2.microsoft.com/windowsserver /en/library/ea8d5585-1b64-44d7-8077-b7721247eca31033.mspx?mfr=true.

Microsoft Corporation. "Server Security Policy Management in Windows Server 2008." Available on the web at http://technet2.microsoft.com/windowsserver2008/en/library/6a85b0ac-2e0a-4a53-9379-b0b3140179601033.mspx?mfr=true.

Herold, R. "Meeting Compliance Needs Through Windows Log Management." Available on the web at http://searchwinit.techtarget.com/tip/0,289483,sid1_gci1306260,00.html?track=NL-118&ad=629344&asrc=EM_NLN_3338484&uid=64259.

Chapter 8

Microsoft Corporation. "Step-by-Step Guide for Windows Server 2008 AD DS Backup and Recovery." Available on the web at http://technet2.microsoft.com/windowsserver2008/en/library/778ff4c7-623d-4475-ba70-4453f964d4911033.mspx?mfr=true.

Microsoft Corporation. "How to Restore Deleted User Accounts and Their Group Memberships in Active Directory." Available on the web at http://support.microsoft.com/kb/840001/en-us.

Microsoft Corporation. "Group Policy Management Console Scripting Examples." Available on the web at http://msdn2.microsoft.com/en-us/library/aa814151(vs.85).aspx.

Microsoft Corporation. "Windows Server 2008 Restartable AD DS Step-by-Step Guide." Available on the web at http://technet2.microsoft.com/windowsserver2008/en/library/caa05f49-210f-4f4c-b33f-c8ad50a687101033.mspx?mfr=true.

Kirkpatrick, G. "What's New in Active Directory Domain Services." Available on the web at http://technet.microsoft.com/en-us/magazine/ cc194387.aspx.

Microsoft Corporation. "Ntdsutil." Available on the web at http://technet2.microsoft.com/windowsserver2008/en/library/199cebb9-967c-4307-a9d7-1c0bb50dc75b1033.mspx?mfr=true.

Microsoft Corporation. "Compact the Directory Database File (Offline Defragmentation)." Available on the web at http://technet2.microsoft.com/windowsserver/en/library/5dd6f9eb-0533-4474-ac52-dca78c5471dd1033.mspx?mfr=true.

Microsoft Corporation. "Microsoft Windows Server Code Name 'Longhorn' Windows System Resource Manager Step-by-Step Guide." Available on the web at http://technet2.microsoft.com/windowsserver2008/zh-CHS/library/1c61547d-497b-4bd7-b9da-3f11bc4031a42052.mspx?mfr=true.

Microsoft Corporation. "Step-by-Step Guide for Performance and Reliability Monitoring in Windows Server 2008." Available on the web at http://technet2.microsoft.com/windowsserver2008/en/library/7e17a3be-f24e-4fdd-9e38-a88e2c8fb4d81033.mspx?mfr=true.

Microsoft Corporation. "Create an LDIF File for Recovering Back-Links for Authoritatively Restored Objects." Available on the web at http://technet2.microsoft.com/windowsserver/en/library/5ec3a3b1-c4b2-4c74-9d8a-61f7cb555f821033.mspx?mfr=true.

Chapter 9

Microsoft Corporation. "Windows Server 2008 Security Guide." Chapter 9, "Hardening Active Directory Certificate Services." Available on the web at http://technet.microsoft.com/en-us/library/cc264455.aspx.

Microsoft Corporation. "Active Directory Certificate Services." Available on the web at http://technet2.microsoft.com/windowsserver2008/en/servermanager/activedirectorycertificateservices.mspx.

Microsoft Corporation. "Documenting Certificate Policies and Practices." Available on the web at http://technet2.microsoft.com/windowsserver/en/library/e0d00680-475a-47a8-8060-5a2ccc7098561033.mspx?mfr=true.

Microsoft Corporation. "Windows Server 2008 Step-by-Step Guides." Available on the web at http://go.microsoft.com/fwlink/?LinkId=90856.

Microsoft Corporation. "Implementing and Administering Certificate Templates in Windows Server 2008." Available on the web at http://www.microsoft.com/downloads/thankyou.aspx?familyId=3c670732-c971-4c65-be9c-c0ebc3749e24&displayLang=en.

Microsoft Corporation. "Key Archival and Recovery." Available on the web at http://technet2.microsoft.com/windowsserver/en/library/ff78185d-815d-4669-98e3-668c9a46cf8f1033.mspx?mfr=true.

Microsoft Corporation. "AD CS: Network Device Enrollment Service." Available on the web at http://technet2.microsoft.com/windowsserver2008/en/library/569cd0df-3aa4-4dd7-88b8-227e9e3c012b1033.mspx?mfr=true.

Microsoft Corporation. "Active Directory Certificate Server Enhancements in Windows Server Code Name 'Longhorn.'" Available on the web at http://www.microsoft.com/downloads/thankyou.aspx?familyId= 9bf17231-d832-4ff9-8fb8-0539ba21ab95&displayLang=en.

Microsoft Corporation. "Specify Certificate Revocation List Distribution Points in Issued Certificates." Available on the web at http://technet2.microsoft.com/windowsserver/en/library/6c95826e-8c8d-4138-bae6-a92e8612499f1033.mspx?mfr=true.

Microsoft Corporation. "Online Responder Installation, Configuration, and Troubleshooting Guide." Available on the web at http://technet2.microsoft.com/windowsserver2008/en/library/045d2a97-1bff-43bd-8dea-f2df7e270e1f1033.mspx?mfr=true.

Appendix C

Microsoft Corporation. "Server Core Installation Option of Windows Server 2008 Step-By-Step Guide." Available on the web at http://technet2. microsoft.com/windowsserver2008/en/library/47a23a74-e13c-46de-8d30-ad0afb1eaffc1033.mspx?mfr=true.

Microsoft Corporation. "Windows Deployment Services Step-by-Step Guide." Available on the web at http://technet2.microsoft.com/windowsserver2008/en/library/7d837d88-6d8e-420c-b68f-a5b4baeb5248 1033.mspx?mfr=true.

A P P E N D I X   B

What's on the CD-ROM

The CD-ROM features an innovative practice test engine powered by MeasureUp, giving you yet another effective tool to assess your readiness for the exam.

Multiple Test Modes

MeasureUp practice tests can be used in Study, Certification, or Custom Modes.

Study Mode

Tests administered in Study Mode allow you to request the correct answer(s) and explanation to each question during the test. These tests are not timed. You can modify the testing environment during the test by selecting the Options button.

You may also specify the objectives or missed questions you want to include in your test, the timer length, and other test properties. In addition, you can modify the testing environment during the test by selecting the Options button.

In Study Mode, you receive automatic feedback on all correct and incorrect answers. The detailed answer explanations are a superb learning tool in their own right.

Certification Mode

Tests administered in Certification Mode closely simulate the actual testing environment you will encounter when taking a certification exam and are timed. These tests do not allow you to request the answer(s) or explanation to each question until after the exam.

Custom Mode

Custom Mode allows you to specify your preferred testing environment. Use this mode to specify the objectives you want to include in your test, the timer length, the number of questions, and other test properties. You can also modify the testing environment during the test by selecting the Options button.

Attention to Exam Objectives

MeasureUp practice tests are designed to appropriately balance the questions over each technical area covered by a specific exam. All concepts from the actual exam are covered thoroughly to ensure you're prepared for the exam.

Installing the CD

System Requirements:

▶ Windows 95, 98, Me, NT 4, 2000, XP, or Vista

▶ 7MB disk space for testing engine

▶ An average of 1MB disk space for each test

▶ Control Panel Regional Settings set to English (United States)

▶ PC only

To install the CD-ROM, follow these instructions:

1. Close all applications before beginning this installation.

2. Insert the CD into your CD-ROM drive. If the setup starts automatically, go to step 6. If the setup does not start automatically, continue with step 3.

3. From the Start menu, select Run.

4. Click Browse to locate the MeasureUp CD. In the Browse dialog box, from the Look In drop-down list, select the CD-ROM drive.

5. In the Browse dialog box, double-click on Setup.exe. In the Run dialog box, click OK to begin the installation.

6. On the Welcome screen, click MeasureUp Practice Questions to begin installation.

7. Follow the Certification Prep Wizard by clicking Next.

8. To agree to the Software License Agreement, click Yes.

9. On the Choose Destination Location screen, click Next to install the software to `C:\Program Files\Certification Preparation`. If you cannot locate MeasureUp Practice Tests through the Start menu, see the section titled "Creating a Shortcut to the MeasureUp Practice Tests," later in this appendix.

10. On the Setup Type screen, select Typical Setup. Click Next to continue.

11. In the Select Program Folder screen, you can name the program folder where your tests will be located. To select the default, simply click Next. The installation continues.

12. After the installation is complete, verify that Yes, I Want to Restart My Computer Now is selected. If you select No, I Will Restart My Computer Later, you cannot use the program until you restart your computer.

13. Click Finish.

14. After restarting your computer, choose Start, Programs, Certification Preparation, Certification Preparation, MeasureUp Practice Tests.

15. On the MeasureUp Welcome Screen, click Create User Profile.

16. In the User Profile dialog box, complete the mandatory fields and click Create Profile.

17. Select the practice test you want to access and click Start Test.

Creating a Shortcut to the MeasureUp Practice Tests

To create a shortcut to the MeasureUp Practice Tests, follow these steps.

1. Right-click on your desktop.

2. From the shortcut menu, select New, Shortcut.

3. Browse to `C:\Program Files\MeasureUp Practice Tests` and select the `MeasureUpCertification.exe` or `Localware.exe` file.

4. Click OK.

5. Click Next.

6. Rename the shortcut **MeasureUp**.

7. Click Finish.

After you complete step 7, use the MeasureUp shortcut on your desktop to access the MeasureUp products you ordered.

Technical Support

If you encounter problems with the MeasureUp test engine on the CD-ROM, please contact MeasureUp at 800-649-1687 or email support@measureup.com. Support hours of operation are 7:30 a.m. to 4:30 p.m. EST. Additionally, you can find Frequently Asked Questions (FAQ) in the "Support" area at www.measureup.com. If you would like to purchase additional MeasureUp products, call 678-356-5050 or 800-649-1687 or visit www.measureup.com.

Installing Windows Server 2008

Before you can even begin to work with Active Directory in Windows Server 2008, you must install a copy of the server software on your computer. This appendix provides guidance on the server installation procedure, which is not covered in any current Microsoft server exam but nevertheless is an essential topic you must master.

Windows Server 2008 Hardware Requirements

As with previous Windows versions, your hardware must meet certain requirements for Windows Server 2008 to function properly. Table C.1 outlines the minimum and recommended hardware requirements for Windows Server 2008 as provided by Microsoft for Release Candidate (RC) 1.

TABLE C.1   Windows Server 2008 Hardware Requirements

Component	Minimum Requirement	Microsoft Recommended
Processor	1GHz (x86 processor) or 1.4GHz (x64 processor)	2GHz or faster
Memory	512MB RAM	2GB RAM or greater
Available Hard Disk Space	10GB	40GB or greater
Optical Drive	DVD-ROM drive	DVD-ROM drive
Display	Super VGA (800×600) monitor	XGA (1024×768) monitor

In addition, you must have the usual input/output (I/O) peripherals, including a keyboard and mouse or compatible pointing device, and a wired or wireless network interface card (NIC). If you can connect to a network location where you have copied the contents of the Windows Server 2008 DVD-ROM, you are not required to have a DVD-ROM drive on your computer. As with any other operating system installation, you will receive improved performance if you have a faster processor and additional memory on your system.

Manually Installing Windows Server 2008

As with other Microsoft operating systems, you can perform a manual or automated installation of Windows Server 2008. Automated installation of Windows Server 2008 simplifies the task of installing multiple servers and uses a technology such as Sysprep or Windows Deployment Services (WDS). The end of this appendix presents a brief summary of these techniques.

Installing a Complete Server

The procedure for installing Windows Server 2008 is the same whether you're installing directly from a DVD-ROM or a network share, except that you must have some type of network client installed on your computer to access a network share. The following procedure outlines installation from a DVD-ROM:

1. Insert the Windows Server 2008 DVD-ROM and turn on your computer. You should see a message informing you that Windows is loading files; if not, access the BIOS setup program included with your computer and modify the boot sequence so that the computer boots from the DVD.

2. After a few minutes, you should see the Install Windows screen shown in Figure C.1. Ensure that the options displayed are correct, and then click Next.

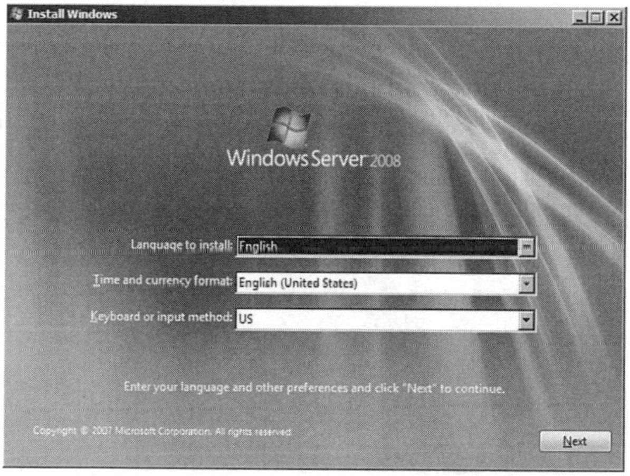

FIGURE C.1 Starting the installation of Windows Server 2008.

3. On the next Install Windows screen, click Install Now.

4. When requested, type your product key, and then click Next.

5. You receive the options shown in Figure C.2, which enables you to install the complete version of Windows Server 2008 or Windows Server 2008 Core. Select the complete installation, and then click Next.

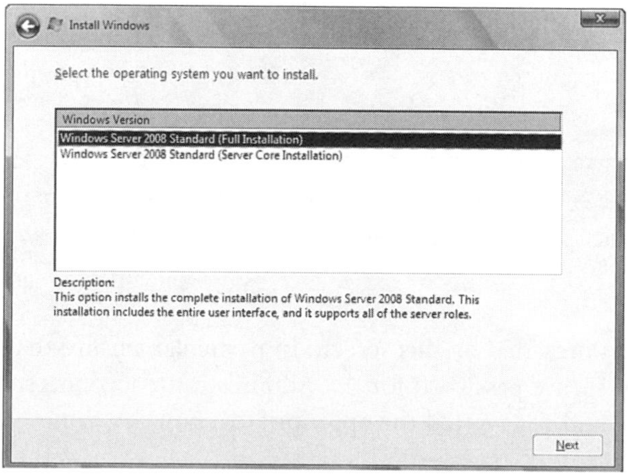

FIGURE C.2 This screen enables you to select either the complete installation of Windows Server 2008 or the Server Core option.

6. Read and accept the licensing terms, and then click Next.

7. You receive the option to upgrade or install a clean copy of Windows Server 2008. Select Custom (advanced) to install a clean copy of Windows Server 2008. The upgrade option is available only if you have started the installation from within Windows Server 2003.

8. Select the disk on which you want to install Windows, and then click Next.

9. Take a coffee break while the installation proceeds. This takes some time (particularly when installing on a virtual machine), and the computer restarts several times.

10. After 30 to 60 minutes (depending on your hardware), Windows restarts one last time and prepares your desktop. Then you are automatically logged on as the default administrator with no password. The Initial Configuration Tasks screen shown in Figure C.3 appears.

FIGURE C.3 The Initial Configuration Tasks screen enables you to perform a basic set of configuration tasks on your new server.

11. Follow the instructions provided by this screen. In particular, ensure that you have configured a secure password for the Administrator account, set the correct time zone, and configured the appropriate computer name and domain settings.

After you have performed the initial configuration steps, you are prompted to press Ctrl+Alt+Delete and enter your password when you restart your server.

> **TIP**
>
> When you shut down a Windows Server 2008 computer, it displays the Shutdown Event Tracker dialog box, which asks you for a reason for shutting down the server. For learning purposes, it is helpful to disable this item so that you do not need to enter a reason every time you shut down or restart your server. You can do so by typing **gpedit.msc** to open the Local Group Policy Object Editor. Navigate to Computer Configuration\Administrative Templates\System, right-click the Display Shutdown Event Tracker policy, and click Properties. On the dialog box that appears, click Disabled, and then click OK.

Using Sysprep to Prepare a Virtual Server

Windows Server 2008 contains the System Preparation tool (sysprep.exe), which prepares your server for the creation of multiple copies. This utility is useful when you are installing several copies of your server as virtual machines on a single host computer without the need to go through a complete server installation.

After you have installed your server as described in the previous section, follow this procedure:

1. Click Start, Command Prompt.

2. Change to the %systemroot%\system32\sysprep folder, type **sysprep /OOBE /generalize /shutdown**, and then press Enter.

3. Sysprep displays a Sysprep is working message box while it performs its tasks, and then the computer shuts down automatically. After this has occurred, navigate to the folder containing virtual images on your host computer, and create as many copies of your server image as desired.

4. From the Virtual PC (or other virtualization program) console, create instances of your server for each copy you have made.

5. Start each virtual server in turn. Windows displays a message asking you to wait while Windows prepares to start for the first time.

6. After several minutes, the server restarts and displays the Set Up Windows screen. Ensure that the options displayed are correct, and then click Next.

7. Type your product key when prompted, and then click Next.

8. Accept the license terms, and then click Next.

9. Type a unique computer name, and then click Start.

10. Press Ctrl+Alt+Delete, and log on using the username and password you configured originally.

Installing a Windows Server Core Computer

As explained in Chapter 1, "Getting Started with Windows Server 2008 Active Directory," Windows Server Core is a new feature of Windows Server 2008 that installs a minimal version of the server software without the GUI; you perform all configuration tasks from the command prompt. Follow this procedure to install Windows Server Core and perform initial configuration tasks:

1. Follow the procedure outlined earlier for installing a full version of Windows Server 2008 until you receive the screen previously shown in Figure C.2.

2. Select the Windows Server Standard Core option, and then click Next.

3. Complete steps 6 through 9 of the earlier procedure. Installation takes 20 to 45 minutes, depending on your hardware.

4. When installation completes, the computer reboots. As instructed, press Ctrl+Alt+Delete to log on, and log on as Other User.

5. Type **administrator** and click the arrow provided to complete the logon. After a minute or so, the desktop appears, containing a command window but no Start menu, taskbar, or desktop icons. This is the standard Windows Server Core interface.

6. To set the correct time, type **control timedate.cpl**. By default, Server Core sets the time zone to Pacific Time. If you are in a different time zone, you need to change this. Set the appropriate time zone, change the date and time if necessary, and then click OK.

7. To set an administrator password, type **net user administrator ***. Follow the prompts to type and confirm a secure password for this account.

8. Windows installs Server Core with a randomly generated computer name. To set a name of your choice, type **netdom renamecomputer %computername% /newname:***ServerC1* (where, in this instance, *ServerC1* is the name you're assigning; substitute your desired server name).

9. Windows warns you that the rename process might have an adverse effect on some services. Type **Y** to proceed, and then type **shutdown** /r /t **0** to reboot your server.

10. After the server reboots, press Ctrl+Alt+Delete, and log on using the password you set in step 7.

If you want to create multiple virtual copies of Server Core, follow the procedure described previously to run `sysprep` and perform initial configurations.

Useful Server Core Commands

All configuration, management, and troubleshooting of Windows Server Core is done from the command line. Available utilities enable you to perform almost all regular configuration tasks in this fashion. Table C.2 describes some of the more useful available commands.

TABLE C.2   Useful Windows Server Core Commands

Command	Meaning
`Netdom join computername /domain:domainname`	Joins an Active Directory domain. You are prompted for the username and password of a user with domain administrator privileges.
`Cscript scregedit.wsf`	Enables automatic updates.
`Oclist`	Displays roles currently installed on the server.
`Ocsetup`	Adds or removes roles.
`Dcpromo`	Installs Active Directory. See Chapter 1 for more information.
`ServerManagerCmd`	Installs and removes roles, role services, and features. Also lists installed and available roles, role services, and features.
`Netsh interface IPv4`	Includes a series of subcommands that enable you to configure IPv4 networking.
`Netsh advfirewall`	Includes subcommands that enable you to configure the Windows firewall.
`Help`	Provides a list of all available Windows Server Core commands.

Available commands also include most commands formerly used with MS-DOS and previous Windows versions. For additional information on installing Windows Server Core, as well as any of these commands or other commands available in Windows Server Core, type the command name followed by /? or consult "Server Core Installation Option of Windows Server 2008 Step-by-Step Guide" in Appendix A, "Need to Know More?"

▶ **Sysprep**—As already discussed, Sysprep prepares a Windows installation for copying to additional computers. It removes computer-specific information such as the server name. You can use third-party disk imaging software to prepare multiple copies for distribution to new servers. In addition to the Windows Server 2008 installation, images can include installations of a common set of software to be used on all servers.

▶ **Windows Deployment Services (WDS)**—WDS is an upgrade to Remote Installation Services (RIS), which was used for deploying installations of Windows 2000/XP/Server 2003 in a domain environment. Similar to RIS, you must have an Active Directory domain, a Dynamic Host Configuration Protocol (DHCP) server, and Domain Name System (DNS) to use WDS. WDS can deploy images of either Windows Vista or Windows Server 2008. For more information, refer to "Windows Deployment Services Step-byStep Guide" in Appendix A.

For more information on Windows Server 2008 deployment, refer to any preparation book for Exam 70-646, PRO: Windows Server 2008, Server Administrator, or Exam 70-647, PRO: Windows Server 2008, Enterprise Administrator.

Glossary

A

access control entry (ACE) An entry within an access control list (ACL) that grants or denies permissions to users or groups for a given resource.

access control list (ACL) A set of access control entries that define an object's permission settings. ACLs enable administrators to explicitly control access to resources.

account partner In AD FS, an organization that has been granted access to a resource partner's web-based application. Users in the account partner can access this application without the need for a separate user account in the resource partner's domain.

ACE *See* access control entry (ACE).

ACL *See* access control list (ACL).

Active Directory (AD) The Windows Server 2008 directory service that replaces the antiquated Windows NT domain structure. Active Directory forms the basis for centralized network management on Windows Server 2008 networks, providing a hierarchical view of network resources. Also known in Windows Server 2008 as Active Directory Domain Services (AD DS).

`auditpol.exe` A command-line tool that enables you to configure audit policy settings and directory service auditing subcategories.

authentication The process by which a server validates a user's logon credentials so that access to a network resource can be granted or denied.

Authority Information Access (AIA) A certificate extension that points to URLs where you can retrieve an issuing CA's certificate.

autoenrollment The ability to automatically enroll users and computers for certificates, retrieve existing certificates, and renew expired certificates without user intervention.

AXFR *See* full zone transfer (AXFR).

B

backup domain controller (BDC) A Windows NT 3.x or 4.0 server that contains a backup read-only copy of the domain security accounts manager (user account and security information). BDCs take the load off the primary domain controller (PDC) by servicing logon requests. Periodic synchronizing ensures that data between the PDC and BDCs remains consistent.

baseline A term associated with performance monitoring, this is the initial result of monitoring typical network and server performance under a normal load. All future results are measured against the baseline readings. A baseline will typically have performance readings for the processor(s), memory, disk subsystem, and network subsystem.

BDC *See* backup domain controller (BDC).

BitLocker A new feature of Windows Server 2008 and Windows Vista that enables you to encrypt the entire contents of your system partition. It is useful for protecting sensitive data on computers such as laptops or branch office domain controllers that are susceptible to theft.

bridgehead server The contact point for the exchange of directory information between Active Directory sites. The bridgehead server receives information replicated from other sites and replicates it to its site's other domain controllers. It ensures that the greatest portion of replication occurs within sites rather than between them.

built-in account A user account that is created by default when Windows is installed on a computer. An example is the local Administrator account.

C

CA *See* certification authority (CA).

CDP *See* CRL distribution point (CDP).

certificate enrollment   The process by which users and computers can be given permission to make requests for certificates, retrieve existing certificates, and renew expired certificates. Each CA that is installed on a server has web pages that users can access to submit basic and advanced certificate requests.

Certificate Revocation List (CRL)   A document published by a CA that lists certificates that have been issued but are no longer valid. By default, the CA publishes the CRL on a weekly basis.

certificate template   Provided by AD CS to simplify the process of requesting and issuing certificates for various purposes. Each template contains the rules and settings that must be in place to create a certificate of a certain type. Certificate templates are available only on enterprise root and subordinate CAs.

certification authority (CA)   A trusted authority either within a network or a third-party company that manages security credentials such that it guarantees the user object holding a certificate is who it claims to be.

checkpoint file   Indicates the location of the last information successfully written from the transaction logs to the database. In a data-recovery scenario, the checkpoint file indicates where the recovery or replaying of data should begin.

circular logging   When a log file fills up, it is overwritten with new data rather than a new log file being created. This conserves disk space but can result in data loss in a disaster-recovery scenario.

claim   In AD FS, a statement made by a server about a client, such as its name, identity, key, group, privilege, or capability. You can enable specific claim types that are accepted by the account partner; claims that fail to match these types will be rejected. Claim types can include identity claims, group claims, or custom claims, and identity claims can include UPN claims, email claims, and common name claims.

claim mapping   In AD FS, the act of processing incoming claims to the resource application hosted by the resource federation service.

Computer Configuration   The portion of a Group Policy object that allows for computer policies to be configured and applied.

conditional forwarding   The relaying of a DNS request for zone information for specific domains from one server to another when the first server is unable to process the request.

connection object   An Active Directory object stored on domain controllers that is used to represent inbound replication links. Domain controllers create their own connection objects for intrasite replication through the Knowledge Consistency

Checker (KCC), whereas only a single domain controller in a site creates connection objects for intersite replication, through the Intersite Topology Generator.

container   An object in Active Directory that is capable of holding other objects. An example of a container would be the Users folder in Active Directory Users and Computers.

convergence   The process of stabilization after network changes occur. Often associated with routing or replication, this ensures each router or server contains consistent information.

counters   The metrics used in performance monitoring, these are what you are actually monitoring. An example of a counter for a CPU object would be %Processing Time.

credential caching   The storing of a limited set of passwords on an RODC. You can configure credential caching to store only those passwords of users who are authorized to log on at a given RODC.

CRL   *See* Certificate Revocation List (CRL).

CRL distribution point (CDP)   A certificate extension that indicates URL locations where a CRL can be retrieved. Multiple HTTP, FTP, FILE, or LDAP locations can be included.

csvde   A utility that imports comma-separated text files into the AD DS database. You can use this utility to automate the bulk creation of user or group accounts.

D

DC   *See* domain controller (DC).

DCPROMO   The command-line utility used to promote a Windows Server 2008 system to a domain controller. DCPROMO can also be used to demote a domain controller to a member server.

DDNS   *See* Dynamic Domain Name System (DDNS).

delegation   The process of offloading the responsibility for a given task or set of tasks to another user or group. Delegation in Windows Server 2008 usually involves granting permission to someone else to perform a specific administrative task such as creating computer accounts.

delta CRL   A CRL that includes the list of certificates revoked since the issuance of the most recent complete (base) CRL. Its use optimizes bandwidth usage when certificates are frequently revoked.

DFS   *See* Distributed File System (DFS).

DHCP   *See* Dynamic Host Configuration Protocol (DHCP).

directory A database that contains any number of different types of data. In Windows Server 2008, Active Directory is a database that contains information about objects in the domain, such as computers, users, groups, and printers.

directory service (DS) Provides the methods of storing directory data and making that data available to other directory objects. A directory service makes it possible for users to find any object in the directory given any one of its attributes.

Directory System Agent (DSA) Makes data within Active Directory accessible to applications that want it, acting as a liaison between the directory database and the applications.

disk quota An administrative disk space limitation set on the server storage space, on a per-volume basis, that can be used by any particular user.

distinguished name The name that uniquely identifies an object. A distinguished name is composed of the relative distinguished name, the domain name, and the container holding the object. An example would be CN=AnyUser, CN=Examcram,CN=COM. This refers to the AnyUser user account in the examcram.com domain.

Distributed File System (DFS) A Windows Server 2008 service that allows resources from multiple server locations to be presented through Active Directory as a contiguous set of files and folders, resulting in more ease of use of network resources for users.

distribution group An Active Directory group of user accounts or other groups used strictly for email distribution. A distribution group cannot be used to grant permissions to resources. That type of group is called a security group.

DNS *See* Domain Name System (DNS).

dnscmd A command-line tool that can perform most of the DNS server administrative tasks in Windows Server 2008.

DNS Notify A process in which the master DNS server for a zone notifies secondary servers of changes so that the secondary servers can determine whether they need to initiate a zone transfer.

domain A logical grouping of Windows Server 2008 computers, users, and groups that share a common directory database. Domains act as a security boundary and are defined by an administrator.

domain controller (DC) A server that is capable of performing authentication. In Windows Server 2008, a domain controller holds an editable copy of the Active Directory database.

domain functional level Windows Server 2008 domains can operate at one of three functional levels: Windows 2000 native, Windows

Server 2003 native, or the Windows Server 2008 functional level. Each functional level has different trade-offs between features and limitations.

domain local group   A domain local group can contain other domain local groups from its own domain, as well as global groups from any domain in the forest. A domain local group can be used to assign permissions to resources located in the same domain as the group.

Domain Name System (DNS)   A hierarchical name-resolution system that resolves host names (fully qualified domain names, FQDNs) into IP addresses and vice versa. DNS also makes it possible for the distributed Active Directory database to function, by allowing clients to query the locations of services in the forest and domain.

Domain Naming Master   One of the two forestwide flexible single-master operations (FSMO) roles, the Domain Naming Master's job is to ensure domain name uniqueness within a forest.

domain user account   A user account that is stored in the AD DS database. It permits a user to log on to any computer in the domain where it is located or a trusted domain.

DS   *See* directory service (DS).

DSA   *See* Directory System Agent (DSA).

dsadd   A command-line tool that enables you to add objects such as users, groups, contacts, or computers to the AD DS database.

Dynamic Domain Name System (DDNS)   An extension of DNS that allows Windows 2000 and later systems to automatically register their A records (by themselves or by the DHCP server) with DNS at the time they obtain an IP address from a DHCP server.

Dynamic Host Configuration Protocol (DHCP)   A service that allows an administrator to specify a range of valid IP addresses to be used on a network, as well as exclusion IP addresses that should not be assigned (for example, if they were already statically assigned elsewhere). These addresses are automatically given out to computers configured to use DHCP as they boot up on the network, thus saving the administrator from having to configure static IP addresses on each network device.

E

enrollment agents   A user who has been issued a special certificate that grants him the authority to enroll users into advanced security and issue certificates on behalf of the users.

enrollment station The physical workstation or server where the enrollment agent certificate is installed and used by the authorized person to enroll users and issue certificates.

enterprise CA A CA that is integrated with AD DS. Enterprise CAs replicate certificates with AD DS replication and require that users be authenticated.

ESE *See* Extensible Storage Engine (ESE).

Extensible Storage Engine (ESE) The Active Directory database engine, ESE is an improved version of the older Jet database technology. The ESE database uses the concept of discrete transactions and log files to ensure the integrity of Active Directory. Each request to the DSA to add, modify, or delete an object or attribute is treated as an individual transaction. As these transactions occur on each domain controller, they are recorded in a series of log files that are associated with each Ntds.dit file.

external trust A trust relationship created between a Windows Server 2008 Active Directory domain and a Windows NT 4 domain, or between Active Directory domains in different forests.

F

federated application In AD FS, a web-based application that is configured so that users in an organization connected by means of a federation trust can be authenticated to access this application without the need for a separate AD DS user account.

federation trust In AD FS, a relationship between two organizations that allows for access to web-based applications without establishing an external or forest trust between the organizations' domains.

File Replication Service (FRS) A service that provides multimaster replication between specified domain controllers within an Active Directory tree.

File Transfer Protocol (FTP) A standard TCP/IP utility that allows for the transfer of files from an FTP server to a machine running the FTP client.

fine-grained password policies A new feature of Windows Server 2008 that enables you to configure password policies that apply only to specific users or groups within a domain.

firewall A hardware and software security system that limits access to network resources across subnets. Typically, a firewall is used between a private network and the Internet to prevent outsiders from accessing the private network. The firewall also limits what Internet services users of the private network can access.

flat namespace   A namespace that cannot be partitioned to produce additional domains. Windows NT 4 and earlier domains were examples of flat namespaces, as opposed to the Windows Server 2008 hierarchical namespace.

flexible single-master operations (FSMO)   Five roles that are required by Windows Server 2008 not to follow the typical multimaster model and instead are hosted on only a single domain controller in each domain, in the case of the Infrastructure Master, PDC Emulator, and RID Master, or on only a single domain controller in the forest, in the case of the Domain Naming Master and the Schema Master.

folder redirection   A Windows Server 2008 feature that allows special folders, such as My Documents, on local Windows XP Professional or Vista Business/Enterprise/ Ultimate system hard drives to be redirected to a shared network location.

forest   A grouping of Active Directory trees that have a trust relationship between them. Forests can consist of a noncontiguous namespace and, unlike domains and trees, do not have to be given a specific name.

forest functional level   The three forest functional levels are Windows 2000, Windows Server 2003, and Windows Server 2008. The default forest functional level is Windows 2000. When the forest functional level is raised to Windows Server 2003 or Windows Server 2008, advanced forestwide Active Directory features are available according to the level chosen.

forest root   The first domain created in a forest.

forest trust   A trust relationship established between two Active Directory forests.

forward lookup query   A DNS name-resolution process by which a hostname is resolved to an IP address.

forwarding   The relaying of a DNS request from one server to another, when the first server is unable to process the request.

FQDN   *See* fully qualified domain name (FQDN).

FRS   *See* File Replication Service (FRS).

FSMO   *See* flexible single-master operations (FSMO).

FTP   *See* File Transfer Protocol (FTP).

full zone transfer (AXFR)   A zone transfer in which the master server transmits the entire zone database to that zone's secondary servers.

fully qualified domain name (FQDN)   A DNS domain name that unambiguously describes the location of the host within a domain tree. An example of an FQDN would be the computer www.examcram.com.

functional level A concept introduced in Windows Server 2003 that determines what level of features and interoperability with other Windows operating systems is available in a domain or forest. In Windows 2000, functional levels were referred to as modes.

G

GC *See* Global Catalog (GC).

Global Catalog (GC) Contains a partial replica of every Windows Server 2008 domain object within the Active Directory, enabling users to find any object in the directory. The partial replica contains the most commonly used attributes of an object, as well as information on how to locate a complete replica elsewhere in the directory, if needed.

Global Catalog server The Windows Server 2008 server that holds the Global Catalog for the forest.

global group A global group can contain users from the same domain in which the group is located, and global groups can be added to domain local groups to control access to network resources.

globally unique identifier (GUID) A hexadecimal number supplied by the manufacturer of a product that uniquely identifies the hardware or

software. A GUID is in the form of eight characters, followed by three sets of four characters, followed by 12 characters. For example, {15DEF489-AE24-10BF-C11A-00BB844CE637} is a valid format for a GUID (braces included).

GPO *See* Group Policy object (GPO).

gpresult A command-line utility that displays information about the current effect Group Policy has had on the local computer and logged-in user account.

Group Policy The Windows Server 2008 feature that allows for policy creation, which affects domain users and computers. Policies can be anything from desktop settings to application assignments to security settings and more.

Group Policy Management Editor The Microsoft Management Console (MMC) snap-in that is used to modify the settings of a Group Policy object.

Group Policy object (GPO) A collection of policies that apply to a specific target, such as the domain itself (Default Domain Policy) or an Organizational Unit (OU). GPOs are modified through the Group Policy Editor to define policy settings.

GUID *See* globally unique identifier (GUID).

H

hierarchical namespace A namespace, such as with DNS, that can be partitioned out in the form of a tree. This allows great flexibility in using a domain name because any number of subdomains can be created under a parent domain.

Hyper-V The new virtualization tool included with the 64-bit editions of Windows Server 2008 that enables you to run multiple instances of the operating system on a single server.

I

incremental zone transfer (IXFR) A zone transfer in which the master server transmits only the modified portion of each zone file to that zone's secondary servers.

Infrastructure Master The FSMO role that is responsible for receiving replicated changes from other domains within the forest and replicating these changes to all domain controllers within its domain. Each domain has one Infrastructure Master; it also is responsible for tracking what Active Directory container an object is located in.

inheritance The process by which an object obtains settings information from a parent object.

Intersite Topology Generator (ISTG) The Windows Server 2008 server that is responsible for evaluating and creating the topology for intersite replication.

issuing CA A CA server that is involved in the day-to-day issuing of certificates for computers and users on the network.

ISTG *See* Intersite Topology Generator (ISTG).

IXFR *See* incremental zone transfer (IXFR).

J

Just-In-Time (JIT) Technology that allows software features to be updated when they are accessed. Whereas in the past, missing application features needed to be manually installed, JIT technology allows the features to be installed on the fly as they are accessed, with no other intervention required.

K

KCC *See* Knowledge Consistency Checker (KCC).

Kerberos An Internet standard security protocol that has largely replaced the older LAN Manager user-authentication mechanism from earlier Windows NT versions.

Knowledge Consistency Checker (KCC) A Windows Server 2008 service that ensures consistent database information is kept across all domain controllers. It attempts to ensure that replication can always take place.

L

LAN *See* local area network (LAN).

latency The delay that occurs in replication from the time a change is made to one replica and the time that change is applied to all other replicas in the directory.

LDAP *See* Lightweight Directory Access Protocol (LDAP).

ldifde A utility that enables you to import data formatted in the LDAP Data Interchange Format (LDIF) format to the AD DS database. You can use this tool to automate the creation of user, computer, or group accounts.

Ldp.exe A GUI-based tool that enables you to perform several types of administrative actions on any LDAP directory service, including AD DS and AD LDS.

Lightweight Directory Access Protocol (LDAP) The protocol that allows access to Active Directory. LDAP is an Internet standard for accessing directory services.

linked policy A Group Policy that exists in one object and is linked to another object. Linked policies are used to reduce administrative duplication in applying the same policies to multiple OUs.

local area network (LAN) A network where all hosts are connected over fast connections (4MBps or greater for Token Ring; 10MBps or better for Ethernet). LANs typically do not involve outside data carriers (such as Frame Relay lines or T1 circuits) and are generally wholly owned by the organization.

local group A security group that exists on a local workstation or server and is used for granting permissions to local resources. Typically, global groups from a domain are placed inside a local group to gain access to resources on a local machine.

local Group Policy objects Objects that exist on the local Windows Server 2008 system. Site-, domain-, and OU-applied GPOs take precedence over local GPOs.

local user account A user account that is stored in the SAM of a member server or client computer. Such an account can be used to log on to that computer only and does not possess domain privileges.

M

member server   A server that is a member of a domain but is not a domain controller. A Windows Server 2008 domain can have Windows NT, Windows 2000, Windows Server 2003, and Windows Server 2008 member servers, regardless of the domain functional level.

Microsoft Management Console (MMC)   An extensible management framework that provides a common look and feel to all Windows Server 2008 utilities.

MMC   *See* Microsoft Management Console (MMC).

multihomed   A server that has two or more network cards. This allows a server either to function as a router or to belong to more than one subnet simultaneously. Alternatively, multiple network adapters can be used for load balancing or fault tolerance.

multimaster replication   A replication model in which any domain controller will replicate data to any other domain controller. This is the default behavior in Windows Server 2008. It contrasts with the single-master replication model of Windows NT 4, in which a PDC contained the master copy of everything and BDCs contained backup copies.

N

name resolution   The process of resolving a hostname into a format that computers can understand. This is typically resolving a DNS name or NetBIOS name to an IP address but could also be a MAC address on non-TCP/IP networks.

NetBIOS   An application programming interface (API) used on Windows NT 4 and earlier networks by services requesting and providing name resolution and network data management.

Network Monitor   A utility that enables you to capture, view, and analyze frames transmitted across the network to network adapter cards on your computer. It is useful for detecting incursions by unauthorized users and tracing their activity on the network.

nonlocal Group Policy objects   GPOs that are stored in Active Directory rather than on the local machine. These can be site-, domain-, or OU-level GPOs.

Nslookup   A TCP/IP utility used in troubleshooting DNS name-resolution problems.

Ntdsutil   A command-line utility that provides a number of Active Directory management functions.

NTFS   The Windows NT/2000 file system that supports a much more robust feature set than either FAT16 or FAT32 (which was used on Windows 9x). You should use NTFS whenever possible on Windows Server 2008 systems; indeed, the server installation utility automatically creates an NTFS partition during installation.

O

object A distinct entity represented by a series of attributes within Active Directory. An object can be a user, group, computer, folder, file, printer, and so on.

object identifier A number that uniquely identifies an object class or attribute. In the United States, the American National Standards Institute (ANSI) issues object identifiers, which take the form of an x.x.x.x dotted decimal format. Microsoft, for example, was issued the root object identifier of 1.2.840.113556, from which it can create further subobject identifiers.

OCSP *See* Online Certificate Status Protocol (OCSP).

Online Certificate Status Protocol (OCSP) A protocol that enables rapid certificate status validations. AD CS in Windows Server 2008 includes an OCSP Responder role service.

operations master A Windows Server 2008 domain controller that has been assigned one or more of the special Active Directory domain roles, such as Schema Master, Domain Naming Master, PDC Emulator, Infrastructure Master, and Relative Identifier (RID) Master.

Organizational Unit (OU) An Active Directory container object that allows an administrator to logically group users, groups, computers, and other OUs into administrative units.

OU *See* Organizational Unit (OU).

P

package A collection of software compiled into a distributable form, such as a Windows Installer (`.msi`) package created with `WinInstall`.

parent-child trust relationship The relationship whereby a child object trusts its parent object, and the parent object is trusted by all child objects under it. Active Directory automatically creates two-way transitive trust relationships between parent and child objects.

partial attribute set A schema attribute that tracks the internal replication status of partial replicas, such as those found on GC servers.

password settings object (PSO) An object class defined in the AD DS schema that holds attributes for the fine-grained password and account lockout policy settings.

Password Synchronization A new feature of Windows Server 2003 R2 that contributes to better Active Directory and UNIX interoperability by automatically synchronizing passwords between the two.

patching The process of modifying or updating software packages.

PDC *See* primary domain controller (PDC).

PDC Emulator The domain-level FSMO role that replicates data with Windows NT 4 BDCs in a domain, in effect functioning as an NT 4 PDC.

Ping A TCP/IP utility that tests for basic connectivity between the client machine running Ping and any other TCP/IP host.

PKI *See* Public Key Infrastructure (PKI).

policy Settings and rules that are applied to users or computers, usually Group Policy in Windows Server 2008 and System Policy in Windows NT 4.

preferred bridgehead server Rather than letting the KCC decide which server should be a bridgehead server, you can designate preferred bridgehead servers to be used if the primary goes down. Only one preferred bridgehead server can be active at a time.

primary domain controller (PDC) A Windows NT 4 (and earlier) server that contains the master copy of the domain database and the only writable copy of the database. PDCs authenticate user logon requests and track security-related changes within the domain.

primary zone A master copy of DNS zone data hosted on a server that is the primary source of information for records found in this zone.

PSO *See* password settings object (PSO).

Public Key Infrastructure (PKI) An industry standard technology that allows for the establishment of secure communication between hosts based on a public key/private key or certificate-based system.

published applications Through the Software Installation utility in Group Policy, administrators can publish applications to users. Published applications appear in Add/Remove Programs and can be optionally installed by the user.

R

RDN *See* relative distinguished name (RDN).

read-only domain controller (RODC) A new Windows Server 2008 feature in which the domain controller is installed with a read-only directory database. You cannot perform directory updates directly from the RODC. It is especially suitable in reduced security environments such as branch offices.

realm trust A trust relationship in Windows Server 2008 that is created between an Active Directory domain and a UNIX realm.

Registry A data repository on each computer that contains information about that computer's configuration. The Registry is organized into a hierarchical tree and is made up of hives, keys, and values.

relative distinguished name (RDN) The part of a DNS name that defines the host. For example, in the FQDN www.examcram.com, www is the relative distinguished name.

relative identifier (RID) The part of the security identifier (SID) that uniquely identifies an account or group within a domain.

Reliability and Performance Monitor A Microsoft Management Console application that contains several tools for monitoring your computer's performance.

Reliability Monitor A component of the Reliability and Performance Monitor that provides a trend analysis of your computer's system stability with time. It shows how events such as hardware or application failures, software installations or removals, and so on affect your computer's stability.

replica A copy of any given Active Directory object. Each copy of an object stored on multiple domain controllers is a replica.

replication The process of copying data from one Windows Server 2008 domain controller to another. Replication is a process managed by an administrator and typically occurs automatically whenever changes are made to a replica of an object.

Request for Comments (RFC) Official uniquely numbered documents that specify Internet standards for the TCP/IP protocol.

resource partner In AD FS, an organization that hosts a server containing a web-based application that has been configured for access by users in the trusted organization.

resource records Standard database record types used in DNS zone database files. Common types of resource records include Address (A), Mail Exchanger (MX), Start of Authority (SOA), and Name Server (NS), among others.

Resultant Set of Policy (RSoP) A Windows Server 2008 Group Policy tool that lets you simulate the effects of Group Policies without actually implementing them. RSoP has two modes: logging mode and planning mode. Logging mode determines the resultant effect of policy settings that have been applied to an existing user and computer based on a site, domain, or organizational unit. Planning mode simulates the resultant effect of policy settings that are applied to a user and computer.

return on investment (ROI) A business term that seeks to determine the amount of financial gain that occurs as a result of a certain expenditure. Many IT personnel today are faced with the prospect of justifying IT expenses in terms of ROI.

reverse lookup query A DNS name-resolution process by which an IP address is resolved to a hostname.

RID *See* relative identifier (RID).

RID Master The domain-level FSMO role that is responsible for managing pools of RIDs and ensuring that every object in the domain gets a unique RID.

RODC *See* read-only domain controller (RODC).

ROI *See* return on investment (ROI).

root CA The topmost CA in a PKI hierarchy, this is the most authoritative certificate server. You should protect this server with the highest level of security possible, such as storing it offline in a vault. If it is compromised, the entire PKI hierarchy is compromised.

root hints A list of the names and IP addresses of DNS servers that are authoritative for the Internet root domains. Used by a DNS server to forward queries for Internet domains that it is unable to resolve from its own database.

round robin A load-balancing mechanism that DNS servers use to distribute name resolution activity among all available DNS servers.

router A dedicated network hardware appliance or a server running routing software and multiple network cards. Routers join dissimilar network topologies (such as Ethernet to Frame Relay) or simply segment networks into multiple subnets.

RSoP *See* Resultant Set of Policy (RSoP).

S

scalability Measurement (often subjective) of how well a resource such as a server can expand to accommodate growing needs.

scavenging The process by which a DNS server searches for and deletes aged (stale) resource records.

schema In Active Directory, a schema is a database that contains the description of object classes and the attributes that the object classes must possess and can possess.

Schema Master The Windows Server 2008 domain controller that has been assigned the Operations Master role to control all schema updates within a forest.

SDDNS *See* secure dynamic DNS (SDDNS).

secondary zone   An additional copy of DNS zone data hosted on a DNS server that is a secondary source for this zone information.

secure dynamic DNS (SDDNS)   An enhancement to DNS that enables you to permit dynamic updates only from authorized client computers in an Active Directory–integrated zone.

security group   A type of group that can contain user accounts or other groups and can be used to assign levels of access (permissions) to shared resources.

security identifier (SID)   A number that uniquely identifies a user, group, or computer account. Every account is issued one when created. If the account is later deleted and re-created with the same name, it will have a different SID. Once an SID is used in a domain, it can never be used again.

security templates   Collections of standard settings that can be applied administratively to give a consistent level of security to a system.

seizing a role   The act of moving an operations master role from one domain controller to another when the original role holder is no longer available on the network. You cannot seize a role if the original role holder is available; you must transfer it instead. Once you have seized a role, you cannot bring back the original role holder without reinstalling Active Directory in most cases.

Server Core   A new feature of Windows Server 2008 that enables you to install a minimal version of the server without a GUI, Start menu, taskbar, or many ancillary components. A Server Core computer can hold most of the roles that an ordinary Windows Server 2008 computer holds, but with a smaller network footprint and fewer points of attack.

Server for NIS   A new feature of Windows Server 2003 R2 that helps integrate Active Directory and UNIX by enabling an Active Directory domain controller to function as a UNIX NIS server.

Server Performance Advisor   A utility that provides an in-depth view of current server performance and suggestions for making improvements.

shortcut trust   A Windows Server 2008 trust relationship between two domains within the same forest. Shortcut trusts are used to reduce the path authentication needs to travel by directly connecting child domains.

SID   *See* security identifier (SID).

SID filtering   A mechanism that validates the SIDs of users in a trusted domain that is attempting to authenticate across a trust relationship to a trusting domain. It enhances security by verifying that the authentication request contains only SIDs of security principals in the trusted domain.

single-master operations   Certain Active Directory operations that are only allowed to occur in one place at any given time (as opposed to being allowed to occur in multiple locations simultaneously). Examples of single-master operations include schema modifications, RID assignments, and infrastructure changes.

single sign-on (SSO)   The ideal of having one username and password that works for everything on a network. Windows Server 2008 features like Active Directory Federation Services bring this closer to reality than ever before.

site   A physical component of Active Directory. Sites are created for the purpose of balancing logon authentication with replication. They can have zero (in planning), one, or multiple IP subnets. These subnets should be well connected with fast LAN links.

site link   A connection between sites, it is used to join multiple locations.

site link bridge   A collection of site links that helps Active Directory work out the cost of replicating traffic from one point to another within the network infrastructure that is not directly connected by a single site link. By default, all site links are bridged, but this can be disabled in favor of manually configured site link bridges.

site link cost   A way for AD to determine what path to replicate traffic over on a routed network.

The lower the cost, the more preferable it is for AD to use a particular site link. For example, if you have a T1 and an ISDN site link connecting the same sites, the T1 site link would have a lower cost than the ISDN site link, making it the preferred path for traffic. In other words, the faster the link, the lower the site link cost.

slow link   A connection between sites that is not fast enough to provide full functionality in an acceptable timeframe. Site connections below 512KBps are defined as slow links in Windows Server 2008.

smartcard   A credit card–sized device that is used with an access code to enable certificate-based authentication and single sign-on to the enterprise. Smartcards securely store certificates, public and private keys, passwords, and other types of personal information. A smartcard reader attached to the computer reads the smartcard.

Software Installation   A Group Policy component that allows administrators to optionally assign applications to be available to users and computers or publish applications to users.

snap-in   A component that can be added or removed from a Microsoft Management Console (MMC) console to provide specific functionality. The Windows Server 2008 administrative tools are implemented as snap-ins.

SSO *See* single sign-on (SSO).

standalone CA A CA whose database is stored locally and not integrated with AD DS. Typically, an organization has a standalone root CA coupled with enterprise subordinate CAs. This practice enables the administrator to keep the standalone root CA offline and secured in a safe location such as a vault. It is brought back online only when required for issuing certificates to subordinate CAs.

static IP address Also called a static address, this is where a network device (such as a server) is manually configured with an IP address that doesn't change rather than obtaining an address automatically from a DHCP server.

store Implemented using the Extensible Storage Engine, this is the physical storage of each Active Directory replica.

stub zone A DNS zone that contains source information about authoritative name servers for its zone only. The DNS server hosting the stub zone obtains its information from another server that hosts a primary or secondary copy of the same zone data.

subnet A collection of hosts on a TCP/IP network that are not separated by routers. A basic corporate LAN with one location would be referred to as a subnet when it is connected by a router to another network, such as that of an Internet service provider.

subordinate CA A CA whose certificates come from a root CA. The subordinate CA's job is to issue certificates to users and computers on the network. Each subordinate CA may be dedicated to a single type of certificate, such as smart cards, Encrypting File System (EFS), or a geographical location of a multisite network.

synchronous processing Synchronous processing occurs when one task does not wait for another to complete before it begins. Rather, the two run concurrently. This is typically associated with scripts in Windows Server 2008, such as a user logon script running without waiting for the computer startup script to finish.

syskey A locally stored system key that encrypts the SAM database on Windows 2000 and later computers. It is required for computers to start. For added security, you can remove this key and store it on a floppy disk or specify a password to be entered manually on startup.

System Policies Windows NT 4 Registry–based policy settings that have largely been replaced in Windows Server 2008 by Group Policy. System Policies can still be created using poledit.exe, however, for backward compatibility with pre-Windows 2000 clients.

SYSVOL A shared folder on an NTFS partition on every AD domain controller that contains information (scripts, Group Policy info, and so on) that is replicated to other domain controllers in the domain. The SYSVOL folder is created during the installation of Active Directory.

T

TCP/IP *See* Transmission Control Protocol/Internet Protocol (TCP/IP).

template account A special account created for the sole purpose of copying as needed when creating a large number of user accounts with similar privileges.

Time to Live (TTL) The amount of time a packet destined for a host will exist before it is deleted from the network. TTLs are used to prevent networks from becoming congested with packages that cannot reach their destinations.

transferring a role The act of moving one of the operations masters roles from one domain controller to another when the original role holder is available on the network. You cannot transfer the role if the original holder is not available.

transitive trust An automatically created trust in Windows Server 2008 that exists between domain trees within a forest and domains within a tree. Transitive trusts are two-way trust relationships. Unlike with Windows NT 4, transitive trusts in Windows Server 2008 can flow between domains. This way, if Domain1 trusts Domain2, and Domain2 trusts Domain3, Domain1 automatically trusts Domain3.

Transmission Control Protocol/Internet Protocol (TCP/IP)
The standard suite of networking protocols for communicating on the Internet. It is the default protocol in Windows Server 2008.

tree A collection of Active Directory domains that are connected through transitive trusts and share a common Global Catalog and schema. Domains within a tree must form a contiguous namespace. A tree is contained within a forest, and multiple trees can exist within a forest.

TTL *See* Time to Live (TTL).

U

universal group An Active Directory security group that can be used anywhere within a domain tree or forest, the only caveat being that universal groups can only be used when an Active Directory domain has been converted to native mode.

universal group caching A feature that can be used once a domain has been raised to the Windows Server 2008 functional level, it allows users in universal groups to log on without out the presence of a GC server.

update sequence number (USN)   A 64-bit number that keeps track of changes as they are written to copies of Active Directory. As changes are made, this number increments by one. Every attribute in Active Directory has a USN value.

UPN   *See* user principal name (UPN).

UPN suffix   The portion of the UPN following the @ character. By default, this is the DNS domain name of the domain where the user account is located. However, you can define an alternate UPN suffix that enables you to conceal the actual domain structure of the forest or match the user's email address domain name.

User Configuration   The portion of a Group Policy object that allows for user policy settings to be configured and applied.

user logon name   The name employed by a user to log on to a domain. AD DS uses this name and its associated password to authenticate the user.

user principal name (UPN)   An alternate username that is formatted in a manner similar to that of an email address (for example, user@domain.com). Its use enables a user to more easily log on to a domain in the forest other than the domain she belongs to.

user principal name (UPN) suffix
See UPN suffix.

user profile   Contains settings that define the user environment, typically applied when the user logs on to the system.

USN   *See* update sequence number (USN).

W

WAN   *See* wide area network (WAN).

Wbadmin.exe   A command-line tool that enables you to perform backups and restores. In Windows Server 2008, this is the only tool that you can use to perform system state backups and restores.

well-connected network   A network that contains only fast connections between domains and hosts. The definition of "fast" is somewhat subjective and may vary from organization to organization.

wide-area network (WAN)   Multiple networks connected by slow connections between routers.

Windows 2000 functional level   The default functional level that exists when you install AD DS on Windows Server 2008. In this functional level, you can have any combination of domain controllers running Windows 2000, Windows Server 2003, or Windows Server 2008.

Windows Internet Name Service (WINS) A dynamic name-resolution system that resolves NetBIOS names to IP addresses on Windows TCP/IP networks. With Windows Server 2008, WINS has been kept in place as a feature so that any legacy clients or applications on the network can use it.

Windows Management Instrumentation (WMI) A Windows Server 2008 management infrastructure for monitoring and controlling system resources. WMI filters are commonly used in Group Policy to modify the scope of a GPO according to the attributes of destination computers.

Windows Script Host Enables the running of VBScript or JavaScript scripts natively on a Windows system, offering increased power and flexibility over traditional batch files.

Windows Server 2003 functional level The functional level of either the domain or forest that you can select after you have removed or upgraded all Windows 2000 domain controllers. This functional level implements all the features of Windows Server 2003 Active Directory but at the expense of some backward compatibility; it does not implement new features of Windows Server 2008 Active Directory.

Windows Server 2008 functional level The highest functional level of the domain or forest that you can select after you have removed or upgraded all Windows 2000 and Windows Server 2003 domain controllers. This functional level implements all the features of Windows Server 2008 Active Directory but at the expense of backward compatibility with older Windows servers.

Windows Server virtualization The capability of running multiple copies of different operating systems on a single server. The 64-bit edition of Windows Server 2008 contains a built-in virtualization capability known as Hyper-V. You can use Microsoft Virtual Server 2005 on 32-bit editions of Windows Server 2008 or on older Windows Server versions.

Windows System Resource Manager (WSRM) An administrative feature that enables you to control how processor and memory resources are allocated to applications, services, and processes running on the server.

WinInstall An optional utility that ships with Windows Server 2008 and can be used to create Windows Installer packages.

WINS *See* Windows Internet Name Service (WINS).

WMI *See* Windows Management Instrumentation (WMI).

workgroup A group of workstations and servers that are networked but not within the concept of a domain. In a workgroup, each machine maintains its own local accounts database and can be difficult to administer as the number of computers in the workgroup grows.

WScript   The Windows interface to Windows Script Host (WSH).

WSRM   *See* Windows System Resource Manager (WSRM).

X

X.500   A set of standards developed by the International Standards Organization (ISO) that defines distributed directory services.

Z

zone   A discrete portion of the local or Internet-based DNS namespace, for which a single DNS server is authoritative.

zone delegation   The act of dividing the DNS namespace into a series of zones and delegating their management by creating resource records in other zones that point to the authoritative DNS servers for the zone being delegated.

Index

A

Register this book!

Register this book at
www.quepublishing.com
and
unlock benefits
exclusive to the owners
of this book.

What you'll receive with this book:

- ► Hidden content
- ► Additional content
- ► Book errata
- ► New templates, spreadsheets, or files to download
- ► Increased membership discounts
- ► Discount coupons
- ► A chance to sign up to receive content updates, information on new editions, and more

Book registration is free and only takes a few easy steps.

1. Go to www.quepublishing.com/bookstore/register.asp.
2. Enter the book's ISBN (found above the barcode on the back of your book).
3. You will be prompted to either register for or log-in to Quepublishing.com.
4. Once you have completed your registration or log-in, you will be taken to your "My Registered Books" page.
5. This page will list any benefits associated with each title you register, including links to content and coupon codes.

The benefits of book registration vary with each book, so be sure to register every Que Publishing book you own to see what else you might unlock at Quepublishing.com!

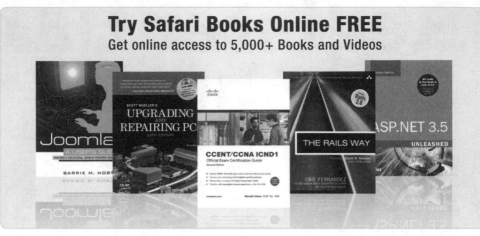

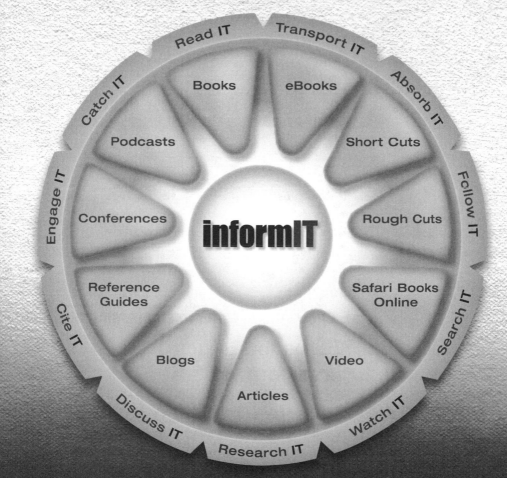

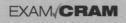

FREE Online Edition

Your purchase of **MCTS 70-640 Exam Cram: Windows Server 2008 Active Directory, Configuring** includes access to a free online edition for 120 days through the Safari Books Online subscription service. Nearly every Exam Cram book is available online through Safari Books Online, along with over 5,000 other technical books and videos from publishers such as Addison-Wesley Professional, Cisco Press, IBM Press, O'Reilly, Prentice Hall, Que, and Sams.

SAFARI BOOKS ONLINE allows you to search for a specific answer, cut and paste code, download chapters, and stay current with emerging technologies.

Activate your FREE Online Edition at www.informit.com/safarifree

> **STEP 1:** Enter the coupon code:45KT-3A2I-41WY-SLJL-DI88.

> **STEP 2:** New Safari users, complete the brief registration form.
> Safari subscribers, just login.

Safari
Books Online